THIRTEENTH EDITION
1984

A CATALOG

of

MODERN WORLD COINS

1850-1964

by
R. S. YEOMAN

Revised and Edited by
Arthur L. Friedberg
and Ira S. Friedberg

THE COIN & CURRENCY INSTITUTE, INC.
102 Linwood Plaza
Fort Lee, New Jersey 07024

No. 9053

Printed in U.S.A.

PRINCIPAL CONTRIBUTORS

Arthur S. Goldenberg, *Associate Editor*

Many illustrations and data herein are based on
Wayte Raymond's standard works on 20th Century World Coins, and on
Robert Friedberg's GOLD COINS OF THE WORLD.
Library of Congress Catalog Card No. 83–72378
ISBN: 0-87184-713-2
Printed with the permission and under license from
Western Publishing Co., Inc., Racine, Wisconsin
Copyright 1983 by
WESTERN PUBLISHING COMPANY, INC.
RACINE, WISCONSIN 53404

New photographs and "Friedberg" numbering system
Copyright 1983 by Arthur L. Friedberg and Ira S. Friedberg

PREFACE

FOREWORD BY RICHARD S. YEOMAN

It seems hard to believe that collecting modern world coins could have changed so substantially since the first edition of this book was published in 1957.

It almost seems incredible that prior to that time, Americans seemed to little more than dabble in the world of collecting the monies of foreign lands, whose exotic jingle has proved to be so fascinating with time.

That the book has grown in size and scope is readily apparent, but perhaps the most important additions are those which changing economic conditions have wrought, together with the dramatic increase in the popularity of collecting type coins of the world.

Back in 1957, when the first edition was issued, and even in 1974, when the 11th edition was published, the prices of gold and silver did not make a substantial difference in the way that coins were valued. Gold, after all, had remained stable at $35.00 per ounce from 1837 to 1971; even in 1974, when (on December 31st) Americans were finally able to own gold legally, prices remained at affordable levels. (In January of 1974, gold opened at $117.00 per ounce, and by year's end, the price rose to $194.00, only to slide again at the start of the following year. Silver, likewise, remained a pillar of stability. From the high price of 91 cents an ounce in 1957, it did not rise above $1.00 an ounce until 1961, and even in 1974, prices averaged only $4.70, hardly enough to encourage the melting of coins, let alone have a major effect on their price structure.

By contrast, the 1980's brought major changes in the way we collected the coins of foreign lands, and major changes in the way these sought-after collectibles are valued. In the first place, one direct consequence of the gold and silver boom is that the price of silver rose to nearly $50.00 an ounce, while the price of gold approached the $800 mark. This was an extraordinary development, one that was not contemplated (at least initially) even by the most daring of seers. Indeed, it is probably fair to say that if such a change had been contemplated aloud in the last edition of this book, no one would have believed it.

What has happened to the precious metals in our coinage is endemic to what has happened to coin collecting; it has risen steadily—in interest and in value.

Two people who have also witnessed this extraordinary increase and chronicled it in GOLD COINS OF THE WORLD are Arthur Friedberg and Ira Friedberg, two brothers, who have revised the work of the late Robert Friedberg, their father, through several different editions since the book was first published in 1958.

This book and the above one are extraordinarily compatible, and they are similar to each other in the descriptive manner in which they catalog coins—by their type, the way most people collect them.

GOLD COINS OF THE WORLD, of course, starts at the year 600 AD, which is 1200 years before the first coin listed in this catalog, but, for those collecting popular gold coins produced between 1850 and the end of the gold boom marked by World War II, MODERN WORLD COINS will now offer an additional invaluable aid, it will use both the Yeoman catalog numbers and the Friedberg numbers, side by side.

The Friedbergs, together with the contributors listed in the front part of this volume, have revised this, the thirteenth edition, and have also undertaken the revision of CURRENT COINS OF THE WORLD, covering modern issues between 1950 and the present, which now (incredibly) covers almost a 35 year time frame.

To those who have followed MODERN WORLD COINS, it is not surprising that CURRENT COINS OF THE WORLD has continued to grow as this volume has. When issued later this year, it too will prove a valuable addition to any library.

One of the major changes in the new edition of MODERN WORLD COINS has been the introduction of multiple conditions. This gives recognition to the fact that, increasingly, modern world coins are collected (and indeed, are available) as specimen coins, and in uncirculated, as well as in circulated states of preservation. Even after the great melts, as well as with the huge price increases of the past dozen years, foreign coins are still available, and widely collected. They show promise on every level, including, most of all, that at which so many found a challenge when filling in the American coin boards of yesteryear.

In prior volumes, I always offered a word to the beginning collector. You may be young, or you may be retired, you may have consulted this book upon the suggestion of a friend, or the reference librarian at your local library. Someone in your family may have returned from overseas or from a tour in foreign lands with a pocketful of strange coins. This book will tell you what those coins are about.

The country of origin, denomination, relative monetary value, government of the ruling nation, and its geography are all part of the fascinating and wonderful world of coin collecting. If you examine these coins, and let this book guide the way for you, it is entirely possible for you to start your own personal coin collection and be assured in the process of a richly rewarding experience that may last your entire lifetime.

If you are a collector of American coins, you may have reached the point of a waning interest in your present specialty. By moving into the realm of foreign coins, you can begin an entirely different collection obtainable at modest cost—and have the entire world to choose from.

It's easy to collect foreign coins, for even today, most are not collected by date and mintmark, the way American coins are, but rather by type. It is for this reason that the numbering systems in this book are so useful. This is how most coins have been collected for years.

There are dozens of different ways that you can collect foreign coins. You can select gold coins of the world; crown-size coins (approximately U.S. silver dollar-size, though actually 39mm and larger) from various countries; type coins of a particular country; commemorative coins; a single coin from each country; all types of coins from a single country or group of countries; coins of a different variety or design, for example, coins with fishes on them, or coins with foreign rulers. As you get into it, you can view and consider many other areas.

After more than half a century of involvement with the coin field, I must confess to having always retained a strong interest in coins of the world, as opposed to those of a particular country. American coins are certainly involved, and in this volume are listed all but the most recent of commemorative issues, of which there are over 66 different designs and varieties. These, as most of the other coins in this book, can be collected by type since a complete set of dates and mintmarks becomes more and more difficult and expensive to obtain.

This book, then, as revised by Arthur and Ira Friedberg, offers a substantial opportunity to any collector or investor in coins. Clearly, it is a book that belongs in your library, not only for the value, but also for the new information that modern research has disclosed about these wonderful coins.

July, 1983   R. S. Yeoman

AN APPRECIATION OF R. S. YEOMAN

To the coin collector, be it of foreign or American coins, the name Richard S. Yeoman is as synonymous to organization and structure as the name Samuel Johnson is to lexicographers.

An examination of the library catalog of the American Numismatic Association discloses the reason why.

The author of eight major titles, Yeoman has been a prolific author of books, as well as magazine articles. Through the years, he has published on a variety of subjects. "Monies of the Bible," a 1961 work, is an illustrated digest of coins of biblical times complete with scriptural references. His first book "Handbook of United States Coins with a Premium List," known as the Blue Book, was first published in 1942. The following year, he authored "Handbook of United States Type Coins," and four years later, in 1947, he authored the classic "A Guidebook of United States Coins," which is now in its 37th edition, having sold more than 15 million copies, and thus classifying it among the best sellers of all time.

A little later came "Buying and Selling United States Coins," with co-author (and editor of the later editions of many of his works), Kenneth Bressett, and of course, CURRENT COINS OF THE WORLD, first published in 1966, and this book, A CATALOG OF MODERN WORLD COINS, first published in 1957.

In many respects, Yeoman is a consummate renaissance man. His articles in "The Numismatist" have included Commemorative Coins, Emergency Coinage of the California Gold Rush, The American Eagle and Half Eagle, the 1848 Quarter Eagle with CAL., and even Lincoln Cents. He found time, as well, to write for The Young Numismatist, and to serve as Editor-in-Chief of the Whitman Numismatic Journal, which started publication in 1964.

For over 40 years he led Whitman Publishing Company (which became part of Western Publishing Co., and then a division of Mattel) to leadership in the coin industry, ultimately becoming vice president and general manager of the Coin Supply Division and a member of the company's Board of Directors.

Born in Milwaukee in 1904, Yeoman went to the University of Wisconsin and, at the age of 28, became a member of the staff of Whitman Publishing Company in Racine. His initial duties were with sales, sales promotion and advertising, and it was not until two years later, in 1934, that Whitman obtained an order to produce coin boards, and then quickly bought the rights to the product and added them to their regular line of books, stationery supplies and children's games.

Yeoman joined the American Numismatic Association in 1941, and in 1957 was awarded its coveted Farran Zerbe Award, the highest honor the Association can give a member for distinguished service. He served as a member of the Board of Governors of the A.N.A. from 1946 to 1951, and probably has done more than any other individual in modern times to popularize coin collecting in all its various forms.

The ultimate gentleman, Yeoman has been much in demand as a speaker for years. Although now semi-retired in Arizona, he remains a consultant to the Whitman Hobby Division.

I have known Dick Yeo (that is his real name, Yeoman is a pen name) for nearly twenty years, since shortly after I began writing about coins. Unfailingly courteous, always a good source for news or information, he has been accessible as well as reliable, and always a good friend. Even more remarkably, his books MODERN WORLD COINS and CURRENT COINS OF THE WORLD were two desk references that I utilized repeatedly, not only for the valuable information that they contained, but also for the convenience of having a slim, easy to carry volume that could be used almost as a checklist.

The last edition of MODERN WORLD COINS was published nearly five years ago, and without question, a number of changes have taken place within what was once called a hobby. Coin Collecting, today, is a growth industry. Millions of dollars are made each year in the buying and selling of coins. Dick Yeoman's numbering system is utilized, widely, in the foreign coin field. Pick up a coin periodical, any of the weekly publications, and the Yeoman numbering system is the shorthand that is used for copper and silver coins.

The Friedberg numbering system for gold coins has a similar unique status. From the time the late Robert Friedberg initiated the system it obtained an international audience, the same way that the Yeoman classic did for foreign minors, as well as silver crowns. Yet there are marked similarities, at least conceptually, in what both the numbering systems have done, the most systematic of which is the categorization, by type, of the coins of the world.

The amalgamate brought together in this book is distinctive.

It is a tribute to Richard Yeoman that this book is now in its 13th edition, more than a quarter of a century after it was first published. It seems obvious that it is a book destined to be revised and remain in print as the true encyclopedia of the field for many years to come.

July, 1983   David L. Ganz

INTRODUCTION

PURPOSE

This is essentially an introductory coin book, intended as an outline or framework for organizing a collection of type coins of the world. As such, it is useful for beginner and advanced collector alike as a handy source of information to supplement more complex books which list all mints, dates and varieties. A single volume such as this does not illustrate all coins, though every effort is made to show as many as possible. All major or popular varieties a collector will find useful are also listed in this catalog. Medals, patterns and tokens are generally excluded, but bullion issues are included for some of the popular series.

GENERAL INFORMATION

Arrangement

A simple alphabetical sequence is employed for finding each country in this book, regardless of geographical location or government affiliation. This arrangement was decided upon to reduce the use of the index.

Illustrations in every instance are adjacent to corresponding listings and descriptions for easy identification.

Historical and geographical data and monetary equivalents are placed at the beginning of each country group.

In conformity with other Whitman coin books, minor coinage is listed first in each period or type group, followed by more precious metals, silver and gold.

The abbreviation "Br." is for "Bronze," always. "Brass" is not abbreviated, but always spelled out.

Scope

Just over a century—from mid-nineteenth century to about 1964—of coinage of the world is the scope of this book. a logical starting and ending date for each country has been selected.

Listing of Dates

In most instances the first and last known dates of issue for each type are shown (viz. 1898–1911). Coinage during intervening years may not necessarily be continuous. Dates shown are those actually appearing on the coins. For some countries they do not always conform to the year of production. See details of unusual dating systems in the following several pages.

Rare Date Listings

For the first time in this catalog, a substantial number of rare dates are shown separately, just beneath their respective type listings. The usual date span for the type remains unaltered.

Valuations

Prices are given opposite each catalog number, in three columns—for coins in very fine, extremely fine and uncirculated conditions. In every instance these values refer to the commonest date and mint mark if coined in several years or at several mints. The omission of a price usually indicates rarity and no recent sale record, but may also mean lack of information about a newly discovered type or variety. As in other coin reference books, values are approximate and intended only as a guide. Latest prices may be obtained from established coin dealers.

The opinions of many dealers and collectors are combined to arrive at each value. The values shown are not offers to buy or sell but are included only as general information.

Each valuation is for a specific grade as indicated in the price columns. Except where a specific grade is mentioned, better dates are priced in Very Fine condition only.

Numbering System

When a coin type is inserted in a previously established sequence, capital letters A, B, etc. are placed before a catalog number to avoid the necessity of renumbering all later issues. A small letter a, b, etc. following a catalog number indicates a minor difference of a re-issued type, such as a change of metal or size only.

There are instances throughout this catalog where numbers and their corresponding listings have been removed. Reasons are numerous but the most likely causes are: combining with earlier types which are identical except for date, coins discovered to be patterns, medals or otherwise unauthorized pieces. We regret that since earlier editions, occasional renumbering or rearranging has been necessary. This is done only to make the continuity more natural and useful, and is kept to a minimum. In cases of complete country renumbering, the old number is included in parenthesis.

A star preceding a listing indicates that it is the coin illustrated at the top of the group.

For the first time, the numbering system used in Robert Friedberg's standard reference work, GOLD COINS OF THE WORLD is included in another publication. In addition to having a Yeoman catalog number, all gold coins in this volume also have the corresponding Friedberg number. These appear in italics (e.g. F23) either next to or underneath the Yeoman number.

HOW TO DETERMINE THE ORIGIN OF A COIN

First of all, a magnifying glass willl prove useful in reading the legends, symbols, dates and other interesting details on your coin specimens.

Sort your coins as best you can, grouping them by countries, or at least by similar types for later checking. Start with the easy ones, which will probably be coins using our own familiar "English" alphabet, with portraits of monarchs familiar to you and languages which you may recognize immediately, such as German, French, Italian, etc. Country names are often similar to the Anglicized spelling such as NEDERLAND for NETHERLANDS, LIBAN for LEBANON, etc. Bear in mind, however, that there are many colonial issues. Thus, a coin with French legends could be issued for such faraway places as French Indo-China (Indo-Chine Francaise), French West Africa (Afrique Occidentale Francaise) etc.

Many countries, especially in Asia, have alphabets strange to us. Until characteristics of such coins become familiar to you, it is best to page through this volume until you locate illustrations which are similar to the coin. Far from being an arduous task, this phase can be intriguing to a reader with the true collector instinct. If the coin was struck during the past 120 years, the chances are it can be located in this book.

The denomination shown on the coin often is a short cut to identification. SHILLING, CENTAVO, FRANC, etc. are more or less familiar to us and it would be natural to conclude that they belong respectively to Great Britain, Mexico and France. The table of denominations, however, might reveal that this is not necessarily so. A more careful inspection of the coins may show that the SHILLING actually was struck for Southern Rhodesia, the CENTAVO for St. Thomas and Prince Islands and the FRANC for Guadeloupe, where the same coin denominations are or have been used. That is the romance of collecting world coins. The quest is the thing.

   Millimeter Scale

ERAS AND DATING SYSTEMS

Most countries show the date more or less prominently on their coins. Little difficulty will be encountered with the coins of Europe, parts of Africa and the Americas. In the Arabic countries and countries of the Near East and the Orient, however, strange symbols and letters pose a difficult problem of translation both of legends and dates. The chart below shows some of the date numerals now in use throughout the world, while other less common systems are shown with their respective countries.

NUMERALS

	1	2	3	4	5	6	7	8	9	0	10	100	1000
WESTERN	1	2	3	4	5	6	7	8	9	0	10	100	1000
ARABIC	١	٢	٣	٤	٥	٦	٧	٨	٩	•	١•	١••	١•••
ARABIC VARIANTS (Persia, etc.)	١	٢	٣	٣	٥	٦	٧	٨	٩	•			
CHINESE, JAPANESE, KOREAN (Ordinary)	一	二	三	四	五	六	七	八	九		十	百	千
CHINESE, JAPANESE, KOREAN (Official)	壹	貳	叁	肆	伍	陸	柒	捌	玖		拾	(半=½)	
DEVANAGARI (India, Nepal)	९	२	३	४	५	६	७	८	९	०			

Many countries using Arabic numerals observe the Mohammedan Era, also known as the Era of the Hegira (AH or SH), dating from Mohammed's flight from Mecca to Medina in AD 622. This era has traditionally been based on a lunar year of 354 days, or about 3% fewer days than the 365 in our Gregorian (AD) solar year. Mohammedan lunar dates are indicated by the letters AH in this volume. The following method may be used for an approximate conversion of AH to AD dates:

> Example: To convert AH 1330 into AD date.
> 3% of 1330 = 39.90 (closest whole number is 40)
> 1330 − 40 = 1290
> 1290 + 622 = 1912 AD

A few countries such as Afghanistan and Iran have adopted a modification of the Mohammedan calendar based on a solar year of normal length. Such dates are indicated by the letters SH, and the corresponding AD year is found by simply adding 621.

The coins of Thailand use the dating systems of three eras:

1. The "Buddhist" era (abbreviated as BE) which dates from 543 BC; subtract 543 for AD dates. Four numerals are found on current issues.

2. The "Bangkok" or Ratanakosind-sok era (abbreviated as RS) which dates from 1782; add 1781 to convert to an AD date. Dates will have three numerals.

3. The "Little" or Chula Sakarat era (abbreviated as CS) which dates from AD 638; add 638 to convert to AD dates. Dates will have four numerals. Example: AD 1910 would be respectively BE 2453, RS 129 and CS 1271.

Several different eras were observed on the coinage of the INDIA NATIVE STATES.

The VIKRAMA Era has its initial point in 57 BC and is observed mainly in northern India. This is also known as the SAMVAT Era. Their year 1957 is our 1900 AD.

The SAKA Era, originating in the Southwest corner of Northern India, is the dominant era and the great historical reckoning of Southern India. It dates from AD 78 but is based on elapsed years, so that AD equivalents are found by adding 78. Thus, Saka 1822 began in AD 1900.

CHINESE dates are correctly read from right to left. Coins of the Republic, when dated, start with the year 1912 AD. Unlike our own system, some coins of the Chinese Empire are dated according to a 60-year (sexagenary) cycle. Such dates are shown in this book by the abbreviation CD.

Coins with NO DATE are indicated by the abbreviation ND, followed by the date of striking in parentheses when known.

AFGHANISTAN

Afghanistan is a mountainous inland country in south-west Asia bordered by the U.S.S.R., Iran, Pakistan and China. An independent kingdom from 1747 to 1973, it was then proclaimed a republic. Principal exports are hides and agricultural products. Area: 250,000 square miles. Official languages: Persian, Pushtu. Capital: *Kabul.*

The traditional reverse design is the national emblem, a mosque with pulpit, generally over crossed arms. Inscriptions have been mostly in Persian; Pushtu was introduced in 1929 and used exclusively after 1950. Islamic era lunar dating (AH) was used until AH 1337 (1919) and during the period AH 1347-50 (1929-31). In 1919, the solar calendar (SH) was introduced, which was about 40 years earlier than the AH calendar at that time. It was restored in 1931 and has been retained since then. To obtain AD dates from AH and SH dates, see the Introductory section at the front of the book.

Monetary System:

Before AD 1926, 10 Dinar = 1 Paisa; 60 Paisa = 12 Shahi = 6 Sanar = 3 Abbasi = 2 Qiran = 1 Kabuli Rupee.

From 1926, with the introduction of a decimal system, 100 Pul = 1 Afghani; 20 Afghani = 1 Amani.

AMIR ABDUR RAHMAN
AH 1297-1319 (1880-1901)

For crude, "dump" issues of this reign, which preceded the machine-struck types, see Craig, "Coins of the World."

Most early issues listed below are extraordinarily difficult to find in Uncirculated condition.

Copper or Brass

1	1 Paisa AH 1309 (1891) 24mm	35.00	45.00	–
2*	1 Paisa 1309-17 (20-21mm)	5.00	10.00	–
3	1 Shahi 1309, brass (31mm)	30.00	60.00	–
4	100 Dinar 1311 (41mm)	200.00	350.00	–

5	1 Paisa 1317, no wreaths (20mm)	7.50	12.50	–

6	1 Paisa 1317, obv. of No. 5, rev. of No. 2	10.00	15.00	

Silver

All silver of this reign has a toughra in wreath on the obverse, and a mosque in wreath on the reverse, but there are many minor varieties of inscriptions, ornamentation such as stars and weapons, and location of date.

7	1 Sanar 1315 (13mm), 2 vars.	12.50	22.50	–
8	1 Abbasi 1313-14 (15-16mm)	7.50	12.50	–
9	1 Qiran 1308-09 (18-20mm)	7.50	12.50	–
A10	1 Rupee 1304	50.00	80.00	–
10*	1 Rupee 1308-18 (23-26mm)	11.00	20.00	–
11	5 Rupee 1314 (39mm, thick)	50.00	100.00	–

12	5 Rupee 1316 (45mm, thin)	50.00	100.00	–

Gold

A13	1 Tilla 1309 (22mm)	150.00	250.00	
13*	F23 1 Tilla 1313-16 (19-21mm)	125.00	150.00	–
14	F22 2 Tilla 1309 (21mm, 9.1 gm.)	250.00	300.00	–

Unless otherwise noted, prices are for coins in very fine, extremely fine, and uncirculated condition.

AMIR HABIBULLAH

AH 1319–1337 (1901–1919)

First Coinage 1319–21, 25

Designs similar to Nos. 8–10, 12–13
Obv: Toughra in wreath
Rev: Mosque in wreath

Silver

15	1 Abbasi AH 1320 (1902), 16mm	25.00	45.00	–
16	1 Qiran 1320–21, 25 (19mm)	12.50	20.00	–
17*	1 Rupee 1319–21, 25 (25mm)	15.00	20.00	–
18	5 Rupee 1319 (46mm)	50.00	100.00	–

Gold

19	*F24* 1 Tilla 1319–20 (21mm)	125.00	200.00	–

Second Coinage 1321–1329

Brass

Design similar to No. 2

20	1 Paisa AH 1329 (1911), 20mm	12.50	25.00	–

Silver

Obv: Inscription in wreath
Rev: Mosque in wreath

21	1 Sanar 1325–29 (13mm)	10.00	20.00	–
22	1 Abbasi 1324–28 (17mm)	12.50	22.50	–
23	1 Qiran 1323–29 (19mm)	7.50	12.50	–
24*	1 Rupee 1321–29 (25mm)	15.00	20.00	–

25	5 Rupee 1322–29 (45mm)	50.00	100.00	–

Third Coinage 1329–1337

Copper or Brass

Obv: Inscription
Rev: Mosque in sunburst

26	1 Paisa AH 1329–37 (1911–19), 19–22mm	4.50	10.00	–

Silver

27	1 Sanar 1329–37 (13mm)	7.50	15.00	–

Obv: Inscription in wreath
Rev: Mosque in sunburst in wreath

28	1 Abbasi 1329–37 (17mm)	8.00	11.00	–
29*	1 Qiran 1329–37 (20mm)	5.00	9.00	–
30	1 Rupee 1329–37 (25mm)	15.00	20.00	–

Gold

31	*F25* 1 Tilla 1336–37 (21mm)	135.00	200.00	–

AMIR AMANULLAH

AH 1337, SH 1298-1307
(1919-1929)

First Coinage 1337, 1298-1300

Copper or Brass

Obv: Inscription in wreath
Rev: Mosque in sunburst

32 1 Paisa AH 1337, SH
    1298 (1919), 20mm   8.00   15.00   –

Obv: Inscription in stars
Rev: Mosque in sunburst in stars

33 1 Paisa SH 1299-1303
    (20mm)   6.00   12.00   –
34* 1 Shahi AH 1337 (25mm)   20.00   40.00   –
35 1 Sanar AH 1337
    (29-30mm)   15.00   25.00   –
36 3 Shahi AH 1337, SH
    1298-1300 (33mm)   7.50   12.50   –

Billon

37* 1 Abbasi SH 1298
    (20mm)   65.00   95.00   –
38 1 Abbasi SH 1299
    (25mm)   22.50   40.00   –

Silver

Design similar to Nos. 28-31

39* 1 Qiran AH 1337, SH
    1298-1300 (20mm)   6.50   9.50   –

40 1 Rupee AH 1337, SH
    1298-99 (25mm)   15.00   20.00   –

Gold

Design similar to No. 31

41 F27 1 Tilla AH 1337
    (21mm)   85.00 150.00   –
42* F26 2 Tilla SH 1298
    (23mm)   150.00 225.00   –

Second Coinage

Copper

Obv: Toughra in stars
Rev: Mosque in sunburst in stars

43 3 Shahi SH 1300-01
    (33mm)   5.50   7.50   –

Billon

44 1 Abbasi 1299-1303
    (25mm)   4.00   7.00   –

Silver

Obv: Toughra in wreath
Rev: Mosque in sunburst in wreath

45 1 Qiran SH 1300-03
    (20mm)   7.50   10.00   –

46* 1 Rupee 1299–1303
    (27mm)   15.00 20.00   –
47 2½ Rupee 1298–1303
    (34mm)   25.00 40.00   –

Gold

48 *F32* ½ Amani SH 1299
    (16mm)   75.00 125.00   –
49 *F31* 1 Amani 1299
    (22mm)   90.00 150.00   –
50 *F30* 2 Amani 1299–1303
    (24mm)   175.00 250.00   –
51* *F29* 5 Amani 1299
    (34mm)   500.00 850.00   –

Decimal System 1926–
100 Pul = 1 Afghani

Third Coinage

Copper

52 2 Pul SH 1304–05
    (1926–27), 18mm   3.00   5.00   7.00
53 5 Pul 1304–05 (22mm)   3.50   5.50   7.50
54* 10 Pul 1304–06 (24mm)   4.00   5.00   8.00

Silver

55 20 Pul 1304, ND (19mm)   65.00 100.00 175.00

56 ½ Afghani 1304–07
    (25mm)   6.00   7.50 10.00
57* 1 Afghani 1304–07
    (29mm)   12.00 15.00 20.00
58 2½ Afghani 1305–06
    (38mm)   27.50 35.00 60.00

Gold

59* *F35* ½ Amani 1304–06
    (18mm)   50.00 75.00 100.00
60 *F34* 1 Amani 1304–06
    (23mm)   100.00 125.00 175.00
61 *F33* 2½ Amani 1306
    (29mm)   450.00 600.00 900.00

HABIBULLAH GHAZI

(BACHA-I-SAQAO)
AH 1347–1348 (1929)
Lunar Dating Resumed

First Coinage

Copper or Brass

Obv: Horizontal legend

62 20 Paisa AH 1347
    (1929), 25mm   6.00 10.00   –

Silver

63	1 Qiran 1347 (21mm)	10.00	15.00	–
64*	1 Rupee 1347 (25mm)	15.00	20.00	–

Gold

65	*F36* 1 Habibi 1347 (21mm)	225.00 350.00 –

Second Coinage
Copper

Obv: Circular legend

66	10 Paisa 1348 (22mm)	15.00	22.50	–

Silver

67	1 Qiran 1348 (21mm)	25.00	35.00	–
68*	1 Rupee 1347 (26mm)	35.00	50.00	–

MUHAMMAD NADIR SHAH
AH 1348–50, SH 1310–12 (1929–33)
First Coinage-Lunar Dating
Copper or Brass

69	1 Pul AH 1349 (1930), 15mm	1.50	2.00	3.00

70	2 Pul 1348 (18mm)	2.50	3.00	5.00
71	5 Pul 1349–50 (22mm)	2.00	3.00	5.00
72	10 Pul 1348–49 (25mm)	4.00	6.00	9.00
73*	20 Pul 1348–49 (25mm)	4.50	6.50	9.50
74	25 Pul 1349 (25mm)	4.00	6.00	9.00

Silver

75*	½ Afghani 1348–50 (24mm)	6.00	7.50	10.00
76	1 Afghani 1348–50 (30mm)	12.00	15.00	20.00

Gold

78	*F37* 20 Afghani 1349–50 (22mm)	185.00 200.00 250.00

Second Coinage
Solar Dating Resumed
Brass

80	2 Pul SH 1311–14 (1932–35), 18mm	3.00	4.00	5.00
81	5 Pul 1311–14 (21mm)	3.50	5.50	7.50
82*	10 Pul 1311–14 (23mm)	3.75	5.00	8.00

Nos. 80–82 do not bear the name of the ruler and were continued into the reign of Muhammad Zahir.

Unless otherwise noted, prices are for coins in very fine, extremely fine, and uncirculated condition.

Silver

83 ½ Afghani 1310–12
    (24mm)   6.00   7.50   10.00
84 1 Afghani 1310 (27mm) 80.00 100.00 150.00

MUHAMMAD ZAHIR SHAH

SH 1312–1352 (1933–1973)

First Coinage
Also see Nos. 80–82 above

Copper or Brass

85 25 Pul SH 1312–16
    (1933–37), 24–25mm   2.75   5.00   6.50

Silver

86 ½ Afghani 1312–16
    (24mm)   6.00   7.50   10.00

Gold

87 *F39* 1 Tilla 1313 (6gm,
    22mm)   165.00 175.00 200.00

88 *F41* 4 Gram (1 Tilla)
    1315,17 (19mm)   125.00 150.00 175.00
89* *F40* 8 Gram (2 Tilla)
    1314–17 (22mm)   150.00 175.00 225.00

Second Coinage

Bronze

90 2 Pul SH 1316 (1937),
    15mm   .50   1.00   2.00
91 3 Pul 1316 (16mm)   .75   1.50   2.50
92* 5 Pul 1316 (17mm)   .40   .50   .70

Cupro-Nickel

93 10 Pul 1316 (18mm)   .75   1.00   1.50

94 25 Pul 1316 (20mm)   .60   1.00   2.00

Later Issues

Bronze

95 25 Pul SH 1330–32
    (1951–53), 20mm   .30   .50   .75

96 50 Pul 1330 (22mm)   .30   .50   .75

Nickel-Clad Steel

95a 25 Pul 1331–34, edge
    plain or reeded   .30   .50   .75
96a 50 Pul 1331–34   .30   .50   .75

Gold

A102 *F44* 4 Gram (1 Tilla)
  1339/1380   125.00 150.00 200.00
B102 *F42* 8 Gram (2 Tilla)
  1339/1380   250.00 300.00 400.00

Later issues in *Current Coins of the World.*

97 50 Pul 1331   .50   .75   1.00

Aluminum

98* 2 Afghani 1337 (1958)   .75   1.25   2.00

99 5 Afghani 1337   1.00   2.00   3.00

Nickel-Clad Steel

100 1 Afghani 1340 (1961)   .20   .30   .50

101 2 Afghani 1340   .35   .45   .75

102 5 Afghani SH 1340/AH
  1381   .50   1.00   1.50

ALBANIA
(Shqipni, Shqiperi)

The smallest of the Balkan states, Albania lies between Greece and Yugoslavia on the Adriatic coast. It declared independence from the Ottoman Empire in 1912, but underwent many political changes before coming under communist control in 1944. Mountainous terrain has hindered both agriculture and industry, making it Europe's poorest nation. Area: 11,097 square miles. Language: Albanian. Capital: *Tirane.*

Monetary Systems:
1925–31:
100 Qindar Leku = 1 Frang Ar
5 Lek = 1 Frang Ar
1935–38:
100 Qindar Ar = 1 Frang Ar

REPUBLIC 1912–1918

Bronze

1 5 Qindar Leku 1926   10.00 20.00 35.00

2 10 Qindar Leku 1926   15.00 25.00 45.00

Nickel

3 ¼ Leku 1926–27   5.00 10.00 20.00

Gold

Obv: President Zogu. Rev: Eagle

9	F3	10 Franga Ar 1927	–	– 175.00
10	F2	20 Franga Ar		
		1926–27	–	– 250.00

4	½ Lek 1926	3.00	5.00	15.00

5	1 Lek 1926–31	4.00	8.00	15.00

Silver

6	1 Frang Ar 1927–28	50.00	75.00	150.00

11	F1	100 Franga Ar 1926	–	– 950.00
11a	F1	100 Franga Ar 1927	–	– 950.00

(Modified reverse die)

7	2 Franga Ar 1926–28	65.00	110.00	190.00

Obv: George Kastrioti, "Skanderbeg" (1404–68), national hero

12	F4–6	20 Franga Ar		
		1926–27	–	– 350.00

KINGDOM 1928–1939

Amet Zogu as King Zog I

First Coinage

Nickel

Obv: President Amet Zogu

8	5 Franga Ar 1926–27	150.00	225.00	350.00

13	½ Lek 1930–31	2.25	3.50	9.00

No. 5 was also struck during this period.

Second Coinage

Bronze

14	1 Qindar Ar 1935	2.00	4.00	8.00
15	2 Qindar Ar 1935	3.00	5.00	10.00

20	*F12* 20 Franga Ar 1937	–	–	450.00
21	*F11* 100 Franga Ar 1937	–	–	1450.

Silver

16	1 Frang Ar 1935, 37	7.50	15.00	35.00
17	2 Franga Ar 1935	15.00	25.00	60.00

Marriage of King Zog

Gold

25th Anniversary
of Independence

Silver

Dated 28 XI (Nov 28) 1912–37

18*	1 Frang Ar 1937	9.50	17.50	37.50
19	2 Franga Ar 1937	17.50	35.00	65.00

Gold

Dated 27 IV (April 27) 1938

22	*F14* 20 Franga Ar 1938	–	–	450.00

23	*F13* 100 Franga Ar 1938	–	–	1450.

Unless otherwise noted, prices are for coins in very
fine, extremely fine, and uncirculated condition.

10th Anniversary of Reign

Gold

Dated 1 IX (Sept. 1) 1928–38

24	F17	20 Franga Ar 1938	–	– 450.00
25	F16	50 Franga Ar 1938	–	– 950.00
26	F15	100 Franga Ar 1938	–	– 1450.

VITTORIO EMANUELE III
of Italy,
as King of Albania 1939–43

1 Lek = 1 Lira

Aluminum-Bronze

27	0.05 Lek 1940–41	1.50	2.50	5.00
	1941 . . . 4			

28	0.10 Lek 1940–41	2.00	3.50	5.00
	1941 . . . 40			

Stainless Steel

Two different alloys were used for Nos. 29–32: non-magnetic in 1939 and part of 1940, and magnetic in the balance of 1940 through 1941.

29	0.20 Lek 1939–41	1.25	2.00	4.00

30	0.50 Lek 1939–41	1.50	2.25	4.00
31	1 Lek 1939–41, like			
	No.29	1.50	2.50	6.00
32	2 Lek 1939–41, Like No.			
	30	2.00	4.00	8.00

Dates after 1939 of Nos. 31–32 not for circulation.

Silver

33	5 Lek 1939	10.00	15.00	25.00
34	10 Lek 1939, head right	30.00	40.00	80.00

PEOPLE'S REPUBLIC 1946–

Zinc

35	½ Leku 1947, 57	.50	.75	1.50
36	1 Lek 1947, 57	.50	.75	1.75
37	2 Leke 1947, 57	.50	1.00	1.75
38	5 Leke 1947, 57	.75	1.50	2.25

Later issues in *Current Coins of the World.*

ALGERIA (Algerie)

An Islamic state on the Mediterranean coast of north Africa, Algeria was nominally part of the Ottoman Empire until being colonized by France in the 19th century. It became an independent republic in 1962. Although much of the country is desert, it has petroleum and other minerals, while the coastal plain is highly agricultural. Area: 919,951 square miles. Languages: Arabic, French, Berber dialects. Capital: *Algiers.*

Monetary System:
100 Centimes = 1 Franc

French Colony 1830–1962
France No. 89 (2 Francs 1944) was also issued in Algeria during World War II.

Postwar Issues

Cupro-Nickel

1	20 Francs 1949, 56	.35	1.00	3.50
2	50 Francs 1949	.35	1.00	4.00
3	100 Francs 1950, 52	.50	1.25	6.00

Later issues in *Current Coins of the World.*

ANGOLA

A large territory on the west coast of Africa, Angola was under Portuguese control from the 1500's to 1975. Following a civil war, a people's republic was proclaimed that year. Having important mineral resources, it exports coffee, petroleum, diamonds, and iron ore. Area: 481,-351 square miles. Languages: Portuguese, many native tongues. Capital: *Luanda.*

Monetary System:
5 Centavos = 1 Macuta to 1928
100 Centavos = 1 Angolar 1926–52
100 Centavos = 1 Escudo 1914–26; 1952–75

Bronze

12	1 Centavo 1921	8.00	20.00	50.00
13	2 Centavos 1921	25.00	30.00	75.00
14	5 Centavos 1921–24	7.00	15.00	35.00
	1924 Unc . . . 100			

Cupro-Nickel

15	10 Centavos 1921–23	5.00	10.00	35.00
	1921 Unc . . . 60			
16	20 Centavos 1921–22	5.00	8.50	35.00

Nickel

17*	50 Centavos 1922–23	6.00	12.50	27.50

Nickel-Bronze
Value in centavos and macutas

18	5 Centavos 1927	3.00	8.00	22.50
19	10 Centavos 1927–28	3.00	7.50	18.00
20*	20 Centavos 1927–28	4.00	8.00	27.50
21	50 Centavos 1927–28	7.00	15.00	60.00

New Coinage System

Bronze

22	10 Centavos 1948–49	.50	1.00	5.00
23	20 Centavos 1948–49	.50	1.00	5.00

Nickel-Brass

24	50 Centavos 1948, 50	1.00	2.00	7.50

Decree of Jan. 21, 1952
COLONIA DE Omitted
Bronze

23a	20 Centavos 1962	.20	.25	1.00

Unless otherwise noted, prices are for coins in very fine, extremely fine, and uncirculated condition.

25	50 Centavos 1953–62	.10	.20	1.00
26	1 Escudo 1953–74	.20	.50	1.50

Cupro-Nickel

27	2½ Escudos 1953–74	.25	.50	1.50

Silver

28	10 Escudos 1952, 55	2.00	4.00	7.50
29	20 Escudos 1952, 55	3.50	6.00	11.00

Later issues in *Current Coins of the World.*

ANNAM

Now part of Vietnam, formerly one of the states of French Indo-China; located along the coast of the South China Sea. Produces spices, silk, rice, rubber and minerals. Language: Khmer. Capital: *Hue.*

THANH THAI 1889–1907

Cast Coins

1	1 Sapeque Brass (rev. blank)	5.00	10.00	15.00
2*	10 Sapeque Copper or Brass (rev. value)	3.00	5.00	10.00
A3	1 Lang Silver	400.00	600.00	800.00

Gold

A4	*F75*	1 Tien	400.00	600.00	800.00
A5	*F76*	3 Tien	500.00	750.00	900.00
A6	*F79*	4 Tien	500.00	750.00	900.00
A7	*F74*	1 Lang	1000.	1250.	1750.
A8	*F73*	1 Lang Bar	800.00	1000.	1250.

DUY TAN 1907–1916

Brass

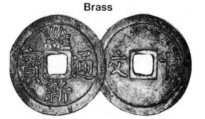

3	10 Sapeque (rev. value)	1.00	3.00	5.00

KHAI DINH 1916–1926

Copper Alloy

4	1 Sapeque (cast)	2.00	3.00	5.00
5*	1 Sapeque (struck)	1.00	2.00	3.00

BAO DAI 1926–1945

Brass

6	1 Sapeque (rev. blank), small planchet	3.00	5.00	10.00

6a	1 Sapeque (rev. blank), large planchet	1.00	3.00	5.00

ARABIAN SULTANATES (Hadhramaut)

Small semi-independent sultanates under British control in the former East Aden protectorate, now part of the Southern Yemen Republic. At one time these sultanates were sovereign states, extending along the lower coast of the Arabian Peninsula and into the "Empty Quarter." Languages: Arabic and English.

QUAITI STATE
Sultan Monasar bin Abdullah

Coinage of East Africa, British East India Company, and Maria Theresa Thalers counterstamped in Arabic, both copper and silver (dated 1307).

c/s = counterstamp

Prices in this section are for counter-stamps in Very Fine condition.
Copper

A1	¹/₁₂ Anna size, small c/s	20.00
1*	¼ Anna size, small c/s	15.00
1a	¼ Anna size, large c/s	15.00
2*	½ Anna size, large c/s	25.00
2a	½ Anna size, small c/s	20.00

Silver
3	½ Rupee size, small c/s	27.50
4	½ Rupee size, large c/s	30.00
5	1 Rupee size, small c/s	32.50
6	1 Rupee size, large c/s	35.00
7	1 Ryal (Crown), small c/s	50.00
7a	1 Ryal (Crown). large c/s	55.00

The following prices are for coins in Very Fine condition.

Sultan Nawaz Bin Omer
Copper

8	5 Chomsihs AH 1315 (1897)	20.00

9	5 Chomsihs 1318 (1900)	22.50

SULTANATE OF MUKALLA
Sultan Al Nakib Salah

1	½ Chomsihs Ah 1276 (1859)	90.00
2*	1 Chomsihs 1276	80.00

LAHEJ
Small semi-independent Sultanate just north of the city of Aden in the former West Aden Protectorate.

Monetary System:
128 Pessa (Pice) = 1 Indian Rupee

Sultan Ali Mohasan 1849–1863
Copper

1	½ Pessa ND (1860)	20.00

Sultan Fazal Bin Ali 1874–1898

2	½ Pessa ND (1896)	22.50

Date AH 1291 (1874) on coin is accession date.

TARIM AND GHURFAH (Cities)
Located in the Hadhramaut in the southern part of Arabia (East Aden Protectorate). This has been a passageway rather than a developed country. Most of the area is desert wadies which in earlier times were used by wandering tribes.

Monetary System:
120 Chomsih (Chamsi) = 1 Riyal (Maria Theresa Thaler)

For TARIM
Copper

A1	1 Chomsih AH 1258 (1842), thin	22.50
A2*	3 Chomsih AH 1258, thick	37.50

Silver

A3 30 Chomsih AH 1258, thick 37.50
Several die varieties exist for Nos. A1–A3.
A4 4 Chomsih AH 1270 (1853) 70.00
A5 8 Chomsih 1270 75.00
A6 16 Chomsih 1270 100.00

1 6 Chomsih AH 1315 (1897),
11.5mm 6.00
2 12 Chomsih 1315 (17mm) 8.50
3* 24 Chomsih 1315 (21mm) 16.00
Nos. 1–3 were occasionally struck to 1926.

For GHURFAH,

A town in Kathiri State 30 miles southwest of Tarim.

Silver

4 4 Chomsih AH 1344 (1926),
11.5mm 37.50
6 8 Chomsih 1344 (14mm) 45.00
8 15 Chomsih 1344 (18mm) 30.00
10* 30 Chomsih 1344 (22mm) 30.00
11 45 Chomsih 1344 (24.5mm) 300.00
12 60 Chomsih 1344 (27.5mm)

ARGENTINA

Republic occupying the major portion of southern South America. One of the world's largest exporters of meats and linseed; ranks high in the production of corn, wool, wheat, hides and skins. Area: 1,072,067 square miles. Language: Spanish. Capital: *Buenos Aires.*

Monetary System:
100 Centavos = 1 Peso
5 Pesos = 1 Argentino

Bronze

1 1 Centavo 1882–96 .50 2.00 10.00
2 2 Centavos 1882–96 .50 2.50 15.00

Silver

3 10 Centavos 1881–83 1.50 3.00 12.00
   1881 . . . 250.
4 20 Centavos 1881–83 3.00 6.00 20.00
   1881 . . . 100.
5 50 Centavos 1881–83 6.00 12.00 45.00
   1881 . . . 450.
6 1 Peso 1881–83 65.00 125.00 350.00

Gold

10 *F16* ½ Argentino 1884 500.00 1000. 2000.
11* *F14* 1 Argentino
   1881–96 130.00 165.00 275.00

Cupro-Nickel

7 5 Centavos 1896–1942 .15 .75 3.00
8 10 Centavos 1896–1942 .15 1.00 4.00
9 20 Centavos 1896–1942 .15 1.25 5.00

Nickel

14 50 Centavos 1941 .25 .75 2.00

Bronze

12 1 Centavo 1939–44 .25 .50 2.00
13 2 Centavos 1939–47 .35 .75 2.00

Copper, Crude

12a 1 Centavo 1945–48 .35 .75 3.00
13a 2 Centavos 1947–50 .35 .75 3.00

Aluminum-Bronze

15 5 Centavos 1942–50 .20 .50 3.00
16 10 Centavos 1942–50 .20 .50 3.00
17 20 Centavos 1942–50 .30 .60 4.00

Centennial Death of San Martin
Cupro-Nickel

18	5 Centavos 1950	.25	1.00	5.00
19	10 Centavos 1950	.25	1.00	5.00
20	20 Centavos 1950	.50	2.00	6.00

Regular Issues
Cupro-Nickel

Edge: Reeded

21	5 Centavos 1951–53	.15	.40	1.00
22	10 Centavos 1951–52	.15	.40	1.00
23	20 Centavos 1951–52	.20	.45	2.00

Copper-Nickel Clad Steel
Edge: Plain

21a	5 Centavos 1953–56	.10	.15	.30
22a	10 Centavos 1952–56	.10	.15	.40
23a	20 Centavos 1952–56	.10	.20	.50
24	50 Centavos 1952–56	.15	.30	1.00

Note: Smaller bust on Nos. 21a–23a, 1954 and later.

Nickel-Clad Steel

25	5 Centavos 1957–59	–	–	.25
26	10 Centavos 1957–59	–	–	.25
27	20 Centavos 1957–61	–	–	.25
28	50 Centavos 1957–61	–	–	.35
29	1 Peso 1957–62	–	–	.50

Sesquicentennial of Provisional Government

30	1 Peso 1960	–	–	1.00

Regular Issues

31	5 Pesos 1961–68	–	–	.35

32	10 Pesos 1962–68	–	–	.50

33	25 Pesos 1964–68	–	–	.80

Sesquicentennial of Independence

34	10 Pesos 1966	–	–	.80

80th Anniversary Death of Sarmiento

35	25 Pesos 1968	–	–	1.00

Later issues in *Current Coins of the World.*

AUSTRALIA

An island continent between the Pacific and Indian Oceans, Australia is a dominion of the British Commonwealth. Industrial development is strong; exports include wheat, wool and minerals. Most of the people live in a few major cities, and large areas of the arid interior are uninhabited. Area: 2,967,909 square miles. Language: English. Federal capital: *Canberra*.

Monetary System:
12 Pence = 1 Shilling
2 Shillings = 1 Florin
5 Shillings = 1 Crown
20 Shillings = 1 Pound (Sovereign)

Gold
Australian mints at Melbourne, Perth and Sydney struck Sovereigns and ½ Sovereigns from 1871 to 1931 with mintmarks M, P, and S. The designs are standard British types.

VICTORIA 1837–1901
Young Head
Designs like Great Britain Nos. 13–15

A1	*F13–14* ½ Sovereign 1871–87	250.00	500.00	900.00

B1	*F11–12* 1 Sovereign 1871–87 (Rev. Shield)	130.00	150.00	225.00
C1	*F15–16* 1 Sovereign 1871–87 (Rev. St. George)	130.00	150.00	225.00

JUBILEE HEAD
Designs of Great Britain Nos. 28–29

D1	*F21–22* ½ Sovereign 1887–93	70.00	100.00	150.00
E1	*F 19–20* 1 Sovereign 1887–93	130.00	140.00	200.00

OLD HEAD
Designs as Great Britain Nos. 42–43

F1	*F26–29* ½ Sovereign 1893–1901	75.00	100.00	140.00
G1	*F23–25* 1 Sovereign 1893–1901	130.00	140.00	160.00

EDWARD VII 1901–1910
Silver

1	3 Pence 1910	15.00	35.00	95.00
2	6 Pence 1910	25.00	70.00	200.00
3	1 Shilling 1910	50.00	125.00	325.00
4	1 Florin/2 Shillings 1910	200.00	400.00	1500.

Gold
Designs like Great Britain Nos. 56–57

A5	*F35–37* ½ Sovereign 1902–10	90.00	105.00	140.00
B5	*F32–34* 1 Sovereign 1902–10	150.00	165.00	180.00

GEORGE V 1910–1936
Bronze

5	½ Penny 1911–36	1.00	10.00	70.00
			Proof . . . 750.00	
6	1 Penny 1911–36	1.00	15.00	75.00
	1930 . . . Rare		Proof . . . 750.00	

Silver

9	3 Pence 1911–36	5.00	15.00	50.00
10	6 Pence 1911–36	5.00	15.00	75.00
11	1 Shilling 1911–36	15.00	35.00	100.00
12	1 Florin 1911–36	15.00	50.00	200.00
	1932 . . . 650			

Gold
Designs like Great Britain Nos. 77–78

A13	*F41–43* ½ Sovereign 1911–18	65.00	70.00	110.00
	1918 . . . Rare			
B13	*F38–40* 1 Sovereign 1911–31	125.00	135.00	165.00

COMMEMORATIVE ISSUES
Establishment of Parliament at Canberra
Silver

7	1 Florin 1927	15.00	25.00	50.00
		Proof . . . 1500.		

Centennial of Victoria and Melbourne

8	1 Florin "1934–35" on coin	300.00	400.00	500.00

GEORGE VI 1936–1952
Bronze

13	½ Penny 1938–39	.50	5.00	25.00
		Proof . . . 350.00		

14	½ Penny 1939–48	.25	3.00	15.00
		Proof 500.00		

15	1 Penny 1938–48	.25	3.00	15.00
		Proof . . . 750.00		

Silver

Note: In 1946, the fineness was reduced from .925 to .500

16	3 Pence 1938–44	.75	1.50	3.00
16a	3 Pence 1947–48	1.00	2.50	5.00

17	6 Pence 1938–45	1.50	3.00	15.00
17a	6 Pence 1946, 48	2.00	5.00	15.00
18	1 Shilling 1938–44	4.00	7.50	15.00
18a	1 Shilling 1946, 48	5.00	10.00	25.00

19	1 Florin 1938–45	5.00	10.00	20.00
19a	1 Florin 1946–47	4.00	7.50	15.00

20	1 Crown 1937–38	15.00	35.00	100.00
		Proof . . . 1250.		

Unless otherwise noted, prices are for coins in very fine, extremely fine, and uncirculated condition.

IND: IMP: omitted from obv. legend

Bronze

21	½ Penny 1949–52	.25	2.50	10.00
		Proof . . . 500.00		
22	1 Penny 1949–52	.25	2.00	5.00
		Proof . . . 500.00		

Fifty Year Jubilee

Silver

23	1 Florin 1951	5.00	10.00	20.00

Regular Issues
Designs like Nos. 16–19

24	3 Pence 1949–52	.75	2.50	5.00
25	6 Pence 1950–52	2.50	5.00	15.00
26	1 Shilling 1950, 52	3.00	6.00	15.00
27	1 Florin 1951–52	7.00	15.00	30.00

ELIZABETH II 1952–

Bronze

28	½ Penny 1953–56	.50	3.00	10.00

29	1 Penny 1953	1.00	3.00	15.00

Silver

30	3 Pence 1953–54	2.50	5.00	10.00
31	6 Pence 1953–54	1.50	3.00	6.00
32	1 Shilling 1953–54	3.00	6.00	15.00

33	1 Florin 1953–54	5.00	10.00	20.00

Royal Visit Commemorative

34	1 Florin 1954	3.50	7.00	15.00

Regular Issues

Obv: F: D: added to legend

Bronze

35	½ Penny 1959–64	.25	.75	2.00
		Proof . . . 50.00		
36	1 Penny 1955–64	.25	.75	2.00
		Proof . . . 75.00		

Silver

37	3 Pence 1955–64	.50	1.00	2.00
		Proof . . . 40.00		
38	6 Pence 1955–63	1.00	2.00	4.00
		Proof . . . 40.00		
39	1 Shilling 1955–63	1.75	3.50	7.00
		Proof . . . 40.00		
40	1 Florin 1956–63	4.00	6.00	10.00
		Proof . . . 40.00		

Later issues in *Current Coins of the World.*

AUSTRIA (Oesterreich)

A republic in central Europe, Austria is noted for both industrial and agricultural production. Tourism is an important industry. Chief exports include metals and metal products, chemicals, textiles, paper, and machinery. Area: 32,369 square miles. Language: German. Capital: Vienna.

Monetary System:
100 Kreuzer = 1 Florin (Gulden) 1857–92
1½ Florin = 1 Vereinsthaler
100 Heller = 1 Krone 1892–1923
10,000 Kronen = 1 Schilling 1923–24
100 Groschen = 1 Schilling 1924–

FRANZ JOSEPH I
1848–1916
I. Vereinsmunzen (1857–68)

"Convention Money" struck for circulation throughout the Austrian and German states observing the monetary agreement of 1857.

Regular Issues

First Obv: portrait with light sideburns

Silver

1*	1 Vereinsthaler 1857–65	40.00	75.00	110.00
2	2 Vereinsthaler 1865	1000.	1500.	2250.

Gold

4	F413–416 ½ Krone 1858–65	350.00	600.00	900.00
5*	F408–412 1 Krone 1858–65	450.00	750.00	1250.

Second obv: portrait with heavier beard

Silver

1a*	1 Vereinsthaler 1866–67	40.00	75.00	125.00
2a	2 Vereinsthaler 1866–67	400.00	750.00	1250.

Gold

4a	F413 ½ Krone 1866	750.00	1250.	1750.
5a	F408 1 Krone 1866	1000.	1750.	2500.

COMMEMORATIVE ISSUES

Silver

Opening of Vienna-Trieste Railway

3	2 Vereinsthaler 1857	1000.	1500.	2000.

3rd German Shooting Fest

A16	1 Thaler 1868	75.00	125.00	175.00
			Proof . . .	200.00

Unless otherwise noted, prices are for coins in very fine, extremely fine, and uncirculated condition.

Opening of Mt. Raxalpe Inn

A20 1 Thaler 1877 2000. 3000. 3750.
No. A20 was issued strictly for presentation, and was struck long after the formal end of the Vereinsthaler system.

II. Landesmunzen (1857–92)

Subsidiary coinage for circulation within the Austro-Hungarian Empire alone. Note that after 1868 Hungary had a separate coinage, but that the money of the two countries continued interchangeable.

Regular Issues

Copper

6	⁵⁄₁₀ Kreuzer 1858–91	1.00	4.00	10.00
7	1 Kreuzer 1858–91	.75	1.50	3.00
8	4 Kreuzer 1860–64	5.00	12.50	20.00

First obv: portrait with light sideburns
Billon

9	5 Kreuzer 1858–64	2.00	5.00	10.00
10	10 Kreuzer 1858–65	4.00	10.00	40.00

Silver

13	¼ Florin 1857–59, large eagle	10.00	15.00	25.00

14	¼ Florin 1859–65, small eagle	7.50	12.50	20.00

15	1 Florin 1857–65	7.50	15.00	25.00
16	2 Florin 1859–65	75.00	110.00	175.00
	1860A . . . 1000			

Gold

23*	*F393–396* 1 Dukat 1860–65	60.00	100.00	150.00
25	*F382–383* 4 Dukaten 1860–65	500.00	800.00	1100.

Similar gold types dated 1852–59 with a younger portrait were issued both before and after the Monetary Convention of 1857.

Second obv: portrait with heavier beard
(as No. 11)
Billon

9a	5 Kreuzer 1867	100.00	175.00	275.00
10a	10 Kreuzer 1867	100.00	175.00	275.00

Silver

14a	¼ Florin 1866	125.00	200.00	350.00
15a	1 Florin 1866	60.00	110.00	150.00
16a	2 Florin 1866–67	110.00	175.00	250.00

Gold

23a	*F397–400* 1 Dukat 1866	75.00	140.00	190.00
25a	*F384* 4 Dukaten 1866	400.00	700.00	1100.

New Reverse Legend:
LOMB. ET VEN. omitted
Billon

11	10 Kreuzer 1868–72	.75	2.00	5.50
12	20 Kreuzer 1868–72	2.75	7.00	12.00

Silver
Designs similar to Nos. 14a–25a

14b	¼ Florin 1867–71	50.00	90.00 150.00
15b	1 Florin 1867–72	20.00	35.00 55.00
16b	2 Florin 1867–72	85.00	140.00 200.00

Gold

23b	*F397–399* 1 Dukat		
	1867–72	65.00	90.00 130.00
25b	*F384* 4 Dukaten		
	1867–72	400.00	700.00 1100.

Silver
Third obv: older head

14c	¼ Florin 1872–75	85.00	150.00 240.00
15c	1 Florin 1872–92	6.50	13.00 20.00
16c	2 Florin 1872–92	50.00	90.00 160.00

Gold

23c	*F401–403* 1 Dukat		
	1872–1915	65.00	80.00 100.00
25c	*F385–386* 4 Dukaten		
	1872–1915	225.00	275.00 325.00

Nos. 23c and 25c dated 1915 are official restrikes. These trade at only a slight premium over their bullion value. In 1915, the mint, in error, struck some ducats dated 1951.

Trade Coinage
Gold

21	*F420* 4 Florin/10 Francs	
	1870–92	90.00 150.00 190.00
22	*F419* 8 Florin/20 Francs	
	1870–92	100.00 120.00 140.00

Nos. 21–22 were struck on the standard of the Latin Monetary Union to facilitate foreign trade. Coins dated 1892 have been officially restruck in recent years.

COMMEMORATIVE SERIES
Silver
Pribram Mine

17	1 Florin 1875	250.00 425.00 525.00

Vienna Shooting Fest

18	2 Florin 1873	1100. 1600. 2000.

Unless otherwise noted, prices are for coins in very fine, extremely fine, and uncirculated condition.

A18 *F417* 4 Dukaten gold
1873   2000. 2500. 3250.
             Proof . . . 5000.

Silver Wedding Anniversary

Rev: Date in Roman numerals
19 2 Gulden (on edge) 1879   30.00 50.00 70.00

Reopening of Kuttenberg Mines

Rev: Date in Roman numerals
20 2 Florin 1887   1400. 1750. 2500.
             Proof . . . 3000.

50th Anniversary of Reign

Gold

24 *F387* 1 Dukat 1848–51,
date 1898 below eagle   250.00 350.00 475.00

KRONE STANDARD
Regular Issues

Bronze

26	1 Heller 1892–1916	.30	.60	1.50
	1892 . . . 175			
28	2 Heller 1892–1915	.30	.60	1.75
	1892 . . . 175			

Nickel

29*	10 Heller 1892–1911	.40	.60	1.50
	1892 . . . 250			
30	20 Heller 1892–1914	.60	1.25	2.25

Silver

Obv: Laureate head

35	1 Krone 1892–1907	2.75	6.00	13.00
	1892 . . . 150			
39	5 Kronen 1900, 07	15.00	35.00	60.00

Gold

42	*F422–423* 10 Kronen			
	1892–1906	50.00	65.00	75.00
	1892 . . . 750			
43	*F421* 20 Kronen			
	1892–1905	100.00	115.00	125.00
	1900 . . . 400			

Silver
Obv: Small plain bust (as No. 36)

41	5 Kronen 1909	20.00	45.00	85.00

Gold

47	*F423* 10 Kronen 1909	50.00	65.00	75.00
48	*F421* 20 Kronen 1909	650.00	900.00	1250.

Silver
Obv: Large plain head by Schwartz

37	1 Krone 1912–16	2.50	3.50	7.50

38	2 Kronen 1912–13	4.00	4.50	9.00
A41	5 Kronen 1909	20.00	40.00	75.00

Gold

49	*F428* 10 Kronen			
	1909–12	50.00	65.00	75.00
50	*F425–426* 20 Kronen			
	1909–16	120.00	160.00	200.00

51 *F424* 100 Kronen
1909–15   650.00 800.00   1250.
                                            Proof . . . 1500.

No. 49 dated 1912 and Nos. 50–51 dated 1915 are official restrikes.

60th Anniversary of Reign

Silver

36	1 Krone 1908	3.25	7.00	14.00

40	5 Kronen 1908	17.50	27.50	60.00
				Proof . . . 450.00

Gold

44	*F431* 10 Kronen 1908	50.00	75.00	90.00
45	*F430* 20 Kronen 1908	140.00	175.00	250.00

46	*F429* 100 Kronen 1908	700.00	1100.	1600.
				Proof . . . 1800.

Unless otherwise noted, prices are for coins in very fine, extremely fine, and uncirculated condition.

World War I Issues
Copper-Nickel-Zinc

31 10 Heller 1915–16 .25 .50 1.00

Obv: Eagle with Austrian shield
Bronze

27 1 Heller 1916 .25 .75 1.50

Copper-Nickel-Zinc
32 10 Heller 1916 .90 1.50 5.00

Iron

33 2 Heller 1916–18 .20 .50 1.00
34 20 Heller 1916–18 .25 .75 1.50

Gold

52 *F427* 20 Kronen 1916 450.00 800.00 1200.

Trade Coin
Silver

55 1 Thaler 1780 11.50 12.00 15.00
Proof . . . 17.50
An unofficial "trade dollar," the final date of the famous Maria Theresa Thaler has been struck intermittently to modern times at many world mints. It has been used in many areas that lacked a firm local coinage, particularly in north and east Africa and the Near East.

REPUBLIC 1918–38
Monetary Law of December 21, 1923

Bronze

56 100 Kronen 1923–24 .75 1.25 3.00

57 200 Kronen 1924 1.50 2.25 3.50

Cupro-Nickel

58 1000 Kronen 1924 2.75 4.75 8.00

Bullion Coins
Gold

80	F434 20 Kronen
	1923-24

850.00 1250. 1500.

81	F433 100 Kronen
	1923-24

1300. 1750. 2250.
Proof . . . 2750.

Coinage Reform
of December 20, 1924
Silver

59 1 Schilling 1924   3.25   5.00   8.00

Bronze

60 1 Groschen 1925-38   .75   1.25   3.00
    1931 . . . 15 1938 . . . 6

61 2 Groschen 1925-38   .75   1.25   3.00
    1934 . . . 15 1938 . . . 6

Cupro-Nickel

62 5 Groschen 1931-38   .60   1.10   2.25
    1937 . . . 45 1938 . . . 250

63 10 Groschen 1925,
    28-29   .75   1.25   2.75

Silver

67 ½ Schilling 1925-26   2.00   3.75   7.00

68 1 Schilling 1925-26, 32 2.00   4.25   6.00
    1932 . . . 60

Cupro-Nickel

64 50 Groschen 1934   40.00   55.00   75.00
    Proof . . . 150.00

65 50 Groschen 1935-36   2.25   3.50   8.00
    1936 . . . 70   Proof . . . 65.00

Unless otherwise noted, prices are for coins in very
fine, extremely fine, and uncirculated condition.

Mozart

66 1 Schilling 1934–35   2.00   3.50   7.00
                                    Proof . . . 100.00

72 2 Schilling 1931   20.00 30.00 50.00
                                 Proof . . . 225.00

COMMEMORATIVE SERIES
1928–1937

Silver

Franz Schubert

Haydn

73 2 Schilling 1932   50.00 70.00 100.00
                                 Proof . . . 325.00

69 2 Schilling 1928   6.50   11.00   14.00
                                 Proof . . . 300.00

Dr. Seipel

Dr. Theodor Billroth

74 2 Schilling 1932   30.00 45.00 65.00
                                 Proof . . . 250.00

70 2 Schilling 1929   14.00 20.00 35.00

von der Vogelweide

Dr. Dollfuss

71 2 Schilling 1930   8.00 17.50 27.50
   Also see Germany No. 71   Proof . . . 140.00

75 2 Schilling 1934   15.00 22.50 35.00
                                 Proof . . . 150.00

Dr. Lueger

76 2 Schilling 1935   17.50 25.00 40.00
                                            Proof . . . 150.00

Prince Eugen

77 2 Schilling 1936   12.50 17.50 32.50
                                            Proof . . . 140.00

Karlskirche in Vienna

78 2 Schilling 1937   12.50 17.50 27.50
                                            Proof . . . 140.00

Regular Issues

79 5 Schilling 1934–36   25.00 35.00 55.00
        1936 . . . 110   Proof . . . 250.00

Gold

82 *F435* 25 Schilling
        1926–34   95.00 125.00 150.00
                                            Proof . . . 200.00

83 *F436* 100 Schilling
        1926–34   375.00 450.00 525.00
                                            Proof . . . 650.00

Rev: St. Leopold
84 *F439–440* 25 Schilling
        1935–38   450.00 600.00 750.00
        1938 . . . 8000   Proof . . . 950.00

Rev: Madonna of Maria Zell
85 *F437–438* 100 Schilling
        1935–38   900.00 1350. 1750.
        1938 . . . 9500   Proof . . . 2000.

REPUBLIC
RE-ESTABLISHED 1945–

Zinc

86 1 Groschen 1947   .20   .35   .85

87 5 Groschen 1948–   .10   .15   .25
                                          Proof 50

88 10 Groschen 1947–49   .25   1.75   3.00
                                          Proof . . . 5.00

Aluminum

89 2 Groschen 1950–   .10   .15   .20
                                          Proof 50

90 10 Groschen 1951   .10   .15   .20
                                          Proof 50

91 50 Groschen 1946–55   .25   .60   1.25
                                          Proof . . . 25.00

92 1 Schilling 1946–57   .40   .90   2.50
                                          Proof . . . 30.00

93 2 Schilling 1946–52   1.25   2.50   6.00
        1952 . . . 225   Proof . . . 45.00

94 5 Schilling 1952, 57   1.75   4.00   7.00
        1957 . . . 300   Proof . . . 45.00

Aluminum-Bronze

95 20 Groschen 1950–54   .40   .75   2.25
                                          Proof . . . 17.50

103 50 Groschen 1959–   .10   .15   .20
                                          Proof 50

104 1 Schilling 1959–   .10   .20   .30
Proof 50

Silver

106 5 Schilling 1960–68   1.75   1.85   2.50
Proof . . . 2.50

99 10 Schilling 1957–73   2.50   2.75   3.50
Proof . . . 3.50

COMMEMORATIVE ISSUES
Reopening of Bundestheater

96 25 Schilling 1955   10.00   15.00   22.50
Proof . . . 85.00

Bicentennial Birth of Mozart

97 25 Schilling 1956   5.00   6.00   7.50
Proof . . . 300.00

8th Centennial
Maria Zell Cathedral

98 25 Schilling 1957   5.00   6.00   7.50
Proof . . . 300.00

Centennial Birth of von Welsbach

100 25 Schilling 1958   5.00   6.00   7.50
Proof . . . 1350.

Tirol Sesquicentennial

Rev: Andreas Hofer
101 50 Schilling 1959   9.00   10.00   12.50
Proof . . . 450.00

Centennial Death of Archduke Johann

102 25 Schilling 1959   5.00   6.00   8.00
Proof . . . 275.00

Unless otherwise noted, prices are for coins in very
fine, extremely fine, and uncirculated condition.

40th Anniversary
Carinthian Plebiscite

105 25 Schilling 1960   6.00   8.00 12.00
Proof . . . 375.00

40th Anniversary-Burgenland

107 25 Schilling 1961   5.00   8.00 12.00
Proof . . . 250.00

Anton Bruckner

108 25 Schilling 1962   5.00   7.00   8.00
Proof . . . 175.00

300th Anniversary
Birth of Prince Eugen

109 25 Schilling 1963   5.00   6.00   7.50
Proof . . . 140.00

600th Anniversary
Union with Tirol

110 50 Schilling 1963   9.00 10.00 13.50
Proof . . . 140.00

Franz Grillparzer

112 25 Schilling 1964   5.00   6.00   7.50
Proof . . . 12.00

112a 25 Schilling 1964 (error) old
obv., large numerals
Proof only . . . 425.00

Winter Olympic Games

111 50 Schilling 1964   9.00 11.00 15.00
Proof . . . 25.00

Technical School Sesquicentennial

113 25 Schilling 1965   5.00   6.00   7.50
Proof . . . 20.00

600th Anniversary Vienna University

114 50 Schilling 1965   9.00   10.00   12.50
Proof . . . 20.00

Later issues in *Current Coins of the World*

AZORES

Group of islands, part of the Republic of Portugal, lying in the North Atlantic about 1,000 miles west of Lisbon. Chief products are fruits, wines and other agricultural crops. The chief export item is pineapple. There is an extensive tourist trade. Area: 883 square miles. Language: Portuguese. Chief city: Ponta Delgada.

LUIS I 1861–1889

Copper

#				
1	5 Reis 1865, 66, 80	3.00	6.00	11.00
2	10 Reis 1865–66	4.00	7.00	12.00
3	20 Reis 1865–66	4.00	7.00	14.00

Countermarked Issues

In 1887, various foreign coins were countermarked with a crowned GP (Governo Portugues) in a circular indent to authorize local circulation. This stamp is found most often on Brazilian coins. Values below are for common varieties.

Copper or Bronze

C1	on various issues	30.00	40.00	–

Silver

C2	on small coin	25.00	45.00	–
C3	on ¼ dollar size	25.00	45.00	–
C4	on ½ dollar size	50.00	80.00	–
C5	on 1 dollar size	85.00	125.00	–

CARLOS I 1889–1908

Copper

| 4 | 5 Reis 1901 | 4.00 | 7.00 | 12.00 |
| 5 | 10 Reis 1901 | 4.00 | 7.00 | 12.00 |

Note: Bright red uncirculated specimens of Nos. 1–5 are worth double the uncirculated prices listed.

6	1 Franc 1887–96	30.00	60.00	150.00
7	2 Francs 1887–96	50.00	90.00	250.00
8	5 Francs 1887–96	175.00	325.00	750.00

Cupro-Nickel

9	5 Centimes 1906,08	3.00	5.00	25.00
10	10 Centimes 1906,08	4.00	8.00	45.00
11	20 Centimes 1906,08	5.00	10.00	30.00

BELGIAN CONGO (Belgisch Congo, Congo Belge)

Former Belgian colony in equatorial Africa; became independent in 1960; short coastline where the Congo River empties into the Atlantic. Languages: Bantu, French. Capital: *Leopoldville (renamed Kinshasa).* Now the republic of Zaire.

Monetary System:
100 Centimes = 1 Franc

I. CONGO Free State 1885–1908.

LEOPOLD II of Belgium, as owner, 1885–1908

Copper

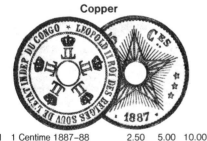

1	1 Centime 1887–88	2.50	5.00	10.00
2	2 Centimes 1887–88	3.00	6.00	12.50
3	5 Centimes 1887–88,94	4.00	8.00	20.00
4	10 Centimes 1887–89,94	7.00	12.50	30.00

Silver

| 5 | 50 Centimes 1887–96 | 20.00 | 35.00 | 100.00 |

II. BELGIAN CONGO 1908–1952.

LEOPOLD II as King, 1908–09

New Legend:
CONGO BELGE-BELGISCH CONGO
Cupro-Nickel

12	5 Centimes 1909	8.00	20.00	60.00
13	10 Centimes 1909	10.00	25.00	75.00
14	20 Centimes 1909	20.00	35.00	150.00

ALBERT I, 1909–1934

Copper

| 15 | 1 Centime 1910,19 | 1.00 | 3.00 | 10.00 |
| 16 | 2 Centimes 1910,19 | 5.00 | 10.00 | 25.00 |

Cupro-Nickel

17	5 Centimes 1910–28	1.00	2.00	8.00
18	10 Centimes 1910–28	1.00	2.00	12.00
19	20 Centimes 1910–11	3.00	5.00	20.00

20	50 Centimes 1921–29	3.00	5.00	22.50
21	1 Franc 1920–30	2.50	5.00	25.00

Nos. 20–21 have either French or Flemish legends.

LEOPOLD III 1934–1950

Nickel-Bronze

26	5 Francs 1936–37	10.00	20.00	90.00

Brass

24	2 Francs 1943	4.00	7.50	35.00

22	1 Franc 1944,46,49	1.50	3.00	8.50
23	2 Francs 1946–47	2.00	4.00	10.00

25	5 Francs 1947–48	5.00	10.00	40.00

Silver

27	50 Francs 1944	45.00	60.00	145.00

III. WITH RUANDA-URUNDI 1952–60.

BAUDOUIN I 1951–1960

Aluminum-Bronze

28	5 Francs 1952	1.00	3.00	10.00

Aluminum

29	50 Centimes 1954–55	.25	.50	2.50
30	1 Franc 1957–60	.35	.75	3.00
31	5 Francs 1956–59	1.00	2.00	5.00

For later issues see Katanga, also Rwanda & Burundi.

BELGIUM
(Belgique, Belgie)

A constitutional monarchy lying on the North Sea between France and the Netherlands. Chiefly a manufac-

Unless otherwise noted, prices are for coins in very
fine, extremely fine, and uncirculated condition.

turing nation, producing iron and steel, textiles and chemicals; agriculture is intensive with every useful acre under cultivation. Area: 11,800 square miles. Languages: Flemish and French. Capital: *Brussels*.

Monetary System:
100 Centimes = 1 Franc, Frank
5 Francs = 1 Belga

French and Flemish Inscriptions

The population of Belgium is divided into well-defined groups, the Flemings and the Walloons (French). Since 1886 all coins have been minted in approximately equal numbers of French (Belgique) and Flemish (Belgie) specimens, or where not, the coin is inscribed with both languages.

LEOPOLD II 1865–1909
First Coinage
Copper

1	1 Centime 1869–1907	3.00	6.00	10.00
	1869,70,73,76 . . . 8			
2	2 Centimes 1869–1909	2.00	4.00	10.00
	1869 . . . 35			

Cupro-Nickel

3	5 Centimes 1894–1901	6.00	12.00	20.00
	1898–1901 . . . 30			
4	10 Centimes 1894–1901	5.00	10.00	18.00
	1895Fr . . . 75 1901 . . . 110			

Silver

5	50 Centimes 1866–99	15.00	40.00	65.00
	1867 . . . 40 1868,81 . . . 125			
6	1 Franc 1866–87	15.00	40.00	65.00
	1868 . . . 700 1869 . . . 40			
	1881 . . . 200			
7*	2 Francs 1866–87	40.00	80.00	150.00
	1887 . . . 200			

8	5 Francs 1865–76	20.00	40.00	60.00
	1865–66 . . . 400			

Gold

19	*F8* 20 Francs 1867–82	100.00	110.00	120.00

50th Anniversary of Independence

9	1 Franc 1880	35.00	75.00	150.00
10	2 Francs 1880	125.00	200.00	300.00

Second Coinage
Cupro-Nickel

12	5 Centimes 1901–07	1.00	4.00	10.00
	1901 . . . 60			
13	10 Centimes 1901–06	1.00	4.00	10.00
	1901 . . . 18			
14	25 Centimes 1908–09	5.00	10.00	15.00

Silver

15	50 Centimes 1901	12.00	25.00	40.00

16	50 Centimes 1907,09	6.00	10.00	15.00

17	1 Franc 1904,09	6.00	10.00	15.00
	1904 . . . 12			

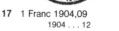

| 18 | 2 Francs 1904,09 | 10.00 | 20.00 | 30.00 |
| | 1904 . . . 25 | | | |

ALBERT I 1909–1934

Copper

| 22 | 1 Centime 1912,14 | 1.50 | 3.00 | 5.00 |
| 23 | 2 Centimes 1910–19 | 1.00 | 2.00 | 4.00 |

Cupro-Nickel

24	5 Centimes 1910–32	.20	.50	1.00
	1914Fr . . . 10 1932 . . . 20			
25	10 Centimes 1920–29	.20	.50	1.00
26	25 Centimes 1910–29	.50	1.00	2.50

Nickel-Brass

Rev: Star over value for change of alloy

24a	5 Centimes 1930–32	.75	1.50	3.00
25a	10 Centimes 1930–32	3.00	6.00	10.00
	1930Fr,31,32 . . . 100			

Nickel

27	50 Centimes 1922–34	.50	1.00	2.00
	1934 . . . 140			
28	1 Franc 1922–35	.50	1.00	2.00
	1933Fl . . . 600			
29	2 Francs 1923–30	3.00	6.00	10.00
	1924,30 . . . 35			

30	5 Francs/1 Belga			
	1930–34	4.00	10.00	20.00
	1934Fr . . . 120			

Centennial of Independence

Nickel

| 31 | 10 Francs/2 Belgas 1930 | 100.00 | 140.00 | 200.00 |

Regular Issues

| 32 | 20 Francs/4 Belgas | | | |
| | 1931–32 | 75.00 | 90.00 | 120.00 |

Unless otherwise noted, prices are for coins in very
fine, extremely fine, and uncirculated condition.

Silver

33	50 Centimes 1910–14	4.00	8.00	15.00
34	1 Franc 1910–18	2.00	3.00	5.00
	1917,18 . . . 250			
35	2 Francs 1910–12	10.00	20.00	30.00
	1912Fr . . . 20			

No. 34 dated 1917–18 not issued to circulation

36	20 Francs 1933–34	3.00	5.00	10.00
	1933 . . . 45			

Gold

37	*F13* 20 Francs 1914	120.00	130.00	140.00

GERMAN OCCUPATION 1914–1918

Zinc

38	5 Centimes 1915–16	1.50	3.00	5.00
39	10 Centimes 1915–17	1.50	3.00	5.00
	1917 . . . 55			
40	25 Centimes 1915–18	5.00	8.00	10.00

41	50 Centimes 1918	7.50	12.50	17.50

LEOPOLD III 1934–1950

All Leopold III coins minted in both Flemish and French varieties except Nos. 49 and 56.

Legend: BELGIE-BELGIQUE or BELGIQUE-BELGIE
Nickel-Brass

42	5 Centimes 1938–40	.30	.60	1.00
43	10 Centimes 1938–39	.20	.40	.70
	1939Fr . . . 3			
44	25 Centimes 1938–39	.20	.40	.70

Nickel

45	1 Franc 1939–40	.20	.40	.70
46	5 Francs 1938–39	1.50	3.00	5.00

47	5 Francs 1936–37	18.00	35.00	50.00

Brussels Exposition/Railway Centennial

Silver

48 50 Francs 1935   170.00 200.00 250.00

Regular Issues

49 20 Francs 1934–35   4.00   7.00   10.00
    1934 . . . 10

50 50 Francs 1939–40   15.00   18.00   20.00
    1940 . . . 22.50

GERMAN OCCUPATION 1940–45

Zinc

51	5 Centimes 1941–43	1.00	2.50	5.00
52	10 Centimes 1941–46	1.00	2.50	5.00
53	25 Centimes 1942–47	1.00	2.50	5.00
	1947 . . . Rare			
54	1 Franc 1941–47	1.00	2.50	5.00
	1947 . . . 85			
55	5 Francs 1941–47	3.00	6.00	10.00
	1944,46 . . . 10 1947Fr . . . 90			
	1947Fl . . . 300			

ALLIED ISSUE

Zinc-coated Steel
(U.S. 1943 Cent planchet)

56 2 Francs 1944   .75   1.50   3.00

POSTWAR ISSUES

Cupro-Nickel

57	1 Franc 1950–	.10	.15	.20
58	5 Francs 1948–	.10	.15	.30

Silver

59 20 Francs 1949–55   4.00   6.00   10.00
    1954 . . . 40 1955fr . . . 400
    1955Fl . . . 90
60 50 Francs 1948–54   6.00   9.00   15.00
    1954Fr . . . 15

61 100 Francs 1948–54   10.00   14.00   20.00
    1949Fr . . . 40

Unless otherwise noted, prices are for coins in very
fine, extremely fine, and uncirculated condition.

BAUDOUIN I 1951–

Bronze

62	20 Centimes 1953–63	.10	.15	.25
	1962 . . . 8			
63	50 Centimes 1952–	.10	.15	.25

Brussels Fair

Silver

64	50 Francs 1958	14.00	17.00	20.00

Marriage Commemorative

Obv: Latin legend only

65	50 Francs MCMLX (1960)	14.00	17.00	20.00

Cupro-Nickel

66	25 Centimes 1964–76	.10	.15	.25

Later issues in *Current Coins of the World*

BERMUDA

This group of islands, 677 miles southeast of New York City, is the oldest self-governing British colony. Settled by Sir George Somers who was shipwrecked there in 1609. Tourism is a thriving industry. Area: 18.5 square miles. Capital: *Hamilton.*

British coins used to 1970.

ELIZABETH II 1952–
350th Anniversary of Founding
Silver

1	1 Crown 1959	9.00	12.50	20.00

Regular Issue

2	1 Crown 1964	3.00	4.00	6.50
			Proof . . . 12.50	

Later issues in *Current Coins of the World*

BHUTAN

A semi-independent kingdom in the eastern Himalayas. India controls its external relations. Area: 19,305 square miles. Capital: *Thimbu*.

Some modern Bhutanese coins use cyclical dates which appear as the top line in the reverse square as shown below:

ཞི་ས་འབྲུག   ༡༢ལྕགས་སྟག

(1928) Yr. of Earth-Dragon   (1950) Yr. of Iron-Tiger

MAHARAJAH JIGME WANGCHUK 1926–1952
DORJI WANGCHUK 1952–72

Copper Alloy

5 1 Pice ND (ca. 1800–1930)   5.00 10.00 25.00

Bronze

1 1 Pice CD 1928 (design as No. 4)   30.00 45.00 65.00

Silver

Obv: Jigme Wangchuk
4 ½ Rupee CD 1928   12.50 20.00 30.00

Second Coinage

Bronze

3 1 Pice ND (1951–55)   1.00 1.50 2.25

Nickel

Obv: Jigme Wangchuk (king 1926–52)
4a ½ Rupee CD 1928, 50 (5.83 grams)   2.00 3.00 4.50

4b ½ Rupee CD 1950 (5.0 grams)   1.00 1.50 2.25

No. 4a was struck 1951–55 to the weight standard of the India rupee; No. 4b was struck 1967–68 to the standard of the new (decimal) Indian rupee. Weights may vary slightly.

Later issues in *Current Coins in the World*

BOLIVIA

A landlocked country in central South America containing the highest heavily populated areas in the world, with over half the inhabitants living at altitudes above 10,000 feet. Chief industry is mining and the major product is tin. Area: 424,162 square miles. Languages: Spanish, Indian. Capitals: La Paz (administrative) and Sucre (constitutional).

I. PRE-DECIMAL COINAGE TO 1863

Monetary System:
16 Soles (Sueldos, Reales) = 1 Scudo

A. Potosi Mint

Mmk: PTS monogram in reverse legend.
Silver

Rev: Llama in plain field
1 (¼ Sol) 1852   10.00 18.00 30.00

Rev: Llama between branches
1a (¼ Sol) 1853   200.00 350.00 –
No. 1a is usually found holed.

Obv: Laureate head of Bolivar, name on neck
Rev: No value shown

Unless otherwise noted, prices are for coins in very fine, extremely fine, and uncirculated condition.

2	(½ Sol) 1853–56 (17mm)	7.00	15.00	50.00
3	(1 Sol) 1853–54 (20mm)	15.00	35.00	–
4	(2 Soles) 1853 (25mm)	35.00	100.00	–
5*	(4 Soles) 1853 (32mm)	25.00	75.00	–
6	(8 Soles) 1852–54, 56			
	(37mm)	50.00	100.00	400.00

Obv: Like Nos. 2–6
Rev: Value in legend

2a	½ Sol 1856–58	6.00	15.00	35.00
3a*	1 Sol 1855–58	8.00	20.00	75.00
4a	2 Soles 1854–58	25.00	100.00	–
5a	4 Soles 1853–58	7.00	15.00	40.00
6a	8 Soles 1854–55	25.00	75.00	400.00

Obv: Name below neck
Rev: Like Nos. 2a–6a

2b	½ Sol 1859	40.00	100.00	250.00
3b	1 Sol 1859	50.00	125.00	300.00
4b	2 Soles 1859	60.00	200.00	–
5b*	4 Soles 1859	8.00	20.00	55.00
6b	8 Soles 1859	2500.	4000.	7500.

Obv: PESO (weight) in legend
Rev: Fineness in legend, no value shown

7	PESO 25 Gs (½ Sol)			
	1859	40.00	100.00	250.00
8	PESO 50 Gs (1 Sol) 1859	40.00	100.00	250.00

9*	PESO 100 Gs (2 Soles)			
	1859	75.00	250.00	–
11	PESO 400 GS (8 Soles)			
	1859	40.00	100.00	400.00
11a	Po 400 Gs 1859	2000.	3000.	–
11b	Po 400 Gs 1860, rev. like No.			
	11d (mule)			Rare

Obv: Weight in legend, PESO omitted
Rev: Fineness above llamas

7a	25 Gs (½ Sol) 1860–63	6.00	12.00	35.00
8a	50 Gs (1 Sol) 1860–63	8.00	15.00	50.00
9a*	100 Gs (2 Soles)			
	1860–63	10.00	25.00	75.00
10	200 Gs (4 Soles) 1860	75.00	200.00	500.00
11c	400 Gs (8 Soles) 1859,			
	rev. like No. 11 (mule)	600.00	1200.	–
11d	400 Gs 1859–63	15.00	30.00	100.00
	1859 . . . 600.			

Gold

12	F36	½ Escudo 1852–56	80.00	125.00	200.00
13*	F35	1 Escudo 1852–56	125.00	200.00	300.00
14	F34	8 Escudos 1852–57	700.00	1000.	1500.

B. La Paz Mint
Mmk: PAZ in reverse legend
Silver

Obv: Bare head of Bolivar
Rev: Value in legend

| 15 | 2 Soles 1853 | 2000. | 3000. | – |
| 16 | 4 Soles 1853 | 250.00 | 500.00 | 1000. |

Obv: "Potosi style" laureate head (general style of Nos. 2–6)

18	1 Sol 1855	20.00	60.00	–
19	2 Soles 1854	200.00	450.00	–
20*	4 Soles 1853–55	15.00	35.00	100.00

Obv: Crude "La Paz style" head

17	½ Sol 1855–56	25.00	65.00	200.00
18a	1 Sol 1855–56	25.00	65.00	200.00
19a	2 Soles 1855–56	300.00	700.00	–
20a	4 Soles 1855–58	14.00	32.00	85.00

Obv: Crude so-called "ugly head"

17b	½ Sol 1858	35.00	100.00	300.00
18b	1 Sol 1857, 59	30.00	85.00	300.00
20b	4 Soles 1859	75.00	125.00	250.00

Note: The three styles listed for Nos. 17–20 are general groups only; considerable variation exists from die to die. Dates are often crude on the two smaller values, making attribution of some years difficult or uncertain.

II. MELGAREJO ISSUES 1865–68

Silver

Obv: Melgarejo and Munoz

21*	(¼ Melgarejo) 1865	15.00	40.00	–
22	(½ Melgarejo) 1865, 68	10.00	25.00	50.00
	1868 . . . Very Rare.			

Obv: Mariano Melgarejo, President 1864–71

| 23 | (1 Melgarejo) 1865–66 | 40.00 | 125.00 | 500.00 |
| | 1866 . . . Very Rare. | | | |

III. DECIMAL COINAGE 1864–1962

Monetary System:
100 Centavos or Centecimos = 1 Boliviano
2 Bolivianos = 1 Escudo
8 Escudos = 1 Onza

First Coinage

Copper

| 24 | 1 Centecimo 1864 | 80.00 | 225.00 | 500.00 |
| 25 | 2 Centecimos 1864 | 100.00 | 250.00 | 500.00 |

Silver

26	¹⁄₂₀ Boliviano 1864–65	12.00	25.00	75.00
27	¹⁄₁₀ Boliviano 1864–67	12.00	25.00	100.00
28	⅕ Boliviano 1864–66	10.00	25.00	150.00

Unless otherwise noted, prices are for coins in very fine, extremely fine, and uncirculated condition.

29	1 Boliviano 1864–68, obv. 9 stars	18.00	35.00	125.00
29a	1 Boliviano 1866–69, 11 stars	16.00	30.00	100.00

Gold
Designs like Nos. 26–29a

30	*F39*	½ Escudo 1868	250.00	375.00	500.00
31	*F38*	1 Escudo 1868	275.00	450.00	700.00
32	*F37*	1 Onza 1868	4000.	7000.	9750.

Second Coinage

Legend: LA UNION HACE LA FUERZA
Silver

Obv: 11 stars at bottom, rococo shield
Rev: With weight in grams

33	5 Centavos 1871	25.00	60.00	150.00
34	10 Centavos 1870–71	8.00	20.00	50.00
35	20 Centavos 1870–71	45.00	100.00	–
36	1 Boliviano 1870, large legend and wreath	17.00	35.00	75.00
36a	1 Boliviano 1870–71, small legend and wreath	17.00	35.00	65.00

Obv: 11 stars at bottom
Rev: Without weight

33a	5 Centavos 1871–72	6.00	15.00	40.00
34a	10 Centavos 1871	6.00	15.00	45.00
35a	20 Centavos 1871	55.00	125.00	–

Obv: 9 stars at bottom

33b	5 Centavos 1872	6.00	12.00	35.00
34b	10 Centavos 1872	4.00	8.00	25.00
35b*	20 Centavos 1871–72	6.00	15.00	100.00
36b	1 Boliviano 1871–72	17.00	30.00	50.00

Third Coinage
Copper

Obv: Date at bottom
Rev: Value in wreath

37	1 Centavo 1878	75.00	150.00	–
38	2 Centavos 1878	60.00	150.00	–

Obv: Value at bottom
Rev: Legend in wreath, date below

37a	1 Centavo 1878	500.00	900.00	–
38a	2 Centavos 1878	400.00	800.00	–

Bronze

39	1 Centavo 1883	3.00	10.00	25.00
40	2 Centavos 1883	4.00	15.00	35.00

Cupro-Nickel

41	5 Centavos 1883	4.00	15.00	35.00
42	10 Centavos 1883	3.00	15.00	30.00

41a	5 Centavos 1883	3.00	15.00	35.00
42a	10 Centavos 1883	3.00	15.00	30.00

Nos. 41a–42a were converted from Nos. 41–42 by officially punching a center hole to prevent confusion with the silver 10 and 20 Centavos.

43 5 Centavos 1892   3.00 10.00 40.00
44 10 Centavos 1892   3.00 10.00 40.00

45 5 Centavos 1893–1919   1.00 5.00 15.00
46 10 Centavos 1893–1919   1.00 5.00 10.00

Silver
Legend: LA UNION ES LA FUERZA

Rev: Fineness below value
47 5 Centavos 1872–84   4.00 8.00 20.00
48 10 Centavos 1872–84   4.00 8.00 25.00
49* 20 Centavos 1872–85   4.00 8.00 30.00
50 ½ Boliviano 1879   350.00 550.00 1250.
Rev: Weight and fineness below value
51 ½ Boliviano/50 Centavos
    1873   15.00 30.00 125.00
52 1 Boliviano 1872–93   17.00 27.00 45.00
    1877 . . . 350. 1879 . . . 400. 1893 . . . 1500.

Slightly modified dies, both sides
47a 5 Centavos 1885–1900   4.00 8.00 20.00
48a 10 Centavos 1885–1900   6.00 10.00 30.00
    1887, 88 . . . 30.
49a* 20 Centavos
    1885–1907   5.00 8.00 30.00
    1907 . . . Rare.
51a ½ Boliviano/50 Centavos
    1891 weight below value   400.00 600.00 1250.
51b ½ Boliviano/50 Centavos
    1891–1900 weight omit-
    ted   6.00 12.00 30.00
Nos. 47a–51a dated 1884 are patterns, as are probably
all 1884–93 dates of the 1 Boliviano.

Daza Commemorative

Obv: Hilarion Daza, President 1876–80
53 20 Centavos 1879   35.00 60.00 200.00

Obv: Stars above arms
Rev: Fineness "9 Ds"
54 50 Centavos 1900–08.
    Potosi   7.00 13.00 30.00
54a 50 Centavos 1900. San-
    tiago   8.00 15.00 40.00

Obv: Stars below arms
Rev: Fineness "$^{10}/_{12}$"
55 20 Centavos 1909   5.00 6.00 10.00
56 ½ Boliviano/50 Centavos
    1909   8.00 10.00 15.00

Fourth Coinage

Cupro-Nickel

Like Nos. 45–46 but reduced size
57 5 Centavos 1935   .25 .50 3.00
58 10 Centavos 1935–36,
    39   .25 .50 2.00
59 50 Centavos 1939   .25 .50 2.00

Unless otherwise noted, prices are for coins in very
fine, extremely fine, and uncirculated condition.

| 60 | 10 Centavos 1937 | 1.00 | 2.00 | 6.00 |
| 61 | 50 Centavos 1937 | 30.00 | 45.00 | 75.00 |

Zinc

| 57a | 10 Centavos 1942 (17mm) | 1.00 | 2.00 | 8.00 |
| 58a | 20 Centavos 1942 (21mm) | 1.00 | 2.00 | 8.00 |

Bronze

| 59a | 50 Centavos 1942 | 1.00 | 2.00 | 3.50 |
| 59b | 50 Centavos 1942, restrike, poor detail | 1.00 | 2.00 | 3.50 |

Fifth Coinage

Bronze

| 62 | 1 Boliviano 1951 | .50 | 1.00 | 1.75 |

| 63 | 5 Bolivianos 1951 | .50 | 1.00 | 2.00 |

| 64 | 10 Bolivianos 1951 | 1.00 | 2.00 | 4.00 |

Later issues in *Current Coins of the World.*

BRAZIL (Brasil)

Brazil is the largest country in South America, covering over half the continent. From 1549 to 1822 it was a royal colony of Portugal. It produces a wealth of tropical products including timber, rubber, fruits, cocoa, wax and much of the world's coffee. Vast mineral resources are being increasingly developed and industry is growing rapidly, with manufacturing comprising over 60% of the total production. Area: 3,286,470 square miles. Language: Portuguese. Capital: *Brasilia.*

Monetary System:
1000 Reis = 1 Milreis to 1942
100 Centavos = 1 Cruzeiro 1942–

PEDRO II 1831–1889
DECIMAL ISSUES
First Coinage

Silver

A1	500 Reis 1849–52	6.00	12.00	40.00
A2	1000 Reis 1849–52	8.00	15.00	50.00
	1849 . . . 750.			
A3	2000 Reis 1851–52	14.00	22.00	65.00

Dates not shown above are either counterfeits or patterns.

Gold

| A4* | F120 10,000 Reis 1849–51 | 300.00 | 500.00 | 650.00 |
| A5 | F119 20,000 Reis 1849–51 | 350.00 | 500.00 | 750.00 |

Second Coinage

Silver

A6	200 Reis 1854–67	4.00	8.00	15.00
A7	500 Reis 1853–67	4.00	8.00	15.00
A8	1000 Reis 1853–66	5.00	8.00	20.00
A9	2000 Reis 1853–67	14.00	22.00	50.00
	1859,66,67 . . . 750.			

Gold

A10 *F121* 20,000 Reis
1851–52   350.00 500.00 650.00

Rev: "Decreto de 1870" added

A23 500 Reis 1876–89	5.00	9.00	20.00
1887 . . . 750.			
A24 1000 Reis 1876–89	8.00	20.00	50.00
1885, 87, 89 . . . 40.			
A25 2000 Reis 1886–89	14.00	20.00	40.00
1886 . . . 500.			

Third Coinage

Bronze

A11 10 Reis 1868–70	.50	2.00	8.00
A12 20 Reis 1868–70	1.00	4.00	10.00
A13 40 Reis 1873–80	3.00	10.00	50.00

Cupro-Nickel

A14 100 Reis 1871–85	1.00	3.00	12.00
1872 . . . 750.			
A15* 200 Reis 1871–84	3.00	6.00	20.00
A16 50 Reis 1886–88	3.00	6.00	20.00
A17 100 Reis 1886–89	3.00	6.00	20.00
A18 200 Reis 1886–89	4.00	10.00	40.00

Silver

A19 200 Reis 1867–69	4.00	8.00	15.00
A20 500 Reis 1867–68	5.00	9.00	20.00
A21 1000 Reis 1869	17.00	40.00	125.00
A22 2000 Reis 1868–69,			
75–76	20.00	40.00	125.00

Gold

A26 *F123* 5,000 Reis			
1854–89	125.00	200.00	400.00
A27 *F122* 10,000 Reis			
1853–89	140.00	250.00	500.00
A28 *F121a* 20,000 Reis			
1853–89	300.00	400.00	650.00

REPUBLIC 1889–

Bronze

1 20 Reis 1889–1912	1.00	2.00	15.00

2 40 Reis 1889–1912	1.00	2.00	10.00

Unless otherwise noted, prices are for coins in very
fine, extremely fine, and uncirculated condition.

Cupro-Nickel

3	100 Reis 1889–1900	1.00	3.00	15.00
4	200 Reis 1889–1900	3.00	10.00	35.00

Silver

5	500 Reis 1889	4.00	8.00	20.00
6	1000 Reis 1889	10.00	25.00	80.00
7	2000 Reis 1891–97	500.00	800.00	1200.
	1891, 96 . . . 1250.			

400th Anniversary of Discovery

8	400 Reis 1900	30.00	45.00	75.00

9	1000 Reis 1900	60.00	90.00	150.00

10	2000 Reis 1900	100.00	175.00	275.00

11	4000 Reis 1900	325.00	500.00	800.00

Cupro-Nickel

12	100 Reis MCMI (1901)	1.00	3.00	10.00
13	200 Reis MCMI	1.00	5.00	12.00
14	400 Reis MCMI	2.00	8.00	25.00

B14	400 Reis 1914	100.00	150.00	250.00

No. B14 was not issued to circulation. Some authorities
consider it to be a pattern.

Silver

15	500 Reis 1906–12	3.00	6.00	15.00
	1912 . . . 50.			
16	1000 Reis 1906–12	5.00	8.00	20.00
17	2000 Reis 1906–12	8.00	15.00	30.00

Obv: Dashes between stars
Rev: Divided legend

18	500 Reis 1912	5.00	10.00	50.00
19	1000 Reis 1912–13	5.00	9.00	30.00
20	2000 Reis 1912–13	10.00	25.00	75.00

Obv: No dashes between stars
Rev: Continuous legend

21	500 Reis 1913	3.00	6.00	15.00
22	1000 Reis 1913	5.00	8.00	20.00
23	2000 Reis 1913	10.00	20.00	60.00

Silver

24	2000 Reis 1924–34	3.00	4.00	8.00

Gold

25	F125 10,000 Reis			
	1889–1922	400.00	600.00	1000.

26	F124 20,000 Reis			
	1889–1922	400.00	600.00	1000.

Cupro-Nickel

27	20 Reis 1918–35	.15	.50	2.00
	1935 UNC . . . 500.			
28	50 Reis 1918–35	.15	.50	3.00
	1935 UNC . . . 500.			
29	100 Reis 1918–35	.15	.50	3.00
30	200 Reis 1918–35	.25	1.00	6.00
31	400 Reis 1918–35	.40	2.00	10.00

Nos. 27–28 dated 1935 were not issued to circulation.

Aluminum-Bronze

32	500 Reis 1924–30	.50	1.00	5.00
33	1000 Reis 1924–31	.50	1.50	7.00

COMMEMORATIVE ISSUES
Independence Centennial

Obv: Dom Pedro I and Pres. Pessoa

34	500 Reis 1922	1.00	2.00	5.00
35	1000 Reis 1922	1.00	2.50	10.00
34a	500 Reis 1922 (BBASIL error)	35.00	60.00	125.00
35a	1000 Reis 1922 (BBASIL error)	4.00	8.00	15.00

Unless otherwise noted, prices are for coins in very
fine, extremely fine, and uncirculated condition.

Silver

38 2 Milreis 1922   3.00   4.00   10.00

400th Anniversary of Colonization

Obv: Cazique Tiberica, 16th century Indian leader
39 100 Reis 1932   1.00   2.00   6.00

40 200 Reis 1932   1.00   3.00   8.00

41 400 Reis 1932   2.00   4.00   10.00

Aluminum-Bronze

Obv: Joao Ramalho, first settler
42 500 Reis 1932   4.00   10.00   20.00

Obv: Martim Alfonso da Sousa, first governor 1530-33
43 1000 Reis 1932   4.00   8.00   20.00

Silver

Obv: Joao III, king 1521-57
44 2000 Reis 1932   3.00   4.00   8.00

NATIONAL HEROES SERIES 1935-1938

Cupro-Nickel

Obv: Tamandare
45 100 Reis 1936-38   .50   1.00   3.00

Obv: Maua
46 200 Reis 1936-38   .75   2.00   4.00

Obv: Carlos Gomes
47 300 Reis 1936-38   1.00   2.00   4.00

Obv: Oswaldo Cruz

48	400 Reis 1936–38	1.00	2.00	6.00

Aluminum-Bronze

Obv: Diego Feijo

49	500 Reis 1935 (4 gr.)	6.00	10.00	17.00
50	500 Reis 1936–38 (5 gr.)	1.00	2.00	6.00

Obv: Jose de Anchieta

51	1000 Reis 1935 (26mm)	2.00	4.00	10.00
52	1000 Reis 1936–38 (24mm)	2.00	3.00	8.00

Obv: Duke of Caxias

53	2000 Reis 1936–38	2.00	3.00	10.00
54	2000 Reis (polygonal) 1938	2.00	4.00	15.00

Silver

Obv: Caxias

55	2000 Reis 1935	3.00	4.00	6.00

Obv: Santos Dumont

56	5000 Reis 1936–38	3.00	4.00	6.00

NEW GOVERNMENT
Cupro-Nickel

Obv: Getulio Vargas

57	100 Reis 1938–42	.35	.75	2.00
58	200 Reis 1938–42	.35	.75	2.00
59	300 Reis 1938–42	.35	1.00	3.00
60	400 Reis 1938–42	.35	1.00	4.00

The 1942 issues have a yellow color due to higher copper content.

Famous Men Series 1939
Aluminum-Bronze

Obv: Joachim Machado de Assis

61	500 Reis 1939	.50	1.00	3.00

Obv: Tobias Barreto

62	1000 Reis 1939	.50	1.00	3.00

Obv: Floriano Peixoto

Unless otherwise noted, prices are for coins in very fine, extremely fine, and uncirculated condition.

63 2000 Reis 1939 .50 1.00 4.00

CURRENCY REFORM OF 1942
100 Centavos = 1 Cruzeiro

Cupro-Nickel

Obv: Getulio Vargas

64 10 Centavos 1942-43 .25 .50 2.00
65 20 Centavos 1942-43 .25 .60 3.00
66 50 Centavos 1942-43 .25 .75 4.00

Aluminum-Bronze

64a 10 Centavos 1943-47 .25 .50 2.00
65a 20 Centavos 1943-48 .25 .60 3.00
66a 50 Centavos 1943-47 .25 .75 4.00

67 1 Cruzeiro 1942-56 .25 .65 2.00
68 2 Cruzeiros 1942-56 .25 .60 2.00
69 5 Cruzeiros 1942-43 3.00 5.00 8.00

Obv: Jose Bonifacio

73 10 Centavos 1947-55 .10 .25 1.00

Obv: Rui Barbosa

74 20 Centavos 1948-56 .10 .25 1.00

Obv: Eurico Dutra

75 20 Centavos 1948-56 .10 .25 1.00

Aluminum

76 10 Centavos 1956-61 .10 .20 .30
77 20 Centavos 1956-61 .10 .20 .35

Aluminum-Bronze

78 50 Centavos 1956 .10 .20 .35
79 1 Cruzeiro 1956 .20 .40 .85
80 2 Cruzeiros 1956 .15 .50 1.25

Aluminum

81 50 Centavos 1957-61 .10 .20 .30
82 1 Cruzeiro 1957-61 .10 .20 .30
83 2 Cruzeiros 1957-61 .20 .30 .60

84 10 Cruzeiros 1965 .10 .20 .30
85 20 Cruzeiros 1965 .10 .20 .30

Cupro-Nickel

86 50 Cruzeiros 1965 .20 .30 .60
Later issues in *Current Coins of the World*.

BRITISH CARIBBEAN TERRITORIES (Eastern Group)

The combined territories of the Leeward Islands, British Guiana, Barbados, Windward Islands, Trinidad and Tobago comprised the Eastern Group of the British Caribbean Territories. The coinage issue was intended to replace regular British coins in these territories.

Monetary System:
100 Cents = 1 British West Indies Dollar

ELIZABETH II 1952–

Bronze

1	½ Cent 1955, 58	.35	.60	.75
	1958 Proof . . . 175		Proof . . . 1.50	

2	1 Cent 1955–65	.15	.20	.35
	1958 Proof . . . 200		Proof . . . 2.25	
3	2 Cents 1955–65	.10	.15	.35
	1958 Proof . . . 225		Proof . . . 3.00	

Nickel-Brass

4	5 Cents 1955–65	.10	.15	.35
			Proof . . . 4.00	

Cupro-Nickel

5	10 Cents 1955–65	.15	.25	.45
			Proof . . . 4.00	
6	25 Cents 1955–65	.40	.65	.95
			Proof . . . 5.50	

7	50 Cents 1955, 65	1.00	1.50	2.75
			Proof . . . 7.00	

For later issues see Barbados, East Caribbean Territories, Guyana and Trinidad and Tobago in this volume and in *Current Coins of the World*.

BRITISH GUIANA

A former crown colony on the north shore of South America which gained independence as the Republic of Guyana in May, 1966. The agricultural area along the coast produces sugar, rum, rice, molasses and copra. Interior jungle produces timber. Exports mineral products including gold, diamonds manganese and bauxite. The escarpment rising behind the coastal plain is the site of many famous waterfalls. Area: 83,000 square miles. Language: English. Capital: *Georgetown*.

Monetary System:
50 Pence = 1 British Guiana Dollar

VICTORIA 1837–1901

Silver

A1	4 Pence 1838–55	5.00	15.00	40.00
	(Same as Gr. Brit. No. 4) 1851–53 . . . 75			

B2	4 Pence 1888	10.00	22.50	55.00

(Struck for B.G. & W.I. only)

Legend: BRITISH GUIANA AND WEST INDIES

1	4 ence 1891–1901	3.00	5.00	15.00

EDWARD VII 1901–1910

2	4 Pence 1903–10	5.00	15.00	35.00

Unless otherwise noted, prices are for coins in very fine, extremely fine, and uncirculated condition.

GEORGE V 1910-1936

3   4 Pence 1911, 13, 16   7.50   15.00   35.00

Legend: BRITISH GUIANA Only

4   4 Pence 1917-36   2.00   4.00   12.50
    1923 . . . 15   Proof . . . 175.00

GEORGE V1 1936-1952

5   4 Pence 1938-45   1.75   2.50   5.00
                                   Proof . . . 150.00
For later issues see GUYANA in *Current Coins of the World.*

BRITISH HONDURAS

British Honduras, on the Caribbean coast of Central America, was settled in the 1600's and prospered despite Spanish opposition. It was administered as part of Jamaica from 1862 to 1884, when it became a separate Crown colony. Upon independence in 1973, it took the name Belize. Until recent years forestry was the most important industry. Area: 8,866 square miles. Languages: English, Spanish. Capital: *Belize City (to 1970).*

Monetary System:
100 Cents = 1 Dollar

VICTORIA 1837-1901

Bronze

1   1 Cent 1885-94   8.00   15.00   45.00
                                   Proof . . . 175.00

Silver

2   5 Cents 1894   10.00   25.00   65.00
                                   Proof . . . 225.00
3   10 Cents 1894   15.00   30.00   75.00
                                   Proof . . . 300.00
4   25 Cents 1894-1901   15.00   50.00 150.00
                                   Proof . . . 225.00
5   50 Cents 1894-1901   15.00   60.00 250.00
                                   Proof . . . 450.00

EDWARD VII 1901-1910

Bronze

6   1 Cent 1904-09   20.00   30.00   50.00
    1909 . . . 275

Cupro-Nickel

7   5 Cents 1907, 09   35.00   75.00 150.00

Silver

8   25 Cents 1906-07   15.00   65.00 175.00
9   50 Cents 1906-07   25.00 100.00 275.00

GEORGE V 1910–1936
Bronze

10	1 Cent 1911–13	75.00	150.00	550.00

11	11 Cent 1914–36	3.50	15.00	45.00
			Proof . . . 75.00	

Cupro-Nickel

12	5 Cents 1911–36	3.00	10.00	40.00
			Proof . . . 75.00	

Silver

13	10 Cents 1918–36	7.50	15.00	60.00
			Proof . . . 75.00	
14	25 Cents 1911, 19	10.00	35.00	125.00
15	50 Cents 1911, 19	15.00	60.00	200.00
			Proof . . . 350.00	

GEORGE VI 1936–52
Bronze

16	1 Cent 1937–47	.75	5.00	15.00
			Proof . . . 50.00	

Cupro-Nickel

17	5 Cents 1939	3.00	15.00	35.00
			Proof . . . 75.00	

Nickel-Brass

17a	5 Cents 1942–47	3.00	9.50	35.00
			Proof . . . 125.00	

Silver

18	10 Centa 1939–46	2.00	3.50	15.00
			Proof . . . 75.00	

New Legend:
KING GEORGE THE SIXTH
Bronze

19	1 Cents 1949–51	.75	2.00	4.00
			Proof . . . 50.00	

Nickel-Brass

20	5 Cents 1949–52	.50	2.00	12.50
			Proof . . . 200.00	

Cupro-Nickel

21	25 Cents 1952	2.00	10.00	75.00
			Proof . . . 200.00	

ELIZABETH II 1952–1973
Bronze

22	1 Cent 1954	.50	1.50	4.00
			Proof . . . 45.00	

Unless otherwise noted, prices are for coins in very fine, extremely fine, and uncirculated condition.

23 1 Cent 1956–73   .05   .10   .20
                                              Proof . . . 35.00

Nickel-Brass

24 5 Cents 1956–73   .05   .10   .25
                                              Proof . . . 75.00

Cupro-Nickel

25 10 Cents 1956–70   .10   .25   .50
          1959 . . . 1   Proof . . . 65.00
26 25 Cents 1955–73   .15   .35   .75
          1960 . . . 1   Proof . . . 90.00
27 50 Cents 1954–71   .35   .90   2.00
          1965,66 . . . 1.50   Proof . . . 125.00

BRITISH NORTH BORNEO

A former colony on the northern tip of the island of Borneo, now known as Sabah. It is part of the Federation of Malaysia. Languages: various. Capital: *Jesselton (now Kota Kinabalu).*

Monetary System:
100 Cents = 1 Straits Dollar

Legend:
BRITISH NORTH BORNEO CO.
Bronze

1 ½ Cent 1885–1907   7.00   15.00   40.00
          1907 . . . 30   Proof . . . 100.00

2 1 Cent 1882–1907   5.00   15.00   35.00
          1894–1907 . . . 25.00   Proof . . . 75.00

New Legend:
STATE OF NORTH BORNEO
Cupro-Nickel

3 1 Cent 1904–41   3.00   7.00   15.00
4 2½ Cents 903, 20   4.50   15.00   35.00
5 5 Cents 1903–41   2.50   6.00   9.50
          1920 . . . 7   1903–28 . . . 4

Silver

6 25 Cents 1929   12.50   20.00   35.00
                                              Proof . . . 85.00

For later issues see **Malaya.**

BRITISH WEST AFRICA

An administrative grouping of four separate British colonies on the west coast of Africa: The Gambia, Sierra Leone, Gold Coast (now Ghana), and Nigeria. They gained independence between 1957 and 1965, and each now has its own coinage. **Monetary System:**

12 Pence = 1 Shilling

EDWARD VII 1901–1910

Legend:
NIGERIA-BRITISH WEST AFRICA
Aluminum

3 ¹⁄₁₀ Penny 1907–08   3.00   6.00   11.50

Cupro-Nickel

1	1/10 Penny 1908–10	.50	1.00	3.50
2	1 Penny 1907–10	3.00	6.50	12.50

GEORGE V 1910–1936

Cupro-Nickel
Designs similar to Nos. 1–3

4	1/10 Penny 1911	3.00	6.50	11.50
5	½ Penny 1911	10.00	20.00	50.00
6	1 Penny 1911	30.00	50.00	85.00

New Legend:
BRITISH WEST AFRICA
Cupro-Nickel

7	1/10 Penny 1912–36	1.50	3.00	6.00
	1916 . . . 100 1919 . . . 20 1925 . . . 12			
8	½ Penny 1912–36	2.50	6.00	10.00
	1913 . . . 175 1914 . . . 15 1922,31 . . . 750			
9	1 Penny 1912–36	2.00	4.50	10.00
	1913 . . . 15 1914H . . . 60 1922 . . . 600			
	1927 . . . 25			

Silver

Rev: Value and wreath

14	3 Pence 1913–20	3.00	6.00	12.50
	1915–16 . . . 15			
15	6 Pence 1913–20	4.00	7.50	20.00

16	1 Shilling 1913–20	8.50	10.00	35.00
	1915H, 19 . . . 12.50 1919H,20 . . . 30			
17	2 Shillings 1913–20	10.00	15.00	35.00
	1914,15H,17H,20 . . . 27.50			

Nickel-Brass

14a	3 Pence 1920–36	3.00	6.00	22.50
	1926 . . . 15 1927,36H . . . 40			
	1928,36KN . . . 25			
15a	6 Pence 1920–36	4.50	10.00	27.50
	1924,33,36 . . . 25 1928 . . . 50			
16a	1 Shilling 1920–36	5.00	10.00	35.00
	1920G . . . Rare 1924H,28,36H . . . 25			
17a	2 Shillings 1920–36	5.00	12.50	40.00
	1928 . . . Rare 1936H . . . 35 1936KN . . . 20			

EDWARD VIII 1936

Cupro-Nickel

18	1/10 Penny 1936	.50	1.00	2.50
	1936H . . . 125			
19	½ Penny 1936	.75	1.25	2.50
20	1 Penny 1936	1.00	2.00	3.00
21	10 Cents 1936, obv. of			
	East Africa No. 26 (mule) 225.00 400.00 500.00			

GEORGE VI 1936–1952

Cupro-Nickel

22	1 Penny 1938–47	.50	1.00	2.50
	1938H . . . 15 1947KN . . . Rare			
23	½ Penny 1937–47	1.00	2.00	3.00
24	1 Penny 1937–47	.75	1.50	3.00
	1946SA . . . Rare			

Unless otherwise noted, prices are for coins in very fine, extremely fine, and uncirculated condition.

| 25 | 3 Pence 1938–47 | 1.50 | 3.00 | 5.00 |

Brass

| 26 | 6 Pence 1938–47 | 1.25 | 2.50 | 7.50 |
| | 1944–46 . . . 5 | | | |

27	1 Shilling 1938–47	2.00	3.50	11.50
	1945H . . . 8			
28	2 Shillings 1938–47	2.00	4.50	22.50

New Legend:
without IND. IMP.
Cupro-Nickel

Designs similar to Nos. 22–28

29	$^1/_{10}$ Penny 1949–50	1.00	1.50	2.00
	1949KN . . . 6			
30	½ Penny 1949–51	3.00	6.00	20.00
31	1 Penny 1951	10.00	20.00	32.50

Bronze

29a	$^1/_{10}$ Penny 1952	1.00	2.00	5.00
30a	½ Penny 1952	.25	.50	2.00
31a	1 Penny 1952	1.25	3.00	7.50

Nickel-Brass

32	6 Pence 1952	9.00	15.00	30.00
33	1 Shilling 1949–52	1.00	2.00	5.00
34	2 Shillings 1949–52	2.00	5.00	20.00

ELIZABETH II 1952–

Bronze

38	$^1/_{10}$ Penny 1954–57	1.00	2.00	5.00
39	1 Penny 1956–58	1.00	2.00	5.00
A39	1 Penny 1956, George VI obverse legend (mule)	100.00	150.00	350.00

Cupro-Nickel

| 40 | 3 Pence 1957 | 30.00 | 75.00 | 150.00 |

For later issues see each of the four former colonies.

BRUNEI

A sultanate on the northwest coast of Borneo, under British protection since 1888. It has an important oil industry and also exports rubber. Area: 2,226 square miles. Languages: Malay, English. Capital: *Bandar Seri Begawan (formerly named Brunei).*

Monetary System:
100 Cents = 1 Straits Dollar

Sultan HASHIM JELAL
1885–1906

Bronze

| 1 | 1 Cent AH 1304 (1887) | 15.00 | 25.00 | 50.00 |
| | | | Proof . . . 200.00 | |

Later issues in *Current Coins of the World.*

BUKHARA — see Russian Turkestan

BULGARIA

Bulgaria, on the Balkan peninsula of Europe, gained partial independence from the Ottoman Empire as a principality in 1878, and was proclaimed a kingdom in 1908. After coming under communist control during World War II, it became a republic in 1946. It was primarily agricultural in earlier years, but more recently has had rapid industrial growth. Area: 42,785 square miles. Language: Bulgarian. Capital: *Sofia*.

Monetary System:
100 Stotinki = 1 Lev

ALEXANDER I
Prince 1879–1886
Bronze

1	2 Stotinki 1881	1.00	4.00	8.00
2	5 Stotinki 1881	1.00	5.00	12.00
3	10 Stotinki 1881	1.00	6.00	18.00

Silver

4	50 Stotinki 1883	3.00	15.00	40.00
5	1 Lev 1882	5.00	15.00	45.00
6	2 Leva 1882	10.00	35.00	100.00
7	5 Leva 1884–85	20.00	60.00	200.00

FERDINAND I
Prince 1887–1908
Cupro-Nickel

8	2½ Stotinki 1888	1.00	5.00	15.00

9	5 Stotinki 1888	1.00	5.00	15.00
10	10 Stotinki 1888	1.00	5.00	15.00
11	20 Stotinki 1888	1.00	7.00	20.00

Silver

12	50 Stotinki 1891	5.00	15.00	40.00
13	1 Lev 1891	5.00	25.00	65.00
14	2 Leva 1891	15.00	50.00	125.00
15	5 Leva 1892	25.00	75.00	250.00

Obv: Rearranged legend

13a	1 Lev 1894	5.00	25.00	65.00
14a	2 Leva 1894	15.00	50.00	125.00
15a	5 Leva 1894	25.00	65.00	225.00

Gold

21	F4	10 Leva 1894	100.00	175.00	300.00
22	F3	20 Leva 1894	125.00	200.00	350.00
23	F2	100 Leva 1894	500.00	800.00	2000.

Minor Issues
Bronze

16	1 Stotinka 1901, 12	1.00	4.00	8.00
17	2 Stotinki 1901, 12	1.00	4.00	8.00

Cupro-Nickel

18	5 Stotinki 1906–13	1.00	5.00	10.00
19	10 Stotinki 1906–13	1.00	5.00	10.00
20	20 Stotinki 1906–13	1.00	5.00	15.00

Unless otherwise noted, prices are for coins in very fine, extremely fine, and uncirculated condition.

World War I Issues

Zinc

18a	5 Stotinki 1917	1.00	5.00	20.00
19a	10 Stotinki 1917	1.00	5.00	20.00
20a	20 Stotinki 1917	1.00	5.00	30.00

As Tsar 1908–1918

Silver

24	50 Stotinki 1910	5.00	25.00	50.00
25	1 Lev 1910	5.00	25.00	65.00
26	2 Leva 1910	15.00	65.00	150.00

27	50 Stotinki 1912–16	1.00	3.00	10.00
	1916 . . . 50.			
28	1 Lev 1912–16	2.00	5.00	15.00
	1916 . . . 100.			
29	2 Leva 1912–16	5.00	10.00	25.00
	1916 . . . 150.			

Establishment of Tsardom and 25th Year of Reign

Gold

30	F6 20 Leva 1912	125.00	200.00	350.00
31	F5 100 Leva 1912	500.00	1000.	2500.

BORIS III 1918–1943

Aluminum
Designs like Nos. 34–35

32	1 Lev 1923, "Lev" in 3 letters	1.00	5.00	12.00
32a	1 Lev 1923, "Lev" in 4 letters	–	–	–
33	2 Leva 1923	1.00	7.00	17.00

Cupro-Nickel

34	1 Lev 1925	.50	1.00	2.00
35	2 Leva 1925	.50	1.00	2.00

36	5 Leva 1930	1.00	2.00	10.00
37	10 Leva 1930	1.00	4.00	15.00

Aluminum-Bronze

41	50 Stotinki 1937	.10	.25	1.00

Silver

38	20 Leva 1930	2.00	5.00	15.00
39	50 Leva 1930	4.00	8.00	20.00
40	100 Leva 1930	5.00	10.00	35.00

44	50 Leva 1934	4.00	10.00	25.00

45 100 Leva 1934, 37   6.00   15.00   35.00

Cupro-Nickel

42 20 Leva 1940   .50   1.00   3.00
43 50 Leva 1940   .75   2.00   5.00

WORLD WAR II ISSUES

Iron

Designs like Nos. 34–37

34a 1 Lev 1941   1.00   5.00   15.00
35a 2 Leva 1941   .50   2.00   5.00
36a 5 Leva 1941   1.00   5.00   20.00
37a 10 Leva 1941   2.00   10.00   40.00

A45 2 Leva 1943   1.00   3.00   10.00

Nickel-Clad Steel

36b 5 Leva 1943   1.00   2.00   5.00
37b 10 Leva 1943   1.00   3.00   10.00
43a 50 Leva 1943   1.00   3.00   10.00

PEOPLE'S REPUBLIC 1946–

Brass

46 1 Stotinka 1951   –   –   .10
47 3 Stotinki 1951   .05   .10   .20
48 5 Stotinki 1951   .05   .10   .25

Cupro-Nickel

49 10 Stotinki 1951   .05   .10   .25
A49 20 Stotinki 1952, 54   .10   .15   .35
50 25 Stotinki 1951   .10   .20   .50
51 50 Stotinki 1959   .10   .20   .50

52 1 Lev 1960   .50   .75   1.00

Later issues in *Current Coins of the World.*

BURMA

Located on the Bay of Bengal between India and Thailand, modern Burma was unified in the 1700's. This kingdom ended in 1886 with annexation to British India. It became a separate British colony in 1937, was occupied by Japan in World War II, and gained independence as a republic in 1948. An agricultural nation, it exports rice, lumber, rubber, and ores. Area: 261,789 square miles. Languages: Burmese, English, many others. Capital: *Mandalay (1857–1885), Rangoon (from 1886).*

Monetary System:
16 Annas = 1 Kyat (Rupee)
16 Kyat = 1 Mohur
The denomination 1 Anna may also be referred to as 1 Pe, with 4 Pyas = 1 Pe.

Burmese Numerals

Like Thailand, early coins are dated in the Chula-Sakarat system (see pages 5 and 6).

Unless otherwise noted, prices are for coins in very fine, extremely fine, and uncirculated condition.

MINDON

CS 1214–1240 (1853–1878)
Lead

Obv: Hare to left. Rev: Similar to No. 1

		F	VF	EF
C1	1/32 Anna CS 1231 (1869) (20–21 mm)	20.00	40.00	60.00
D1	1/16 Anna 1231 (21–22 mm)	20.00	30.00	50.00

Copper

		F	VF	EF
1	1/4 Anna CS1227 (1865)	4.00	6.00	12.00
1a	1/4 Anna 1227, Iron	30.00	50.00	90.00

The existence of former Nos. A1 and B1 cannot be confirmed.

		F	VF	EF
2	1/2 Anna CS1231 (1869)	45.00	80.00	100.00

Silver

Accession date CS 1214 on coins

		F	VF	EF
3	1 Anna ND (12mm)	12.50	25.00	50.00
4	1/8 Kyat ND (15mm)	12.50	20.00	40.00
5	1/4 Kyat ND (20mm)	12.50	20.00	40.00
6	1/2 Kyat ND (25mm)	10.00	15.00	35.00
7*	1 Kyat ND (30mm)	15.00	22.50	50.00

Gold

			F	VF	EF
10*	F2	1 Kyat ND (12mm)	90.00	150.00	225.00
11	F3	2 Kyat ND (16mm)	175.00	225.00	350.00

			F	VF	EF
A8	F6	1 Kyat CS 1228 (1866) (12mm)	90.00	150.00	225.00
8*	F5	1/4 Mohur 1228 (18–19mm)	200.00	250.00	375.00
B8	F4	1 Mohur 1228 (25mm)	650.00	850.00	1100.

THIBAW

CS 1240–1248 (1880–1885)
Accession date CS 1240 on coins

Copper

		F	VF	EF
9	1/4 Anna ND	6.50	12.50	20.00

Gold

			F	VF	EF
C8	F7	1 Mohur ND (21mm)	275.00	350.00	500.00

REPUBLIC 1948–1974

Cupro-Nickel

		VF	EF	UNC
13*	1/2 Anna 1949	.50	1.00	2.50
14	1 Anna 1949–51 (scalloped)	1.00	2.00	3.00
15	2 Annas 1949–51 (square)	1.00	2.00	5.00

Nickel

16*	4 Annas 1949–50	2.00	4.50	9.00
17	8 Annas 1949–50	2.50	5.50	12.50

Decimal Coinage System

Bronze

18	1 Pya 1952–65 (round)	.10	.20	.50

Cupro-Nickel

19	5 Pyas 1952–66 (scalloped)	.20	.30	.50
20	10 Pyas 1952–65 (square)	.30	.40	.75
21	25 Pyas 1952–65 (scalloped)	.25	.50	1.00

22*	50 Pyas 1952–66	.50	1.00	2.00
23	1 Kyat 1952–65	1.00	2.00	3.00

1949 Proof Set . . . 400.00 1952 Proof Set . . . 300.00

1962 Proof Set . . . 250.00

Later issues in *Current Coins of the World*.

CAMBODIA
(Cambodge)

The kingdom of Cambodia, on the southeast Asian peninsula, became a French protectorate in 1863, and in 1887 was federated with Annam, Tonkin and Laos to form French Indo-China. It regained full independence as a constitutional monarchy in 1953. The monarchy was abolished in 1970 and Cambodia became the Khmer Republic. Area: 66,000 square miles. Languages: Khmer, French. Capital: *Phnom Penh*.

Monetary System:
100 Centimes = 1 Franc
5 Francs = 1 Piastre
100 Centimes (Sen) = 1 Riel, 1953–

NORODOM I 1859–1904

Brass

1	1 Centime ND (1897)	45.00	90.00	175.00

Bronze

2	5 Centimes 1860	10.00	20.00	50.00
3	10 Centimes 1860	10.00	20.00	35.00

Nos. 2–9 were struck in Phnom Penh ca. 1875–87. The date 1860 on coins is (incorrect) accession date. Pieces with E or ESSAI on obverse are collectors' samples struck in Europe. No. 9 was issued for presentation only, as were strikings in gold of this and other denominations.

Silver

4	25 Centimes 1860	20.00	40.00	100.00
5	50 Centimes 1860	25.00	50.00	125.00
6	1 Franc 1860	35.00	75.00	100.00
7*	2 Francs 1860	50.00	100.00	275.00
8	4 Francs 1860	100.00	200.00	300.00
9	1 Piastre 1860	1000.	2000.	4000.

NORODOM II SIHANOUK

1941–55, 1960–70, 1975–76
Aluminum

11	10 Centimes 1953	1.00	2.00	5.00

Unless otherwise noted, prices are for coins in very fine, extremely fine, and uncirculated condition.

| 12 | 20 Centimes 1953 | 1.50 | 3.50 | 7.00 |
| 13 | 50 Centimes 1953 | 2.00 | 5.00 | 10.00 |

NORODOM SURAMARIT
1955-1960
SEN Replaces CENT
Aluminum

| 11a | 10 Sen 1959 | .50 | 1.50 | 3.00 |

| 12a | 20 Sen 1959 | .50 | 1.75 | 4.00 |
| 13a | 50 Sen 1959 | .75 | 2.00 | 5.00 |

CAMEROUN (Cameroon)

Cameroun became a French territory in 1919 when the former German colony of Kamerun in west central Africa was divided between Britain and France. It attained independence as a republic in 1960. Primarily an agricultural nation, its major exports are food crops, cotton, timber and aluminum. Area: 183,381 square miles. Languages: French, native dialects. Capital: *Yaounde.*

Monetary System:
100 Centimes = 1 Franc

Issues Under French Mandate
Aluminum-Bronze

| 1 | 50 Centimes 1924-26 | 4.00 | 7.50 | 15.00 |

| 2 | 1 Franc 1924-26 | 6.00 | 10.00 | 20.00 |
| 3 | 2 Francs 1924-25 | 7.00 | 15.00 | 25.00 |

Bronze

| 4 | 50 Centimes 1943 | 3.00 | 7.50 | 15.00 |
| 5 | 1 Franc 1943 | 7.50 | 12.50 | 25.00 |

Obv: LIBRE added to legend

| 6 | 50 Centimes 1943 | 8.00 | 15.00 | 30.00 |
| 7 | 1 Franc 1943 | 10.00 | 25.00 | 35.00 |

Aluminum

| 8 | 1 Franc 1948 | .25 | .50 | 1.00 |
| 9 | 2 Francs 1948 | .25 | .50 | 1.00 |

Later issues in *Current Coins of the World*

CANADA

A member of the British Commonwealth occupying most of northern North America. Products of her industrial, agricultural and mineral resources make her one of the world's richest trading nations. Area: 3,851,809 square miles. Languages : English and French. Nearly one-third of the nation is of French origin. Capital: *Ottawa.*

Monetary System:
100 Cents = 1 Dollar

VICTORIA 1837-1901

Bronze

Obv: Laureate head

1	1 Cent 1858–59	2.00	4.00	25.00

1858 . . . 60.

Silver

2	5 Cents 1858–1901	3.00	6.00	200.00

1875, 84 . . . 200. 1887–90, 94, 98 . . . 35.
1858, 70–72, 74, 83, 85 . . . 20.

3	10 Cents 1858–1901	5..00	20.00	275.00

1872 . . . 200. 1875, 84 . . . 450.
1887 . . . 85 1889 . . . 1,250.

4	20 Cents 1858	55.00	100.00	1200.

Bronze

Obv: Head with coronet

5	1 Cent 1876–1901	1.50	3.00	30.00

1890, 94, 1900 . . . 10.
1881, 84, 86–87, 92–93, 95, 98 . . . 6.

Silver

8	25 Cents 1870–1909	7.00	22.00	750.00

1875 . . . 800. 1880 . . . 80.
1885, 87, 89, 91, 93 . . . 250.
1870–71, 82–83, 86, 88, 90, 92, 94 . . . 50.

9	50 Cents 1870–1901	45.00	200.00	3250.

1871 . . . 275. 1888, 99 . . . 400.
1890 . . . 2500. 1894 . . . 1000.

EDWARD VII 1901–1910

Bronze

10	1 Cent 1902–10	1.00	2.50	20.00

Silver

11a	5 Cents 1902, Royal crown on rev.	2.50	5.00	70.00
11	5 Cents 1903–10, imperial crown	2.50	5.00	150.00

1903, 08 . . . 14.

12	10 Cents 1902–10	3.00	11.00	200.00

1903 . . . 35. 1904–05, 09–10 . . . 22.50

13	25 Cents 1902–10	4.00	17.50	400.00

1904 . . . 55. 1908 . . . 35.

14	50 Cents 1902–10	18.00	100.00	3000.

1903 . . . 200. 1904–05 . . . 500.
1908 . . . 150.

Gold

Type of Great Britain No. 57
With Mint Mark ''C'' (Ottawa)

A14	*F1*	1 Sovereign 1908–10	300.00	450.00	800.00

1908 . . . 2000.

GEORGE V 1910–1936

Bronze

Obv: legend omits DEI GRA:

15a	1 Cent 1911	1.50	3.50	30.00

Silver

17a	5 Cents 1911	2.50	7.00	180.00
18a	10 Cents 1911	8.00	25.00	300.00
19a	25 Cents 1911	10.00	50.00	750.00
20a	50 Cents 1911	20.00	50.00	3250.

Bronze

Obv: DEI GRA: added

15	1 Cent 1912–20	.60	1.50	10.00

Silver

17	5 Cents 1912–21	1.50	3.00	75.00

1915 . . . 17. 1921 . . . 3000.

18	10 Cents 1912–36	1.50	4.00	130.00

1915, 33–34 . . . 15. 1935 . . . 20.

Unless otherwise noted, prices are for coins in very
fine, extremely fine, and uncirculated condition.

19	25 Cents 1912–36	3.00	12.00	300.00

1914, 30–35 . . . 17. 1915, 27 . . . 125.
1921 . . . 50.

20	50 Cents 1912–36	10.00	40.00	1000.

1912–13, 34, 36 . . . 100.
1914, 32 . . . 250. 1921 . . . 14,000.

A22	1 Dollar 1936	15.00	20.00	65.00

Gold

23	F4	5 Dollars 1912–14	175.00	275.00	450.00

1914 . . . 650.

24	F3	10 Dollars 1912–14	375.00	650.00	950.00

1914 . . . 750.

*Type of Great Britain No. 78
with Mint Mark "C"*

25	F2	1 Sovereign 1911–19	125.00	175.00	250.00

1913 . . . 900. 1914 . . . 400.
1916 . . . 22,500.

Bronze

16	1 Cent 1920–36	.25	.75	12.00

1922, 25 . . . 20. 1923 . . . 27
1930, 31 . . . 4. 1934–36 . . . 2.

Nickel

21	5 Cents 1922–36	.40	3.50	80.00

1925 . . . 125. 1926 Far 6 . . . 150.

25th Anniversary of Reign
Silver

*Obv: Different bust and legend
Rev: Like No. A22*

22	1 Dollar 1935	15.00	20.00	65.00

GEORGE VI 1936–52
Bronze

26	1 Cent 1937–47	.10	.25	2.00

1937 . . . 2.

Nickel

27	5 Cents 1937–42	.35	2.00	35.00

1937, 39 . . . 4.

Brass

28	5 Cents 1942, 12 sided	.75	2.00	5.00

29	5 Cents 1943	.25	.60	4.00

Chromium-Plated Steel

29a	5 Cents 1944–45	.25	.75	12.00

Nickel
Design like No. 28

28a	5 Cents 1946–47, 12 sided	.25	.75	12.00

Silver

30 10 Cents 1937–47   1.00   2.50   30.00
        1937–39, 41, 47 . . . 4

31 25 Cents 1937–47   2.50   4.50   30.00
        1937–39 . . . 7.

32 50 Cents 1937–47   5.00   10.00   42.50
        1937, 46–47 . . . 15. 1938–39 . . . 20.

33 1 Dollar 1937–47   15.00   20.00   65.00
        1938, 46 . . . 35. 1945 . . . 120.
        1947 . . . 70.

Royal Visit Commemorative

Rev: Parliament Building in Ottawa

---

34 1 Dollar 1939   10.00   12.00   25.00

New Legend: without IND: IMP:
Designs like Nos. 26, 28, 30–33

Bronze

35 1 Cent 1948–52   .10   .20   1.00

Nickel

36 5 Cents 1948–50   .20   .50   6.00
        1948 . . . 2.

Chromium-Plated Steel

36a 5 Cents 1951–52   .20   .50   2.50

Silver

38 10 Cents 1948–52   1.00   1.75   10.00
        1948 . . . 10.
39 25 Cents 1948–52   2.50   4.00   15.00
        1948 . . . 10.
40 50 Cents 1948–52   5.00   7.50   20.00
        1948 . . . 100.
41 1 Dollar 1948–52   10.00   12.50   25.00
        1948 . . . 650. 1949 . . . 20.

Commemorating Province of Newfoundland

Rev: Ship of discoverer John Cabot

42 1 Dollar 1949   12.00   17.00   40.00

200th Anniversary Isolation of Nickel

Nickel

37 5 Cents 1951   .20   .50   2.50

Unless otherwise noted, prices are for coins in very
fine, extremely fine, and uncirculated condition.

ELIZABETH II 1952–

Bronze

43 1 Cent 1953–64   .10 .15 .25

Chromium-Plated Steel

44 5 Cents 1953–54   .20 .75 6.00

Nickel

45 5 Cents 1955–62   .10 .25 1.00

45a 5 Cents 1963–64   .10 .15 .25
Rev: Designs like Nos. 30–33

Silver

46 10 Cents 1953–64	1.00	1.50	2.25
47 25 Cents 1953–64	2.50	3.75	5.00
48 50 Cents 1953–58	4.00	5.00	9.00
49 1 Dollar 1953–63	8.00	10.00	12.50

British Columbia Province

50 1 Dollar 1958   8.00 10.00 15.00

51 50 Cents 1959–64   4.00 5.00 6.00

Centennial of Confederation Conferences

52 1 Dollar 1964   8.00 10.00 12.50
Later issues in *Current Coins of the World.*

CANADA —
NEW BRUNSWICK

Separated from Nova Scotia in 1784, it joined the Canadian federation in 1867. Capital: *Fredericton.*

VICTORIA 1837–1901

Copper

1 ½ Penny 1843   2.50 5.00 35.00
Proof . . . 500.00

2 1 Penny 1843   3.00   6.00 35.00
                              Proof . . . 500.00

3 ½ Penny 1854   2.50   5.00 35.00
                              Proof . . . 500.00
4 1 Penny 1854   3.00   6.00 35.00
                              Proof . . . 500.00

Bronze

5 ½ Cent 1861   45.00 95.00 400.00
                              Proof . . . 1700.
6 1 Cent 1861, 64   1.50   6.50 75.00
                              Proof . . . 600.00

Silver

7 5 Cents 1862, 64   25.00 80.00 1750.
8 10 Cents 1862, 64   25.00 80.00 1700.

9 20 Cents 1862, 64   16.00 45.00 1800.

CANADA — NEWFOUNDLAND

With its dependency, Labrador, it was independently administered by the British government. In 1949, by referendum vote, it united with Canada to become the tenth province. Exports: fish (especially cod), iron and paper. Capital: St. John's.

VICTORIA 1837–1901

Bronze

1 1 Cent 1865–96   2.00   6.00 125.00
     1885, 88 . . . 30.

Silver

2 5 Cents 1865–96   10.00 40.00 1000.
     1876 . . . 250. 1865–73, 81 . . . 100.
     1882, 88, 90, 94 . . . 70. 1885 . . . 300.
3 10 Cents 1865–96   11.00 50.00 1500.
     1865, 72–73, 82, 88 . . . 85.
     1870 . . . 500. 1876, 80 . . . 150.
     1885 . . . 400.
4 20 Cents 1865–1900   7.00 35.00 1800.
     1865, 72–73, 76, 85 . . . 85.
     1870, 80 . . . 125. 1881–82, 88 . . . 55.
5 50 Cents 1870–1900   12.50 50.00 4000.
     1870–74, 81, 85, 88 . . . 80.
     1876, 80 . . . 125.

Gold

6 F1 2 Dollars 1865–88   175.00 250.00 850.00
     1880 . . . 1850.

EDWARD VII 1901–1910

Bronze

7 1 Cent 1904–09   1.50   5.00 150.00
     1904 . . . 15.

Unless otherwise noted, prices are for coins in very fine, extremely fine, and uncirculated condition.

Silver

8	5 Cents 1903–08	6.00	30.00	900.00
9	10 Cents 1903–04	7.00	45.00	2000.
10	20 Cents 1904	17.50	100.00	2500.
11	50 Cents 1904–09	9.00	30.00	1200.

GEORGE V 1910–1936

Bronze

12	1 Cent 1913–36	.75	2.50	60.00

Silver

13	5 Cents 1912–29	3.00	10.00	650.00
14	10 Cents 1912–19	4.00	25.00	1100.
15	20 Cents 1912	5.00	25.00	1500.
16	25 Cents 1917, 19	4.00	12.00	350.00
17	50 Cents 1911–19	8.00	25.00	800.00

GEORGE VI 1936–1952

Bronze

18	1 Cent 1938–47	.40	1.00	15.00
	1940, 44 . . . 5. 1947 . . . 2.			

Silver

Note: In 1944 fineness was reduced from .925 to .800.

19	5 Cents 1938–47	1.00	2.50	60.00
	1946 . . . 375. 1947 . . . 10.			

20	10 Cents 1938–47	2.00	5.00	65.00
	1938, 40 . . . 8. 1946 . . . 25.			
	1947 . . . 1600.			

CANADA — NOVA SCOTIA

First settled by the French. Passed to England in 1621, its possession being contested by both nations until ceded to Britain by Treaty of Utrecht in 1713. Joined the Dominion in 1867. Capital: *Halifax.*

VICTORIA 1837–1901

Copper

3	½ Penny 1840, 43	1.50	6.00	65.00
4	1 Penny 1840, 43	3.00	10.00	70.00

5	½ Penny 1856	2.00	8.00	60.00
6	1 Penny 1856	2.50	9.00	60.00

Bronze

7	½ Cent 1861, 64	6.00	12.00	65.00
8	1 Cent 1861–64	1.50	7.50	65.00

CANADA — PRINCE EDWARD ISLAND

Colonized by the French about 1720, it became a British possession in 1763 and was united with Canada in 1873. It is the smallest Canadian province with an area of only 2,184 square miles. Capital: *Charlottetown.*

Bronze

1 1 Cent 1871   1.50   8.00 15.00

CAPE VERDE ISLANDS
(Cabo Verde)

Until July, 1975, an overseas province of Portugal lying in the North Atlantic about 600 miles off the West African coast. Chief products are coffee and other agricultural goods. The ten islands and five islets comprising the state have a total area of 1,557 square miles. Languages: Portuguese and Crioulo. Capital: *Praia*.

Monetary System:
100 Centavos = 1 Escudo

Bronze

1 5 Centavos 1930   2.00   3.00   7.00
2 10 Centavos 1930   2.00   3.00 12.00
3 20 Centavos 1930   2.00   3.00 12.00

Nickel-Bronze

4 50 Centavos 1930   5.00 17.00 40.00
5 1 Escudo 1930   12.00 25.00 75.00

6 50 Centavos 1949   1.00   2.00   8.00
7 1 Escudo 1949   1.00   3.00 12.00
Obv: COLONIA DE omitted in legend

Bronze

A8 50 Centavos 1968   .10   .25   1.00
8 1 Escudo 1953,68   .50   .75   2.00

Cupro-Nickel

9 2½ Escudos 1953,67   .50 1.00   2.00
A10 5 Escudos 1968   .50 1.00   3.0

Silver
10 10 Escudos 1953   3.00 7.00 15.00

CEYLON

A large island off the southern tip of India, Ceylon came under British control around 1800. Gaining independence within the Commonwealth in 1948, it changed its name to Sri Lanka in 1972. Primarily agricultural, it exports tea, rubber and coconut. Area: 25,332 square miles. Languages: Sinhala, Tamil, English. Capital: *Colombo*.

Monetary System:
4 Farthings = 1 Penny
100 Cents = 1 Rupee

VICTORIA 1837–1901
Copper

Dates 1839–42 for Ceylon
1 ¼ Farthing 1839–53   17.50 35.00 90.00
2 ½ Farthing 1839–56   2.00   4.00 15.00
       1854 . . . 22
In 1842 No. 2 was changed at bottom reverse to conform with English coinage, and was declared current in the United Kingdom. For more on Nos. 1–3, see Great Britain introduction.

Unless otherwise noted, prices are for coins in very fine, extremely fine, and uncirculated condition.

Silver

| 3 | 1½ Pence 1838–62 | 5.00 | 15.00 | 50.00 |

(Also used in Jamaica)
Decimal System
Copper

4	¼ Cent 1870–1901	2.00	6.00	9.50
		Proof . . . 50.00		
5	½ Cent 1870–1901	1.75	3.50	7.00
		Proof . . . 50.00		
6	1 Cent 1870–1901	2.00	5.00	10.00
		Proof . . . 50.00		
7	5 Cents 1870–92	10.00	30.00	65.00
		Proof . . . 75.00		

Silver

8	10 Cents 1892–1900	3.00	7.50	17.50
		Proof . . . 75.00		
9	25 Cents 1892–1900	8.00	15.00	35.00
		Proof . . . 75.00		
10	50 Cents 1892–1900	10.00	25.00	45.00
		Proof . . . 100.00		

EDWARD VII 1901–1910
Copper

11	¼ Cent 1904	3.00	7.00	15.00
		Proof . . . 75.00		
12	½ Cent 1904–09	2.00	5.00	10.00
		Proof . . . 50.00		
13	1 Cent 1904–10	1.00	2.00	5.00
		Proof . . . 50.00		

Cupro-Nickel

| 14 | 5 Cents 1909–10 | 1.75 | 3.00 | 9.00 |

Silver

15	10 Cents 1902–10	2.00	5.00	15.00
		Proof . . . 75.00		
16	25 Cents 1902–10	5.00	10.00	20.00
		Proof . . . 75.00		
17	50 Cents 1902–10	4.50	9.00	20.00
		Proof . . . 100.00		

GEORGE V 1910–1936
Copper

18	½ Cent 1912–26	.50	1.00	3.50
		Proof . . . 45.00		
19	1 Cent 1912–29	.35	1.00	3.00
		Proof . . . 45.00		

Cupro-Nickel

| 20 | 5 Cents 1912–26 | 1.00 | 2.00 | 5.00 |

Silver

In 1919, the fineness was lowered from .800 to .525

21	10 Cents 1911–28	1.25	3.00	7.50
		Proof . . . 75.00		
22	25 Cents 1911–26	2.00	5.00	10.00
		Proof . . . 120.00		
23	50 Cents 1913–29	4.50	10.00	17.50
		Proof . . . 90.00		

GEORGE VI 1936–1952
Copper

24	½ Cent 1937–40	.50	1.00	3.00
			Proof . . . 90.00	
25	1 Cent 1937–42	.25	1.00	2.00
			Proof . . . 50.00	

Bronze
Obv: Larger head

25a	1 Cent 1942–45, thin	.25	.50	1.00
			Proof . . . 15.00	

Nickel-Brass

27	2 Cents 1944	.15	.30	.75

28	5 Cents 1942–43, thick	.50	1.00	3.00
			Proof . . . 25.00	
28a	5 Cents 1944–45, thin	.20	.50	1.00
			Proof . . . 45.00	

29	10 Cents 1944	.35	.50	2.00

30	25 Cents 1943	.35	.50	2.00
31	50 Cents 1943	.50	1.00	2.50

Silver

32	10 Cents 1941	.75	2.00	4.50
33	50 Cents 1942	6.00	12.50	25.00

New Legend:
KING GEORGE THE SIXTH
Nickel-Brass

34	2 Cents 1951	.15	.25	.50
			Proof . . . 15.00	
35	5 Cents 1951, square		Proof . . . 13.50	
36	10 Cents 1951, scalloped	.10	.25	.75
			Proof . . . 10.00	

37	25 Cents 1951	.20	.40	1.00
			Proof . . . 15.00	
38	50 Cents 1951	.25	.50	1.00
			Proof . . . 15.00	

ELIZABETH II 1952–

39	2 Cents 1955,57	.20	.40	.75
			Proof . . . 50.00	
40	1 Rupee 1957	.50	2.00	4.00
			Proof . . . 17.50	
41	5 Rupees 1957	15.00	20.00	30.00
			Proof . . . 225.00	

Later issues in *Current Coins of the World*

CHILE

A republic on the western coastline of South America lying between the Andes and the Pacific. Principal resources are mining and agriculture, mineral exports running about 70% of the total. Area: 292,258 square miles. Languages: Spanish and Indian. Capital: *Santiago.*

Monetary System:
10 Centavos = 1 Decimo
10 Decimos = 1 Peso
10 Pesos = 1 Condor

DECIMAL COINAGE 1851–
First Coinage
Copper

Obv: large flat star, date between stars

1	½ Centavo 1851	5.00	15.00	50.00
2	1 Centavo 1851	5.00	15.00	50.00

Unless otherwise noted, prices are for coins in very fine, extremely fine, and uncirculated condition.

Obv: Star in relief, date between dots

3	½ Centavo 1851	8.00	25.00	75.00
4	1 Centavo 1851	8.00	25.00	75.00

Rev: Different wreath

3a	½ Centavo 1853	4.00	9.00	35.00
4a	1 Centavo 1853	4.00	9.00	40.00

Silver

5	½ Decimo 1851–59 (1.25 gm.)	5.00	12.00	50.00
	1851, 59 . . . 200.			
5a	½ Decimo 1860–62 (1.15 gm.)	12.00	25.00	100.00
6	1 Decimo 1852–59 (2.50 gm.)	8.00	20.00	75.00
6a	1 Decimo 1860–62 (2.30 gm.)	12.00	25.00	100.00
7	20 Centavos 1852–59 (5.00 gm.)	8.00	20.00	75.00
7a	20 Centavos 1860–62 (4.60 gm.)	6.00	15.00	50.00
8	50 Centavos 1853–62	25.00	80.00	300.00

9	1 Peso 1853–62	50.00	100.00	300.00
	1862 . . . 150.			

Second Coinage

Copper-Nickel-Zinc

10	½ Centavo 1871–73	8.00	20.00	40.00
11	1 Centavo 1871–77	4.00	10.00	30.00
12	2 Centavos 1871–77	6.00	15.00	40.00

Bronze

10a	½ Centavo 1883–94	4.00	10.00	25.00
	1890 . . . 40.			
11a	1 Centavo 1878–98	4.00	8.00	25.00
12a	2 Centavos 1878–94	4.00	10.00	40.00

13	2½ Centavos 1886–98	4.00	8.00	35.00

Silver
(.900 fine, not shown on coins)

14	½ Decimo 1865–66	25.00	50.00	100.00
15	1 Decimo 1864–66	8.00	25.00	75.00

16	20 Centavos 1863–67	5.00	15.00	65.00
17	50 Centavos 1862–67	25.00	60.00	200.00
	1862, 67 . . . 50.			
18	1 Peso 1867	2000.	3000.	5000.

Slightly modified dies both sides

14a	½ Decimo 1867–78, 80–81	2.50	5.00	12.00
15a	1 Decimo 1867–78, 80	3.00	6.00	15.00

16a	20 Centavos 1867–79	4.00	8.00	20.00
17a	50 Centavos 1867–72	10.00	20.00	50.00
18a	1 Peso 1867–91	14.00	20.00	60.00

.500 Silver

Obv: "0.5" in legend

14b	½ Decimo 1879–88,			
	92–94	2.00	4.00	9.00
15b	1 Decimo 1879–87,-			
	92–94 (2.5gm.)	2.50	4.50	10.00
15c	1 Decimo 1891 (2.0 gm.)	25.00	75.00	150.00
16b	20 Centavos 1879–81,			
	92–93 (5.0 gm.)	4.00	7.00	14.00
16c	20 Centavos 1891 (4.0			
	gm.)	10.00	25.00	60.00

.200 Silver (Billon)
Obv: "0.2" in legend

| 16d | 20 Centavos 1891 | 100.00 | 200.00 | 400.00 |

Gold

| 19 | F48 | 1 Peso 1860–73 | 35.00 | 60.00 | 100.00 |

20	F47	2 Pesos 1857–75	50.00	85.00	150.00
21	F46	5 Pesos 1851–73	125.00	175.00	250.00
22	F45	10 Pesos 1851–92	250.00	300.00	450.00

Provisional Coinage
City of Copiapo
A. Revolution of 1859
Issues of insurgent leader Pedro Leon Gallo

Silver

Obv: Arms/Value

Rev: Blank

| 23 | 50 Centavos ND | 40.00 | 100.00 | – |
| 24 | 1 Peso ND | 35.00 | 75.00 | – |

B. Provisional Coinage of 1865
Issued during Spanish blockade of Chilean ports.

Silver

| 25 | 50 Centavos 1865 | – | 800.00 | 1000. |
| 26 | 1 Peso 1865 | 40.00 | 80.00 | – |

It is unknown if No. 25 was issued to circulation. Medina (1919) states that a few restrikes were made later from original dies.

Unless otherwise noted, prices are for coins in very fine, extremely fine, and uncirculated condition.

Third Coinage

Bronze

Nos. 11 and 13 were continued briefly into this period.

27	1 Centavo 1904–19	1.00	2.00	4.00
28	2 Centavos 1919	1.50	4.00	8.00
29	2½ Centavos 1904–08	3.50	8.00	25.00

.835 Silver

Obv: No fineness shown

30	5 Centavos 1896	5.00	10.00	25.00
31	10 Centavos 1896	2.00	5.00	10.00
32	20 Centavos 1895	15.00	35.00	75.00
35	1 Peso 1895–97	10.00	25.00	75.00

.500 Silver

Obv: "0.5" in field

30a	5 Centavos 1899–1907	1.00	2.00	6.00
31a	10 Centavos 1899–1907	1.00	2.00	6.00
	1900 . . . 40.			
32a	20 Centavos 1899–1907	1.50	3.00	8.00
	1900 . . . 40.			

.400 Silver (Billon)

Obv: No fineness shown

30b	5 Centavos 1908–13, 19	1.00	2.00	4.00
31b	10 Centavos 1908–13, 19–20	1.00	2.00	5.00
32b	20 Centavos 1907–13, 19–20	1.00	2.50	6.00
33	40 Centavos 1907–08	4.00	10.00	25.00

.450 Silver (Billon)

Obv: "0.45" in field

30c	5 Centavos 1915–19	1.00	2.00	4.00
31c	10 Centavos 1915–18	1.00	2.00	4.00
32c	20 Centavos 1916	1.00	2.00	5.00

.700 Silver

34	50 Centavos 1902–05	4.00	8.00	20.00
35a	1 Peso 1902–05 (35mm)	12.00	35.00	100.00

.900 Silver

35b	1 Peso 1910 (31.5mm)	4.00	9.00	25.00

.720 Silver

35c	1 Peso 1915, 17 (28mm)	2.00	6.00	15.00

Gold

36	F50	5 Pesos 1895–96	75.00	100.00	150.00
37	F49	10 Pesos 1895	125.00	150.00	200.00

38	F53	5 Pesos 1898, 1900	75.00	100.00	150.00
39	F52	10 Pesos 1896, 98, 1901	125.00	150.00	200.00
40	F51	20 Pesos 1896–1917	160.00	190.00	275.00

Fourth Coinage

Cupro-Nickel

41	5 Centavos 1920–38	.25	.50	2.00
	1933 . . . 15.			
42	10 Centavos 1920–41	.25	.50	2.00
43	20 Centavos 1920–41	.35	.65	3.00

.500 Silver

35d	1 Peso 1921–25, value as UN	2.00	5.00	15.00
35e	1 Peso 1927, value as 1/UN	2.00	4.00	12.00

| 45 | 2 Pesos 1927 | 5.00 | 10.00 | 20.00 |

.900 Silver

| 46 | 5 Pesos 1927 | 14.00 | 20.00 | 30.00 |

.400 Silver (Billon)

| 35f | 1 Peso 1932 | 1.50 | 3.00 | 6.00 |

Cupro-Nickel

| 35g | 1 Peso 1933, 40 | .25 | .60 | 3.00 |

Gold

47	F56 20 Pesos 1926, 58–61	65.00	75.00	90.00
48	F55 50 Pesos 1926, 58–74	150.00	160.00	175.00
49	F54 100 Pesos 1926	300.00	325.00	350.00

Modified lettering both sides

| 49a | F54 100 Pesos 1932, 46–63 | 280.00 | 300.00 | 325.00 |

Dates after 1932 of the 20, 50 and 100 Pesos were struck as bullion coins, and not for circulation.

Fifth Coinage

Bronze

50	20 Centavos 1942–53	.25	.35	1.00
51	50 Centavos 1942	1.00	2.00	5.00
52	1 Peso 1942–54	.25	.50	2.00

Aluminum

| 52a | 1 Peso 1954–58 | .15 | .25 | 1.00 |

| 53 | 5 Pesos 1956 | .25 | .75 | 2.00 |
| 54 | 10 Pesos 1956–59 | .20 | .50 | 2.00 |

FIRST MONETARY REFORM 1960

Monetary System:
100 Centesimos (Condores) = 1 Escudo

First Coinage

Aluminum

| 55 | ½ Centesimo 1962–63 | .10 | .25 | 1.00 |
| 56 | 1 Centesimo 1960–63 | .10 | .25 | 1.00 |

Aluminum-Bronze

57	2 Centesimos 1964–70	.05	.10	.25
58	5 Centesimos 1960–70	.10	.20	.35
59	10 Centesimos 1960–70	.15	.25	.50

Later issues in *Current Coins of the World.*

CHINA

A country in eastern Asia, second largest of the world's nations, China was ruled by a succession of emperors before 1912. At that time it became a republic and remained so through several major changes of government. The economy is largely agricultural, though vast mineral resources exist, particularly coal, iron, tin and tungsten. Capital: *Peking.*

Monetary System:
10 Li = 1 Fen (Candareen)
10 Fen = 1 Ch'ien (Mace)
10 Ch'ien = 1 Liang (Tael)
7 Mace and 2 Candareens = 1 Dollar
10 Cash, Wen, Li = 1 Cent, Fen, Hsien
10 Cents = 1 Chio, Hao
100 Cents = 1 Dollar, Yuan

Coins not listed are probably either fantasies or patterns. Beware of often .clever forgeries of the rarer coins, including rare dates.

Cyclical Dates

Many dated coins use the Chinese sexagenary system as shown below. Coins bearing these cyclical dates are

Unless otherwise noted, prices are for coins in very fine, extremely fine, and uncirculated condition.

indicated in this catalog by the abbreviation CD preceding the date.

	1898		1907
戊戊	1898	丁末	1907
己亥	1899	戊申	1908
庚子	1900	己酉	1909
辛丑	1901	庚戊	1910
壬寅	1902	辛亥	1911
癸卯	1903	壬子	1912
甲辰	1904	癸亥	1913
乙巳	1905	甲子	1924
丙午	1906	己巳	1929
		庚午	1930

Mint Names

The first column below shows the abbreviated name used in the center of Tai-Ch'ing-Ti-Kuo coppers. The second column shows the full name as used on most other provincial coins.

皖	Huan for Anhwei	安徽
浙	Che for Chekiang	浙江
直	Chi for Chili	直隸
淮	Huai for Ching-Kiang	清江
閩	Ming for Fukien	福建
奉	Fung for Fengtien	奉天
汴	Bien for Honan	河南
湘	Shiang for Hunan	湖南
鄂	Ngau for Hupeh	湖北
贛	Kung for Kiangsi	江西
寗	Ning for Kiangnan	江南
蘇	Su for Kiangsu	江蘇
吉	Chi for Kirin	吉林
桂	Kuei for Kwangsi	廣西
粤	Yueh for Kwantung	廣東
黔	Ch'ien for Kweichow	貴州
山	Shan for Shansi	山西
陝	Shen for Shensi	陝西
東	Tung for Shantung	山東

川	Ch'uan for Szechuan	四川
雲	Yun for Yunnan	雲南
滇	Dien for Yunnan	雲南
川滇	Dien/Ch'uan for Yunnan/Szechuan	雲南四川

EMPIRE
KUANG HSU 1875–1908
Reign Symbols   on Coins
Legend: HU POO

The Hu Poo (National Board of Revenue) coins were issued about 1903–05 for general circulation. No. 5 was also struck during the early Republican period. Similar silver coins are patterns.

Copper or Brass

3*	5 Cash dragon circled	20.00	30.00	80.00
4	10 Cash dragon uncircled	2.00	3.50	15.00
5a	20 Cash dragon circled	50.00	75.00	200.00
5	20 Cash dragon uncircled	2.00	5.00	15.00

Legend: TAI-CH'ING-TI-KUO
Typical Coin of
Tai-Ch'ing-Ti-Kuo Series

Note: The date characters appear at the top as shown below for all coins dated 1905–06, but for some varieties of later dates they appear at the sides in place of the "Hu-Pu" characters (see No. 11e).

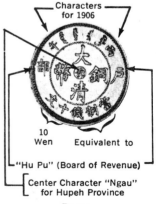

Characters for 1906

10 Wen   Equivalent to

"Hu Pu" (Board of Revenue)

Center Character "Ngau" for Hupeh Province

Brass

7*	1 Wen (Cash) 1908 general	5.00	8.00	20.00

7c	1 Wen 1908 Chihli	7.00	10.00	25.00
7g	1 Wen 1908 Honan	40.00	60.00	150.00
7j	1 Wen 1908 Hupeh	7.00	10.00	25.00
7k	1 Wen 1908 Kiangnan	7.00	10.00	25.00
7t	1 Wen 1908 Szechuan	200.00	250.00	350.00

Copper

Unless otherwise stated, Nos. 8–11 and 19–21 in brass rather than copper are generally contemporary counterfeits, usually cast.

8	2 Wen (Cash) 1905–07 general (blank center)	10.00	15.00	50.00
8b*	2 Wen 1906 Chekiang	15.00	25.00	60.00
8f	2 Wen 1906 Fukien, brass	10.00	15.00	40.00
8j	2 Wen 1906 Hupeh	90.00	120.00	200.00
8k	2 Wen 1906 Kiangnan			Pattern
8n	2 Wen 1906 Kiangsu, brass			Pattern
8s	2 Wen 1906 Shantung	40.00	55.00	140.00

9	5 Wen (Cash) 1905–07, general (blank center)	15.00	25.00	80.00
9b	5 Wen 1906 Chekiang	15.00	25.00	80.00
9c	5 Wen 1906 Chihli	15.00	25.00	80.00
9j*	5 Wen 1906 Hupeh	15.00	20.00	70.00
9k	5 Wen 1906 Kiangnan (vars.)	150.00	250.00	500.00
9n	5 Wen 1906 Kiangsu, brass	150.00	200.00	400.00

10	10 Wen (Cash) 1905–07, general (blank center)	1.50	2.50	15.00
10a	10 Wen 1906 Anhwei	2.00	4.00	30.00
10b	10 Wen 1906 Chekiang	2.00	4.00	25.00
10c	10 Wen 1906 Chihli	1.50	2.50	25.00
10d	10 Wen 1906 Chingkiang	2.00	4.00	25.00
10e	10 Wen 1905–07 Fengtien	5.00	8.00	30.00
10f	10 Wen 1906 Fukien	2.00	4.00	25.00
10g	10 Wen 1906 Honan	4.00	7.00	25.00

10h	10 Wen 1906 Hunan	4.00	7.00	25.00
10j*	10 Wen 1906 Hupeh	1.00	2.00	20.00
10k	10 Wen 1906–08 Kiangnan (vars)	1.00	2.00	20.00
10m	10 Wen 1906 Kiangsi	2.00	4.00	40.00
10n	10 Wen 1906 Kiangsu	2.00	4.00	25.00
10r	10 Wen 1906–08 Kwangtung	1.00	2.00	15.00
10s	10 Wen 1906 Shantung	3.00	5.00	40.00
10t	10 Wen 1906 Szechuan	2.00	4.00	25.00
10u	10 Wen 1906 Yunnan ''Yun'' in ctr.	60.00	85.00	280.00
10v	10 Wen 1906 Yunnan ''Tien'' ctr.	25.00	50.00	200.00
10w	10 Wen 1906 Yunnan-Szechuan	35.00	60.00	200.00

11	20 Wen (Cash) 1905–07, general (blank center)	3.00	5.00	30.00
11a	20 Wen 1906 Anhwei	250.00	350.00	800.00
11b	20 Wen 1906 Chekiang	80.00	120.00	350.00
11c	20 Wen 1906 Chihli	40.00	60.00	200.00
11d	20 Wen 1906 Chingkiang			Rare
11e*	20 Wen 1905–07 Fengtien	15.00	25.00	100.00
11j	20 Wen 1906 Hupeh	250.00	350.00	600.00
11n	20 Wen 1906 Kiangsu	250.00	350.00	600.00
11t	20 Wen 1906 Szechuan	20.00	25.00	120.00
11u	20 Wen 1906 Yunnan ''Yun'' center	100.00	150.00	500.00
11v	20 Wen 1906 Yunnan ''Tien'' ctr.	50.00	70.00	300.00
11w	20 Wen 1906 Yunnan-Szechuan	70.00	100.00	400.00

Silver

12	10 Cents ND (1908)	40.00	60.00	100.00
13*	20 Cents ND	60.00	80.00	120.00
14	1 Dollar ND	20.00	30.00	150.00

Gold

15	*F1–2* 1 Liang (Tael) ND (1906)		Rare

Unless otherwise noted, prices are for coins in very fine, extremely fine, and uncirculated condition.

HSUAN T'UNG 1908–1911

Reign symbols 宣統 on coins
Designs like Nos. 7–11

Brass

18	1 Wen 1909 general	50.00	70.00	120.00
A18	2 Wen 1909			Rare
A18g	2 Wen 1909 Honan			Rare

Copper

19	5 Wen 1909 general (blank ctr.)	200.00	300.00	600.00
19e	5 Wen 1909 Fengtien	200.00	300.00	600.00
19g	5 Wen 1909 Honan			Rare
20	10 Wen 1909 general (blank ctr.)	2.00	4.00	20.00
20a	10 Wen 1909 Anhwei	60.00	90.00	200.00
20e	10 Wen 1909 Fengtien	10.00	20.00	60.00
20f	10 Wen 1909 Fukien	60.00	90.00	200.00
20g	10 Wen 1909, 11 Honan	15.00	25.00	60.00
20j	10 Wen 1909 Hupeh	3.00	5.00	20.00
20p	10 Wen 1909 Kirin	30.00	50.00	120.00
20r	10 Wen 1909 Kwangtung	2.00	4.00	20.00
20t	10 Wen 1909 Szechuan	3.00	6.00	25.00
20x	10 Wen 1909 rosette center (Kirin style dragon)	25.00	40.00	90.00
21	20 Wen 1909 general (blank ctr.)	3.00	5.00	25.00
21e	20 Wen 1909 Fengtien	60.00	90.00	150.00
21g	20 Wen 1909 Honan (Wide flan)			Rare
21p	20 Wen 1909 Kirin	120.00	180.00	400.00
21t	20 Wen 1909 Szechuan	35.00	60.00	130.00

Silver

22	20 Cents 1909 Kirin	40.00	60.00	120.00

23	5 Chio/½ Dollar ND (1910)	60.00	90.00	180.00

Other denominations similar to No. 23 are patterns.

Second Coinage
Brass

25	1 Wen ND	2.00	3.00	6.00
A26	2 Wen ND			Pattern

The origin and date of No. 25 are unknown. Some authorities claim it is not a regular issue; others have it assigned to the series of 1905 or 1909.

Bronze

26	5 Wen Yr. 3 (1911)			Pattern
27*	10 Wen Yr. 3	4.00	6.00	25.00

Silver

28*	1 Chio Yr. 3	15.00	30.00	60.00
29	2 Chio Yr. 3	50.00	80.00	120.00
30	5 Chio Yr. 3	400.00	600.00	1000.

31	1 Dollar Yr. 3	15.00	25.00	80.00

PROVINCIAL COINAGE

Provincial coins, especially the copper 10 Cash pieces, exist in many varieties; only the major types can be listed in this catalog.

Anhwei

Copper or Brass

33 1 Ch'ien ND, struck   150.00 225.00 350.00
For similar cast pieces, more commonly found, see Craig, *Coins of the World.*

Copper

Side view dragon

34	1 "Cen" (10 Cash) ND	80.00	100.00	200.00
34a	1 "Sen" ND	100.00	130.00	250.00
35	5 Cash ND	250.00	350.00	800.00
36	10 Cash ND	4.00	6.00	35.00
36a*	(10 Cash) ND, no English value	3.00	5.00	30.00
37	20 Cash ND	750.00	1000.	1500.

Proof . . . Rare

Front view dragon

38a*	ToENCASH (ND)	30.00	50.00	100.00
38b	(10 Cash) ND, no English value	30.00	50.00	120.00

Coins with a large, single Chinese character on obverse are military award tokens.

Flying dragon (as No. 78)

39	10 Cash ND, AN-HUI	500.00	700.00	1200.
	(2 varieties exist)			

Proof . . . Rare

Silver

41	5 Cents	70.00	100.00	180.00
42	10 Cents	30.00	50.00	90.00
43*	20 Cents	40.00	60.00	130.00
44	50 Cents	100.00	175.00	300.00
45	1 Dollar	80.00	150.00	300.00

Two major varieties of Nos. 41–45: With or without the small letters "A-S-T-C" in Obv. field. The coins are either undated (1897), or variously dated Yrs. 23–27 (1897–1901) and CD 1898.

Chekiang
Brass

48 1 Ch'ien ND, struck   25.00 40.00 80.00
For similar cast pieces, more commonly found, see Craig, *Coins of the World.*

Copper or Brass

49*	(10 Cash) ND (vars.)	2.00	4.00	20.00
49a	(10 Cash) ND, 4 characters on bottom row	10.00	20.00	50.00
50	(20 Cash) ND	250.00	300.00	500.00

Silver

51	5 Cents ND (1902)	25.00	35.00	70.00
52	10 Cents Yr. 22–23 (1896–97), ND	20.00	30.00	60.00
53*	20 Cents Yr. 22–23, ND	35.00	50.00	90.00

Unless otherwise noted, prices are for coins in very fine, extremely fine, and uncirculated condition.

54 50 Cents ND   250.00 400.00 850.00
55 1 Dollar ND   Pattern
Coins inscribed "Che-Kiang" are Birmingham Mint patterns.

Chihli
Legend: PEKING
Silver

58* 10 Cents CD 1900   –
59 20 Cents CD 1900   –
Some authorities claim Nos. 58–59 are patterns. Other denominations are strikings made later from unused dies.

Legend: PEI YANG ARSENAL

61 ½ Chio Yrs. 22–24
        (1896–98)   20.00 35.00 60.00
62 1 Chio Yrs. 22–24   20.00 35.00 60.00
63 2 Chio Yrs. 22–24   25.00 40.00 80.00
64* 5 Chio Yrs. 22–24   60.00 90.00 180.00
65 1 Yuan Yrs. 22–24   25.00 50.00 120.00
The Yr. 22 issue is a major variety without the words "Ta Tsing" in legend. It is rarer than Yrs. 23–24.

Brass

66 1 Wen ND   5.00   8.00 15.00

Copper or Brass

A67 1 Ch'ien ND, struck   25.00 40.00 80.00
For similar cast pieces, more commonly found, see Craig.

Legend: PEI YANG
Copper or Brass

67* 10 Cash ND   3.00   6.00 25.00
68 20 Cash ND   25.00 45.00 120.00

Silver

69 5 Cents Yrs.25–26
        (1899–1900)   35.00 55.00 90.00
70 10 Cents Yr. 25   45.00 65.00 100.00
71* 20 Cents Yrs. 25–26   70.00 100.00 200.00
71a 20 Cents Yr. 31, dragon
        circled   90.00 150.00 300.00
72 50 Cents Yr. 25   120.00 200.00 400.00
73 1 Dollar Yrs. 25–34   13.00 18.00 60.00
74 1 Liang (Tael) Yr. 33   2500. 3500. 6000.

Chingkiang or Tsingkiang
Legend: CHING/KIANG
Copper or Brass

77 (10 Cash) ND   4.00   8.00 35.00

Legend: TSING/KIANG
Copper or Brass

78 10 Cash ND   3.00   6.00 30.00
Note: This was a city in Kiangsu Province.

Fengtien (Fung-Tien)

Despite inscriptions on the following coins, Fengtien was not a province, but the capital city of Shengking.

First Coinage
Copper

81 10 Ch'ien (Cash) ND   40.00 65.00 100.00

Silver

83	½ Chio Yr. 25 (1899)	25.00 45.00 90.00
84	1 Chio Yr. 24	20.00 40.00 90.00
85*	2 Chio Yr. 24	30.00 50.00 90.00
86	5 Chio Yrs. 24–25	200.00 350.00 500.00
87	1 Yuan Yrs. 24–25	150.00 250.00 450.00

Second Coinage
Legend: FEN-TIEN PROVINCE
Brass

88 10 Cash CD 1903   80.00 120.00 160.00

Legend: FUNG-TIEN PROVINCE

89	10 Cash CD 1903–06	5.00 10.00 30.00
90	20 Cash CD 1903–05	15.00 25.00 70.00

Nos. 88–90 struck in copper are patterns or trial strikes.

Silver

91*	20 Cents CD 1904 (2 vars.)	10.00 20.00 50.00
92	1 Dollar CD 1903 (2 vars.)	120.00 200.00 350.00

Undated silver coins, and the 1 Liang coin are patterns.

For later Fengtien issues
see Manchurian Provinces

Formosa —
see Taiwan

Fukien
Brass

95 1 Wen ND   25.00 35.00 60.00

No. 95 is attributed to Fukien by the Manchu character at right on the reverse. Do not confuse this with Nos. 191 and 204.

Unless otherwise noted, prices are for coins in very fine, extremely fine, and uncirculated condition.

Copper or Brass
Legend: F.K. CUSTOM-HOUSE

97	10 Cash ND	3.00	5.00	20.00

Legend: FOO-KIEN CUSTOM
98	10 Cash ND	150.00	250.00	400.00

Legend: FOO-KIEN

99	5 Cash ND	15.00	25.00	80.00
100*	10 Cash ND	2.00	4.00	20.00
101	20 Cash ND	50.00	80.00	150.00

Silver

102	5 Cents ND (1898–1902)	7.00	12.00	25.00
103	10 Cents ND	5.00	8.00	25.00
104*	20 Cents ND	6.00	9.00	25.00
105	1 Dollar ND (1898)	4500.	5500.	8000.
			Proof . . . Rare

The 1898 coins have 5 characters at the top of the obverse (illustrated), while the 1902 issues have only 4.

Hsuan T'ung Reign
Brass

Different characters at top-bottom
(see illus. above No. 18).

106	1 Wen ND	50.00	70.00	100.00

See note below No. 95.

Honan
Copper or Brass

108	10 Cash ND, dragon cir-cled	3.00	6.00	30.00
108a	10 Cash ND, dragon un-circled	3.00	6.00	30.00

Hunan
Copper or Brass

Side view dragon

112	10 Cash ND (vars.)	2.00	4.00	25.00

Flying dragon

113	10 Cash ND (Vars.)	10.00	15.00	35.00

Silver

115	10 Cents CD 1898–99, ND (1902)	25.00	35.00	75.00
116*	20 Cents ND	250.00	350.00	600.00

Other denominations are patterns.

Hupeh

Brass

119 1 Ch'ien ND, struck
(vars.)　　　　35.00　50.00　90.00
For similar cast pieces, more commonly found, see
Craig.

Copper

Side view dragon
120 10 Cash ND, dragon circled　　　　10.00　15.00　40.00
120a 10 Cash ND, dragon uncircled　　　2.00　3.00　20.00
(many varieties)

Front view dragon
121 1 Cash ND　　8.00　12.00　20.00

122 10 Cash ND (vars.)　1.00　2.00　15.00
Extremely rare patterns exist in brass; these are very
heavy, unlike the cast brass counterfeits.
122a 10 Cash ND, circled
front view dragon　200.00 250.00 450.00

Silver

123 5 Cents ND (1896)　　120.00 200.00 300.00
124 10 Cents ND (1895–96)　3.00　6.00　15.00
125* 20 Cents ND (1895–96)　5.00　8.00　20.00
126 50 Cents ND (1896)　35.00　50.00 100.00
127 1 Dollar ND (1895–96)　15.00　20.00　70.00
The 1895 issue (extremely rare) is an experimental series with two Chinese characters added at the sides of
the dragon.
128 1 Tael Yr. 30 (1904)　150.00 250.00 400.00

Hsuan T'ung Reign
Different characters at top-bottom
(See illus. above No. 18)
129 10 Cents ND (1909)　30.00　45.00　90.00
130 20 Cents ND　400.00 500.00 700.00
131 1 Dollar ND　15.00　20.00　70.00

Kiangnan
A region consisting of Kiangsu, Anhwei, and Kiangsi
provinces.

Copper or Brass

Flying dragon
135 10 Cash ND, CD
1902–1905　　2.00　4.00　20.00

Front view dragon
138* 10 Cash CD 1905 (2
vars.)　　2.00　3.00　20.00
140 10 Cash CD 1906, Obv.
of No. 10k, rev. of No.
138.　　3.00　5.00　25.00

Unless otherwise noted, prices are for coins in very
fine, extremely fine, and uncirculated condition.

Other mules of Kiangnan coppers exist, especially with Kiangsu No. 160.

Silver
Dragon circled

141	5 Cents ND (1897)	25.00	45.00	90.00
142	10 Cents ND, CD 1898	20.00	40.00	80.00
143	20 Cents ND, CD 1898	35.00	55.00	100.00
144	50 Cents ND	500.00	700.00	1000.
145	1 Dollar ND	100.00	200.00	400.00

Dragon not circled

141a	5 Cents ND, CD 1899–1901	10.00	15.00	35.00
142a	10 Cents CD 1898–1905	5.00	8.00	25.00
143a*	20 Cents CD 1898–1905	5.00	8.00	20.00
144a	50 Cents CD 1899–1900	1800.	2200.	3000.
		Proof . . . Rare		
145a	1 Dollar CD 1898–1905	15.00	20.00	80.00

The 20 Cents and Dollar have a different dragon (illustrated) starting in 1899. Most coins dated 1901–05 have small English initials on the obverse.

Hsuan T'ung Reign
Different characters at top-bottom
(see illus. above No.18)

146	10 Cents ND (1909)	15.00	35.00	70.00
147	20 Cents ND	40.00	65.00	100.00

Kiangsi
Copper or Brass

Side view dragon

149	10 Cash KIANG-SEE, dragon circled or uncir-cled	10.00	20.00	40.00
150	10 Cash KIANG-SI	2.00	3.00	20.00

Front view dragon

152	10 Cash KIANG-SI	4.00	8.00	35.00
153*	10 Cash KIANG-SEE PROVINCE	4.00	7.00	30.00
	Flying dragon			
154	10 Cash KIANG-SI	70.00	90.00	180.00

Kiangsu
Copper or Brass

157	1 Ch'ien ND, struck	25.00	40.00	70.00

For similar cast pieces, more commonly found, see Craig.

Side view dragon

158	EIVE (= 5) CASH ND	35.00	55.00	100.00
	Front view dragon			
160	10 Cash ND	3.00	5.00	30.00

Flying dragon

159	2 Cash ND	300.00	400.00	500.00
161	5 Cash ND	300.00	400.00	500.00
162	10 Cash ND, CD 1902–03, 05	2.00	3.00	15.00
163	20 Cash ND	40.00	55.00	100.00

Some authorities consider Nos. 159 and 161 to be patterns or later strikings from unused dies.

Kirin
First Coinage
Silver

169	1 Ch'ien (Mace) Yr. 10			
	(1885)	500.00	650.00	800.00
170	3 Ch'ien Yr. 10	500.00	650.00	800.00
171*	5 Ch'ien Yr. 10	500.00	650.00	800.00
172	7 Ch'ien Yr. 10	700.00	850.00	1000.
173	1 Liang (Tael) Yr. 10	1000.	1300.	1500.

Second Coinage
Copper

175*	2 Wen ND	80.00	110.00	200.00
174	10 Wen ND	400.00	550.00	800.00

Copper or Brass
Side view dragon

176	10 Cashes ND	80.00	120.00	200.00
A176	20 Cashes ND	300.00	400.00	500.00
B176	50 Cashes CD 1901	–		

The authenticity of No. B176 is doubtful.

Flying dragon
Many varieties exist of Nos. 177–178

177	10 Cashes ND	6.00	10.00	35.00
178	20 Cashes ND	80.00	120.00	220.00

Silver

Obv. center: Flower vase

179	5 Cents ND (1896–98),			
	CD 1899–1908	10.00	20.00	50.00
180	10 Cents ND, 1899–1907	10.00	20.00	50.00
181*	20 Cents ND,			
	1899–1908	15.00	25.00	60.00
182	50 Cents ND, 1899–1908	35.00	50.00	100.00
183	1 Dollar ND, 1899–1908	55.00	85.00	200.00

Obv. center: Yin-Yang

179a	5 Cents CD 1900–05	12.00	25.00	60.00
180a	10 Cents CD 1900–05	10.00	20.00	50.00
181a*	20 Cents CD 1900–05	12.00	25.00	60.00
182a	50 Cents CD 1900–05	35.00	50.00	100.00
183a	1 Dollar CD 1900–05	55.00	85.00	200.00

Obv. center: two Manchu characters

181b*	20 Cents CD 1908	100.00	150.00	250.00
182b	50 Cents CD 1908	250.00	350.00	600.00
183b	1 Dollar CD 1908	350.00	550.00	900.00

Obv. center: Arabic number

180c	10 Cents CD 1908 ''1''			
	in center	55.00	80.00	150.00
181c*	20 Cents CD 1908 ''2''			
	in ctr.	40.00	70.00	120.00
183c	1 Dollar CD 1908 ''11''			
	in ctr.	300.00	500.00	800.00

Kwangtung
Nos. 189–191 and 204 are attributed to Kwangtung by the Manchu character on the reverse — at left on 189, at right on 190–91.

Brass

189 1 Ch'ien ND (1889–90)   .50   .70 1.00

190 (1 Ch'ien) ND (1892–94)   .30   .50   .80

191 1 Wen ND   .20   .30   .50

Copper

192 1 Cent ND (1900)   1.00 2.00 10.00
193 10 Cash ND   1.00 2.00 10.00

Silver

Obv. with English legend

194 5 Cents ND (1889)   350.00 500.00 750.00
195 10 Cents ND   200.00 350.00 500.00
196* 20 Cents ND   275.00 425.00 650.00
197 50 Cents ND   600.00 850.00 1200.
198 1 Dollar ND   1000. 2000. 3000.
Two varieties of Nos. 194–198: The first slightly heavier and inscribed with higher weights, the second (illus.) of normal weight for provincial silver.

Rev. with English legend
(regular provincial type)

199 5 Cents ND (1890)   4.00 6.00 12.00
200 10 Cents ND   3.00 5.00 7.00
201* 20 Cents ND   3.00 5.00 8.00
202 50 Cents ND   30.00 45.00 100.00
203 1 Dollar ND   15.00 20.00 80.00

Hsuan T'ung Reign
Different characters at top-bottom
(see illus. above No. 18)

Brass

204* 1 Wen ND (as No. 191)   .50 1.00 2.00

Silver

205 20 Cents ND (1909)   5.00 8.00 15.00
206 1 Dollar ND   20.00 30.00 150.00

Manchurian Provinces

(Fengtien, Heilungkiang, Kirin)
Silver

209 10 Cents Yr. 33 (1907)   20.00 35.00 70.00
210* 20 Cents Yr. 33   10.00 15.00 40.00
211 50 Cents Yr. 33   150.00 250.00 400.00
212 1 Dollar Yr. 33   200.00 300.00 450.00

Hsuan T'ung Reign
Different characters in obv. center
(See illus. above No. 18)

213 20 Cents Yr. 1 (1909)   5.00 10.00 25.00

213a *20 Cents ND (1909–10)   5.00 10.00 25.00
No. 213 is inscribed either "1st Year" or "First Year."
Do not confuse No. 213a with 217.

Peiyang — see
Chihli

Shansi
Silver

217 20 Cents ND   250.00 450.00 650.00
The obverse of No. 217 bears Chinese characters for
Shansi, but the reverse is a crude copy of No. 213a.
Several varieties exist, all struck in the early years of the
Republic.

Shantung
Copper

Side view dragon
220 10 Cash ND   10.00 20.00 50.00

Flying dragon
221 10 Cash ND SHANTUNG   8.00 15.00 40.00
221a 10 Cash ND SHANG-
TUNG   3.00   5.00 25.00
Dragon coins of Shensi province are patterns.

Sinkiang — see
Chinese Turkestan

Szechuan
Copper or Brass

Side view dragon
225 5 Cash ND   200.00 300.00 500.00
226* 10 Cash ND   80.00 120.00 350.00
227 20 Cash ND   150.00 250.00 500.00

Flying dragon
228 5 Cash ND   100.00 150.00 250.00
229 10 Cash ND   8.00 15.00 50.00
230 20 Cash ND   35.00 55.00 120.00

Front view dragon
231 10 Cash ND   150.00 250.00 500.00
233 30 Cash ND   Rare
Some authorities believe Nos. 231–233 are patterns.

Silver

234 5 Cents ND (1897)   15.00 25.00 50.00
235 10 Cents ND   15.00 25.00 50.00
236 20 Cents ND   15.00 25.00 50.00
237* 50 Cents ND   30.00 45.00 100.00
238 1 Dollar ND   18.00 25.00 150.00

Unless otherwise noted, prices are for coins in very
fine, extremely fine, and uncirculated condition.

Hsuan T'ung Reign

Different characters at top-bottom
(see illus. above No. 18)

239	5 Cents ND (1909)	30.00	50.00	100.00
240	10 Cents ND	25.00	45.00	90.00
242	50 Cents ND	100.00	150.00	300.00
243	1 Dollar ND	25.00	60.00	250.00

Taiwan (Formosa)

Silver

246	5 Cents ND (ca. 1890)	180.00	250.00	450.00
247*	10 Cents ND (2 vars.)	40.00	75.00	120.00
248	20 Cents ND (2 vars.)			Rare

Tsingkiang — see

Chingkiang

Turkestan — see

Chinese Turkestan

Yunnan

Silver

Regular provincial type

252*	20 Cents ND (1907)	20.00	35.00	70.00
253	50 Cents ND	8.00	15.00	30.00
254	1 Dollar ND	30.00	45.00	120.00

No English legends

255	10 Cents ND (1908)	30.00	40.00	60.00
256	20 Cents ND	15.00	25.00	50.00
257*	50 Cents ND	4.00	7.00	20.00
258	1 Dollar ND	15.00	25.00	60.00

Hsuan T'ung Reign

Different characters in obv. center
(see illus. above No. 18)
Regular provincial type

259	50 Cents ND (1909)	15.00	25.00	60.00
260	1 Dollar ND, CD 1910	35.00	65.00	150.00

The CD 1910 date is extremely rare.

REPUBLIC 1911–1949
General Coinage 1911–26
Copper or Brass

301	10 Cash ND (vars.)	1.00	2.00	12.00

302	10 Wen (Cash) ND (vars.)	2.00	4.00	20.00

303*	10 Cash ND	1.00	2.00	12.00
304	10 Wen ND, obv. of 303, rev. 302	40.00	70.00	100.00

No. 304 is listed by Woodward as No. 1086.

305	10 Cash ND	65.00	95.00	150.00

306* 10 Cash ND, 4 charac-
ters at bottom (3 vars.) 1.00 2.00 12.00
306a 10 Cash ND, 5 char. at
bottom 10.00 15.00 40.00

311 10 Wen Yr. 13 (1924) 150.00 250.00 400.00
312* 2 Mei (Cents) Yr. 13 10.00 25.00 70.00
Some authorities believe No. 311 is a pattern.

Obv: striped flag at right
307 1 Mei (10 Cash) ND 1.00 2.00 20.00
308 20 Wen (20 Cash) Yr. 8
(1919) 2.00 5.00 25.00

Silver

Obv: Sun Yat-sen
317 (20 Cents) ND (1912) 25.00 40.00 60.00

Obv: Ornate flag at right
307a*1 Mei ND 2.00 4.00 20.00
308a 20 Wen Yr. 10 sim 2.00 5.00 25.00

309* 10 Cash ND 20.00 35.00 80.00
310 20 Cash ND, English at
bottom of both sides 30.00 60.00 120.00

318 1 Yuan ND (1912) 150.00 250.00 350.00
No. 318 has stars on rev. (see arrows). Do not confuse
with the common 1927 issue, No. 318a.

**Unless otherwise noted, prices are for coins in very
fine, extremely fine, and uncirculated condition.**

319 1 Dollar ND, obv. as No.
318.   80.00 120.00 200.00

Obv: Li Yuan Hung
320 1 Dollar ND (1912)   200.00 300.00 450.00

321 1 Dollar ND (1912)   35.00 60.00 120.00

Obv: Yuan Shih-kai

322 1 Dollar ND (1914)   100.00 160.00 250.00

Bronze

323 5 Li Yr. 5 (1916)   15.00 25.00 50.00
324* 1 Fen Yr. 5   3.00   5.00 12.00
Also see similar 1933 issues, Nos. 324a and 325a
below. The 2 Fen Yr. 5 is a pattern.

Silver

Obv: Yuan Shih-kai
326 1 Chio Yrs. 3–5
   (1914–16)   4.00   6.00 12.00
327* 2 Chio Yrs. 3–9   2.50   4.00 12.00
   Yr. 9 . . . Rare
328 ½ Yuan Yr. 3   15.00 25.00 50.00
329 1 Yuan Yrs. 3–10   12.00 15.00 20.00
The 5 Fen in nickel is a pattern.

Gold

330 *F5* 10 Yuan Yr. 8 (1919) 1500. 2000. 3500.
331 *F4* 20 Yuan Yr. 8   1800. 2500. 4000.

HUNG HSIEN Reign 1915–16
Title assumed by Yuan Shih-kai
Also see No. 401

Silver

332 (1 Yuan) Yr. 1, obv. as
   322, rev. as 333   250.00 350.00 600.00

Gold

333 *F3* 10 Yuan Yr. 1   2000. 3000. 4500.

Republican Issues Resumed
Silver

334 1 Chio Yr. 15 (1926)   5.00   8.00   20.00
335* 2 Chio Yr. 15   7.00 10.00   25.00
336 1 Yuan Yr. 12   250.00 350.00 550.00

Nationalist Coinage 1927–49

Brass "Ration" Coins

Rev: Nationalist sun

337 1 Fen Yr. 17 (1928)   150.00 250.00 400.00
338 2 Fen Yr. 17   250.00 350.00 500.00
Nos. 337–338 always have a small incuse punch mark on both sides. Similar 5 and 10 Fen are patterns.

Silver

Obv: Sun Yat-Sen

339 1 Chio Yr. 16 (1927)   30.00 45.00 70.00
340* 2 Chio Yr. 16   25.00 40.00 60.00

As 318, but rosettes on rev.

318a 1 Yuan ND (1927–32) 12.50 15.00 20.00

Bronze

324a 1 Fen Yr. 22 (1933)   30.00 50.00 80.00
325a 2 Fen Yr. 22   120.00 150.00 200.00

Rev: Birds over junk, sun at right
344 1 Yuan Yr. 21 (1932)   90.00 130.00 180.00

Rev: No birds or sun
345 1 Yuan Yrs. 22–23   12.00 15.00 20.00
Other coins of various denominations similar to No. 345 are patterns.

Currency Reform Nov. 1935
First Coinage
Bronze

346 ½ Fen Yr. 25 (1936)   2.00   4.00   8.00
347* 1 Fen Yrs. 25–28   1.00   2.00   5.00

Unless otherwise noted, prices are for coins in very fine, extremely fine, and uncirculated condition.

Nickel, Plain Edge

348 5 Fen Yrs. 25-28
   (1936-39)   1.00   2.00   4.00
349* 10 Fen Yrs. 25-28   1.00   1.50   3.00
350 20 Fen Yrs. 25-28   1.00   2.00   4.00
Unlisted denominations, dates, and coins with extra Chinese characters on either side are patterns.

World War II Provisional Issues
Brass

353* 1 Hsien (Cent) Yr. 28
   (1939)   60.00   90.00 150.00
354 2 Hsien Yr. 28   10.00   15.00   25.00

Aluminum

355 1 Fen Yr. 29 (1940)   .30   .50   1.00

356 5 Fen Yr. 29   .20   .50   1.00
Coins dated Yr. 28 and other denominations are patterns.

Second Coinage
Brass

357* 1 Fen Yr. 29   .50   .80   1.20
358 2 Fen Yr. 29   .50   1.00   1.50

Cupro-Nickel, Reeded Edge

359 5 Fen Yrs. 29-30   1.00   2.00   4.00
360* 10 Fen Yrs. 29-31   1.50   2.00   3.00
361 20 Fen Yr. 31 (1942) 1.00   2.00   4.00
362 ½ Yuan Yrs. 31-32   1.50   2.00   3.00
Unlisted dates are patterns.

Third Coinage
Bronze

363 1 Fen Yr. 37 (1948)   10.00   15.00   20.00
For Nationalist issues on Taiwan (Formosa), see Nos. 531-536.

Provincial and Regional Issues
Chekiang

Silver

371* 10 Cents Yr. 13 (1924)   6.00   9.00   15.00
372 20 Cents Yr. 13, similar   Patterns
373 20 Cents Yr. 13, large 20 500.00 700.00 1000.

Fukien
Cast Brass

374 1 Wen ND (1911)   80.00 150.00   –
375* 2 Wen ND (2 vars.)   35.00 50.00   –

Silver

377 20 Cents CD 1911   15.00   25.00   60.00

Copper

379 10 Cash ND (1912)   5.00   10.00   25.00

Silver

380 10 Cents ND (1912), CD
1924   50.00   70.00 120.00
381* 20 Cents ND, CD
1923–24   7.00   10.00   25.00

382 10 Cents ND (1913)   4.00   7.00   15.00
383* 20 Cents ND   4.00   8.00   20.00
383a 20 Cents Yr. 13 (1924)   40.00   55.00   80.00

Northern Expedition Commemoratives

384* 2 Hao (20 Cents) Yr. 16
(1927)   250.00 350.00 550.00

385 2 Hao Yr. 16, obv. center
4 characters   350.00 500.00 800.00

Canton Martyrs Commemoratives

388 10 Cents Yrs. 17,20
(1928,31)   5.00   10.00   25.00
389* 20 Cents Yrs. 17, 20   3.00   6.00   15.00
390 10 Cents Yr. 21 (1932)
obv. flags   150.00 250.00 350.00
391 20 Cents Yr. 21, similar   50.00   70.00 100.00

Honan

Copper or Brass

Obv: Value in center
A392 10 Cash ND   2.00   3.00   15.00

Obv: flower in center
392* 10 Cash ND (1912) 2
vars.   1.00   2.00   15.00
393 20 Cash ND (2 vars.)   2.00   5.00   25.00
394 50 Cash ND (38mm)   5.00   10.00   30.00
395 100 Cash ND (40mm)   6.00   15.00   40.00
396 200 Cash ND (42mm)   6.00   15.00   40.00

New Legend: CHINA replaces HO-NAN
393a 20 Cash ND   60.00 100.00 200.00
394a 50 Cash ND   40.00   80.00 150.00
396 20 Cash Yr. 20 (1931), star replaces China   Rare

Unless otherwise noted, prices are for coins in very
fine, extremely fine, and uncirculated condition.

397 50 Wen Yr. 20 (1931)   100.00 150.00 200.00
398* 100 Wen Yr. 20   40.00 80.00 150.00

Hunan

Copper

399 10 Cash ND (2 vars.)   3.00   6.00 20.00

Copper or Brass

400 20 Cash ND, value
TWENTY spelled out
(many vars.)   1.00   3.00 20.00
400a 20 Cash ND, value "20" 150.00 250.00 400.00

Hung Hsien Reign

401 10 Cash Yr. 1 (1915)   25.00 35.00 80.00
Also see Nos. 332–333 for this reign.

Provincial Constitution Commemoratives
Copper

402 10 Cash Yr. 11 (1922) 2
vars.   20.00 30.00 60.00
403 20 Cash Yr. 11   25.00 45.00 80.00

Silver

404 1 Dollar Yr. 11   275.00 350.00 550.00

Hupeh

Copper or Brass

A405 20 Ch'ien (Cash) ND   100.00 150.00 250.00
Attribution to Hupeh is uncertain.
Design similar to No. 449
405 50 Wen Yrs. 3, 7 (1914,
18)   600.00 800.00   –
Two varieties exist of the 1918 issue, one crude, the
other as No. 449.

Silver

406 2 Chio Yr. 9 (1920)   150.00 250.00 350.00
As No. 327, but two characters for Hupeh added at sides of head.

Kansu

Silver

Obv: Yuan Shih-kai

407 1 Yuan Yr. 3 (1914)   250.00 400.00 1000.
As No. 329, but two characters for Kansu added at sides of head.

Copper

408* 50 Wen Yr. 15 (1926)   60.00 100.00 200.00
409 100 Wen Yr. 15   40.00 80.00 150.00

Silver

Obv: Sun Yat-Sen
410 1 Yuan Yr. 17 (1928)   200.00 350.00 700.00

Kiangsi

Copper

Obv: similar to No. 10m
Rev: stylized Republican star (design of balls and arcs)
411 10 Wen CD 1911   Rare

412 10 Cash CD 1912   200.00 350.00   –
412a 10 Cash CD 1912,
different obverse legends   4.00   7.00 25.00

Kwangsi

Legend: KWANG SEA
Brass

413* 1 Cent Yr. 8 (1919)   80.00 120.00 250.00

Unless otherwise noted, prices are for coins in very
fine, extremely fine, and uncirculated condition.

Silver

415 20 Cents Yr. 8–13   60.00 80.00 150.00

Legend: KWANG-SI
Brass

413a 1 Cent Yr. 8   30.00 50.00 100.00

Silver

414 10 Cents Yr. 9 (1920)   120.00 150.00 200.00
415a 20 Cents Yrs. 8–14   8.00 12.00 20.00

Wreath added on reverse
415b 20 Cents Yrs. 15–16
(1926–27)   4.00 6.00 10.00

416 2 Chio Yr. 38 (1949)   100.00 150.00 300.00

Kwangtung
Brass or Copper

417 1 Cent Yrs. 1–7
(1912–18)   2.00 5.00 12.00

418 2 Cents Yr. 7   60.00 80.00 130.00

Cupro-Nickel

420* 5 Hsien/5 Cents Yr. 8
(1919)   1.00 2.00 4.00
420a ½ Hao/5 Cents Yr. 12   1.00 2.00 4.00

421 5 Cents Yr. 10   3.00 5.00 10.00

Silver

422 10 Cents Yrs. 2–11
(1913–22)   2.00 3.00 6.00
423 20 Cents Yrs. 1–13   3.00 5.00 8.00

424 2 Hao Yr. 13 (1924)   20.00 30.00 50.00

425 1 Hao Yr. 18 (1929)   1.00 2.00 6.00
426* 2 Hao Yrs. 17–18   2.50 3.50 6.00
Coins dated Yr. 19 are patterns.

Copper

427 1 Hsien (Cent) Yr. 25
(1936)   250.00 350.00 500.00
Some authorities claim No. 427 is a pattern.

431 20 Fen Yr. 38, rev. "20"   250.00 350.00   –
432 ½ Yuan Yr. 38, rev. "50"   350.00 450.00   –

Kweichow

First Road in Kweichow
Silver

Obv: Pagoda
433 1 Yuan Yr. 38, rev. 3
bamboo stems   700.00 1000.   –

428 1 Yuan Yr. 17 (1928)   250.00 350.00 1000.
This is the famous "Auto Dollar."

Antimony

429 10 Fen Yr. 20 (1931)   300.00   –   –

Manchurian Provinces

Copper

Silver
Some authorities consider Nos. 431–432 to be patterns.

434 1 Fen Yr. 18 (1929)   2.00   4.00 12.00

Obv: similar to No. 429, ornate border
430 20 Fen Yr. 38 (1949),
rev. 3 seal characters   150.00 250.00   –

Shansi

Copper
A435 1 Mei (10 Cash) ND   200.00 250.00 400.00
As No. 307, but two characters for Shansi replace stars
on obverse. Some authorities consider this coin a pattern, but most known pieces are well-circulated.

Unless otherwise noted, prices are for coins in very
fine, extremely fine, and uncirculated condition.

Shensi

Copper

435* 1 Fen ND (ca. 1924) IM-TYPIF   180.00 250.00   –
436 2 Fen ND, IMTYPEF (vars.)   50.00   80.00 200.00

Silver

453 1 Chio Yr. 1	35.00	50.00	100.00
454* 2 Chio Yr. 1	50.00	80.00	150.00
455 5 Chio Yrs. 1–2	20.00	35.00	100.00
456 1 Yuan Yrs. 1, 3	12.00	15.00	80.00

Cupro-Nickel

457 5 Fen Yr. 14   300.00 350.00 500.00

Copper or Brass

459* 200 Cash Yr. 2 (vars.)   10.00   15.00   50.00

Szechuan

Copper or Brass

441 (5 Wen) Yr. 1 (1912)   80.00 120.00 200.00

443 5 Wen Yr. 1   80.00 120.00 200.00

446 5 Wen Yr. 1	150.00	200.00	350.00
447* 10 Wen Yrs. 1–2	3.00	5.00	12.00
448 20 Wen Yrs. 1–3 (32mm)	4.00	6.00	15.00
449 50 Wen Yrs. 1–3 (36mm)	5.00	8.00	15.00
450 100 Wen Yrs. 2–3 (39mm)	5.00	8.00	15.00

462 50 Wen Yr. 15 (1926)	50.00	75.00	120.00
463 100 Wen Yr. 15	10.00	20.00	45.00
464 200 Wen Yr. 15	10.00	25.00	60.00

Brass

466* 100 Wen Yrs. 15, 19
(1926, 30)   350.00 400.00 600.00

Various Metals

468 1 Chio ND (ca. 1926)   –
No. 468 exists in silver, brass and several other minor
metals. See Kann No. 825.

Silver

Obv: Sun Yat-sen facing

473* 5 Chio Yr. 17 (1928)   350.00 500.00 800.00
474 1 Yuan Yr. 17   500.00 800.00 1500.
Many other legitimate coins in silver and minor metals
were circulated widely; often these coins lack provincial
designations. Warlords (or Chinese communists) copied
Yuan Shih-kai and Sun Yat-sen dollars, the latter with
spelling errors in the English inscription. Crudely struck
or cast copies of Nos. 446–450 are not necessarily
counterfeit, but often warlord issues.

Copper or Brass

476 2 Cents Yr. 19 (1930)   350.00 500.00 800.00

Yunnan

Copper or Brass

Obv: Governor T'ang Chi-yao
478 50 Wen ND (ca. 1916)   25.00 50.00 90.00

Silver

479 50 Cents ND (1916)   5.00   8.00 15.00

480 50 Cents ND (1917)   30.00 45.00 90.00

Gold

481* F12 5 Dollars ND
(1919)   500.00 650.00 900.00
482 F10–11 10 Dollars ND (2
vars.)   600.00 800.00 1200.

493 2 Chio Yr. 38 (1949)   6.00   8.00   30.00

There are two other sets of Yunnan gold $5 and $10 (struck about 1917 and 1925), bearing Chinese inscriptions only, but their authenticity is uncertain.

See Friedberg, *Gold Coins of the World*, Nos. 8–9 and 13–14.

World War II Issues
Silver

Cupro-Nickel

485 5 Cents Yr. 12 (1923)   40.00   60.00 100.00
486* 10 Cents Yr. 12   2.00   4.00   15.00

Brass

495* ½ Liang (Tael) ND
(1942–43)   15.00   25.00   40.00
496 1 Liang ND   30.00   50.00   80.00

488 1 Hsien (Cent) Yr. 21 (1932)   Rare
489 2 Hsien Yr. 21   350.00 500.00   –
490 5 Hsien Yr. 21   200.00 350.00   –

Silver

491* 2 Chio Yr. 21   8.00   12.00   20.00
492 ½ Yuan Yr. 21   4.00   6.00   12.00

497 1 Liang ND   45.00   65.00 120.00
The exact origin of these so-called "Yunnan-Burma Taels" is uncertain. They are said to have been paid to Chinese troops in southern Yunnan, eastern Burma, or the Laotian area of northern Indo-China.

Communist Army Issues 1930–34
Note: All dated Communist coins bear western dates, usually expressed in Chinese numerals. Dates are written either right-to-left or left-to-right.

A. Hunan
Silver

Obv: As No. 504
Rev: Sim. to No. 504, but with garbled Russian legend
503 1 Yuan 1932   700.00 900.00   –

504 1 Yuan 1932   400.00 600.00   –

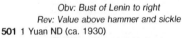

Obv: Bust of Lenin to right
Rev: Value above hammer and sickle
501 1 Yuan ND (ca. 1930)   –
Obv: Hammer and sickle in star
Rev: Value in wreath
502 1 Yuan 1931   –
Nos. 501 and 502 are controversial. Most authorities consider them bogus.

C. Chinese Soviet Republic (Kiangsi).
Modern copies exist of Nos. 506,507, 511 and 512

Copper

506 1 Fen ND (1932)   35.00   50.00   –

507 5 Fen ND (Vars.)   80.00 120.00   –

Unless otherwise noted, prices are for coins in very fine, extremely fine, and uncirculated condition.

Modern Copies

506a 1 Fen   – – 5.00
507a 5 Fen   – – 10.00

Silver

508 2 Chio 1932–33   90.00 150.00 –

512 500 Wen 1934 (vars.) 180.00 250.00 –
512a 500 Wen, modern copy – – 15.00

D. Szechuan and Shensi
Copper

510 200 Wen 1933 (many
  vars., crude)   200.00 500.00 –

511 200 Wen 1934   120.00 180.00 –
511a 200 Wen, modern copy – – 15.00

Silver

513 1 Yuan 1934 (vars.) 250.00 350.00 –

"Puppet State" Issues

Japanese-controlled regional governments

Also see Manchukuo

A. Chi-Tung (Eastern Hopei)
Bronze

516 5 Li (½ Cent) Yr. 26
  (1937)   15.00 25.00 45.00
517 1 Fen Yr. 26   5.00 8.00 20.00

Cupro-Nickel

518 5 Fen Yr. 26   4.00   6.00   12.00

519* 1 Chio Yr. 26   4.00   6.00   12.00
520 2 Chio Yr. 26   8.00   12.00   25.00

B. Meng-Chiang (Inner Mongolia)
Cupro-Nickel

521 5 Chio Yr. 27 (1938)   4.00   6.00   15.00

C. Hua Hsing Bank (Shanghai)
Bronze

A521 1 Fen Yr. 29 (1940)   70.00 100.00 200.00

Cupro-Nickel

522 10 Fen Yr. 29   1.00   2.00   4.00
Other denominations (with different reverse designs), and the 1 Fen in cupro-nickel are patterns.

D. Federal Reserve Bank of China
(North China district — Peking)
Aluminum

523 1 Fen Yrs. 30–32
    (1941–43)   1.00   2.00   5.00
524 5 Fen Yrs. 30–32   2.00   4.00   10.00
525* 1 Chio Yrs. 30–32   1.00   2.00   5.00

NATIONALIST ISSUES 1949–

on Taiwan (Formosa)
First Coinage
Bronze

531* 1 Chio Yr. 38 (1949)   .20   .30   2.00

Silver

532 5 Chio Yr. 38   3.00   4.00   7.50

Second Coinage
Aluminum

533 1 Chio Yr. 44 (1955)   .10   .20   .50
534* 2 Chio Yr. 39   1.00   2.00   5.00

Brass

535 5 Chio Yr. 43   .20   .30   .50

Nickel-Silver

536 1 Yuan Yr. 49– (1960–)   .05   .10   .20
Many patterns of all Republican coins exist, including portrait coins.

Later issues in *Current Coins of the World.*

Unless otherwise noted, prices are for coins in very fine, extremely fine, and uncirculated condition.

CHINA, PEOPLE'S REPUBLIC of

Second largest of the world's nations, China became a republic in 1911. The present government was established in 1949 after Communist forces drove out the former (Nationalist) regime. Area: 3,691,502 square miles. Language: Chinese.

Capital: Peking.

Monetary System:
100 Fen = 1 Yuan

Aluminum

1	1 Fen 1955–	.20	.50	1.00
2	2 Fen 1956–	.20	.50	1.00
3	5 Fen 1955–	.20	.50	1.00

CHINESE TURKESTAN (Sinkiang, Hsin-Chiang)

Claimed by China for 2,000 years and under sporadic control for 500. Though declared autonomous in 1953, it is under Soviet influence. It is China's richest mineral region and is located in Central Asia. Principal cities: Tihwa (Urumchi) and Kuldja.

Monetary System:
10 Fen = 1 Misqal (Mithqal, Mace, Ch'ien)
10 Misqal = 1 Sar (Liang, Tael)

CHINESE EMPIRE
KUANG HSU 1875–1908
and
HSUAN T'UNG 1908–1912
I. Coins Struck in China for General Use in Turkestan

Copper

1	1 Fen 5 Li ND (Kuang Hsu)	80.00 120.00	–

2	10 Wen ND, CD 1910–11 (Hsuan T'ung legend)	20.00 35.00	–

Note: Varieties exist for Nos. 1 and 2.

Modern Copies

1a	1 Fen 5 Li	–	–	25.00
2a	10 Wen	–	–	25.00

Silver

3	1 Misqal ND	150.00 200.00	–
4*	2 Misqal ND	80.00 120.00	–
5	4 Misqal ND	300.00 450.00	–
6	5 Misqal ND	15.00 25.00	–
7	1 Tael ND	25.00 50.00	–

Many varieties, including circled and uncircled dragon, with or without Turkic script, etc.

A7	5 Fen ND, AH 1295 (1878)	30.00 45.00	–
B7	1 Misqal 1292–95	100.00 180.00	–

"Ration Gold"

8	F4 1 Misqal ND	800.00	1000.	1500.
9	F3 2 Misqal ND	1000.	1200.	1800.

Silver

With Title SUNGAREI

10*	1 Mace ND	500.00 700.00	1000.	
11	2 Mace ND	600.00 800.00	1200.	
12	1 Yuan Yr. 38 (1949)	Rare		
12a	1 Yuan 1949	Rare		

The similarly dated 3, 4 and 5 Mace are patterns and/or fantasies.

II. Coins Struck at Various Mints in Turkestan

A. Aksu Mint
Silver

Kuang Hsu legends

A13	1 Misqal AH 1311 (1894) 18mm		Rare	
13	2 Misqal 1311–12 (23mm)	25.00	50.00	–
14	3 Misqal 1311, 13 (26mm)	20.00	40.00	–
15*	5 Misqal 1310–12 (31mm)	15.00	30.00	–

B. Kashghar Mint
Silver

Kuang Hsu legends

16	1 Misqal ND, 1309–10	100.00	190.00	–
17	2 Misqal 1310–22 (1892–1904) 23mm	25.00	50.00	–
18*	3 Misqal 1310–22	20.00	40.00	–
19	5 Misqal 1310–22	15.00	30.00	–

A20	1 Misqal 1323 (1905)	250.00	400.00	–
B20	2 Misqal 1323 (23mm)	200.00	350.00	–
20*	3 Misqal 1323 (27mm)	250.00	400.00	–
21	5 Misqal 1323 (32mm)	40.00	80.00	–

Dragon and Ta Ch'ing legends

23*	2 Misqal 1325–26 (1907–08) 24mm	80.00	150.00	–
25	5 Misqal ND, 1325–28	25.00	50.00	–
26	1 Liang 1325 (40mm)	250.00	400.00	–

Dragon and Hsuan T'ung legend

27	5 Misqal 1327–29 (1909–11)	40.00	70.00	

Dragon and Silver Coin legend

29	2 Misqal 1329 (2 vars.)	40.00	70.00	–
30*	3 Misqal 1329	150.00	250.00	–

Dragon and Ration Silver legend

31	5 Misqal 1329–31 (1911–13)	30.00	50.00	–

C. Urumchi Mint
Silver

Kuang Hsu legends

33	2 Misqal 1321–25 (1903–07) 24mm	30.00	60.00	–

Unless otherwise noted, prices are for coins in very fine, extremely fine, and uncirculated condition.

34*	3 Misqal 1321–25	25.00	50.00	–
35	5 Misqal 1321–25	20.00	40.00	–

REPUBLIC OF CHINA

I. Coins Without Mint Name
Copper

A39 10 Wen CD 1912 (2 vars.)	40.00	70.00	–

Silver

Rev: Crossed five-striped flags

41	5 Misqal 1912 (2 stripes with arabesques)	60.00	120.00	–
42*	1 Tael 1912, similar	100.00	180.00	–
41a	5 Misqal 1912 (4 stripes with arabesques)	50.00	100.00	–
42a	1 Tael 1912, similar	100.00	180.00	–

Copper

B39*	10 Wen ND (vars.)	30.00	70.00	–
39	20 Wen ND, similar	30.00	70.00	–
	Obv: Similar to No. B38			
	Rev: Nationalist flags			
40	10 Wen CD 1929–30 (vars.)	15.00	25.00	–

II. Aksu Mint
Cast Copper

37 10 Wen ND	80.00	150.00	–

III. Kashghar Mint
Copper

A36	5 Wen ND	80.00	150.00	–
B36*	10 Wen ND	35.00	80.00	–

36*	5 Wen AH 1331 (1913)	80.00	150.00	–
38	10 Wen ND, 1331–32 (vars.)	15.00	30.00	–

Silver

43 5 Misqal 1331-34   20.00   40.00   –

HUNG HSIEN Reign 1915-1916
Copper

A38 10 Wen AH 1334 (1916)   50.00 100.00   –

Republican Issues Resumed
Design similar to No. 38

38a 10 Wen Yrs. 10-11
(1921-22) rearranged
obv. legend (vars.)   20.00   40.00   –

B38* 10 Wen CD 1928, rev.
Chinese legend   35.00   70.00   –
B38a 10 Wen CD 1929, rev.
Uighur legend   60.00 100.00   –
*Design similar to No. A37
but Nationalist flags*

C38 20 Wen ND (42mm)   80.00 150.00   –

Uighuristan Republic 1933-34

D38* 10 Wen AH 1352 (1933) 100.00 200.00   –
E38 20 Wen 1352   200.00 350.00   –

IV. Tihwa (Urumchi) Mint
Silver

45 1 Liang (Tael) Yr 6-7
(1917-18)   40.00   80.00 250.00

COLOMBIA

Mountainous republic, northernmost of the South American countries. Products are agricultural and mineral; coffee comprises 80% of Colombian exports. Language: Spanish. Capital: *Bogota.*

Monetary System:
10 Decimos or Reales = 1 Peso
100 Centavos = 1 Peso

Note: Most silver and gold coins 1862-1908 bear mint names BOGOTA, POPAYAN or MEDELLIN. The many minor variations in size and style of portraits, lettering, dates, etc. are beyond the scope of this catalog.

ESTADOS UNIDOS DE
COLOMBIA 1862-1886

I. 10 Reales = 1 Peso
Silver

A4 2 Reales 1880   250.00 400.00   –

II. 10 Decimos = 1 Peso
Silver

1 ¼ Decimo 1863-81   6.00   12.00   35.00

Unless otherwise noted, prices are for coins in very fine, extremely fine, and uncirculated condition.

2* ½ Decimo 1863–65 (.900
   fine)   25.00 50.00 150.00
2a ½ Decimo 1867 (.666
   fine)   50.00 100.00   –
3 1 Decimo 1863–66 (.900
   fine)   25.00 50.00 150.00
3a 1 Decimo 1866 (.835
   fine)   40.00 75.00 200.00

4 2 Decimos 1865 (.900
   fine)   200.00 400.00   –
4a* 2 Decimos 1866–67
   (.835 fine)   25.00 60.00 150.00

5 1 Peso 1862–68   50.00 100.00 400.00

6 ½ Decimo 1868–76 (.666
   fine)   20.00 40.00 150.00
6a ½ Decimo 1870–75 (.835
   fine)   15.00 30.00 100.00
7 1 Decimo 1868–74 15.00 40.00   –
8* 2 Decimos 1870–74 12.00 40.00   –
A9 ½ Peso 1868   1500.   2500.   –
9 5 Decimos 1868–86
   (.835 fine)   7.00 15.00 65.00
Popayan issues of No. 9 are rare.
9a 5 Decimos 1886 (.500
   fine)   125.00 200.00 400.00

10 1 Peso 1868–71   125.00 250.00 600.00
       1868 . . . 600.
No. 9 now includes the former No. 11

III. 100 Centavos = 1 Peso
Cupro-Nickel

18 1¼ Centavos 1874   2.00   5.00 20.00

19 2½ Centavos 1881
   (14mm)   1.00   2.00   6.00
20 2½ Centavos 1881
   (18mm)   1.00   2.00   8.00
21* 2½ Centavos 1886
   (15mm)   1.00   2.00   8.00

Copper

22 2½ Centavos 1885   6.00 12.00 40.00

Silver

12 2½ Centavos 1872–81 6.00 12.00 30.00

A12* 5 Centavos 1872–74 10.00 25.00 50.00
B12 10 Centavos 1872–74 10.00 25.00 75.00
16 50 Centavos 1872–74,
   "50" in numerals 15.00 35.00 100.00

13 5 Centavos 1874 (.835
   fine)   40.00 100.00   –
13a 5 Centavos 1875–85
   (.666 fine)   5.00 10.00 25.00
14 10 Centavos 1875–85 5.00 10.00 15.00
       1885 M . . . 100.
15 20 Centavos 1874–82,
   weight GRAM. 5   8.00 20.00 75.00

15b 20 Centavos 1875–85,
weight GRAMOS 5   8.00   20.00   75.00

17 50 Centavos 1874–85,
value CINCUENTA spelled
out   7.00   15.00   45.00

       1885 . . . 50.

.500 Silver

14a 10 Centavos 1885–86   100.00 200.00 350.00
15a 20 Centavos 1886   400.00 750.00 1000.
17a 50 Centavos 1885–86   10.00   22.00   75.00

.900 Gold
Obv: Liberty head
Rev: Value in wreath

A37 *F95, 98* 1 Peso 1863–64 100.00 150.00 200.00
B37 *F97* 2 Pesos 1863   125.00 175.00 250.00
C37 *F94, 96* 5 Pesos
1862–64   300.00 400.00 600.00

32 *F108–109* 1 Peso
1872–75   75.00 100.00 150.00

37 *F107* 1 Peso 1872–73   75.00 100.00 150.00
38 *F106* 2 Pesos 1871–76 100.00 150.00 250.00
40 *F102–104* 10 Pesos
1862–76   350.00 600.00 1000.

41* *F99–101* 20 Pesos
1862–78   1000.   1500.   2250.
Nos. 40–41 include the former Nos. 33–34 and 35–36.

.666 Gold

39 *F105* 5 Pesos 1885   2000.   3000.   4000.
40a 10 Pesos 1886   – 7000.   –

REPUBLICA DE COLOMBIA
1886–
Cupro-Nickel

23 2½ Centavos 1902   200.00 350.00 600.00
No. 23 dated 1900 is now thought to be a pattern. Nos.
23 and 25 dated 1902 probably were not released to
circulation.

24 5 Centavos 1886, 88 (2
vars.)   .50   1.00   5.00

25 5 Centavos 1886, 1902,
value between branches   .50   1.00   5.00

Silver

26 5 Decimos 1887–88,
head similar to No. 46   100.00 200.00 400.00
26a* 5 Decimos 1888–89,
large ugly head   100.00 200.00 400.00
      1889 . . . 500.

27 50 Centavos 1887–88   30.00   60.00 125.00
      1888 . . . Rare.

Unless otherwise noted, prices are for coins in very
fine, extremely fine, and uncirculated condition.

28 50 Centavos 1888 (.500
   fine)   150.00 300.00 500.00
28a 50 Centavos 1889–99,
   1906–08, (.835 fine)   20.00 40.00 80.00
   1899 . . . 300.

Fourth Centennial
Discovery of America

Obv: Bust of Columbus

29 50 Centavos 1892   10.00 20.00 50.00
   1891 Proof . . . 3500.

30 10 Centavos 1897   1.50   3.00   6.00
31 20 Centavos 1897   2.50   5.00 10.00

SANTANDER
Revolutionary issues by General Ramon Gonzales Va-
lencia. Struck in thin brass on one side only. Impression
shows through on reverse (incuse).

Brass

S1 10 Centavos 1902   20.00 35.00   –
S2 20 Centavos 1902   15.00 30.00   –

S3 50 Centavos 1902   8.00 15.00   –

Cupro-Nickel

42 1 Peso p/m (paper
   money) 1907–16   2.00   5.00 15.00
43 2 Pesos p/m 1907–14   4.00   9.00 25.00
44 5 Pesos p/m 1907–14   3.00   6.00 20.00

Silver

45 5 Centavos 1902   3.00   5.00   8.00

46 50 Centavos 1902   20.00 30.00 60.00

47 10 Centavos 1911–42   1.50   2.50   4.00
48* 20 Centavos 1911–42   3.00   5.00 10.00
   1922 . . . 50.
49 50 Centavos 1912–33,
   narrow hd.   5.00   7.00 20.00
49a 50 Centavos 1916–34,
   round hd.   5.00   7.00 12.00

Gold

50 *F111* 2½ Pesos 1913   60.00 100.00 125.00
51* *F110* 5 Pesos 1913–19 120.00 125.00 130.00
   Obv: Bolivar portrait

52 *F114* 2½ Pesos
1919–20   80.00 100.00 125.00
53 *F113* 5 Pesos 1919–24   120.00 125.00 130.00
54 *F112* 10 Pesos 1919,24 200.00 250.00 350.00

Obv: Smaller head of Bolivar
55 *F116* 2½ Pesos
1924–28   100.00 125.00 150.00
56* *F115* 5 Pesos 1924–30   120.00 125.00 130.00

Cupro-Nickel

57 1 Centavo 1918–48   .50   1.00   2.00
          1918, 19 . . . 20.
59 2 Centavos 1918–47   .50   1.00   2.00
          1918, 19 . . . 20.
60 5 Centavos 1918–50   .50   2.00   3.00

Nickel-clad Steel
57a 1 Centavo 1952–58   .10   .25   .75

Bronze

61 1 Centavo 1942–66   .10   .20   .40
62 2 Centavos 1948–50   1.00   2.00   5.00
63 5 Centavos 1942–66   .15   .25   .50

Silver

Obv: Santander
64 10 Centavos 1945–52   1.00   2.00   5.00
65 20 Centavos 1945–52   2.00   3.00   6.00

Obv: Simon Bolivar
66 50 Centavos 1947–48   6.00 15.00 40.00

Aluminum-Bronze

67 2 Centavos 1952, 65, Di-
         vided legend   .05   .15   .30
67a 2 Centavos 1955–65,
         Continuous legend   .05   .15   .30

Cupro-Nickel

68 10 Centavos 1952–53
        (18mm)   .30   1.00   3.00
68a 10 Centavos 1954–67
        (18.5mm)   .15   .35   .50

Billon

69 20 Centavos 1953   .50   1.50   4.00

Cupro-Nickel

70 20 Centavos 1956–66   .15   .30   .50

Unless otherwise noted, prices are for coins in very
fine, extremely fine, and uncirculated condition.

71 50 Centavos 1958–66   .50   .75   1.50

200th Anniversary of Milled Coinage

Silver

72 1 Peso 1956   12.00   14.00   20.00

Uprising Commemoratives 1810–1960

Same as Nos. 61, 63, 67a, 70 and 71 with dates "1810–1960."

73	1 Centavo Bronze	2.00	4.00	8.00
74	2 Centavos Aluminum-Bronze	3.00	5.00	10.00
A74	5 Centavos Bronze	4.00	7.00	15.00

Cupro-Nickel

75 10 Centavos   1.00   3.00   10.00

76	20 Centavos	2.00	5.00	15.00
77	50 Centavos	4.00	10.00	25.00

Jorge Eliecer Gaitan Commemoratives

78	20 Centavos 1965	.50	1.00	2.00
79	50 Centavos 1965	.50	1.00	3.00

Later issues in *Current Coins of the World.*

COMORO ISLANDS (Grand Comore)

A former French overseas territory located in the Mozambique Channel off the coast of Africa. Achieved autonomy in 1961, and proclaimed independence unilaterally in 1975. Area: 693 square miles. Languages: French, Swahili. Capital: *Moroni.*

Monetary System:
100 Centimes = 1 Franc

Bronze

1*	5 Centimes AH 1308 (1890)	5.00	15.00	100.00
2	10 Centimes 1308	7.50	20.00	125.00

Silver

3 5 Francs 1308   450.00 650.00   1250.
Later issues in *Current Coins of the World*.

COSTA RICA

Republic in southern Central America. Chief products: coffee, bananas, cocoa and abaca. There is some mineral export and local manufacturing. Area: 19,653 square miles. Language: Spanish. Capital: *San Jose*.

Monetary System:
8 Reales = 1 Peso
2 Pesos = 1 Escudo
8 Escudos = 1 Onza to 1864
100 Centavos = 1 Peso 1865–96
100 Centimos = 1 Colon 1896–

Silver

5	¹⁄₁₆ Peso 1850–55, 62	35.00	75.00	200.00
	1862 . . . 200.			
6	⅛ Pesos 1850–55	30.00	75.00	150.00
7	¼ Pesos 1850–55	25.00	65.00	140.00
	1855 . . . 100.			

Gold

22	*F10* ½ Escudo 1850–64	60.00	90.00	175.00
23	*F9* 1 Escudo 1850–55	80.00	175.00	350.00
24	*F8* 2 Escudos 1850–63	150.00	250.00	450.00
25	*F7* ½ Onza 1850	350.00	600.00	1000.

Decimal System 1864–1896

Cupro-Nickel

32 ¼ Centavo ND (1865)   100.00 150.00 250.00
There are many counterfeits of No. 32.

30 1 Centavo 1865–68   8.00   15.00   50.00

31 1 Centavo 1874   7.00   14.00   30.00

Silver

9	5 Centavos 1865–75	8.00	20.00	75.00
	1870–72 . . . 40.			
10	10 Centavos 1865–72 (19.5mm)	25.00	60.00	150.00
	1868, 72 . . . 200.			
10a	10 Centavos 1875 (18mm)	15.00	40.00	100.00
11	25 Centavos 1864, sm. "25Cs"	40.00	90.00	250.00

Unless otherwise noted, prices are for coins in very fine, extremely fine, and uncirculated condition.

11a 25 Centavos 1864–75, lg.
  "25Cs"   25.00 60.00 150.00
    1864 . . . 100.

12 50 Centavos 1865–75   50.00 150.00 500.00
    1867, 70 . . . 150.

Gold

20 50 Centavos of Colombia
    countermarked on both
    sides (1889)   45.00 75.00   –

26 *F15–16* 1 Peso 1864–72   50.00 75.00 100.00
27 *F14* 2 Pesos 1866–68   75.00 125.00 200.00
27a *F14a* 2 Pesos 1876   500.00 700.00 1000.

NEW COINAGE SYSTEM 1896–

Cupro-Nickel

28 *F12* 5 Pesos 1867–70   150.00 250.00 450.00
28a *F13* 5 Pesos 1873–75   225.00 350.00 550.00
29 *F11* 10 Pesos 1870–72 200.00 275.00 500.00
29a *F11a* 10 Pesos 1876   750.00 1000. 1500.

46 2 Centimos 1903   1.00   2.00   6.00

.900 Silver

Designs as Nos. 26–29

LEI 0.900 G.W. added to rev. legend
33 *F18* 5 Pesos 1873   1500. 2000. 3500.
34 *F17* 10 Pesos 1873   6000. 12,000. 20,000.

39 5 Centimos 1905–14   1.00   3.00   6.00
40 10 Centimos 1905–14   1.50   3.00   8.00
41 50 Centimos 1902–14   30.00 60.00 125.00
    1914 . . . 1000.

Silver

.500 Silver
42 10 Centavos 1917   1.00   3.00   6.00
A42 50 Centimos 1917–18   – 3000. 4000.
(All No. A42 were counterstamped as No. 44 except for
ten presentation pieces.)

.650 Silver

13 5 Centavos 1885–87   4.00 10.00 25.00
14 10 Centavos 1886–87   5.00 15.00 40.00
15 20 Centavos 1886–87   6.00 20.00 50.00
16 50 Centavos 1880–90   12.00 30.00 75.00

HEATON BIRMm on reverse
17 5 Centavos 1889–92   2.00   5.00 10.00
18 10 Centavos 1889–92   2.00   5.00 15.00
19 20 Centavos 1889–93   4.00   6.00 20.00

45 25 Centimos 1924   2.00   4.00 10.00

Revaluation 1923

43	50 CENTIMOS 1923 stamped on various 25c pieces	3.00	5.00	10.00
44	UN COLON 1923 stamped on 50c pieces of various dates	5.00	8.00	15.00

Banco Internacional de Costa Rica

Initials B.I.C.R. on Coins
Cupro-Nickel

55	25 Centimos 1935	2.00	5.00	20.00
56	50 Centimos 1935	3.00	8.00	35.00
57	1 Colon 1935	5.00	10.00	50.00

Banco Nacional de Costa Rica

Initials B.N.C.R. on Coins

Gold

35	*F22* 2 Colones 1900–28	25.00	50.00	75.00
36	*F21* 5 Colones 1899–1900	75.00	100.00	150.00
37	*F20* 10 Colones 1897–1900	100.00	135.00	200.00
38*	*F19* 20 Colones 1897–1900	275.00	350.00	500.00

58	5 Centimos 1942, struck over 2c, No. 46	1.00	3.00	5.00

Brass

A58	5 Centimos 1942–47	1.00	2.00	5.00
B58	10 Centimos 1942–47	1.00	2.00	5.00

47	5 Centavos 1917–19	4.00	10.00	40.00

Cupro-Nickel

59	25 Centimos 1937–48	.50	1.00	2.00
60	50 Centimos 1937	2.00	5.00	15.00
60a	50 Centimos 1948, larger	.25	.50	2.00
61	1 Colon 1937–48	.75	2.00	5.00
62	2 Colones 1948	.75	2.00	6.00

Brass

48	10 Centavos 1917–19	3.00	8.00	25.00
49	5 Centimos 1920–41	1.00	3.00	5.00
50	10 Centimos 1920–22	2.00	6.00	20.00
54	10 Centimos 1936–41	1.00	3.00	6.00

Bronze

51	5 Centimos 1929	2.00	5.00	15.00
52	10 Centimos 1929	2.00	4.00	15.00
63	25 Centimos 1944–46	.50	2.00	8.00

Unless otherwise noted, prices are for coins in very fine, extremely fine, and uncirculated condition.

Banco Central de Costa Rica

Initials B.C.C.R. on Coins
Cupro-Nickel

A64 5 Centimos 1951 BC/CR
divided   .25   1.00   4.00

64 5 Centimos 1951, 69–78   .05   .10   .25
65 10 Centimos 1951,
    69–75   .05   .10   .25

Stainless Steel

66 5 Centimos 1953–67   .05   .10   .35
67 10 Centimos 1953–79   .05   .10   .25

68 1 Colon 1954   .50   2.00   10.00
69 2 Colones 1954   .50   2.00   15.00
Later issues in *Current Coins of the World.*

CRETE

Under Greek Administration
1898–1906

Largest of the Greek islands, its area being 3,234 square miles. Its history, government and coinage are closely identified with that of Greece from earliest times. Capital: Canea.

Monetary System:
100 Lepta = 1 Drachma

Bronze

1 1 Lepton 1900–01   2.00   7.00   22.50
2 2 Lepta 1900–01   2.00   10.00   25.00

Cupro-Nickel

3 5 Lepta 1900   3.50   15.00   65.00
4 10 Lepta 1900   3.50   15.00   65.00
5 20 Lepta 1900   3.50   15.00   65.00
For similar coins dated 1894–95, see Greece Nos. 16–18.

Silver

Obv: Prince Georgios of Greece
(High Commissioner 1898–1906)
6 50 Lepta 1901   25.00   40.00   275.00

CUBA

Republic occupying the largest of the Caribbean islands. Sugar cane and its products, including rum, were the principal industry before the Castro regime, with tobacco growing and its manufacture into cigars and cigarettes ranking second. Area: 44,218 square miles. Language: Spanish. Capital: *La Habana (Havana).*

Monetary System:
100 Centavos = 1 Peso

Silver

1 Souvenir Peso 1897 (3 vars)   50.00 80.00 125.00

2 1 Peso 1898   450.00 800.00 1500.

Cupro-Nickel

3 1 Centavo 1915–38, ("2.5 G.")   .50   1.00   5.00
                                             Proof . . . 50.00
4 2 Centavos 1915–16   1.00   2.00 15.00
                                             Proof . . . 75.00
5 5 Centavos 1915–20 ("5.0 G")   .50   1.50 10.00
                                             Proof . . . 100.00

Brass

3a 1 Centavo 1943   .25   ..50   2.00
5a 5 Centavos 1943   .50   1.00   5.00

Cupro-Nickel

3b 1 Centavo 1946, 61   .15   .30   .75
5b 5 Centavos 1946, 60, 61   .15   .30   1.00

Silver

6 10 Centavos 1915–49   1.50   2.00   3.00
                                             Proof . . . 100.00
7* 20 Centavos 1915–49   3.00   4.00   5.00
       1932 . . . 20.   Proof . . . 200.00
8 40 Centavos 1915–20   6.00 20.00 50.00
       1916 . . . 35.   Proof . . . 300.00
9 1 Peso 1915–34   14.00 20.00 50.00
       1916 . . . 35.   Proof . . . 600.00

Gold

Obv: Jose Marti (1853–95), writer and patriot

10 F7 1 Peso 1915–16   175.00 250.00 400.00
                                             Proof . . . 1000.
11 F6 2 Pesos 1915–16   60.00 75.00 90.00
                                             Proof . . . 1500.
12 F5 4 Pesos 1915–16   110.00 125.00 150.00
                                             Proof . . . 2000.
13 F4 5 Pesos 1915–16   115.00 125.00 150.00
                                             Proof . . . 2500.
14 F3 10 Pesos 1915–16   225.00 250.00 300.00
                                             Proof . . . 3500.
15* F1–2 20 Pesos 1915–16 475.00 500.00 600.00
        1916 Proof . . . 30,000.   Proof . . . 6000.

Unless otherwise noted, prices are for coins in very
fine, extremely fine, and uncirculated condition.

Silver

16 1 Peso 1934–39   25.00 60.00 125.00
      1937 . . . 400.

50th Anniversary of Republic

17 10 Centavos 1952   1.50   2.00   3.00
18 20 Centavos 1952   2.00   3.00   6.00
19 40 Centavos 1952   4.00   6.00   12.00

Jose Marti Centennial–1953
Nos 20–23

Brass

20 1 Centavo 1953   .20   .50   1.00
                                    Proof . . . 10.00

Silver

21 25 Centavos 1953, rev.
      Liberty cap   3.00   5.00   8.50

22 50 Centavos 1953, rev.
      scroll   7.50   10.00   15.00

23 1 Peso 1953, rev. sun
      and key   15.00   20.00   27.50

Regular Issue

Cupro-Nickel

24 1 Centavo 1958   .10   .50   1.00
Later issues in *Current Coins of the World.*

CURACAO

One of the Leeward Islands in the West Indies, off the
coast of Venezuela. Discovered by Spain in 1499, it
passed to the Dutch in 1624, and was a colony until becoming part of the Netherlands Antilles in 1954. Too dry
for agriculture, it has an economy based on oil refining
and tourism. Area: 174 square miles. Languages:
Dutch, Papiamento, English, Spanish. Capital: *Willemstad.*

Monetary System
100 Cent = 1 Gulden

WILHELMINA 1890–1948
First Coinage
Silver

1	¹/₁₀ Gulden 1901	60.00	80.00	110.00
2	¼ Gulden 1900	60.00	80.00	110.00

Second Coinage
Bronze

3	1 Cent 1944,47	2.00	3.00	5.00
4	2½ Cents 1944–48	3.00	4.00	5.00

Silver

5	¹/₁₀ Gulden 1944,47	4.00	6.00	10.00
6	¼ Gulden 1944,47	5.00	8.00	12.00

7	1 Gulden 1944	20.00	40.00	60.00
10	2½ Gulden 1944	10.00	14.00	18.00

For other World War II issues, see Netherlands Nos. 34a, 36b, 43a, 44a.

Third Coinage
Cupro-Nickel

9	5 Cent 1948	6.00	8.00	12.00

Silver

8	¹/₁₀ Gulden 1948	4.00	6.00	10.00

For issues since 1952, see Netherlands Antilles.

CYPRUS

Island located in the eastern Mediterranean Sea. Four-fifths of the population is of Greek ancestry, the rest of Turkish. The principal industries are agriculture and mining. Until August, 1960, Cyprus was a British Crown Colony, after which it became an independent republic within the British Commonwealth. Area: 3,572 square miles. Languages: Greek, Turkish, English. Capital: *Nicosia*.

Monetary System:
9 Piastres = 1 Shilling to 1955
1000 Mils = 1 Pound 1955–

VICTORIA 1878–1901
Bronze

1	¼ Piastre 1879–1901	10.00	20.00	75.00
			Proof . . . 225.00	
2	½ Piastre 1879–1900	10.00	25.00	100.00
	1884,89,96 . . . 40		Proof . . . 250.00	
3	1 Piastre 1879–1900	10.00	45.00	120.00
	1882H,84 . . . 150		Proof . . . 400.00	

Silver

4	3 Piastres 1901	10.00	30.00	100.00
			Proof . . . 250.00	

5	4½ Piastres 1901	15.00	35.00	100.00
			Proof . . . 250.00	

Unless otherwise noted, prices are for coins in very fine, extremely fine, and uncirculated condition.

6	9 Piastres 1901	20.00	45.00	120.00
		Proof . . . 500.00		
7	18 Piastres 1901	30.00	100.00	275.00
		Proof . . . 700.00		

EDWARD VII 1901–1910
Bronze

8	¼ Piastre 1902–08	12.50	25.00	75.00
	1908 . . . 50			
9	½ Piastre 1908	75.00	200.00	375.00
10	1 Piastre 1908	100.00	200.00	375.00

Silver

| 11 | 9 Piastres 1907 | 65.00 | 225.00 | 400.00 |
| 12 | 18 Piastres 1907 | 75.00 | 200.00 | 375.00 |

GEORGE V 1910–1936
Bronze
Rev. design like Nos. 8–10

13	¼ Piastre 1922,26	15.00	25.00	50.00
		Proof . . . 150.00		
14	½ Piastre 1922–31	7.50	15.00	45.00
	1922 . . . 30	Proof . . . 175.00		
15	1 Piastre 1922–31	20.00	40.00	75.00
		Proof . . . 600.00		

Cupro-Nickel

16	½ Piastre 1934	2.00	5.00	20.00
		Proof . . . 175.00		
17	1 Piastre 1934	2.00	5.00	20.00
		Proof . . . 175.00		

Silver
Rev. design like Nos. 5–7

18	4½ Piastres 1921	10.00	25.00	45.00
19	9 Piastres 1913–21	10.00	25.00	50.00
	1913 . . . 20			
20	18 Piastres 1913,21	10.00	50.00	225.00
	1913 . . . 40			

50th Anniversary of British Rule

| 21 | 45 Piastres 1928 | 22.50 | 35.00 | 100.00 |
| | | Proof . . . 600.00 | | |

GEORGE VI 1936–1952
Cupro-Nickel

22	½ Piastre 1938	1.25	3.50	8.00
		Proof . . . 150.00		
23	1 Piastre 1938	1.25	4.00	12.50
		Proof . . . 200.00		

Bronze

22a	½ Piastre 1942–45	.25	3.50	10.00
		Proof . . . 150.00		
23a	1 Piastre 1942–46	.75	2.75	7.50
		Proof . . . 225.00		

Silver

28	4½ Piastres 1938	3.00	5.00	10.00
		Proof . . . 225.00		
29	9 Piastres 1938,40	4.50	6.00	12.00
		Proof . . . 175.00		
30	18 Piastres 1938,40	10.00	12.00	17.50
		Proof . . . 225.00		

Cupro-Nickel

| 26 | 1 Shilling 1947 | 2.50 | 4.00 | 10.00 |

| 27 | 2 Shillings 1947 | 1.00 | 3.50 | 13.50 |
| | | | Proof . . . | 200.00 |

**New Legend:
GEORGIUS SEXTUS
DEI GRATIA REX
Bronze**

31	½ Piastre 1949	.50	1.00	3.50
			Proof . . .	100.00
32	1 Piastre 1949	.75	1.75	3.50
			Proof . . .	100.00

Cupro-Nickel

33	1 Shilling 1949	3.00	5.00	9.00
			Proof . . .	175.00
34	2 Shillings 1949	1.50	3.00	10.00
			Proof . . .	200.00

**ELIZABETH II 1952–1960
Decimal Currency 1955–
Bronze**

| 35 | 3 Mils 1955 | .05 | .10 | .20 |
| | | | Proof . . . | 5.00 |

| 36 | 5 Mils 1955–56 | .10 | .15 | .25 |
| | | | Proof . . . | 8.00 |

Cupro-Nickel

37	25 Mils 1955	.15	.20	.40
			Proof . . .	10.00
38	50 Mils 1955	.25	.40	.75
			Proof . . .	12.00

| 39 | 100 Mils 1955,57 | .25 | .50 | 1.00 |
| | 1957 . . . 125 | | Proof . . . | 12.50 |

Later issues in *Current Coins of the World.*

CZECHOSLOVAKIA
(Republika Ceskoslo-
venska)

Republic of central Europe created in 1918 through the dissolution of the old Austro-Hungarian Empire. A country of great mineral and agricultural wealth, it is also famous for a variety of products such as munitions, glass, textiles, furniture and ceramics. Area: 49,371 square miles. Languages: Czech and Slovak. Capital: *Praha (Prague).*

Monetary System:
100 Haleru = 1 Koruna

Zinc

| 1 | 2 Halere 1923–25 | 3.00 | 5.00 | 10.00 |

Bronze

| 2 | 5 Haleru 1923–38 | .40 | .75 | 1.50 |
| 3 | 10 Haleru 1922–38 | .40 | .75 | 1.75 |

Cupro-Nickel

| 4 | 20 Haleru 1921–38 | .35 | .60 | 2.00 |
| | 1933 . . . 5 | | | |

5 25 Haleru 1932–33   1.50   2.50   4.00

6 50 Haleru 1921–31   .50   .75   2.00
    1930 . . . Rare

7 1 Koruna 1922–38   .50   .75   1.75

8* 5 Korun 1925–27 (30mm)   3.50   5.00   7.50

Silver
8a 5 Korun 1928–32 (27mm)   2.50   5.00   10.00

Nickel
8b 5 Korun 1937–38 (27mm)   3.50   5.00   6.50
    1937 . . . 75

10th Anniversary of Independence
Silver

Obv: Thomas G. Masaryk, President 1918–35

11 10 Korun 1928   5.00   7.50   12.50

Regular Issues

12 10 Korun 1930–33   5.00   7.50   10.00

13 20 Korun 1933–34   5.00   10.00   15.00

Death of President Masaryk

14 20 Korun 1937   5.00   10.00   15.00

TRADE COINS
(Nos. A15–18)

Fifth Anniversary of the Republic

Gold
Design as No. 15
A15 *F3* 1 Dukat 1923   200.00 475.00 700.00

All pieces of No. A15 were serially numbered (from 1 to 1000) below the figure on reverse.

Regular Issues

Gold

Rev: St. Wenceslas
15* *F2* 1 Dukat 1923–39,51   75.00 100.00 150.00
16 *F1* 2 Dukaty 1923–38,51 200.00 300.00 400.00

17* *F5* 5 Dukatu 1929–38,51 350.00 500.00 950.00
18 *F4* 10 Dukatu 1929–38,
51   650.00 1100. 1850.

WORLD WAR II ISSUES
SLOVAKIA
German Protectorate 1939–45
100 Halierov = 1 Koruna

Zinc

S19b 5 Halierov 1942   5.00 10.00 15.00

Bronze

S20 10 Halierov 1939,42   2.00 4.00 7.50

S21 20 Halierov 1940–42   2.00 3.00 5.00

Cupro-Nickel

S22 50 Halierov 1940–41   2.00 2.50 4.50
1940 . . . 50

S23 1 Koruna 1940–45   2.00 2.75 7.50

Aluminum
S21a 20 Halierov 1942–43   2.00 2.50 4.00
S22b 50 Halierov 1943–44   2.00 4.50 6.50

Nickel

Rev: Father Hlinka, Slovakian patriot
S24 5 Korun 1939   3.50 6.00 12.50

Silver

Rev: Prince Pribina and two allegorical figures
S25 10 Korun 1944   4.00 5.00 10.00

Unless otherwise noted, prices are for coins in very fine, extremely fine, and uncirculated condition.

Election of President Tiso

S26 20 Korun 1939   10.00 15.00 30.00

Regular Issues

*Rev: Sts. Cyril and Methodius, 9th century mission-
aries.*
S27 20 Korun 1941   5.50   7.50 12.50

5th Anniversary of
Independent Slovakia

S28 50 Korun 1944   10.00 12.50 17.50

BOHEMIA-MORAVIA
German Protectorate 1939–45
Zinc

B29 10 Haleru 1940–44   .75   1.00   3.00

B30 20 Haleru 1940–44   .75   1.25   4.00

B31 50 Haleru 1940–44, rev.
as No. 6   1.00 1.50   5.50

B32 1 Koruna 1941–44   1.00   2.00   5.00

REPUBLIC 1945–1960

Bronze

33 20 Haleru 1947–50
(18mm)   .25   .50   1.00
        1947 . . . 125

35 50 Haleru 1947–50   .20   -.40   1.00

Cupro-Nickel

37 1 Koruna 1946–47   .50   .75   1.50
        1947 . . . 3.50

39 2 Koruny 1947–48   .50   1.00   2.00

Aluminum

34 20 Haleru 1951–52
(16mm)   .20   .30   .50

36	50 Haleru 1951–53			
	(18mm)	.50	.75	1.00
38	1 Koruna 1947–53	.40	.75	1.00
	1947 . . . 100			

A39 5 Korun 1952   25.00   40.00   50.00
No. A39 was not released for circulation because of the 1953 currency reform.

Third Anniversary Slovak National Uprising

Silver

40 50 Korun 1947   3.00   5.00   7.50

Third Anniversary Prague Uprising

41 50 Korun 1948   3.00   5.00   7.50

6th Centennial Karlovy University at Prague

42 100 Korun 1948   3.00   6.50   12.50

30th Anniversary of Indepedence

43 100 Korun 1948   3.00   6.50   12.50

7th Centennial Mining Privileges of Jihlava

44 100 Korun 1949   3.00   6.50   12.50

70th Birthday of Stalin

45 50 Korun 1949   3.00   5.00   7.50
46 100 Korun 1949   3.00   6.00   12.50

30th Anniversary of Communist Party

Rev: Klement Gottwald

47 100 Korun 1951   3.00   6.50   12.50

Unless otherwise noted, prices are for coins in very fine, extremely fine, and uncirculated condition.

CURRENCY REFORM 1953

Aluminum

48	1 Haler 1953–60	.10	.15	.25
49	3 Halere 1953–54	.10	.15	.25
50	5 Haleru 1953–55	.15	.25	.50
51	10 Haleru 1953–58	.10	.20	.30
52	25 Haleru 1953–54	.20	.30	.55

56 25 Korun 1955   5.00   7.50 12.50
Proof . . . 17.50

Aluminum-Bronze

61 1 Koruna 1957–60   .30   .50   1.25

10th Anniversary
Slovak National Uprising

57 50 Korun 1955   12.50 17.50 27.50

Silver

53 10 Korun 1954   4.00   6.00 10.00
                              Proof . . . 17.50
54 25 Korun 1954   10.00   15.00 25.00
                              Proof . . . 20.00

58 100 Korun 1955   17.50 25.00 55.00

10th Anniversary Liberation
From Nazis, May 9, 1945

250th Anniversary Technical
High Schools in Prague

Silver

Rev: J. Willenberg, founder

55 10 Korun 1955   3.00   5.00   7.50
                              Proof . . . 17.50

59 10 Korun 1957   3.00   6.50 12.50
                              Proof . . . 17.50

Komensky Commemorative

60 10 Korun 1957   3.00   6.50   12.50
                                   Proof . . . 17.50

Later issues in *Current Coins of the World*.

DANISH WEST INDIES (Dansk Vestindien)

A group of about fifty islands lying southeast of Puerto Rico in the Caribbean. They were purchased by the U.S. in 1917 and became the U.S. Virgin Islands. Tourism is the main industry. Area: 133 square miles. Principal town: Charlotte Amalie.

Monetary System:
20 Cents = 1 Franc
5 Bit = 1 Cent
5 Francs = 1 Daler

CHRISTIAN IX 1863–1906

Bronze

1 1 Cent 1868–83   5.00   15.00   75.00
         1879 . . . 45   Proof . . . 125.00

Silver

2 5 Cents 1878–79   22.50   35.00 175.00
                                   Proof . . . 300.00

3 10 Cents 1878–79   20.00   35.00 175.00
         1879 . . . 35   Proof . . . 225.00

4 20 Cents 1878–79   25.00   50.00 225.00
         1879 . . . 120   Proof . . . 375.00

Bronze

5 ½ Cent–2½ Bit 1905   7.00   10.00   50.00
6 1 Cent–5 Bit 1905   5.00   10.00   50.00
7 2 Cents–10 Bit 1905   12.50   22.50 100.00

Nickel

8 5 Cents–25 Bit 1905   7.00   15.00   60.00

Silver

9 10 Cents–50 Bit 1905   9.00   14.50   65.00

10 20 Cents–1 Franc 1905   25.00   50.00 250.00
11 40 Cents–2 Francs 1905 75.00 125.00 600.00
Note: All proof issues of 1905 (Nos. 5–11) are rare.

Unless otherwise noted, prices are for coins in very fine, extremely fine, and uncirculated condition.

Gold

12 *F2* 4 Daler–20 Francs
1904–05 — – 595.00
13 *F1* 10 Daler–50 Francs
1904 – 2500. 4500.

FREDERIK VIII 1906–1912

Silver

14 20 Cents–1 Franc 1907 45.00 75.00 400.00
15 40 Cents–2 Francs 1907 125.00 200.00 950.00
Note: Proofs of Nos. 14 and 15 are rare.

CHRISTIAN X 1912–1917
Bronze

16 1 Cent–5 Bit 1913 20.00 35.00 175.00

DANZIG
(Freie Stadt Danzig)

A major port on the Baltic Sea, it was created a free city
by the Treaty of Versailles in 1919, and was brought
within the Polish Customs Frontier in 1922. Danzig
struck its own coinage until it was proclaimed part of the
German Reich in 1939. It is now under Polish administration as the city of Gdansk.

Monetary System:
100 Pfennig = 1 Mark to 1923
100 Pfennige = 1 Gulden 1923–39

Emergency Issues (Notgeld)

Zinc

1* 10 Pfennig 1920 18.00 28.00 45.00
2 10 Pfennig 1920, rev.
large 10 250.00 350.00 450.00

Regular Issues
First Coinage

Bronze

3 1 Pfennig 1923–37 2.00 3.00 9.00
Proof . . . 40.00
4 2 Pfennige 1923–37 3.00 5.00 15.00
Proof . . . 45.00

Cupro-Nickel

5 5 Pfennige 1923, 28 2.00 3.00 9.00
Proof . . . 50.00

6 10 Pfennige 1923 2.50 3.50 10.00
Proof . . . 60.00

Silver

7 ½ Gulden 1923, 27 18.00 30.00 50.00
1927 . . . 30 Proof . . . 85.00

Second Coinage

Aluminum-Bronze

13 5 Pfennig 1932   2.00   3.00   9.00

14 10 Pfennig 1932   3.00   4.00   10.00

Nickel

15 ½ Gulden 1932   17.50   22.50   40.00

16 1 Gulden 1932   17.50   25.00   45.00

Silver

17 2 Gulden 1932   200.00 300.00 425.00

8 1 Gulden 1923   22.50   32.50   60.00
Proof . . . 120.00

9 2 Gulden 1923   50.00   70.00 135.00
Proof . . . 185.00

10 5 Gulden 1923, 27   125.00 185.00 300.00
    1927 . . . 125   Proof . . . 375.00

Gold

11 *F43* 25 Gulden 1923   Proof . . . 3950.

12 *F44* 25 Gulden 1930, diff. rev.
arms   Proof . . . 9500.

No. 12 was not issued to circulation.

18 5 Gulden 1932   325.00 450.00 750.00

19 5 Gulden 1932   375.00 525.00 900.00

Third Coinage

Nickel

20 5 Gulden 1935   175.00 225.00 350.00

21 10 Gulden 1935   500.00 800.00 1100.

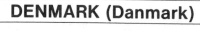

DENMARK (Danmark)

A constitutional monarchy occupying the Jutland peninsula and about 500 islands between the Baltic and the North Seas. Exports large quantities of agricultural produce, especially dairy products. Fisheries are also important. Area: 16,615 square miles. Language: Danish. Capital: *Copenhagen.*

Monetary System:
96 Skilling = 1 Rigsdaler
10 Rigsdaler = 1 Christian d'Or to 1873
100 Ore = 1 Krone (Crown) 1873–

CHRISTIAN IX 1863–1906
Death of Frederik VII and
Accession of Christian IX

Silver

3 2 Rigsdaler 1863   175.00 275.00 600.00

Regular Issues

Bronze

1 ½ Skilling 1868   4.00   8.50   20.00
2 1 Skilling 1867–72   3.00   6.00   15.00

Silver

4 4 Skilling 1867–74   6.50   16.00   40.00
    1874 . . . 35

5 2 Rigsdaler 1864–72   275.00 450.00 900.00

Gold

6 *F294* 1 Christian d'Or
     1869   1800. 2800. 4000.
7 *F293* 2 Christian d'Or
     1866–70   1400. 2000. 3200.

Decimal System 1873–

Bronze

8 1 Ore 1874–1904   3.00   3.50   7.00
    1876 . . . 325 1878 . . . 50 1881 . . . 400
    1886 . . . 35 1892..70 1874–88 . . . 10

---

9 2 Ore 1874–1906   2.00   3.50   7.50
    1875,80–81,86 . . . 10 1876 . . . 95
    1887 . . . 50 1892 . . . 30
10 5 Ore 1874–1906   8.00   15.00   45.00
    1875,82 . . . 30 1884,98,1901,04 . . . 20
    1890 . . . 45 1894–99,1902,06 . . . 15

Silver

11 10 Ore 1874–1905   4.00   7.00   15.00
    1874,75,89 . . . 10 1882–84 . . . 30
    1886 . . . 50 1888 . . . 90 1904 . . . 17
12 25 Ore 1874–1905   7.00   12.00   22.50
    1904 . . . 10

13 1 Krone 1875–98   15.00   40.00 150.00
    1898 . . . 40 1876,92 . . . 20
14 2 Kroner 1875–99   12.00   45.00 100.00
    1897,99 . . . 50

Gold

18 *F296* 10 Kroner
     1873–1900   125.00 145.00 225.00
19 *F295* 20 Kroner
     1873–1900   165.00 185.00 250.00

25th Anniversary of Reign

Silver

15 2 Kroner 1888   25.00   45.00 125.00

Unless otherwise noted, prices are for coins in very
fine, extremely fine, and uncirculated condition.

Golden Wedding

16 2 Kroner 1892   25.00 45.00 125.00

40th Anniversary of Reign

17 2 Kroner 1903   20.00 35.00 60.00

FREDERIK VIII 1906–1912
Death of Christian IX and
Accession of Frederik VIII

Silver

25 2 Kroner 1906   10.00 20.00 45.00

Regular Issues

Bronze

20	1 Ore 1907–12	1.50	2.50	5.00
21	2 Ore 1907–12	2.00	4.00	7.00
22	5 Ore 907–12	6.00	14.00	30.00

Silver

23	10 Ore 1907–12	4.00	7.00	12.00
	1911 . . . 25			
24	25 Ore 1907–11	6.00	10.00	18.00

Gold

26	*F298* 10 Kroner			
	1908–09	125.00	145.00	200.00
27	*F297* 20 Kroner			
	1908–12	165.00	185.00	225.00

CHRISTIAN X 1912–1947
Death of Frederik VIII and
Accession of Christian X

Silver

40 2 Kroner 1912   12.00 20.00 40.00

Regular Issues

Bronze

28	1 Ore 1913–23	1.00	2.00	4.00
	1917 . . . 12 1920 . . . 7			
29	2 Ore 1913–23	2.00	4.00	8.00
	1913 . . . 25 1917 . . . 14			
30	5 Ore 1913–23	3.00	5.00	9.00
	1913 . . . 55 1923 . . . 95			

Iron

28a	1 Ore 1918–19	1.00	2.00	10.00
	1919 . . . 6			

29a	2 Ore 1918–19	2.00	4.00	20.00
	1919 . . . 12			
30a	5 Ore 1918–19	5.00	11.00	35.00
	1919 . . . 11			

Cupro-Nickel

31	10 Ore 1920–23	4.00	6.00	12.00
	1922 . . . 16 1923 . . . 240			
32	25 Ore 1920–22	4.00	6.00	12.00
	1922 . . . 20			

Aluminum-Bronze

33	½ Krone 1924–40	5.00	7.00	15.00
	1926 . . . 15 1939 . . . 50			
34	1 Krone 1924–41	2.00	5.00	16.00
	1924 . . . 160 1930,35,38 . . . 17			
35	2 Kroner 1924–41	4.00	8.00	35.00
	1924,41 . . . 30 1938 . . . 17			

Silver

Design like Nos.31–32

36	10 Ore 1914–19	1.50	3.00	6.00
	1915 . . . 5			
37	25 Ore 1913–19	1.50	2.50	5.00
	1914 . . . 95 1917 . . . 30			

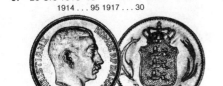

38	1 Krone 1915–16	5.00	8.00	16.00
39	2 Kroner 1915–16	12.00	14.00	20.00
	1915 . . . 20			

Silver Wedding Anniversary

41	2 Kroner 1923	8.00	12.00	25.00

King's 60th Birthday

42	2 Kroner 1930	7.50	11.00	22.50

25th Year of Reign

43	2 Kroner 1937	7.50	11.00	22.50

Regular Issues

Gold

44	F300 10 Kroner			
	1913–17	125.00	145.00	200.00
45	F299 20 Kroner			
	1913–31	165.00	185.00	225.00
	1926–31 . . . 675			

Unless otherwise noted, prices are for coins in very fine, extremely fine, and uncirculated condition.

Bronze

46	1 Ore 1926–40	.10	.50	2.00
	1926,27N . . . 5			
47	2 Ore 1926–40	.10	.50	2.00
	1926 . . . 30			
48	5 Ore 1926–40	.20	.50	3.00
	1926 . . . Unique			

For similar coins dated 1941, see Faeroe Islands.

Cupro-Nickel

49	10 Ore 1924–47	.50	1.50	5.00
	1947 . . . 80			
50	25 Ore 1924–47	.50	3.00	6.00
	1933 . . . 28 1925,37,47 . . . 5			
	1935,39 . . . 11			

For similar coins dated 1941 without mintmark and initials, see Faeroe Islands.

Aluminum

52	2 Ore 1941	.50	2.00	9.00
53	5 Ore 1941	.50	4.00	18.00

Zinc

51	1 Ore 1941–46	.25	2.00	10.00
	1946 . . . 4			
52a	2 Ore 1942–47	.25	1.50	18.00
	1945 . . . 4			
53a	5 Ore 1942–45	.50	3.00	10.00
	1945 . . . 4			
49a	10 Ore 1941–45	.50	3.00	14.00
	1945 . . . 25			
50a	25 Ore 1941–45	1.00	2.00	7.00

Aluminum-Bronze

54	1 Krone 1942–47	.50	2.50	10.00
	1943 . . . 7			

75th Birthday

Silver

55	2 Kroner 1945	8.00	12.00	25.00

FREDERIK IX 1947–1972

Zinc

56	1 Ore 1948–72	.10	.15	.25
	1949 . . . 3			
57	2 Ore 1948–72	.10	.15	.25
58	5 Ore 1950–64	.10	.25	1.50
	1950 . . . 4			

Cupro-Nickel

59	10 Ore 1948–60	.10	.25	2.00
	1959 . . . 80			
60	25 Ore 1948–60	.25	.50	2.00
	1948 . . . 3			

Aluminum-Bronze

61	1 Krone 1947–60	.50	2.00	4.00
	1954,59 . . . 12 1960 . . . 750			
62	2 Kroner 1947–59	1.00	2.00	4.00
	1949,53–55 . . . 4			

Silver Wedding

65	5 Kroner 1960	6.50	7.00	10.00

Later issues in *Current Coins of the World.*

Greenland Commemorative
Silver

63	2 Kroner 1953	8.00	16.00	50.00

18th Birthday of
Princess Margrethe

64	2 Kroner 1958	6.50	8.00	15.00

DOMINICAN REPUBLIC

Occupies the eastern two-thirds of the island of Hispaniola, which lies between Cuba and Puerto Rico. The land is extremely fertile and supports a variety of tropical agricultural crops. Mining and cattle raising are also important. Area: 18,704 square miles. Language: Spanish. Capital: *Santo Domingo.*

Monetary System:
100 Centesimos = 1 Franco
100 Centavos = 1 Peso

Brass or Bronze

A1	¼ Real 1844, 48	10.00	22.00	150.00

Brass

1	1 Centavo 1877	3.00	6.00	12.00

Cupro-Nickel

4	2½ Centavos 1877	15.00	28.00	100.00

Unless otherwise noted, prices are for coins in very fine, extremely fine, and uncirculated condition.

5   5 Centavos 1877   20.00   40.00 150.00

6   1¼ Centavos 1882, 88   10.00   20.00   65.00
     1882 Proof . . . 300.
7   2½ Centavos 1882, 88   3.00   6.00   50.00
     1882 Proof . . . 350.

Bronze

2   5 Centesimos 1891   6.00   12.00   50.00
3   10 Centesimos 1891   6.00   14.00   60.00

Silver

8   50 Centesimos 1891   12.00   25.00   75.00
9*   1 Franco 1891   18.00   35.00 120.00
10   5 Francos 1891   75.00 125.00 600.00

Billon

11   10 Centavos 1897   5.00   15.00 150.00
12   20 Centavos 1897   6.00   20.00 200.00

13   ½ Peso 1897   12.00   35.00 400.00
14   1 Peso 1897   35.00   85.00 700.00

Bronze

15   1 Centavo 1937–61   .25   .50   1.00
     1937 Proof . . . 200.

Cupro-Nickel

16   5 Centavos 1937–74   .25   .50   .75
     1937 Proof . . . 400.
16a 5 Centavos 1944, silver
     alloy   5.00   10.00   25.00

Silver

17   10 Centavos 1937–61   1.25   1.50   4.00
     1937 Proof . . . 250.
18   25 Centavos 1937–61   3.00   4.00   6.00
     1937 Proof . . . 300.
19   ½ Peso 1937–61   6.00   7.00   10.00
     1937 Proof . . . 600.

20   1 Peso 1939, 52   12.00   16.00   22.50
     1939 Proof . . . 3000.

25th Year of
Trujillo Government
Silver

Silver

25	10 Centavos 1963	.95	1.00	1.25
26	25 Centavos 1963	1.85	2.00	3.00
27	½ Peso 1963	3.75	4.00	6.00
28	1 Peso 1963	10.00	12.00	15.00

No. 28 was not released to circulation.

Later issues in *Current Coins of the World.*

EAST AFRICA

An administrative grouping of five separate British territories: Kenya, Uganda, Tanganyika (now Tanzania), British Somaliland (now part of the Somali Republic), and the Sultanate of Zanzibar and Pemba (now part of Tanzania). All became independent between 1960 and 1963, and each now has its own coinage. The East African coinage was also legal tender in Ethiopia and Aden (now Democratic Yemen).

Monetary System:
64 Pice = 1 India Rupee to 1905
100 Cents = 1 Rupee 1905–20
100 Cents = 1 Florin 1920–21
100 Cents = 1 Shilling 1921–63

VICTORIA 1837–1901
Legend:
EAST AFRICA PROTECTORATE
Bronze

21	1 Peso 1955	15.00	30.00	60.00

Gold

22	*F1* 30 Pesos 1955	300.00	325.00	350.00

Centennial
Restoration of Republic

Bronze

23	1 Centavo 1963	.10	.15	.25

Cupro-Nickel

24	5 Centavos 1963	.15	.25	1.00

1	1 Pice 1897–99	5.00	12.50	30.00

Proof . . . 150.00

EDWARD VII 1901–1910
Legend:
EAST AFRICA & UGANDA
PROTECTORATE
Aluminum

2	½ Cent 1908	15.00	30.00	50.00

Unless otherwise noted, prices are for coins in very
fine, extremely fine, and uncirculated condition.

3	1 Cent 1907–08	2.50	6.00	17.50

Cupro-Nickel

2a	½ Cent 1909	15.00	25.00	55.00
3a	1 Cent 1909–10	1.25	4.00	10.00
6	10 Cents 1907, 10	4.00	11.00	25.00

The similar 5 Cents 1908 is a pattern.

Silver

7	25 Cents 1906, 10	10.00	25.00	70.00
8	50 Cents 1906–10	17.50	45.00	150.00

GEORGE V 1910–1936
First Coinage

Cupro-Nickel

9	1 Cent 1911–18	1.50	3.00	12.50
10	5 Cents 1913–19	3.00	8.00	30.00
	1919 . . . 25			
11	10 Cents 1911–18	2.50	7.50	42.50
	1913 . . . 25			

Silver

12	25 Cents 1912–18	10.00	25.00	70.00
	1918 . . . 75			
13	50 Cents 1911–19	12.50	25.00	95.00
	1918H . . . 65 1919 . . . 200			

Second Coinage

Cupro-Nickel

14	1 Cent 1920–21	50.00	125.00	300.00
	1921 . . . Rare			
15	5 Cents 1920	50.00	100.00	200.00

16	10 Cents 1920	125.00	225.00	425.00

Silver

17	25 Cents 1920	30.00	70.00	100.00
18	50 Cents/1 Shilling 1920			Rare
19	1 Florin 1920	30.00	50.00	125.00

No. 18 was not issued to circulation.

Third Coinage

Bronze

20	1 Cent 1922–35	.50	1.50	4.00
	1925 . . . 50			
21	5 Cents 1921–36	1.00	3.00	9.00
22	10 Cents 1921–36	1.00	5.00	15.00

Billon

23	50 Cents/½ Shilling			
	1921–24	2.00	5.00	20.00
24	1 Shilling 1921–25	2.00	3.00	10.00

EDWARD VIII 1936

Bronze

25	5 Cents 1936	1.00	2.50	4.00

| **26** | 10 Cents 1936 | 1.00 | 2.50 | 4.00 |

GEORGE VI 1936–1952

Bronze

27	1 Cent 1942	.25	1.00	2.00
28	5 Cents 1937–43	1.00	2.00	3.00
29	10 Cents 1937–45	1.00	2.00	3.00

Nos. 28 and 29 dated 1942 or later are reduced in weight about 15%.

Billon

30	50 Cents 1937–44	2.00	5.00	20.00
31	1 Shilling 1937–46	2.00	5.00	17.50
	1943 . . . Rare			

New Legend:
GEORGIUS SEXTUS REX
Bronze

32	1 Cent 1949–52	.25	.75	1.50
33	5 Cents 1949–52	.50	2.00	4.00
34	10 Cents 1949–52	.50	2.00	5.00

Cupro-Nickel

| **35** | 50 Cents 1948–52 | .50 | 1.50 | 5.00 |
| **36** | 1 Shilling 1948–52 | 1.00 | 2.00 | 7.50 |

ELIZABETH II 1952–1963

Bronze

| **37** | 1 Cent 1954–62 | .20 | .50 | 1.00 |

| **38** | 5 Cents 1955–63 | .30 | .75 | 1.50 |

| **39** | 10 Cents 1956 | 1.00 | 3.00 | 10.00 |

Cupro-Nickel

| **40** | 50 Cents 1954–63 | .25 | 1.00 | 2.00 |

INDEPENDENT COINAGE

Bronze

| **41** | 5 Cents 1964 | .10 | .20 | .50 |

Unless otherwise noted, prices are for coins in very fine, extremely fine, and uncirculated condition.

42 10 Cents 1964   .10   .20   .50

13 5 Francs 1858   450.00 650.00 2000.

ECUADOR

A republic on the northwest coast of South America. The country is divided into three distinct areas (coastal, plateau and eastern) by two chains of the Andes Mountains. Rich mineral resources are being worked, and Ecuador exports many agricultural products, especially coffee, cacao and balsa wood. Area: 105,685 square miles. Language: Spanish. Capital: *Quito.*

Monetary System:
16 Reales = 1 Escudo to 1856
10 Centavos = 1 Decimo
10 Decimos = 1 Sucre
25 Sucres = 1 Condor

Silver

Obv: Draped bust of Liberty, fineness "8Ds"

8	¼ Real 1849–62 (vars.)	20.00	40.00	100.00
	1862 . . . 500.			
9	½ Real 1848–49	25.00	50.00	100.00
10*	2 Reales 1847–52	25.00	75.00	250.00
10a	2 Reales 1857	2500.	4000.	–
11	4 Reales 1855,57	50.00	200.00	600.00
12	8 Reales 1846	1500.	2750.	4500.

Obv: Fineness ".666"

10b	2 Reales 1862	3500.	5000.	–
11a	4 Reales 1862	1000.	2000.	–

14	2 Reales 1862	2500.	4000.	–
15*	4 Reales 1862	200.00	500.00	–

Proof . . . 2500.

No. 14 probably was not issued to circulation.

Gold

Obv: Simon Bolivar

19 F8 8 Escudos 1847–56 900.00 1400. 2750.

| 26 | 10 Cents 1936 | 1.00 | 2.50 | 4.00 |

ELIZABETH II 1952–1963

Bronze

GEORGE VI 1936–1952

Bronze

| 37 | 1 Cent 1954–62 | .20 | .50 | 1.00 |

27	1 Cent 1942	.25	1.00	2.00
28	5 Cents 1937–43	1.00	2.00	3.00
29	10 Cents 1937–45	1.00	2.00	3.00

Nos. 28 and 29 dated 1942 or later are reduced in weight about 15%.

| 38 | 5 Cents 1955–63 | .30 | .75 | 1.50 |

Billon

30	50 Cents 1937–44	2.00	5.00	20.00
31	1 Shilling 1937–46	2.00	5.00	17.50
	1943 . . . Rare			

| 39 | 10 Cents 1956 | 1.00 | 3.00 | 10.00 |

New Legend:
GEORGIUS SEXTUS REX
Bronze

32	1 Cent 1949–52	.25	.75	1.50
33	5 Cents 1949–52	.50	2.00	4.00
34	10 Cents 1949–52	.50	2.00	5.00

Cupro-Nickel

| 40 | 50 Cents 1954–63 | .25 | 1.00 | 2.00 |

Cupro-Nickel

INDEPENDENT COINAGE

Bronze

| 35 | 50 Cents 1948–52 | .50 | 1.50 | 5.00 |
| 36 | 1 Shilling 1948–52 | 1.00 | 2.00 | 7.50 |

| 41 | 5 Cents 1964 | .10 | .20 | .50 |

Unless otherwise noted, prices are for coins in very fine, extremely fine, and uncirculated condition.

42   10 Cents 1964   .10   .20   .50

ECUADOR

A republic on the northwest coast of South America. The country is divided into three distinct areas (coastal, plateau and eastern) by two chains of the Andes Mountains. Rich mineral resources are being worked, and Ecuador exports many agricultural products, especially coffee, cacao and balsa wood. Area: 105,685 square miles. Language: Spanish. Capital: *Quito.*

Monetary System:
16 Reales = 1 Escudo to 1856
10 Centavos = 1 Decimo
10 Decimos = 1 Sucre
25 Sucres = 1 Condor

Silver

Obv: Draped bust of Liberty, fineness "8Ds"

8	¼ Real 1849–62 (vars.)	20.00	40.00	100.00
	1862 . . . 500.			
9	½ Real 1848–49	25.00	50.00	100.00
10*	2 Reales 1847–52	25.00	75.00	250.00
10a	2 Reales 1857	2500.	4000.	–
11	4 Reales 1855,57	50.00	200.00	600.00
12	8 Reales 1846	1500.	2750.	4500.

Obv: Fineness ".666"

10b	2 Reales 1862	3500.	5000.	–
11a	4 Reales 1862	1000.	2000.	–

13   5 Francs 1858   450.00 650.00 2000.

14	2 Reales 1862	2500.	4000.	–
15*	4 Reales 1862	200.00	500.00	–

Proof . . . 2500.
No. 14 probably was not issued to circulation.

Gold

Obv: Simon Bolivar

19   *F8*   8 Escudos 1847–56   900.00   1400.   2750.

Decimal System

Copper

20	½ Centavo 1890	7.00	20.00	100.00
21*	1 Centavo 1872, 90	7.00	20.00	100.00
23	2 Centavos 1872	15.00	35.00	150.00

Cupro-Nickel

24	½ Centavo 1884	8.00	20.00	40.00
			Proof . . . 150.00	
25*	1 Centavo 1884, 86	8.00	20.00	60.00
			Proof . . . 175.00	
26	½ Decimo 1884, 86	8.00	20.00	75.00
			Proof . . . 250.00	

Silver

Obv: Bust of Sucre

27	½ Decimo 1893–1915	1.50	4.00	10.00
28	1 Decimo 1884–1916	2.00	5.00	12.00
			Proof . . . 300.00	
29*	2 Decimos 1884–1916	4.00	6.00	12.00
			Proof . . . 400.00	
30	½ Sucre 1884	25.00	80.00	750.00
			Proof . . . 1000.	
31	1 Sucre 1884–97	20.00	45.00	125.00
			Proof . . . 1250.	

Gold

| 32 | *F10* 10 Sucres | | | |
| | 1899–1900 | 175.00 | 225.00 | 300.00 |

Cupro-Nickel

33	½ Centavo 1909	4.00	10.00	40.00
34	1 Centavo 1909	6.00	12.00	60.00
35*	2 Centavos 1909	8.00	25.00	100.00
37	5 Centavos 1909	8.00	25.00	100.00

Rev: Values spelled out

36*	2½ Centavos 1917	4.00	15.00	100.00
37a	5 Centavos 1917–18, thin	2.00	5.00	15.00
39	10 Centavos 1918	10.00	25.00	100.00

Rev: Values in numerals

| 38 | 5 Centavos 1919 | 2.00 | 5.00 | 15.00 |
| 40 | 10 Centavos 1919 | 3.00 | 7.00 | 25.00 |

Obv: Simon Bolivar

| 41 | 5 Centavos 1924 | 2.00 | 5.00 | 15.00 |
| 42 | 10 Centavos 1924 | 2.00 | 5.00 | 15.00 |

New Coinage

Bronze

| 44 | 1 Centavo 1928 | 1.00 | 2.00 | 4.00 |

Nickel

| 45 | 2½ Centavos 1928 | 4.00 | 10.00 | 40.00 |

| 46 | 5 Centavos 1928 | 1.00 | 2.00 | 6.00 |
| 47 | 10 Centavos 1928 | 1.00 | 2.00 | 8.00 |

Unless otherwise noted, prices are for coins in very
fine, extremely fine, and uncirculated condition.

Silver

48	50 Centavos 1928, 30	1.50	3.00	10.00
49*	1 Sucre 1928–34	2.50	5.00	12.50
50	2 Sucres 1928, 30	5.00	10.00	25.00

Gold

43	F11 1 Condor 1928	175.00	225.00	400.00

Nickel

51	5 Centavos 1937	.25	.60	3.00
52	10 Centavos 1937	.50	1.00	3.00
53	20 Centavos 1937	1.00	2.00	5.00

54	1 Sucre 1937	1.00	3.00	6.00

Brass

51a	5 Centavos 1942, 44	1.00	2.00	5.00
52a	10 Centavos 1942	1.00	2.00	8.00
53a	20 Centavos 1942, 44	1.00	2.00	10.00

Silver

55*	2 Sucres 1944	2.00	4.00	7.00

56	5 Sucres 1943–44	9.00	12.00	15.00

Cupro-Nickel

51b	5 Centavos 1946	.25	.50	2.00
52b	10 Centavos 1946	.25	.50	2.00
53b	20 Centavos 1946	.25	.50	3.00

Nickel

54a	1 Sucre 1946	.25	1.00	4.00

Later issues in *Current Coins of the World*.

EGYPT (Misr)

Egypt, one of the world's oldest civilized lands, occupies the northeast corner of Africa. It was a province of the Ottoman (Turkish) Empire from 1517 to 1914, when it became a British protectorate. It became an independent kingdom in 1922 and a republic in 1953. In 1958 it joined Syria to form the United Arab Republic; this union was dissolved in 1961 but Egypt retained the U.A.R. name to 1971. Despite being mostly desert, its economy is agricultural, centered along the Nile River. Area: 386,-000 square miles. Languages: Arabic, English, French. Capital: *al-Qahiral (Cairo)*.

Monetary Systems:
 – to 1916:
  40 Para = 1 Ghirsh (Piastre)
 – 1916 on:
  10 Millim (Milliemes) = 1 Ghirsh (Piastre)
  100 Ghirsh = 1 Jiniah (Pound)

OTTOMAN PROVINCE to 1914

MISR (in Arabic)

Most coins issued before 1916 are similar to Turkish types but are distinguished by the Arabic word Misr (Egypt) on the reverse.

ABDUL AZIZ 1861–1876

(Accession Date AH 1277 on Coins)

A. Locally Struck Issues

Copper

Obv: Toughra and flower, value below

		VG	F	VF
2a	10 Para Yrs. 8–11 (11 Rare)	300.00	450.00	750.00
3a	20 Para Yrs. 8–11 (11 Rare)	12.00	20.00	35.00
4a	40 Para Yrs. 9–11 (9, 11 Rare)	500.00	750.00	1000.

Silver

Obv: Toughra and flower, value below.

		F	VF	EF
5	10 Para Yrs. 2–16	5.00	12.50	17.50
6*	20 Para Yrs. 1–15 (1 Rare)	6.00	15.00	20.00
7	1 Ghirsh Yrs. 1–16	4.00	10.00	17.50
8a	2½ Ghirsh Yrs. 8–15	150.00	250.00	375.00
9a	5 Ghirsh Yrs. 1–10	150.00	250.00	375.00
10a	10 Ghirsh Yrs. 2–11 (11 Rare)	300.00	500.00	750.00
11	20 Ghirsh Yrs. 1–2, (11 Rare)	600.00	1000.	1500.

Gold

		F	VF	EF
A11	*F16* 5 Ghirsh Yrs. 2–16	20.00	30.00	75.00
B11	*F15* 10 Ghirsh Yrs. 10–14	45.00	65.00	100.00
C11	*F14* 25 Ghirsh Yrs. 8–15	60.00	90.00	150.00
D11	*F13* 50 Ghirsh Yrs. 11–16	110.00	160.00	225.00
E11	*F11* 100 Ghirsh Yrs. 1–16	110.00	150.00	250.00
F11	*F10* 500 Ghirsh Yrs. 8–15		13,500.	15,000.

B. Issues Struck in Europe

Bronze

		VF	EF	UNC
1	4 Para Yr. 4	15.00	27.50	60.00
2*	10 Para Yrs. 4–10 (29mm)	2.00	5.00	20.00
3	20 Para Yrs. 3–10 (32mm)	2.25	6.00	20.00
3b	20 Para Yr. 7 (29mm, thick)	250.00	350.00	Rare
4	40 Para Yr. 10	12.50	35.00	100.00

No. 3b may have been struck in Egypt

Silver

Obv: No flower at right of toughra

		F	VF	EF
8	2½ Ghirsh Yr. 4	50.00	75.00	225.00
9*	5 Ghirsh Yr. 4	60.00	110.00	225.00
10	10 Ghirsh Yr. 4	90.00	150.00	300.00

Gold

		F	VF	EF
A10	*F12* 100 Ghirsh Yr. 4	750.00	1,250.	2,500.

Other gold coins dated Yr. 4, without flower are thought to be patterns.

MURAD V 1876

(Accession Date AH 1293 on Coins)
Silver

		F	VF	EF
G11	1 Ghirsh Yr. 1	150.00	225.00	350.00

No. G11 can be distinguished from No. 18a dated Yr. 1 only by details of the toughra (a stylized calligraphic design containing the Sultan's name and titles).

Gold

Like Nos. C22–D22, but toughra without flower

		F	VF	EF
H11	*F18* 50 Ghirsh Yr. 1	1,000.	1,500.	3,000.
J11	*F17* 100 Ghirsh Yr. 1	1,000.	1,500.	3,000.

ABDUL HAMID II
1876–1909

(Accession Date AH 1293 on Coins)

A. First Coinage, locally struck

Silver

Obv: Tughra and flower, value below

		VF	EF	UNC
A17	10 Para Yrs. 1–3	75.00	125.00	225.00
B17	20 Para Yrs. 1–3	100.00	160.00	275.00
18a	1 Ghirsh Yrs. 1–5	7.50	15.00	50.00
20a	5 Ghirsh Yr. 2			Rare
22a	20 Ghirsh Yrs. 1,5	750.00	1,250.	Rare

Gold

Obverse like silver coins

		F	VF	EF
A22	*F20* 5 Ghirsh Yrs. 2–7	40.00	65.00	90.00
D22	*F19a* 100 Ghirsh Yrs. 1, 8	115.00	125.00	175.00
E22	*F19* 500 Ghirsh Yrs. 1, 6	2000.	3000.	5000.

The existence of former No. C22 cannot be confirmed.

Obv: "al-Ghazi" (the Victorious) to right of toughra
A22a *F23* 5 Ghirsh Yrs.
    16–34   35.00 50.00 75.00
B22 *F22* 10 Ghirsh Yrs.
    17–34   45.00 60.00 90.00

B. Second Coinage, struck in Europe

Bronze

		VF	EF	UNC
12	¹⁄₄₀ Ghirsh Yrs. 10–35	.60	1.50	4.25
	Yr. 18 . . . 45			
13*	¹⁄₂₀ Ghirsh Yrs. 10–35	.75	1.25	6.50
	Yr. 18 . . . 15			

Cupro-Nickel

14	¹⁄₁₀ Ghirsh Yrs. 10–35	1.00	2.75	7.50
	Yr. 18 . . . 15			
15*	²⁄₁₀ Ghirsh Yrs. 10–35	1.00	3.50	15.00
16	⁵⁄₁₀ Ghirsh Yrs. 10–33	.85	2.50	8.00

17	1 Ghirsh Yrs. 22–33	2.00	7.50	25.00
	Yr. 22 . . . 15			

Silver

18	1 Ghirsh Yrs. 10–33	2.25	6.00	15.00
19	2 Ghirsh Yrs. 10–33	2.25	5.50	15.00
20*	5 Ghirsh Yrs. 10–33	7.50	15.00	35.00
21	10 Ghirsh Yrs. 10–33	12.50	22.50	50.00
22	20 Ghirsh Yrs. 10–33	22.50	55.00	175.00

Gold

Floral borders both sides
F22 *F21* 100 Ghirsh Yr. 12   140.00 180.00 250.00

MOHAMMED V 1909–1914
(Accession Date 1327 on Coins)
Designs similar to Nos. 12–22

Bronze

23	¹⁄₄₀ Ghirsh Yrs. 2–6	1.00	3.50	12.50
24	¹⁄₂₀ Ghirsh Yrs. 2–6	.75	2.00	5.50

Cupro-Nickel

25	¹⁄₁₀ Ghirsh Yrs. 2–6	1.25	2.75	7.00
	Yr. 3 . . . 7.50			
26	²⁄₁₀ Ghirsh Yrs. 2–6	2.50	7.50	20.00
	Yr. 3 . . . 10			
27	⁵⁄₁₀ Ghirsh Yrs. 2–6	2.00	7.50	17.50
	Yr. 3 . . . 15			
28	1 Ghirsh Yrs. 2–6	3.00	7.50	20.00
	Yr. 3 . . . 20			

Silver

29	1 Ghirsh Yrs. 2–3	4.00	12.50	25.00
30	2 Ghirsh Yrs. 2–3	15.00	35.00	75.00
31	5 Ghirsh Yrs. 2–6	6.00	12.50	35.00
	Yr. 2 . . . 25			
32	10 Ghirsh Yrs. 2–6	12.50	22.50	50.00
	Yr. 2 . . . 20			
33	20 Ghirsh Yrs. 2–6	22.50	55.00	150.00

II. BRITISH PROTECTORATE
1914–1922
Sultan HUSSEIN KAMIL
1915–1917

Bronze

34	½ Millieme 1917	2.25	5.00	10.00

Cupro-Nickel

35	1 Millieme 1917	1.25	3.25	7.50

36	2 Milliemes 1916–17	1.25	4.00	15.00
37	5 Milliemes 1916–17	1.00	2.00	15.00
38	10 Milliemes 1916–17	1.50	3.50	20.00

Silver

39	2 Piastres 1916–17	2.25	5.50	12.50
40	5 Piastres 1916–17	3.00	7.50	27.50
41	10 Piastres 1916–17	10.00	17.50	55.00
42	20 Piastres 1916–17	25.00	55.00	160.00
		Proof . . . 400.00		

Gold

43	*F24* 100 Piastres 1916	140.00	160.00	225.00

FUAD, as Sultan 1917–1922

Silver

44	2 Piastres 1920	45.00	85.00	225.00
45	5 Piastres 1920	27.50	65.00	125.00
46	10 Piastres 1920	35.00	75.00	140.00

All proofs of Nos. 44–46 are rare.

III. INDEPENDENT KINGDOM
1922–1952
FUAD, AS KING FUAD I
1922–1936
First Coinage

Bronze

47*	½ Millim 1924	2.50	6.00	15.00

48	1 Millim 1924	2.00	7.50	20.00

Cupro-Nickel

49	2 Millim 1924	1.50	7.50	15.00
50	5 Millim 1924	1.25	4.50	15.00
51	10 Millim 1924	3.50	10.00	25.00

Silver

52	2 Ghirsh 1923	4.25	10.00	17.50
53*	5 Ghirsh 1923	5.50	17.50	35.00
54	10 Ghirsh 1923	10.00	27.50	65.00
55	20 Ghirsh 1923	22.50	55.00	200.00

Gold

56	*F30* 20 Ghirsh 1923	40.00	75.00	90.00
57	*F29* 50 Ghirsh 1923	70.00	90.00	125.00
58	*F27–28* 100 Ghirsh 1922	140.00	175.00	225.00
59*	*F25–26* 500 Ghirsh 1922	700.00	900.00	1400.
		Proof . . . 2000.		

Second Coinage

Bronze

60	½ Millim 1929, 32	5.00	12.50	27.50
61*	1 Millim 1929–35	.75	1.50	5.00
	1929 . . . 7.50			

Cupro-Nickel

62	2 Millim 1929	1.00	2.75	7.50
64	5 Millim 1929–35	1.50	3.50	10.00
65	10 Millim 1929–35	1.25	4.50	13.50

Unless otherwise noted, prices are for coins in very fine, extremely fine, and uncirculated condition.

| 63 | 2½ Millim 1933 | 2.50 | 5.00 | 12.50 |

Silver

66	2 Ghirsh 1929	1.75	4.00	7.50
67*	5 Ghirsh 1929, 33	6.00	15.00	25.00
68	10 Ghirsh 1929, 33	15.00	27.50	60.00
69	20 Ghirsh 1929, 33	20.00	45.00	160.00

Gold
Rev. designs like Nos. 56–59

70	F34	20 Ghirsh 1930	45.00	60.00	95.00
71	F33	50 Ghirsh 1929–30	85.00	125.00	175.00
72	F32	100 Ghirsh 1929–30	140.00	160.00	275.00
73	F31	500 Ghirsh 1929–32	750.00	1100.	1750.
				Proof . . .	2000.

FAROUK I 1936–1952
First Coinage

Bronze

| 74 | ½ Millim 1938 | 3.50 | 6.50 | 15.00 |

Cupro-Nickel

| 79 | 1 Millim 1938 | 2.00 | 7.50 | 15.00 |

80	2 Millim 1938	1.00	2.50	15.00
81*	5 Millim 1938, 41	.35	1.00	2.50
82	10 Millim 1938, 41	.40	1.25	3.25

Silver

83	2 Ghirsh 1937–42	1.50	2.75	5.50
84*	5 Ghirsh 1937,39	3.00	5.50	12.50
85	10 Ghirsh 1937,39	6.00	12.50	35.00
86	20 Ghirsh 1937,39	22.50	40.00	100.00

Royal Wedding
Gold

Rev. designs similar to Nos 83–86

88	F38	20 Ghirsh 1938	45.00	70.00	85.00
89	F37	50 Ghirsh 1938	70.00	90.00	145.00
90	F36	100 Ghirsh 1938	140.00	160.00	200.00
91	F35	500 Ghirsh 1938	750.00	2000.	2500.
				Proof . . .	3250.

Second Coinage
Bronze

| 75 | 1 Millim 1938–50 (round) | .30 | .75 | 2.50 |
| | | | Proof . . . | 50.00 |

77*	5 Millim 1938, 43	.30	.65	2.25
				Proof . . .	50.00
78	10 Millim 1938, 43	.40	.75	2.75
				Proof . . .	50.00

Nos. 77–78 dated 1938 were struck in 1942.

Silver

87   2 Ghirsh 1944   1.25   2.50   5.50

IV. REPUBLIC 1953–1958

Aluminum-Bronze

Obv: Small bust of Sphinx				
92	1 Millim 1954–56	.20	.40	1.00
93*	5 Millim 1954–56	.35	1.25	5.50
94	10 Millim 1954–55	.45	1.75	7.50
Obv: Large bust of Sphinx				
92a	1 Millim 1956–58	.20	.30	.75
93a	5 Millim 1957–58	.35	.85	3.50
94a	10 Millim 1955–58	.45	1.00	3.50

Silver

95	5 Ghirsh 1956–57	1.50	3.25	5.50
96*	10 Ghirsh 1955–57	2.75	4.50	7.50
97	20 Ghirsh 1956	7.50	13.50	25.00

Nationalization of Suez Canal

Silver

98   25 Ghirsh 1956   7.50   13.50   25.00

Evacuation of the British

99   50 Ghirsh 1956   15.00   25.00   45.00

Inauguration of National Assembly

102 25 Ghirsh 1957   7.50   13.50   25.00

3rd and 5th Anniversaries of the Revolution

Gold

103*	F40,42 1 Pound 1955, 57	135.00	145.00	175.00
				Proof . . . 200.00
104	F39,41 5 Pounds 1955, 57	600.00	700.00	900.00
				Proof . . . 1000.

V. UNITED ARAB REPUBLIC 1958–1971

This Republic was composed of Egypt and Syria which joined together February 21, 1958. Syria broke away and resumed independence on September 29, 1961. For other U.A.R. issues, see Syria Nos. A19–23.

Unless otherwise noted, prices are for coins in very fine, extremely fine, and uncirculated condition.

Agriculture and Industry Fair
Aluminum-Bronze

105 20 Milliemes 1958   1.75   2.75   6.50

Founding of the U.A.R.
Gold

106 *F43* ½ Pound 1958   75.00 110.00 125.00
Proof . . . 150.00

Silver

107 10 Ghirsh 1959   3.50   6.00   12.50

Aswan Dam
Gold

108* *F45* 1 Pound 1960   125.00 145.00 175.00
Proof . . . 250.00

109 *F44* 5 Pounds 1960   600.00 700.00 875.00
Proof . . . 1000.

National Assembly
Silver

110 25 Ghirsh 1960   7.50   10.00   25.00

Regular Issues
Aluminum-Bronze

111 1 Millieme 1960, 66	.10	.15	.30
112 2 Milliemes 1962, 66	.20	.35	.60
113* 5 Milliemes 1960, 66	.20	.40	.85
A113 10 Milliemes 1960, 66	.20	.45	.85

Silver

114 5 Ghirsh 1960, 66	2.25	2.75	3.25
115 10 Ghirsh 1960, 66	3.00	4.00	5.50
116 20 Ghirsh 1960, 66	10.00	12.50	22.50

1966 Set Nos.111–116 Proof only . . . 100.00

Later issues in *Current Coins of the World.*

EL SALVADOR

The smallest of the Central American countries. Lying in the tropics, its economy is based on its coffee plantations, which produce 80% of all exports. Area: 8,259 square miles. Language: Spanish. Capital: *San Salvador.*

Monetary System:
100 Centavos = 1 Peso
100 Centavos = 1 Colon

Cupro-Nickel

Obv: Francisco Morazan,
Federation President, 1830–39

1	1 Centavo 1889, 1913	2.00	5.00	15.00
2	3 Centavos 1889, 1913	3.00	8.00	20.00

Copper

3	1 Centavo 1892–93	85.00	140.00	250.00
	1893 . . . 500.			

Silver

8	5 Centavos 1892–93	15.00	30.00	50.00
9	10 Centavos 1892	60.00	140.00	300.00
10*	20 Centavos 1892	20.00	50.00	150.00

4	50 Centavos 1892	50.00	150.00	300.00
5	1 Peso 1892	125.00	250.00	600.00

Rev: Columbus

6	50 Centavos 1892–94	25.00	75.00	250.00
7*	1 Peso 1892–1911	15.00	30.00	60.00
	1892 . . . 50.			
7a	1 Peso 1904–14 (heavier portrait)	14.00	25.00	50.00

Gold

11	F4 2½ Pesos 1892	400.00	650.00	1000.
12	F3 5 Pesos 1892	550.00	800.00	1200.
13	F2 10 Pesos 1892	1000.	2000.	2800.
14	F1 20 Pesos 1892	2000.	4000.	6000.

Copper

15	¼ Real 1909	35.00	55.00	100.00

Unless otherwise noted, prices are for coins in very
fine, extremely fine, and uncirculated condition.

Silver

22	5 Centavos 1911	5.00	12.00	25.00
23	10 Centavos 1911	6.00	15.00	40.00
24	25 Centavos 1911	7.00	20.00	75.00

Legend: with DEL SALVADOR
Cupro-Nickel

16	1 Centavo 1915–36	2.00	6.00	10.00
17	3 Centavos 1915	3.00	10.00	25.00
18	5 Centavos 1915–25	3.00	10.00	20.00

New Legend:
with DE EL SALVADOR

19	1 Centavo 1940	2.00	5.00	15.00
20	5 Centavos 1940–74	.10	.20	.50
21	10 Centavos 1921–72	.10	.30	.65

Bronze

19a	1 Centavo 1942–72	.05	.10	.20

Copper-Nickel-Zinc

20a	5 Centavos 1944–52	.25	1.00	3.00
21a	10 Centavos 1952	.25	1.00	3.00

Silver

25	5 Centavos 1914	3.00	8.00	20.00
26	10 Centavos 1914	4.00	10.00	30.00
27	25 Centavos 1914	5.00	15.00	50.00
28	25 Centavos 1943–44			
	(design similar to No. 21)	3.00	5.00	8.00

400th Anniversary of San Salvador
Silver

30	1 Colon 1925	100.00 200.00 300.00

Gold

29	F5 20 Colones 1925	1000. 2000. 3000.

Silver

31	25 Centavos 1953	.75	1.00	4.00
32	50 Centavos 1953	1.50	2.00	5.00

Later issues in *Current Coins of the World.*

ERITREA

A former Italian colony on the Red Sea, Eritrea became federated with Ethiopia in 1952 by an act of her parliament. Products are chiefly agricultural. Languages: Amharic, various. Capital: *Asmara.*

Monetary System:
100 Centesimi = 1 Lira
5 Lire = 1 Tallero

UMBERTO I 1878-1900

Silver

1	50 Centesimi 1890	40.00	75.00	190.00
2	1 Lira 1890-96	35.00	55.00	175.00
	1896 . . . 75			
3	2 Lire 1890, 96	45.00	75.00	275.00
4	5 Lire/1 Tallero 1891, 96	180.00	350.00	900.00

VITTORIO EMANUELE III
1900-1946

Silver

5 1 Tallero 1918   45.00 75.00 300.00
Average diameter 40mm. Diameter varies because
coins were struck without a collar.

ESTONIA (Eesti Vabariik)

Now part of the U.S.S.R., Estonia was a short-lived republic which existed between the two World Wars. Products are chiefly those of farm and forest. Furniture manufacture and precision industries are also important.

Area: 18,357 square miles. Language: Estonian. Capital: *Tallinn*.

Monetary Systems:
100 Penni = 1 Mark 1918-27
100 Senti = 1 Kroon 1928-41

Bronze

1	1 Sent 1929	2.00	3.00	6.00

1a	1 Sent 1939	12.50	17.50	35.00
2	2 Senti 1934	3.00	5.00	10.00
3	5 Senti 1931	3.00	6.00	15.00

Cupro-Nickel

4	1 Mark 1922	5.00	7.50	12.50
5	3 Marka 1922	6.00	8.50	15.00
6	5 Marka 1922	7.00	12.00	25.00

Nickel-Bronze

4a	1 Mark 1924	6.00	9.00	17.50
5a	3 Marka 1925	7.50	12.50	32.50
6a	5 Marka 1924	7.50	12.50	32.50
7	10 Marka 1925	10.00	17.50	40.00

8	1 Mark 1926	7.50	12.00	30.00
9	3 Marka 1926	40.00	50.00	100.00
10	5 Marka 1926	200.00	275.00	400.00
A10	10 Marka 1926	750.00	1000.	1250.
B10	25 Marka 1926			Rare

Nos. A10 and B10 were not issued to circulation.

11	10 Senti 1931	4.00	7.50	15.00
12	20 Senti 1935	3.50	6.50	15.00

Unless otherwise noted, prices are for coins in very
fine, extremely fine, and uncirculated condition.

13 25 Senti 1928   12.00 20.00 40.00

14 50 Senti 1936   15.00 22.50 45.00

Aluminum-Bronze

15 1 Kroon 1934   10.00 15.00 32.50

Silver

Rev: Tallinn Castle
16 2 Krooni 1930   15.00 20.00 35.00

Tercentenary University of Tartu

17 2 Krooni 1932   20.00 40.00 80.00

Tenth Singing Festival

18 1 Kroon 1933   25.00 50.00 75.00

ETHIOPIA

A volcanic mountain country in northeast Africa, Ethiopia is one of the world's oldest Christian nations (since 330 A.D.) Following a leftist military development in 1974, the emperor was deposed. In 1975 Ethiopia was proclaimed a socialist country. Area: 457,142 square miles. Language: Amharic. Capital: *Addis Ababa.*

Monetary Systems:

a. to EE 1889 (1897): 16 Mahalek or Gersh = 1 Ber

b. EE 1889: 100 Matona = 20 Gersh (Mahalek, Piastres) = 1 Ber (Talari, Taler)

c. ca. EE 1890–1925 (AD 1898–1933): 32 Besa = 16 Gersh = 1 Ber

d. EE 1925–37: 100 Matona = 1 Ber

e. EE 1937– : 100 Santeem = 1 Ber

Dating System: Dates on coins are in the Ethiopian Era (EE), which commenced September, AD 7. To convert from EE to AD dates, add 7 years and 8 months to the EE date.

Numeral Chart:

1	2	3	4	5
$\underline{\delta}$	$\bar{B}$	$\bar{\Gamma}$	$\bar{\Omega}$	$\bar{\mathcal{E}}$
6	7	8	9	0
$\bar{3}$	$\bar{Z}$	$\bar{\mathcal{I}}$	$\bar{\Theta}$	♦
10	20	30	40	50
$\underline{I}$	$\bar{\lambda}$	$\bar{\mathcal{W}}$	$\bar{?}$	$\bar{Y}$
60	70	80	90	100
$\bar{?}$	$\bar{G}$	$\bar{\mathbb{T}}$	$\bar{?}$	$\bar{Q}$

MENELIK II
EE 1881–1906 (1889–1913)
First Coinage
Silver

A1 1 Mahalek EE 1885   175.00 250.00 450.00

Second Coinage

Nos. 1–10 were struck in Paris, all with the usual Paris Mint privy marks and (except for No. 10) an "A" mint mark on the reverse.

Copper

1 $^1/_{100}$ Ber EE 1889 (1897)   8.00 15.00 45.00

Brass
Designs like No. 1

2 ¼ Gersh EE 1888 (1896),
     26mm   1000. 1500. 2500.
3 ½ Gersh 1888 (30mm)   800.00 1200. 1800.
4 1 Gersh 1888 (38mm)   900.00 1400. 2000.

Nos. 2–4 appear to have been struck only for presentation sets.

Silver

Rev: Lion's left leg raised

5 1 Gersh EE 1889–95
     (16mm)   1.00   3.00   15.00
6 ⅛ Ber 1887–88 (20mm) 35.00   60.00 250.00
7* ¼ Ber 1887–95 (24mm) 10.00 25.00 100.00
8 ½ Ber 1887–89 (30mm) 17.50   35.00 150.00
9 1 Ber 1887–89 (40mm) 40.00   75.00 250.00

Coins dated EE 1888 were struck only for presentation. Final dates of Nos. 5, 7 and 8 were occasionally restruck to 1928.

Obv: Slightly modified portrait.
Rev: Lion's right leg raised.

10 1 Ber EE 1892, 95
      (1889,1903)   45.00 90.00 275.00

Third Coinage

Nos. 17–20 and 11–13 were struck in Addis Ababa ca. 1903–33, all with frozen date EE 1889. Dies, although made in Paris, lack the mint marks and privy marks used on Nos. 1–10.

Copper

17 ($^1/_{32}$ Ber) EE 1889   2.00   5.00 45.00

17a $^1/_{32}$ Ber 1889   2.00   5.00 35.00

Unless otherwise noted, prices are for coins in very fine, extremely fine, and uncirculated condition.

No. 17 was struck from dies intended for a silver ⅛ Ber as Nos. 18–20, and the incorrect value below the lion was defaced or removed. No. 17a is identical in design but the correct value appears at the bottom. Nos. 17 and 17a occur with edges either reeded or plain.

Silver

Rev: Lion's right leg raised, no mint marks

18	1 Gersh EE 1889 (17mm)	85.00	150.00	300.00
19*	¼ Ber 1889 (25mm)	25.00	50.00	100.00
20	½ Ber 1889 (30mm)	75.00	125.00	350.00

Gold

11	F22 ¼ Wark EE 1889 (16mm)	125.00	175.00	300.00
12	F21 ½ Wark 1889 (18mm)	150.00	225.00	350.00
13	F20 1 Wark 1889 (20mm)	175.00	275.00	500.00

Nos. 11–13 were issued for presentation rather than circulation. Their weights vary widely, with no relationship to the values shown on the coins. Nos. 18–20 were also struck in gold for presentation, usually with value defaced on reverse. (See illustration of the Zauditu piece below).

EMPRESS ZAUDITU
EE 1909–23 (1916–30)

Gold

21	F26 1 Wark EE 1917 (1925)	700.00	1200.	2000.
A21	F25 2 Warks 1917	900.00	1500.	2500.
22	F24 4 Warks 1917	2000.	3000.	4500.

These issues were presentation strikings from dies intended for silver coins. Values were usually defaced after striking. Weights of all are very irregular.

HAILE SELASSIE
EE 1923–66 (1930–74)
First Coinage

Gold

28	F29 ½ Wark EE 1923 (1931), 18mm	350.00	600.00	1250.
29*	F28 1 Wark 1923 (20mm)	500.00	750.00	1500.

Nos. 28–29 were issued for presentation in varying weights. Similar silver coins with lion reverse are patterns, as are silver and gold coins dated EE 1921 (1928).

Second Coinage

Copper
Design like No. 26

23	1 Matona EE 1923 (1931)	2.00	3.00	15.00
24	5 Matona 1923	2.50	4.00	25.00

Nickel

25	10 Matona 1923	1.50	2.50	17.50
26	25 Matona 1923	1.50	2.50	20.00
27	50 Matona 1923	2.00	3.50	25.00

Third Coinage

Bronze

30	1 Santeem EE 1936 (1944), 17mm	.10	.15	.50
31*	5 Santeem 1936 (20mm)	.15	.20	.75
32	10 Santeem 1936 (23mm)	.20	.25	1.00
33	25 Santeem 1936 (26mm, round)	15.00	30.00	45.00

35 25 Santeem 1936 (scal-
      loped)   .50   1.00   2.00
Most specimens of No. 33 were converted to No. 35 by
crimping the edge so as to avoid confusion with No. 34.

Nos. 30–32 and 35 were struck with date unchanged
for many years.

Silver
34 50 Santeem EE 1936   3.00   5.00   12.50
Later issues in *Current Coins of the World.*

FAEROE ISLANDS
(Faeroerne)

A group of 18 volcanic islands located about 300 miles
northwest of the Shetlands in the North Atlantic. Though
they are a Danish possession, they have extensive home
rule. Area: 540 square miles. Language: Danish. Capital: *Thorshavn.*

Monetary System:
100 Ore = 1 Krone

CHRISTIAN X 1912–1947

Bronze

1	1 Ore 1941	15.00	25.00	40.00
2	2 Ore 1941	3.50	8.00	12.00
3	5 Ore 1941	3.50	7.50	12.00

Cupro-Nickel

4	10 Ore 1941	4.50	9.00	20.00
5	25 Ore 1941	5.00	9.00	20.00

Nos. 1–5 are identical to Denmark Nos. 46–50 except
that they do not bear mint mark or mintmaster's initials.

FIJI

A group of about 320 islands in the South Pacific
Ocean. Fiji was a British colony from 1874 to 1970,
when it became an independent nation within the British
Commonwealth. Its forests furnish valuable woods. Capital: *Suva.*

Monetary System:
12 Pence = 1 Shilling
2 Shillings = 1 Florin
20 Shillings = 1 Pound

GEORGE V 1910–1936

Cupro-Nickel

1	½ Penny 1934	4.50	8.00	10.00
2	1 Penny 1934–36	1.50	6.00	25.00
	1936 . . . 5			

Silver

3	6 Pence 1934–36	3.00	15.00	60.00
	1936 . . . 15		Proof . . . 600.00	

4	1 Shilling 1934–36	7.00	20.00	100.00
	1936 . . . 12		Proof . . . 700.00	

51	Florin 1934–36	10.00	30.00	125.00
	1936 . . . 15		Proof . . . 900.00	

Unless otherwise noted, prices are for coins in very
fine, extremely fine, and uncirculated condition.

EDWARD VIII 1936

Cupro-Nickel

6	1 Penny 1936	1.50	4.00	10.00

GEORGE VI 1936–1952

7	½ Penny 1940–41	3.00	7.00	20.00
	1940 . . . 15			
8	1 Penny 1937–41, 45	2.00	4.00	9.00
	1940 . . . 4			

Brass

7a	½ Penny 1942–43	1.50	4.50	18.50
8a	1 Penny 1942–43	2.00	8.50	25.00

Silver

Obv: EMPEROR to right of head
Rev: Designs like Nos. 3–5

11	6 Pence 1937	15.00	30.00	100.00
			Proof . . . 250.00	
12	1 Shilling 1937	7.50	60.00	150.00
			Proof . . . 350.00	
13	1 Florin 1937	15.00	70.00	250.00
			Proof . . . 425.00 ·	

Obv: KING EMPEROR to right of head

11a	6 Pence 1938–41	12.00	25.00	100.00

12a	1 Shilling 1938–41	7.50	35.00	195.00
13a	1 Florin 1938–45	25.00	65.00	300.00

Nickel-Brass

17	3 Pence 1947	2.00	4.50	20.00
			Proof . . . 250.00	

New Legend:
KING GEORGE THE SIXTH
Cupro-Nickel

18	½ Penny 1949–52	.50	1.00	3.00
			Proof . . . 225.00	
19	1 Penny 1949–52	.75	1.50	6.00
			Proof . . . 250.00	

ELIZABETH II 1952–
Cupro-Nickel

21	½ Penny 1954	.25	.75	2.00
			Proof . . . 225.00	
22	1 Penny 1954–68	.20	.40	.75
			Proof . . . 300.00	

Nickel-Brass

23	3 Pence 1955–67	.10	.40	2.00
	1955–61 . . . 1			Proof . . . 125.00

Cupro-Nickel

24	6 Pence 1953–67	.25	.45	2.00
			Proof . . . 250.00	

25 1 Shilling 1957–65   .25   1.00   3.00

26 1 Florin 1957–65   .75   1.25   3.50
                   Proof . . . 650.00

Later issues in *Current Coins of the World.*

FINLAND
(Suomi,
Suomen Tasavalta)

A republic at the northeastern end of the Baltic Sea. Forests cover much of the country and the principal industry is lumbering and paper manufacture; other important exports include iron and steel, furs, chemicals and textiles. The Finns are a progressive people with the world's highest literacy rate, 99%. Area: 130,160 square miles. Languages: Finnish, Swedish. Capital: *Helsinki.*

Monetary System:
100 Pennia = 1 Markka

UNDER RUSSIAN EMPIRE
1809–1917
General Coinage

Nos. 1–6 do not bear the name of the ruler, and were struck without change through three reigns.

Silver

1	25 Pennia 1865–71	20.00	35.00	75.00
	1867,68 . . . 200.			
2	50 Pennia 1864–71	25.00	45.00	75.00
	1868 . . . 100.			

3	1 Markka 1864–67	15.00	35.00	100.00
4	2 Markka 1865–70	25.00	50.00	150.00
	1867 . . . Rare			

Modified Dies

1a	25 Pennia 1872–1917	15.00	25.00	75.00
	1876 . . . 1500.			
2a	50 Pennia 1872–1917	15.00	25.00	75.00
	1876 . . . 1500.			
3a	1 Markka 1872–1915	10.00	20.00	50.00
4a	2 Markka 1872–1908	15.00	25.00	75.00
	1905 EF . . . 200			

Gold

5	F4–6 10 Markkaa			
	1878–1913	150.00	250.00	350.00
	1904 EF . . . 500 1905 EF . . . 2000			
6	F1–3 20 Markkaa			
	1878–1913	175.00	275.00	375.00
	1880 EF . . . 500			

ALEXANDER II 1855–1881

Copper

7	1 Penni 1864–71	5.00	15.00	35.00
	1864 EF . . . 500			
8	5 Pennia 1865–70	10.00	20.00	40.00
9	10 Pennia 1865–67	10.00	20.00	50.00

Modified Dies

7a	1 Penni 1872–76	5.00	15.00	35.00
8a	5 Pennia 1872–75	5.00	15.00	45.00

Unless otherwise noted, prices are for coins in very fine, extremely fine, and uncirculated condition.

9a 10 Pennia 1875–76　　10.00　20.00　50.00
　　1875 EF . . . 150

ALEXANDER III 1881–1894

Copper

10	1 Penni 1881–94	5.00	10.00	25.00
	1882,84 EF . . . 100			
11	5 Pennia 1888–92	5.00	10.00	35.00
12	10 Pennia 1889–91	30.00	75.00	150.00

NIKOLAI II 1894–1917

Copper

13	1 Penni 1895–1916	5.00	10.00	25.00
14	5 Pennia 1896–1917	5.00	10.00	35.00
	1910 EF . . . 75			
15	10 Pennia 1895–1917	5.00	10.00	50.00
	1898 EF . . . 150			

CIVIL WAR 1917–1918
A. Official Government Issues.

Copper
Obv: No crown over eagle

16	1 Penni 1917	5.00	10.00	20.00
17	5 Pennia 1917	5.00	10.00	20.00
18	10 Pennia 1917	5.00	10.00	20.00

Silver

19 25 Pennia 1917　　6.00　12.00　25.00

20 50 Pennia 1917　　6.00　12.00　25.00

B. Communist Government Issue.

Copper

21 5 Pennia 1918　　25.00　45.00　65.00

REPUBLIC 1918–
First Coinage

Bronze

22	1 Penni 1919–24	.50	.75	2.00
23	5 Pennia 1918–40	.50	.75	2.00
24	10 Pennia 1919–40	.50	.75	2.00

Iron
23a 5 Pennia 1918　　250.00　450.00　750.00

Cupro-Nickel

25	25 Pennia 1921–40	.50	1.00	3.00
26	50 Pennia 1921–40	.50	2.00	5.00
27	1 Markka 1921–24			
	(24mm)	2.00	5.00	10.00

27a* 1 Markka 1928–40
　　(21mm)　　1.00 · 4.00　7.50

Aluminum-Bronze

28 5 Markkaa 1928–42　　5.00　15.00　40.00
　　1928,29 . . . 35.

28a	5 Markkaa 1946–52	1.00	2.00	5.00
	1952 . . . 20.			
29	10 Markkaa 1928–39	5.00	15.00	40.00
30	20 Markkaa 1931–39	5.00	20.00	50.00
	1931–32 . . . 50.			

Dates after 1946 of No.28a vary in composition.

Gold

31	*F8* 100 Markkaa 1926	500.00	750.00	1,000.
32	*F7* 200 Markkaa 1926	650.00	850.00	1,250.

Second Coinage
Bronze

33	5 Pennia 1941–43	1.00	2.00	5.00
34	10 Penniä 1941–43	1.00	2.00	5.00

Designs like Nos. 25–27a.

25a	25 Pennia 1940–43	.50	2.00	5.00
	1940 . . . 15			
26a	50 Pennia 1940–43	.50	2.00	5.00
	1940 . . . 15			
27b	1 Markka 1940–51	.50	2.00	5.00
	1949 . . . 750			

Iron

34b	10 Pennia 1943–45	3.00	5.00	7.00
25b	25 Pennia 1943–45	1.00	2.00	5.00
26b	50 Pennia 1943–48	1.00	2.00	5.00
27c	1 Markka 1943–52	.50	1.00	3.00

15th Olympic Games
Silver

35	500 Markkaa 1951–52	35.00	45.00	65.00
	1951 UNC . . . 450			

Third Coinage
Iron

36	1 Markka 1952–53	.50	.75	1.00
37	5 Markkaa 1952–53	.50	1.00	1.50

Nickel-Plated Iron

36a	1 Markka 1953–62	.25	.50	1.00
	1953 . . . 10			
37a	5 Markkaa 1953–62	.35	.50	1.00
	1953 . . . 35			

Aluminum-Bronze

38	10 Markkaa 1952–62	.25	.50	1.00
39	20 Markkaa 1952–62	.50	1.00	3.00
	1952 . . . 25			
40	50 Markkaa 1952–62	1.00	2.00	3.00
	1958,60 . . . 20			

Silver

41	100 Markkaa 1956–60	3.00	5.00	7.00
42	200 Markkaa 1956–59	4.00	6.00	10.00
	1958 . . . 200			

Centennial of
Markka Currency System

7	5 Francs 1848–49	12.00	20.00 175.00
	1849-D . . . 225		Proof 2500.

Gold

43 1000 Markkaa 1960   12.00 18.00 25.00
Later issues in *Current Coins of the World*.

8	*F329* 20 Francs	
	1848–49	110.00 135.00 600.00

FORMOSA —
See China

FRANCE
(Republique Francaise)

France is located in Western Europe and has widely diversified resources of industry and agriculture. The Second Empire under Napoleon III succeeded the Second Republic in 1852 and lasted until the Franco-Prussian War of 1870. The Third Republic was formed Sept. 4, 1870 and lasted until World War II. A four-year period of Nazi occupation followed. After the Allied victory in 1945, a new constitution established the Fourth Republic. Area: 212,973 square miles. Capital: *Paris*.

Monetary System:
100 Centimes = 1 Franc

Except where noted, prices are for the most common dates and mints. Usually coins bearing other than "A" (Paris) or "BB" (Strasbourg) mintmarks sell for more than the prices stated.

REPUBLIC 1848–1852
First Coinage

Copper

1	1 Centime 1848–51	3.00 10.00 25.00

Second Coinage
Silver

2	20 Centimes 1849–51	8.00 20.00 100.00
	1849A . . . 175	
3	50 Centimes 1849–51	18.00 40.00 150.00
	1849A . . . 400	
4	1 Franc 1849–51	40.00 75.00 250.00
5	2 Francs 1849–51	175.00 450.00 1000.00
6	5 Francs 1849–51	20.00 35.00 300.00

Gold

9	*F332* 10 Francs	
	1850–51	225.00 400.00 750.00

10 *F331* 20 Francs
1849–51   110.00 135.00 400.00

THIRD COINAGE
Silver

Obv: President Bonaparte (1851–52)
Rev: value in wreath

11 50 Centimes 1852   50.00 125.00 400.00
12 1 Franc 1852   100.00 175.00 500.00
13 5 Francs 1852   40.00 150.00 700.00

Gold
Obv: head to right
A13 *F305* 20 Francs 1852   110.00 135.00 500.00

SECOND EMPIRE
Bonaparte as
EMPEROR NAPOLEON III
1852–1870
First Coinage
Bronze

Obv: Bare head to left
14 1 Centime 1853–57   2.00   6.00   15.00
15 2 Centimes 1853–57   1.00   5.00   20.00
16* 5 Centimes 1853–57   2.00   5.00   25.00
17 10 Centimes 1852–57   3.00   8.00   50.00

Silver

22 20 Centimes 1853–63   10.00   20.00   90.00
23 50 Centimes 1853–63   15.00   30.00 225.00
                                       Proof . . . 500.00
24 1 Franc 1853–64   20.00   75.00 300.00
      1863A . . . 600
25 2 Francs 1853–59   275.00 500.00   2000.
      1858A,59A . . . Rare
26 5 Francs 1854–59, rev.
      like No. 30   50.00 175.00 1000.00
      1854,57,58A EF . . . 900 1859A . . . Rare

Gold

Obv: like Nos. 35–37
Rev: value in wreath
Nos. 33A (16.5mm) and 34A (19mm) are each 2mm
larger than their prior type.

33 *F315–316* 5 Francs
1854–55   150.00 200.00 375.00
33A *F315–316* 5 Francs
1856–60   75.00 125.00 350.00
34 *F313–314* 10 Francs
1854–55   150.00 300.00 850.00
34A *F313–314* 10 Francs
1855–60   90.00 125.00 400.00

Obv: Bare head to right
35 *F310–312* 20 Francs
1853–60   110.00 115.00 250.00
36* *F308–309* 50 Francs
1855–60   300.00 450.00 1200.
37 *F306–307* 100 Francs
1855–60   600.00 700.00 1500.

Commemorative Issues

Bronze

Visit of Royal Couple
to Paris Bourse
A16 (5 Centimes) 1853   25.00 75.00 125.00
A17 (10 Centimes) 1853   25.00 75.00 125.00

Emperor's Visit to Bourse
B17 (10 Centimes) 1854   25.00 75.00 125.00

Dedication of
Napoleon I Monument
C17 (10 Centimes) 1854   25.00 75.00 145.00
Nos. A16–C17 were struck on 5 and 10 centime flans,

using the normal obverse with special reverse legends. Although bearing no denominations, they circulated with regular issues.

SECOND COINAGE

Bronze

Obv: Laureate head to left

18	1 Centime 1861–70	1.00	4.00	10.00
19	2 Centimes 1861–62	1.00	2.00	20.00
20*	5 Centimes 1861–65	3.00	8.00	25.00
21	10 Centimes 1861–65	6.00	15.00	60.00

Silver

27	20 Centimes 1864,66 (15mm)	7.00	15.00	65.00
	1864T . . . 50			
28	20 Centimes 1867–69 (16mm)	3.00	7.00	45.00
	1869 BB . . . Rare			
29	50 Centimes 1864–69	4.00	10.00	85.00
	1869 BB . . . 125			

30	1 Franc 1866–70	7.00	15.00	100.00
31	2 Francs 1866–70	15.00	40.00	300.00
32	5 Francs 1861–70	15.00	25.00	225.00
	1861–66	400.00	800.00	2000.

Gold

Obv: laureate head to right
Rev: value in wreath

38	F325–326 5 Francs			
	1862–69	50.00	75.00	300.00
39	F323–324 10 Francs			
	1861–69	60.00	85.00	300.00

Rev: like Nos. 35–37

40	F321–322 20 Francs			
	1861–70	110.00	115.00	275.00
A40	F319–320 50 Francs			
	1862–69	300.00	525.00	1800.
B40	F317–818 100 Francs			
	1862–70	675.00	1000.	2200.
	1870-A . . . 8000		Proof . . . 18,000.	

REPUBLIC 1870–1940

Bronze

41	1 Centime 1872–97	1.00	3.00	9.00
42	2 Centimes 1877–97	1.00	4.00	10.00
43	5 Centimes 1871–98	1.00	3.00	10.00
	1871-K . . . 100 1878-K . . . 60			
44	10 Centimes 1870–98	2.00	5.00	20.00
	1871-K . . . 100			

Silver

Rev: Without motto

45	2 Francs 1870–71	60.00	125.00	450.00
46	5 Francs 1870–71	145.00	250.00	850.00

Rev: Like Nos. 2–6
Proofs of the below listed coins dated 1878 and 1889 are very rare.

47	20 Centimes 1878 (30 pcs.), 1889 (100	pcs.) Proof Only	

48	50 Centimes 1871–95	3.00	8.00	50.00
			Proof . . .	250.00
49	1 Franc 1871–95	6.00	10.00	75.00
			Proof . . .	375.00
50	2 Francs 1870–95	15.00	30.00	200.00
			Proof . . .	550.00
51	5 Francs 1870	70.00	125.00	500.00

52	5 Francs 1870–78	12.00	20.00	75.00
	1878-A . . . 1100			
52a	5 Francs 1871, rev. small trident symbol (Commune issue)	400.00	700.00	1500.

Gold
Design like No. 9

54	F334 10 Francs 1895–99	75.00	125.00	250.00

55	F330 20 Francs 1871–98	110.00	115.00	130.00
56	F328 50 Francs 1878–1904	1000.	1500.	2200.
	1889-A EF . . . 4500 1900-A EF . . . 4000			
57	F327 100 Francs 1878–1914	575.00	650.00	750.00
	1887,94 EF . . . 4000 1878,89 Proof only . . . Rare			

Second Coinage

Note: From 1898 to 1920 all proofs were struck with matte surfaces.

Bronze

58	1 Centime 1898–1920	1.50	2.00	6.00
	1898,1900 Proof . . . 350 1910 . . . 45			
59	2 Centimes 1898–1920	2.00	4.00	12.00
	1900 . . . 75 1898,1900 Proof . . . 450			
60	5 Centimes 1898–1921	1.00	4.00	15.00
	1921 . . . 150 1898,1900 Proof . . . 300			
61	10 Centimes 1898–1921	2.00	4.00	20.00
	1905 . . . 35 1898,1900 Proof . . . 200			

Nickel

69	25 Centimes 1903	2.00	4.00	25.00

70	25 Centimes 1904–05, polygonal	2.00	4.00	25.00

Silver

62	50 Centimes 1897–1920	1.50	3.00	15.00
	1897 . . . 75		Proof . . .	375.00

All dates before 1911 are scarcer

63	1 Franc 1898–1920	2.00	4.00	20.00
	1900 . . . 300 1903 . . . 250 1914-C . . . 175			
	Proof . . . 500.00			

All dates before 1915 are scarcer

64	2 Francs 1898–1920	10.00	15.00	50.00
	1900, 13 . . . 100		Proof . . .	650.00

All dates before 1915 are scarcer

Gold

65 *F337* 10 Francs
1899–1914   60.00   65.00   70.00
                                          Proof . . . 650.00

66 *F336* 20 Francs
1899–1906, edge DIEU
PROTEGE LA FRANCE   110.00 115.00 125.00
                                          Proof . . . 950.00

66a *F336* 20 Francs
1907–1914, edge LI-
BERTE EGALITE FRA-
TERNITE   110.00 115.00 125.00

No. 66a has been officially restruck in recent years.

Third Coinage

Nickel

73 10 Centimes 1914   700.00 1100.   1500.
76 25 Centimes 1914–17   7.00   15.00   35.00

Cupro-Nickel

71 5 Centimes 1917–20
        (19mm)   1.00   2.00   7.00
72 10 Centimes 1920–38
        (17mm)   .50   1.00   3.00
73a 10 Centimes 1917–38   .50   1.00   3.00
76a 25 Centimes 1917–37   1.00   1.50   5.00

Nickel-Bronze

72a 5 Centimes 1938–39   .50   1.00   3.00

73c 10 Centimes 1938–39   .50   1.00   3.00
76b 25 Centimes 1938–40   1.00   2.00   6.00

Aluminum-Bronze

77 50 Centimes 1921–29   .50   1.00   8.00
78 1 Franc 1920–28   1.00   2.00   12.00
        1920 . . . 10
79 2 Francs 1920–27   1.50   3.00   20.00
        1927 . . . 250

80 50 Centimes 1931–41,
        47   .50   .75   3.00
        1947 . . . 200
81 1 Franc 1931–41   1.00   2.00   7.00
        1935 . . . 30
82 2 Francs 1931–41   1.00   2.00   15.00
        For similar aluminum-bronze coins dated 1944,
        see French West Africa.

Nickel

83 5 Francs 1933   4.00   8.00   25.00

84 5 Francs 1933–38   1.00   1.50   12.00
        1936,39 . . . 500

Aluminum-Bronze

84a 5 Francs 1938–40,
        45–47   2.00   3.00   15.00
        1947 . . . 300

Silver

86	10 Francs 1929–39	3.00	7.00	20.00
	1937 . . . 150			
87	20 Francs 1929–38	7.00	12.00	40.00
	1936,39 . . . 400			

Gold

88	*F338* 100 Francs			
	1929–36	500.00	700.00	1000.
1929,34 . . . Rare				

WORLD WAR II ISSUES
A. German Occupation (Vichy) Government 1940–44
First Coinage

Zinc

73b	10 Centimes 1941	1.00	1.50	5.00

Aluminum

80a	50 Centimes 1941,			
	44–47	.25	.50	2.00
81a	1 Franc 1941, 44–59	.20	.50	2.00
	1943 . . . Rare			
82a	2 Francs 1941,44–59	.35	.75	5.00

Nos. 80a–82a were struck under this government in 1941, then were resumed by the DeGaulle government after German withdrawal in 1944.

Second Coinage

Zinc

Rev: Value written out

V90	VINGT (20) CENTIMES			
	1941	3.00	7.00	20.00

Rev: Value in numerals

V91	10 Centimes 1941–43			
	(21mm)	.50	1.00	5.00

V93	10 Centimes 1943–44			
	(17mm)	1.00	2.00	7.00
V92	20 Centimes 1941–44	1.00	2.00	8.00

Iron

V92a	20 Centimes 1944	60.00	125.00	200.00

Aluminum

V94	50 Centimes 1942–44	.25	.50	3.00
V95	1 Franc 1942–44	.40	.75	10.00
V96	2 Francs 1943–44	.75	2.00	15.00

Cupro-Nickel

Obv: Philippe Petain, Chief of State 1940–44

V97	5 Francs 1941	100.00	125.00	200.00

No. V97 was not issued to circulation.

B. Allied Provisional Issues

Zinc

81b	1 Franc 1943	500.00	700.00	1000.

No. 81b was struck for use in North Africa, but probably was never issued to circulation.

Brass

89	2 Francs 1944	5.00	10.00	25.00

No. 89 is said to have circulated in Algeria and Southern France.

POSTWAR ISSUES

Zinc

74	10 Centimes 1945–46			
	(17mm)	2.00	3.00	10.00
75	20 Centimes 1945–46	6.00	10.00	35.00
	1945B, 46B . . . 100			

Aluminum

84b	5 Francs 1945–52	.50	1.00	7.00

Nos. 80a–82a were resumed in this period.

Unless otherwise noted, prices are for coins in very fine, extremely fine, and uncirculated condition.

Cupro-Nickel

86a 10 Francs 1945–47,
    large head   1.00   4.00   12.00

86b 10 Francs 1947–49,
    small head   .40   .75   5.00

Aluminum-Bronze

98   10 Francs 1950–58   .35   .75   5.00
99   20 Francs 1950, designer
     GEORGES GUIRAUD   2.00   6.00   15.00
99a* 20 Francs 1950–53, de-
     signer G. GUIRAUD   .40   1.00   7.00
100 50 Francs 1950–58   1.00   2.00   10.00
         1950 . . . 125   1958 . . . 75

Cupro-Nickel

101 100 Francs 1954–58   .75   2.00   10.00
         1958 (owl) . . . 50
Later issues in *Current Coins of the World.*

FRENCH COCHIN CHINA
(Cochinchine Francaise)

Southernmost of the Indo-China states, corresponding
generally to former South Vietnam. Saigon, the major
port of Vietnam, was also the administrative seat.

Monetary System:
5 Sapeque (Cash) = 1 Centime
100 Centimes = 1 Piastre

Bronze

A1 (1 Sapeque) 1875   35.00   50.00   75.00
No. A1 is a France 1 Centime 1875-K (No. 41) punched
with a center hole.

1   2 Sapeque 1879, 85   4.50   12.00   27.50
     1885 Proof . . . 500

2   1 Centime 1879–85   15.00   50.00 125.00
    1885 . . . 50   Proof . . . 525.00

Silver

3   10 Centimes 1879–85   45.00 135.00 300.00
     1885 Proof . . . 875
4   20 Centimes 1879–85   70.00 150.00 300.00
     1885 Proof . . . 900
5* 50 Centimes 1879–85   300.00 375.00 650.00
6   1 Piastre 1885   Rare
No. 6 dated 1879, and all coins dated 1885 except No.
2, were issued only in specimen sets.

For later issues see French Indo-China.

FRENCH EQUATORIAL AFRICA
(Afrique Equatoriale Francaise)

This area consisted of the four territories of Gabon, Middle Congo, Tchad and Ubangi-Shari (now Central African Empire). It was held by France from the mid–19th century until 1960, when each territory was given independence. Area: 970,000 square miles. Languages: French, native tongues. Capital: *Brazzaville*.

Monetary System:
100 Centimes = 1 Franc

Semi-Official Tokens
5 Francs = 1 Unit

Brass

Rev: Identical to obv.

A6	1 Unit 1883	–	–	–
A7	5 Units 1883	–	–	–
A8	10 Units 1883	–	–	–

Regular Issues

Brass

1	50 Centimes 1942	2.00	4.00	9.50
2	1 Franc 1942	3.00	5.00	12.50

Bronze

1a	50 Centimes 1943	3.00	7.00	17.50
2a	1 Franc 1943	5.00	7.50	15.00

Aluminum

3	1 Franc 1948	.25	1.00	2.25
4	2 Francs 1948	1.00	2.00	5.00

FRENCH EQUATORIAL AFRICA — CAMEROUN

In the 1950's, the neighboring French territory of Cameroun was added to the monetary union of the Equatorial African possessions. The following pieces were formerly listed as Cameroun Nos. 10–12.

Aluminum-Bronze

5	5 Francs 1958	.25	.50	1.00
6	10 Francs 1958	.50	1.00	1.50
7	25 Francs 1958	1.00	1.50	3.00

For later coinage see Equatorial African States in *Current Coins of the World*.

FRENCH INDO–CHINA
(Indo-Chine Francaise)

A federation in southeast Asia formed in 1887 from the French colony of Cochin China and the protectorates of Annam, Cambodia and Tongking (Tonkin). Laos was added in 1898. When the Japanese occupying forces departed at the close of World War II, the Communists under Ho Chi Minh came to control much of this area. They were ousted by the returning French, but commenced guerilla activity which eventually led to the departure of the French. By the Geneva Conference, Indo-China was partitioned in 1953 into North Vietnam (Communist), Cambodia, Laos and South Vietnam.

Monetary System:
5 Sapeque (Cash) = 1 Centime
100 Centimes = 1 Piastre

Bronze

1	2 Sapeque 1887–1902	5.00	10.00	35.00
	1889,1900 Proof . . . 300		Proof . . . 200.00	

2	1 Centime 1885–94	3.50	7.00	27.50
	1889 . . . Rare 1893,94 . . . 30 Proof . . . 400.00			

Unless otherwise noted, prices are for coins in very fine, extremely fine, and uncirculated condition.

2a 1 Centieme 1895   150.00 250.00 450.00

3 1 Centime 1896–1906
   (27.5mm)   2.00   5.00 10.00
     1900 . . . Rare 1898,1906 . . . 15
                                   Proof . . . 400.00
4 1 Centime 1908–39
   (26mm)   .75   1.50   4.50
     1921 . . . 75
All dates before 1921 are worth more.

Cupro-Nickel

5 5 Centimes 1923–37 (5
gr.)   .75   3.50   7.00
     1938 . . . 25   Proof . . . 200.00

Nickel-Brass

5a 5 Centimes 1938–39
   (3.8–4.5 gr.)   .50   1.25   3.00

.900 Silver

Rev: Weight in legend, 27.215 grams to Piastre
6 10 Centimes 1885–95
   (2.721 gr.)   10.00 30.00 75.00
     1889 Proof . . . 650 1892 . . . 100

7 20 Centimes 1885–95
   (5.443 gr.)   25.00 75.00 125.00
1885 is the only common date

1892 . . . 125 1889 Proof . . . 800
  8 50 Centimes 1885–95
     (13.607 g.)   100.00 225.00 500.00
       1885 . . . 200 1889 Proof . . . 1500
  9* 1 Piastre 1885–95
     (27.215 gr.)   25.00 50.00 100.00
       1889 Proof . . . 1200 1890 . . . 2800
Rev: Slightly reduced weight, 27.0 grams to Piastre
6a 10 Centimes 1895–96
   (2.7 gr.)   50.00 100.00 300.00
     1895 . . . Rare
7a 20 Centimes 1895–97
   (5.4 gr.)   125.00 250.00 500.00
8a 50 Centimes 1896–1936
   (13.5 g.)   4.50   8.00 15.00
     1896 . . . 200 1900 Proof . . . 1100
9a 1 Piastre 1895–1928 (27
   gr.)   12.00 40.00 75.00
     1900 Proof . . . 1500 1910 . . . 65

.835 Silver

14 10 Centimes 1898–1919 10.00 25.00 40.00
     1898,1908,09,19 . . . 75 1900 Proof . . . 550
15 20 Centimes 1898–1916 10.00 40.00 100.00
     1900 Proof . . . 800

Billon
.400 silver, not shown on coins

14a 10 Centimes 1920   17.50 35.00 75.00
15a 20 Centimes 1920   40.00 75.00 125.00

.680 Silver

16 10 Centimes 1921–37   2.00   4.00   9.00
     1928 . . . 40
17 20 Centimes 1921–37   2.00   4.50   8.00
     1928 . . . 25

.900 Silver

18 1 Piastre 1931   15.00 25.00 40.00

Bronze

20	½ Centime 1935–40	.75	1.50	5.00
	1940 . . . 7.50			

Zinc

20a	½ Centime 1939, 40	350.00	450.00	650.00

Nickel (magnetic)

21	10 Centimes 1939–40 Reeded Edge	1.00	1.50	3.00
22	10 Centimes 1939 Security Edge	12.50	27.50	45.00

Cupro-Nickel (non-magnetic)
Edge: Reeded

21a	10 Centimes 1939, 41	.50	1.75	4.00
	1939 . . . 10			
22a	20 Centimes 1939, 41	.75	1.25	3.00

VICHY GOVERNMENT

Zinc

V30	1 Centime 1940–41	3.50	7.00	12.00
	1940 . . . 10			
V31	¼ Centime 1942–44	7.50	15.00	40.00
	1944 . . . 300			

Aluminum

V32	1 Centime 1943	.45	.75	2.00
V33	5 Centimes 1943	.75	1.25	2.50

POSTWAR ISSUES
Aluminum

26	5 Centimes 1946	.45	.75	2.00
27	10 Centimes 1945	1.25	2.25	4.00
28	20 Centimes 1945	.75	2.00	5.50

Cupro-Nickel

23	50 Centimes 1946	3.50	7.00	15.00

24	1 Piastre 1946–47, security edge	10.00	40.00	75.00
	1947 . . . 35			
24a	1 Piastre 1947, reeded edge	1.50	2.50	6.50

For later issues see Cambodia, Laos and Vietnam.

FRENCH OCEANIA (Etablissements Francais de l'Oceanie)

Made up of a widely scattered group of islands in the South Pacific. Government headquarters are at Papeete, Tahiti. It is now French Polynesia. Area: 1,544 square miles.

Monetary System:
100 Centimes = 1 Franc

Aluminum

1	50 Centimes 1949	.50	1.50	4.00
2	1 Franc 1949	.30	.50	2.00
3	2 Francs 1949	.50	2.00	4.50
4	5 Francs 1952	1.25	3.00	5.50

For later issues see French Polynesia in *Current Coins of the World.*

FRENCH SOMALILAND
(Cote Francaise des Somalis)

Area in northeast Africa. Became the French Territory of the Afars and Issas in 1967, then gaining indepndence as the Republic of Djibouti in 1977. Area: 8,996 square miles. Languages: Hamitic, Arabic, French. Capital: *Djibouti.*

Monetary System:
100 Centimes = 1 Franc

Aluminum

1	1 Franc 1948–49	1.00	3.00	6.00
2	2 Francs 1948–49	1.00	3.00	6.00
3	5 Francs 1948	1.00	3.00	6.00

Aluminum-Bronze

4	20 Francs 1952	1.25	3.00	9.00

UNION FRANCAISE omitted
Aluminum

5	1 Franc 1959,65	1.00	2.00	4.00
6	2 Francs 1959,65	1.00	2.00	4.00
7	5 Francs 1959,65	1.00	2.00	4.00

Aluminum-Bronze

8	10 Francs 1965	1.00	2.00	5.00
9	20 Francs 1965	1.00	2.00	5.00

For later issues see French Afars and Issas in *Current Coins of the World.*

FRENCH WEST AFRICA
(Afrique Occidentale Francaise)

On the northwest coast of Africa extending eastward to the Sudan. It is now broken up into a number of independent states. Languages: Sudanese, Hamitic, Arabic and French. Capital: *Dakar.*

Monetary System:
100 Centimes = 1 Franc

Aluminum-Bronze

1	50 Centimes 1944	2.00	5.00	10.00
2	1 Franc 1944	2.00	5.00	10.00

Aluminum

3	1 Franc 1948, 55	.30	.75	1.25
4	2 Francs 1948, 55	.50	1.00	2.00

Unless otherwise noted, prices are for coins in very fine, extremely fine, and uncirculated condition.

Aluminum-Bronze

5	5 Francs 1956	.50	.75	1.50
6	10 Francs 1956	.75	1.00	2.25
7	25 Francs 1956	.75	1.25	4.50

FRENCH WEST AFRICA-TOGO (1957)
Integrated Coinage

8	10 Francs 1957	1.00	1.50	4.50
9	25 Francs 1957	1.00	1.50	3.00

For later coinage see West African States in *Current Coins of the World.*

GERMAN STATES

When the states of Germany were unified into an Empire in 1871, a new decimal coinage system was established. Coins of 1 Pfennig through 1 Mark were issued for the Empire as a whole (see GERMANY), while the individual states were permitted to issue their own types of 2 through 20 Mark. These states are included in this section.

During the 1871–73 transition to the new unified coinage, some states continued to issue coins using older monetary systems. Such older series may be found in Craig, "Coins of the World."

Note: Through the period 1871–1918 covered by this section, three standard reverse designs were used. They are identified in the listings as follows:

REVERSE STYLE A: Small eagle; date and value at bottom (1871–73)

REVERSE STYLE B: Small eagle; date and value in legend (1874–1889

REVERSE STYLE C: Large eagle; date and value in legend (1890–1918)

Exceptions: A few commemoratives 1910–1915 used special reverses. See Nos. 98–99, 130–133, 136, 177.

ANHALT, Duchy

Friedrich I 1871–1904
First Coinage

Silver

1	2 Mark 1876	175.00	1000.	1750.

Gold

2	*F1* 20 Mark 1875	850.00	1250.	1750.

Second Coinage

Silver

3	2 Mark 1896	275.00	600.00	1000.
4	5 Mark 1896	725.00	1500.	2250.

Unless otherwise noted, prices are for coins in very fine, extremely fine, and uncirculated condition.

Gold

5	*F3* 10 Mark 1896, 1901	500.00	1200.	1700.
6	*F2* 20 Mark 1896, 1901	475.00	1100.	1600.

Friedrich II 1904–18

Silver

7	2 Mark 1904	250.00	500.00	800.00
8*	5 Mark 1909, 11	50.00	90.00	150.00

Gold
Obv: Like No. 7

9	*F4* 20 Mark 1904	750.00	1200.	1750.

Silver Wedding Anniversary

Silver

10*	3 Mark 1914	35.00	50.00	70.00
11	5 Mark 1914	125.00	200.00	290.00

BADEN, Grand Duchy

Friedrich I 1852–1907
First Coinage

Silver

Rev: Style B
Varieties exist with and without a cross-bar in the "A"
of Baden

12*	2 Mark 1876–88	120.00	250.00	500.00
13	5 Mark 1875–88	65.00	500.00	1700.
	Rev: Style C			
12a	2 Mark 1892–1902	60.00	250.00	500.00
13a	5 Mark 1891–1902	60.00	250.00	875.00

Gold
Rev: Style A

15	*F8* 10 Mark 1872–73	150.00	200.00	325.00
16	*F5* 20 Mark 1872–73	150.00	250.00	335.00
	Rev: Style B			
14	*F12* 5 Mark 1877	250.00	400.00	600.00
15a	*F9* 10 Mark 1875–88	140.00	225.00	325.00
	1880 . . . Rare			
16a	*F6* 20 Mark 1874	350.00	475.00	725.00
	Rev: Style C			
15b	*F10* 10 Mark 1890–1901	200.00	250.00	325.00
16b	*F7* 20 Mark 1894–95	175.00	250.00	400.00

Second Coinage

Silver

17	2 Mark 1902–07	30.00	60.00	175.00
18	5 Mark 1902–07	40.00	140.00	450.00

Gold

10	*F11* 10 Mark 1902–07	200.00	250.00	325.00

Commemorative Issues
50th Year of Reign

Silver

20*	2 Mark 1902	15.00	30.00	40.00
21	5 Mark 1902	100.00	150.00	225.00

Golden Wedding Anniversary

22*	2 Mark 1906	20.00	35.00	45.00
23	5 Mark 1906	100.00	175.00	225.00

Death of Friedrich I

| 24* | 2 Mark 1907 | 20.00 | 50.00 | 80.00 |
| 25 | 5 Mark 1907 | 135.00 | 200.00 | 250.00 |

Friedrich II 1907–18

Silver

26*	2 Mark 1911, 13	250.00	400.00	800.00
27	3 Mark 1908–15	12.50	25.00	40.00
28	5 Mark 1908, 13	45.00	100.00	350.00

Gold

| 29 | F14 | 10 Mark 1909–13 | 475.00 | 650.00 | 1000. |
| 30 | F13 | 20 Mark 1911–14 | 150.00 | 245.00 | 325.00 |

BAVARIA (Bayern), Kingdom

Ludwig II 1864–86

Silver

Rev: Style B
| 31* | 2 Mark 1876–83 | 70.00 | 275.00 | 800.00 |
| 32 | 5 Mark 1874–76 | 50.00 | 200.00 | 550.00 |

Gold
Rev: Style A
| 34 | F17 | 10 Mark 1872–73 | 150.00 | 235.00 | 300.00 |
| 35 | F15 | 20 Mark 1872–73 | 150.00 | 250.00 | 325.00 |

Rev: Style B
33	F19	5 Mark 1877–78	200.00	350.00	550.00
		1878 . . . 900.			
34a	F18	10 Mark 1874–81	125.00	175.00	250.00
35a	F16	20 Mark 1874–78	150.00	250.00	300.00
		1875 . . . 1750. 1878 . . . 650.			

Otto III 1886–1913

(Under regency of Prince Luitpold)
Silver

Rev: Style B
| 36 | 2 Mark 1888 | 325.00 | 800.00 | 1500. |
| 38 | 5 Mark 1888 | 350.00 | 1200. | 1750. |

Rev: Style C
36a	2 Mark 1891–1913	20.00	32.50	75.00
37*	3 Mark 1908–13	15.00	20.00	30.00
38a	5 Mark 1891–1913	30.00	55.00	140.00

Gold
Rev: Style B
| 39 | F21 | 10 Mark 1888 | 250.00 | 400.00 | 600.00 |

Rev: Style C
39a	F22	10 Mark 1890–1900	140.00	175.00	200.00
39b	F23	10 Mark 1900–12,			
		rearranged obv. legend	150.00	200.00	265.00
40	F20	20 Mark 1895–1913	150.00	195.00	250.00
		1913 . . . 1750.			

90th Birthday of Regent

Silver

41*	2 Mark 1911	15.00	30.00	40.00
42	3 Mark 1911	17.50	30.00	40.00
43	5 Mark 1911	70.00	120.00	150.00

Unless otherwise noted, prices are for coins in very fine, extremely fine, and uncirculated condition.

Ludwig III 1913–1918

Silver

44*	2 Mark 1914	55.00	95.00	125.00
45	3 Mark 1914	22.50	35.00	60.00
46	5 Mark 1914	120.00	225.00	265.00

Gold

47	*F24* 20 Mark 1914	2000.	2500.	3000.

Golden Wedding Anniversary

Silver

48	3 Mark 1918	Rare

Ernst August 1913–18
Wedding Commemorative

Silver

Obv: Legend ends BRAUNSSCHWEIG

54*	3 Mark 1915	800.00	1500.	2000.
55	5 Mark 1915	1100.	1800.	2400.

Obv: U. LUNEB. added

54a	3 Mark 1915	80.00	170.00	225.00
55a	5 Mark 1915	320.00	475.00	700.00

BREMEN, Free City

Silver

49*	2 Mark 1904	35.00	85.00	120.00
50	5 Mark 1906	140.00	250.00	325.00

Gold

51	*F26* 10 Mark 1907	550.00	850.00	1200.
52	*F25* 20 Mark 1906	750.00	1100.	3200.

BRUNSWICK

(Braunschweig-Wolfenbuttel),

Duchy

Wilhelm 1831–84

Gold

53	*F27* 20 Mark 1875–76	600.00	1100.	1600.

HAMBURG, Free City

First Coinage

Gold

Obv: Arms not supported

56	*F30* 10 Mark 1873, rev. A	1200.	1750.	2400.
56a	*F31* 10 Mark 1874, rev. B	650.00	950.00	1300.

Second Coinage

Silver

Obv: Lions support arms
Rev: Style B

57	2 Mark 1876–88	45.00	300.00	625.00
59	5 Mark 1875–76, 88	50.00	500.00	1000.

Rev: Style C

57a	2 Mark 1892–1914	25.00	50.00	125.00
58	3 Mark 1908–14	20.00	25.00	40.00
59a	5 Mark 1891–1913	30.00	80.00	150.00

Gold

Rev: Style B

60	*F34*	5 Mark 1877	200.00	325.00	425.00
61	*F32*	10 Mark 1875–88	140.00	175.00	225.00
62	*F28*	20 Mark 1875–89	135.00	160.00	200.00

Rev: Style C

61a*	*F33*	10 Mark 1890–1913	140.00	175.00	225.00
62a	*F29*	20 Mark 1893–1913	140.00	175.00	225.00

HESSE (Hessen-Darmstadt), Grand Duchy
Ludwig III 1848–77

Silver
Rev: Style B

63	2 Mark 1876–77		300.00	2000.	3500.
64	5 Mark 1875–76		160.00	1750.	3000.

Gold
Rev: Style A

66	*F37*	10 Mark 1872–73	200.00	400.00	700.00
67	*F35*	20 Mark 1872–73	200.00	400.00	500.00

Rev: Style B

65	*F39*	5 Mark 1877	475.00	875.00	1200.
66a	*F38*	10 Mark 1875–77	175.00	235.00	275.00
67a	*F36*	20 Mark 1874	400.00	625.00	800.00

Ludwig IV 1877–92

Silver
Rev: Style B

68	2 Mark 1888		900.00	1750.	4000.
69	5 Mark 1888		1300.	2250.	4000.

Rev: Style C

68a	2 Mark 1891		600.00	1000.	2000.
69a	5 Mark 1891		600.00	1600.	3000.

Gold
Rev: Style B

70	*F44*	5 Mark 1877	700.00	850.00	1000.
71	*F41–42*	10 Mark 1878–88	400.00	650.00	1200.

Rev: Style C

71a	*F43*	10 Mark 1890	600.00	900.00	1200.
72	*F40*	20 Mark 1892	1000.	1500.	2000.

ERNST LUDWIG 1892–1918
First Coinage

Gold

73	*F48*	10 Mark 1893	600.00	900.00	1200.
74	*F45*	20 Mark 1893	900.00	1000.	1250.

Second Coinage

Silver

75	2 Mark 1895–1900		250.00	600.00	900.00
76	5 Mark 1895–1900		200.00	450.00	900.00

Gold

77	*F49*	10 Mark 1896, 98	200.00	375.00	550.00
78*	*F46*	20 Mark 1896–1903, obv. GROSHERZOG	200.00	350.00	500.00
78a	*F47*	20 Mark 1905–11, obv. GROSSHERZOG	200.00	325.00	450.00

Third Coinage

Silver

79	3 Mark 1910		50.00	100.00	150.00

Commemorative Issues
400th Anniversary Birth of Philipp the Generous

Silver

80*	2 Mark 1904		40.00	70.00	100.00
81	5 Mark 1904		100.00	175.00	250.00

25th Anniversary of Reign

82	3 Mark 1917. Proof only.		4000.

Unless otherwise noted, prices are for coins in very fine, extremely fine, and uncirculated condition.

LIPPE (Lippe-Detmold), Principality

Leopold IV 1905–18

Silver

83*	2 Mark 1906	175.00	275.00	400.00
84	3 Mark 1913	250.00	400.00	500.00

LUBECK, Free City

Silver
Obv: Small eagle

85	2 Mark 1901	150.00	250.00	375.00

Obv: Large eagle

85a	2 Mark 1904–12	80.00	125.00	175.00
86*	3 Mark 1908–14	60.00	110.00	150.00
87	5 Mark 1904–13	250.00	400.00	625.00

Gold
Obv: Small eagle

88	F50 10 Mark 1901, 04	600,00	850.00	1200.

Obv: Large eagle

88a	F51 10 Mark 1905–10	550.00	825.00	1100.

MECKLENBURG-SCHWERIN, Grand Duchy

Friedrich Franz II 1842–83

Silver
Rev: Style B

89	2 Mark 1876	225.00	1000.	2000.

Gold
Rev: Style A

90	F53 10 Mark 1872	1200.	1750.	2000.
91	F52 20 Mark 1872	750.00	950.00	1200.

Rev: Style B

90a	F54 10 Mark 1878	625.00	850.00	1100.

Friedrich Franz III 1883–97

Gold

92	F55 10 Mark 1890	350.00	720.00	900.00

Friedrich Franz IV 1897–1918

Silver

93	2 Mark 1901	250.00	450.00	800.00

Gold

94	F57 10 Mark 1901	1000.	1500.	2000.
95	F56 20 Mark 1901	1500.	2500.	3500.

Commemorative Issues
Wedding of Grand Duke

Silver

96*	2 Mark 1904	40.00	65.00	90.00
97	5 Mark 1904	110.00	200.00	350.00

Centennial Elevation
to Grand Duchy

98 3 Mark 1915   85.00 160.00 225.00
99* 5 Mark 1915   325.00 650.00 850.00

Second Coinage
Silver

106 3 Mark 1913   350.00 800.00 1200.

MECKLENBURG-STRELITZ,
Grand Duchy
Friedrich Wilhelm 1860–1904
Silver
Rev: Style B

100 2 Mark 1877   275.00 1700. 3000.

Gold
Rev: Style A

101 *F60* 10 Mark 1873   5500.   –   –
102 *F58* 20 Mark 1873   3500.   –   –
Rev: Style B
101a *F61* 10 Mark 1874,80   4500.   –   –
102a *F59* 20 Mark 1874   3000.   –   –

Adolf Friedrich V 1904–14
First Coinage
Silver

103 2 Mark 1905   350.00 575.00 800.00

Gold

104 *F63* 10 Mark 1905   3500.   –   –
105 *F62* 20 Mark 1905   4250.   –   –

OLDENBURG, Grand Duchy
Nicolaus Friedrich Peter
1853–1900
First Coinage
Gold

107 *F64* 10 Mark 1874   2000.   –   –

Second Coinage
Silver

108 2 Mark 1891   225.00 400.00 600.00

Friedrich August 1900–18
Silver

109 2 Mark 1900–01   175.00 400.00 800.00
110* 5 Mark 1900–01   500.00 1400. 2200.

Unless otherwise noted, prices are for coins in very
fine, extremely fine, and uncirculated condition.

PRUSSIA (Preussen), Kingdom

Wilhelm I 1861–88

Rev: Style B

111* 2 Mark 1876–84   40.00 200.00 500.00
     1879 . . . 250. 1880 . . . 80. 1883–84 . . . 150.
112 5 Mark 1874–76   40.00 250.00 500.00

Gold
Rev: Style A
114 *F71–73* 10 Mark
    1872–73   150.00 200.00 250.00
115 *F65–67* 20 Mark
    1871–73   160.00 180.00 220.00
Rev: Style B
113 *F77–79* 5 Mark 1877–78 175.00 250.00 325.00
114a *F74–76* 10 Mark
    1874–88   140.00 180.00 220.00
115a *F68–70* 20 Mark
    1874–88   150.00 180.00 225.00

Friedrich III 1888

Silver

116* 2 Mark 1888   30.00 50.00 75.00
117 5 Mark 1888   80.00 125.00 200.00

Gold

118 *F81* 10 Mark 1888   140.00 180.00 220.00
119 *F80* 20 Mark 1888   150.00 175.00 200.00

Wilhelm II 1888–1918
First Coinage

Silver

Rev: Style B
120 2 Mark 1888   350.00 450.00 700.00
122 5 Mark 1888   475.00 950.00 1300.
Rev: Style C
120a*2 Mark 1891–1912   35.00 40.00 80.00
    1892, 1901 . . . 115.
121 3 Mark 1908–12   17.50 20.00 27.50
122a 5 Mark 1891–1908   25.00 50.00 200.00

Gold
Rev: Style B
123 *F86* 10 Mark 1889   2500. 3500.   –
124 *F82* 20 Mark 1888–89   140.00 150.00 200.00
Rev: Style C
123a *F87* 10 Mark
    1890–1912   130.00 160.00 200.00
124a *F83–84* 20 Mark
    1890–1913   135.00 140.00 175.00

Second Coinage

Silver

125* 3 Mark 1914   17.50 20.00 32.50
126 5 Mark 1913–14   27.50 35.00 45.00

Gold

127 *F85* 20 Mark 1913–15   135.00 145.00 175.00
    1915 . . . Rare.

Commemorative Issues
Bicentennial of Kingdom
Silver

128* 2 Mark 1901	12.50	17.50	22.50
129 5 Mark 1901	45.00	70.00	90.00

Centennial Founding
of Berlin University

130 3 Mark 1910	35.00	70.00	110.00

Centennial Founding
of Breslau University

131 3 Mark 1911	30.00	50.00	80.00

Centennial Defeat of Napoleon

132* 2 Mark 1913	12.50	17.50	20.00
133 3 Mark 1913	17.50	20.00	25.00

25th Year of Reign

134* 2 Mark 1913	15.00	17.50	20.00
135 3 Mark 1913	17.50	20.00	27.50

Centennial Absorption of
Mansfeld

136 3 Mark 1915	250.00	400.00	550.00

REUSS-GREIZ
(Reuss alterer Linie),
Principality
Heinrich XXII 1859–1902
First Coinage
Silver
Rev: Style B

137 2 Mark 1877	325.00	1750.	3500.

Unless otherwise noted, prices are for coins in very
fine, extremely fine, and uncirculated condition.

Rev: Style C
137a 2 Mark 1892   375.00 750.00 1200.

Gold

Rev: Style B
138 *F88* 20 Mark 1875   Rare

Second Coinage

Silver
139 2 Mark 1899, 1901   150.00 300.00 500.00

Heinrich XXIV 1902–18

Silver
140 3 Mark 1909   220.00 400.00 600.00

REUSS-SCHLEIZ

(Reuss Jungerer Linie),

Principality

Heinrich XIV 1867–1913

Silver
141 2 Mark 1884   275.00 800.00 1500.

Gold
142 *F90* 10 Mark 1882   4000.   –   –
143 *F89* 20 Mark 1881   1800. 3200. 4000.

SAXE-ALTENBURG, Duchy

Ernst 1853–1908

Silver

Rev: Style C
144 2 Mark 1901   225.00 400.00 650.00
145* 5 Mark 1901   350.00 850.00 1300.

Gold
Rev: Style B
146 *F102* 20 Mark 1887   1000. 1500. 2000.

50th Year of Reign

Silver

147 5 Mark 1903   150.00 325.00 450.00

SAXE-COBURG-GOTHA, Duchy

Ernst II 1844–93

Gold
Rev: Style A
148 *F103* 20 Mark 1872   Rare
Rev: Style B
148a *F104* 20 Mark 1886   1000. 1500. 2000.

Alfred 1893–1900

Silver

149 2 Mark 1895   550.00 1000. 1500.
150* 5 Mark 1895   1750. 2000. 3000.

Gold

151 *F105* 20 Mark 1895   1250. 1900. 2500.

Carl Eduard 1900–18

Silver

152 2 Mark 1905, 11	325.00	600.00	1000.	
1911 . . . Rare.				
153 5 Mark 1907	700.00	1100.	1750.	

Gold

154 *F107* 10 Mark 1905	725.00	1300.	1800.
155 *F106* 20 Mark 1905	725.00	1250.	1750.

SAXE-MEININGEN, Duchy

Georg II 1866–1914
First Coinage

Gold

Rev: Style A
156 *F108* 20 Mark 1872		Rare

Rev: Style B
156a *F109* 20 Mark 1882	4000.	–	–

Second Coinage

Gold

Rev: Style B
158 *F110* 20 Mark 1889	600.00	–	–

Rev: Style C
157 *F113* 10 Mark 1890, 98	3500.	–	–
158a*F111* 20 Mark 1900, 05	5000.	–	–

Third Coinage

Silver

159* 2 Mark 1901	180.00	325.00	650.00
160 5 Mark 1901	200.00	450.00	700.00

Nos. 159–160 celebrate the Duke's 75th birthday, but are not marked as commemoratives.

Fourth Coinage

Silver

161* 2 Mark 1902, 13	200.00	300.00	600.00
162 3 Mark 1908, 13	80.00	125.00	200.00
163 5 Mark 1902, 08	120.00	200.00	325.00

Gold

164 *F114* 10 Mark 1902, 09, 14	2000.	3750.	–
165 *F112* 20 Mark 1910, 14	4500.	–	–

Death of Georg

Silver

166 2 Mark 1915	60.00	120.00	200.00
167* 3 Mark 1915	75.00	150.00	225.00

Unless otherwise noted, prices are for coins in very fine, extremely fine, and uncirculated condition.

SAXE-WEIMAR, Grand Duchy

Carl Alexander 1853–1901

Silver

168* 2 Mark 1892, 98   140.00 300.00 500.00

Gold

169 *F115* 20 Mark 1892, 96   1200. 1500. 2250.

Wilhelm Ernst 1901–18

Silver

170 2 Mark 1901   220.00 400.00 750.00

Gold

171 *F116* 20 Mark 1901   1700. 2500. 3500.

Commemorative Issues
First Marriage

Silver

172* 2 Mark 1903   60.00   80.00 120.00
173 5 Mark 1903   100.00 200.00 275.00

350th Anniversary Founding
of Jena University

174 2 Mark 1908   50.00   90.00 120.00
175* 5 Mark 1908   100.00 200.00 250.00

Second Marriage

176 3 Mark 1910   30.00   55.00 250.00

Centennial Elevation
to Grand Duchy

177 3 Mark 1915   80.00 140.00 180.00

SAXONY (Sachsen), Kingdom

Johann 1854–73

Gold

178 *F92* 10 Mark 1872–73   125.00 175.00 220.00
179 *F91* 20 Mark 1872–73   130.00 200.00 250.00

Albert 1873–1902

Silver

Rev: Style B
180 2 Mark 1876–88   110.00 425.00 1200.
181 5 Mark 1875, 76, 89   40.00 600.00 1500.
Rev: Style C
180a*2 Mark 1891–1902   50.00 120.00 225.00
181a 5 Mark 1891–1902   35.00 175.00 550.00

Gold

Rev: Style B
182 *F97* 5 Mark 1877   240.00 300.00 450.00
183 *F95* 10 Mark 1874–88   175.00 220.00 250.00
184 *F93* 20 Mark 1874–78   175.00 220.00 300.00
Rev: Style C
183a *F96* 10 Mark
      1891–1902   180.00 220.00 275.00
184a *F94* 20 Mark 1894–95 145.00 220.00 275.00

Death of Albert

Silver

185* 2 Mark 1902   32.50 50.00 120.00
186 5 Mark 1902   60.00 145.00 200.00

Georg 1902–04

Silver

187* 2 Mark 1903–04   40.00 145.00 275.00
188 5 Mark 1903–04   40.00 250.00 650.00

Gold

189 *F99* 10 Mark 1903–04   175.00 225.00 280.00
190 *F98* 20 Mark 1903   185.00 240.00 325.00

Death of Georg

Silver

191* 2 Mark 1904   24.00 60.00 80.00
192 5 Mark 1904   100.00 200.00 275.00

Friedrich August III 1904–18

Silver

193* 2 Mark 1905–14   25.00 45.00 110.00
194 3 Mark 1908–13   14.00 20.00 35.00
195 5 Mark 1907–14   30.00 60.00 140.00

Gold

196 *F101* 10 Mark 1905–12   200.00 245.00 350.00
197 *F100* 20 Mark 1905, 13,
     14   160.00 200.00 245.00

Unless otherwise noted, prices are for coins in very
fine, extremely fine, and uncirculated condition.

Commemorative Issues
500th Anniversary Founding
of Leipzig University

Silver

198* 2 Mark 1909	35.00	55.00	80.00
199 5 Mark 1909	85.00	160.00	225.00

Centennial Battle of Leipzig
200 3 Mark 1913	17.50	25.00	30.00

400th Anniversary Protestant
Reformation
201 3 Mark 1917. Proof only.   Rare

Gold

205 *F118* 20 Mark 1898,
1904   1200. 1800. 2250.

Death of Georg

Silver

206 3 Mark 1911   60.00 100.00 150.00

SCHAUMBURG-LIPPE,
Principality
Adolf Georg 1860–93

Gold

202 *117* 20 Mark 1874   6500.   –   –

Albrecht Georg 1893–1911

Silver

203* 2 Mark 1898, 1904	300.00	650.00	1100.
204 5 Mark 1898, 1904	850.00	1350.	1800.

SCHWARZBURG–RUDOLSTADT,
Principality
Gunther 1890–1918

Silver
207 2 Mark 1898   200.00 425.00 600.00

Gold

208 *F119* 10 Mark 1898   1300. 1700. 2200.

SCHWARZBURG–SONDERSHAUSEN,
Principality
Karl Gunther 1880–1909

Silver
209 2 Mark 1896   200.00 500.00 750.00

Gold
210 *F120* 20 Mark 1896   1400. 2400. 2750.

25th Year of Reign

Silver

211 2 Mark 1905 (2 vars.)   40.00 90.00 120.00

Death of Karl Gunther

212 3 Mark 1909   50.00 95.00 120.00

WALDECK-PYRMONT,

Principality

Friedrich 1893–1918

Silver
213 5 Mark 1903   1000. 2750. 3750.

Gold
214 *F121* 20 Mark 1903   1750. 3000. 4000.

WURTTEMBERG, Kingdom

Karl 1864–91

Silver
Rev: Style B
215 2 Mark 1876–88   100.00 700.00 1800.
216 5 Mark 1874–88   40.00 800.00 2250.

Gold
Rev: Style A
218 *F124* 10 Mark 1872–73 140.00 200.00 400.00
219 *F122* 20 Mark 1872–73 120.00 180.00 300.00
Rev: Style B
217 *F127* 5 Mark 1877–78   250.00 325.00 475.00
          1878 . . . 1000.
218a *F125* 10 Mark
          1874–88   120.00 180.00 200.00
219a *123* 20 Mark 1874–76 160.00 170.00 475.00

Rev: Style C
218b *F126* 10 Mark
          1890–91   180.00 220.00 300.00

Wilhelm II 1891–1918

Silver

220* 2 Mark 1892–1914   20.00 35.00 85.00
221 3 Mark 1908–14   15.00 20.00 27.50
222 5 Mark 1892–1913   27.50 45.00 120.00

Gold
223 *F129* 10 Mark
          1893–1913   130.00 180.00 250.00
224 *F128* 20 Márk
          1894–1914   135.00 160.00 220.00

Silver Wedding

Silver

225 3 Mark 1911   17.50 35.00 50.00

25th Year of Reign
226 3 Mark 1916. Proof only.   5000.

GERMANY (Deutschland)

The German Empire was formed by Bismarck in 1871, finally uniting the various states of this north central European country. After World War I it became a republic, but many factors combined to lead to the rise of Adolf Hitler in 1933. He formed the totalitarian Third Reich; World War II ended in disaster for him and his regime. Germany was divided into western and eastern areas, each becoming autonomous in 1949.

Monetary System:
100 Pfennig = 1 Mark

Unless otherwise noted, prices are for coins in very fine, extremely fine, and uncirculated condition.

I. EMPIRE 1871–1918
First Coinage
Copper

Rev: Small eagle

1 1 Pfennig 1873–89   2.00   12.50   20.00
        1873, . . . 200. 1874H,75H,76H,85E . . . 50.
        1874G,86G . . . 45. 1876J,77A . . . 100.
2 2 Pfennig 1873–77   1.00   12.50   25.00
        1873B, C . . . 50. 1873A, D,74B-G,76J . . . 6.
        1873F,77B . . . 200.

Cupro-Nickel

5 5 Pfennig 1874–89   2.00   8.00   25.00
        1874E . . . 8. 1875H . . . 35.
6 10 Pfennig 1873–89   2.00   10.00   37.50
        1873H . . . 120. 1873B, C, F, G, 74D, E, H, 75H,
        76H . . . 20.
        1873A, 88E-G . . . 6.

7 20 Pfennig 1887–88   20.00   37.50   70.00

Silver

Rev: Small eagle in plain field

12 20 Pfennig 1873–77   6.00   8.00   17.50
        1873B-D,74C, E, G, H,75B, E, H, J . . . 15.
        1873E . . . 400. 1873H . . . 85.
        1877F . . . 150.
13 50 Pfennig 1875–77   12.50   27.50   45.00
        1875E, H . . . 150. 1877H, J . . . .55.
17 1 Mark 1873–87, obv.
        like No.18   5.00   25.00   40.00

Obv: Like No. 18
Rev: Small eagle in wreath
14 50 Pfennig 1877–78   40.00   80.00 150.00

Second Coinage
Copper

Rev: Large eagle

3 1 Pfennig 1890–1916   .50   .75   3.50
        1891D,93G,95D, E,97G . . . 17.
        1902J . . . Rare 1891E, G . . . 45.
        1913A . . . 150.
4 2 Pfennig 1904–16   .50   1.25   4.00
        1904E, G, J,08E,10E . . . 4.
        1913E,15E . . . 12. 1914F . . . 40.

Cupro-Nickel

8 5 Pfennig 1890–1915   .25   .50   2.00
Dates pre-1905 are worth more.

        1891E,10J . . . 30.
        1891G,92E-G,93G,13J . . . 10.
        1892J . . . 80.
9 10 Pfennig 1890–1916   .25   .50   2.25
        1891G,94E,96G,10E . . . 12.
        1909E-J . . . 2.

10 20 Pfennig 1890–92   32.50   60.00   85.00

Nickel

11 25 Pfennig 1909–12   5.00   10.00   20.00
    1909E, 12J . . . 20. 1909J . . . Rare.

Silver

Rev: Large eagle in wreath
15 50 Pfennig 1896–1901   165.00 225.00 300.00
16 ½ Mark 1905–19   4.00   6.00   10.00
Part of the 1917 issue and all of the 1918–19 were artificially blackened to discourage hoarding.
18 1 Mark 1891–1916   3.00   4.00   12.00

Higher Denominations
The right to issue coins larger than 1 Mark belonged to the individual states of the German Empire. See GERMAN STATES for these 1871–1918 coins of 2, 3 and 5 Mark silver and 5, 10 and 20 Mark gold.

WORLD WAR I and INFLATION 1915–1923
This period marks the end of the German Empire and the rise of the Weimar Republic in 1919. Silver coins were retained unchanged until stopped, while the lower denominations were made in aluminum, zinc and iron.

Occupation Issue
Struck for use in German-occupied territories of eastern Europe (Baltic states, eastern Poland, northwest Russia.)

Iron

A18 1 Kopek 1916   2.00   5.00   10.00
B18 2 Kopeks 1916   2.25   6.00   12.00
C18 3 Kopeks 1916   3.00   7.50   15.00

Regular Issues

Aluminum

19 1 Pfennig 1916–18   2.00   3.25   5.00
    1916 . . . 125. 1918D . . . 12.

Iron

Rev: large eagle (like No. 8)
21 5 Pfennig 1915–22   .50   1.00   2.00
    1915D, E,16E,17E,20E,21E, 22E,22J . . . 8.

Rev: Small eagle in beaded border
22 10 Pfennig 1915–22   .50   2.00   4.00
    1915A . . . 225. 1922E, G . . . 35.
    1918D . . . 425. 1922D . . . 6
    1921A,22F, J . . . 3.

Zinc
22a 10 Pfennig 1916–17, rev.
like No. 22   •   125.00 180.00 275.00
    1916 . . . Rare.
25 10 Pfennig 1917–22, rev.
like No. 21   .50   1.00   2.00

II. WEIMAR REPUBLIC 1919–33
Nos. 21, 22 and 25 were continued into this period.

Aluminum

26 50 Pfennig 1919–22   .25   .50   1.00
    1919A-D,20E, G, J,21E,22E, J . . . 1
    1919E-F . . . 10. 1919G-J . . . 4

Unless otherwise noted, prices are for coins in very fine, extremely fine, and uncirculated condition.

Third Anniversary Weimar Constitution

28 3 Mark 1922–23   2.00   4.00   8.00
    1922D . . . 250. 1922F . . . 10.
    1923E . . . 30.

Regular Issues

29 3 Mark 1922, no. obv.
legend   2.00   4.00   8.00
    1923E . . . 120.

30 200 Mark 1923   .50   1.50   2.00
31 500 Mark 1923   .75   1.50   2.00

Coinage Law of Nov. 8, 1923

Bronze

32 1 Rentenpfennig
1923–24, 29   .50   1.25   5.00
    1925, 29 . . . Rare
33 2 Rentenpfennig
1923–24   .50   2.50   5.00
    1923F, J . . . 4.

Aluminum-Bronze

34 5 Rentenpfennig
1923–25   .50   1.00   5.00
    1923F . . . 80. 1923G, J . . . 40.
35 10 Rentenpfennig
1923–25   .50   1.00   5.00
    1923F . . . 80. 1923A, D . . . 3.
    1925F . . . Rare.
36 50 Rentenpfennig
1923–24   6.00   12.00   27.50
    1923F . . . 75. 1923J . . . Rare. 1923G . . . 25.

Coinage Reform of 1924

Bronze
Designs like Nos. 32–33

37 1 Reichspfennig 1924–36   .40   .80   2.50
    1924E . . . 125. 1925D, 30E . . . 10.
38 2 Reichspfennig 1924–36   .25   .60   3.00
    1924E,25G,36A . . . 1 1936E . . . 18.

39 4 Reichspfennig 1932   7.50   13.50   22.50

Aluminum-Bronze
Designs like Nos. 34–36

40 5 Reichspfennig 1924–36   .50   1.50   3.00
All dates except 1925A, D; 1935A; and 1936 A, D are
worth more than the prices listed.
41 10 Reichspfennig
1924–36   .40   .75   4.00
    1924F,28A,30E-F,32D, F,33J,34D . . . 6.
    1925J,26G,30G-J,31F,32E,33G . . . 11.
    1928G . . . 80. 1931D,33A,34E-G . . . 40.
    1931G,32G . . . 450.
42 50 Reichspfennig 1924–25   Rare

Nickel

43 50 Reichspfennig
    1927–38   1.00   3.50   6.00
      1927D-J,30D,31D, F,35J,38E-J . . . 4.
      1930E, G-J,36D-G . . . 12.
      1930F . . . 50. 1931G . . . 275.
      1932G . . . Rare. 1933G, J,36J,37J . . . 75.

Silver

44 1 Mark 1924–25   10.00 20.00 35.00
      1925A . . . 25. 1924D,25D . . . 15.
47 3 Mark 1924–25   40.00 55.00 100.00
      1925D . . . 100.

45 1 Reichsmark 1925–27   12.00 20.00 30.00
      1926J . . . 70. 1927A . . . 175.
      1927F, J . . . 40.
46 2 Reichsmark 1925–31   9.00 25.00 50.00
      1925G-J . . . 20 1927D, E . . . 275.
      1927F, J . . . 85. 1931E-J . . . 45.
48 3 Reichsmark 1931–33 250.00 350.00 450.00
      1932F, G,33G . . . Rare

49 5 Reichsmark 1927–33   75.00 100.00 200.00

COMMEMORATIVE ISSUES
Silver
Millennium Unification of Rhineland

50 3 Reichsmark 1925   20.00 40.00 50.00
                                 Proof . . . 150.00
51 5 Reichsmark 1925   60.00 100.00 150.00
                                 Proof . . . 250.00

700th Anniversary Freedom of Lubeck

52 3 Reichsmark 1926   110.00 195.00 250.00
                                 Proof . . . 275.00

Centennial City of Bremerhaven

53 3 Reichsmark 1927   100.00 150.00 200.00
                                 Proof . . . 375.00

Unless otherwise noted, prices are for coins in very
fine, extremely fine, and uncirculated condition.

54 5 Reichsmark 1927   350.00 550.00 950.00
Proof . . . 1000.

Millennium City of Nordhausen

55 3 Reichsmark 1927   100.00 200.00 300.00
Proof . . . 400.00

400th Anniversary
University of Marburg

56 3 Reichsmark 1927   85.00 150.00 195.00
Proof . . . 235.00

450th Anniversary
University of Tubingen

57 3 Reichsmark 1927   300.00 450.00 650.00
Proof . . . 775.00
58 5 Reichsmark 1927   350.00 500.00 700.00
Proof . . . 800.00

400th Anniversary
Death of Durer

59 3 Reichsmark 1928   275.00 450.00 550.00
Proof . . . 650.00

900th Anniversary
City of Naumburg

60 3 Reichsmark 1928   125.00 175.00 225.00

Millennium City of Dinkelsbuhl

61 3 Reichsmark 1928   400.00 650.00 900.00
Proof . . . 1200.

Bicentennial Birth of Lessing

62 3 Reichsmark 1929   45.00 70.00 100.00
Proof . . . 125.00
63 5 Reichsmark 1929   75.00 120.00 200.00
Proof . . . 275.00

Waldeck-Prussia Union

64 3 Reichsmark 1929   75.00 150.00 200.00
Proof . . . 300.00

10th Anniversary of Constitution

65	3 Reichsmark 1929	27.50	40.00	60.00
			Proof . . . 170.00	
66	5 Reichsmark 1929	80.00	150.00	2000.
			Proof . . . 375.00	

Millennium City of Meissen

67	3 Reichsmark 1929	35.00	70.00	110.00
			Proof . . . 300.00	
68	5 Reichsmark 1929	300.00	550.00	800.00
			Proof . . . 1100.	

World Flight of Graf Zeppelin

69	3 Reichsmark 1930	45.00	80.00	125.00
			Proof . . . 200.00	
70	5 Reichsmark 1930	100.00	175.00	225.00
			Proof . . . 350.00	

700th Anniversary Death of von der Vogelweide

| 71 | 3 Reichsmark 1930 | 55.00 | 85.00 | 125.00 |
| | Also see Austria No. 71. | | Proof . . . 225.00 | |

End of Occupation of Rhineland

72	3 Reichsmark 1930	27.50	47.50	75.00
			Proof . . . 175.00	
73	5 Reichsmark 1930	110.00	200.00	265.00
			Proof . . . 425.00	

300th Anniversary Rebuilding of Magdeburg

| 74 | 3 Reichsmark 1931 | 150.00 | 250.00 | 325.00 |
| | | | Proof . . . 500.00 | |

Centennial Death of von Stein

| 75 | 3 Reichsmark 1931 | 100.00 | 150.00 | 225.00 |
| | | | Proof . . . 400.00 | |

Centennial Death of Goethe

76	3 Reichsmark 1932	70.00	100.00	150.00
			Proof . . . 250.00	
77	5 Reichsmark 1932	2000.	3000.	3500.
			Proof . . . 3750.	

Unless otherwise noted, prices are for coins in very fine, extremely fine, and uncirculated condition.

III. THIRD REICH (NAZI STATE)
1933–1945
Commemorative Issues

Silver

450th Anniversary
Birth of Martin Luther

78	2 Reichsmark 1933	10.00	20.00	40.00
			Proof . . . 175.00	
79	5 Reichsmark 1933	75.00	100.00	200.00
			Proof . . . 275.00	

First Anniversary of Nazi Rule

Obv: With date "21 Marz 1933"

83	2 Reichsmark 1934	7.50	17.50	60.00
			Proof . . . 100.00	
84	5 Reichsmark 1934	12.50	27.50	75.00
			Proof . . . 150.00	

175th Anniversary
Birth of Schiller

86	2 Reichsmark 1934	35.00	50.00	100.00
			Proof . . . 200.00	
87	5 Reichsmark 1934	140.00	225.00	325.00
			Proof . . . 475.00	

Regular Issues
First Coinage

Nos. 37, 38, 40, 41 and 43 were continued into this period.

Nickel

81	1 Reichsmark 1933–39	2.00	6.00	10.00
	1933E-G,34G,35J,36D-F, J,37F-J . . . 5.			
	1936G,38J,39E . . . 75.			
	1937E,38E-G,39A, D . . . 15.			
	1939F, J . . . 40. 1939G . . . 100.			

Silver

Obv: Like No. 84 but commemorative date omitted

85	5 Reichsmark 1934–35	10.00	12.50	20.00

Obv: Paul von Hindenburg, President 1925–34

82	5 Reichsmark 1935–36	10.00	12.50	17.50

Second Coinage

Bronze

88	1 Reichspfennig 1936–40	.25	.40	2.00
	1936A,38B,40G . . . 6. 1936E, F . . . 45.			
	1936G, J . . . 20.			
89	2 Reichspfennig 1936–40	.35	.75	2.35
	1936A, D,37G, J,38B,40J . . . 5.			
	1936F,37E . . . 17. 1940E . . . 8			
	1940G . . . 40.			

Aluminum-Bronze

90	5 Reichspfennig 1936–39	.50	1.00	2.50
	1936A . . . 20. 1936G . . . 75.			

91 10 Reichspfennig
1936–39   .75   1.50   4.00
   1936A,37E . . . 12. 1936E, G . . . 125.
   1937G,39E, G . . . 4.

Nickel

93 50 Reichspfennig
1938–39   12.50   25.00   50.00
   1938G, J,39G, J . . . 25.00

Silver

96 2 Reichsmark 1936–39   6.50   8.00   10.00
   1936E,39E . . . 35.   1936G . . . 15.
   1936J . . . 55.

97 5 Reichsmark 1936–39   8.00   10.00   20.00

Third Coinage

Zinc

A92 1 Reichspfennig 1940–45   .40   .75   2.00
B92 5 Reichspfennig 1940–44   .50   1.00   2.50
   1942E,44A . . . 15. 1943B . . . 25.
   1944G . . . 60. 1943E . . . 6.

C92 10 Reichspfennig
1940–45   .40   1.00   2.75
   1943B, G . . . 6. 1943E,45A . . . 10.
   1943J,45E . . . 32.

Aluminum

80 50 Reichspfennig 1935   .50   2.00   4.00
No. 80 was coined in 1935 but withheld from circulation
until 1939.

92 50 Reichspfennig
1939–44   1.00   2.00   8.00
   1939D, G, J,40E, G, J,42B, G,43G, J . . . 7.
   1939E,41B, D, J42D, E,43B . . . 5.
   1944G . . . 55.

German Army Issues

Zinc

94 5 Reichspfennig 1940–41   4.00   8.00   20.00
95 10 Reichspfennig
1940–41   4.00   8.00   20.00

IV. ALLIED OCCUPATION
1945–1950
First Coinage

Zinc

Rev: Swastika omitted

98 1 Reichspfennig 1944–46   10.00   12.50   30.00
   1944 . . . Rare. 1946F . . . 25. 1946G . . . 65.
99 5 Reichspfennig 1947–48   4.00   7.50   12.00
   1948A . . . 14. 1948E . . . Rare.

100 10 Reichspfennig
1945–48   8.00   14.00   20.00
   1946F,47A,48A . . . 15.
   1946G . . . 120. 1947E . . . 140.

Second Coinage

Legend:
BANK DEUTSCHER LANDER
Bronze-Clad Steel

101 1 Pfennig 1948–49   1.75   7.50   20.00

Unless otherwise noted, prices are for coins in very
fine, extremely fine, and uncirculated condition.

Brass-Clad Steel

102	5 Pfennig 1949	2.50	12.00	24.00
103	10 Pfennig 1949	2.50	12.00	24.00

Cupro-Nickel

104	50 Pfennig 1949–50	.50	4.00	17.50

GERMANY — FEDERAL REPUBLIC (West Germany)

In 1949, the three western zones of occupied Germany had their civil government restored, and united as a federal republic. Area: (with West Berlin): 95,815 square miles. Capital: *Bonn.*

Monetary System:
100 Pfennig = 1 Deutsche Mark (DM)

New Legend:
BUNDESREPUBLIK DEUTSCHLAND
Designd similar to Nos. 101–104

Bronze-Clad Steel

105	1 Pfennig 1950–	.25	.40	1.25

Bronze

106	2 Pfennig 1950–68	.10	.20	.50
	1950 UNC . . . 4.			

Brass-Clad Steel

107	5 Pfennig 1950–	.20	.80	2.00
108	10 Pfennig 1950–	.20	.80	2.00

Cupro-Nickel

109	50 Pfennig 1950–71	.25	1.00	2.50

110	1 DM 1950–	2.00	4.00	15.00

111	2 DM 1951	15.00	25.00	60.00

117	2 DM 1957–71	2.00	4.00	17.50

Silver

112	5 DM 1951–74	6.00	15.00	40.00
			Proof . . . 275.00	

All issues before 1964 are worth more than the above prices.

COMMEMORATIVE ISSUES

Silver

Nurnberg Museum Centennial

113	5 DM 1952	325.00	600.00	700.00
			Proof . . . 4000.	

150th Anniversary Death of
Friedrich von Schiller

114 5 DM 1955   175.00 350.00 500.00
                              Proof . . . 1350.

300th Anniversary Birth of
Ludwig von Baden

115 5 DM 1955   150.00 325.00 475.00
                              Proof . . . 1350.

Centennial
Death of von Eichendorff

116 5 DM 1957   150.00 325.00 475.00
                              Proof . . . 1350.

Later issues in *Current Coins of the World.*

GERMAN DEMOCRATIC REPUBLIC
(East Germany)

East Germany was proclaimed a democratic republic in 1949 and became sovereign as such in 1954. Area: 40,646 square miles. Capital: *East Berlin.*

Monetary System:
100 Pfennig = 1 Mark

First Coinage

Aluminum

1	1 Pfennig 1948–50	.50	1.00	8.00
2	5 Pfennig 1948–50	1.00	2.00	5.00
3	10 Pfennig 1948–50	1.00	2.50	5.50

Aluminum-Bronze

4	50 Pfennig 1949–50	3.00	5.00	10.00
	1949 . . . Rare.			

Second Coinage

Aluminum

5	1 Pfennig 1952–53	.50	1.00	5.00
6	5 Pfennig 1952–53	.50	1.00	2.00
7	10 Pfennig 1952–53	1.00	2.00	5.00

Later issues in *Current Coins of the World*

GERMAN EAST AFRICA
(Deutsch Ostafrika)

In 1884, Germany gained control of this east African territory and retained it until after World War I. At that time, the colony was split between Britain (administering Tanganyika), Belgium (Ruanda-Urundi), and Portugal. Principal products include sisal, cotton, hides and ivory. Capital: *Dar-es-Salaam.*

Monetary System:
64 Pesa (Pice) = 1 Rupie to 1902
100 Heller = 1 Rupie 1902–17

Unless otherwise noted, prices are for coins in very fine, extremely fine, and uncirculated condition.

WILHELM II 1888–1918
German East Africa Co.
Copper

1	1 Pesa 1890–92	4.00	8.00	17.50
			Proof . . . 125.00

Silver

2	¼ Rupie 1891–1901	12.50	25.00	75.00
			Proof . . . 225.00
3	½ Rupie 1891–1901	25.00	45.00	125.00
			Proof . . . 350.00
4	1 Rupie 1890–1902	20.00	35.00	90.00
	1894 . . . 75		Proof . . . 250.00
5*	2 Rupien 1893–94	200.00	350.00	850.00
			Proof . . . 1750.

New Legend:
DEUTSCH OSTAFRIKA only
Bronze

6	½ Heller 1904–06	3.00	8.00	25.00
			Proof . . . 150.00
7	1 Heller 1904–13	1.00	3.00	15.00
			Proof . . . 75.00
8	5 Heller 1908–09	20.00	35.00	150.00
			Proof . . . 450.00

Cupro-Nickel

11	5 Heller 1913–14	7.50	20.00	50.00
			Proof . . . 150.00
12	10 Heller 1908–14	8.00	17.50	60.00
			Proof . . . 175.00

Silver

13	¼ Rupie 1904–14	15.00	30.00	100.00
			Proof . . . 275.00
14	½ Rupie 1904–14	30.00	50.00	150.00
	1906 . . . 75		Proof . . . 400.00
15	1 Rupie 1904–14	20.00	40.00	120.00
			Proof . . . 300.00

World War I
Provisional Issues

9	5 Heller Brass 1916	3.00	10.00	40.00
10	10 Heller Copper 1916	5.00	15.00	45.00
10a	10 Heller Brass 1916	4.00	8.00	35.00

4 varieties each of Nos. 10 and 10a (differences in size and shape of lettering and crown).

Gold

16	*F1* 5 Rupien 1916	650.00	950.00	1200.

Nos. 9, 10, 10a and 16 were struck at Tabora.

GERMAN NEW GUINEA (Neu-Guinea)

German New Guinea comprised the northern part of eastern New Guinea. The territory was annexed by Germany in 1884. After World War I it was mandated to Australia by the League of Nations. In 1973 it became part of Papua New Guinea, which is now independent. Capital: *Herbertshohe (now Kokopo).* **Monetary System:**.

100 Pfennig = 1 Mark

Copper

1	1 Pfennig 1894	45.00	65.00	100.00
			Proof . . . 200.00	
2	2 Pfennig 1894	75.00	125.00	200.00
			Proof . . . 350.00	

Designs like No. 8

3	10 Pfennig 1894	60.00	100.00	150.00
			Proof . . . 250.00	

Silver
Designs like No. 8

4	½ Mark 1894	125.00	200.00	350.00
			Proof . . . 500.00	
5	1 Mark 1894	100.00	175.00	400.00
			Proof . . . 750.00	
6	2 Mark 1894	150.00	300.00	750.00
			Proof . . . 1500.	
7	5 Mark 1894	650.00	900.00	1500.
			Proof . . . 2500.	

Gold

8	F2 10 Mark 1895	5000.	7000.	11000.
			Proof . . . 14000.	
9	F1 20 Mark 1895	6000.	8500.	12500.
			Proof . . . 16000.	

GHANA

Situated in West Africa on the Gulf of Guinea, this was the former British colony taken over in 1821 from the British merchant company which had developed the Gold Coast. Ghana was given its independence in 1957, and became a Republic within the British Commonwealth in 1960. Area: 92,100 square miles. Capital: *Accra.*

Monetary System:
12 Pence = 1 Shilling
For earlier issues, see BRITISH WEST AFRICA.

Bronze

1	½ Penny 1958	.05	.10	.20
2	1 Penny 1958	.10	.20	.30

Cupro-Nickel

3	3 Pence 1958	.15	.25	.50
4	6 Pence 1958	.25	.35	.75
5	1 Shilling 1958	.50	.75	1.50

6	2 Shillings 1958	.75	1.50	3.00

Silver

7	10 Shillings 1958	10.00	15.00	25.00

Proof Set, Nos. 1–7 in case . . . 30.00

Later issues in *Current Coins of the World.*

GREAT BRITAIN

The United Kingdom of Great Britain and Northern Ireland is separated from the European mainland by the North Sea and the English Channel. London, its capital, is the hub of the British Commonwealth of Nations, which includes more than one fourth of the world's population. It is also one of the world's largest seaports. More important British exports include iron and steel, woolens, textiles and machinery. Area: 94,214 square miles.

Monetary System:
4 Farthings = 1 Penny
12 Pence = 1 Shilling
2 Shillings = 1 Florin
5 Shillings = 1 Crown
20 Shillings = 1 Pound
20 Shillings = 1 Sovereign (Gold)

Unless otherwise noted, prices are for coins in very fine, extremely fine, and uncirculated condition.

TRADE COIN
Silver

T1 1 Dollar 1895–1935   15.00   35.00   75.00
                                    Proof . . . 1000.
    1895–6 . . . 60   1900,00–C . . . 125
    1901–C,02–C . . . 30
    1904–B . . . 75   1913–B . . . 100
    1921–B . . . 1500.
    1934 . . . 50   1935 . . . 1000.

The British Trade Dollar was legal tender in Hong Kong and the Straits Settlements, but was created primarily to facilitate British commerce throughout the Orient. The value ONE DOLLAR appears in English, Chinese and Malay.

SPECIAL ISSUES
FOR COLONIAL USE

During the 19th century, several new denominations were created to help adapt the British monetary system to the local systems used in various colonies. They resemble regular British issues and do not bear the names of the colonies, but are easily distinguishable by their unusual denominations. The following guide indicates the location of such pieces in this catalog:

Copper

Denomination	Location
¼ Farthing 1839–53	Ceylon Y–1
⅓ Farthing 1844	Malta Y–1
½ Farthing 1839–56	Great Britain Y–C2,
	Ceylon Y–2

Bronze

⅓ Farthing 1866–1913	Malta Y–2,3,4

Silver

1½ Pence 1838–62	Great Britain Y A5,
	Ceylon Y–3,
	Jamaica Y–A3
4 Pence 1838–55	Great Britain Y–4,
	British Guiana Y–A1
4 Pence 1888	British Guiana Y–B2

REGULAR ISSUES
VICTORIA 1837–1901
A. Young Portrait Types

Copper

C2 ½ Farthing 1839–56 (2 var.)   3.00   6.00   15.00
    1847–56 . . . 6

1 1 Farthing 1838–60
    (22mm)   4.00   12.00   25.00
       1842,46,49,52,59 . . . 12   1844 . . . 50
       1860 . . . 700
2* ½ Penny 1838–59
    (28mm)   4.00   12.00   40.00
       1843 . . . 15   1845 . . . 60   1846–48 . . . 8
       1860 . . . 400
3 1 Penny 1841–60
    (34mm)   6.00   12.00   45.00
       1849 . . . 125   1856 . . . 60

Bronze

16 1 Farthing 1860–95   1.00   3.00   12.00
      1863 . . . 40   1876,95 . . . 10   1892 . . . 4
17 ½ Penny 1860–94   2.00   8.00   30.00
      1864,69,70,73,74 . . . 10   1871 . . . 35
      1878 . . . 25

18* 1 Penny 1860–94						4.00	13.00	30.00
    1864 . . . 30 1865,67 . . . 13 1866 . . . 8
    1868,70 . . . 22
    1869,71,75H..65 1878,80,81 . . . 8
    1882 . . . 250

Silver

A5 1½ Pence 1838–62					3.00	10.00	25.00
    1840 . . . 8

No. A5 was issued only for colonial use in Ceylon, Jamaica, and many other colonies.

A3 3 Pence 1838–87					3.00	15.00	30.00
    1838–72 . . . 5
    1839,44,46,49,53,55,57,63,65 . . . 10
    1869 . . . 200

4 4 Pence (Groat) 1838–62				5.00	16.00	40.00
    1841,51 . . . 12 1853 . . . 50

5 6 Pence 1838–87					6.00	20.00	40.00
    1848,62–3,67–70,76 . . . 30 1850–1,82 . . . 16
    1854 . . . 60
6 1 Shilling 1838–87					8.00	30.00	65.00
    1840,48 . . . 50 1850–1,54 . . . 150
    1862–3 . . . 75

9* ½ Crown 1839–87
    (32mm)						30.00	90.00	160.00
    1839 . . . 600 1840–1,43 . . . 75 1848 . . . 100
10 1 Crown 1839–47					60.00	350.00	1200.
    1839 Proof . . . 3000.

Maundy Money

Maundy Money is the term for a special set of silver coins distributed by the Monarch to certain poor persons each year on Maundy Thursday. The set consists of 1, 2, 3 and 4 pence coins.

The 3 pence used in the sets was of the regular type until 1927; regular issues after this date use different reverse designs.

Silver

A12 1 Penny 1838–87			10.00	15.00	20.00
B12 2 Pence 1838–87			10.00	15.00	30.00
C12 3 Pence 1838–87			10.00	15.00	30.00
D12 4 Pence 1838–87			10.00	15.00	30.00

Gold

13 *F254* ½ Sovereign
    1838–85, rev. arms			80.00	125.00	225.00
  1839 Proof . . . 2000.
14* *F252* 1 Sovereign
    1838–74, rev. Arms in
    wreath					125.00	150.00	225.00
        1839 . . . 600 1841 . . . 1500
        1874 . . . 1300
        Rev: St. George and Dragon
15 *F253* 1 Sovereign
    1871–85					130.00	150.00	225.00
    1874 . . . 175 1879 . . . 300

B. Gothic Types

Silver

7 1 Florin 1849				20.00	75.00	150.00

Unless otherwise noted, prices are for coins in very fine, extremely fine, and uncirculated condition.

No. 7 omits DEI GRATIA from the legend, and is popularly known as the "Godless" Florin.

Rev: Date in Roman numerals

8 1 Florin 1851–87   25.00   75.00   170.00
    1851 Proof . . . 5000   1854 . . . 750
    1862-3,67 . . . 75
11 1 Crown 1847,53   500.00   750.00   1250.
    1853 Unc . . . 6500

C. Golden Jubilee Type

Silver

A18 3 Pence 1887–93   2.00   10.00   15.00
    1893 . . . 40

For 4 Pence 1888 with rev. like No. 4, see British Guiana.

19* 6 Pence 1887   4.00   6.00   8.00
20 1 Shilling 1887–89, small
    bust   5.00   10.00   20.00
    1889 . . . 50
21 1 Shilling 1889–92, large
    bust   6.00   30.00   50.00

22 6 Pence 1887–93   3.00   10.00   25.00
    1893 . . . 200

23* 1 Florin 1887–92 (29mm)   6.00   15.00   25.00
    1890 . . . 35   1891-2 . . . 50
25 2 Florins 1887–90
    (36mm)   17.00   25.00   65.00
                 Proof . . . 175.00

24* ½ Crown 1887–92
    (32mm)   10.00   15.00   50.00
                 Proof . . . 200.00

26 1 Crown 1887–92   20.00   50.00   110.00
                 Proof . . . 500.00

Maundy Coins

A27 1 Penny 1888–92   10.00   15.00   20.00
B27 2 Pence 1888–92   10.00   15.00   20.00
C27 3 Pence 1888–92   5.00   15.00   25.00
D27 4 Pence 1888–92   10.00   15.00   20.00

Gold

Proofs were struck only in 1887

28 *F258* ½ Sovereign
    1887–93, rev. arms
    (19mm)   70.00   100.00   150.00
29 *F257* 1 Sovereign
    1887–92 (22mm)   130.00   140.00   200.00
30 *F256* 2 Pounds 1887
    (28mm)   300.00   450.00   550.00
31 *F255* 5 Pounds 1887
    (36mm)   600.00   850.00   1100.

D. Aged Portrait Types

Bronze

32 1 Farthing 1895–1901   1.00   2.00   5.00

| 33 | ½ Penny 1895–1901 | 2.00 | 4.00 | 10.00 |
| 34 | 1 Penny 1895–1901 | 1.00 | 4.00 | 10.00 |

Silver
Rev: Value in wreath

| 35 | 3 Pence 1893–1901 | 1.00 | 4.00 | 10.00 |
| 36 | 6 Pence 1893–1901 | 4.00 | 10.00 | 22.50 |

| 37 | 1 Shilling 1893–1901 | 4.00 | 18.00 | 35.00 |
| 38 | 1 Florin 1893–1901 | 6.00 | 30.00 | 60.00 |

| 39 | ½ Crown 1893–1901 | 10.00 | 40.00 | 65.00 |

Rev: Like No. 26

| 40 | 1 Crown 1893–1900 | 30.00 | 40.00 | 200.00 |
| | 1898 . . . 45 | | | |

Maundy Coins

A41	1 Penny 1893–1901	5.00	10.00	15.00
B41	2 Pence 1893–1901	5.00	10.00	20.00
C41	3 Pence 1893–1901	4.00	5.00	20.00
D41	4 Pence 1893–1901	5.00	10.00	20.00

Gold

Proofs were struck only in 1893.

42	*F262* ½ Sovereign			
	1893–1901	75.00	100.00	140.00
43*	*F261* 1 Sovereign			
	1893–1901	130.00	140.00	160.00
44	*F260* 2 Pounds 1893	300.00	500.00	700.00
45	*F259* 5 Pounds 1893	600.00	1000.	1400.

EDWARD VII 1901–1910

Bronze
Obv: Like No. 51
Rev: Like Nos. 32–34

| 46 | 1 Farthing 1902–10 | 1.00 | 3.00 | 12.00 |

| 47 | ½ Penny 1902–10 | 1.00 | 5.00 | 15.00 |
| 48 | 1 Penny 1902–10 | 1.00 | 5.00 | 15.00 |

Silver
Obv: Like No. 51
Rev: Value in wreath

49	3 Pence 1902–10	2.00	7.00	12.00
	1904–6 . . . 5			
50	6 Pence 1902–10	4.00	15.00	25.00
	1903–9 . . . 8			

| 51 | 1 Shilling 1902–10 | 5.00 | 20.00 | 30.00 |
| | 1903,4,07–9 . . . 12 1905 . . . 55 | | | |

| 52 | 1 Florin 1902–10 | 12.00 | 30.00 | 60.00 |
| | 1903–4,09 . . . 40 1906–8 . . . 25 1905 . . . 65 | | | |

Rev: Like No. 69

53	½ Crown 1902–10	10.00	40.00	80.00
	1903 . . . 60 1904 . . . 40			
	1905 . . . 180 1906–9 . . . 20			

| 54 | 1 Crown 1902 | 50.00 | 125.00 | 185.00 |

Maundy Coins

A55	1 Penny 1902–10	8.00	11.00	15.00
B55	2 Pence 1902–10	8.00	11.00	15.00
C55	3 Pence 1902–10	8.00	11.00	15.00
D55	4 Pence 1902–10	8.00	11.00	15.00

Unless otherwise noted, prices are for coins in very
fine, extremely fine, and uncirculated condition.

Gold

56	*F266* ½ Sovereign 1902–10	90.00	105.00	140.00
			Proof . . . 200.00	
57*	*F265* 1 Sovereign 1902–10	150.00	165.00	180.00
			Proof . . . 325.00	
58	*F264* 2 Pounds 1902	300.00	425.00	600.00
			Proof . . . 675.00	
59	*F263* 5 Pounds 1902	600.00	850.00	1200.
			Proof . . . 1350.	

68	1 Florin 1911–26	5.00	10.00	22.00
	1925 . . . 50		Proof . . . 75.00	

GEORGE V 1910–36

Bronze

60	1 Farthing 1911–36	.50	1.00	2.00
61	½ Penny 1911–27	.50	3.00	7.00
62	½ Penny 1928–36	.50	1.00	4.00
63	1 Penny 1911–27	.50	3.00	7.50
64	1 Penny 1928–36	.50	.75	4.00
	1933 . . . Rare			

During the period 1925–27 the effigy was reduced in size. The difference is greatest on Nos. 62 and 64.

69	½ Crown 1911–27	6.50	12.00	20.00
	1925 . . . 18		Proof . . . 90.00	

70	3 Pence 1927–36	.75	1.50	3.50
	1928 . . . 3		Proof . . . 55.00	
71	6 Pence 1927–36	1.00	1.50	6.00
			Proof . . . 22.00	

Silver

The silver coins were debased to .500 fine during 1920, but this change was not denoted on the coins.

65	3 Pence 1911–26	.75	3.00	7.00
			Proof . . . 30.00	
66	6 Pence 1911–27	1.50	4.50	10.00
			Proof . . . 25.00	
67	1 Shilling 1911–27	2.50	5.00	15.00
			Proof . . . 30.00	

72	1 Shilling 1927–36	1.50	3.00	8.00
			Proof . . . 30.00	
73	1 Florin 1927–36	3.00	4.50	15.00
	1932 . . . 25		Proof . . . 70.00	

74	½ Crown 1927–36	3.50	4.50	15.00
	1930 . . . 15		Proof . . . 40.00	

75 1 Crown 1927–36   80.00 150.00 200.00
          1932,36 . . . 150   Proof . . . 200.00

Silver Jubilee

76 1 Crown 1935   9.00 12.00 18.00
                              Proof . . . 375.00

Maundy Coins

First Issue
Silver

A81 1 Penny 1911–20	5.00	10.00	15.00
B81 2 Pence 1911–20	5.00	10.00	20.00
C81 3 Pence 1911–20	2.00	5.00	20.00
D81 4 Pence 1911–20	5.00	10.00	20.00

Second Issue

E81 1 Penny 1921–36	5.00	10.00	15.00
F81 2 Pence 1921–36	5.00	10.00	20.00
G81 3 Pence 1921–36	2.00	5.00	20.00
H81 4 Pence 1921–26	5.00	10.00	20.00

Gold

77 *F270* ½ Sovereign 1911–15	65.00	70.00	110.00
78* *F269* 1 Sovereign 1911–25	125.00	135.00	165.00
79 *F268* 2 Pounds 1911			1250.
80 *F267* 5 Pounds 1911			2250.

EDWARD VIII 1936
Some 3 Pence were minted as patterns and a few
escaped into circulation. These are very rare.

GEORGE VI 1936–1952
First Coinage

Bronze

82 1 Farthing 1937–48   .15   .50   1.50
                                   Proof . . . 4.50

83 ½ Penny 1937–48   .15   .50   2.00
                                Proof . . . 6.00

Rev: Similar to Nos. 32–34

84 1 Penny 1937–48   .15   .50   2.00
                                Proof . . . 7.50

Nickel-Brass

85 3 Pence 1937–48   .25   2.00   4.00
          1946 . . . 9   Proof . . . 4.50

Silver

86 3 Pence 1937–44   .50   1.00   3.00
          1942–44 . . . 4   Proof . . . 7.50
87 6 Pence 1937–46   .50   1.00   3.00
                                Proof . . . 7.50

A. English Crest   B. Scottish Crest

88 1 Shilling 1937–46, rev.
A   .50   1.00   4.00
                                Proof . . . 12.00

*Unless otherwise noted, prices are for coins in very
fine, extremely fine, and uncirculated condition.*

89 1 Shilling 1937–46, rev.
B   .50   1.00   4.00
Proof . . . 12.00

A93	1 Penny 1937–48	5.00	15.00	20.00
B93	2 Pence 1937–48	5.00	15.00	20.00
C93	3 Pence 1937–48	5.00	15.00	20.00
D93	4 Pence 1937–48	5.00	15.00	20.00

90   2 Shllings 1937–46   .50   1.00   4.50
Proof . . . 12.00

Cupro-Nickel
Designs like Nos. 87–91

95	6 Pence 1947–48	.15	.50	2.00
96	1 Shilling 1947–48, rev.			
	A	.15	.50	2.00
97	1 Shilling 1947–48, rev.			
	B	.15	.50	2.00
98	2 Shillings 1947–48	.25	.50	3.00
99	½ Crown 1947–48	.25	.50	3.00

Gold

100	F274	½ Sovereign 1937	Proof 250.00
101	F273	1 Sovereign 1937	Proof 525.00
102*	F272	2 Pounds 1937	Proof 650.00
103	F271	5 Pounds 1937	Proof 1250.

91   ½ Crown 1937–46   1.00   2.00   6.00
Proof . . . 15.00

Second Coinage
Obv: IND. IMP. omitted
Rev: Like Nos. 82–85

Bronze

92   1 Crown 1937   14.50   16.00   20.00
Proof . . . 50.00

104	1 Farthing 1949–52	.15	.50	2.00
			Proof . . . 3.00	
105	½ Penny 1949–52	.15	.50	1.00
			Proof . . . 4.50	
106	1 Penny 1949–51	.15	.25	1.00
	1950 . . . 9 1951 . . . 10		Proof . . . 18.00	

Maundy Coins

Nickel-Brass

107 3 Pence (12 sided)

1949–52	.25	1.00	4.00
1949 . . . 7		Proof . . . 7.50	

Cupro-Nickel

Obv: Like Nos. 86–91
Rev: sim., IND. IMP. omitted

108 6 Pence 1949–52	.25	.75	3.00
1952 . . . 3		Proof . . . 6.00	
109 1 Shilling 1949–51, rev. A	.25	.50	7.00
		Proof . . . 9.00	
110 1 Shilling 1949–51, rev. B	.25	.50	7.00
		Proof . . . 9.00	
111 2 Shillings 1949–51	.50	2.00	5.00
		Proof . . . 12.00	
112 ½ Crown 1949–52	.50	2.00	9.00
1952 . . . Rare		Proof . . . 12.00	

Maundy Coins

Silver

A113 1 Penny 1949–52	8.00	12.00	20.00
B113 2 Pence 1949–52	8.00	12.00	20.00
C113 3 Pence 1949–52	8.00	12.00	20.00
D113 4 Pence 1949–52	8.00	12.00	20.00

Cupro-Nickel

114 5 Shillings 1951   Prooflike . . . 7.50

ELIZABETH II 1952–
1953 Coronation Coins

Bronze

116 1 Farthing 1953	.10	.20	1.00
		Proof . . . 8.00	
117 ½ Penny 1953	.15	.25	3.00
		Proof . . . 4.50	
118 1 Penny 1953	2.00	3.00	5.00
		Proof . . . 7.50	

Nickel-Brass

119 3 Pence 1953	.25	.50	2.00
		Proof . . . 5.00	

Cupro-Nickel

120* 6 Pence 1953	.10	.25	1.00
		Proof . . . 4.00	
121 1 Shilling 1953, rev. A	.10	.25	2.00
		Proof . . . 5.00	
122* 1 Shilling 1953, rev. B	.50	1.00	3.00
		Proof . . . 5.00	

123 2 Shillings 1953	.25	.50	3.00
		Proof . . . 8.00	
124 ½ Crown 1953	.25	.50	3.00
		Proof . . . 10.00	

Unless otherwise noted, prices are for coins in very
fine, extremely fine, and uncirculated condition.

125 5 Shillings 1953   .75   2.00   7.50
       Proof . . . 20.00

Maundy Coins

Silver

A126 1 Penny 1953		65.00
B126 2 Pence 1953		65.00
C126 3 Pence 1953		65.00
D126 4 Pence 1953		65.00

Second Coinage
Obv: BRITT: OMN: omitted

Bronze

127 1 Farthing 1954–56   .25   .50   1.25

128 ½ Penny 1954–67   .10   .15   .25
       Proof . . . 1.75

A128 1 Penny 1954–70   .10   .15   .25
     1954 . . . Unique   Proof . . . 3.50

Nickel-Brass
129 3 Pence 1954–70   .10   .20   .50
       Proof . . . 3.50

Cupro-Nickel

Coins dated 1970 were struck in proof only.

130 6 Pence 1954–70	.10	.20	.50
		Proof . . . 2.50	
131* 1 Shilling 1954–70, rev. A	.10	.20	.50
		Proof . . . 2.50	
132 1 Shilling 1954–70, rev. B	.10	.20	.50
		Proof . . . 3.50	
133 2 Shillings 1954–70	.15	.25	.60
		Proof . . . 3.00	
134 ½ Crown 1954–70	.25	.50	2.00
		Proof . . . 3.00	
136 5 Shillings 1960	.50	2.00	7.50
		Polished Die . . . 9.00	

Maundy Coins

Silver

A135 1 Penny 1954–	25.00
B135 2 Pence 1954–	25.00
C135 3 Pence 1954–	25.00
D135 4 Pence 1954–	25.00

Gold

137 *F275* 1 Sovereign
     1957–68   125.00 130.00 140.00

No. 137 was issued for overseas distribution only.

Later issues in *Current Coins of the World*

GREECE

Southernmost of the Balkan states in eastern Europe, extending down into the Mediterranean Sea. An agricultural nation, it exports tobacco, citrus fruits, currants, olives, leather and hides. Area: 50,547 square miles. Capital: *Athens*.

Monetary System:
100 Lepta = 1 Drachma

GEORGIOS I 1863–1913
First Coinage

Copper

Obv: Young head

1	1 Lepton 1869–70	5.00	15.00	35.00
2	2 Lepta 1869	7.00	20.00	50.00
3	5 Lepta 1869–70	5.00	15.00	45.00
4	10 Lepta 1869–70	10.00	20.00	65.00

Silver

5	20 Lepta 1869–83	5.00	25.00	60.00
6	50 Lepta 1868–83	5.00	20.00	45.00
	1868 . . . Rare.			

7	1 Drachma 1868–83	12.00	45.00	125.00
8	2 Drachmai 1868–83	75.00	375.00	750.00

Gold

24	F8 5 Drachmai 1876	450.00	850.00	1500.
25	F7 10 Drachmai 1876	450.00	750.00	1000.

A25	F6 20 Drachmai 1876	200.00	375.00	600.00

Second Coinage
Copper

Obv: Older head

10	1 Lepton 1878–79	1.00	10.00	30.00
11	2 Lepta 1878	2.00	10.00	40.00
12	5 Lepta 1878–82	2.00	10.00	40.00
13	10 Lepta 1878–82	5.00	15.00	50.00

Silver

14	5 Drachmai 1875–76	30.00	75.00	175.00

Gold

26	F9 20 Drachmai 1884	100.00	150.00	275.00
27	F5 50 Drachmai 1876	4500.	7000.	10,000.
28	F4 100 Drachmai 1876	7500.	15,000.	20,000

Unless otherwise noted, prices are for coins in very
fine, extremely fine, and uncirculated condition.

Third Coinage

Cupro-Nickel

16	5 Lepta 1894–95	1.00	5.00	17.00
17	10 Lepta 1894–95	2.00	7.00	20.00
18	20 Lepta 1893–95	2.00	7.00	20.00

For similar coins dated 1900, see CRETE.

Nickel

19	5 Lepta 1912	1.00	5.00	15.00
20	10 Lepta 1912	1.00	5.00	15.00

21	20 Lepta 1912	1.00	7.00	35.00

Silver

22	1 Drachma 1910–11	5.00	20.00	65.00
23	2 Drachmai 1911	10.00	40.00	100.00

KONSTANTINOS I
Second Reign 1920–22

Aluminum

29	10 Lepta 1922	1.00	5.00	15.00

Cupro-Nickel

30	50 Lepta 1921	500.00	800.00	1250.

No. 30 was not issued to circulation.

REPUBLIC 1924–1935

Cupro-Nickel

31	20 Lepta 1926	1.00	5.00	15.00
32	50 Lepta 1926	1.00	5.00	15.00
33	1 Drachma 1926	1.00	5.00	25.00
34	2 Drachmai 1926	1.00	7.00	40.00

Nickel

35	5 Drachmai 1930	1.00	5.00	50.00

Silver

36	10 Drachmai 1930	5.00	20.00	75.00

37	20 Drachmai 1930	5.00	20.00	75.00

GEORGIOS II
Second Reign 1935–47
Restoration Commemoratives

Silver

Rev: Like Nos. 7–8

A37 100 Drachmai 1935   – 400.00 –
Proof . . . 700.00

Gold

B37 *F11* 20 Drachmai 1935   Proof . . . 5000.00
C37 *F10* 100 Drachmai 1935   Proof . . . 7500.00
Nos. A37, B37 and C37 were struck in 1939 and were
not issued to circulation.

GENERAL COINAGE

Aluminum

38 5 Lepta 1954, 71	.05	.10	.25

39 10 Lepta 1954–71	.05	.10	.25
40 20 Lepta 1954–71	.05	.10	.25

PAULOS I 1947–1964

Cupro-Nickel

41 50 Lepta 1954–65	.10	.25	1.00
1957 . . . 10.			
42 1 Drachma 1954–65	.20	.30	1.00
43 2 Drachmai 1954–65	.50	1.00	4.00
44 5 Drachmai 1954, 65	.50	1.00	3.00

Nickel

45 10 Drachmai 1959, 65	.50	1.00	3.00

Silver

46 20 Drachmai 1960, 65	3.00	5.00	10.00

Centennial of Royal Greek Dynasty

47 30 Drachmai 1963	6.00	8.00	12.00

Later issues in *Current Coins of the World.*

GREENLAND
(Gronland)

An integral part of Denmark; a large island between the
North Atlantic and the Polar Sea. About four-fifths of the
island is ice-capped. Exports: cryolite, fish and fur.
Area: 840,000 square miles. Capital: *Godthaab.*

Monetary System:
100 Ore = 1 Krone

Unless otherwise noted, prices are for coins in very
fine, extremely fine, and uncirculated condition.

Cupro-Nickel

5	25 Ore 1926	1.75	3.75	7.50
6	25 Ore (center hole) 1926	9.50	15.00	35.00

Aluminum-Bronze

7	50 Ore 1926	3.00	4.50	10.00
8	1 Krone 1926	2.50	5.00	12.50

Brass

9	5 Kroner 1944	25.00	40.00	60.00

Aluminum-Bronze

10	1 Krone 1957	4.50	7.00	12.50

Cupro-Nickel

10a	1 Krone 1960, 64	3.50	4.50	6.00

GUADELOUPE

Two large islands in the Caribbean near Antigua. They have been French possessions since 1634. Exports: sugar, rum, cacao, vanilla and bananas. Area: 686 square miles. Capital: *Basse-Terre.*

Monetary System:
100 Centimes = 1 Franc

Cupro-Nickel

Obv: Indian Chief Karukera

1	50 Centimes 1903, 21	6.00	18.50	50.00
2	1 Franc 1903, 21	12.00	27.50	60.00

GUATEMALA

North Central America, with Mexico bounding it on the north. The main port is Puerto Barrios on the Atlantic. Four-fifths of all exports is coffee. Language: Spanish. Area: 42,042 square miles. Capital: *Guatemala City.*

Monetary System:
8 Reales = 1 Peso
100 Centavos = 1 Peso to 1924
100 Centavos = 1 Quetzal 1924–

REPUBLIC 1839–
First Coinage

Silver

1	¼ Real 1859–69	4.00	8.00	20.00
	1859 . . . 500. 1864–65 . . . 40.			

Obv: Rafael Carrera, President 1851–65

2	½ Real 1859–61	15.00	50.00	100.00
	1859 . . . 35.			
3	1 Real 1859–60	15.00	50.00	200.00
4	2 Reales 1859	300.00	700.00	2500.
5	2 Reales 1860–61, modi-			
	fied dies	15.00	35.00	150.00
6	4 Reales 1860–61	15.00	60.00	400.00
7	1 Peso 1859	250.00	750.00	3500.
	Modified dies both sides			
8	½ Real 1862–65	6.00	15.00	50.00
9	1 Real 1861–65	5.00	12.00	20.00
10*	2 Reales 1862–65	6.00	15.00	75.00
11	4 Reales 1863, 65	15.00	40.00	200.00
12	1 Peso 1862–65	22.00	50.00	400.00
	1862 . . . 75.			

Gold

| 13 | F37 | 4 Reales 1860–64 | 30.00 | 40.00 | 50.00 |
| 14 | F36 | 1 Peso 1859–60 | 45.00 | 55.00 | 75.00 |

15	F35	2 Pesos 1859	150.00	225.00	400.00
16*	F34	4 Pesos 1861–62	500.00	700.00	1000.
17	F33	8 Pesos 1864	750.00	1000.	1500.
18	F31	16 Pesos 1863 (36mm)		3500. 7000.	10,000
19	F32	16 Pesos 1865 (33mm)		4500. 8000.	12,000

Second Coinage

New Legend:
R. CARRERA FUNDADOR
Silver
Designs similar to Nos. 8–19

20	½ Real 1867–69	6.00	15.00	35.00
21	1 Real 1866–67	9.00	20.00	80.00
22	1 Real 1868–69, modified arms	12.00	30.00	80.00
23	2 Reales 1866–69	7.00	15.00	50.00
24	4 Reales 1867–68	10.00	30.00	150.00
25	1 Peso 1866–69, fineness "10D 20G"	18.00	40.00	250.00

Gold

| 26 | F43 | 4 Pesos 1866–69 | 225.00 | 350.00 | 600.00 |

| 27 | F41 | 8 Pesos 1869 | | Very Rare |
| 28 | F39 | 16 Pesos 1867, 69 | 650.00 | 900.00 | 1500. |

No. 27 is probably not a regular issue.

Third Coinage
100 Centimos = 1 Peso 1869–70
100 Centavos = 1 Peso 1870–71

Bronze

| 34 | 1 Centavo 1871 | 5.00 | 9.00 | 18.00 |

Silver
Designs like Nos. 23–25

| 29 | 25 Centimos 1869–70 | 20.00 | 60.00 | 350.00 |
| 30 | 1 Peso 1869–71, fineness "0.900" | 16.00 | 30.00 | 150.00 |

| 35 | 50 Centavos 1870 | 15.00 | 40.00 | 150.00 |

Gold
Designs like Nos. 26–28

31	F42	5 Pesos 1869	175.00	250.00	400.00
32	F40	10 Pesos 1869	225.00	350.00	700.00
33	F38	20 Pesos 1869	450.00	650.00	1000.

Fourth Coinage
After 1871 the silver coinage returned to the Real system while gold was struck in the decimal system.

8 Reales = 1 Peso

.900 Silver

Obv: Short-rayed sun

| 36 | ¼ Real 1872–78 | 2.00 | 4.00 | 8.00 |

| 37 | ½ Real 1872–73 | 5.00 | 12.00 | 50.00 |

Unless otherwise noted, prices are for coins in very fine, extremely fine, and uncirculated condition.

38	1 Real 1872–78	8.00	20.00	75.00
39	2 Reales 1872–73	6.00	15.00	75.00

No fineness indicated

36a	¼ Real 1878, G on rev.	2.00	5.00	15.00

No. 36a has three minor varieties: large (illus.), medium or small G.

37a	½ Real 1878, 93	5.00	15.00	40.00
38a	1 Real 1878	15.00	35.00	100.00

.835 Silver
Obv: Like No. 36

36b	¼ Real 1878, rev. as No. 36	4.00	8.00	25.00
36c	¼ Real 1878–79, rev. as No.42	3.00	7.00	20.00

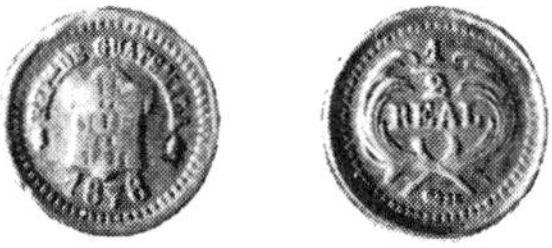

37b	½ Real 1878–79	4.00	6.00	15.00

Obv: Long-rayed sun
Rev: Modified wreath

42	¼ Real 1879–86	2.00	4.00	8.00
	1883, 85 . . . 15.			

No fineness indicated
Obv: Like No. 36

45	¼ Real 1887–88, rev. lion	2.00	4.00	6.00
46	¼ Real 1889, G below mountains, date below wreath	3.00	5.00	10.00
47	¼ Real 1889–91, 5 stars below wreath	2.00	4.00	6.00

Obv: Like No. 42

48	¼ Real 1892–93, rev. lion	2.00	4.00	6.00
	1892 . . . 100.			
49	¼ Real 1893–94, 3 stars below wreath	2.00	3.00	5.00
	1894 . . . 20.			

Seated Liberty Design
.900 Silver

Obv: Arms with small wreath
Rev: Seated Liberty

54	4 Reales 1873–79	50.00	125.00	400.00
56	1 Peso 1872–73, date at bottom	35.00	75.00	400.00
57*	1 Peso 1878–79, date at top	300.00	500.00	1500.

Obv: Arms with large wreath

52	1 Real 1879	25.00	60.00	250.00
53	2 Reales 1879	8.00	35.00	250.00
58	1 Peso 1879	300.00	500.00	1500.
58a	1 Peso 1888–93, modified Liberty	500.00	1000.	2500.
	1893 . . . 1000.			

.835 Silver

59	½ Real 1879–80, "½ RL"	3.00	7.00	35.00
60	½ Real 1880–90, "MEDIO REAL"	3.00	5.00	8.00
52a	1 Real 1883–93	4.00	8.00	18.00
53a*	2 Reales 1881, 92–93	15.00	35.00	125.00
	1892 . . . 150. 1893 . . . Rare.			
54a	4 Reales 1892	200.00	400.00	750.00

No fineness indicated

64*	½ Real 1893, sm. wreath	50.00	100.00	200.00
65	½ Real 1893, lg. wreath	3.00	6.00	15.00

Gold

66 *F45* 5 Pesos 1872–78   250.00 375.00 600.00
67* *F44* 20 Pesos 1877–78 5000. 10,000. 15,000.

73 1 Peso 1882, 89   40.00 100.00 250.00
       1889 . . . 250.

Second Decimal System
1881–1882

Bronze

68 1 Centavo 1881 (all
       struck over No. 34)   5.00 10.00 25.00

Silver
Design similar to No. 62

69 25 Centavos 1881–91   5.00 10.00 25.00
69a 25 Centavos 1890–93,
       larger rev. lettering   5.00   7.00 15.00
           1890 . . . 40.

70 5 Centavos 1881   20.00 40.00 100.00
71 10 Centavos 1881   25.00 50.00 150.00

72 25 Centavos 1882   225.00 400.00   –

Real System Continued

New Dies 1894
Silver

74 ¼ Real 1894–99   1.00   2.00   4.00
Coins dated 1893 are patterns.

75 ½ Real 1894–97, .835
       fine   1.00   2.00   4.00
76 ½ Real 1899, .600 fine   2.00   4.00 10.00
77 1 Real 1894–98, .835
       fine   1.50   3.00   6.00
78 1 Real 1899, no fineness 3.00   7.00 15.00
79 1 Real 1899, .750 fine 100.00 175.00 500.00
80 1 Real 1899, .600 fine   3.00   5.00 10.00
81* 1 Real 1899–1900, .500
       fine   1.50   3.00   5.00
82 2 Reales 1894–99, .835
       fine   2.50   3.00   5.00
           1899 . . . 40.
83 4 Reales 1894, .900 fine 8.00 12.00 40.00
84 1 Peso 1894–97, .900
       fine   10.00 15.00 40.00

Cupro-Nickel
Designs similar to Nos. 74, 75, 77

85 ¼ Real 1900–01   .50   2.00   5.00
86 ½ Real 1900–01   .75   2.00   5.00
87 1 Real 1900–12   1.00   2.00   5.00

Counterstamped Issues

Silver

Dies of No. 75 (½ Real) dated 1894 stamped on Pesos
of Chile, Soles of Peru and others.

**Unless otherwise noted, prices are for coins in very
fine, extremely fine, and uncirculated condition.**

88* (1 Peso) on Peru Sol
   1864–94   25.00   30.00   60.00
88a (1 Peso) on Chile Peso
   1867–91   28.00   37.00   85.00
88b (1 Peso) on Peru 5 Pe-
   setas 1880   100.00 200.00 500.00
This counterstamp is known on several other Latin
American crowns. All are very rare.

PROVISIONAL ISSUES
Bronze

89	12½ Centavos 1915	2.00	4.00	7.00
90	25 Centavos 1915	2.00	4.00	7.00

Aluminum-Bronze

91	50 Centavos 1922	2.00	5.00	15.00

92	1 Peso 1923	2.00	5.00	15.00

93	5 Pesos 1923	3.00	10.00	50.00

COINAGE REFORM
November 26, 1924
Bronze

95	1 Centavo 1925	4.00	12.00	25.00
96	1 Centavo 1929, larger arms	4.00	12.00	25.00

Brass

94	½ Centavo 1932, 46	.25	1.00	2.00
97	1 Centavo 1932–49	.35	1.00	5.00
98	2 Centavos 1932	2.00	6.00	30.00

Silver

Obv: Long-tailed quetzal on scroll

99	5 Centavos 1925, 44–49	1.50	3.00	6.00
100	10 Centavos 1925, 44–49	2.00	3.00	8.00

Obv: Short-tailed quetzal on scroll

99a	5 Centavos 1928–43	1.50	3.00	7.00
100a	10 Centavos 1928–43, 47	2.00	3.00	8.00
	1934, 36 . . . 8.			
101	¼ Quetzal 1925, lettered edge	6.00	15.00	50.00
102	¼ Quetzal 1926–29, diff. dies	5.00	10.00	40.00
102a	¼ Quetzal 1946–49, reeded edge	4.00	8.00	22.00

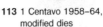

113 1 Centavo 1958–64,
modified dies .10 .20 .50

103	½ Quetzal 1925	20.00	40.00	125.00
104	1 Quetzal 1925	500.00	800.00	2000.

Gold

105	*F50* 5 Quetzales 1926	200.00	275.00	400.00
106	*F49* 10 Quetzales 1926	300.00	450.00	700.00
107	*F48* 20 Quetzales 1926	450.00	650.00	1000.

Wartime Issues

Brass

108	1 Centavo 1943–44	3.00	10.00	25.00
109	2 Centavos 1943–44	3.00	10.00	35.00

Silver

110	25 Centavos 1943	5.00	10.00	50.00

New Designs

Brass

No. 111   No. 112

111 1 Centavo 1949–54, sm.
hd. .15 .50 5.00
112 1 Centavo 1954–58, lg.
hd. .10 .30 2.00

Silver

No. 114   No. 115
Obv: Short-tailed quetzal on scroll
Rev: Ceiba tree

114 5 Centavos 1949, sm.
tree 3.00 8.00 20.00
115 5 Centavos 1950–58, lg.
tree .50 1.50 3.00

Obv: Short-tailed quetzal on scroll
Rev: Mayan monolith

117 10 Centavos 1949–58,
small monolith 1.00 1.50 4.00
117a 10 Centavos 1957–58,
large monolith 1.00 1.50 5.00
Obv: Long-tailed quetzal on scroll
115a 5 Centavos 1958–59,
rev. like No. 115 .50 1.00 3.00
117b 10 Centavos 1958–59,
rev. like No. 117 1.00 2.00 4.00

119 25 Centavos 1950–59 2.50 5.00 7.00

Modified Dies

116 5 Centavos 1960–64 .50 .75 1.00
118 10 Centavos 1960–64 .75 .85 1.00

Unless otherwise noted, prices are for coins in very
fine, extremely fine, and uncirculated condition.

120 25 Centavos 1960–64   1.00   2.00   4.00

121 50 Centavos 1962–63   2.00   6.00   8.00
Later issues in *Current Coins of the World.*

GUERNSEY

One of the Channel Islands, 30 miles off the coast of France, famous for its cattle. Though a dependency of the British monarch, Guernsey is administered by its own laws. Area: 29 square miles. Capital: *St.* Peter Port.

Monetary System:
8 Doubles = 1 Penny

Copper

A1	1 Double 1830	3.00	8.50	17.50
			Proof . . . 75.00	
B1	2 Doubles 1858	20.00	45.00	75.00
C1	4 Doubles 1830,58	5.00	10.00	25.00
			Proof . . . 125.00	

D1	8 Doubles 1834, 58	10.00	30.00	75.00
			Proof . . . 200.00	

Bronze

1	1 Double 1868–1911	1.00	2.00	7.00
			Proof . . . 50.00	
2	2 Doubles 1868–1911	3.00	6.00	17.50
	1868,74,1906,08 . . . 15		Proof . . . 60.00	
3	4 Doubles 1864–1911	3.00	6.50	17.50
	1864, 1908 . . . 15		Proof . . . 60.00	

4	8 Doubles 1864–1911	1.50	5.00	10.00
	1868,74,1911 . . . 10		Proof . . . 85.00	

Obv: Leaf cluster above shield

1a	1 Double 1911–38	1.00	2.00	7.00
2a	2 Doubles 1914–29	3.00	4.50	10.00
	1917 . . . 60			
3a	4 Doubles 1914–49	1.00	2.50	8.00
5	8 Doubles 1914–49	.75	1.25	4.50
	1934 Proof only . . . 50			

6	4 Doubles 1956–66	.75	1.25	7.50
	1966 Proof Only . . . 3		Proof . . . 9.00	

7	8 Doubles 1956, 59, 66	.15	.35	1.50
	1966 Proof Only . . . 3		Proof . . . 9.00

4	1 Franc 1962	.25	.75	1.75

Cupro-Nickel

5	5 Francs 1962	1.00	2.00	3.00

8	3 Pence 1956, thin	.20	.75	3.00
			Proof . . . 9.00
8a	3 Pence 1959, 66, thick	.15	.40	1.50
	1966 Proof Only . . . 3.25			

6	10 Francs 1962	2.00	5.00	7.50

900th Anniversary
Norman Conquest

9	10 Shillings 1966	.75	1.25	4.00
			Proof . . . 6.50

Later issues in *Current Coins of the World*.

7	25 Francs 1962	2.50	5.00	9.50
8	50 Francs 1969, Obv. like			
	No. 6	–	–	80.00

No. 8 was not released to circulation.

Later issues in *Current Coins of the World*.

GUINEA

A former French overseas territory on the west coast of Africa, which became an independent republic in 1958. Area: 94,925 square miles. Language: French. Capital: *Conakry*.

Monetary System:
100 Centimes = 1 Franc 1958–1971

HAITI

Located west of the Dominican Republic on the Caribbean island of Hispaniola, Haiti was originally a prosperous French colony. The lengthy war which gained it independence in 1803 disrupted its agricultural economy to a point from which it has never fully recovered. Coffee is the most important export crop. Most of the inhabitants are descendants of African slaves brought in during the 1700's. Area: 10,714 square miles. Languages: French, Creole. Capital: *Port-au-Prince*.

Aluminum-Bronze

Obv: President Toure

1	5 Francs 1959	3.00	5.00	10.00
2	10 Francs 1959 (Head to left)	4.00	7.50	12.50
3	25 Francs 1959	7.50	10.00	17.50

Monetary System:
100 Centimes = 1 Gourde

Unless otherwise noted, prices are for coins in very fine, extremely fine, and uncirculated condition.

Bronze

Obv: President Geffrard (1859–67)

A1	5 Centimes 1863	2.50	5.00	15.00
B1*	10 Centimes 1863	2.00	5.00	15.00
C1	20 Centimes 1863	2.50	7.50	22.50

Design similar to Nos. 6–9

1	1 Centime 1881	4.00	6.00	15.00
2	2 Centimes 1881	4.00	6.00	15.00

3	1 Centime 1886, 94, 95	3.00	5.00	12.00
4	2 Centimes 1886, 94	3.00	5.00	12.50

Silver

6	10 Centimes 1881–94	2.00	5.00	15.00
7	20 Centimes 1881–95	4.00	7.50	20.00
8	50 Centimes 1882–95	10.00	15.00	30.00
9	1 Gourde 1881–95	25.00	50.00	100.00

Insurrection 1889

Cupro-Nickel

A5	5 Centimes 1889	30.00	50.00	75.00

Bronze

Rev: Blank

5	1 Gourde ND	200.00	300.00	375.00

No. 5 is counterstamped B.P. 1G/GLH

(Bon pour 1 Gourde/General Hippolyte.)

Regular Issues

Cupro-Nickel

Obv: President Nord Alexis (1902–08)

10	5 Centimes 1904–05	.50	3.00	10.00
11	10 Centimes 1906	.65	3.50	11.00
12	20 Centimes 1907	1.00	4.00	12.00
13	50 Centimes 1907–08	1.50	5.00	13.00

14	5 Centimes 1904	5.00	10.00	35.00

Obv: President Estime (1946–50)

15	5 Centimes 1949	.25	.50	1.50

16	10 Centimes 1949	.35	.75	1.75

Copper-Nickel-Zinc

Obv: President Magloire (1950–56)

17	5 Centimes 1953	.10	.20	.40
18	10 Centimes 1953	.15	.30	.60
19	20 Centimes 1956	.50	.75	1.75

Obv: President F. Duvalier (1957–71)

20	5 Centimes 1958, 70	.05	.10	.15
21	10 Centimes 1958, 70	.10	.15	.25
22	20 Centimes 1970	.20	.30	.85

Later issues in *Current Coins of the World.*

HAWAII

Became the 50th of the United States in 1959. It was a kingdom from 1791 until 1894 when a republic was proclaimed. The Spanish-American War brought about its annexation to the United States. Mauna Loa, on Hawaii, is the largest active volcano in the world. A great tourist center, Hawaii is also noted for its sugar and pineapple production. Capital: *Honolulu.*

Monetary System:
10 Cents = 1 Dime
100 Cents = 1 Dollar (Dala)

KAMEHAMEHA III
1825–1854

Copper

1	1 Cent 1847	100.00 200.00 600.00

Note: Many souvenir replicas exist of No. 1.

KALAKAUA I 1874–1891

Silver

2	1 Dime 1883	25.00 70.00 250.00

3	¼ Dollar 1883	20.00 45.00 175.00
4	½ Dollar 1883	65.00 90.00 750.00
5	1 Dollar 1883	150.00 350.00 2000.

Proofs exist of Nos. 2–5. All are very rare.

HEJAZ (Al-Hijaz)

The Hejaz, meaning "barrier," is the district of the rugged Mountain range lying along the northern Red Sea coast of the Arabian peninsula. It contains the Islamic holy cities of Mecca and Medina. In 1916 it gained independence from the Ottoman Empire, but was conquered by Nejd in 1925. The two countries were united in 1932 to form Saudi Arabia. Language: Arabic. Capital: *Mecca.*

Monetary System:
40 Para = 1 Ghirsh
20 Ghirsh = 1 Riyal
100 Ghirsh = 1 Dinar

HUSAIN IBN ALI
1916–1924

(Accession Date AH 1334 on Coins)
Nickel or Cupro-Nickel

Counterstamp incuse "al-Hijaz" in Arabic

1	on Turkish 10 Para	VF . . . 40.00
2	on Turkish 20 Para	VF . . . 12.50
3*	on Turkish 40 Para	VF . . . 15.00

Nos. 4–5 in previous editions are now believed to be counterfeits.

Silver

8	on Turkish or Egyptian 2 Ghirsh	VF . . . 50.00
9	on similar 5 Ghirsh	VF . . . 40.00

Unless otherwise noted, prices are for coins in very fine, extremely fine, and uncirculated condition.

10	on similar 10 Ghirsh	VF . . . 40.00
11	on similar 20 Ghirsh	VF . . . 60.00
12	on Austria No. 55	VF . . . 50.00

Copies of the Hejaz counterstamps on some or all of the above silver types are believed to have been produced in recent years.

Regular Issues
Copper

16	⅛ Ghirsh Yr. 5 (1920) 12–13mm	15.00	20.00	–
17	¼ Ghirsh Yr. 5 (16mm)	7.50	10.00	–
18*	½ Ghirsh Yr. 5 (18–19mm)	7.50	11.00	–
19	1 Ghirsh Yr. 5 (21–22mm)	10.00	15.00	–

Nos. 16–19 are of variable thickness. They are sometimes found with light silver wash.

20*	¼ Ghirsh Yr. 8 (1923) 17mm	6.50	9.00	–
21	½ Ghirsh Yr. 8 (19mm)			Rare
22	1 Ghirsh Yr. 8 (21mm)	8.50	15.00	–

Silver

23	5 Ghirsh Yr. 8 (24mm)	30.00	50.00	–
24*	10 Ghirsh Yr. 8 (28mm)	100.00	150.00	–
25	20 Ghirsh Yrs. 8–9 (37mm)	50.00	95.00	–

Gold

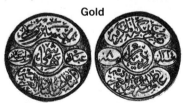

| 26 | *F1* 1 Dinar Yr. 8 | 175.00 | 275.00 | – |

For later issues see SAUDI ARABIA.

HONDURAS

A Central American republic bounded on the north by Guatemala and on the south by Nicaragua. Fertile soil, rich forests and abundant mineral resources have not been developed. Exports mostly to the United States are bananas (65%), coconuts, and hardwoods. Area: 43,-277 square miles. Language: Spanish. Capital: *Tegucigalpa.*

Monetary System:
8 Reales = 1 Peso to 1871
100 Centavos = 1 Peso 1871–1926
100 Centavos = 1 Lempira 1926–

Provisional Issues
Bronze

P1	1 Peso 1862	12.00	25.00	100.00
P2	2 Pesos 1862	15.00	30.00	150.00
P3	4 Pesos 1862	18.00	40.00	200.00
P4	8 Pesos 1862	35.00	100.00	500.00

Regular Issues
Cupro-Nickel

1	⅛ Real 1869–70	6.00	15.00	30.00
2	¼ Real 1869–70	3.00	8.00	15.00
3	½ Real 1869–71	5.00	12.00	22.00
	1871 . . . 100.			
4	1 Real 1869–70	10.00	25.00	75.00
	1869 . . . 25.			

Decimal Issues
First Coinage
Bronze

| 9 | 1 Centavo 1878–80 | 40.00 | 100.00 | 500.00 |
| | 1878 . . . 400. | | | |

Silver

10	5 Centavos 1879	2000.	3500.	–
11*	10 Centavos 1878	1750.	3000.	–
12	50 Centavos 1879	1000.	1500.	–

1 Peso 1878 is a pattern.

Second Coinage

Silver

5	5 Centavos 1871	400.00	800.00	2000.
6	10 Centavos 1871	45.00	150.00	600.00
7*	25 Centavos 1871	10.00	25.00	150.00
8	50 Centavos 1871	15.00	45.00	200.00

Nos. 5-8 were struck ca. 1879-82.

Third Coinage

Bronze

Standard Obv: Large pyramid

13	½ Centavo 1881-91	30.00	50.00	150.00
	1891 . . . 300.			

14	1 Centavo 1881-1907	8.00	20.00	60.00

Obv: Die of No. 14

15	1 Centavo 1890-1908,			
	rev. altered from No. 21	6.00	10.00	15.00

Obv: Die of No. 14

16	1 Centavo ND, rev. of No.			
	9	500.00	800.00	–

Obv: Arms in wreath (die of No. 21)

17	1 Centavo 1890-1908,			
	rev. altered from No. 21.	10.00	25.00	75.00

Obv: Die of No. 6

18	1 Centavo 1895, rev. of			
	No. 9	1000.	2000.	–

Silver

Standard obv: Arms in wreath

19	5 Centavos 1884-1902	20.00	50.00	150.00
	1902 . . . 200.			
21	10 Centavos 1884-1900	15.00	40.00	200.00
	1900 . . . 200.			

Obv: Die of No. 13

20	5 Centavos 1886, 95-96	12.00	25.00	50.00
	1895 . . . 75.			

Obv: Die of No. 6

22	10 Centavos 1886, 95,			
	ND, rev. like No. 21			
	(vars.)	80.00	250.00	–

.900 Silver

23	25 Centavos 1883-1912	9.00	20.00	80.00
	1912 . . . 300.			
24	50 Centavos 1883-1910	15.00	50.00	150.00
	1896 . . . 500. 1910 . . . 1000.			

Obv: Without weight
Rev: Small lettering

25	1 Peso 1881-83	75.00	150.00	400.00

Obv: Weight above UN PESO
Rev: Large lettering

25a 1 Peso 1883–1914   35.00   70.00 200.00
         1883 . . . 200. 1893 . . . 500. 1899 . . . 2000.
         1904 . . . 100. 1914 . . . 900.
25b 1 Peso 1894–96, obv. of
         No. 25, rev. of No. 25a   40.00   90.00 300.00

.835 Silver

23a* 25 Centavos
         1899–1913   10.00   30.00 150.00
         1904 . . . 60.
24a 50 Centavos 1908   125.00 250.00 500.00

Gold

26 *F3* 1 Peso 1871, obv. of
        No. 5   1000.   1400.   2000.
27 *F7* 1 Peso 1888–1922   200.00 325.00 650.00
28* *F6* 5 Pesos 1888–1913 800.00 1750.   3000.
29 *F5* 10 Pesos 1889   Very Rare
30 *F4* 20 Pesos
        1888–1908   7000. 12,500. 25,000.
        1908 . . . 12,500.

Reduced Size Bronze

Obv: Dies of Nos. 13–14
Rev: Altered from Nos. 19–20
36 1 Centavo 1910   60.00 100.00 200.00
31* 2 Centavos 1908   125.00 250.00 500.00

Obv: Dies of Nos. 13–14
Rev: Altered from Nos. 13–14
32 1 Centavo 1910–11   25.00   60.00   –
33* 2 Centavos 1910–13   5.00   10.00 50.00

Obv: Die of No. 19
34* 1 Centavo 1910, rev. al-
        tered from No. 13   25.00   60.00   –
        "1610" . . . 75.
35 1 Centavo 1910–11, rev.
        altered from No. 19   10.00   25.00 75.00

Obv: Dies of Nos. 13–14
Rev: Altered from Nos. 13–14
37* 1 (Centavo) 1919–20   10.00   40.00   –
38 2 (Centavos) 1919–20   3.00   10.00 65.00

New Coinage System
Bronze

39 1 Centavo 1935–57   .05   .10   .25
40 2 Centavos 1939–56   .05   .15   .50

Cupro-Nickel
41 5 Centavos 1931–72   .15   .30   2.00
42 10 Centavos 1932–67   .50   1.50   5.00

Silver

43 20 Centavos 1931–58   1.50   3.00   5.00
44 50 Centavos 1931–51   3.00   7.00   20.00
45 1 Lempira 1931–37   6.00   8.00   20.00
Later issues in *Current Coins of the World.*

HONG KONG

A British Crown Colony at the mouth of the Canton
River, 90 miles south of Canton, China. Often called the
"Gateway between East and West," it is an important

trans-shipment port and British naval station. Hong Kong is one of the most densely populated locations in the world. Area: 398 square miles. Languages: English, Cantonese.

Monetary System:
10 Mils = 1 Cent
100 Cents = 1 Dollar

VICTORIA 1837-1901

Bronze

1 1 Mil 1863–65, (1 Wen in
   Chinese)   3.00   5.00 10.00
       1864 . . . 750   Proof . . . 200.00
1a 1 Mil 1866, (1 Ch'ien in
   ·Chinese)   3.00   5.00 12.00

2 1 Cent 1863–1901   1.50   7.50 20.00
There are several minor die varieties of No. 2. Dates before 1900 are worth approximately twice the listed prices.

Silver

3 5 Cents 1866–1901   .75   1.50 10.00
    1866–83 . . . 6 84–98 . . . 1.50Proof . . . 200.00
4 10 Cents 1863–1901   3.00   4.50 20.00
    1864 . . . 300 1866–83 . . . 7.50 72–H . . . 35
    Proof . . . 150.00

5 20 Cents 1866–98   13.00 30.00 100.00
    1879 . . . 400 1880 . . . 150 1881 . . . 325
                      Proof . . . 300.00

6 ½ Dollar 1866–68   300.00 450.00 950.00
    1867 . . . 900   Proof . . . 1800.
8 1 Dollar 1866–68   50.00 120.00 375.00
                      Proof . . . 750.00

7 50 Cents 1890–94   25.00 65.00 150.00
    1892 . . . 75   Proof..450.00
No. 7 of 1891–92 with H mintmark has a slightly larger diameter than the other dates.

EDWARD VII 1901-1910

Bronze
9 1 Cent 1902–05   1.50   3.00 15.00

Silver

Rev: Like Nos. 3–5
10 5 Cents 1903–05   1.00   1.75   3.00
                      Proof . . . 150.00
11 10 Cents 1902–05   2.50   3.00 15.00
    1905 . . . 650   Proof . . . 100.00

Unless otherwise noted, prices are for coins in very fine, extremely fine, and uncirculated condition.

| 12 | 20 Cents 1902–05 | 35.00 | 50.00 | 150.00 |
| | 1905 . . . 450 | | Proof . . . 350.00 | |

| 13 | 50 Cents 1902–05 | 15.00 | 25.00 | 45.00 |
| | | | Proof . . . 125.00 | |

GEORGE V 1910–1936

Bronze

14	1 Cent 1919–26 (28mm)	.75	2.00	6.00
			Proof . . . 100.00	
15*	1 Cent 1931–34 (22mm)	.25	.50	1.75
			Proof . . . 45.00	

Silver

| 18 | 5 Cents 1932–33 | 1.00 | 1.50 | 3.00 |
| | | | Proof . . . 75.00 | |

Cupro-Nickel

16	5 Cents 1935	2.00	2.75	5.00
			Proof . . . 50.00	
17	10 Cents 1935–36	.40	.75	2.50
			Proof . . . 50.00	

GEORGE VI 1936–1952

Nickel

20	5 Cents 1937	.75	1.25	3.00
			Proof . . . 50.00	
21	10 Cents 1937	.50	.75	2.50
			Proof . . . 50.00	

Bronze
Obv: Larger Head

| 19 | 1 Cent 1941 | 1200. | 1500. | 2000. |

No. 19 was not issued to circulation.

Proof . . . 3500.

Nickel

22	5 Cents 1938–41	.20	.50	1.50
	1941-H . . . 300 1941-KN . . . 100			
23	10 Cents 1938–39	.20	.35	1.50
			Proof . . . 25.00	

New Legend:
KING GEORGE THE SIXTH
Nickel-Brass

24	5 Cents 1949–50	.10	.20	3.00
			Proof . . . 125.00	
25	10 Cents 1948–51	.15	.25	1.50
			Proof . . . 25.00	

Cupro-Nickel

| 26 | 50 Cents 1951 | .35 | .75 | 4.50 |
| | | | Proof . . . 75.00 | |

ELIZABETH II 1952–

Nickel-Brass

Edge: With security groove

27	5 Cents 1958–68	.10	.15	.20
	1964 . . . 5			
28	10 Cents 1955–68	.10	.15	.20
			Proof . . . 25.00	

Cupro-Nickel

| 29 | 50 Cents 1958–70 | .15 | .20 | .35 |

| 30 | 1 Dollar 1960, 70 | .25 | .45 | 1.00 |

Later issues in *Current Coins of the World.*

HUNGARY

A republic in Central Europe, formerly part of the Austro-Hungarian Empire. Allied with Germany in World War II, it was taken by Russia in 1945. Declared a republic in 1946, under Communist control industry has been nationalized and collective farming established. Area: 35,-900 square miles. Capital: *Budapest*.

Restrikes of many issues for the period covered in this book have been made at the Budapest Mint. These reportedly include dates not originally issued and pieces from mismatched dies.

Monetary System:
100 Krajczar = 1 Forint 1857–92
100 Filler = 1 Korona 1892–1921
100 Filler = 1 Pengo 1925–45
100 Filler = 1 Forint 1946–

FERENCZ JOZSEF I

(Franz Joseph of Austria)

as King of Hungary 1867–1916

Copper or Bronze

1	1 Krajczar 1868–73	1.00	2.00	7.00
	1873 . . . 60			
2	4 Krajczar 1868	6.50	15.00	25.00

3	5/10 Krajczar 1882	3.50	6.00	8.00
4	1 Krajczar 1878–88	5.00	10.00	15.00
4a*	1 Krajczar 1891–92, modified arms	4.00	6.00	9.00

Billon

Obv: Legend ends KIRALYA
Rev: Legend VALTO PENZ only

6	10 Krajczar 1868	20.00	35.00	60.00
8	20 Krajczar 1868	18.00	30.00	50.00

Obv: As Nos. 6, 8
Rev: MAGYAR KIRALYI added

7	10 Krajczar 1868–69	16.00	27.50	45.00
9	20 Krajczar 1868–69	18.00	30.00	55.00

Silver

12	1 Forint 1868–69	16.00	22.00	40.00

Gold
Obv: Emperor standing
Rev: Like No. 12

21	F84–85 1 Dukat			
	1868–70	250.00	300.00	350.00

Billon

Obv: Legend ends KIR.
Rev: As Nos. 6, 8

10	10 Krajczar 1870–88	12.00	18.00	35.00
	1868 . . . 50			
11	20 Krajczar 1870–72	35.00	60.00	100.00
	1868 . . . 50			

Nos. 10 and 11 dated 1868 are modern restrikes using reverses of Nos. 6 and 8.

Silver

13	1 Forint 1870–81 (2 vars.)	12.00	16.00	22.50

Unless otherwise noted, prices are for coins in very fine, extremely fine, and uncirculated condition.

14 1 Forint 1882–90   10.00 14.00 20.00

Gold
Rev. As No. 13

22	*F86*	1 Dukat 1877–81	900.00	1100.	1300.
		1881 . . . Rare (43 pcs.)			
22a	*F86R*	1 Dukat 1870 (Restrike) Proof . . . 100.00			
17	*F89–90*	4 Forint/10			
		Francs 1870–90	100.00	135.00	175.00
18	*F87–88*	8 Forint/20			
		Francs 1870–90	125.00	150.00	200.00

Silver
Rev: Modified arms

15 1 Forint 1890–92   12.00 17.50 30.00

Gold

19	*F89*	4 Forint/10 Francs			
		1890–92	275.00	350.00	500.00
		1892 . . . 2000 (20 pcs.)			
20	*F87*	8 Forint/20 Francs			
		1890–92	100.00	130.00	150.00

Most experts now consider the No. 16 in prior editions, the 1 Forint of 1878 commemorating the reopening of the Jozsef II mine at Selmeczbanya to be a medal. It was struck in gold and bronze, as well as silver.

KORONA SYSTEM 1892–1921

Bronze

23	1 Filler 1892–1914	.50	1.25	4.00
	1892 . . . 30 1906 . . . 150			
24	2 Filler 1892–1915	.50	1.50	4.50
	1900 . . . 110			

Nickel

25	10 Filler 1892–1914	.50	.75	3.50
27	20 Filler 1892–1914	1.00	2.00	5.00

Silver

32	1 Korona 1892–1906, lg. head	3.00	5.00	10.00
	1906 . . . 200			
32a*	1 Korona 1912–16, sm. head	3.50	6.00	12.00
	1913 . . . 65			
33	2 Korona 1912–14	5.00	8.00	15.00
34	5 Korona 1900–09	17.50	40.00	100.00

Gold

36	*F94*	10 Korona 1892–1915	70.00	80.00	90.00
	1895, 1915 . . . 2000				
A36	*F92*	20 Korona 1892–1915	95.00	120.00	135.00
B36	*F93*	20 Korona 1914, 16. Bosnian arms added to rev.	200.00	350.00	400.00
D36*	*F91*	100 Korona 1907–08	1000.	1500.	1750.

Note: All but No. B36 exist as restrikes.

Millenium Founding of Kingdom

Silver

Rev: Duke Arpad (875–907)

31 1 Korona 1896   6.00 8.00 12.50

40th Anniversary of Coronation

35 5 Korona 1907   25.00   35.00   55.00

Gold

C36 *F95* 100 Korona 1907   900.00   1000.   1200.
Restrikes of this coin are commonly found.

World War I Issues

Copper-Nickel-Zinc

26 10 Filler 1914–16   .50   1.00   4.00
     1914 . . . 200

Iron

28 2 Filler 1916–18   2.00   4.00   10.00
29 10 Filler 1915–20   15.00   20.00   35.00
30 20 Filler 1916–22   1.25   3.00   7.00
The 20 Filler 1922 struck in brass, in proof, is a modern
restrike. If in UNC it is a trial strike, worth about $15.00

REGENCY 1920–1945

Bronze

37 1 Filler 1926–39   .40   .60   1.50
38 2 Filler 1926–40   .40   .60   1.50

Cupro-Nickel

39 10 Filler 1926–40   .35   .65   2.00
40 20 Filler 1926–40   .50   .80   3.00
41 50 Filler 1926–40   .90   1.50   4.00

Silver

42 1 Pengo 1926–39   2.50   4.00   6.00

43 2 Pengo 1929–39   3.00   5.00   8.00
     1931 . . . 60

COMMEMORATIVE ISSUES
10th Year of Regency

Obv. Admiral Horthy, Regent 1920–44
Rev: Like No. 57
44 5 Pengo 1930   14.00   17.00   20.00

300th Anniversary Founding of
Pazmany University

45 2 Pengo 1935   6.00   9.00   13.50

Bicentennial
Death of Ferenc Rakoczi

46 2 Pengo 1935   5.50   8.00   11.00

50th Anniversary Death of Liszt

47 2 Pengo 1936   5.00   7.00   10.00

900th Anniversary
Death of St. Stephan

48 5 Pengo 1938   15.00   17.00   25.00

Horthy Government
Commemorative
Obv: Admiral Horthy
Rev: Like No. 57

49 5 Pengo 1939   14.00   17.00   20.00

WORLD WAR II COINAGE

Steel

50 2 Filler 1940, plain rim   2.50   4.50   6.00
50a* 2 Filler 1940–42,
    toothed rim   .30   .75   3.00

Zinc

51 2 Filler 1943–44   .30   .75   3.00

Steel

52 10 Filler 1940–42   .35   .75   2.00

53 20 Filler 1941–44   .35   .75   2.50

Aluminum

54 1 Pengo 1941–44   .35   .70   2.00
55 2 Pengo 1941–43   .50   .90   2.00

75th Birthday of Regent

57 5 Pengo 1943   2.00   3.50   5.00

PROVISIONAL
GOVERNMENT 1944–1946

Aluminum

56 5 Pengo 1945   2.00   3.00   4.00

REPUBLIC 1946–1949

Legends:
MAGYAR ALLAMI VALTOPENZ
or
MAGYAR KOZTARSASAG
Bronze

58	2 Filler 1946–47	.15	.25	.35

Aluminum

59	5 Filler 1948–51	.30	.40	.50

ALuminum-Bronze

60	10 Filler 1946–50	.40	.50	.60

10 Filler 1946, 50 in aluminum were trial strikes.

61	20 Filler 1946–50	.40	.50	.60

Aluminum

62	50 Filler 1948	1.00	1.25	1.50

63	1 Forint 1946–49	.60	.80	1.00
64	2 Forint 1946–47	1.00	1.25	1.50

Silver

Obv: Lajos Kossuth

65	5 Forint 1946, thick	7.00	8.00	10.00
66	5 Forint 1947, thin	2.25	3.50	4.50

COMMEMORATIVE ISSUES
Centennial of 1848 Revolution
Silver

Obv: Sandor Petofi

67	5 Forint 1948	3.50	6.00	8.00

Obv: Istvan Szechenyi

68	10 Forint 1948	6.00	9.00	12.00

Unless otherwise noted, prices are for coins in very fine, extremely fine, and uncirculated condition.

Obv: Mihaly Tancsics
69 20 Forint 1948   15.00 18.00 22.50

PEOPLE'S REPUBLIC 1949–
Legend:
MAGYAR NEPKOZTARSASAG
Aluminum

70 2 Filler 1950–74   .10   .15   .20
    Designs similar to Nos. 59–62
71 5 Filler 1953–74   .10   .15   .20
72 10 Filler 1950–66   .20   .25   .35
73 20 Filler 1953–66   .20   .35   .40
74 50 Filler 1953–66   .35   .60   .75

75 1 Forint 1949–52   .50   .75   1.00

Cupro-Nickel

76 2 Forint 1950–52   .50   .80   1.25

Aluminum

Obv: Different arms
80 1 Forint 1957–66   .35   .50   .75

Cupro-Nickel
81 2 Forint 1957–61   .50   .60   1.00

Copper-Nickel-Zinc
81a 2 Forint 1962–66   .40   .50   .90

10th Anniversary of Forint
Silver

Hungarian National Museum
77 10 Forint 1956   14.00 20.00 25.00

Chain Bridge, Budapest
78 20 Forint 1956   14.00 20.00 25.00

Hungarian Parliament

79   20 Forint 1956   15.00   22.00   27.50

150th Anniversary
Birth of Liszt

Silver

82   25 Forint 1961   25.00
83   50 Forint 1961   35.00

Gold

84   F103 50 Forint 1961   175.00
85   F102 100 Forint 1961   225.00
86   F101 500 Forint 1961   800.00

80th Anniversary
Birth of Bartok

Silver

87   25 Forint 1961   25.00
88   50 Forint 1961   35.00

Gold

89   F106 50 Forint 1961   175.00
90   F105 100 Forint 1961   225.00
91   F104 500 Forint 1961   800.00

Later issues in *Current Coins of the World*.

ICELAND (Island)

Island in the North Atlantic near the Arctic Circle. Now a republic, it was until 1944 a sovereign state united with Denmark under King Christian X. It is governed by the Althing (Parliament), the world's oldest parliamentary assembly. Area: 39,758 square miles. Language: Icelandic. Capital: *Reykjavik*.

Monetary System:
100 Aurar = 1 Krona

CHRISTIAN X 1912–1944

NOTES:

1. The 1930 commemorative issues (former Nos. 8–10) are considered to be medals by most authorities.

2. Some coins of 1940 and all of 1942 were struck in Great Britain without the customary Copenhagen mint marks.

Bronze

1   1 Eyrir 1926–42   2.50   5.00   7.50
2   2 Aurar 1926–42   2.50   5.00   10.00
3   5 Aurar 1926–42   7.50   12.50   30.00
    1926,31 . . . 8 1940 (no mintmark),42 . . . 1

Cupro-Nickel

4   10 Aurar 1922–40   4.00   8.00   15.00
    1925–33 . . . 20
5   25 Aurar 1922–40   2.00   4.00   12.50
    1933 . . . 8

Note: Nos. 4–5 dated 1940 are very common, and worth $3.00 each in UNC.

Aluminum-Bronze

6   1 Krona 1925–40   1.50   3.00   7.50
    1925,29 . . . 6
7   2 Kronur 1925–40   10.00   20.00   75.00
    1940 . . . 1

World War II Issues

Zinc

4a 10 Aurar 1942   2.00   4.00   12.50
5a 25 Aurar 1942   1.50   3.00   12.50

Unless otherwise noted, prices are for coins in very fine, extremely fine, and uncirculated condition.

REPUBLIC 1944–

Bronze

11	1 Eyrir 1946–66	.15	.35	.75

12	5 Aurar 1946–66	.25	.50	1.00

Cupro-Nickel

13	10 Aurar 1946–69	.05	.10	.20
14	25 Aurar 1946–67	.05	.10	.20

Aluminum-Bronze

15	1 Krona 1946	.10	.20	.30
16	2 Kronur 1946	.25	.50	1.00

Jon Sigurdsson Sesquicentennial

Gold

17	*F1* 500 Kronur 1961	–	– 250.00

Later issues in *Current Coins of the World*.

INDIA

The largest country of the south Asian subcontinent, India extends from the Himalaya Mountains into the the the Indian Ocean. Formerly under British control, it attained independence in 1947 and became a republic within the Commonwealth in 1950. As the world's second most populous nation it is still largely agricultural. Area: ca. 1,-230,000 square miles. Languages: English, Hindi, many others. Capital: *New Delhi.*

Monetary System:
3 Pies = 1 Pice (Paisa)
4 Pice = 1 Anna
16 Annas = 1 Rupee
15 Rupees = 1 Mohur (Gold)

Prices are for coins in Very Fine condition unless otherwise indicated.

I. British East India Company to 1858
VICTORIA 1837–1901

Legend: EAST INDIA COMPANY

For similar copper coinage 1845–62, see Straits Settlements.

Proof restrikes exist for most of these issues.

Silver
Continuous legend on obverse

1	2 Annas 1841	7.50
2	¼ Rupee 1840	5.00
3	½ Rupee 1840	7.50
4	1 Rupee 1840	15.00

Gold

A4	*F3* 1 Mohur 1841	350.00

Divided legend on obverse

Silver

1a	2 Annas 1841	4.00
2a	¼ Rupee 1840	6.00
3a	½ Rupee 1840	7.50
4a	1 Rupee 1840	15.00

Gold

A4a	*F3* 1 Mohur 1841	350.00

II. British India 1857–1947
New Legend: INDIA only
Copper

5	$^1/_{12}$ Anna 1862, 74–76	1.00
6	½ Pice 1865, 75	2.00
7	¼ Anna 1862, 74–76	2.00
8	½ Anna 1862, 75–76	10.00

Silver
9	2 Annas 1862, 74–76	5.00
10	¼ Rupee 1862, 74–76	6.00
11	½ Rupee 1862, 74–76	10.00
12	1 Rupee 1862–76	15.00

Gold

Obv: young portrait, thin face
13	F6 5 Rupees 1870–76	450.00
14	F5 10 Rupees 1870–76	300.00
15	F4 1 Mohur 1862, 75	400.00

Nos. 13–14 were not issued to circulation.
Obv: Mature portrait, plump face
13a	F9 5 Rupees 1870	Proof 275.00
14a	F8 10 Rupees 1870	Proof 300.00
15a	F7 1 Mohur 1870	Proof 300.00

No. 15a was not issued to circulation.

New Obverse Legend:
VICTORIA EMPRESS
Designs Sim to Nos. 5–12, 13a–15a
Copper
16	$^1/_{12}$ Anna 1877–1901	1.00
17	½ Pice 1885–1901	2.00
18	¼ Anna 1877–1901	1.00
19	½ Anna 1877	15.00

Silver

20	2 Annas 1877–1901	3.00

21	¼ Rupee 1877–1901	5.00
22*	½ Rupee 1877–1900	7.50
23	1 Rupee 1877–1901	10.00

Gold
24	F11,13 5 Rupees 1879	300.00
25	F12 10 Rupees 1879	300.00
26	F10 1 Mohur (15 Rupees) 1877–91	300.00

No. 24 was not issued to circulation.

EDWARD VII 1901–1910

Copper, Thick Planchet

27	$^1/_{12}$ Anna 1903–06	.75
28	½ Pice 1903–06	1.50
29	¼ Anna 1903–06	1.00

Bronze, Thin Planchet
27a	$^1/_{12}$ Anna 1906–10	.50
28a	½ Pice 1906–10	1.00
29a	¼ Anna 1906–10	1.00

Cupro-Nickel

30	1 Anna 1907–10	1.00

Silver

31	2 Annas 1903–10	2.50
32	¼ Rupee 1903–10	3.00
33	½ Rupee 1904–10	6.00
34	1 Rupee 1903–10	10.00

Unless otherwise noted, prices are for coins in very fine, extremely fine, and uncirculated condition.

GEORGE V 1910–1936

Bronze

35	$^1/_{12}$ Anna 1912–36	.50
36	½ Pice 1912–36	.50
37	¼ Anna 1911–36	.50

Cupro-Nickel

38	1 Anna 1912–36	1.00
39	2 Annas 1918–36 (square)	2.00

40	4 Annas 1919–21	4.00

41	8 Annas 1919–20	8.00

Silver

42	2 Annas 1911–17	2.00
43	¼ Rupee 1911–36	2.50
44	½ Rupee 1911–36	5.00
45	1 Rupee 1911–36	10.00

1935–36 proof only.

Gold

46	*F14* 15 Rupees 1918	300.00
A46	*F15* 1 Sovereign 1918, rev.	
	St. George and Dragon	150.00

No. A46 is identical to Great Britain No. 78 but has I mint mark above date.

GEORGE VI 1936–1947

First Coinage
Bronze

Obv: first portrait (high-relief head)

47	$^1/_{12}$ Anna 1939	.75
49*	½ Pice 1938–40	1.00
50	¼ Anna 1938–40	.75

Cupro-Nickel

53	1 Anna 1938–40	1.00
54	2 Annas 1939–40 (square)	1.50

Silver

55	¼ Rupee 1938–40	4.00
56	½ Rupee 1938–39	6.00

Second Coinage
Bronze

Obv: second portrait (low-relief head)

47a	$^1/_{12}$ Anna 1939–42	.75
49a	½ Pice 1939, 42	1.00
50a	¼ Anna 1939–42	.75

51*	1 Pice 1943, small legend	.60
51a	1 Pice 1943–47, large legend	.20

Cupro-Nickel

52a	½ Anna 1946–47	.15

53b 1 Anna 1940–41, 46–47 (scalloped) .25
54b 2 Annas 1939–41, 46–47 (square) .35

Nickel-Brass

52 ½ Anna 1942–45 .15
53a 1 Anna 1942–45 .25
54a 2 Annas 1942–45 .35

Silver

Obv: second portrait
Edge: reeded
55a ¼ Rupee 1940–43 2.00
56a ½ Rupee 1939–40 5.00
57 1 Rupee 1938–39 10.00
   1939 . . . 150.00.
   Edge: with security groove
55b ¼ Rupee 1943–45 2.00
56b ½ Rupee 1941–45 4.00
57b 1 Rupee 1939–45 5.00
   1939 . . . Rare.

Nickel

58 ¼ Rupee 1946–47 2.00
59 ½ Rupee 1946–47 3.50
60 1 Rupee 1947 5.00

III. REPUBLIC 1950–

Bronze

61 1 Pice 1950, thick .25

61a 1 Pice 1951–55, thin .10

Cupro-Nickel

62 ½ Anna 1950–55 .10

63 1 Anna 1950–55 .30
64 2 Annas 1950–55 (square) .30

Nickel

65 ¼ Rupee 1950–55, large lion .20
65a ¼ Rupee 1954–56, small lion .20
66 ½ Rupee 1950–56 .35
67 1 Rupee 1950–54 1.00

Decimal System 1957

100 Naye (new) Paise = 1 Rupee 1957–63

100 Paise = 1 Rupee 1963–

First Coinage

Bronze

68 1 Naya Paisa 1957–62 .10

Nickel-Brass

68a 1 Naya Paisa 1962–63 .10

Cupro-Nickel

69 2 Naye Paise 1957–63 (scalloped) .15
70 5 Naye Paise 1957–63 (squared) .20

Unless otherwise noted, prices are for coins in very fine, extremely fine, and uncirculated condition.

71 10 Naye Paise 1957–63 (scalloped) .25

Nickel

72 25 Naye Paise 1957–63 .35
73 50 Naye Paise 1960–63 .60
74 1 Rupee 1962, 70–74 1.25

Cupro-Nickel

74a 1 Rupee 1975 .75

Second Coinage

Nickel-Brass

75 1 Paisa 1964 .15

Cupro-Nickel

76 2 Paise 1964 .15

78 5 Paise 1964–65 .20
79 10 Paise 1964–65 .25

Nickel

80 25 Paise 1964–68 •.35
81 50 Paise 1964–71 .50

Nehru Commemoratives

82 50 Paise 1964 .75
82a* 50 Paise 1964, Nagari Script
on obv .60
83 1 Rupee 1964 1.50
Later issues in *Current Coins of the World.*

INDIA — NATIVE STATES

Unless otherwise noted, prices are for coins in Very Fine condition.

ALWAR
Sheodan Singh 1857–74

Copper

Obv: Queen Victoria legend
Rev: Sheodan Singh legend
Dump planchets
1* 1 Paisa 1859–74 (19–23mm) 5.00
Broad, thin planchets
1a 1 Paisa 1871/Yr. 15 (33mm) –

Silver
Dump planchets
2 1 Rupee 1859–74 (20–24mm) 25.00

Broad, thin planchets
2a* 1 Rupee 1859–74
(28–33mm) 60.00

Mangal Singh 1874-92

Copper
Obv: like No. 1
Rev: Mangal Singh legend
Broad, thin planchets

3 1 Paisa 1874-91   25.00

Silver
Design like No. 3
Broad, thin planchets

4 1 Rupee 1874-76   60.00

Rev: with title Raja

5* 1 Rupee 1788 (error),
   1877-82   15.00

Rev: with title Maharaja

5a* 1 Rupee 1891   15.00

AMRELI

Khande Rao of Baroda
AH 1273-87 (1856-70)

Copper
Design like No. 1a
Dump planchets

1 1 Paisa ND   6.00

Obv: Nagari "Sri Kha Ga," jhar
Rev: Mint-date legend
Broad, thin planchets

1a* 1 Paisa AH 1277 (1861)   6.00

Sayaji Rao III of Baroda
AH 1292-1357 (1875-1939)
Copper
Obv: Nagari "Sa Ga", sun, scimitar
Rev: debased mint-date legend

2 ½ Paisa AH 1312 (1894)   5.00
3 1 Paisa 1312-13   10.00
3a 1 Paisa ND, with additional
   marks Latin "S" on obv.,
   sword on rev.   15.00

BAHAWLPUR

Anonymous Issues
Copper

Round or square planchets

1* 1 Falus AH 1248-81
   (1832-65), 14-16mm   6.00

2* 1 Paisa AH 1302-25
   (1885-1907)   10.00

Silver
Rev: Ahmadpur mint legend
3 1 Rupee 1275-84 (7 gr.)   20.00
Rev: Bahawalpur mint legend
4 1 Rupee 1272-73 (11.5 gr.)   35.00
4a 1 Rupee 1280-81 (7 gr.)   27.50
Rev: Khanpur mint legend
5 1 Rupee 1280 (7 gr.)   27.50

Muhammad Bahawal Khan V
AH 1317-25 (1899-1907)

Copper

Obv: Ruler's legend
Rev: Date-mint legend

6* 1 Paisa AH 1324 (1906)   9.00

Unless otherwise noted, prices are for coins in very
fine, extremely fine, and uncirculated condition.

Sadiq Muhammad Khan V
AH 1325–66 (1907–1947)

Copper
Design similar to No. 6

7	1 Paisa AH 1326–27 (1908–09)	8.00

8*	1 Paisa 1342–43	15.00

9*	1 Paisa AH 1343 (1925)	30.00

Silver

10*	1 Rupee 1343	Unc 400.00

Gold

11*	F42 Ashrafi 1343	–

Nos. 10 and 11 were probably struck for presentation only.

Copper

12*	½ Pice 1940	.75
13	¼ Anna 1940	1.00

BANSWARA

Anonymous Issues
First Coinage

Copper
Obv. and rev: state symbol in circles

1	½ Paisa ND (18–19mm)	6.00
2	1 Paisa ND (21mm)	6.00

Second Coinage

Copper
Obv. and rev: state symbol in stylized legend

3	½ Paisa ND (17–19mm)	10.00
4	1 Paisa ND (22–25mm)	4.00

Third Coinage
Copper
Obv. and rev: more complex symbol in circular legend

5	1 Paisa ND (18–20mm)	4.00

Silver

Obv. and rev: more complex symbol in stylized legend

6	⅛ Rupee ND (10mm)	25.00
7	¼ Rupee ND (13mm)	25.00
8*	½ Rupee ND (17mm)	25.00
9	1 Rupee ND (21mm)	30.00

Gold

10	1 Mohur ND	–

BARODA

Khande Rao
AH 1273–87 (1856–70)
First Coinage

Copper
Obv: Muhammad Akbar II legend
Rev: mint-date legend, pomegranate, Nagari "Kha"

1	½ Paisa ND (4 gr.)	4.50
2	1 Paisa Yr. 52 (8 gr.)	4.50

Silver

Obv: Muhammad Akbar II legend
Rev: like No. 11

3	¼ Rupee AH 1273 (13–14mm)	9.00
4	½ Rupee ND (16–17mm)	10.00
5	1 Rupee Yr. 53 (21–22mm)	15.00

Second Coinage

Copper

Obv: Gaekwar's titles
Rev: mint-date legend, scimitar, "Kha Ga"

6	½ Paisa AH 1274–76 (1857–59), 3.5 gr.	4.00
7*	1 Paisa 1274–77 (7–8 gr.)	5.00

Obv: like No.7
Rev: similar, horse hoof added

6a	½ Paisa 128x	12.50
7a	1 Paisa 1281–85	7.00
8	2 Paise 1282–84	7.00

Silver

Obv: like No. 7
Rev: mint-date legend, sword, Nagari "Kha"

9	⅛ Rupee 1282	6.00
10	¼ Rupee 1274–86	7.00
11*	½ Rupee 1274–86	8.00
12	1 Rupee 1274–87	15.00

Obv: Khande Rao legend in Nagari
Rev: mint-date legend

13	½ Rupee AH 1287 (1870)	100.00
14*	1 Rupee 1287	100.00

Malhar Rao
AH 1287–92 (1870–75)

Copper

Obv: like No. 7
Rev: like No. 7 but "Ma Ga", plus ball

15	½ Paisa AH 1288, 90 (4 gr.)	4.00
16*	1 Paisa 1288–90 (7–9 gr.)	4.00
17	2 Paisa 1288–89 (16 gr.)	4.00

Silver

Obv: like No. 7
Rev: like No. 11 but "Ma Ga"

18	⅛ Rupee ND	7.00
19	¼ Rupee 1290	6.50
20	½ Rupee 1287–90	6.50
21	1 Rupee 1287–90	10.00
22*	2 Rupees 1288	–

Sayaji Rao III
AH 1292–1357/VS 1932–96
(1875–1939)
First Coinage

Copper

Obv: Nagari "Sa Ga"/ball, scimitar
Rev: date/value
Dump planchets

23	½ Paisa VS 1937, 48 (1880, 91)	4.50

Unless otherwise noted, prices are for coins in very fine, extremely fine, and uncirculated condition.

24*	1 Paisa 1937–48	4.00
25	2 Paisa 1937–48	5.00

Round planchets

24a	1 Paisa VS 1949	6.00
25a	2 Paisa 1949	10.00

Silver

Obv: like No. 7
Rev: like No. 11 but "Sa"

26	⅛ Rupee AH 1294–95 (1877–78), 10mm	5.00
27	¼ Rupee 1299 (13mm)	4.50
28*	½ Rupee 1294–1301 (15–16mm)	10.00
29	1 Rupee 1292–1302 (20mm)	15.00

Second Coinage

Copper

Thick planchet

30	1 Pai VS 1944–47 (1887–90)	1.50
31	1 Paisa 1940–47	1.00
32	2 Paisa 1940–47	1.50

Thin planchet

30a	1 Pai 1948–50	1.50
31a*	1 Paisa 1948–50	1.00
32a	2 Paisa 1948–50	1.25

Nos. 30–32a have several minor varieties of wreath style and arrangement of legends.

Silver

Designs like Nos. 37–39

33	2 Annas VS 1949 (1892), 16mm	10.00
34*	¼ Rupee 1949 (19mm)	6.00
35	½ Rupee 1948–49 (24mm)	30.00
36	1 Rupee 1948–49 (30mm)	15.00

Reduced size

33a	2 Annas 1951–52 (14mm)	7.00
34a	¼ Rupee 1951–52 (17mm)	7.00
35a	½ Rupee 1951–52 (22mm)	15.00
36a	1 Rupee 1951–56 (28mm)	15.00

Gold

37*	F46 ⅙ Mohur VS 1943–59 (1886–1902)	200.00
38	F45 ⅓ Mohur 1942–59	225.00

39*	F44 1 Mohur 1945–59	300.00

Pratap Singh
VS 1995–2008 (1939–51)

Gold

40	⅓ Mohur VS 1995 (18mm)	250.00
41*	1 Mohur 1995 (21mm)	275.00

BHARTPUR
Mints: Braj Indrapur (Bhartpur), Dig.

Jaswant Singh 1852–93
Copper

Designs like No. 3

1	½ Paisa 1858/VS 1910 (9 gr.)	–
2	1 Paisa 1858/1910 (18 gr.)	–

Silver

Obv: Victoria portrait and legend
Rev: Braj Indrapur — Jaswant Singh legend

3*	1 Rupee 1858/VS 1910 (21–24mm)	40.00

Obv: Victoria portrait and title, no name
Rev: Victoria titles/Braj indrapur

4	1 Rupee 1858–61/VS 1914–17	50.00

Obv: like No. 4
Rev: similar to No. 4 but Dig mint
5 1 Rupee 1858/VS 1910   50.00
For similar issues with katar (dagger) at left of head, see
Bindraban State.

Gold
Design like No. 4
6 *F53* 1 Mohur 1858–59/vs 1915–19 (21mm) 350.00

Rearranged legends both sides
11 ⅛ Rupee AH 1294–1306   5.00
12 ¼ Rupee 1294–1304   6.00
13 ½ Rupee 1294–1306   10.00
14* 1 Rupee 1293–1306   15.00

BHOPAL

Sikandar Begam
AH 1261–85 (1844–68)
Shah Jahan Begam
Ah 1285–1319 (1868–1901)
Anonymous Issues

Copper

Obv: date/Bhopal legend
Rev: Value
1* ¼ Anna AH 1266–79 (7–8 gr.)   3.00
2 ½ Anna 1276, 78 (15–16 gr.)   5.00
3 1 Anna 1276 (30–32 gr.)   10.00

Obv: Persian "Sh/Bhopal"
Rev: date/value
4 ¼ Anna AH 1285–99   3.00
5 ½ Anna 1286–1300   4.00
6* 1 Anna 1285–1300   10.00

Silver

Obv: Formal date legend
Rev: mint legend
7 ⅛ Rupee AH 1275, 88   4.00
8 ¼ Rupee AH 1275–88   4.00
9 ½ Rupee 1275–92   10.00
10* 1 Rupee 1271–93   15.00

Obv: Shah Jahan Begam/value
Rev: date/Bhopal legend
15 ½ Paisa AH 1305 (1888)   4.00
16 ¼ Anna 1302–06 (7–8 gr.)   1.50
17* ½ Anna 1302–06 (15 gr.)   2.50
18 1 Anna 1302–06 (30–32 gr.)   7.50

BIKANIR

Sardar Singh 1851–72
For pre-Victorian coins of this reign, Craig, *Coins of the
World*.

Copper
Design like No. 5
1 1 Paisa 1859/VS 1916 (7–8
gr.)   2.00

Silver

Obv: Queen Victoria legend
Rev: date/regnal symbols
Dump planchets
2 ⅛ Rupee 1859/VS 1916
(11mm)   7.00
3 ¼ Rupee 1959/1916 (15mm)   8.00
4 ½ Rupee 1859/1916 (18mm)   10.00
5* 1 Rupee 1859/1916 (22mm)   15.00
Broad, thin planchets
5a 1 Rupee 1859/1916 (30mm)   75.00

Dungar Singh 1872–87

Copper
Design like No. 10

6 1 Paisa 1859/VS 1916 (7–8 gr.) 2.50

Silver

Rev: Dungar Singh symbol added
Dump planchets

7 ⅛ Rupee 1859/VS 1916 (12mm) 7.00
8 ¼ Rupee 1859/1916 (14mm) 10.00
9 ½ Rupee 1859/1916 (16–19mm) 10.00
10* 1 Rupee 1859/1916 (22mm) 15.00
    Broad, thin Planchets
10a 1 Rupee 1859/1916 (30mm) 75.00

Ganga Singh 1887–1943
First Coinage

Copper
Design like No. 15

11 1 Paisa 1859/VS 1916 .... 5.00

Silver

Rev: Ganga Singh symbol added
Dump planchets

12 ⅛ Rupee 1859/VS 1916 (12mm) 7.00
13 ¼ Rupee 1859/1916 (14mm) 9.00
14 ½ Rupee 1859/1916 (16–19mm) 10.00
15* 1 Rupee 1859/1916 (20–22mm) 15.00
    Broad, thin planchets
15a 1 Rupee 1859/1916 (30mm) 75.00

Second Coinage

Copper

16* ½ Pice 1894 .... 10.00
17 ¼ Anna 1895 .... 10.00

Silver

18* 1 Rupee 1892, 97 .... 15.00

50th Year of Reign

Silver

19* 1 Rupee VS 1994 .... 15.00

Gold

20 F56 ½ Mohur 1994 .... 125.00
21* F55 1 Mohur 1994 .... 225.00

BINDRABAN

Silver
Obv: like Bhartpur No. 4
Rev: Victoria titles/Bindraban

1 ¼ Rupee 1858–67/VS 1915–24 .... 40.00

2 ½ Rupee 1858–67/VS
   1915–25   50.00
3 1 Rupee 1858/VS 1915   60.00
This series is further distinguished from Bhartpur by mint marks: katar and sword on obverse, umbrella on reverse.

BUNDI

A. In name of Queen Victoria.

Nos. 1–6 have AD dates on obverse and Samvat dates on reverse. Coins with both dates indentifiable usually command higher prices.

Copper

Obv: horizontal English legend

1 ¼ Paisa 1867/VS 1924   7.50
2* ½ Paisa 1858, 67/VS 1915,
   24   6.00
3 1 Paisa 1862–99/VS 1919–56   1.75

Silver

Round planchets

4 ¼ Rupee 1858–79/VS
   1915–36   8.00
5 ½ Rupee 1858–86/VS
   1915–43   9.00
6* 1 Rupee 1858–86/VS
   1915–43   15.00
Square planchets
6a 1 Rupee 1858–77/VS
   1915–34   45.00

Obv: katar (dagger) in center
Round planchets

7 ¼ Rupee VS 1944–55
   (1887–98)   7.50
8 ½ Rupee 1946–55   6.50
9* 1 Rupee 1943–57   15.00
Square planchets
9a 1 Rupee 1945–52   75.00

Obv: seated figure in center
10* 1 Rupee VS 1958 (1901)   75.00

B. In name of Edward VII.

Silver

Obv: seated figure in center
B11 ¼ Rupee VS 1958, 61 (1901,
    04)   35.00
A11 ½ Rupee 1958   35.00
11* 1 Rupee 1958–63 (21–25mm)   10.00

Copper

Obv: katar (dagger) in center
A12* 1 Paisa VS 1963, 65 (1906,
    08)   7.50

Silver

Small round planchets
12 ¼ Rupee VS 1963–66
   (1906–09)   6.00
13 ½ Rupee 1963–66   5.00
14* 1 Rupee 1963–69 (18–21mm)   6.00
Square planchets
14a 1 Rupee 1966–69   75.00
Broad round planchets
14b 1 Rupee 1967–68 (26mm)   75.00

C. In name of George V.

Copper

Obv: katar (dagger) in center
15* 1 Paisa VS 1973–87
    (1916–30)   2.00

Silver

Round planchets
16* ¼ Rupee VS 1972–82
    (1915–25)   3.50

17* ½ Rupee 1972–84   7.00
18 1 Rupee 1972–89   15.00
Square planchets
18a 1 Rupee 1974–87   85.00

Obv: AD date in center
Round planchets
19 ½ Rupee AD 1925   60.00
20* 1 Rupee 1925   40.00
Square planchets
20a 1 Rupee 1925   60.00

CAMBAY

Hussain Ja'afar
AH 1257–97 (1841–80)

Silver
Obv: Shah Alam II legend
Rev: mint-date legend
1 1 Rupee AH 1282, 94 (20mm)   20.00

Ja'afar Ali
AH 1297–1333/VS 1937–72
(1880–1915)

Copper
Obv: Persian "Shah"
Rev: Date legend
2 ¼ Paisa VS 1962 (1905)   7.50
3 ½ Paisa 1962   7.50
4 1 Paisa 1962   3.00
Dates of Nos. 2–4 are rarely on planchets.

Obv: state name
Rev: value/date
5 ½ Paisa VS 1963–64, rev.
    value in words   9.00
5a ½ Paisa 1965–66, value in nu-
    merals   7.50
6* 1 Paisa 1963–70   2.50

Silver

Obv: Ja'afar Ali legend
Rev: mint legend
7 ⅛ Rupee AH 1313 (1895),
    11mm   10.00
8 ¼ Rupee ND (14mm)   12.00
9 ½ Rupee 1313 (15–16mm)   15.00
10* 1 Rupee 1313–19 (19–20mm)   25.00

CHHOTA UDAIPUR

Jitsinghji
Saka 1773–1803/VS 1908–38
(1851–81)

Copper

Obv. and rev: crude Gujerati legend
1* 1 Paisa Saka 1787 (7 gr.)   6.00
2 2 Paisa 1787 (14 gr.)   7.00

Obv: sword and legend
3   2 Paisa VS 1919, 24   10.00

Motisinghji
VS 1938-62 (1881-1905)

Copper
Obv: date in circular legend
Rev: value/sword in circular legend
4   1 Paisa VS 1948 (15mm)   6.50
5   2 Paisa 1948 (20-22mm)   7.00

COOCH BEHAR
Dating system: Coins of this state are dated in a local era beginning in AD 1510.

Narendra Narayana 1863-1911

Silver
Four-line legends both sides
1   ½ Rupee ND (20-22mm)   40.00

Gold
2   F71 1 Mohur ND   400.00

Nrpendra Narayana 1847-63

Silver
Obv: Nrpendra legend (style of No. 8)
Rev: 4-line legend in square
3   ½ Rupee Yr. 354 (1864)   30.00

Gold

4   F71 1 Mohur Yr. 354   275.00

Rajendra Narayana 1911-13

Silver
Like No. 8 but Rajendra legend
5   ½ Rupee Yr. 402 (1912)   35.00

Gold
6   F72 1 Mohur Yr. 402   250.00

Jitendra Narayana 1913-22

Silver
7   ½ Rupee Yr. 404 (1914)   30.00

Gold

Obv: Jitendra legend
Rev: state arms
8* F72 1 Mohur Yr.404   250.00

Jagaddipendra Narayana 1922-49

Silver
Like No. 8 but Jagaddipendra legend
9   ½ Rupee Yr. 413 (1923)   50.00

DATIA
Govind Singh 1907-48

Gold
Obv: bust slightly right
Rev: state arms
1   F73 ½ Mohur ND   400.00

DEWAS, Senior Branch
Krishnaji Rao 1860-99

Copper
Obv: bust of Victoria
Rev: DEWAS STATE S.B.
1   ¹⁄₁₂ Anna 1888   Proof 10.00
2   ¼ Anna 1888   Proof 10.00

Vikrama Simha Rao 1937-48

Copper
Obv: bust of ruler
3   1 Paisa 1944   65.00

DEWAS, Junior Branch
Narayan Rao 1864-92

Copper

Rev: DEWAS STATE J.B.
1   ¹⁄₁₂ Anna 1888   17.50
3* ¼ Anna 1888   15.00

Unless otherwise noted, prices are for coins in very fine, extremely fine, and uncirculated condition.

DHAR

Anand Rao III
AH 1276-1316 (1860-98)

Copper

Obv: Hanuman (monkey god)

A1 ½ Paisa AH 1289 (1872),
16mm 12.50
B1* 1 Paisa 1289 (17-20mm) 5.00

1 ¹⁄₁₂ Anna 1887 5.00
2* ½ Pice 1887 6.50
3 ¼ Anna 1887 8.00

Anand Rao IV 1943-48

Gold
Obv: bust
Rev: state arms
4 1 Mohur 1943 200.00

DUNGARPUR

Udai Singh
VS 1901-55 (1844-98)

Copper
Obv: date/sword
Rev: state legend
A1 1 Paisa VS 1916-17
(1859-60) 7.00

Lakshman Singh
VS 1975-2005 (1918-48)

Copper

Obv: state arms
Rev: state name/value/date
1* 1 Paisa VS 2001 (1944) 30.00

FARIDKOT

Harindar Sing 1918-49

Gold

1 ⅓ Mohur 1941 (20mm) 300.00

GWALIOR

I. Handmade Issues
A. Bhilsa mint

Mint marks: frozen date AH (12) 25, bow and arrow.

Jayaji Rao 1843-86

Silver

Obv: Shah Alam II legend, "25"
Rev: debased mint legend, bow and arrow,
Nagari "Ji" for Jayaji
1 ⅛ Rupee AH (12) 25 7.00
2 ¼ Rupee (12) 25 (12-14mm) 8.00
3 ½ Rupee (12) 25 (14-16mm) 10.00
4* 1 Rupee (12) 25 (17-18mm) 15.00

Madho Rao II 1886-1925

Silver

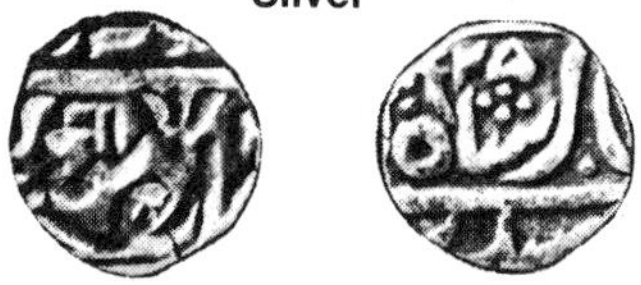

Obv: like No. 4
Rev: similar but Nagari "M" for Madho
5 ⅛ Rupee AH (12) 25
(9-10mm) 8.00
6 ¼ Rupee (12) 25 (12-13mm) 8.00
7 ½ Rupee (12) 25 (14mm) 10.00
8* 1 Rupee (12) 25 (17-18mm) 15.00

B. Gwalior Fort mint

Mint marks: 5-petal rosette, bow and arrow, frozen Yr.
23 (silver), frozen AH 1130/Yr. 2 (gold).

Jayaji Rao 1843–86

Silver
Designs like No.13a
Dump planchets

9	¹/₁₆ Rupee Yr. 23 (9mm)	5.00
10	⅛ Rupee Yr. 23 (11mm)	5.00
11	¼ Rupee Yr. 23 (13mm)	5.00
12	½ Rupee Yr. 23 (15mm)	10.00
13	1 Rupee Yr. 23 (17–19mm)	12.00

Obv: Muhammad Akbar II legend
Rev: mint-date legend, Nagari "Ji"
Broad thin planchets

13a*	1 Rupee AH 125x/Yr. 23 (25–27mm)	50.00

Gold
Obv: Muhammad Shah legend
Rev: mint-date legend, Nagari "Ji"

14	F135a ⅓ Mohur AH 1130/Yr. 2	200.00

Madho Rao II 1886–1925

Gold
Obv: like No. 14
Rev: similar but Nagari "M" for Madho

15	F135a ⅓ Mohur AH 1130/Yr. 2	200.00

C. Jhansi mint

Mint marks: figure resembling "99111", Persian (not Nagari) "Ji" for Jayaji.

Jayaji Rao 1843–86

Silver

Obv: Shah Alam II legend
Rev: mint-date legend, Persian "Ji"

16	⅛ Rupee ND	12.50
19*	1 Rupee AH 1282, 84 (1865, 67)	7.50

D. Lashkar mint (Gwalior city)

Mint marks: bow and arrow, snake, single or double trident, frozen Yr. 23.

Jayaji Rao 1843–86

Copper

Obv: Shah Alam II legend
Rev: degenerate legend, double trident

20	½ Paisa Yr. 23 (5 gr.)	5.00
21*	1 Paisa Yr. 23 (10 gr.)	5.00
22	2 Paisa Yr. 23 (20 gr.)	7.50

Silver

Obv: Shah Alam II legend
Rev: mint marks, Nagari "Ji"

23	¹/₁₆ Rupee Yr. 23 (8–9mm)	5.00
24	⅛ Rupee Yr. 23 (9–11mm)	5.00
25	¼ Rupee Yr. 23 (12–13mm)	5.00
26	½ Rupee Yr. 23 (15–16mm)	6.00
27*	1 Rupee Yr. 23 (18–21mm)	10.00

Anonymous Issues

Copper

28	½ Paisa VS 1926 (1869), 3 gr.	10.00
29*	1 Paisa 1926 (6 gr.)	1.00

Nos. 28–29 were struck 1869–99 with no change of date.

Madho Rao II 1886–1925

Silver
Obv: like No. 27
Rev: similar but Nagari "M" for Madho

30	⅛ Rupee Yr. 23	2.50
31	¼ Rupee Yr. 23	2.50
32	½ Rupee Yr. 23	5.00
33	1 Rupee Yr. 23	10.00

Unless otherwise noted, prices are for coins in very fine, extremely fine, and uncirculated condition.

E. Ujjain mint
Jayaji Rao
AH 1259–1302 (1843–86)

Copper

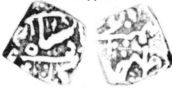

Obv: Shah Alam II legend

35* 1 Paisa AH 1262–95   2.50

Madho Rao II
AH 1302–45 (1886–1925)

Silver

Obv: Shah Alam II legend

36	$^1/_{16}$ Rupee AH 1313 (8–9mm)	6.00
37	$^1/_8$ Rupee 1310, 12 (9–10mm)	5.00
38	¼ Rupee 1310–14 (12–13mm)	5.00
39	½ Rupee 1310–14 (14–15mm)	8.00
40	1 Rupee 1310–14 (18–20mm)	10.00

II. Machine-struck Issues.
Madho Rao II
VS 1943–82 (1886–1925)
First Coinage

Copper

41	1 Pai VS 1946 (1889), 14mm	–
42	½ Paisa 1946 (20mm)	55.00
43*	¼ Anna 1945–46 (25mm)	40.00
44	½ Anna 1946 (31mm)	65.00

45*	½ Paisa VS 1956–58 (1899–1901)	1.25
46	¼ Anna 1953–58	1.00

Gold

Obv: bust to right
Rev: state arms

47   F136   ⅓ Mohur VS 1959 (1902)   275.00

Second Coinage

Copper

48	¼ Anna VS 1970 (1913), thick	1.25
48a*	¼ Anna 1970, 74, thin	1.00

Jivaji Rao III
VS 1982–2005 (1925–48)

Copper

Obv: young bust

49*	¼ Anna VS 1986 (1929), thick	.60
49a	¼ Anna 1986, 99, thin	1.00

Obv: older bust

50*   ¼ Anna VS1999 (1942)   .50

Brass

51   ½ Anna 1999 (19mm)   .50

III. Local Issues
A. Dohad (Dahod)

Copper

1*   1 Paisa VS 1912 (1855), 6.4 gr.   6.50

B. Jawad
Jayaji Rao 1843–86
Copper

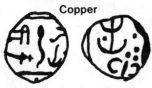

Obv: snake, other symbols, Nagari "Ji"
1* 1 Paisa ND   5.50

Madho Rao 1886–1925
Copper
Obv: like No. 1 but Nagari "M"
Rev: similar to No. 1
2 1 Paisa ND   6.50

C. Mandisor
Mint mark: trident.

Jayaji Rao
VS 1900–43 (1843–86)
Copper

Obv: complex design
Rev: trident, date
1* 1 Paisa VS 1921–27
    (1864–70)   4.00

Obv: Nagari "Ji" in circular legend
Rev: like No. 1
2* 1 Paisa VS 1937 (1880)   4.00

D. Rajod
Mint marks: trefoil, yuni (female symbol) or snake at right on obverse.

Copper

Obv: Hanuman (monkey god), trefoil at right
Rev: date/ Rajod

1* 1 Paisa VS 1930 (1873)   10.00
    Like No. 1 but obv. yuni at right
2 1 Paisa VS 1936 (1879)   10.00
    Like No. 1 but obv. snake at right
3 1 Paisa VS 1940 (1883)   10.00

HYDERABAD

Afzal ad-Daula
AH 1273–85 (1857–69)
Early issues of this reign are listed in Craig, *Coins of the World.*

Copper
Design like No. 11 but crude
1 1 Paisa (Dub) AH 1278–83
    (1861–66)   5.00

Silver
2	1/16 Rupee 1275 (9mm)	10.00
3	1/8 Rupee 1278–79 (11–13mm)	5.00
4	1/4 Rupee 1276–83 (15–16mm)	7.00
5	1/2 Rupee 1275–85 (19–20mm)	7.00
6	1 Rupee 1275–85 (22–25mm)	8.00

Gold

Obv: Asaf Jah legend (dynastic founder) Persian "A"
for Afzal in center
Rev: mint-date legend
8	*F222*	1/8 Mohur 1279–81 (11mm)	40.00
9	*F221*	1/4 Mohur 1281 (14mm)	55.00
10	*F220*	1/2 Mohur 1281 (16mm)	80.00
11*	*F219*	1 Mohur 1281 (22mm)	125.00

Mir Mahbub Ali Khan II
AH 1285–1329 (1869–1911)
First Coinage
Copper

Design like No. 16 but crude
12* 1 Paisa (Dub) AH 1289–1313
    (1872–95)   1.50

Unless otherwise noted, prices are for coins in very fine, extremely fine, and uncirculated condition.

Silver

Designs like No. 11 but Persian "M" for Mir Mahbub in center

13	$^1\!/_{16}$ Rupee AH 1299–1321 (1882–1903), 7–9mm	2.00
14	$^1\!/_8$ Rupee 1286–1321 (10–13mm)	3.00
15	$^1\!/_4$ Rupee 1286–1321 (13–16mm)	4.00
16*	$^1\!/_2$ Rupee 1286–1317 (17–19mm)	5.00
17	1 Rupee 1286–1318 (22–24mm)	7.00

Gold

18	F223 $^1\!/_{16}$ Mohur 1321 (7mm)	25.00
19*	F222 $^1\!/_8$ Mohur 1306–21 (10mm)	40.00
20	F221 $^1\!/_4$ Mohur 1301–21 (14mm)	55.00
21	F220 $^1\!/_2$ Mohur 1306–19 (17mm)	100.00
22	F219 1 Mohur 1286–1314 (22mm)	200.00

Second Coinage

Machine-struck silver coins dated AH 1305–07 and copper coins dated 1312–16 are believed to be patterns.

Silver

Obv: Asaf Jah legend
Rev: mint-date legend

29	2 Annas AH 1318 (1900), 15mm	25.00
30	4 Annas 1318 (19mm)	20.00
31*	8 Annas 1312, 18 (24mm)	20.00
32	1 Rupee 1312–18 (30mm)	17.50

Gold

33	1 Ashrafi (Mohur) 1311 (24mm)	200.00
33a	1 Ashrafi (Mohur) 1311 (30mm)	200.00

Third Coinage

Copper

Obv: Persian "M" for Mahbub in loop of tughra

34	1 Pai AH 1326–29 (1908–11)	5.00
35*	2 Pai 1322–29	1.00
36	$^1\!/_2$ Anna 1324–29	3.00

Silver

Obv: Persian "M" in doorway

37	2 Annas 1323 (15mm)	2.00
38	4 Annas 1323–29 (20mm)	4.00
39*	8 Annas 1322–29 (24mm)	10.00
40	1 Rupee 1321–29 (30mm)	15.00

Gold

41	$^1\!/_8$ Ashrafi 1325	55.00
42	$^1\!/_4$ Ashrafi 1325, 29	60.00
43	$^1\!/_2$ Ashrafi 1325–29	100.00
44	1 Ashrafi 1325, 29	250.00

Mir Usman Ali Khan
AH 1329–67 (1911–48)
First Coinage

Bronze
Design like No. 46a
Obv: short intitial "Ain" in loop of tughra

46	2 Pai 1329–30	10.00

Silver

Obv: short initial "Ain" in doorway

53*	1 Rupee 1330	10.00

Gold

57	1 Ashrafi 1330	275.00

Second Coinage

Bronze

Obv: full intitial "Ain" in loop of Tughra

45	1 Pai 1338-53	.75
46a*	2 Pai 1330-49	.50
47	½ Anna 1332-48	1.00

Cupro-Nickel

48*	1 Anna 1338-54	.75

49*	1 Anna 1356-61	.50

Silver

Obv: full initial "Ain" in doorway

50	2 Annas 1335-58	1.75
51*	4 Annas 1337-58	2.25
52	8 Annas 1337-54	4.50
53a	1 Rupee 1330-43	8.00

Gold

54	⅛ Ashrafi 1337-54	55.00
55	¼ Ashrafi 1337-57	60.00
56	½ Ashrafi 1337-57	100.00
57a*	1 Ashrafi 1331-54	200.00

Third Coinage

Bronze

58*	2 Pai AH 1362-68 (1943-49)	.20

59*	1 Anna 1361-68	.30

Silver

60	2 Annas 1362 (15mm)	.50
61	4 Annas 1362-65 (20mm)	.75
62*	8 Annas 1363 (24mm)	5.00
63	1 Rupee 1361-65 (30mm)	7.50

Nickel

64	2 Annas AH 1366,68 (1947, 49)	.25
65	4 Annas 1366, 68	.50
66*	8 Annas 1366	.85

INDORE

Dating system: Most coins bear Vikrama dates (VS = AD + 57); exceptions use Saka dates (Saka + 78 = AD) or Fasli Era dates (FE + 590 = AD).

Tukoji Rao II
VS 1901–43 (1844–86)
First Coinage

Copper
Design like No. 3

1	½ Paisa Saka 1780, 88 (1858,-66)	40.00
2	1 Paisa Saka 1780,88	35.00

Silver

3* 1 Rupee Saka 1780, 88   60.00
Nos. 1–3 dated Saka 1788 also bear VS date 1923.
Obv: like No. 3
Rev: similar but sword and lance below sunface
4 1 Rupee FE 1287/VS 1934
    (1877), 20mm   60.00

Obv: sword and lance/date
5 ½ Rupee FE 1289   75.00
6* 1 Rupee FE 1289, 95
    (17–18mm)   60.00

Second Coinage

Copper
Obv: Bull
Rev: sunface
Dump planchets
7 ½ Anna VS 1942 (1885), 16
gr.   –
Obv: seated bull
Rev: legend
Machine-struck planchets
8 ½ Anna VS 1942 (1885), 13
gr.   –

Shivaji Rao
VS 1943–60 (1886–1903)

Copper
Obv: without ruler's name
9 ½ Paisa VS 1944 (21mm)   25.00
10 ¼ Anna 1943–44 (25mm)   5.00
11 ½ Anna 1943 (31mm)   3.00

Obv: Shivaji Rao legend
9a ½ Paisa VS 1946 (1889)   25.00
10a* ¼ Anna 1945–59   1.00

11a ½ Anna 1944–59   1.50
Nos. 9–11a occur in several minor varieties, differing in
arrangement of legends.

Silver
Obv: Shah Alam II legend
Rev: like No. 4
12 ¼ Rupee FE 1295/VS 1945
    (1888)   40.00
13 ½ Rupee 1296/1947   35.00
14 1 Rupee 1294–97/1945–48   25.00

Obv: Shah Alam II legend in wreath
Rev: sunface
15 ⅛ Rupee VS 1947–51 (10mm)   3.25
16 ¼ Rupee 1947–54 (12mm)   3.00
17 ½ Rupee 1947–54 (16mm)   4.00
18* 1 Rupee 1947–55 (22mm)   8.00

19* 1 Rupee VS 1956, 58 (1899,
    1901)   150.00

Yeshwant Rao
VS 1983–2005 (1926–48)

Copper

20* ¼ Anna VS 1992 (1935)   2.00
21 ½ Anna 1992   4.00

JAIPUR

Ram Singh 1835–80

For pre-Victorian coins of this reign, see Craig, *Coins of the World*

Copper

Obv: Queen Victoria legend
Rev: Ram Singh legend
Dump planchets

1* 1 Paisa Yrs. 36–45 (6 gr.),
    17–20mm   1.50

Broad thin planchets

1a 1 Paisa 1858–80/Yrs. 23–45
    (28mm)   7.50

Silver

Designs like No. 1
Dump planchets

3 ⅛ Rupee Yrs. 22–42 (14mm)   3.50
4 ¼ Rupee Yrs. 21–44
   (15–17mm)   2.50
5 ½ Rupee Yrs. 21–45
   (18–20mm)   3.50
6 1 Rupee Yrs. 20–45
   (21–23mm)   7.50

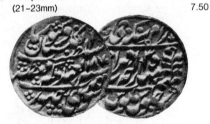

Broad thin planchets

6a* 1 Rupee Yrs. 24–35
    (27–29mm)   15.00

Gold

7* F233a 1 Mohur Yrs. 21–45
   (18–20mm)   200.00

Madho Singh II 1880–1922

Copper

Obv: Queen Victoria legend
Rev: Madho Singh legend
Dump planchets

8* 1 Paisa Yrs. 4–39 (16–20mm)   .50

Broad thin planchets

8a* 1 Paisa Yrs. 1–37 (32–36mm)   15.00

Silver

Designs like No. 8
Dump planchets

9   1/16 Rupee Yrs. 2, 10 (1881,
    90), 10mm   3.50
10 ⅛ Rupee Yrs. 4–42 (13mm)   2.50
11* ¼ Rupee Yrs. 1–44 (16mm)   2.50
12 ½ Rupee Yrs. 1–37 (18mm)   3.50
13 1 Rupee Yrs. 1–42 (21mm)   4.00

Broad thin planchets

13a 1 Rupee Yrs. 1–5, plain bor-
    ders (30–31mm)   25.00
13b* 1 Rupee Yrs. 5–37, wreath
    borders (36–37mm)   7.50

Unless otherwise noted, prices are for coins in very
fine, extremely fine, and uncirculated condition.

Gold
Dump planchets
14	F233a 1 Mohur Yrs. 16–42	
	(18mm)	200.00

Broad, thin planchets
14a	F233a 1 Mohur Yrs. 1–8	
	(29–36mm)	400.00

Man Singh II 1922–49
First Coinage

Silver

Second Coinage

Copper

Obv: George VI legend
Rev: Man Singh legend
Round thin planchets
16*	½ Paisa Yrs. 21–23 (17mm)	.75
17	1 Paisa 1949/Yr. 28 (32mm)	10.00

Brass

18*	1 Anna 1943–44	.50

19*	1 Anna 1944	.50

20*	2 Annas 1942/Yr. 21	3.50

Silver
Broad thin planchets
21	1 Rupee Yrs. 17–20, plain borders (27–30mm)	17.50
21a	1 Rupee Yrs. 18–28, borders as No. 13b (37–38mm)	10.00

Gold
Dump planchets
22	F233a 1 Mohur Yrs. 20–22	
	(19–21mm)	225.00

JAISALMIR

Silver

Obv: Queen Victoria legend
Rev: degenerate mint-date legend
1	⅛ Rupee Yr. 22 (12mm)	4.00
2	¼ Rupee Yr. 22	4.00
3	½ Rupee Yr. 22 (18mm)	5.00
4*	1 Rupee Yr. 22	15.00
4a	1 Rupee Yr. 22, Square	75.00

Obv: like Nos. 1–4a
Rev: Sim., mmks., bird and umbrella added
5	⅛ Rupee Yr. 22	2.50
6	¼ Rupee Yr. 22 (14–15mm)	2.50
7	½ Rupee Yr. 22 (17–19mm)	4.00
8	1 Rupee Yr. 22 (20–23mm)	5.00
8a	1 Rupee Yr. 22, square	75.00
8b	1 Rupee Yr. 22, round (35mm)	150.00

Gold
9	⅛ Mohur Yr. 22	100.00
10	¼ Mohur Yr. 22	150.00
11	½ Mohur Yr. 22	175.00
12	1 Mohur Yr. 22	250.00

JAMMU

Ranbir Singh
VS 1914–42 (1857–85)
Pertab Singh
VS 1942–82 (1885–1925)

Copper
Obv: mint legend in persian, leaf mmk.
Rev: Gurmukhi legend
1	1 Paisa VS 1914–22 (7 gr.), var.	1.00

Obv: like No. 1
Rev: Takari legend
Round machine-made planchets
2	1 Paisa VS 1935 (1878), 15mm	7.50

Thin dump planchets
2a	1 Paisa VS 1935–49 (3 gr.)	1.50

Gold
Obv: mint legend, leaf, date in wreath
Rev: 3-line Nagari legend
3 ⅓ Mohur VS 1921 (1864),
  19mm   300.00

JAORA

Muhammad Ismail
AH 1282-1313 (1865-95)

Copper
Obv: wheat, pennant/mint legend
Rev: date/Jaora legend
A1 1 Paisa AH 1282-85   75.00
Obv: without wheel
B1 1 Paisa 1295   7.50

1* 1 Paisa 1893-96   3.00
2 2 Paisa 1893-94   5.00
Nos. 1-2 bear dates in three systems: AD dates on obverse, AH and VS dates on reverse. Overlapping dates and incorrect combinations exist.

JHALAWAR

Prithvi Singh 1847-75
Zalim Singh 1875-96

Copper
Designs like No. 2a
Rectangular dump planchets
1 ½ Paisa ND (9 gr.)   15.00
2 1 Paisa Yrs. 1-34 (18 gr.)   15.00

Obv: Queen Victoria legend
Rev: mint-date legend
Broad square planchets
2a* 1 Paisa Yrs. 9, 21   20.00

Silver
Designs like No. 2a
Round dump planchets
3 ⅛ Rupee Yrs. 1-37   10.00

---

4 ¼ Rupee Yrs. 1-35   8.00
5 ½ Rupee Yrs. 1-35   15.00
6 1 Rupee Yrs. 1-41   20.00

Broad thin planchets
6a* 1 Rupee Yrs. 2-39
  (27-28mm)   75.00
6b 1 Rupee Yrs. 3, 15 (37-38mm)   100.00

JIND

Mint marks: (on reverse of No. 1) stylized "4" in Persian "S", Quatrefoil at lower right. Compare Maler-Kotla, Nabha, Patiala.

Raghbir Singh 1864-87

Silver
Obv: Couplet of Ahmad Shah Durrani
Rev: mint-date legend, stylized 4
Dump planchets
1 1 Rupee Yr. 4   30.00

Ranbir Singh
VS 1943- (1887-)
50th Year of Reign

Silver
Obv: like No.1
Rev: Commemorative legend
Broad thin planchets
2 1 Rupee VS 1993 (1937),
  30mm   80.00

JODHPUR

Takhat Singh 1843-73
First Coinage

Silver
Obv: Queen Victoria legend
Rev: Takhat Singh legend
1 1 Rupee Yrs. 16, 22, 52, mint
  name on obv.   15.00
1a 1 Rupee Yrs. 16, 22, 52, mint
  name on rev.   15.00
Nos. 1 and 1a were struck at both Jodhpur and Sujat, but all bear Jodhpur mint name.

Unless otherwise noted, prices are for coins in very fine, extremely fine, and uncirculated condition.

Gold

2 *F238* 1 Mohur Yr. 22, like No.
1   285.00

Second Coinage

Silver

Designs like No. 1a
Rev: Nagari legend added
3* 1 Rupee Yr. 22   15.00

Third Coinage

Silver

Obv: "Queen of India" legend
Rev: Takhat Singh legend, mint name below
4* 1 Rupee VS 1926–28   15.00
Mint names on No. 4 are Jodhpur (shown), Nagore, Pali,
and Sujat.

Jaswant Singh 1873–95

Copper

Obv: Queen Victoria legend
Rev: Victoria-mint legend
5* 1 Paisa VS 1940–47, AH
1293–1305 (ca. 20 gr.)   2.50

Silver
Obv: Queen Victoria legend
Rev: Jaswant Singh legend

6 ⅛ Rupee ND (11mm)   20.00
7 ¼ Rupee ND   20.00
8 ½ Rupee VS 1945 (17mm)   25.00

9* 1 Rupee VS 1924–50, AH
1291–93 (19–22mm)   15.00
Mint names: on No. 9 Jodhpur, Pali, and Sujat, on Nos.
6–8 Jodhpur only.

Gold

10 *F238c* ¼ Mohur AH 1293
(1876), 13mm   150.00
11 *F238b* ½ Mohur 1293
(17–18mm)   200.00
12 *F238a* 1 Mohur 1293 (20mm) 285.00

Sardar Singh 1895–1911
First coinage

Silver
Obv: Queen Victoria legend
Rev: Sardar Singh legend
13 ⅛ Rupee ND   15.00
14 ¼ Rupee ND   15.00
15 ½ Rupee ND   15.00
16 1 Rupee ND   25.00

Gold

17 *F238c* ¼ Mohur VS 1952
(1895), 15mm   150.00
18 *F238b* ½ Mohur 1952 (18mm) 200.00
19 *F238a* 1 Mohur 1952 (21mm) 300.00

Second Coinage

Copper

Obv: Edward VII legend
Rev: Sardar Singh legend
20 ¼ Anna 1901–10 (16mm)   5.00
21* ½ Anna 1906, 08   10.00

Silver
22 ¼ Rupee VS 1965 (1908),
19mm   25.00

Gold
23 *F238c* ¼ Mohur 1906 (13mm) 150.00
24 *F238b* ½ Mohur 1906 (18mm) 200.00
25 *F238a* 1 Mohur 1906 (20mm) 285.00

Sumar Singh 1911–18
First Coinage

Gold
Obv: Edward VII legend
Rev: Sumar Singh legend
26 *F238b* ½ Mohur ND (19mm)   450.00

Second Coinage

Copper
Obv: George V legend
Rev: Sumar Singh legend

27	¼ Anna 1911, 14 (16–18mm)	5.00
28	½ Anna 1914, 18 (25mm)	9.00

Silver

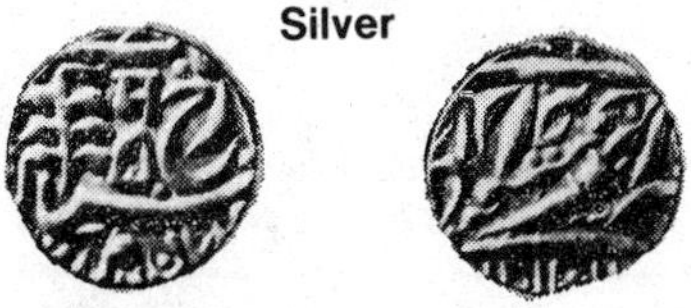

29	⅛ Rupee ND (13mm)	25.00
30	¼ Rupee ND (14mm)	25.00
31*	½ Rupee ND (18mm)	25.00
32	1 Rupee ND (21mm)	30.00

Gold
33	*F238a*	1 Mohur ND (18mm)	300.00

Umaid Singh (1918–47)
First Coinage

Copper
Obv: George V legend
Rev: Umaid Singh legend

34	¼ Anna ND (19–20mm)	5.00

Silver
35	¼ Rupee ND	35.00

Gold
36	*F238c*	¼ Mohur ND (16mm)	150.00
37	*F238b*	½ Mohur ND (18mm)	200.00
38	*F238a*	1 Mohur ND (18–20mm)	285.00

Second Coinage

Copper

Obv: Edward VIII legend
Rev: Umaid Singh legend

39	¼ Anna 1936	5.00

Third Coinage

Copper
Obv: George VI legend
Rev: Umaid Singh legend

40	¼ Anna 1937–39, VS 1996 (thick, 10gr.)	1.00
41*	¼ Anna VS 2000–02 (thin, 3gr.)	.60

Gold
42	*F238a*	1 Mohur ND (18mm)	285.00

Hanwant Singh 1947

Copper
Obv: George VI legend
Rev: Hanwant Singh legend

43	¼ Anna ND (16mm)	25.00

Gold
44	*F238a*	1 Mohur ND (18mm)	350.00

JUNAGADH

Mahabat Khan II 1851–1882

Early issues of this reign are continuations of older anonymous types.

Copper

Obv: Mahabat Khan legend
Rev: Value-mint legend

1*	1 Dokdo VS 1931,35 (1874, 78)	40.00

Silver

2*	1 Kori AH 1292–99/VS 1932–38 (1875–82)	3.00

Gold
3	*F238d*	1 Kori 1292/1932	150.00

Unless otherwise noted, prices are for coins in very fine, extremely fine, and uncirculated condition.

Bahadur Khan III 1882–1892

Gold

4*	F240 ½ Kori AH 1309/VS 1947 (1891)	200.00
5	F239 1 Kori 1309/1947 (18mm)	275.00

Rasal Khan 1892–1911

Copper

6*	1 Dokdo ND, VS 1963–67 (1906–10), vars.	5.00

7*	2 Dokda VS 1964	15.00

Silver

8	1 Kori VS 1966 (15mm)	30.00

Mahabat Khan III 1911–1948

Copper

9	1 Dokdo 1985, 90	30.00

KALAT (Qalat)

Khudadad Khan, Second Reign
AH 1281–1311 (1864–93)

Copper

Obv: Mahmud Khan legend
Rev: Mint legend

1*	1 Falus AH 1186 (error), 1293–95	5.00

KARAULI

Madan Pal 1853–69

Most coins of this reign are dated 1852 (error for 1859.)

Copper

1	1 Paisa 1852/Yr. 13'	8.00

Silver

Obv: Queen Victoria legend

2	¼ Rupee 1852/Yrs. 7–14	15.00
3	½ Rupee 1852/Yr. 13	15.00
4*	1 Rupee 1852–59/Yrs. 7–14	15.00

Arjun Pal 1875–86

Copper

5	¼ Paisa Yr. 11	15.00
6	½ Paisa 1886/Yr.11 (9 gr.)	6.00
7	1 Paisa 1881–86/Yrs. 9–11 (18 gr.)	6.00

Silver

Obv: Empress Victoria legend
Rev: Nagari A (rjun)

8*	1 Rupee 1882–86/Yrs. 10–11	20.00

Bhanwar Pal 1886–1927

Copper

9	½ Paisa 1886–87/Yrs. 1–2 (9 gr.)	6.50
10	1 Paisa 1886–93/Yrs. 1–8 (18 gr.)	6.50

Silver

Obv: Like No. 8
Rev: Nagari BH (anwar)

11	¼ Rupee 1893, 96/Yrs. 8, 11	15.00
12	½ Rupee 1893, 96/Yrs. 8, 10	15.00
13*	1 Rupee 1882–97/Yrs. 1–11	20.00

The 1882 date is an error for 1886.

KASHMIR
Mint: Srinagar

Gulab Singh
VS 1903–13 (1846–56)
Ranbir Singh
VS 1914–42 (1857–85)
Pertab Singh
VS 1942–79 (1885–1925)
First Coinage

Copper

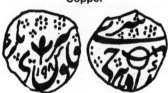

Obv: Mint legend, leaf or flower
Rev: Gadadharji legend

1*	1 Falus (Paisa) VS 1904–08, vars.	4.50

Silver
Obv: Symbols, sword and leaf, no initials
Rev: Mint-date legend

2	⅛ Rupee VS 1903–05 (10–12mm)	10.00
3	¼ Rupee 1903–04 (13–15mm)	10.00
4	½ Rupee 1903–05 (17–19mm)	15.00
5	1 Rupee 1903–06 (20–23mm)	20.00

Second Coinage

Copper
Obv: Mint legend
Rev: Like No. 1, date in frame

6	½ Paisa VS 1920–28 (1863–71), 15–18mm	6.00
7	1 Paisa 1920–31 (18–20mm)	3.00

Obv: Mint legend, sword
Rev: Value, leaf

8	½ Anna VS 1920 (19–20mm)	10.00
9	1 Anna 1920 (24mm)	15.00

Silver

Obv: Persian legends both sides
Obv: Latin JHS added

10	⅛ Rupee VS 1914, 25 (1857, 68), 13 mm	15.00
11	¼ Rupee 1914–25 (14–15mm)	15.00

12	½ Rupee 1914, 22 (16–17mm)	15.00
13*	1 Rupee 1907–27 (20–22mm)	15.00

Reduced Weight Silver
Obv: Persian legend, Latin IHS
Rev: Takari legend
Machine struck in collar

16	1 Rupee VS 1927 (1870), date at bottom	20.00
	Hand-struck on round planchets	
14	¼ Rupee 1928 (15mm)	20.00
15	½ Rupee 1928 (17mm)	20.00
16a	1 Rupee 1927–29 (22mm), date at top	15.00
	Hand struck on crude planchets	
16b	1 Rupee VS 1929–32 (1872–75)	16.00

Third Coinage

Copper
Obv: Persian mint-Raganatha legend, JHS
Rev: Same legend in Takari

17	¼ Paisa 1935–41 (1878–84), 10mm	4.50
18	½ Paisa 1932–41 (14–16mm)	1.00
19	1 Paisa 1936–41 (19mm)	6.50

Silver
Obv: persian legend, Latin JHS
Rev: Takari legend

20	½ Rupee VS 1946–51 (1889–94), 16mm	12.00
21	1 Rupee 1932–52 (18–21mm)	10.00

KISHANGARH

Prithvi Singh 1840–79

Silver

Obv: Queen Victoria legend
Rev: Prithvi Singh legend

1*	1 Rupee 1858–59/Yr. 24	16.50

Sardul Singh 1879–1900

Silver
Obv: Queen Victoria legend

2	1 Rupee 1880/Yr. 24	25.00

Madan Singh 1900–26

Silver
Obv: Edward VII legend

3	½ Rupee 1904/Yr.24	20.00

Unless otherwise noted, prices are for coins in very fine, extremely fine, and uncirculated condition.

Yagyanarain 1926–38

Obv: George (V or VI) legend
Rev: Yagyanarain legend

4	¼ Rupee Yr. 24	22.50
5	½ Rupee Yr. 24	25.00
6	1 Rupee Yr. 24	30.00

Gold

7	½ Mohur Yr. 24 (18mm)	250.00
8	1 Mohur Yr. 24 (19mm)	300.00

Anonymous Issues

Silver

Obv: mint-date legend
Rev: Nagari word

9	⅛ Rupee Yr. 24 (12mm)	20.00
10	¼ Rupee Yr. 24 (15mm)	20.00
11	½ Rupee Yr. 24 (17–18mm)	25.00
12	1 Rupee Yr. 24 (20–24mm)	27.50

Obv: Mint-date legend
Rev: Value in Hindi/Urdu

13	2 Annas Yr. 24 (11mm)	25.00
14	4 Annas Yr. 24 (12–13mm)	20.00
15	8 Annas Yr. 24 (16mm)	20.00

KOTAH

Ram Singh 1828–66
Chattar Sal 1866–89
Umed Singh 1889–1945

Copper

Designs like No. 2a
Rectangular dump planchets

1	½ Paisa Yrs. 37,39 (9 gr.)	3.00
2	1 Paisa Yrs. 15–51 (18 gr.)	3.00

Obv: Queen Victoria legend
Date-mint legend
Broad square planchets

2a*	1 Paisa Yrs. 15, 28	15.00

Silver

Dump planchets

3	⅛ Rupee Yrs. 27–38 (9mm)	3.00
4	¼ Rupee Yrs. 1–38 (12mm)	3.00
5	½ Rupee Yrs. 1–38 (13–15mm)	6.00
6	1 Rupee Yrs. 1–44 (18–20mm)	7.50
7	1 Rupee VS 1956 (1899), 20mm	30.00

Broad, thin planchets

6a*	1 Rupee Yrs. 1–44 (26–30mm)	35.00
7a	1 Rupee VS 1956 (30mm)	50.00

Gold

6	F251b 1 Mohur Yrs. 1–44 (dump, 18mm)	300.00

KUCHAWAN

Kersi Singh 1857–

Silver

Obv: Queen Victoria legend
Rev: "Kuchawan, dependency of Jodhpur"

1	¼ Rupee 1863 (13mm)	20.00
2	½ Rupee 1863 (15–16mm)	20.00
3*	1 Rupee 1863 (19–20mm)	10.00

KUTCH

Monetary System:

48 Trambiyo = 24 Dokda = 16 Dhingla = 1 Kori.

100 Kori = 1 Muhr (Mohur)

Pragmalji II 1860–1875

Copper

Obv: Queen Victoria legend
Rev: Mint/Pragmalji legend

1	1 Trambiyo 1865 (16mm)	3.00

Obv: Value/mint in Urdu
Rev: Same in Nagari

5	1 Trambiyo 1767 (error), 1865–68 (16mm)	1.50
6*	1 Dokdo 1865–69	1.50

8* 3 Dokda 1868   3.00

Obv: Queen Victoria legend
Rev: Pragmalji legend

9   1 Trambiyo 1869 (14mm)   2.00
10* 1 Dokdo 1869–74   1.50
11 1½ Dokda 1869–75 (23mm)   1.50
12 3 Dokda 1863–69 (32mm)   4.50

Silver

13 ½ Kori 1862–63   2.50
14* 1 Kori 1862–63   2.50
Designs similar to Nos. 36–37
15 2½ Kori 1875   5.00
16 5 Kori 1863–75   12.50

Gold
Designs like No. 14
17 F70 25 Kori 1862–70 (16mm)   90.00
Designs similar to Nos. 36–37
18 F69 50 Kori 1866–74 (24mm)   200.00
19 F68 100 Kori 1866 (29mm)   400.00

Khengarji III 1876–1942
First Coinage
Copper

Obv: Queen Victoria legend
Rev: Khengarji legend

22 1 Dokdo 1878   20.00
23* 1½ Dokda 1876–79   2.00

Silver
Designs like Nos. 35, 37
26 1 Kori 1876   100.00
28 5 Kori 1876   30.00

Second Coinage

Copper

Obv: Empress Victoria legend
Rev: Khengarji legend
30* 1 Trambiyo 1881–83   1.00

31* 1 Dokdo 1882–99 (2 vars.),
         21–22mm   1.00
32 1½ Dokda 1882–99 (3 vars),
        23–25mm   1.25
33 3 Dokda 1883–99 (2 vars),
        33–34mm   2.00

Silver

34* ½ Kori 1898–1900 (13mm)   5.00
35 1 Kori 1881–1900 (2 vars.),
        16.5mm   2.00

36* 2½ Kori 1881–99 (3 vars)   7.50

37* 5 Kori 1880–99 (4 vars)   12.50

Unless otherwise noted, prices are for coins in very
fine, extremely fine, and uncirculated condition.

Third Coinage

Copper

Obv: Edward VII legend
Rev: Khengarji legend

38	1 Trambiyo 1908–10 (16mm)	1.00
39*	1 Dokdo 1909 (20.5mm)	1.25
40	1½ Dokda 1909	100.00
41	3 Dokda 1909	100.00

Silver

45*	5 Kori 1902–09	200.00

Fourth Coinage

Copper

Obv: George V legend
Rev: Khengarji legend

46	1 Trambiyo 1919–20 (16mm)	.50
47	1 Dokdo 1920 (21mm)	1.00
48*	1½ Dokda 1926 (23.5mm)	1.50
49	3 Dokda 1926 (33mm)	2.50

Silver

51*	1 Kori 1913–27	1.75

52	2½ Kori 1916–26	5.00
53*	5 Kori 1913–27	10.00

Modified Dies

Copper

54	1 Trambiyo 1928 (16mm)	.75
55	1 Dokdo 1928–29 (21mm)	1.25
56*	1½ Dokda 1928–32 (23mm)	1.00
57	3 Dokda 1928–35 (33mm)	1.50

Silver

58	½ Kori 1928 (14mm)	1.75
59	1 Kori 1928–36 (17mm)	1.75
52a	2½ Kori 1927–35	5.00
53a	5 Kori 1928–36	10.00

Fifth Coinage

Copper

Obv: Edward VIII legend
Rev: Khengarji legend

63*	3 Dokda 1936	7.50

Silver

65*	1 Kori 1936	2.50

Borders like No. 53

66	2½ Kori 1936	15.00
67	5 Kori 1936	8.00

Sixth Coinage

Copper

Obv: George VI legend
Rev: Khengarji legend

71*	3 Dokda 1937	2.00

Silver

73	1 Kori 1937–40	2.50
74	2½ Kori 1937–39	6.00
75	5 Kori 1936–41	12.00

Vijayarajji 1942–1947

Copper

Obv: George VI legend
Rev: Vijayarajji legend

76*	1 Trambiyo 1943–44	.35
77	1 Dhinglo (1½ Dokda) 1943–47 (21mm)	.40

78*	1 Dhabu (3 Dokda) 1943–44 (23mm)	.50
79	1 Payalo (¼ Kori) 1943–47 (27mm)	.75
80	1 Adhio (½ Kori) 1943–46 (36mm)	1.00

Silver

81*	1 Kori 1942–44	3.00
82	5 Kori 1942–43	12.50

Madanasinhji 1947

Copper

Obv: "India Victory" legend
Rev: Madanasinhji legend

83*	1 Dhabu VS 2004	1.25

Silver

Legends like No. 83

84*	1 Kori 2004	10.00

85	5 Kori VS 2004	125.00

LADAKH (Botaan)

Monetary System:

1 Timasha (3 Masha) = Tibet ½ Sho

= approx. ¼ Rupee

Gulab Singh
VS 1903–13 (1846–56)

Silver

Obv: Gulab Singh legend
Rev: Mint legend

1*	1 Timasha (3 Masha) ND (1846–56)	12.00

Unless otherwise noted, prices are for coins in very
fine, extremely fine, and uncirculated condition.

Ranbir Singh
VS 1914–42 (1857–85)
Copper

Obv: Persian legend
Rev: Nagari legend
2* 1 Paisa VS 1924–31   8.00

Silver
Obv: Persian legend
Rev: Tibetan legend
3 1 Timasha VS 1928 (1871)   40.00

LUNAVADA

Wakhat Singhji 1867–1929
Copper
1 1 Paisa ND, obv. 2 swords   7.50
2 1 Paisa ND, obv. cannon   7.50

Obv: Lotus blossom
3* 1 Paisa ND   3.50

Obv: Hand
A4 ½ Paisa ND   5.00
4* 1 Paisa ND   3.50

Obv: Hand in square
7 ½ Paisa VS 1942 (1885)   4.50
8* 1 Paisa 1942   3.00

Obv: Lion to right
5 ½ Paisa VS 1949 (1892)   4.50
6* 1 Paisa 1949   3.00

Obv: Sun symbols
9* 1 Paisa ND   3.00
No. 9 was formerly listed as Banswara No. 1. It has also been attributed to Rampura.

Nos. 1–9 are crude and vary greatly in shape and size. Later coins were usually struck over earlier types, often causing two or more designs to show.

MAKRAI

Bharat Singh 1866–1920
Copper
Obv: Katar (dagger) in lozenge
Rev: Nagari "Makrai"
1 1 Paisa ND (17–22mm)   5.00

MALER-KOTLA
Mint marks on Rev: Stylized "4" in Persian "S", trefoil at lower right, flower at left (Nos. 7–9 omit trefoil and flower). Ruler's name or initial above "4." Compare Jind, Nabha, Patiala.

Sikandar Ali Khan 1859–71
Silver
Obv: Couplet of Ahmad Shah Durrani
Rev: Mint-date legend, Persian "S" above 4
1 ¼ Rupee Yr. 4   15.00
2 ½ Rupee Yr. 4   15.00
3 1 Rupee Yr. 4   10.00

Ibrahim Ali Khan 1871–1908
Silver
Obv: Designs like No. 3
Rev: Persian "BA" above 4
4 ¼ Rupee Yr. 4   12.50
5 ½ Rupee Yr. 4   12.50
6 1 Rupee Yr. 4   10.00

Ahmad Ali Khan 1908–23

Copper
Obv: like No. 3
Rev: Ruler's name spelled out above 4

7	½ Paisa Yr. 4	17.50
8	1 Paisa Yr. 4	15.00

Silver

9	1 Rupee Yr. 4	10.00

MEWAR
Mint: Udaipur.

Anonymous Issues
First Coinage

Silver

1	$^1/_{16}$ Rupee ND (8–9mm)	4.50
2	⅛ Rupee ND (10–11mm)	3.00
3	¼ Rupee ND (12–14mm)	2.50
4	½ Rupee ND (15–17mm)	4.50
5*	1 Rupee ND (18–20mm)	4.50

Gold

6	*F273* 1 Mohur ND (17–19mm)	125.00

Nos. 1–6, known as the "New Chandori" series, were struck ca. 1842–90.

Second Coinage

Silver

7	$^1/_{16}$ Rupee ND (8–9mm)	2.50
8	⅛ Rupee ND (11–12mm)	6.50
9*	¼ Rupee ND (14–15mm)	2.00
10	½ Rupee ND (17–18mm)	5.00

11*	1 Rupee ND (22–24mm)	5.00

Gold

12	*F274* 1 Mohur ND (23–24mm)	200.00

Nos. 7–12, known as the "Swarupshahi" series, were struck ca. 1851–1930.

Provisional Issues

Copper
Obv: Nagari "Udaipur"
Rev: Nagari "Chitor," date

13	1 Pai VS 1975 (1918), 16mm	15.00

Legends like No. 13, ornamental borders

14	1 Pai VS 1978 (1921)	8.00

Third Coinage
Machine Struck Issues

Copper

15*	¼ Anna VS 1999 (1942)	.50

16*	½ Anna VS 1999	.50

17*	1 Anna VS 2000 (1943)	.50

Silver

18	1 Anna VS 1985 (1928), 12mm	1.50
19	2 Annas 1985 (15mm)	2.00
20*	¼ Rupee 1985 (19mm)	2.50
21	½ Rupee 1985 (24mm)	5.00
22	1 Rupee 1985 (30mm)	8.00

Nos. 18–22 were struck in 1931. Other silver coins dated VS 1985, but without city walls on obverse, are believed to be patterns and restrikes.

Local Coinage for Umarda

Copper
Random lines and dots both sides
Thin dump planchets

23	1 Paisa ND (late 19th century?)	1.25

Designs like No. 23
Very thin square planchets

Unless otherwise noted, prices are for coins in very fine, extremely fine, and uncirculated condition.

24 1 Paisa ND (ca. 1938–41?)   .75
Nos. 23–24 are commonly known as "dhingla paisa."

NABHA
Mint mark on reverse: Stylized "4" in Persian "S," spiky flower (with or without stem) at lower right. Ruler's symbol at left. Compare Jind, Maler-Kotla, Patiala.

Bharpur Singh
VS 1903–20 (1846–63)

Silver
Obv: Like No. 2
Rev: Similar but leaf at left
1 1 Rupee VS 1907–20/Yr. 4   25.00

Hira Singh
VS 1927–68 (1870–1911)

Silver

Obv: Govind Singh legend (Sikh saint), date
Rev: Mint-date legend with "4," katar at left
2* 1 Rupee VS 1927–29/Yr. 4   25.00

NAVANAGAR
Nos. 1–10 are basically degenerate copies of the Gujerati coinage of Muzaffar Shah III (1560–84). All but No. 1 bear the frozen date AH 1178, degenerated from 978 (1570).

Mint mark: Ruler's title, "Sri Jamji" on reverse of Nos. 2–10.

Vibhaji
VS 1909–51 (1852–94)
First Coinage

Copper
Obv: Like No. 3
Rev: Similar, but true date replaces legend
Thin dump planchets
1 1 Dokdo VS 1909, 17 (1852, 60)   7.50

Second Coinage
Style: Nos. 2–8 have relatively fine engraving and thin planchets, and probably date from the mid to late 19th century. Earlier issues, with heavier engraving and thick dump planchets (style of No. 1 but dated AH 1178) are listed in Craig, "Coins of the World."

Copper

Obv: Stylized Persian legend
Rev: Nagari "Sri Jamji," date
Thin planchets
2* ½ Dokdo AH 1178 (14–16mm)   3.00

3* 1 Dokdo 1178 (17–19mm)   2.00
4 1½ Dokda 1178 (20–21mm)   1.50

Silver
5 ½ Kori 1178 (12–13mm)   2.50
6 1 Kori 1178 (14–16mm)   2.00

Gold
7 F293a ½ Kori 1178   150.00
8 F293 1 Kori 1178   175.00

Third Coinage

Style: Nos. 9–12 were all struck in collars by machine.
Copper

Designs like No. 3
9 ½ Dokdo AH 1178   5.00
10* 1 Dokdo AH 1178   5.00

11* 3 Dokda VS 1928 (1871)   10.00

Silver

12* 1 Kori VS 1934-36 (1877-79)   10.00

Fourth Coinage

Style: Coinage on dump planchets resumed.

Copper

13* 2 Dokda VS 1943 (1886)   10.00

14* 3 Dokda VS 1942   6.50

Silver

15* 2½ Kori VS 1949-50
    (1892-93), 17-21mm   15.00
16   5 Kori 1945-50 (22-27mm)   15.00

Jaswant Singh
VS 1951-64 (1894-1907)

Copper

17   ½ Dokdo VS 1956 (1899)   30.00
18   1 Dokdo 1956   20.00
19* 1½ Dokda 1956   15.00
20   2 Dokda 1956   30.00
21   3 Dokda 1956   40.00

PARTABGARH (Pratapgarh)

Udaya Singh
VS 1921-47 (1864-90)

Copper

Obv: Sunface with hands
Rev: Nagari legend
1* 1 Paisa VS 1935 (1878), 7.5
    gr.   3.00
Obv: Sunface/2 swords
Rev: legend, date in oval
2   1 Paisa VS 1942-43
    (1885-86)   3.00

Silver

Obv: Shah of London (Victoria) legend
Round dump planchets
3   ⅛ Rupee AH 1236/Yr. 45   3.00
4   ¼ Rupee 1236/Yr. 45   3.00
5   ½ Rupee 1236/Yr. 45   4.00
6* 1 Rupee 1236/Yr. 45   7.00
Square planchets
6a 1 Rupee 1236/Yr. 45   75.00

Raganath Singh
VS 1947-86 (1890-1929)

Copper

Obv: Curved legend/ornament
Rev: 4-line legend
7   1 Paisa VS 1953 (1896)   4.00

PATIALA

Mint marks on reverse: Stylized "4" in Persian "S," floral ornament at lower right. Ruler's symbol at left. (These marks occur on silver, but may differ on gold.) Compare Jind, Maler-Kotla, Nabha.

NARINDAR SINGH 1845-62

Silver

Obv: Couplet of Ahmad Shah Durrani
Rev: mint-date legend with "4," spearhead at left
1   1 Rupee Yr. 4   30.00

Unless otherwise noted, prices are for coins in very
fine, extremely fine, and uncirculated condition.

Gold

2	*F301* 1 Mohur Yr. 4	200.00

Mahindar Singh 1862–76

Silver

Obv: like No. 1
Rev: Similar but different style spearhead

3	1 Rupee Yr. 4	40.00

Rajindar Singh 1876–1900

Silver

Obv: Like No. 1
Rev: Similar but katar at left
Dump planchets

4	¼ Rupee Yr. 4	25.00
5	½ Rupee Yr. 4	25.00
6	1 Rupee Yr. 4	15.00
	Broad thin planchets	
6a	1 Rupee Yr. 4	–

Gold

7	⅓ Mohur Yr. 4 (3.7 gr.)	250.00
8	⅔ Mohur Yr. 4 (7.4 gr.)	300.00
9	*F301* 1 Mohur Yr. 4 (11 gr.)	350.00

PUDUKKOTTAI (Pudukota)

Copper

A1*	1 Amman Cash ND (native issue ca, 1810–90)	1.50

Martanda Bhairava 1886–1928
Rajagopala 1928–47

Bronze

1*	1 Amman Cash ND (1889–1934)	1.50

RADHANPUR

Anonymous Issues

Copper

Obv: Nagari "Go"
Rev: Blank

1	1 Paisa ND	2.50
	Obv: Nagari "Ji"	
	Rev: Blank	
2	1 Paisa ND	1.50

The meaning of the Nagari initials on Nos. 1–2 is unknown, but it has been tentatively suggested that they

can attributed to Zorawar Khan and Bismilla Khan respectively.

Zorawar Khan
AH 1240–91 (1825–74)

Silver

Designs like No. 8

3	50 Falus 1867/AH 1284	40.00
4	100 Falus 1284–86	45.00

Obv: Victoria-mint legend
Rev: Value-Zorawar legend

5	2 Anna 1871/AH 1288 (15mm)	35.00
6	4 Anna 1869–72/AH 1287–88 (18mm)	30.00
7	8 Anna 1869, 71/AH 1287–88 (23mm)	27.50
8*	1 Rupee 1871–72/AH 1287, 89 (28mm)	30.00

Gold

9	*F310* 1 Mohur 1860/AH 1277	250.00

Bismilla Khan
AH 1291–1313 (1874–95)

Silver

Obv: Victoria Empress legend

10	2 Anna 1880	40.00
11	2 Anna 1880	32.50
12	8 Anna 1880–81/AH 1297, 99	32.50
13	1 Rupee 1881, 94	30.00

RAJKOT

Dharmendra Singhji
1930–1948

Gold

1*	*F311* 1 Mohur 1945	UNC 200.00

No. 1 was struck for presentation only.

Silver

1a 1 Mohur 1945   7.50

No. 1a is said to have been struck as a pattern for No. 1, but a quantity of restrikes was made for collectors ca. 1964. It is sometimes called a ½ Rupee.

RATLAM (Rutlam)

Ranjit Singh
VS 1921–50 (1864–93)

Copper

1 1 Paisa VS 1921 (1864)   10.00

Obv: Gujerati "Ratlam"/katar
Rev: Date/star

2* 1 Paisa VS 1927–28 (1870–71)   3.50

3* 1 Paisa 1885   4.50

4* 1 Paisa VS 1945, 47 (1888, 90)   1.75

4a* 1 Paisa VS 1947 (thin, crude restrike of No. 4)   .75

REWAH (Rewa)

Gulab Singh
VS 1975–2003 (1918–46)

Gold

1 *F311a* 1 Mohur VS 1975 (1918)   300.00

SAILANA

Dule Singh
VS 1907–47 (1850–90)

Copper

Obv: Banner
Rev: Date/sword

1* 1 Paisa VS 1937 (1880)   2.50

Obv: Like No. 1
Rev: Date/sword. jhar

2 1 Paisa VS 1940 (1883)   4.00

Obv: Like No.1
Rev: Persian "Sailana," date

3 1 Paisa VS 1941   5.00

Obv: Like No. 1
Rev: Trident in circular Nagari legend

4 1 Paisa VS 1944 (1887)   4.00

Jaswant Singh 1895–1919

Bronze

Obv: head of Edward VII
Rev: Like No. 6

5 ¼ Anna 1908   8.00

6* ¼ Anna 1912   6.00

Unless otherwise noted, prices are for coins in very
fine, extremely fine, and uncirculated condition.

SIKKIM

Thotab Namgyel
VS 1931–68 (1874–1911)

Copper

Obv: Ruler's title, date
Rev: State legend

| 1 | 1 Paisa VS 1940–42 (1883–85) | 8.00 |

SITAMAU

Bahadur Singh
VS 1942–56 (1885–99)

Copper

| 1* | 1 Paisa VS 1942 (1885) | 5.00 |

Sardul Singh
VS 1956–57 (1899–1900)

Copper

| 2 | 1 Paisa VS 1956 (1889) | 8.00 |

TONK

Mints: Sironj (to ca. 1896), Tonk (ca. 1873–1934).

State symbols: 5-petal flower (see No. 2) before AH 1280, fly-whisk (leaf-like symbol) thereafter.

Types: The descriptions given are general guides only. Much variation occurs in wording and arrangement of legends, particularly for Nos. 8–28.

Wazir Muhammad Khan
AH 1250–80 (1834–64)

Copper
Designs like No. 2

| 1 | 1 Paisa AH 1278 (1861) | 15.00 |

Silver

Obv: Victoria-Sironj legend
Rev: Wazir-Muhammad legend

| 2* | 1 Rupee 1276–80/Yr. 23 | 20.00 |

Muhammad Ali Khan
AH 1280–84 (1864–67)

Copper
Obv: Like No. 2
Rev: Muhammad Ali legend

| 3 | 1 Paisa AH 1283–89/Yr. 23 | 10.00 |

Silver

4	⅛ Rupee ND (12mm)	20.00
5	¼ Rupee ND (14–15mm)	20.00
6	½ Rupee ND (16–17mm)	25.00
7	1 Rupee 1282–89/Yr. 23 (20–23mm)	25.00

Coins of this series were struck into the following reign (to 1872/AH 1289).

Muhammad Ibrahim Ali Khan
AH 1284–1349 (1868–1930)
First Coinage

Copper
Obv: Queen Victoria-Tonk legend
Rev: Md. Ibrahim Ali legend

| 8 | 1 Paisa AH 1290 (1873) | 15.00 |

Silver

| 10 | 1 Rupee 1873–77/AH 1290–94 | 20.00 |

Second Coinage

A. Sironj Mint
Copper
Obv: Empress of India-Sironj legend
Rev: Like No. 8

| 11 | 1 Pai AH 1314 (1896) | – |
| 12 | 1 Paisa 1298–1302 (1881–85) | 15.00 |

Silver

13	⅓ Rupee 1896/1314	20.00
14	½ Rupee 1893, 96/1310, 14	30.00
15	1 Rupee 1892–93/1309–10	35.00

B. Tonk Mint
Copper
Obv: Ruler of England-Tonk legend
Rev: Like No. 8

| 16 | 1 Paisa 1876–96/AH 1290–1303 | 5.00 |

Silver

Obv: Like No. 12, but Tonk
Rev: Like No. 8
Dump planchets

17	⅛ Rupee 1892, 99/AH 1309, 17	10.00
18	¼ Rupee 1888–99/1305–18	10.00
19	½ Rupee 1888–99/1305–17	12.50
20*	1 Rupee 1878–97/1293–1315	12.50
	Broad thin planchets	
21	2 Rupees 1880–81/1297–98 (32mm)	175.00

Gold
Dump planchets

22	F324 1 Mohur 1880/AH 1297–98 (19mm)	–
	Broad, thin planchets	
23	F323 2 Mohurs 1880/1297 (31mm)	–

Third Coinage
Copper

Obv: George V legend
Rev: Like No. 8

24*	1 Paisa 1911–28/AH 1329–45	4.00

Silver

25	⅛ Rupee 1928/1346	15.00
26	¼ Rupee 1928/1346	15.00
27	½ Rupee 1928/1346	20.00
28	1 Rupee 1912–30/1330–48	15.00

Muhammad Sa'adat Ali Khan AH 1349–68 (1930–49)
Bronze

Obv: George V legend
Rev: Md. Sa'adat Ali legend

29	1 Paisa 1932/AH 1350 (26mm)	1.25

29a*	1 Paisa 1932/1350 (21mm, struck 1934)	.75

Silver
Obv: George V legend
Rev: Md. Sa'adat Ali legend
Dump planchets

30	⅛ Rupee 1934/1351–53	7.50

TRAVANCORE
Monetary System:

15 Cash = 1 Chuckram

4 Chuckram = 1 Fanam

2 Fanam = 1 Anantaraya

52½ Fanam = 1 Pagoda

Dates are expressed in the Malabar Era (ME), which began in AD 824. For AD date, add 824 or 825 to ME date. Example: ME 1114 + 824–25 = AD 1938–39.

Martanda Varma II 1847–1860
Copper

1*	1 Cash ND (1848–60), 8–10mm	1.00
2	2 Cash ND (1848–49), 10–11mm	2.00

3*	4 Cash ND (13–14mm)	7.00
A3	8 Cash ND (18–19mm)	15.00

Gold
Obv: 3–line legend in beaded circle
Rev: Blank

4	F334 ¼ Pagoda ND (1850), 13mm, 0.64 gm.	75.00
5	F333 ½ Pagoda ND (14.5mm, 1.27 gm.)	100.00
6	F332 1 Pagoda ND (17mm, 2.55 gm.)	150.00
7	F331 2 Pagoda ND (20mm, 5.10 gm.)	225.00

Rama Varma IV 1860–1880
Copper

1a*	1 Cash ND (1860–85)	.40

No. 1a is a slightly degenerate form of No.1, often with no features on face or body.

Unless otherwise noted, prices are for coins in very fine, extremely fine, and uncirculated condition.

Silver

Obv: Leaf sprays at sides
8* 1 Chuckram ND (1860–1901) .50
Similar coins without leaf sprays are earlier issues.

9* 1 Velli Fanam ND (1860–61) 3.00

10* 1 Velli Fanam ND (1864) 3.00

Gold

Obv: leaf sprays at sides
11* *F325* 1 Anantaraya ND
(1860–90) 12.50
Similar coins without leaf sprays are earlier issues.
Obv: similar to No. 10
Rev: Similar to Nos. 29–34
16 *F336* 1 Pagoda 1877 (17mm) 150.00
17 *F335* 2 Pagoda 1877 (19mm) 200.00

Rama Varma V 1880–1885
Note: Nos. 1a, 8 and 11 were continued through this reign.

Silver

18* 1 Viraraya Fanam ND (1881) 3.00

Gold

19* *F325* 1 Viraraya Fanam ND
(1881) 12.50

20 *F340* ½ Sovereign 1881/ME
1057 (20mm) 350.00
21* *F339* 1 Sovereign 1881/1057
(22mm) 450.00
Nos. 20–21 are presentation coins struck to the British gold standard.

Rama Varma VI 1885–1924
First Coinage
Note: Nos. 8 and 11 were continued into this reign.

Copper

1b* 1 Cash ND (1885–95 .35
No. 1b is a yet more degenerate version of No. 1.

22 ¼ Chuckram ND (1888–89),
13mm 3.50
23* ½ Chuckram ND (17–20mm) 4.00

24* 1 Kali Fanam ND (1890–95) 7.50

Second Coinage
Bronze

Obv: RV monogram
29 CASH 1 ND (1901) 8.00
30 CASH FOUR ND 2.00
31* CASH EIGHT ND (1901–03) 3.00
32 CHUCKRAM ONE ND 3.50
30a FOUR CASH ND (1924–30) 1.25
31a EIGHT CASH ND 1.75
32a ONE CHUCKRAM ND 2.50

Silver

33 CH (uckram) s 2 ND (1901) 3.00
33a 2CHS. ND (1928) 2.50
34 ONE FANAM ND (1889) 5.00
34a* FANAM ONE ND (1911), ME
1087–1106 (1912–30) 1.50
The undated variety of No. 34a has edge either plain or reeded.

35* 1 Rupee AD 1889, ME
1083–1106 (1903–30)   5.00
36 ½ Rupee 1889, ME
1086–1107   7.50

Bala Rama Varma II 1924–1949

Bronze

41* 1 Cash ND (1938–45)   .20
        Obv: BRV monogram
42 4 Cash ND   .30
43 8 Cash ND   .35

44* 1 Chuckram ME 1114 (1938),
        ND (1939–45)   .75

Silver

45 1 Fanam ME 1112 (1936)   1.85
45a* 1 Fanam 1116–21, modified
        dies   1.35
46 ¼ Rupee ME 1112   3.25
46a ¼ Rupee 1116–21, modified
        dies   3.25
47 ½ Rupee 1112   7.50
47a "Chitra" ½ Rupee 1114,
        reeded edge   6.50
47b "Chitra" ½ Rupee 1116–21,
        security edge   4.00

INDO–CHINA
see French Indo-China

INDONESIA

A group of four large and some 3,000 small islands extending along the Equator between southeast Asia and Australia. The area came under Dutch control in the 17th century, and was known as the Netherlands Indies. Following Japanese occupation in World War II, it became independent in 1945. Although still primarily agricultural, it exports oil, timber, rubber and metals. Area: 736,000 square miles. Languages: Indonesian, English. Capital: *Jakarta (formerly Batavia).*

Monetary System:
100 Sen = 1 Rupiah

Aluminum

1 1 Sen 1952	.25	.50	1.00
2 5 Sen 1951, 54	.25	.50	.75

3 10 Sen 1951, 54	.25	.50	.75
4 25 Sen 1952	.25	.50	.75

English inscription INDONESIA over eagle

3a 10 Sen 1957	.50	1.00	1.50
4a 25 Sen 1955, 57	.20	.40	.60

Cupro-Nickel

5 50 Sen 1952	.20	.40	.75

Unless otherwise noted, prices are for coins in very
fine, extremely fine, and uncirculated condition.

Malayan word behind head omitted
5a 50 Sen 1954–57   .25   .40   .60

Aluminum

7 50 Sen 1958–61   .25   .40   .75

RIAU ARCHIPELAGO
Area composed of small islands between Singapore and Sumatra.

Inscription on Edge:
KEPULAUAN RIAU
Aluminum

8 1 Sen 1962   .50   1.25   2.00
9 5 Sen 1962   .40   1.00   1.50

10 10 Sen 1962   .40   1.00   1.75

11 25 Sen 1962   .50   1.25   2.00
12 50 Sen 1962   1.00   1.50   3.00

WEST NEW GUINEA
(West Irian, Irian Barat)
Formerly Netherlands New Guinea. Came under administration of Indonesia May 1, 1963. Area: 182,308 square miles.

No Inscription on Edge
Nos. 8–10a have plain edge; 11a–12a have reeded edge.

Aluminum

8a 1 Sen 1962   .75   1.00   1.75
9a 5 Sen 1962   .75   1.00   1.75
10a 10 Sen 1962   .75   1.50   2.50
11a 25 Sen 1962   1.00   1.50   3.00
12a 50 Sen 1962   1.00   1.75   3.50
Later issues in *Current Coins of the World.*

IRAN (Persia)

Between the Tigris and Indus Rivers in southwest Asia. It is one of the oldest countries in the world, being mentioned in the Bible as the Land of the Persians. Use of the name Iran became widespread in the 1920's. Agriculture is the most important industry, but large oil fields and other mineral wealth provide considerable revenue. Languages: Persian, Arabic, Kurdish. Area: 628,060 square miles. Capital: *Tehran.*

Monetary System:
50 Dinar = 1 Shahi
1000 Dinar = 20 Shahi = 1 Qiran (Kran)
10 Qiran = 1 Toman (Tuman)

Prices in this section are for coins in Very Fine condition.

NASIR AL-DIN SHAH
AH 1264–1313 (1848–1896)

Copper

Obv: Value in Dinar
1 12 Dinar ND, AH 1301 (1884),
    15mm   8.00
2 25 Dinar ND, 1293–1307
    (20mm)   1.50
4* 50 Dinar ND, 1293–1305,
    1330 (error), 25mm   1.00

5 100 Dinar ND, 1297–1313,
1330 (error), 30mm 2.50

6 200 Dinar 1300–01 .... 17.50
Obv: Value in Shahi
4a 1 Shahi ND, 1305 (25mm) 25.00
5a 2 Shahi ND, 1305 (30mm) 50.00

New Year Issues
Silver

These pieces, although having a monetary value, were
primarily exchanged as New Year tokens among
friends. Valued at 3 Shahi by weight, they bear only the
word "Shahi" and often are known as "Shahi Sefid," or
"White Shahi."

Designs like Nos. 9–12

7 (3 Shahi) 1296, date in wreath
(17mm, thin) 15.00
7a* (3) Shahi ND, 1297–1309,
date at bottom 2.50
7b (3) Shahi 1313, date in lion's
legs 3.00
Obv: Like No.11
Rev: Like No. A25
8 (3 Shahi) ND 3.50

Regular Issues
Silver
A. Values in Qiran and Dinar,
date at bottom

Obv: Short Nasir legend (3 lines)

9 ¼ (Qiran) ND, 1296–1311
(1879–94), 15mm 2.00
10 500 Dinar ND, 1296–1311
(18mm) 4.50
11* 1000 Dinar ND, 1296–1306
(23mm) 2.00
12 2000 Dinar 1296–98 (27mm) 2.25
Value and date on obv.
13 5000 Dinar 1296–97 .... 75.00

Obv: Long Nasir legend (4 lines)
11a 1000 Dinar 1298–1303 .... 2.00
12a 2000 Dinar 1298–1308 .... 3.00

B. Value in Qiran, date at bottom
Obv: Like No. 11a
12b 2 Qiran 1310 .... 8.00

C. Values in Shahi and Qiran
Obv: Like Nos. 9–12
Rev: Like No. 10c
10b 10 Shahi 1310 .... 12.50

Obv: Like No. 11a
Rev: Date in lion's legs
10c* 10 Shahi 1310–11 .... 10.00
11c 1 Qiran 1310–11 (23mm) 2.50
12c 2 Qiran 1310–11 (27mm) 4.00
Obv: Like No. 13
13c 5 Qiran 1311 .... 125.00

D. Qiran-Dinar values resumed,
date in lion's legs

Obv: Like Nos. 9–12
9d ¼ (Qiran) 1311–12 (15mm) 4.00
10d* 500 Dinar 1311–13 .... 10.00
Obv: Like No. 11a
11d 1000 Dinar 1311 (23mm) 8.50
12d 2000 Dinar 1311–12 (27mm) 2.50

Unless otherwise noted, prices are for coins in very
fine, extremely fine, and uncirculated condition.

Gold
Designs like Nos. 9–12
A16 *F57* ⅕ Toman 1295 (11.5mm)   100.00
B16 ¼ Toman 1295 (14mm)   –
C16 *F56* 5000 Dinar 1296, 98
(17mm)   –
D16 *F55* 1 Toman 1296 (19mm)   –
Nos. B16–D16 may be patterns.
Obv: Like No. 18 but no legend
Rev: Like No. 18
16 *F64* ⅕ Toman 1297–1301,
date on rev. (13mm)   25.00
17 *F63* 5000 Dinar ND,
1297–1305, date on obv.
(16.5mm)   45.00
A18 *F61* 1·Toman ND, 1297
(19mm)   –
No. A18 may be a pattern.

Obv: First portrait with legend
Rev: Like obv. of No. 11a
18* *F62* 1 Toman 1297–1312
(19mm, 2.9 gm.)   60.00

19* *F60* 2 Toman 1297–1309 (21mm, 5.7 gm.) 90.00

Nos. 18–19 bear accession date AH 1264 at lower
right. Actual date (sometimes blundered) appears at
upper left, or divided at upper left and right.
21 *F59* 10 Toman 1296–1311
(36mm, 28.6 gm.)   650.00

Obv: Second portrait
22 *F62* 1 Toman 1310, rev. 3 line
legend   –
22a* *F62* 1 Toman 1311, rev. 4
line legend   300.00
Obv: Like No. 22a but no legend
Rev: Like No.21
A23 *F59* 10 Toman 1311   2000.

Largesse Issue

Silver

15 1 Toman (10 Qiran) 1301
(1884)   350.00
Some authorities consider No. 15 a medal rather than a
coin.

Commemorating Shah's Return from Europe

Silver

A15 500 Dinar 1307 (1889)   200.00

Gold
Obv: Like Nos. 18–19
Rev: Like obv. of No. A15
D15 *F66* 1 Toman 1307   –
B15 *F65* 2 Toman 1307   –

Bank Official's Mint Visit

Gold
Obv: Like No. 19
Rev: Legend in wreath
E15 *F67* 2 Toman 1308   –

50 Years of Reign
Silver

C15 2000 Dinar 1313   3000.
No. C15 may not have been released to circulation due to the assassination of the Shah. Silver and gold pieces dated 1313 with portraits are medals.

GENERAL COINAGE
Nos. 23–24 were issued without the name of the ruler through several successive reigns.

Cupro-Nickel

23	50 Dinar AH 1318–37 (1900–19) 19mm	1.00
24*	100 Dinar 1318–37	1.00

MUZAFFAR AL-DIN SHAH
AH 1314–1324 (1897–1907)

New Year Issues
Silver

Obv: Muzaffar legend
Rev: Date in lion's legs

25*	(3) Shahi ND, 1314–20 (16–17mm, thin)	2.00
25a	(3 Shahi) ND, no value below lion	2.00

Obv: Like No. 25
Rev: In name of Sahib al-Zaman

A25	(3 Shahi) ND	2.00

Regular Issues
Some coins in this series are characterized by poor dies, weak strikes, blundered dates and variable date positions.

First Coinage
Silver
Obv: Muzaffar legend, no crown at top
Rev: Date in lion's legs

26	¼ (Qiran) ND, AH 1316–19 (1898–1901), 15mm	2.00
27	500 Dinar ND, 1313–22 (18–19mm)	4.00
A27	1000 Dinar 1313–14 (23mm)	10.00
28	2000 Dinar 1313–14	2.50

Obv: Crown added at top

A27a*	1000 Dinar 1317–22	10.00
28a	2000 Dinar 1314–20	2.50
28b	2 Qiran 1320–22	6.00

29	5000 Dinar 1320	15.00

Gold

Obv: Like Nos. 26–28
Rev: Date at bottom

A38	*F77* ⅕ Toman 1309 (error)	–
38	*F76* ½ Toman 1314–15	–
39	*F75* 1 Toman 1314	–
A39*	*F74* 2 Toman 1311 (error)	–

No. A39 is presumably the same size as No. 39 but double the weight. Verification of sizes and weights for this series is requested.

Second Coinage

Silver

30	500 Dinar 1319, 23 (1901, 05)	10.00
31	1000 Dinar 1319, 23	12.50
32*	2000 Dinar 1319, 23	5.00
33	5000 Dinar 1319, 24	100.00

Nos. 30–33 dated 1319 are probably patterns.

Gold

Obv: First portrait, no legend
Rev: Like obv. of Nos. 26–28

A34	¼ Toman ND, 1317, date on rev. (15mm)	–
40	*F73* 2 Toman 1322, date on obv. (19mm, 5.7 gm.)	200.00

No. 40 is said to be 1 Toman size but double thick. It bears no value, and may also exist in 1 Toman weight (2.9 gm.).

Rev: Like No. 21 but Muzaffar legend

B34	*F68* 10 Toman 1314 (29 gm.)	–

No. B34 bears value "dah tuman" at top of reverse, but pieces of only 5 Toman weight (14.6 gm.) are said to exist also.

Obv: Value and date added

A34a	¼ Toman 1319	–

Obv: Second portrait, no legend

34	¼ Toman 1323–24	100.00
35*	*F71* ½ Toman 1316–23	50.00
35a	½ Toman 1323, rev. of No. A25 (mule)	–

Obv: Legend added

36	*F70* 1 Toman 1316–24 (19mm, 2.9 gm.)	65.00

Commemorating Royal Birthday

Silver

Like No. 33, legend at sides of head

A40	5000 Dinar 1322 (1904)	750.00

Gold

Like No. 40, legend at sides of head

41	*F73* 2 Toman 1322 (19mm, 5.8 gm.)	250.00

MUHAMMAD ALI SHAH
AH 1324–1327 (1907–1909)
New Year Issues

Silver

Obv: Muhammad Ali legend
Rev: Date in lion's legs

44	(3) Shahi AH 1325–27, 17mm, thin	3.50

Obv: Like No. 44
Rev: Like No. A25

A44	(3 Shahi) ND	3.00

Obv: Like rev. of No. A25
Rev: Like rev. of No. 44

B44	(3) Shahi 1326	3.50

Regular Issues

First Coinage
Silver

Obv: Muhammad Ali legend
Rev: Date in lion's legs

45	¼ (Qiran) AH 1325–27 (15mm)	5.00
46*	500 Dinar 1325–26 (18mm)	10.00
A47	1000 Dinar 1325–26 (23mm)	35.00
47	2 Qiran 1325–27 (28mm)	3.00

Gold

56*	*F81* 5000 Dinar 1324–25 (17mm)	–
A56	*F80* 1 Toman 1324 (19mm)	–

Second Coinage
Silver

48	500 Dinar 1326–27	10.00
49*	1000 Dinar 1326–27	17.50
50	2000 Dinar 1326	350.00
A50	5000 Dinar 1327	175.00

Gold
Obv: like Nos. 48–A50, but no legend or wreath
Rev: Like obv. of Nos. 45–47

53	*F79* ½ Toman 1327, 62 (error), 17mm, 1.4 gm.	250.00
54	*F78* 1 Toman 1327	–

Similar ⅕ and 2 Toman pieces have been reported.

AHMAD SHAH
AH 1327–44 (1909–25)
First Coinage
New Year Issue

Silver

Obv: Ahmad legend

64	(3) Shahi AH 1328–30 (1910–12), date at bottom	2.00
A64	(3) Shahi 1332, date in lion's legs	3.50

Mules exist from various dies of Nos. 64, A70 and B70

Regular Issues

Obv: Ahmad legend
Rev: Date at bottom

65	¼ (Qiran) 1327–31 (15mm)	1.50
66	500 Dinar 1327–30 (18mm)	2.25
67*	1000 Dinar 1327–30 (23mm)	1.50
68	2 Qiran 1327–29 (28mm)	2.25
68a	2000 Dinar 1330	2.25

Rev: Date in lion's legs

68b	2000 Dinar 1330–31	3.00

Gold
Designs like Nos. 65–68a

75	⅕ Toman 1329 (14mm)	–
76	*F82* ½ Toman 1329	–

A similar 1 Toman has been reported.

Second Coinage
New Year Issues

Mules exist from various dies of Nos. 64, A70 and B70.

Silver

Obv: Ahmad legend, date at bottom
A70 (3) Shahi 1333–42   1.00

Obv: : Like rev. of No. A25
Rev: Date in lion's legs
B70 (3) Shahi ND, 1332–42   1.00
No. B70 without date cannot be definitely assigned to this reign.

Regular Issues
Silver

Obv: Ahmad legend
Rev: Date in lion's legs
C70 ¼ (Qiran) AH 1327 (error),
32–43 (1914–25)   1.50

70 500 Dinar 1331–43   3.50
71* 1000 Dinar 1331–44   1.35
72 2000 Dinar 1330–44   2.50
69 5000 Dinar 1331–44   8.00

Gold

79 *F84* 2000 Dinar 1335–41
(14mm)   20.00
80 *F85* 5000 Dinar 1333–37
(17mm)   35.00
80a 5000 Dinar 1340, 42 rev. of
No. A25 (mule)   85.00
81* *F86* 1 Toman 1337–43
(19mm, 2.9 gm.)   125.00

A81 2 Toman 1332, size and weight
of No. 81   –
Gold coins similar to Nos. 70–72, with values of 2, 5, and 15 Ashrafi are believed to be patterns. Other gold pieces larger than 2 Toman bear no values, have variable weights and appear to be medals only.

Tenth Year Jubilee Issues
Silver

Obv: Legends at sides of head
73 1000 Dinar 1337 (1919)   35.00
74* 2000 Dinar 1337   40.00

REZA SHAH PAHLAVI
SH 1304–20 (1925–41)

Solar year adopted S.H. 1304, Started March 21, 1925
10,000 Dinar = 1 Pahlavi 1926–30

New Year Issue
Gold
Obv: 4 line legend, no wreath
Rev: Date below lion
119 *F91* 1 Toman SH 1305 (1926)
19mm   50.00

Regular Issues
First Coinage
Cupro-Nickel
95 50 Dinar SH 1305–07
(1926–28)   1.00
96 100 Dinar 1305–07   .75
Nos. 95–96 are identical to Nos. 23–24 except for the use of the solar dating system.

Silver

Obv: In the name of Kingdom of Iran
Rev: Date below lion
100 ¼ (Qiran) SH 1304 (1925),
15mm   7.50

Gold

A101* 500 Dinar 1304   2500.
101 1000 Dinar 1304–05   2.00
102 2000 Dinar 1304–05   2.50
103 5000 Dinar 1304–05   12.50

120 *F94* 1 Pahlavi SH 1306–08
   (1927–29)   20.00
121* *F93* 2 Pahlavi 1306–08   45.00
122 *F92* 5 Pahlavi 1306–08   300.00

Second Coinage

Silver

Fourth Coinage

5 Dinar = 1 Shahi
100 Dinar = 1 Rial
100 Rial = 1 Pahlavi

Bronze

Obv: In name of Reza
Rev: Date at bottom

105 500 Dinar 1305   35.00
106 1000 Dinar 1305–06   2.00
107* 2000 Dinar 1305–06   2.50
108 5000 Dinar 1305–06   10.00

93 1 Dinar SH 1310 (1931)   1.50
94* 2 Dinar 1310   1.50

Gold

Cupro-Nickel

No. 116   *No. 117*
116 *F90* 1 Pahlavi SH 1305 (1926)   75.00
117 *F89* 2 Pahlavi 1305   200.00
118 *F88* 5 Pahlavi 1305   400.00

97 5 Dinar 1310 (18.5mm)   1.50
98* 10 Dinar 1310 (21mm)   1.50
99 25 Dinar 1310 (24mm)   5.00

Third Coinage

Copper

97a 5 Dinar 1314   15.00
98a 10 Dinar 1314   5.00
99a 25 Dinar 1314   15.00
92 10 Shahi (50 Dinar) 1314
   (24.5mm)   2.00

Silver

Silver

Obv: Like No. 100
Rev: Date at bottom

104 ¼ (Rial) 1315   1.00

A109 500 Dinar 1306–08   3.00
109 1000 Dinar 1306–08   2.00
110* 2000 Dinar 1306–08   2.50
111 5000 Dinar 1306–08   6.00

Unless otherwise noted, prices are for coins in very
fine, extremely fine, and uncirculated condition.

Obv: In name of Reza

112 ½ Rial 1310–15 (1931–36),
18mm 1.00
113 1 Rial 1310–13 (22.5mm) 2.50
114* 2 Rial 1310–13 (26mm) 5.00
115 5 Rial 1310–13 (37mm) 10.00

Gold

123* F96 ½ Pahlavi 1310–15 125.00
124 F95 1 Pahlavi 1310 400.00

GENERAL COINAGE

Nos. 125–128 were issued without the name of the ruler through the last years of Reza Shah and continued into the following reign. The listings have been combined with former Nos. A129–E129.

Aluminum-Bronze

125 5 Dinar SH 1315–21
(1936–42), 16mm .20
126* 10 Dinar 1315–21 (18mm) .25
127 25 Dinar 1326–29 (19mm) 2.00
128 50 Dinar 1315–32 (1936–53),
20mm .30

Bronze

128a 50 Dinar 1322 (1943) 1.25

MOHAMMAD REZA PAHLAVI
1941–1979
First Coinage
Silver

Obv: In the name of Mohammad Reza
Rev: Lion in full wreath

129 1 Rial SH 1322–30 (1943–51),
18mm .35
130* 2 Rial 1322–30 (22mm) .75
131 5 Rial 1322–28 (26mm) 2.00
132 10 Rial 1323–26 (32mm) 3.00

Gold

133 F98 ½ Pahlavi SH 1322–23
(1943–44) 40.00
134* F97 1 Pahlavi 1322–24 60.00

Obv: Head in high relief

135 ½ Pahlavi SH 1324–30
(1945–51) 40.00
136* 1 Pahlavi 1324–30 60.00

Second Coinage

Aluminum-Bronze
Design like No. 128

137 50 Dinar 1332–54 (1954–76),
thin .40

Cupro-Nickel

Obv: No crown at top
Rev: Lion in small wreath

138* 1 Rial (13) 31–36 (18.5mm) .50
139 2 Rial 1331–36 (2 vars.),
22.5mm .60
140 5 Rial 1331–36 (26mm) .75

No. 138 uses only the last two digits of the date.

Gold

Obv: Head in lower relief

141* F103 ¼ Pahlavi 1332–35
(14mm) 15.00

141a *F104* ¼ Pahlavi 1336–55
(16mm)   14.00

142* *F102* ½ Pahlavi SH1333–55   35.00
143 *F101* 1 Pahlavi 1333–55   35.00
144 *F100* 2½ Pahlavi 1339–55   125.00
145 *F99* 5 Pahlavi 1339–55   250.00
Later issues in *Current Coins of the World.*

IRAQ

Western Asia, bounded by Turkey, Iran, Syria, Jordan, Kuwait and Saudi Arabia; its only seacoast is on the Persian Gulf. Extending along the Tigris and Euphrates valleys, it encompasses the area of the oldest world civilization known. In modern times it has been held by Turkey, been a British mandate under the League of Nations, and became a sovereign state in 1932. It is one of the great oil producing countries of the world. Area: 172,000 square miles. Languages: Arabic, Kurdish. Capital: *Baghdad.*

Monetary System:
50 Fils = 1 Dirham
200 Fils = 1 Riyal
1000 Fils = 1 Dinar (Pound)

Except where noted, prices are for coins in Very Fine condition.

FAISAL I 1921–1933

Bronze

1* 1 Fils 1931, 33   .75
2 2 Fils 1931, 33   1.25

Nickel
3 4 Fils 1931, 33 (scalloped)   1.50
4 10 Fils 1931, 33 (scalloped)   2.00

Silver

5* 20 Fils 1931, 33   2.50
6 50 Fils 1931, 33   4.00
7 1 Riyal 1932   18.00

GHAZI I 1933–1939

Bronze

8* 1 Fils 1936, 38   .50
No. 8 dated 1938 was struck to 1952.

Nickel
9 4 Fils 1938–39   1.50
10 10 Fils 1937–38   2.50

Cupro-Nickel

9a* 4 Fils 1938   .50
10a 10 Fils 1938   1.00
Nos. 9a–10a were struck 1941–42.

Bronze
9b 4 Fils 1938   .50
10b 10 Fils 1938   .75
Nos. 9b–10b were struck 1942–44.

Silver

11 20 Fils 1938   1.75
12* 50 Fils 1937–38   3.50

FAISAL II 1939–1958

Bronze

13 4 Fils 1943   2.50
14* 10 Fils 1943   5.00

Unless otherwise noted, prices are for coins in very fine, extremely fine, and uncirculated condition.

15* 1 Fils 1953   .25
16 2 Fils 1953   .85

Cupro-Nickel

17* 4 Fils 1953 (scalloped)   .35
18 10 Fils 1953   .50

Silver

19 20 Fils 1953   40.00
20 50 Fils 1953   60.00
21 100 Fils 1953   6.50

Redesigned reverse, slightly reduced size

22 20 Fils 1955   2.00
23* 50 Fils 1955   3.25
The 100 Fils 1955 is thought to be a pattern.

REPUBLIC 1958–

The following valuations are for Uncirculated coins.
Bronze

24 1 Fils 1959   .50

Cupro-Nickel

25* 5 Fils 1959   .50
26 10 Fils 1959   .60

Silver

27* 25 Fils 1959   1.00
28 50 Fils 1959   2.00
29 100 Fils 1959   3.00
Former No. 30, the so-called "500 Fils" 1959, bears no
denomination and is officially considered a medal.

Later issues in *Current Coins of the World.*

IRELAND (Eire)

Formerly a part of the United Kingdom but became a
self-governing Dominion of the British Commonwealth in
1922. Adopted a republican form of government in
1949. Area: 27,137 square miles. Languages: English,
Gaelic. Capital: *Dublin.*

Monetary System:

4 Farthings = 1 Penny	5 Shillings = 1 Crown
12 Pence = 1 Shilling	20 Shillings = 1 Pound
2 Shillings = 1 Florin	

Gaelic Legend:
SAORSTAT EIREANN
Bronze

1   1 Farthing 1928–37   .65   3.25   13.00
        1931,32 . . . 3 1935,36 . . . 8

2   ½ Penny 1928–37   1.25   3.50   20.00
        1933 . . . 25

3   1 Penny 1928–37   .65   4.00   25.00
        1933 . . . 2

Nickel

4 3 Pence 1928–35   1.00   2.50   10.50
    1933 . . . 6   1935 . . . 3
5 6 Pence 1928–35   6.50   13.00   32.50

Silver

6 1 Shilling 1928–37   6.50   13.00   32.50
   1930,33 . . . 30   1931,35 . . . 12   1937 . . . 100

7 1 Florin 1928–37   9.00   15.00   45.00
   1930,33,37 . . . 33   1934 . . . 85   1935 . . . 20

8 ½ Crown 1928–37   12.00   25.00   45.00
   1930-33 . . . 26   1937 . . . 200

New Legend: EIRE only
Bronze

9 1 Farthing 1939–66   .15   .30   1.00
   1940 . . . 4   Proof . . . 225.00

10 ½ Penny 1939–67   .10   .15   .50
   1946 . . . 3   Proof . . . 250.00
11 1 Penny 1940–68   .10   .15   .25
   1940 . . . 5   Proof . . . 80.00

Nickel

12 3 Pence 1939–40   1.25   5.00   32.50
   1939 . . . 6   Proof . . . 1000.
13 6 Pence 1939–40   1.25   6.50   32.50
    Proof . . . 625.00

Silver

14 1 Shilling 1939–42   6.50   12.00   25.00
    Proof . . . 450.00
15 1 Florin 1939–43   8.00   15.00   40.00
   1943 . . . 3500   Proof..525.00
16 ½ Crown 1939–43   12.00   16.00   45.00
   1943 . . . 325   Proof . . . 525.00

Cupro-Nickel

12a 3 Pence 1942–68   .10   .15   .25
    Proof . . . 325.00
13a 6 Pence 1942–69   .10   .15   .30
   1945-47 . . . 650   Proof . . . 400.00

14a 1 Shilling 1951–68   .15   .35   1.00
    Proof . . . 325.00

15a 1 Florin 1951–68   .25   1.00   2.00
    Proof . . . 400.00
16a ½ Crown 1951–67   .65   1.00   2.50
   1954 . . . 4   Proof . . . 400.00

Unless otherwise noted, prices are for coins in very fine, extremely fine, and uncirculated condition.

50th Anniversary of
1916 Uprising

Silver

Obv: Padraig Pearse

17 10 Shillings 1966   8.00   9.00 12.50
                                 Proof . . . 20.00

1928 Proof Set . . . 200.00

Later issues in *Current Coins of the World.*

Aluminum

1 25 Mils 5708-09
       (1948-49)   12.00 18.00 30.00
            5708 . . . 100

ISRAEL

Situated in the Middle East, bordering the Mediterranean Sea, Israel is a republic created by U.N. resolution in 1948. With the Nazi persecution of Jews during World War II, a great exodus began toward Palestine, which is now part of Israel. The largest export crop is citrus fruits, but a gradual increase in manufactured commodities is seen. Area: 7,993 square miles. Languages: Hebrew, Arabic. Capital: *Jerusalem.*

Monetary System:
1000 Mils = 1 Lira (Pound)
1000 Pruta = 1 Pound to 1960
100 Agorot = 1 Pound 1960-1980

HEBREW DATES ON ISRAELI COINS

Dates on regular coins are from the ancient Hebrew calendar, and appear only in Hebrew. On commemoratives, the AD date is also included, as are Arabic numerals.

Note: The style of date may vary slightly on some denominations.

A.D. Date	Equivalent Hebrew Date	Hebrew Date on Coin
1948	5708	תש"ח
1949	5709	תש"ט
1952	5712	תשי"ב
1954	5714	תשי"ד
1955	5715	תשט"ו
1957	5717	תשי"ז

New Coinage System

On coins dated 5709, varieties exist with and without a small pearl at the bottom of the bar on the reverse.

2 1 Prutah 5709   .50   1.00   2.00
       w/o Pearl   2.00   5.00 12.00

Bronze

3 5 Prutah 5709   .50   1.00   2.00
       w/o Pearl   2.00   4.00   9.00

4 10 Prutah 5709   10.00 20.00 40.00
       w/o pearl   1.00   2.50   5.00

Aluminum

5	10 Prutah 5712	.50	1.00	2.00
5a	10 Prutah 5717, round	.50	1.00	2.00

Anodized Aluminum (Brown)

5b	10 Prutot 5717, round	.50	1.00	2.00

Cupro-Nickel

6	25 Pruta 5709	.50	1.00	2.00
	w/o Pearl	10.00	20.00	35.00

8	50 Pruta 5709,14 (reeded edge)	10.00	20.00	40.00
	w/o Pearl	1.00	2.00	3.00
	5714 . . . 15			
8a	50 Pruta 5714 (plain edge)	1.00	2.00	5.00

10	100 Pruta 5709, 15 (28.5mm)	1.00	2.00	3.00

12	250 Pruta 5709	5.00	10.00	15.00

Silver

12a	250 Pruta 5709	6.00	10.00	12.50

14	500 Pruta 5709	10.00	15.00	25.00

Nos. 12a and 14 were issued only in Mint Sets.

Nickel-Clad Steel
Edge: Plain

6a	25 Pruta 5714	1.00	2.00	3.00
8b	50 Pruta 5714	1.00	2.00	3.00
10a	100 Pruta 5714 (25.6mm)	1.00	2.00	3.00

COMMEMORATIVE ISSUES

Proofs can be distinguished by the presence of the Hebrew letter "Mem" on all issues except those of 1958, which have no special markings.

Tenth Anniversary of Republic

Silver

Unless otherwise noted, prices are for coins in very fine, extremely fine, and uncirculated condition.

	UNC	PROOF
16 5 Pounds 1958	20.00	500.00

Law is Light (Chanuka)
Cupro-Nickel

17 1 Pound 1958	4.00	60.00

Ingathering of Exiles
Silver

18 5 Pounds 1959	40.00	75.00

Deganya
Cupro-Nickel

19 1 Pound 1960	7.50	60.00

Dr. Theodore Herzl
Silver

20* 5 Pounds 1960	35.00	85.00

Gold
21 *F1* 20 Pounds 1960	550.00	–

Henrietta Szold —
Hadassah Medical Center

Cupro-Nickel

27 1 Pound 1960	50.00	300.00

Bar Mitzvah
Silver

28 5 Pounds 1961	80.00	100.00

Feast of Purim
Cupro-Nickel

29 ½ Pound (Half Shekel)
1961–62   15.00   18.00

Heroism and Sacrifice

30 1 Pound 1961   18.00   30.00

Industrialization of the Negev
Silver

31 5 Pounds 1962   85.00 125.00

10th Anniversary
Death of Chaim Weizman
Gold

32 *F3* 50 Pounds 1962   —   500.00
33 *F2* 100 Pounds 1962   —   900.00

Chanuka-Italian Lamp
Cupro-Nickel

34 1 Pound 1962   60.00   80.00

Seafaring
Silver

35 5 Pounds 1963   500.00 550.00

Chanuka-North African Lamp
Cupro-Nickel

38 1 Pound 1963   60.00   80.00

Unless otherwise noted, prices are for coins in very
fine, extremely fine, and uncirculated condition.

Israel Museum
Silver

39 5 Pounds 1964   90.00 135.00

Tenth Anniversary
Bank of Israel
Gold

40 *F4* 50 Pounds 1964   500.00 3000.

Later issues in *Current Coins of the World.*

ITALIAN SOMALILAND

The southeastern coast of the Somali region, on the eastern "horn" of Africa, became an Italian colony in the late 1800's. It came under British administration during World War II, but was returned to Italy under U.N. trusteeship in 1950 with ten years to prepare for independence. In 1960, Italian and British Somaliland joined to form the independent Somali Republic. Most of the native population were nomadic herdsmen; Italian colonists practiced agriculture. Area: 246,155 square miles. Languages: Somali, Arabic, Italian. Capital: *Mogadiscio (Mogadishu).*

Monetary System:
100 Bese (Pice) = 1 Rupia
100 Centesimi = 1 Lira

VITTORIO EMANUELE III
1900–1946
Bronze

1	1 Besa 1909–21	15.00	30.00 75.00
2	2 Bese 1909–24	15.00	30.00 85.00
3	4 Bese 1909–24	22.50	45.00 125.00

Silver

4	¼ Rupia 1910, 13	30.00	50.00 100.00
	1913 EF . . . 80		
5	½ Rupia 1910–19	30.00	55.00 125.00
	1915 EF . . . 80		
6	1 Rupia 1910–21	45.00	75.00 150.00
	1920,21 . . . 2000		

New Coinage System

7	5 Lire 1925	90.00 140.00 235.00
8	10 Lire 1925	115.00 175.00 300.00

For later issues see SOMALIA.

ITALY

Italy, a boot-shaped European peninsula into the Mediterranean, was a collection of independent states from the Middle Ages until gradual unification from 1815 to 1870. A kingdom was proclaimed in 1861. It became a republic by referendum in 1946. Highly industrialized, it imports raw materials and exports finished products. Area: 116,000 square miles. Language: Italian. Capital: *Roma (Rome).*

Monetary System:
100 Centesimi = 1 Lira

VITTORIO EMANUELE II
1861–1878
Italian Unification

Silver

5	5 Lire 1861	300.00	500.00	1000.

Regular Issues

Copper

6	1 Centesimo 1861–67	1.00	2.00	10.00
	1867T . . . 50			
7	2 Centesimi 1861–67	1.00	2.00	10.00
8	5 Centesimi 1861–67	2.00	5.00	20.00
	1861B . . . 30			
9	10 Centesimi 1862–67	1.00	5.00	50.00

Silver

Rev: Arms in wreath

10	20 Centesimi 1863		Rare

11	50 Centesimi 1861–63	5.00	15.00	40.00
	1861M . . . 1500 1861T . . . 600 1861F . . . 150			
	1862N, T . . . 50			
12*	1 Lira 1861–67	5.00	15.00	40.00
	1861T . . . 1000 1861F,62T, N . . . 100			
	1867T . . . 60			
13	2 Lire 1861–63	20.00	40.00	100.00
	1861T,62N . . . 1000			
14	5 Lire 1861–78	25.00	30.00	100.00
	1861 . . . 1000 1862 . . . 200			
	1866 . . . 1500 1872–73 . . . 900			

Rev: Value above branches

15	20 Centesimi 1863–67	5.00	15.00	30.00
	1867T . . . 60			
16	50 Centesimi 1863–67	5.00	15.00	60.00
	1867T . . . 200			
17	1 Lira 1863	5.00	15.00	30.00
18	2 Lire 1863	20.00	50.00	150.00

Gold

A18	*F16* 5 Lire 1863, 65	80.00	100.00	150.00
B18	*F14–15* 10 Lire 1861–65			
	(vars.)	80.00	100.00	150.00
	1861 . . . 5000			
19	*F11–13* 20 Lire 1861–78	80.00	100.00	135.00
	1861,70–71 . . . 300			
	1873 . . . 5000 1873R . . . 1500			
20	*F10* 50 Lire 1864	10000.	20000.	30000.
21	*F8–9* 100 Lire 1864–78	5000.	8000.	10000.

UMBERTO I 1878–1900

Copper

22	1 Centesimo 1895–1900	1.00	5.00	10.00
	1897 . . . 30			
23	2 Centesimi 1895–1900	1.00	5.00	10.00
	1896 . . . 50			
24	5 Centesimi 1895–96	10.00	20.00	40.00

Unless otherwise noted, prices are for coins in very
fine, extremely fine, and uncirculated condition.

| 25 | 10 Centesimi 1893–94 | 1.00 | 5.00 | 20.00 |
| | 1893, 94R . . . 40 | | | |

Cupro-Nickel

| 26 | 20 Centesimi 1894–95 | 1.00 | 5.00 | 10.00 |

Silver

27	50 Centesimi 1889, 92	40.00	80.00	150.00
28	1 Lira 1883–1900	5.00	10.00	50.00
	1883, 92 . . . 2000			
29	2 Lire 1881–99	5.00	20.00	80.00
	1885, 98 . . . 100			
30	5 Lire 1878–79	25.00	40.00	250.00
	1878 . . . 700			

Gold

32	F21	20 Lire 1879–97	100.00	130.00	150.00
	1884 . . . 600 1889 . . . 300				
33	F19–20	50 Lire 1884–91	1000.	1500.	2000.
	1891 . . . 3000				
34	F17–18	100 Lire			
	1880–91	2000.	4000.	5000.
	1880 . . . 7000 1891 . . . 4000				

VITTORIO EMANUELE III
1900–1946
First Coinage

Bronze

| 35 | 1 Centesimo 1902–08 | 1.00 | 5.00 | 15.00 |
| | 1902 . . . 400 | | | |

| 36 | 2 Centesimi 1903–08 | 1.00 | 5.00 | 15.00 |
| | 1905, 07 . . . 100 | | | |

Nickel

| 37 | 25 Centesimi 1902–03 | 15.00 | 25.00 | 40.00 |

Silver

38	1 Lira 1901–07	10.00	15.00	40.00
	1905 . . . 100			
39	2 Lire 1901–07	30.00	60.00	150.00
	1901,03,04 . . . 175			
40	5 Lire 1901	10000.	15000.	25000.

No. 40 has been extensively counterfeited.

Gold

41	F23–24	20 Lire 1902–10	300.00	600.00	1000.
	1902, 08, 10 . . . 10,000				
42	F22	100 Lire 1903, 05	3000.	5000.	8000.

Dates of No. 41 after 1905 were not for circulation.

Second Coinage

Bronze

43	1 Centesimo 1908–18	5.00	10.00	15.00
	1908 . . . 150			
44	2 Centesimi 1908–17	1.00	5.00	15.00
	1908 . . . 100			
45	5 Centesimi 1908–18	5.00	20.00	60.00
46	10 Centesimi 1908	5000.	7000.	10000.

Nickel

47 20 Centesimi 1908–35   1.00   3.00   10.00
         1919 . . . 20
Dates after 1922 were not for circulation.

Silver

48 1 Lire 1908–13   5.00   15.00   30.00
         1908 . . . 50
49 2 Lire 1908–12   10.00   20.00 100.00
         1910 . . . 100 1911 . . . 300

50 1 Lira 1915–17   5.00   10.00   25.00
51 2 Lire 1914–17   10.00   15.00   35.00
52 5 Lire 1914   1000.   2000.   4000.
No. 52 has been extensively counterfeited.

Gold

53 *F29* 10 Lire 1910–27   1000. 1500. 2500.
54 *F28* 20 Lire 1910–27 300.00 400.00 600.00
55 *F27* 50 Lire 1910–27 700.00 1000. 1500.
56 *F26* 100 Lire 1910–27 1500. 2500. 3500.
Dates other than 1912 of Nos. 53–56 were not for circulation.

50th Anniversary of Kingdom
Nos. 57–60

Bronze
57 10 Centesimi 1911   5.00   15.00   25.00

Silver

58 2 Lire 1911   15.00   25.00   80.00
59 5 Lire 1911   200.00 400.00 700.00

Gold

60 *F25* 50 Lire 1911   300.00 500.00 800.00

Third Coinage
Bronze

61 5 Centesimi 1919–37   1.00   3.00   10.00
         1937 . . . 15

62 110 Centesimi 1919–37   1.00   5.00   10.00
         1919 . . . 50

Unless otherwise noted, prices are for coins in very
fine, extremely fine, and uncirculated condition.

Cupro-Nickel

63 20 Centesimi 1918–20,
overstruck on No. 26
1920 . . . 10   1.00   3.00   10.00

Nickel

64 50 Centesimi 1919–28,
plain edge   1.00   5.00   20.00
1919 . . . 40   1924 . . . 200
64a 50 Centesimi 1919–35,
reeded edge   1.00   10.00   100.00
Dates after 1925 of Nos. 64–64a were not for circulation.

65 1 Lire 1922–35   1.00   5.00   10.00
1926, 27 . . . Rare
Dates after 1928 were not for circulation.

66 2 Lire 1923–35   1.00   5.00   10.00
1926 . . . 50   1927 . . . 80
Dates after 1927 not for circulation.

Silver

67 5 Lire 1926–35   5.00   10.00   20.00
Dates after 1930 not for circulation

68 10 Lire 1926–34   10.00   20.00   50.00
1926 . . . 100   1930 . . . 100
Dates after 1930 not for circulation.

69 20 Lire 1927–34   50.00   80.00   150.00
Dates after 1928 not for circulation.

Gold

70 *F34* 50 Lire 1931–33   100.00   200.00   300.00
1933 . . . 300

71 *F33* 100 Lire 1931–33   200.00   300.00   400.00
1933 . . . 400

First Anniversary of Fascist Government 1922–23

Gold

72	F31 20 Lire 1923	300.00 400.00 600.00
73	F30 100 Lire 1923	600.00 800.00 1500.

75 20 Lire 1928   50.00   80.00 200.00

Dual Commemorative

25th Anniversary of Reign and 10th Anniversary of Entry into World War I

Fourth Coinage

Title: RE E IMPERATORE
Bronze

77 5 Centesimi 1936–39   .50   1.00   5.00
      1936 . . . 5

78 5 Centesimi 1936–39   .50   1.00   5.00
      1936 . . . 5

74 F32 100 Lire 1925   1500. 2000. 3500.

Nickel

79 20 Centesimi 1936–38   20.00   40.00 100.00

10th Anniversary Ending of World War I

Silver

80	50 Centesimi 1936–38	10.00 20.00 50.00
81	1 Lira 1936–38	10.00 20.00 50.00

Unless otherwise noted, prices are for coins in very fine, extremely fine, and uncirculated condition.

82 2 Lire 1936–38   10.00 20.00 50.00
Dates after 1936 of Nos. 79–82 not for circulation.

91 20 Lire 1936–41   200.00 400.00 700.00
Dates after 1936 not for circulation.

No. 91 has been extensively counterfeited.

Aluminum-Bronze
77a 5 Centesimi 1939–43   1.00   2.00   3.00
78a 10 Centesimi 1939–43   1.00   2.00   3.00

Gold

Stainless Steel
79a 20 Centesimi 1939–43   1.00   2.00   5.00
80a 50 Centesimi 1939–43   1.00   2.00   5.00
    1943 . . . 20
81a 1 Lira 1939–43   1.00   2.00   5.00
    1943 . . . 25
82a* 2 Lire 1939–43   1.00   2.00   5.00
    1942 . . . 100 1943 . . . 50
Two different alloys were used for Nos. 79a–82a:
"Niox" (non-magnetic) in 1939 and part of 1940; and
"Acmonital" (magnetic) in the balance of 1940 through
1943.

92 *F37* 50 Lire 1936   1000. 2000. 3000.
93 *F35* 100 Lire 1936
    (24mm)   2000. 2500. 4000.

Reduced Size

93a *F36* 100 Lire 1937
    (21mm)   4000. 6000. 10000.

Silver

89 5 Lire 1936–41   10.00 15.00 30.00
    1937 . . . 50
Dates after 1937 not for circulation.

REPUBLIC 1946–
First Coinage

Aluminum

90 10 Lire 1936–41   10.00 20.00 40.00
Dates after 1936 not for circulation.

95 1 Lira 1946–50   1.00   2.50 10.00
    1946, 47 . . . 30

96 2 Lire 1946–50   1.50   3.00   12.50
1946 . . . 40   1947 . . . 75

97 5 Lire 1946–50   2.00   4.00   15.00
1946 . . . 100   1947 . . . 200

98 10 Lire 1946–50   2.00   7.50   25.00
1946 . . . 100   1947 . . . 600

Second Coinage

99 1 Lira 1951–   1.00   2.00   5.00

100 2 Lire 1953–   1.00   2.00   5.00
1958 . . . 80

101 5 Lire 1951–   1.00   2.00   5.00

102 10 Lire 1951–   1.00   2.00   5.00

Aluminum-Bronze

A102 20 Lire 1957–59   1.00   2.00   10.00

Stainless Steel

103 50 Lire 1954–   1.00   2.00   10.00
1958 . . . 10

104 100 Lire 1955   1.00   2.00   10.00

Silver

105 500 Lire 1958–82, date
on edge   5.00   7.00   10.00
Later issues in *Current Coins of the World.*

Unless otherwise noted, prices are for coins in very
fine, extremely fine, and uncirculated condition.

JAMAICA

Former colony of the British West Indies in the Caribbean Sea south of Cuba. Achieved national independence and membership in the British Commonwealth in 1962. Exports: sugar, coffee, bananas, rum. Tourism is a thriving industry. Area: 4,411 square miles. Languages: English, Creole. Capital: *Kingston*.

Monetary System:
4 Farthings = 1 Penny

VICTORIA 1837–1901

Cupro-Nickel

1	1 Farthing 1880–1900	2.50	5.00	25.00
	1891 . . . 4		Proof . . . 150.00	
2	½ Penny 1869–1900	3.50	7.00	35.00
	1882 . . . 6		Proof . . . 200.00	
3	1 Penny 1869–1900	4.50	10.00	40.00
	1882 . . . 12		Proof . . . 100.00	

Silver

A3	1½ Pence 1838–62	5.00	15.00	50.00
(See Ceylon No. 3)				

EDWARD VII 1901–1910

Cupro-Nickel

Rev: Horizontal shading in arms

4	1 Farthing 1902–03	3.00	5.00	25.00
5	½ Penny 1902–03	3.50	9.00	30.00
6	1 Penny 1902–03	3.50	9.00	35.00

Rev: Vertical shading in arms

7	1 Farthing 1904–10	1.50	3.00	18.50
			Proof . . . 150.00	
8	½ Penny 1904–10	2.50	5.00	15.00
	1904 . . . 8			
9	1 Penny 1904–10	2.50	6.00	20.00
	1904 . . . 10		Proof . . . 250.00	

GEORGE V 1910–1936

Cupro-Nickel

10	1 Farthing 1914–34	1.00	2.00	9.00
	1914 . . . 6		Proof . . . 100.00	
11	½ Penny 1914–28	1.00	3.00	10.00
	1914 . . . 8		Proof . . . 55.00	
12	1 Penny 1914–28	1.00	3.00	12.00
	1914,16 . . . 30		Proof . . . 55.00	

GEORGE VI 1936–1952

Nickel-Brass

13	1 Farthing 1937	1.00	3.00	7.00
			Proof . . . 100.00	
14	½ Penny 1938	1.50	3.00	8.00
			Proof . . . 125.00	
15	1 Penny 1937	2.00	4.00	8.00
			Proof . . . 150.00	

Larger Head

16	1 Farthing 1938–47	.30	.50	1.00
			Proof . . . 125.00	
17	½ Penny 1938–47	.45	1.00	4.50
			Proof . . . 125.00	
18	1 Penny 1938–47	.50	1.25	3.00
			Proof . . . 150.00	

New Legend:
KING GEORGE THE SIXTH

19	1 Farthing 1950, 52	.10	.20	.75
			Proof . . . 100.00	
20	½ Penny 1950, 52	.15	.25	1.00
			Proof . . . 125.00	
21	1 Penny 1950, 52	.25	1.00	2.00
			Proof . . . 150.00	

ELIZABETH II 1952–

Nickel-Brass

22	½ Penny 1955–63	.10	.25	.40
		Proof . . . 60.00		
23	1 Penny 1953–63	.15	.20	.40
		Proof . . . 75.00		

Later issues in *Current Coins of the World*.

JAPAN

Islands in the North Pacific off the coast of China. After its defeat in World War II, Japan's area was reduced to four main islands, a fifth being returned to it in 1953. Total area is now 147,470 square miles. Important industries are agriculture, the making of silk, steel manufacture, and motor vehicles. Language: Japanese. Capital: *Tokyo*.

Monetary System:
10 Rin = 1 Sen
100 Sen = 1 Yen

MEIJI REIGN
1868–1912 (Years 1 to 45)

Reign Symbols 治 明 on Coins

First Coinage

Silver

1	5 Sen Yrs. 3–4			
	(1870–71)	80.00	120.00	250.00
2	10 Sen Yr. 3	10.00	15.00	60.00
3*	20 Sen Yrs. 3–4	10.00	15.00	60.00
4	50 Sen Yrs. 3–4 (32mm)	25.00	35.00	90.00
4a	50 Sen Yr. 4 (30.5mm)	30.00	50.00	120.00
5	1 Yen Yr. 3	150.00	200.00	400.00

6	5 Sen Yr. 4	20.00	35.00	100.00

Gold

9	*F49*	1 Yen Yr. 4	250.00	300.00	400.00
10	*F48*	2 Yen Yr. 3	550.00	700.00	1000.
11	*F47*	5 Yen Yrs. 3–4	700.00	900.00	1200.
12	*F46*	10 Yen Yr. 4	2000.	2500.	3000.
13	*F45*	20 Yen Yr. 3	–	–	–

Second Coinage

Copper

15	1 Rin Yrs. 6–17			
	(1873–84)	2.00	4.00	10.00
	Yrs. 9, 13 . . . Rare Yr. 10 . . . 125			

16	½ Sen Yrs. 6–21	1.00	4.00	20.00
	Yr. 10 . . . 35			
17*	1 Sen Yrs. 6–21	1.00	3.00	30.00
	Yr. 6 . . . 4			
18	2 Sen Yrs. 6–17	2.00	5.00	60.00
	Yr. 6 . . . 15			

Bronze

20	1 Sen Yrs. 31–35			
	(1898–1902)	2.00	5.00	50.00

Unless otherwise noted, prices are for coins in very fine, extremely fine, and uncirculated condition.

Cupro-Nickel

19 5 Sen Yrs. 22–30
(1889–97)   2.00   6.00   40.00
Yr. 28 . . . 40

21 5 Sen Yrs. 30–38
(1897–1905)   4.00   10.00   60.00
Yr. 36 . . . 75

Sllver

22 5 Sen Yrs. 6–13
(1873–80)   8.00   12.00   25.00
Yr. 7 . . . 65 Yr. 13 . . . Rare
23 10 Sen Yrs. 6–39   3.00   5.00   15.00
Yr. 7 . . . 85 Yr. 13 . . . Rare
Yr. 34 . . . 60 Yr. 35 . . . 40
24* 20 Sen Yrs. 6–38   5.00   8.00   18.00
Yr. 8 . . . 90 Yr. 7, 13 . . . 20
Yr. 21 . . . 35 Yr. 34 . . . 100
25 50 Sen Yrs. 6–38   12.00   15.00   60.00
Yrs. 7–13 . . . Rare Yr. 18 . . . 60   Yr. 35 . . . 40
A25 1 Yen Yrs. 7–45   20.00   25.00   60.00
Yrs. 7, 12 . . . 450 Yr. 8 . . . Rare

Gold
Reduced size

9a* *F48* 1 Yen Yrs. 7–13   1200.   1400.   1800.
10a *F47* 2 Yen Yrs. 7–13   –   –   –
11a *F46* 5 Yen Yrs. 5–30   800.00 1000.   1300.
Same size, smaller design
12a *F45* 10 Yen Yrs. 9–13   –   –   –
13a *F44* 20 Yen Yrs. 9–13   –   –   –

Third Coinage
Silver

29 10 Sen Yrs. 40–45
(1907–1912)   1.00   2.00   5.00
30* 20 Sen Yrs. 39–44   2.00   4.00   30.00
Yr. 44 . . . 35
31 50 Sen Yrs. 39–45   3.00   7.00   40.00

Gold

32 *F52* 5 Yen Yrs. 30–45   450.00 550.00 750.00
33* *F51* 10 Yen Yrs. 30–43 400.00 500.00 750.00
34 *F50* 20 Yen 30–45   800.00 900.00   1400.

Trade Coins
Silver

14 Trade Dollar Yrs. 8–10
(1875–77)   300.00 450.00 900.00
Coins dated Yr. 7 are patterns

An expanding trade forced Japan to call in the old one yen pieces (Nos. 5 and A25), counterstamp them with a Japanese character "Gin," (meaning "silver") in a small circle, and circulate them principally in Taiwan (Formosa).

28 "Gin" stamp (1897) on
No. 5 – – –
28a* "Gin" stamp on No.
A25, Yrs. 7–30 20.00 25.00 60.00
28b "Gin" stamp on No. 14 400.00 500.00 1000.

TAISHO REIGN
1912–1926 (Years 1 to 15)
正大
Reign Symbols on Coins
First Coinage

Like Nos. 20, A25 and 29–34 except for
symbols of Taisho Reign
Bronze
35 1 Sen Yrs. 2–4 (1913–15) 2.00 4.00 20.00

Silver
36 10 Sen Yrs. 1–6
(1912–17) 1.00 1.50 5.00
37 50 Sen Yrs. 1–6
Yrs. 3–4 . . . 12.50 3.00 6.00 30.00
38 1 Yen Yr. 3 (1914) 18.00 20.00 30.00

Gold

39 F54 5 Yen Yrs. 2, 13 600.00 700.00 900.00
40* F53 20 Yen Yrs. 1–9 800.00 900.00 1400.

Second Coinage
Bronze

41 5 Rin Yrs. 5–8 (1916–19) .50 .80 3.00

42* 1 Sen Yrs. 5–13
(1916–24) .20 .50 2.00

Cupro-Nickel

43 5 Sen Yrs. 6–9
(1917–20) 20mm 4.00 6.00 10.00
44* 5 Sen Yrs. 9–12
(1920–23) 18.5mm .20 .40 1.50

45 10 Sen Yrs. 9–15
(1920–26) .10 .20 1.00

Silver

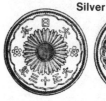

46 50 Sen Yrs. 11–15
(1922–26) 2.00 3.50 12.00

SHOWA REIGN 1926–
和昭
Reign Symbols on Coins

First Coinage

Like Nos. 32–34, 39–42, and 44–46 except for symbols of Showa Reign.
Bronze
47 1 Sen Yrs. 2–13
(1927–38) .20 .40 1.50
Yr. 4 . . . 5

Cupro-Nickel
48 5 Sen Yr. 7 (1932) .30 .60 2.00
49 10 Sen Yrs. 2–7 .10 .20 1.00

Silver
50 50 Sen Yrs. 3–13 2.00 3.50 8.00
Yr. 13 . . . 50

Gold
51 F56 5 Yen Yr. 5 (1930) – – –
52 F55 10 Yen Yrs. 5–7 – – –

Unless otherwise noted, prices are for coins in very
fine, extremely fine, and uncirculated condition.

Second Coinage

Nickel

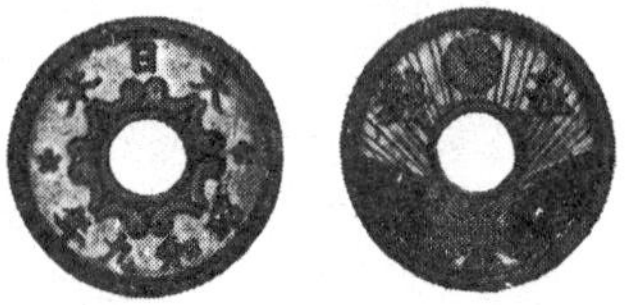

53 5 Sen Yrs. 8–13 (1933–37) .40 .80 2.00

Yr. 13 not released to circulation

54 10 Sen Yrs. 8–12 .20 .40 1.50

Bronze

55 1 Sen Yr. 13 (1938) .10 .20 1.00

Aluminum

56 1 Sen Yrs. 13–15 (1938–40) .10 .30 1.00

Aluminum-Bronze

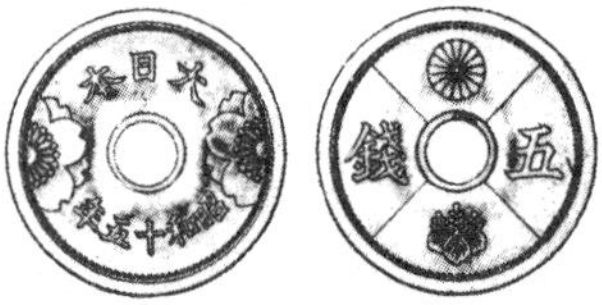

57 5 Sen Yrs. 13–15 .20 .40 1.00

58 10 Sen Yrs. 13–15 .30 .50 2.00

WORLD WAR II ISSUES

Aluminum

59 1 Sen Yrs. 16–18 (1941–43) 0.65 gr .10 .20 .40

59a 1 Sen Yr. 18, 0.55 gr. .15 .25 .60

60 5 Sen Yrs. 15–16 (1940–41) 1.2 gr. .20 .30 1.00

60a 5 Sen Yrs. 16–17, 1.0 gr .20 .30 1.00

60b 5 Sen Yr. 18, 0.8 gr. .10 .20 1.00

61* 10 Sen Yrs. 15–16, 1.5 gr. .10 .20 .80

61a 10 Sen Yrs. 16–17, 1.2 gr. .10 .20 .80

61b 10 Sen Yr. 18, 1.0 gr. .10 .20 .80

Tin

62 1 Sen Yrs. 19–20 (1944–45) .10 .20 .80

63 5 Sen Yr. 19 .20 .40 1.50

64* 1 Sen Yr. 19 .10 .20 1.50

65 5 Sen Yrs. 20–21 (1945–46) .30 .60 1.50

Japan

311

Aluminum

68 10 Sen Yrs. 20–21   .10   .20   .50
Red fiber 1 Sen ND (1945), 5 Sen and 10 Sen Yr. 20 (1945) circulated for only a few days.

POSTWAR ISSUES

Brass

67 50 Sen Yrs. 21–22
(1946–47)   .40   .60   1.50
Yr. 22 not released to circulation.

69 50 Sen Yrs. 22–23
(1947–48)   .10   .30   1.00

Henceforth numerals in Japanese read from left to right

70 1 Yen Yrs. 23–25
(1948–50)   .10   .30   .60

71 5 Yen Yrs. 23–24
(1948–49)   .20   .40   8.00

72* 5 Yen Yrs. 24–33
(1949–58)   .10   .30   3.00
with script style characters

72a 5 Yen Yr. 34– (1959–)   .05   .10   .15
with block style characters

10 Yen Yrs. 25–26 (1950–51) in cupro-nickel were not released to circulation.

Bronze

73 10 Yen Yrs. 26–33
(1951–58), reeded edge   .10   .20   10.00
73a 10 Yen Yr. 34– (1959–),
plain edge   .10   .15   .25

Aluminum

74 1 Yen Yr. 30– (1955–)   .05   .10   .15

Nickel

75 50 Yen Yrs. 30–33
(1955–58)   .30   .50   5.00

Unless otherwise noted, prices are for coins in very fine, extremely fine, and uncirculated condition.

76 50 Yen Yrs. 34–41
(1959–66)   1.20   1.50   2.50
Yr. 35 . . . 5

Silver

77 100 Yen Yrs. 32–33
(1957–58)   1.50   2.50   5.00

78 100 Yen Yrs. 34–41
(1959–66)   1.50   2.50   4.00
Later issues in *Current Coins of the World*.

JERSEY

One of the Channel Islands belonging to Britain off the northwest coast of France. It has a lieutenant governor appointed by the Crown, but is not bound by acts of Parliament unless named in the legislation. Area: 45 square miles. Capital: *St.* Helier.

Coinage 1841–1966 in fractional parts of a shilling.

VICTORIA 1837–1901

Copper

1 1/52 Shilling 1841   45.00   75.00 150.00
                                  Proof . . . 300.00
2 1/26 Shilling 1841–61   4.00   15.00   25.00
                                  Proof . . . 200.00

3 1/13 Shilling 1841–61   9.00   25.00   45.00
      1865 Proof only . . . 450   Proof . . . 275.00

Bronze

4 1/26 Shilling 1866–71   5.00   10.00   22.50
                                  Proof . . . 150.00
5 1/13 Shilling 1866–71   4.50   9.00   25.00
                                  Proof . . . 150.00

New System

6 1/48 Shilling 1877   25.00   50.00 100.00
                                  Proof . . . 200.00
7 1/24 Shilling 1877–94   1.50   4.50   15.00
                                  Proof . . . 125.00
8 1/12 Shilling 1877–94   3.00   4.50   15.00
                                  Proof . . . 100.00

EDWARD VII 1901–1910

9 1/24 Shilling 1909   3.50   9.00   28.50
10 1/12 Shilling 1909   2.50   7.50   28.50

GEORGE V 1910–1936

11 1/24 Shilling 1911–23   3.50   7.50   28.50
12 1/12 Shilling 1911–23   1.50   3.50   18.50

13 ¹/₂₄ Shilling 1923, 26   2.50   5.00   12.00
Proof . . . 100.00
14 ¹/₁₂ Shilling 1923, 26   1.50   3.00   15.00

15 ¹/₂₄ Shilling 1931–35   2.50   4.50   12.00
Proof . . . 125.00
16 ¹/₁₂ Shilling 1931–35   1.25   2.50   12.00
Proof . . . 125.00

GEORGE VI 1936–1952

17 ¹/₂₄ Shilling 1937–47   1.50   3.50   6.00
Proof . . . 100.00
18 ¹/₁₂ Shilling 1937–47   .25   1.00   3.50
Proof . . . 125.00

Commemorating
End of German Occupation

Obv: Without IND. IMP.

19 ¹/₁₂ Shilling 1945 (struck
1949–52)   .30   .60   1.50
Proof . . . 100.00

ELIZABETH II 1952–

Bronze

Rev: Like No. 19

20 ¹/₁₂ Shilling 1945 (struck
1954)   .30   .60   1.50
Proof . . . 85.00

New Legend:
BAILIWICK OF JERSEY
Bronze

21 ¹/₁₂ Shilling 1957, 64   .10   .15   .50
Proof . . . 2.50

Nickel-Brass

22 ¼ Shilling 1957, 60   .10   .15   1.00
1960 Proof only . . . 12   Proof . . . 10.00

300th Anniversary Accession
of Charles II

Bronze

23 ¹/₁₂ Shilling 1960   .20   .25   1.00
Proof . . . 7.50

Nickel-Brass

24	¼ Shilling 1964	.25	.50	2.00
			Proof . . . 4.00	

900th Anniversary of
Norman Conquest

Bronze

25	¹⁄₁₂ Shilling 1966	.20	.25	.75
			Proof . . . 2.50	

Nickel-Brass

26	¼ Shilling 1966	.20	.25	1.00
			Proof . . . 2.00	

Cupro-Nickel

27	5 Shillings 1966	1.00	2.00	3.50
			Proof . . . 10.00	

Later issues in *Current Coins of the World.*

JORDAN

An independent kingdom in the Middle East bounded by Israel, Syria, Iraq and Saudi Arabia. The population is mostly Moslem, and one-third are refugees resulting from the division of Palestine. Area: 37,297 square miles. Language: Arabic. Capital: *Amman.*

Monetary System:
1000 Fils = 1 Dinar (Pound)

ABDULLA IBN AL HUSSEIN
1946–1951

Legend:
KINGDOM OF THE JORDAN
Bronze

1	1 "Fil" 1949 (error)	1.00	1.50	2.50
2	1 Fils 1949	.50	.85	1.75
3	5 Fils 1949	.35	.65	1.25
4	10 Fils 1949	.60	1.00	1.75

Cupro-Nickel

5	20 Fils 1949	.60	1.00	1.75
6	50 Fils 1949	.60	1.75	3.00
7	100 Fils 1949	1.75	2.50	4.50

Note: 25 Proof Sets were struck in 1949.

HUSSEIN I 1952–

New Legend:
KINGDOM OF JORDAN
Bronze

8	1 Fils 1955–65	.25	.50	1.00
			Proof . . . 2.50	
9	5 Fils 1955–67	.25	.50	.85
			Proof . . . 4.00	
10	10 Fils 1955–67	.25	.50	1.00
			Proof . . . 2.00	

Cupro-Nickel

A10	20 Fils 1964–65	1.00	2.50	4.50
			Proof . . . 5.00	
11	50 Fils 1955–65	.50	1.00	1.50
			Proof . . . 4.00	
12	100 Fils 1955–65	1.00	1.50	3.50
			Proof . . . 4.00	

No. A10 was not issued to circulation.

Later issues in *Current Coins of the World.*

KATANGA

A province of the Republic of the Congo which gained independence from Belgium June 30, 1960. Katanga seceded from the republic on July 11, 1960, and was not re-integrated into the Congo until January, 1963. Area: 191,873 square miles. Capital: *Elizabethville*.

Monetary System:
100 Centimes = 1 Franc

Gold

1	5 Francs 1961	175.00	200.00	250.00

Bronze
Design as No. 1

2	1 Franc 1961	1.00	1.50	2.50
3	5 Francs 1961	1.75	2.00	3.00

240

KIAO CHAU (Kiautschou)

Formerly a German leased territory on the Shantung peninsula in eastern China; now a district of China. Area: 117 square miles. Capital: *Tsingtao*.

Monetary System:
100 Cents = 1 Dollar

Cupro-Nickel

1	5 Cents 1909	15.00	20.00	70.00
2	10 Cents 1909	15.00	20.00	70.00

KOREA

Peninsula in northeastern Asia extending toward southern tip of Japan. One of the world's oldest nations. During the latter part of the nineteenth century Korea became a pawn between China, Russia and Japan. Finally, in 1910 Japan annexed the country, holding it until 1945. Independent since World War II, the country has been divided into two zones, North and South Korea, as a result of the war of 1950–53. Capitals: Seoul (South), Pyongyang (North).

Monetary Systems:
1000 Mun = 1 Warn before 1892
100 Fun = 1 Yang 1892–1902
5 Yang = 1 Whan 1892–1902
100 Chon = 1 Won 1902–10

Dating Systems:

Dates of Nos. 1–9 are figured from the beginning of Korea's Yi Dynasty in 1392 AD. Nos. 1–3 were actually struck in 1891. Later coins are dated by the year of the current emperor's reign.

EMPEROR KOJONG 1864–1907
Struck Coinage

For earlier coinage of this reign see Mandel, *Cast Coinage of Korea*, and Craig, *Coins of the World*.

Brass

A1	5 Mun ND (1890)	150.00	200.00	450.00

Copper

1	5 Mun Yr. 497 (1888)	45.00	90.00	250.00
2	10 Mun Yr. 497	65.00	120.00	350.00

Silver

3	1 Warn Yr. 497.	3500.	5000.	9000.

Some authorities claim No. 3 is a pattern. Similar coins in silvered or gilt metal, and a 20 Mon in copper dated Yr. 495 are all patterns

New System, 1892
100 Fun = 1 Yang

Unless otherwise noted, prices are for coins in very fine, extremely fine, and uncirculated condition.

Brass

4 1 Fun Yrs. 501–05
(1892–96)   10.00 20.00 45.00

Copper

5 5 Fun Yrs. 501–05   3.00   6.00 20.00

Cupro-Nickel

6 ¼ Yang Yrs. 501–05   8.00 12.00 30.00

Silver

7 1 Yang Yrs. 501–02   60.00 100.00 180.00
8 5 Yang Yr. 501   800.00 1000. 2000.
9 1 Whan Yr. 502   2500. 3500. 7000.

KUANG MU REIGN
1897–1907 (Yrs. 1 to 11)

Reign Symbols 武 光 on Coins
(Title assumed by Emperor Kojong in 1897)

First Coinage
Like Nos. 5–7 except for symbols of Kuang Mu Reign.

Copper

A10 5 Fun Yrs. 2–6
(1898–1902)   2.00   4.00 15.00
    Yr. 3 . . . 400

Cupro-Nickel

B10 ¼ Yang Yrs. 1–5
(1897–1901)   2.00   3.00 10.00
All dates but Yr. 2 are scarce to rare.

Silver
C10 1 Yang Yr. 2 (1898)   80.00 120.00 200.00
(2 varieties)

Second Coinage
100 Chon = 1 Won

Bronze
10 1 Chon Yr. 6 (1902)   800.00 1500. 2800.

Cupro-Nickel

11 5 Chon Yr. 6   800.00 1500. 2800.

Silver
12 ½ Won Yr. 5 (1901)   1500. 2500. 4500.

Third Coinage
Bronze

13 ½ Chon Yr. 10 (1906)   3.00   5.00 25.00
14 1 Chon Yrs. 9–10   7.00 15.00 35.00

Cupro-Nickel

15 5 Chon Yrs. 9–11   5.00 10.00 35.00

Silver

16	10 Chon Yr. 10	15.00	20.00	40.00
17	20 Chon Yrs. 9–10	20.00	35.00	80.00
18	½ Won Yrs. 9–10	50.00	85.00	140.00

Gold

| 20* | F2 10 Won Year 10 | 4500. | 8500. | 12000. |
| 21 | F1 20 Won Year 10 | – | – | – |

Fourth Coinage

Bronze

| B22 | 1 Chon Yr. 11 (1907) | 4.00 | 7.00 | 30.00 |

Silver

C22	10 Chon Yr. 11 (thin)	10.00	15.00	40.00
D22	20 Chon Yr. 11	15.00	25.00	60.00
E22	½ Won Yr. 11	60.00	90.00	160.00

YUNG HI REIGN
1907–1910 (Years 1 to 4)

Reign Symbols 隆 熙 on Coins
Like Nos. B22–E22 except for symbols of reign.

Bronze

22	½ Chon Yrs. 1–4			
	(1907–10)	4.00	8.00	30.00
	Yrs. 1, 4 . . . 100			
23	1 Chon Yrs. 1–4	3.00	7.00	25.00

The cupro-nickel 5 Chon of this reign was not issued to circulation.

Silver

25	10 Chon Yrs. 2–4	7.00	10.00	25.00
	Yr. 3 . . . Rare			
26	20 Chon Yrs. 2–4	10.00	20.00	40.00
27	½ Won Yrs. 2–3	60.00	90.00	160.00
	Yr. 3 . . . Rare			

Gold

| 19 | F3 5 Won Yr. 2 | 5000. | 9000. | 15000. |

Other gold dates and denominations exist, but they are thought to be patterns.

KOREA, NORTH

A communist-formed state established May 1, 1948. Area: 46,768 square miles. Language: Korean. Capital: *Pyongyang*.

Monetary System:
100 Chon = 1 Won

Aluminum

1	1 Chon 1959, 70	1.00	1.50	2.50
2	5 Chon 1959, 74	2.00	3.00	4.00
3	10 Chon 1959	3.00	4.00	6.00

KOREA, SOUTH

A government formed May, 1948. Separated by compromise from North Korea by U.N. negotiation. Language: Korean. Area: 38,031 square miles. Capital: *Seoul*.

Unless otherwise noted, prices are for coins in very fine, extremely fine, and uncirculated condition.

First Coinage
Dates according to Korean calendar

Bronze

| 1 | 10 Hwan 4292, 94 (1959, 61) | .20 | .30 | .60 |

Cupro-Nickel-Zinc

| 2 | 50 Hwan 4292, 94 | .20 | .35 | .80 |

Copper-Nickel

Obv: Pres. Syngman Rhee (1948–60)

| 3 | 100 Hwan 4292 | .50 | 1.00 | 2.00 |

Later issues in *Current Coins of the World*.

KUWAIT — see
Current Coins of the World.

LAOS

One of the three former French Indo-Chinese States. Bounded by China, Vietnam, Cambodia, Thailand and Burma. Became an independent sovereign state in 1949. Area: 91,430 square miles. Languages: Lao, French. Capital: *Vientiane.*

Monetary System:
100 Centimes = 1 Kip

Aluminum

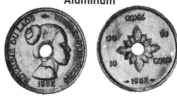

| 1 | 10 Centimes 1952 | .25 | .50 | 1.25 |

| 2 | 20 Centimes 1952 | .25 | .50 | 1.50 |

| 3 | 50 Centimes 1952 | .50 | 1.00 | 2.00 |

LATVIA
(Latvija,
Latvijas Republika)

On the Baltic Sea between Lithuania and Estonia. A Russian province until 1918, it became an independent republic until 1940 when Russia incorporated it into the U.S.S.R. (Latvian S.S.R.). Area: 25,305 square miles. Language: Lettish. Capital: *Riga.*

Monetary System:
100 Santimu = 1 Lats

Bronze

1	1 Santims 1922–35	2.00	4.00	10.00
2	2 Santimi 1922–32	2.00	4.00	10.00
3	5 Santimi 1922	2.00	4.00	10.00

Nickel

4	10 Santimu 1922	3.00	6.00	12.00
5	20 Santimu 1922	3.50	7.50	15.00

6	50 Santimu 1922	5.00	10.00	20.00

Silver

7	1 Lats 1924	4.00	6.50	12.50
8	2 Lati 1925–26	10.00	15.00	20.00

9	5 Lati 1929–32	17.50	25.00	50.00

Bronze

10	1 Santims 1937–39	3.00	6.00	12.00
11	2 Santimi 1937 (19mm)	35.00	50.00	100.00
11a	2 Santimi 1939 (19.5mm)	5.00	12.50	30.00

LEBANON (Grand Liban, Republique Libanaise)

A republic on the east coast of the Mediterranean, 120 miles long and about 30 miles wide, bordering Israel on the south. Under French mandate from 1920 until 1944 when France withdrew. Area: 4,000 square miles. Languages: Arabic and French. Capital: *Beirut*.

Monetary System:
100 Piastres = 1 Lira (Pound)

First Coinage

Aluminum-Bronze

1	2 Piastres 1924	2.50	10.00	40.00
2	5 Piastres 1924	3.00	10.00	35.00

Second Coinage

Cupro-Nickel

5	½ Piastre 1934, 36	2.50	5.00	20.00

6	1 Piastre 1925–36	1.00	2.50	12.50

Aluminum-Bronze

3	2 Piastres 1925	7.50	15.00	50.00
4	5 Piastres 1925–40	2.50	7.50	20.00

Silver

8	10 Piastres 1929	12.50	30.00	75.00

Unless otherwise noted, prices are for coins in very fine, extremely fine, and uncirculated condition.

9	25 Piastres 1929–36	7.50	20.00	65.00
10	50 Piastres 1929–36	12.50	42.50	135.00

Zinc

5a	½ Piastre 1941	1.25	2.75	7.50
6a	1 Piastre 1940	1.00	2.00	7.00

Aluminum-Bronze
Design like No. 6

7	2½ Piastres 1940	2.50	4.00	8.00

WORLD WAR II
PROVISIONAL ISSUES

Brass

11	½ Piastre ND	1.50	4.00	8.00

12	1 Piastre ND	2.00	4.00	10.00

Aluminum

13	2½ Piastres ND	2.00	4.00	12.50

POSTWAR ISSUES

Aluminum

14	5 Piastres 1952	1.00	2.00	5.00

15	10 Piastres 1952	1.00	10.00	25.00

Aluminum-Bronze

16	25 Piastres 1952, 61	.50	.75	1.00

Silver

17	50 Piastres 1952	2.00	3.00	4.50

Aluminum-Bronze

18	1 Piastre 1955	.10	.15	.20
19	2½ Piastres 1955	.15	.20	.25

Aluminum

20	5 Piastres 1954	.35	.75	1.50

Aluminum-Bronze

21	10 Piastres 1955	.50	.75	1.00

22	5 Piastres 1955, 61	.15	.20	.40

Design similar to No. 24

23	10 Piastres 1955	.25	.50	.75

Cupro-Nickel

24 10 Piastres 1961   .10   .25   .50
Later issues in *Current Coins of the World.*

LIBERIA

An independent republic founded in 1847 on the southwest coast of Africa. From its rich tropical forests comes 10% of the United States' rubber imports. It also produces iron ore which is rated as the purest now mined. Area: 43,000 square miles. Capital: *Monrovia.*

Monetary System:
100 Cents = 1 Dollar

Copper

1 1 Cent (token) 1833, is-
     sued by American Coloni-
     zation Society   20.00   35.00   75.00

Regular Issues

2 1 Cent 1847, 62   15.00   25.00   60.00
                              Proof . . . 125.00
3 2 Cents 1847, 62   17.50   30.00   90.00
                              Proof . . . 175.00

Bronze

4 1 Cent 1896, 1906   7.50   15.00   45.00
                              Proof . . . 65.00
5 2 Cents 1896, 1906   8.00   18.00   50.00
                              Proof . . . 75.00

Silver

6 10 Cents 1896, 1906   10.00   30.00 150.00
                              Proof . . . 250.00
7 25 Cents 1896, 1906   15.00   45.00 250.00
                              Proof . . . 350.00
8 50 Cents 1896, 1906   20.00   75.00 450.00
                              Proof . . . 600.00

Brass

9   ½ Cent 1937   .10   .35   1.00
10 1 Cent 1937   1.50   5.00   12.50
11 2 Cents 1937   2.00   6.00   15.00

Cupro-Nickel

9a ½ Cent 1941   .25   .50   1.50
10a 1 Cent 1941   5.00   12.50   35.00
11a 2 Cents 1941   1.00   2.00   5.00

Bronze

12 1 Cent 1960–   .05   .10   .25

Unless otherwise noted, prices are for coins in very
fine, extremely fine, and uncirculated condition.

LIBERIA

Cupro-Nickel

13 5 Cents 1960–   .10   .25   .50

Silver

14	10 Cents 1960–61	1.00	1.50	2.50
15	25 Cents 1960–61	2.00	3.00	5.00
16	50 Cents 1960–61	4.00	4.50	8.00
17	1 Dollar 1961–62	8.00	10.00	17.50

Later issues in *Current Coins of the World*.

Cupro-Nickel

| **4** | 1 Piastre 1952 | .30 | .75 | 1.50 |
| **5*** | 2 Piastres 1952 | .40 | 1.00 | 2.50 |

1952 Proof Set . . . 350.00

Later issues in *Current Coins of the World*.

LIECHTENSTEIN

A small principality between Austria and Switzerland. Tied to the Austrian monetary system until the end of World War I, to the Swiss thereafter. Area: 61 square miles. Language: German. Capital: *Vaduz*.

Monetary System:
1 ½ Florins = 1 Vereinsthaler 1857–68
100 Heller = 1 Krone 1892–1923
100 Rappen = 1 Frank 1924 on

PRINCE JOHANN II 1858–1929

Silver

1 1 Thaler 1862   1000. 1500. 2000.
Modern restrikes of No. 1 have letter "M" above date.

Values in Terms of Kronen

| **2** | 1 Krone 1900–15 | 20.00 | 30.00 | 50.00 |
| **3** | 2 Kronen 1912, 15 | 30.00 | 40.00 | 55.00 |

LIBYA

Libya was formed as a constitutional monarchy in 1951 from former Italian-occupied territories in northern Africa. The king was deposed in 1969 and the country was declared a republic. Much of the land is desert but vast oil fields are now being developed. Language: Arabic. Area: 679,360 square miles. Capital: *Tripoli*.

Monetary System:
10 Milliemes = 1 Piastre
100 Piastres = 1 Pound

IDRIS I 1951–1969

Bronze

1	1 Millieme 1952	.10	.15	.35
2	2 Milliemes 1952	.15	.25	.50
3*	5 Milliemes 1952	.20	.50	1.00

4 5 Kronen 1900–15   100.00 150.00 225.00
      1900 . . . 450

Gold

5	*F14* 10 Kronen 1900	–	– 2500.
6	*F12* 20 Kronen 1898	–	– 2500.

No. 5 dated 1898 is thought to be a pattern.

Values in Terms of Franken

Silver

7	½ Frank 1924	150.00	175.00 225.00
8	1 Frank 1924	50.00	80.00 100.00
9	2 Franken 1924	80.00	150.00 200.00
10	5 Franken 1924	500.00	800.00 1000.

PRINCE FRANZ I 1929–1938

Gold

11	*F16* 10 Franken 1930	–	– 1000.
12	*F15* 20 Franken 1930	–	– 1000.

PRINCE FRANZ JOSEF II 1938–

Gold

13	*F18* 10 Franken 1946	–	– 200.00
14	*F17* 20 Franken 1946	–	– 350.00

15	*F21* 25 Franken 1956	–	– 200.00
16	*F20* 50 Franken 1956	–	– 350.00
17*	*F19* 100 Franken 1952	–	– 2750.

National Bank Centennial
Obv: Head to right. Rev: Arms

18	*F23* 25 Franken 1961	–	–	–
19	*F22* 50 Franken 1961	–	–	–

Nos. 18–19 were not issued to circulation.

LITHUANIA (Lietuva)

A Baltic state between Latvia and Poland. It was incorporated into the U.S.S.R. in 1940 and has changed from an agricultural nation to a highly industrialized one. Area: 25,174 square miles. Capital: *Kaunas*.

Monetary System:
100 Centu = 1 Litas

First Coinage

Aluminum-Bronze

1	1 Centas 1925	4.50	7.50	15.00
2	5 Centai 1925	5.00	10.00	20.00

3	10 Centu 1925	4.00	10.00	20.00
4	20 Centu 1925	5.00	10.00	20.00
5	50 Centu 1925	20.00	30.00	50.00

Silver

6	1 Litas 1925	6.00	12.50	20.00
7	2 Litu 1925	12.50	17.50	37.50
8	5 Litai 1925	12.50	17.50	40.00

Second Coinage

Bronze

| 9 | 1 Centas 1936 | 4.00 | 8.00 | 12.50 |

| 10 | 2 Centai 1936 | 5.00 | 10.00 | 20.00 |
| 11 | 5 Centai 1936 | 5.00 | 10.00 | 20.00 |

Silver

| 12 | 5 Litai 1936 | 12.50 | 15.00 | 22.50 |

| 13 | 10 Litu 1936 | 22.50 | 32.50 | 50.00 |

20th Anniversary of Independence

Obv: President Smetona

| 14 | 10 Litu 1938 | 35.00 | 55.00 | 100.00 |

Other coins dated 1938 are patterns.

LUNDY

These "unlawful coins" have created considerable interest among collectors and for that reason have been included in this volume. Martin Coles Harmon, a London businessman, purchased Lundy Island, off the coast of England, in 1925, for approximately $25,000. He issued the coins shown below in 1929 and was fined by Britain in April, 1930 for issuing unauthorized coins. They were struck in Birmingham, England. The puffin, a sea bird, is shown on the coins; Harmon's portrait appears on the obverse of each piece. The coins circulated briefly but had no exchange value in terms of other currencies.

Lettered Edge:
LUNDY LIGHTS AND LEADS
Bronze

| 1 | ½ Puffin 1929 | 3.00 | 5.00 | 9.00 |
| 2 | 1 Puffin 1929 | 3.00 | 5.00 | 9.00 |

Later issues in *Current Coins of the World.*

LUXEMBOURG
(Letzeburg)

A Grand Duchy, bordered on the south by France, on the east and north by Germany, and on the west and north by Belgium. Although primarily an agricultural country, it has a large output of iron and steel. Area: 999 square miles. Languages: French, German, Luxembourgish. Capital: *Luxembourg*

Monetary System:
100 Centimes = 1 Frang (Franc)

General Coinage

Bronze

1	2½ Centimes 1854–1908	2.00	5.00	10.00
	1870 . . . 20			
2	5 Centimes 1854–70	6.00	10.00	18.00
	1860 . . . 40			
3	10 Centimes 1854–70	6.00	10.00	18.00
	1854 . . . 25			

Zinc

4	5 Centimes 1915	4.00	7.00	10.00
5	10 Centimes 1915	3.00	5.00	8.00
6	25 Centimes 1916	6.00	10.00	15.00

Iron

7	5 Centimes 1918–22	4.00	7.00	10.00
	1922 . . . 30			
8	10 Centimes 1918–23	2.00	4.00	6.00
	1923 . . . 20			
9	25 Centimes 1919–22	3.00	5.00	10.00

Issues with Royal Portraits or Monograms
ADOLPHE 1890–1905

Cupro-Nickel

10	5 Centimes 1901	.40	2.00	4.00
11	10 Centimes 1901	.25	1.50	4.00

GUILLAUME IV 1905–1912

12	5 Centimes 1908	.40	2.00	4.00

CHARLOTTE 1919–1964
First Coinage

Cupro-Nickel

13	5 Centimes 1924	.10	1.00	2.00
14	10 Centimes 1924	.10	1.00	2.00

15	25 Centimes 1927 (C TS)	1.00	3.00	5.00
15a	25 Centimes 1927 (C MES)	2.00	3.50	5.00

Nickel

16	50 Centimes 1930	2.00	3.50	5.00

17	1 Franc 1924–35	1.00	3.00	5.00
18	2 Francs 1924	4.00	7.00	10.00

Unless otherwise noted, prices are for coins in very fine, extremely fine, and uncirculated condition.

19	5 Francs 1929	4.00	7.00	10.00
20	10 Francs 1929	6.00	10.00	18.00

Bronze

21	5 Centimes 1930	.20	1.00	2.00
22	10 Centimes 1930	.20	1.00	2.00

15b	25 Centimes 1930	2.00	4.00	10.00

New Spelling: LETZEBURG
Cupro-Nickel

24	1 Frang 1939	1.00	2.00	4.00

Second Coinage

Bronze

25	25 Centimes 1946–47	.10	.50	2.00

Aluminum

25a	25 Centimes 1954–72	–	–	.10

Cupro-Nickel

26	1 Frang 1946–47 (23mm)	.25	.50	1.00

26a	1 Frang 1952 (21mm)	.25	.50	1.00
26b	1 Frang 1953–64, modi-			
	fied rev. die	.10	.15	.30

27	5 Frang 1949	.40	1.00	2.00

600th Anniversary Death of
John the Blind

Silver

28	20 Francs 1946	15.00	20.00	25.00
29	50 Francs 1946	20.00	25.00	30.00
30	100 Francs 1946	20.00	25.00	30.00

No. 30 without designer's initials on obverse was restruck in 1964.

Cupro-Nickel

31 5 Francs 1962   .15   .25   1.00

Silver

32 100 Francs 1963   10.00 15.00 20.00

Millennium Commemorative

33 250 Francs 1963   70.00 100.00 125.00
No. 33 was struck in both brilliant and antiqued finishes.

Later issues in *Current Coins of the World.*

MACAU (Macao)

Part of an island at the mouth of the Canton River in China covering six square miles. It is a Portuguese overseas province. The trade is mostly transit. Area: 6 square miles. Languages: Portuguese, Cantonese. Capital: *Macao.*

Monetary System:
100 Avos = 1 Pataca

Bronze

1 5 Avos 1952   .50   1.00   3.00

2 10 Avos 1952   .50   1.00   2.00

Cupro-Nickel

3 50 Avos 1952   .50   1.00   4.00

Silver

4 1 Pataca 1952   2.00   4.00   8.00
5 5 Patacas 1952   5.00   8.00 15.00

Later issues in *Current Coins of the World.*

MADAGASCAR

The world's fifth largest island, lying off the southeast coast of Africa, it became a French protectorate in 1890. In 1960 it gained independence and, as the Malagasy Republic, remained a member of the French Community. Main industries are agriculture and cattle raising. Area: 228,000 square miles. Capital: *Tananarive.*

Monetary System:
100 Centimes = 1 Franc

Unless otherwise noted, prices are for coins in very fine, extremely fine, and uncirculated condition.

World War II Issue
Bronze

1	50 Centimes 1943	5.00	10.00	20.00
2	1 Franc 1943	5.00	12.50	40.00

Postwar Issues
Aluminum

3	1 Franc 1948, 58	.25	.50	1.75
4	2 Francs 1948	.25	.50	2.00
5	5 Francs 1953	.50	.75	2.00

Aluminum-Bronze

6	10 Francs 1953	.50	.75	2.00
7	20 Francs 1953	.50	.75	3.50

Later issues in *Current Coins of the World*.

MALAWI

Formerly known as Nyasaland, it became a British protectorate in 1891; was a member of the Federation of Rhodesia and Nyasaland from 1953 until 1963; achieved full independence on July 6, 1964. It is now a republic within the British Commonwealth. Languages: English, Chickewa and others. Area: 45,747 square miles. Capital: *Lilongwe.*

Monetary System:
12 Pence = 1 Shilling
2 Shillings = 1 Florin
5 Shillings = 1 Crown
20 Shillings = 1 Pound

Copper-Nickel-Zinc

Obv: Prime Minister Banda

1	6 Pence 1964, 67	.25	.50	1.00

2	1 Shilling 1964, 68	.50	1.00	1.75

3	1 Florin 1964	1.00	1.50	2.50

4	½ Crown 1964	1.25	2.00	3.50

Republic Day Commemorative

5	1 Crown 1966	Proof . . . 10.00

Bronze

6 1 Penny 1967–68   .50 .65 1.25
1964 Proof Set . . . 15.00

Later issues in *Current Coins of the World*.

MALAYA

A peninsula extending out into the South China Sea from the southeast tip of Asia. Formerly a federation of states under British suzerainty, it became an independent elective kingdom within the Commonwealth on August 31, 1957. Its chief products are rubber and tin. Capital: *Kuala Lumpur*.

Monetary System:
100 Cents = 1 Dollar
For earlier issues, see STRAITS SETTLEMENTS

GEORGE VI 1936–1952

Bronze

1	½ Cent 1940	.75	1.25	2.00
		Proof . . . 125.00		
2	1 Cent 1939–41	.25	.40	.75
		Proof . . . 125.00		

2a	1 Cent 1943, 45 (reduced size)	.15	.30	.50
		Proof . . . 125.00		

Silver

3	5 Cents 1939–45	.45	.95	1.25
		Proof . . . 150.00		

4	10 Cents 1939–45	.75	1.00	1.50
		Proof . . . 175.00		
5	20 Cents 1939–45	2.00	3.00	4.00
	1945 . . . 5	Proof . . . 175.00		

New Legend:
KING GEORGE THE SIXTH
Cupro-Nickel

7	5 Cents 1948–50	.20	.75	1.00
		Proof . . . 150.00		
8	10 Cents 1948–50	.35	.50	.75
		Proof . . . 175.00		
9	20 Cents 1948–50	.50	1.00	3.00
		Proof . . . 175.00		

For later issues see MALAYA AND BRITISH BORNEO.

MALAYA AND BRITISH BORNEO

Issues for Malaya, Singapore, Sarawak, Brunei, and British North Borneo.

ELIZABETH II 1952–1963

Bronze

A1	1 Cent 1956–61	.10	.20	.40
		Proof . . . 100.00		

Cupro-Nickel

1	5 Cents 1953–61	.25	.50	1.00
		Proof . . . 175.00		
2	10 Cents 1953–61	.25	.50	1.00
		Proof . . . 175.00		
3	20 Cents 1954–61	.50	.75	1.75
		Proof . . . 200.00		
4	50 Cents 1954–61	.75	1.25	2.00
		Proof . . . 250.00		

Unless otherwise noted, prices are for coins in very fine, extremely fine, and uncirculated condition.

Bronze

5 1 Cent 1962   .05   .10   .35
                                        Proof . . . 100.00

For later issues see Brunei, Malaysia and Singapore in *Current Coins of the World.*

6 4 Lari AH 1331   2.00   3.00   4.00
Later issues in *Current Coins of the World.*

MALDIVE ISLANDS

Coral atolls southwest of Ceylon. Formerly a dependency of Ceylon, it was later a British Protected State. Became fully independent on July 26, 1965. Chief export: Fish. Area: 115 square miles. Languages: Divehi, Arabic. Capital: *Male.*

Monetary System:
120 Lari = 1 Rupee to ca. 1960
(Nos. 3 and 6 use the plural form "Lariat.")

IBRAHIM NUR AL-DIN
AH 1300–18 (1882–1900)

Copper

A1 ¼ Larin AH 1300
        (10–11mm)   2.50   4.00   5.00

MUHAMMAD IMAD AL-DIN V
AH 1318–22 (1900–04)

1* 1 Larin AH 1311 (error),
        18–19 (10–13mm,
        0.8–2.7 gr.)   1.50   2.25   4.00
3 4 Lari AH 1320 (17mm)   3.00   4.00   6.50

Recent study indicates that former No. 2 (2 Lari 1319) is actually No. 1 struck on heavier planchets. Pieces dated 1319 tend to be heavier and larger than those of 1318.

Nos. 1 and 3 have been reported in brass, silver and gold: all seem to be normal copper pieces unofficially plated for jewelry use.

MUHAMMAD SHAMS AL-DIN III
AH 1322–53 (1904–35)

Copper

5 1 Larin AH 1331 (1913)   1.00   1.50   2.00

MALI — see *Current Coins of the World.*

MALTA

A pair of islands south of Sicily in the Mediterranean Sea. Malta was a British colony from 1814 until gaining independence in 1964. Its economy derived chiefly from its use as the base of British naval operations in the Mediterranean. Area: 121 square miles. Languages: Maltese, English. Capital: *Valetta.*

One-third farthing pieces, called "Granos" (Grains), were were struck especially for Malta beginning in 1827. English coins were also used.

VICTORIA 1837–1901

Copper

1 ⅓ Farthing 1844 (16mm)   25.00 45.00 100.00

Bronze

2 ⅓ Farthing 1866–85   5.50 10.00 30.00

EDWARD VII 1901–1910

3 ⅓ Farthing 1902   2.50   4.00   7.50

GEORGE V 1910–1936

4 ⅓ Farthing 1913 .... 2.50 4.00 7.50

Later issues in *Current Coins of the World*.

MANCHUKUO

Japanese forces invaded the Chinese province of Manchuria in 1931. Shortly thereafter, it became the nominally independent nation of Manchukuo, but under Japanese control. The puppet emperor under the assumed name of Kang Teh was previously the last emperor of China (Pu-Yi, or Hsuan T'ung, 1909–11). After the close of World War II in 1945 the area was returned to China. Rich soil and large mineral deposits make this territory an important possession. Capital: *Hsinking*.

Monetary System:
10 Li (Cash) = 1 Fen
10 Fen = 1 Chio

TA-TUNG REIGN
1932–1934 (Years 1–3)

同大

Reign Symbols on Coins
Bronze

1* 5 Li Yrs. 2–3 (1933–34) 10.00 17.50 35.00
  Yr. 2 . . . 17.50
2 1 Fen Yrs. 2–3 .... 4.00 12.50 25.00

Cupro-Nickel

3 5 Fen Yrs. 2–3 .... 1.50 4.00 12.50
4* 1 Chio Yrs. 2–3 .... 2.50 5.00 12.50

KANG TEH REIGN
1934–1945 (Years 1–12)

Reign Symbols 德康 on Coins
Like Nos. 1–4 except for symbols of Kang Teh reign.

Bronze

5* 5 Li Yrs. 1–6 (1934–39) 6.00 9.00 25.00
  Yr. 3 . . . 35 Yr. 6 . . . Rare
6 1 Fen Yrs. 1–6 .... 2.50 5.00 12.50

Cupro-Nickel

7 5 Fen Yrs. 1–6 .... 2.00 3.50 6.50
8* 1 Chio Yrs. 1–6 .... 1.75 3.00 7.50

Second Coinage

Aluminum

9 1 Fen Yrs. 6–10
  (1939–43) 1.00 2.00 5.00

11 5 Fen Yrs. 7–10
  (1940–43) 1.25 2.50 5.50
12 10 Fen Yrs. 7–10 .... 2.00 3.50 8.00
  Yr. 10 . . . Rare

Cupro-Nickel

10 1 Chio Yr. 7 (1940) 5.00 10.00 25.00

Unless otherwise noted, prices are for coins in very fine, extremely fine, and uncirculated condition.

Third Coinage

Aluminum

13	1 Fen Yrs. 10–11			
	(1943–44)	2.00	4.50	9.00
A13	5 Fen Yrs. 10–11	3.00	6.00	10.00
14	10 Fen Yr. 10	2.50	5.00	10.00

Red Fiber

13a	1 Fen Yr. 12 (1945)	2.50	5.00	7.50
A13a	5 Fen Yr. 11	12.50	17.50	25.00

MARTINIQUE

An island in the West Indies, it has been a French possession since 1635. Principal exports are sugar cane, cocoa, pineapples, and bananas. Area: 431 square miles. Capital: *Fort-de-France.*

Monetary System:
100 Centimes = 1 Franc

Cupro-Nickel

1	50 Centimes 1897, 1922	15.00	35.00	125.00
2	1 Franc 1897, 1922	25.00	45.00	150.00

MAURITIUS

An island east of Madagascar in the Indian Ocean, settled by France in the 18th century. In 1814 it was ceded to the British, who preserved French laws and customs. It became independent within the British Commonwealth in 1968. The economy is based on sugar and other agricultural products. Area: 720 square miles. Languages: French, English, Creole, Hindi. Capital: *Port Louis.*

Monetary System:
100 Cents = 1 Rupee

VICTORIA 1837–1901

Bronze

1	1 Cent 1877–97	4.00	8.00	20.00
2	2 Cents 1877–97	5.00	10.00	25.00
3	5 Cents 1877–97	7.50	20.00	50.00
	1878 . . . 20 1882H . . . 30			

Silver

4	10 Cents 1877–97	7.50	20.00	60.00
	1878 . . . 20 1882H . . . 50			
5	20 Cents 1877–99	8.00	25.00	75.00
	1878 . . . 20 1882H . . . 55			

GEORGE V 1910–1936

Bronze

6	1 Cent 1911–24	2.00	5.00	10.00
7	2 Cents 1911–24	3.00	7.00	20.00
8	5 Cents 1917–24	5.00	15.00	35.00

Silver

9	¼ Rupee 1934–36	5.00	12.00	40.00

Rev: Like No. 21

10	½ Rupee 1934	7.00	15.00	45.00

11 1 Rupee 1934   10.00   18.00   50.00

GEORGE VI 1936–1952

Bronze

12	1 Cent 1943–47	1.00	2.00	8.00
13	2 Cents 1943–47	1.25	2.50	9.00
14	5 Cents 1942–45	1.50	3.00	10.00

Cupro-Nickel

15 10 Cents 1947   2.00   4.00   10.00

Silver
Rev: Designs similar to Nos. 9–11

16	¼ Rupee 1938, 46	4.00	10.00	35.00
17	½ Rupee 1946	15.00	45.00	250.00
18	1 Rupee 1938	12.50	25.00	65.00

New Legend:
KING GEORGE THE SIXTH
Bronze

23	1 Cent 1949, 52	.50	1.00	3.00
24	2 Cents 1949, 52	.50	1.00	3.00

Cupro-Nickel

19	10 Cents 1952 (scal- loped)	1.00	2.00	5.00

20	¼ Rupee 1950–51	1.00	2.00	5.00
21	½ Rupee 1950–51	1.50	3.00	8.00
22	1 Rupee 1950–51	1.25	2.50	6.00

ELIZABETH II 1952–

Bronze

25	1 Cent 1953–78		.25
26	2 Cents 1953–78		.35
27	5 Cents 1956–78		.50

Cupro-Nickel

28 10 Cents 1954–78   .60

29 1 Rupee 1956–78   2.00

30 ¼ Rupee 1960–78   1.00
Later issues in *Current Coins of the World.*

Unless otherwise noted, prices are for coins in very
fine, extremely fine, and uncirculated condition.

MEXICO

A federal republic to the south of the United States. Since its independence from Spain in the early 1800's, Mexico has been torn by many revolutions and civil wars, but in the last 60 years has made great progress. Tourism has become an important industry. Its principal products include cotton, coffee, shrimp, cattle, lead and petroleum. Two-thirds of its exports are made to the United States. Area: 758,259 square miles. Language: Spanish. Capital: *Mexico City.*

Monetary System:
8 Reales = 1 Peso
16 Reales = 1 Escudo
100 Centavos = 1 Peso

Fourteen mints coined silver and gold from 1823 to 1905. Certain issues are much rarer than the values indicated for a common date and mint. For a detailed listing one should refer to any of the numerous specialized catalogs available on the coins of Mexico.

REPUBLICA MEXICANA
1823–1905

Copper

Designs like No. S12

S9	⅛ Real 1829 (27mm)		Fine	250.00
S10	¼ Real 1829 (33mm)	30.00	100.00	500.00

S11	¹⁄₁₆ Real 1831–33	20.00	40.00	180.00
SA11	⅛ Real 1829–35 (21mm)	10.00	25.00	150.00
S12	¼ Real 1829–37 (27mm)	5.00	15.00	125.00

S14	⅛ Real 1841–61	10.00	20.00	150.00

Silver

Obv: "Hooked-neck" eagle

S16*	½ Real 1824	50.00	100.00	250.00
S17	1 Real 1824		Fine	2000.
S18	2 Reales 1824	200.00	450.00	1000.
S19	8 Reales 1823–25	250.00	500.00	2500.

S20	¼ Real 1842–63		7.00 10.00	40.00

Obv: Upright eagle

S21	½ Real 1825–69	3.00	5.00	30.00
S22	1 Real 1825–69	4.00	10.00	100.00
S23*	2 Reales 1825–72	7.00	12.00	200.00
S24	4 Reales 1825–69	25.00	50.00	1000.
S25	8 Reales 1824–69	15.00	20.00	75.00

Gold

S26	*F107–118* ½ Escudo 1825–69	60.00	100.00	200.00
S27	*F97–106* 1 Escudo 1825–70	120.00	175.00	350.00
S28*	*F87–96* 2 Escudos 1825–70	275.00	350.00	800.00
S29	*F77–86* 4 Escudos 1825–69	800.00	1500.	4000.
S30	*F63* 8 Escudos 1823, Obv. as No. S16	6500.	9000.	15000.
S31	*F64–76* 8 Escudos 1825–73	500.00	600.00	1000.

EMPEROR MAXIMILIAN
1864–1867

Legend: IMPERIO MEXICANO
Copper

REPUBLIC 1863–1905

Copper

S32 1 Centavo 1864   75.00 200.00 1250.

S15	1 Centavo 1863	15.00	25.00 300.00

Silver

1	1 Centavo 1869–97	5.00	9.00 20.00

S33	5 Centavos 1864–66	40.00	65.00 200.00
S34	10 Centavos 1864–66.	35.00	50.00 200.00

Obv: Restyled eagle

2	1 Centavo 1898	10.00	20.00 70.00

S35 50 Centavos 1866   50.00 90.00 500.00

3	1 Centavo 1899–1905	1.00	2.00 10.00

Cupro-Nickel

S36 1 Peso 1866–67   40.00 90.00 400.00

Gold

S37 *F62* 20 Pesos 1866   1250. 1600. 4000.

4	1 Centavo 1882–83	.50	1.00	2.00
5	2 Centavos 1882–83	.50	1.00	2.00
6	5 Centavos 1882–83	.50	1.00	2.00

Unless otherwise noted, prices are for coins in very fine, extremely fine, and uncirculated condition.

Silver

7	5 Centavos 1867–69	70.00	100.00	500.00
8	10 Centavos 1867–69	70.00	100.00	500.00

9	5 Centavos 1863–70	70.00	100.00	500.00
10	10 Centavos 1863–70	70.00	100.00	500.00

11	5 Centavos 1869–97	2.00	3.00	15.00
12	10 Centavos 1869–97	2.00	4.00	35.00

11a	5 Centavos 1878–80, 86, 98, obv. of No. 21 (mule)	10.00	20.00	75.00
12a	10 Centavos 1885–86, obv. of No. 22 (mule)	50.00	75.00	250.00

13	25 Centavos 1869–92	5.00	10.00	150.00
14	50 Centavos 1869–95	10.00	25.00	500.00
15	1 Peso 1869–73	15.00	25.00	250.00

Obv: Restyled eagle

16	5 Centavos 1898–1905	1.00	2.00	15.00
17	10 Centavos 1898–1905	2.00	4.00	35.00
18	20 Centavos 1898–1905	5.00	10.00	100.00

19	8 Reales 1869–97	15.00	20.00	70.00

20	1 Peso 1898–1909	15.00	20.00	75.00

Gold

21	*F157–164* 1 Peso 1870–1905	150.00	175.00	250.00

21a	1 Peso 1898, obv. of No. 16 (mule)	160.00	190.00	300.00
22	*F148–156* 2½ Pesos 1870–93	350.00	500.00	1000.

23* *F139–147* 5 Pesos
1870–1905 · 400.00 500.00 1000.

24 *F128–138* 10 Pesos
1870–1905 · 750.00 1200. 2500.

25 *F119–127* 20 Pesos
1870–1905 · 750.00 1200. 2500.

ESTADOS UNIDOS
MEXICANOS 1905–

Bronze

27 1 Centavo 1905–49
(20mm) · .10 .15 .30

28 1 Centavo 1915 (16mm) · 25.00 30.00 50.00

29 2 Centavos 1905–41
(25mm) · .50 1.00 15.00

30 2 Centavos 1915 (20mm) · 5.00 8.00 35.00

Nickel

31 5 Centavos 1905–14 · 1.00 2.00 40.00

Silver

39 10 Centavos 1905–14
(18mm) · 3.00 4.00 10.00

40 20 Centavos 1905–14
(22mm) · 4.00 6.00 40.00

41 50 Centavos 1905–18
(30mm) · 5.00 7.00 16.00

42 1 Peso 1910–14 · 30.00 50.00 200.00
1914 . . . 800
No. 20 was continued briefly into this period.

Gold

55 *F170* 2 Pesos 1919–48 · 30.00

56 *F169* 2½ Pesos 1918–48 · 35.00
1947 . . . 300

57* *F167–168* 5 Pesos 1905–55 · 75.00
1905 . . . 250

Unless otherwise noted, prices are for coins in very
fine, extremely fine, and uncirculated condition.

58 *F165–166* 10 Pesos 1905–59   150.00
1920 . . . 500

59 *F171* 20 Pesos 1917–59   300.00

46 1 Peso 1918–19   20.00 40.00 500.00
1918 . . . 30

Bronze

.720 Silver

Obv: With "0.720"

32 5 Centavos 1914–35   1.00   2.00 15.00
33 10 Centavos 1919–21,
   35   12.00 25.00 75.00

47	10 Centavos 1925–35	1.00	2.00	5.00
48	20 Centavos 1920–43	1.00	2.00	3.00
49	50 Centavos 1919–45	2.00	3.00	4.00
50	1 Peso 1920–45	5.00	6.00	8.00

Billon

34 20 Centavos 1920, 35   5.00   7.00 50.00
1920 . . . 25

Obv: No fineness shown
52 50 Centavos 1935   2.00   3.00   5.00

.800 Silver

Obv: No fineness shown
43 10 Centavos 1919
   (15mm)   8.00 14.00 75.00

Independence Centennial

44 20 Centavos 1919
   (19mm)   20.00 50.00 250.00
45 50 Centavos 1918–19
   (27mm)   7.00 17.50 100.00
1918 . . . 15

Obv: Date in Roman numerals

51 2 Pesos 1921   40.00 75.00 300.00

38 20 Centavos 1943–55   .25   .40   4.00
       1951 . . . 3

Gold

Obv: Like Nos. 55–56

60 *F172* 50 Pesos 1921–47   675.00
1921 UNC . . . 900
60a (50 Pesos) 1943, no value
       shown   700.00
Only the 1921 date of No. 60 is considered a commemorative.

Silver

Rev: Jose Morelos

53 1 Peso 1947–49   3.00   4.00   6.00
       1949 . . . 12

Cupro-Nickel

35 5 Centavos 1936–42   .25   .75   4.00
36 10 Centavos 1936–46   .25   .50   2.00

Bronze

Rev: Josefa Dominguez

37 5 Centavos 1942–55   .10   .15   .35
       1942 . . . 20

Rev: Cuauhtemoc

54 5 Pesos 1947–48   15.00 16.00 22.50

Decree of December 29, 1949

Brass

61 1 Centavo 1950–69   .10

Unless otherwise noted, prices are for coins in very
fine, extremely fine, and uncirculated condition.

Cupro-Nickel

Rev: Josefa Dominguez
62   5 Centavos 1950   .50   1.00   5.00

Billon

63   25 Centavos 1950–53   .50   .75   1.00

Rev: Cuauhtemoc
64   50 Centavos 1950–51   1.00   1.50   2.00

Rev: Jose Morelos
65   1 Peso 1950   2.00   3.00   4.00

Silver

Rev: Miguel Hidalgo
67   5 Pesos 1951–54   10.00   11.00   15.00
     1954 . . . 100

Completion of Southeastern Railway

66   5 Pesos 1950   40.00   50.00   65.00

Bicentennial Birth of Hidalgo

68   5 Pesos 1953   10.00   11.00   15.00

Brass

69   5 Centavos 1954–69   .10
     1954 . . . 7

Bronze

70   10 Centavos 1955–67   .20
     1955 . . . 1

71	20 Centavos 1955–71	.10	.15	.25
	1959 . . . 5			

72	50 Centavos 1955–59	.10	.15	.50
	1955 . . . 1			

Silver Alloys

A72	1 Peso 1957–67 (.100 fine)	.50	.75	1.25

73*	5 Pesos 1955–57 (.720 fine)	6.00	7.00	10.00
74	10 Pesos 1955–56 (.900 fine)	12.00	13.00	15.00

Constitution Centennial
1857–1957

75*	1 Peso 1957 (.100 fine)	2.00	3.00	15.00
76	5 Pesos 1957 (.720 fine)	6.00	8.00	13.00
77	10 Pesos 1957 (.900 fine)	30.00	40.00	60.00

Centennial Birth of Carranza

Silver

78	5 Pesos 1959	6.00	7.00	10.00

Dual Commemorative —
Revolutions of 1810 and 1910

79	10 Pesos 1960	12.00	13.00	15.00

Later issues in *Current Coins of the World.*

REVOLUTIONARY ISSUES
1913–1917
STATE OF AGUASCALIENTES

Copper
Obv: Liberty cap

R1	1 Centavo 1915	50.00	100.00	150.00
R2	2 Centavos 1915	175.00	250.00	400.00

Unless otherwise noted, prices are for coins in very
fine, extremely fine, and uncirculated condition.

R3 5 Centavos 1915, rev. lg.
5c   12.00 25.00 50.00
Rev: Similar to Mexico No.52
R4 5 Centavos 1915   20.00 30.00 50.00
R5 20 Centavos 1915 (vars.) 10.00 15.00 30.00
Nos. R1–R3 and R5 were also struck in silver for presentation purposes.

STATE OF CHIHUAHUA
I. Hidalgo del Parral, city.

Legend:
FUERZAS CONSTITUCIONALISTAS
Copper or Brass
R7 2 Centavos 1913   3.00   5.00 15.00

Silver
R8 50 Centavos 1913   20.00 25.00 45.00

R9 1 Peso 1913, rev. ball in
ctr.   3000. 4000.   –
R10* 1 Peso 1913, without
ball   150.00 200.00 400.00

II. Ejercito Constitucionalista
(Constitutionalist Army).

Copper

R11 5 Centavos 1914–15   .50   .75   1.50
R12 10 Centavos 1914–15   .50   .75   1.50

Brass
R11a 5 Centavos 1914–15   1.00   3.00   5.00
R12a 10 Centavos 1915   1.00   3.00   5.00
The 50 Centavos and 1 Peso with obverse as above are considered patterns, as are two types of 5 Centavos with eagle obverse.

III. Ejercito del Norte
(Army of the North).

Silver

R16 1 Peso 1915   60.00 90.00 175.00

STATE OF DURANGO
Copper
R17 1 Centavo 1914	2.00	5.00	20.00
R18 I Centavo 1914	15.00	30.00	75.00
R19 5 Centavos 1914, ES-			
TADO DE	1.00	2.00	3.00
R20 5 Centavos 1914, E. DE	2.00	5.00	20.00
R21 V Centavos 1914	10.00	15.00	30.00
Obv: 3 stars at bottom			
R22 1 Centavo 1914	15.00	20.00	40.00

Brass

R17a	1 Centavo 1914	100.00	145.00 250.00
R18a	I Centavo 1914	100.00	145.00 250.00
R20a	5 Centavos 1914	100.00	145.00 250.00

Lead

R17b	1 Centavo 1914	30.00	60.00 150.00
R18b	I Centavo 1914	35.00	75.00 175.00
R20b	5 Centavos 1914	50.00	100.00 200.00
R21b	V Centavos 1914	–	– –
R22b	I Centavo 1914	–	– –

Aluminum

R24	1 Centavo 1914	1.00	2.00	5.00

Brass

R25	5 Centavos 1914	1.00	2.00	5.00

Silver

Legend: MUERA HUERTA
("Death to Huerta")
Rev: 6 stars around lower border
Crude lettering both sides

R26	1 Peso 1914	2500.	3000.	4000.

Rev: Without stars

R27*	1 Peso 1914	175.00	225.00 600.00

STATE OF GUERRERO
Mint towns and mintmarks on coins:

ATLIXTAC

CACALOTEPEC

CAMPO MO (rado), CoMo, C.M.

SURIANA

TAXCO, To

G, Go, GRO, G.R.O. = Guerrero

Copper
Obv: Similar to No. R32c
Rev: Similar to Mexico No. 32

R29	2 Centavos 1915	300.00	400.00 600.00
R30	3 Centavos 1915	2000.	3000. –
R31	5 Centavos 1915 C.M.	15.00	20.00 35.00
R31a	5 Centavos 1915 TAXCO GRO	20.00	30.00 50.00
R31b	5 Centavos 1915 GRO	750.00	1250. 2000.

R32	10 Centavos 1915 C.M. GRO	15.00	20.00 30.00
R32a	10 Centavos 1915 TAXCO GRO	25.00	30.00 50.00
R32b	10 Centavos 1915 GRO	5.00	10.00 20.00
R32c	10 Centavos 1915 AT-LIXTAC GRO	4.00	9.00 15.00
R33	20 Centavos 1915 C.M. GRO	50.00	75.00 150.00
R34	50 Centavos 1915 C.M. GRO (vars.)	5.00	7.00 10.00

Obv: Similar to No. R32c
Rev: Date on radiant sun

R35	50 Centavos 1915 TAXCO/GRO	50.00	75.00 125.00

Obv: Eagle, EDO. DE GRO
Rev: Similar to No. R32c

RA36	2 Centavos 1915 To	65.00	100.00 150.00

Type of Mexico No. 32

RA37	5 Centavos 1917 G	75.00	100.00 200.00

Silver
Types of Mexico Nos. 39–40
Obv. legend: MEXICO ESTADO (DE) G.R.O.

RA38	10 Centavos 1914, cast	900.00	– –
RA39	20 Centavos 1914, cast	900.00	– –

Obv: Liberty cap
Crude legends both sides

RA40	25 Centavos 1915 E.D.G.	400.00	500.00 600.00
RA41	50 Centavos 1915 E. deG	2000.	3000. 4000.

Type of No. R35

R35a	50 Centavos 1915 TAXCO/GRO	50.00	90.00 150.00

Unless otherwise noted, prices are for coins in very
fine, extremely fine, and uncirculated condition.

R36 1 Peso 1914–15 GRO	10.00	15.00	30.00
R36b 1 Peso 1914 CAMPO Mo	25.00	35.00	50.00
R36c*1 Peso 1915 TAXCO GRO	15.00	20.00	30.00

Rev: Radiant sun over mountains

R37 2 Pesos 1914–15 GRO	25.00	35.00	75.00
R37a 2 Pesos 1915 CoMo	50.00	75.00	150.00
R37b 2 Pesos 1915 SURIANA	7500.	10000.	15000.

R38 2 Pesos 1915 C.M. GRO	25.00	35.00	75.00

Types of Mexico Nos. 40–41

R39 20 Centavos 1917 G	175.00	250.00	500.00
R39a 20 Centavos 1917 CA-CALOTEPEC/GRO	2000.	2500.	3000.
R40 50 Centavos 1917 GRO	100.00	150.00	250.00

Type of Mexico No. 20

R41 1 Peso 1917 Go	3500.	4500.	6000.

STATE OF JALISCO

Copper

R42 1 Centavo 1915	15.00	20.00	30.00
R43 2 Centavos 1915	10.00	20.00	30.00
R44 5 Centavos 1915	15.00	20.00	30.00

Obv: State arms

R45 10 Centavos 1915	2500.	3000.	4000.

STATE OF MEXICO

I. Amecameca, town.

Copper or Brass

Obv: Incuse eagle
Rev: Incuse value

R47 5 Centavos ND	175.00	250.00	350.00
R48 10 Centavos ND	125.00	175.00	250.00
R49 20 Centavos ND, brass (25mm)	35.00	50.00	75.00
R50 20 Centavos ND (20mm)	15.00	25.00	–
R51 25 Centavos ND	20.00	25.00	–
R52 50 Centavos ND	10.00	20.00	50.00

II. Tenancingo, town.

Copper

R53 5 Centavos 1915	7.00	10.00	20.00
R54 10 Centavos 1916	20.00	30.00	50.00
R55 20 Centavos 1915	60.00	100.00	–

III. Texcoco, town.

Reddish Clay

Type similar to Mexico No. 27

R56 1 Centavo 1915	3500.	–	–

IV. Toluca, city.

Bronze

Counterstamps on Mexico Nos. 27, 29

R57 "20 C" in circle on 1 Cent. 1906	50.00	70.00	100.00
R58 "40 C" in circle on 2 Cent. 1906	75.00	100.00	150.00

Gray Cardboard

R59 5 Centavos 1915	40.00	60.00	100.00

STATE OF MORELOS

Copper

Type similar to No. R69

R60 10 Centavos ND, 1915, crude	30.00	50.00	100.00
R62 2 Centavos 1915	2500.	–	–
R63 5 Centavos 1915	2500.	–	–
R64 10 Centavos 1915	2500.	–	–
R65 20 Centavos 1915	25.00	40.00	75.00
R66 50 Centavos 1915	15.00	25.00	50.00

R69 10 Centavos 1916	15.00	20.00	40.00
R71 50 Centavos 1916	20.00	25.00	35.00

Silver
Type similar to No. R36

R72 1 Peso 1916	2000.	3000.	4000.

STATE OF OAXACA

(Independent State)

Copper

R73 1 Centavo 1915	150.00	200.00	275.00
R74* 3 Centavos 1915	150.00	200.00	275.00

Restrikes or counterfeits of Nos. R73 and R74 are known.

R75 1 Centavo 1915	20.00	25.00	35.00

R76 3 Centavos 1915, lg. flat top 3	10.00	12.00	20.00
R76a 3 Centavos 1915, small, round top 3	10.00	12.00	20.00
R77 5 Centavos 1915	1.00	2.00	3.00
R78 10 Centavos 1915	1.00	2.00	3.00
R79 20 Centavos 1915	1.00	2.00	3.00

Silver

R80 20 Centavos 1915	2000.	2500.	3000.
R81 50 Centavos 1915	20.00	30.00	45.00
R82 1 Peso 1915	10.00	15.00	25.00

R83 2 Pesos 1915	25.00	35.00	50.00

R84* 2 Pesos 1915 value as numeral	20.00	30.00	50.00
R84a 2 Pesos 1915 value as "DOS"	20.00	30.00	50.00

R85 2 Pesos 1915	25.00	35.00	50.00
R86 5 Pesos 1915	125.00	175.00	300.00

Gold

R87 *F177* 5 Pesos 1915	250.00	325.00	450.00

Unless otherwise noted, prices are for coins in very fine, extremely fine, and uncirculated condition.

R88 *F176* 10 Pesos 1915   300.00 350.00 500.00
R89 *F175* 20 Pesos 1915   400.00 500.00 750.00

R90 *F174* 60 Pesos 1916   7500. 10000. 12500.
Specimens of No. R90 in silver and copper are patterns.

STATE OF PUEBLA

I. "Madero Brigade" Coinage.

Copper

R91 X Centavos 1915   12.00 22.00 35.00
R92 20 Centavos 1915   4.00   7.00 12.00

II. Tetela del Oro y Ocampo

Copper

R93 2 Centavos 1915 (17mm)   3.00   5.00 10.00
R94 2 Centavos 1915 (21mm)   25.00 35.00 50.00
R95 5 Centavos 1915   500.00 600.00   –
R96 10 Centavos 1915   400.00 500.00   –
R97 20 Centavos 1915   300.00 400.00   –
Some authorities feel Nos. R95–R97 may be patterns.
They also occur in other metals.

STATE OF SINALOA

Cast Silver

R98 20 Centavos ND (1914),
      copy of Mexico No. 18   400.00   –   –

R99 50 Centavos ND, copy of
      No. 41   350.00   –   –
R100 8 Reales ND, copy of
      No. 19   40.00   –   –
R101 1 Peso ND, copy of No.
      20   40.00   –   –
Nos. R98–R101 are crudely cast copies of earlier national coinage. Legends, when readable, will show dates of various original coins used to make molds.

MOMBASA

Now a seaport in Kenya. This town came under British administration in 1888. It was their first foothold in the present Kenya.

Monetary System:
4 Pice = 1 Anna
16 Annas = 1 Rupee

Bronze

1 1 Pice 1888 (2 vars.)   5.00 12.00 20.00
                                      Proof . . . 100.00

Silver

2 2 Annas 1890   15.00 25.00 50.00
                                      Proof . . . 75.00
3 ¼ Rupee 1890   20.00 40.00 60.00
                                      Proof . . . 100.00
4 ½ Rupee 1890   25.00 40.00 75.00
                                      Proof . . . 100.00

5 1 Rupee 1888   25.00 50.00 100.00
                                      Proof . . . 125.00

For later issues see East Africa.

MONACO

A small principality on the Mediterranean coast bounded by France, famous for its resort areas and Monte Carlo. Area: Less than one square mile. Languages: French, English, Italian, Monagasque. Capital: *Monaco-Ville.*

Monetary System:
100 Centimes = 1 Franc

CHARLES III 1856–1889

Gold

A1	*F12* 20 Francs 1878–79	–	250.00	450.00
B1*	*F11* 100 Francs			
	1882–86	–	–	850.00
1882 . . . Rare				

ALBERT I 1889–1922

Gold

1	*F13* 100 Francs			
	1891–1904	–	–	750.00
1892 . . . Rare				

LOUIS II 1922–1949

Within Inner Circle:
"REMB. JUSQU'AU 31 X BRE 1926"
(Good until 31 December 1926)
Aluminum-Bronze

2	50 Centimes 1924	15.00	30.00	50.00
3	1 Franc 1924	15.00	30.00	50.00
4	2 Francs 1924	20.00	40.00	75.00

Rev: Without inner legend

5	50 Centimes 1926	15.00	32.50	60.00
6	1 Franc 1926	20.00	35.00	75.00
7	2 Francs 1926	25.00	45.00	85.00

8	1 Franc ND (1945)	1.00	3.50	7.00
9	2 Francs ND (1945)	2.00	6.00	12.00

Aluminum

8a	1 Franc ND (1943)	1.00	2.00	5.00
9a	2 Francs ND (1943)	1.50	5.00	10.00

10	5 Francs 1945	1.00	3.00	7.50

Unless otherwise noted, prices are for coins in very fine, extremely fine, and uncirculated condition.

Cupro-Nickel

11	10 Francs 1946	1.50	3.00	8.00
12	20 Francs 1947	3.00	4.00	10.00

RAINIER III 1949–

Aluminum-Bronze

13	10 Francs 1950–51	.50	1.00	3.00
14	20 Francs 1950–51	.50	1.00	3.00

15	50 Francs 1950	2.00	3.50	7.50

Cupro-Nickel

16	100 Francs 1950	2.50	5.00	15.00

17	100 Francs 1956	1.50	3.50	7.50

Later issues in *Current Coins of the World.*

MONGOLIA, Outer

In northeastern Asia, bounded on the north by the U.S.S.R. A Chinese province until 1911, it patterned its People's Republic after the Soviet's. Principal industry: livestock raising. Area; 626,000 square miles. Languages: Mongolian and Russian. Capital: *Ulan Bator.*

Monetary System:
100 Mongo = 1 Tukhrik
Calendar:
Year 1 = 1911

People's Republic
First Coinage

Copper

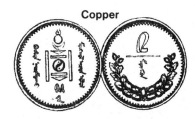

1	1 Mongo Yr. 15 (1925), 21mm	5.50	9.50	20.00
2*	2 Mongo Yr. 15 (24mm)	10.00	12.50	25.00
3	5 Mongo Yr. 15 (32mm)	15.00	20.00	40.00

Silver

4	10 Mongo Yr. 15 (17mm)	6.00	9.00	17.50
5	15 Mongo Yr. 15 (19mm)	6.00	10.00	20.00
6	20 Mongo Yr. 15 (22mm)	8.00	12.50	25.00
7	50 Mongo Yr. 15 (27mm)	12.50	15.00	30.00
8	1 Tukhrik Yr. 15 (34mm)	24.00	35.00	70.00

Second Coinage

Aluminum-Bronze

10*	1 Mongo Yr. 27 (1937)	4.00	6.00	12.50
11	2 Mongo Yr. 27 (22mm)	4.00	6.00	12.50
12	5 Mongo Yr. 27 (28mm)	4.00	6.00	12.50

Cupro-Nickel

13*	10 Mongo Yr. 27 (1937)	4.00	6.00	12.50
14	20 Mongo Yr. 27 (21mm)	4.00	6.00	12.50
15	20 Mongo Yr. 27	6.00	9.00	20.00

Third Coinage
Aluminum-Bronze

16	1 Mongo Yr. 35 (1945)	4.00	7.50	15.00
17	2 Mongo Yr. 35	2.50	4.00	9.00
18	5 Mongo Yr. 35	4.00	5.00	10.00

Cupro-Nickel

19	10 Mongo Yr. 35 (1945)	4.00	6.00	12.50
20	15 Mongo Yr. 35	3.00	5.00	10.00
21	20 Mongo Yr. 35	4.00	6.00	12.50

Fourth Coinage
Aluminum

22	1 Mongo 1959	1.00	1.50	2.50
23	2 Mongo 1959	1.00	1.50	2.50
24	5 Mongo 1959	1.00	1.50	2.50

25	10 Mongo 1959	2.00	3.00	5.00
26	15 Mongo 1959	1.50	2.50	3.50
27	20 Mongo 1959	1.50	2.50	3.50

Later issues in *Current Coins of the World.*

MONTENEGRO
(Crna Gora)

A former kingdom north of Albania, now a part of Yugo-slavia. Capital: *Cetinje.*

Monetary System:
100 Para = 1 Perper

NIKOLA I 1860–1918
as Prince 1860–1910
Bronze

1	1 Para 1906	5.00	15.00	30.00
2	2 Pare 1906, 08	5.00	10.00	20.00

Nickel

3	10 Pare 1906, 08	2.00	7.00	20.00
4	20 Pare 1906, 08	2.00	7.00	20.00

Silver

5	1 Perper 1909	12.00	25.00	75.00
6	2 Perpera 1910	25.00	45.00	125.00
7	5 Perpera 1909	150.00	275.00	400.00

Gold

8	F3	10 Perpera 1910	250.00	300.00	475.00
9	F2	20 Perpera 1910	300.00	450.00	650.00
10	F1	100 Perpera 1910			Rare

as King 1910–1918
Bronze
Rev: New legend

11	1 Para 1913–14	5.00	10.0	20.00
12	2 Pare 1913–14	5.00	10.00	20.00

Nickel

13	10 Para 1913–14	2.50	7.00	20.00
14	20 Para 1913–14	3.00	7.50	20.00

Unless otherwise noted, prices are for coins in very
fine, extremely fine, and uncirculated condition.

Silver

15	1 Perper 1912, 14	12.00	25.00	75.00
16	2 Perpera 1914	25.00	60.00	150.00
17*	5 Perpera 1912, 14	135.00	250.00	450.00

50th Year of Regency

Gold

18	F6	10 Perpera 1910	250.00	350.00	475.00
19	F5	20 Perpera 1910	300.00	450.00	650.00
20	F4	100 Perpera 1910	3000.	5000.	8500.

MOROCCO
(Empire Cherifien, Maroc)

A monarchy on the northwest coast of Africa. It was formerly a French and Spanish protectorate. From this area all northwest Africa and most of the Spanish peninsula were ruled during the seventh century. Area: 171,953 square miles. Languages: Moorish-Arabic and Berber, French and Spanish. Capital: *Rabat.*

Monetary Systems:
500 Muzuna = 1 Dirham
10 Dirham = 1 Rial
100 Centimes = 1 Franc 1921–1959

Prices for Nos. C1 to 45 are for coins in Very Fine condition.

HASAN I 1873–1894

Bronze

C1	½ Muzuna AH 1310 (1893), 15.5mm	350.00
B1	1 Muzuna 1310 (18.5mm)	250.00
1	2½ Muzuna 1310 (23.5mm)	200.00
2*	5 Muzuna 1310–11 (28mm)	75.00
3	10 Muzuna 1310–11 (34mm)	100.00

Other machine-struck bronze coins dated 1301–09 are now thought to be patterns.

Silver

| 4 | ½ Dirham AH 1299–1314 (1882–96), 15mm | 1.75 |
| 5* | 1 Dirham 1299–1314 (17mm) | 2.00 |

6*	2½ Dirham 1299–1314 (26mm)	2.50
7	5 Dirham 1299–1314 (33mm)	6.00
8	10 Dirham 1299	12.50

'ABD AL-AZIZ 1896–1908
First Coinage

Silver

| 9 | ½ Dirham AH 1313–19 (1896–1901) | 3.50 |
| 10* | 1 Dirham 1313–18 | 4.00 |

11* 2½ Dirham 1313–18 6.00
12 5 Dirham 1313–18 10.00
13 10 Dirham 1313 85.00

Nos. 9–22 have variations in Arabic inscriptions, size of numerals, etc., according to the mints which were Fez, Birmingham, Berlin and Paris. (Illustration below is 5 Muzuna of Birmingham Mint.)

Second Coinage

Bronze

14 1 Muzuna 1320-21 (1901-03) 3.00
15 2 Muzuna 1320-23 2.00
16* 5 Muzuna 1320-22 1.00
17 10 Muzuna 1320-23 1.25

No. 14 dated 1319 is probably a pattern.

Silver

18 1/20 Rial 1320-21 (1902-04), 15mm 2.00
19* 1/10 Rial 1320-21 (16.5 mm) 3.50

20* ¼ Rial 1320-21 (25mm) 3.00
21 ½ Rial 1320-23 (32mm) 5.00
22 1 Rial 1320-21 (37mm) 12.50

HAFIZ 1908–1912

Silver

23* ¼ Rial 1329 (1911) 2.00
24 ½ Rial 1329 5.00
25 1 Rial 1329 10.00

YUSUF 1912–1927
First Coinage

Bronze

26 1 Muzuna AH 1330 (1912) 3.50
27 2 Muzuna 1330 2.00
28* 5 Muzuna 1330, 40 (1912, 22) .75
29 10 Muzuna 1330, 40 1.00

Silver

30 1/10 Rial 1331 (1913) 40.00

31* ¼ Rial 1331 40.00
32 ½ Rial 1331, 36 5.00
33 1 Rial 1331, 36 8.50

Unless otherwise noted, prices are for coins in very fine, extremely fine, and uncirculated condition.

Second Coinage
100 Centimes = 1 Franc

Cupro-Nickel

34	25 Centimes ND (1921–26)	2.00

Nickel

35	50 Centimes ND (1921–24)	2.00
36	1 Franc ND	2.00

MUHAMMAD BIN YUSUF
as Sultan
AH 1345–72 (1927–53)
Became King Mohammed V in 1955

First Coinage

Silver

37	5 Franc AH 1347, 52 (1929, 34)	2.00
38	10 Francs 1347, 52	3.50
39	20 Francs 1347, 52	10.00

Second Coinage

Aluminum-Bronze

4i	50 Centimes 1945	.50

41	1 Franc 1945	.50
42	2 Francs 1945	.60

43	5 Francs AH 1365 (1946)	1.00

Cupro-Nickel

44	10 Francs 1366	1.00
45	20 Francs 1366	1.25

Third Coinage
Nos. 46–51 were struck in various years through 1973 with no change of date.

The following prices are for coins in Uncirculated condition.
Aluminum

46	1 Franc 1951	.10
47	2 Francs 1951	.15

48	5 Francs AH 1370 (1951)	.20

Aluminum-Bronze

49	10 Francs AH 1371 (1952)	.30
50	20 Francs 1371	.50

51   50 Francs 1371   .75

Silver

52   100 Francs 1953   2.00
53   200 Francs 1953   3.75

MOHAMMED V
as King 1955–1961
Silver

54   500 Francs 1956   20.00

Monetary Reform 1959
100 Francs = 1 Dirham

55   1 Dirham 1960   2.00
Later issues in *Current Coins of the World.*

MOZAMBIQUE
(Mocambique)

Portuguese East Africa. It is a seacoast country of southeast Africa. About 400 square miles of German East Africa were added to it after World War I. Area: 303,769 square miles. Languages: Portuguese, African dialects, English. Capital: *Lourenco Marques (now Maputo).*

Monetary System:
100 Centavos = 1 Escudo

Counterstamps

Silver

Crowned PM in circle (1889)

A1	on India Rupee	30.00	45.00	–
B1	on Austria No. 55	60.00	95.00	–
	Counterstamp: Large PM in oval (ca. 1889–95)			
C1	on India Rupee	25.00	35.00	–
D1	on Austria No. 55	50.00	75.00	–

Regular Issues

Bronze

1	10 Centavos 1936	1.50	3.50	15.00
2	20 Centavos 1936	2.50	4.50	20.00

Cupro-Nickel

3	50 Centavos 1936	2.50	5.00	27.50
4	1 Escudo 1936	3.00	7.00	40.00

Silver

5	2½ Escudos 1935	3.50	8.00	35.00
6	5 Escudos 1935	4.50	12.50	50.00
7	10 Escudos 1936	9.00	15.00	55.00

Unless otherwise noted, prices are for coins in very fine, extremely fine, and uncirculated condition.

New Reverse Arms

8	2½ Escudos 1938–51	1.50	2.50	7.50
9	5 Escudos 1938, 49	3.00	7.00	15.00
10	10 Escudos 1938	9.00	15.00	50.00

Bronze

11	10 Centavos 1942	.75	2.25	7.50
12	20 Centavos 1941	1.50	5.00	17.50
13	50 Centavos 1945	.75	2.50	9.00
14	1 Escudo 1945	1.50	3.50	10.00
15	20 Centavos 1949–50	.50	1.00	4.00

Nickel-Bronze

16	50 Centavos 1950–51	.75	1.50	4.00
17	1 Escudo 1950–51	1.00	2.00	7.00

Decree of January 21, 1952

COLONIA DE omitted
Bronze

18	50 Centavos 1953, 57	.25	.50	2.00
19	1 Escudo 1953–74	.25	.50	2.00

Cupro-Nickel

20	2½ Escudos 1952–73	.25	.50	1.00

Silver

21	5 Escudos 1960	2.00	3.00	6.00
22	10 Escudos 1952–66	3.00	5.00	8.50
23	20 Escudos 1952–66	4.00	7.00	12.50

Note: in 1966, the fineness of the silver coins was lowered from .720 to .680.

Later issues in *Current Coins of the World*.

MUSCAT AND OMAN

A sultanate on the southeast coast of the Arabian peninsula, consisting of the Oman district, Dhofar province, and capital city, Masqat (Muscat). Independent since 1650, it once owned Zanzibar and other coastal areas of Africa and Asia. Its economy is based on agriculture and nomadic herding, with petroleum becoming important. Area: 82,000 square miles. Language: Arabic

Monetary System:
4 Baisah (Baizah) = 1 Anna
64 Baisah = 1 India Rupee
200 Baisah = 1 Riyal = Maria Theresa Taler

Prices for Nos. 1–11 are for coins in Very Fine condition

FESSUL BIN TURKEE
1888–1913

Copper

1*	1/12 Anna AH 1311 (1894)	60.00
2	¼ Anna 1311	20.00

Copper or Brass

3	¼ Anna 1312–16 (1895–99)	5.00

Many varieties of No. 3 include size and arrangement of lettering and Arabic inscriptions, omission of wreath, etc. Some are less crude than the example shown.

A3	¼ Anna 1315	2.00

SA'ID BIN TAIMUR
1932–1970

Cupro-Nickel

4	10 Baisah AH 1359 (1940)	3.50

5	20 Baisah 1359	5.00
6*	50 Baisah 1359	6.50

7	2 Baisah AH 1365 (1946)	1.00

8*	5 Baisah 1365	1.25
10	20 Baisah 1365	2.00

Nos. 4, 5, 6, 11, 12 and 13 used only in Dhofar Province, Oman.

Silver

11	½ Dhufari Riyal AH 1367 (1948)	25.00

The following prices are for Uncirculated coins.
Bronze

13*	3 Baisah 1378 (1959), 20mm	2.00
14	3 Baisah 1380 (18mm)	.75

Cupro-Nickel

16	5 Baisah 1381	1.50

Silver

15*	½ Riyal 1380-81 (1961-62)	5.00
12	1 Riyal 1378	12.50

Unless otherwise noted, prices are for coins in very fine, extremely fine, and uncirculated condition.

Gold

17 *F1* 15 Riyal 1381   200.00
Later issues in *Current Coins of the World.*

NEJD (Najd)

Occupying the desert highlands of the Arabian peninsula, Nejd was first unified as a sultanate in the late 18th
century. Torn by strife until the early 1900's, it thereafter
became the dominant power in the area. It was proclaimed a kingdom in 1927 and was united with the
Hejaz in 1932 to form Saudi Arabia. Language: Arabic.
Capital: *ar-Riyad (Riyadh).*

Monetary System:
40 Para = 1 Ghirsh
20 Ghirsh = 1 Riyal

Prices are for Fine condition.

'ABD AL-AZIZ IBN SA'UD
as Sultan and King of Nejd
1921-1932

Counterstamp: Incuse "Najd" in Arabic
Copies of the Nejd counterstamps on some or all of
these silver types are believed to have been produced in
recent years.

Silver
1 on Turkish or Egyptian 5
Ghirsh   30.00
2 on similar 10 Ghirsh   30.00
2a on India Rupee   40.00
3 on similar 20 Ghirsh   60.00
3a on Austria No. 55   50.00
For later issues, see SAUDI ARABIA.

NEPAL

An independent kingdom in the Himalaya Mountains between India and Tibet. Nepal is famous for its mountains,
including Mt. Everest. Area: 54,362 square miles. Languages: Newari (Nepali), Magar, Pahari. Capital: *Kat-
mandu.*

Monetary System:
32 Paisa = 16 Dhyak = 8 Ani = 4 Do-Ani = 2 Suka =
1 Mohar

PRITHVI 1881-1911 A.D.
Saka Dates 1803-33
Samvat Dates 1938-68
In the reign of King Prithvi coin dates are expressed in
either the Saka or Samvat eras. (See pages 5 and 6 for
details), while only Samvat dates are used in later
reigns. In the following listings, the term "Saka" is always spelled out in full, and the abbreviation "S" refers
only to Samvat dates.

Copper

1 ¼ Paisa Saka 1818-19,
S 1951-64 (14mm)   10.00 12.50 17.50

Type: Circular legends
3* 1 Paisa Saka 1810, S
1945-51 (21-24mm)   40.00 60.00 90.00
4 2 Paisa S 1948-50
(26mm)   7.50 15.00 25.00

Type: Legends in wreaths
A3 1 Paisa S 1949-64   4.00   8.00 15.00

Type: Legends in squares
B3* 1 Paisa S 1959-68   3.00   6.00 12.50
B4 2 Paisa 1949-50   45.00   –   –

5 ¼ Paisa S (19) 68 (1911)
16mm 5.00   8.00   15.00
6* ½ Paisa (19) 64, 68
(19mm) 5.00   8.00   15.00
7 1 Paisa 1964, 68 (23mm)   8.00   12.00   20.00
8 2 Paisa 1964, 68
(26.5mm) 12.50   20.00   30.00
Nos. 5–8 are said to have been issued only in presentation sets.

Silver

Rev: Incuse mirror image of obverse
A9 ¹/₁₂₈ Mohar ND (6mm)   7.50   12.00   20.00
9 ¹/₆₄ Mohar ND 6.00   10.00   17.50
10* ¹/₃₂ Mohar ND (11mm)   7.00   10.00   15.00
11 ¹/₁₆ Mohar ND (13mm)   8.00   12.00   17.50

12 ⅛ Mohar ND 10.00   15.00   25.00
13 ¼ Mohar Saka 1803–27
(1881–1905) 18mm 20.00   30.00   50.00

13a ¼ Mohar Saka 1833
(15.5mm) 4.00   6.00   10.00
14* ½ Mohar Saka 1803–29
(21mm) 20.00   25.00   35.00
14a ½ Mohar Saka 1833
(19mm) 20.00   25.00   35.00

15 1 Mohar Saka 1803–33
(26mm, 5.5gr.) 7.50   10.00   15.00

16 2 Mohar Saka 1803–31
(26mm, 11gr.) 20.00   25.00   40.00
16a* 2 Mohar 1832–33
(29mm, 11gr.) 10.00   12.50   17.50
17 4 Mohar 1817, 33
(29mm, 22gr.) 100.00 150.00 225.00

Gold

Rev: Incuse mirror image of obverse
18* *F21* ¹/₁₂₈ Mohar ND   15.00   20.00   30.00
19 *F19* ¹/₃₂ Mohar ND 20.00   25.00   35.00
20 *F18* ¹/₁₆ Mohar ND, (18)
33 .... 20.00   25.00   35.00
21 *F17* ⅛ Mohar ND, (18)
33 .... 30.00   40.00   60.00

22 *F16* ¼ Mohar 1808–33   60.00   70.00 100.00
23 *F15* ½ Mohar 1805–33   75.00 100.00 125.00
24 *F14* 1 Mohar 1805–33   125.00 150.00 200.00
25* *F13* 1 Ashrafi 1805–33
(12.4gr.) 300.00 350.00 400.00
26 *F12* 2 Rupees 1811–33
(23.2gr.) .... 750.00 1000.   1500.

QUEEN LAKSMI
DIVYESWARI (Regent)

Silver

A26 ½ Mohar VS 1971 (1914)   5.00   8.00   12.50

B26 1 Mohar 1971 .... 5.00   8.00   12.50

Gold

C26 1 Mohar 1971 ...... 125.00 150.00 200.00

Unless otherwise noted, prices are for coins in very
fine, extremely fine, and uncirculated condition.

TRIVHUVANA, 1st Reign
VS 1968–2007 (1911–50)

Copper

27 1 Paisa VS 1968–77
(1912–20)   3.00   6.00   15.00

28 ½ Paisa 1978, 85 (1921,
28)   20.00 30.00   50.00
29* 1 Paisa 1975–87
(1918–30)   10.00 15.00   30.00
30 2 Paisa 1976–87   5.00   10.00   20.00
31 5 Paisa 1976–88   3.00   4.00   7.00

Silver

Rev: Incuse mirror image of obverse
A32 1/128 Mohar ND   25.00 45.00   75.00

32 ¼ Mohar 1969–70
(16mm)   5.00   8.00   17.50
33* ½ Mohar 1968, 70   3.00   5.00   8.00
Designs similar to Nos. 15–17
34 1 Mohar 1968–71   5.00   7.50   12.50
35 2 Mohar 1968–89
(29mm)   7.00   10.00   20.00
36 4 Mohar 1971   50.00   70.00 125.00

Gold

37 *F22* ½ Mohar 1969 (1912)   –
38 *F23* 1 Mohar 1969–75   100.00 150.00 200.00
39 *F24* 1 Ashrafi 1969–89
(12.4gr.)   300.00 350.00 400.00

Decimal System
VS 1989– (1932–)

100 Paisa = 1 Rupee

Copper

Rev: Trident in center
40 1 Paisa 1990–97
(1933–40) 23mm   1.00   2.50   5.00
41* 2 Paisa 1992   7.50   12.50   20.00
42 5 Paisa 1991–97 (30mm) 2.50   5.00   7.50

Rev: Sword in center
A41* 2 Paisa 1992–97
(27mm)   3.00   4.00   6.00
A41a 2 Paisa 1992–99
(25mm)   1.00   2.00   3.00

Reduced Weight Copper

A42 1 Dam 2000, 04 (14mm) 20.00 30.00   37.50
B42 ½ Paisa 2004 (16mm)   20.00 30.00   37.50
43 1 Paisa 2005 (1948)
20mm   1.00   2.00   3.00
44* 2 Paisa 1999–2003
(23mm)   .50   1.00   2.00

Brass

43a 1 Paisa 2000–06   .50   1.00   1.25
44a 2 Paisa 1999–2010   .75   1.25   2.00

Copper-Nickel-Zinc

45 5 Paisa 2000–10
(1943–53)   1.50   2.25   4.75

Silver

A45 1/16 Rupee (19) 96   20.00 30.00 50.00

46 20 Paisa 1989–2004
(1932–47)   3.00   4.00   6.00

47* 50 Paisa 1989–2005   5.00   7.50 12.50
48 1 Rupee 1989–2005   5.00   7.50 17.50

Billon

46a 20 Paisa 2006–10
(1949–53)   1.00   1.25   2.00
47a 50 Paisa 2005–10   2.00   3.00   5.00
48a 1 Rupee 2005–11   5.00 10.00 15.00

Gold

50 *F28* 1/4 Rupee 1995
(1938)   100.00 150.00 200.00
51 *F27* 1/2 Rupee
1995–2005   125.00 175.00 250.00
52 *F26* 1 Rupee
1995–2005   250.00 300.00 400.00
53 *F25* 2 Rupees 2005 500.00 600.00 700.00

JNANENDRA
VS. 2007 (1950–51)

Billon

54 50 Paisa 2007   200.00 300.00 400.00
55* 1 Rupee 2007   5.00 10.00 15.00

TRIVHUVANA, 2nd Reign
VS. 2007–2011 (1951–55)

Nos. 43–45 and 46a–48a were resumed during this period.

56* 50 Paisa 2010–11
(1953–54)   1.00   2.00   3.00
57 1 Rupee 2010–11   1.00   2.00   3.00

General Coinage
VS. 2010–14 (1953–57)

Nos. 58–65 do not bear the name of the ruler, and were continued unchanged into the reign of Mahendra.

Brass

58 1 Paisa 2010–12 (18mm)   2.00   3.00   4.00
59* 2 Paisa 2010–11 (21mm) 30.00 40.00 60.00
Restrikes exist dated 2011, worth $2.00 in UNC
59a 2 Paisa 2012–14 (20mm)   .50   1.00   2.00

61 4 Paisa 2012   2.00   3.00   5.00

Bronze

62 5 Paisa 2010–14   .50   1.00   1.50

63 10 Paisa 2010–12   .25   .50   1.00

Cupro-Nickel
Designs similar to No. 63

64 20 Paisa 2010–11
(18mm)   25.00 40.00 50.00

| 65 | 25 Paisa 2010–14 (19mm) | 3.00 | 4.00 | 5.00 |

Regular Issues
First Coinage

Brass

| 78 | 1 Paisa 2014–20 (1957–63) 16mm | .20 | .30 | .50 |
| 79* | 2 Paisa 2014–20 | .20 | .30 | .50 |

MAHENDRA
VS. 2012–2028 (1955–72)
Coronation Commemoratives

(Nos. 66–77)
Brass

| 66 | 1 Paisa 2013 | .50 | 1.00 | 1.50 |

| 67 | 2 Paisa 2013 | .50 | 1.00 | 1.50 |

Bronze

| 80 | 5 Paisa 2014–20 (22mm) | .25 | .40 | 1.00 |
| 81* | 10 Paisa 2014–20 (25mm, thick) | .25 | .50 | 1.00 |

Aluminum-Bronze

| 80a | 5 Paisa 2021 | 1.00 | 2.00 | 3.00 |
| 81a | 10 Paisa 2021 | 1.00 | 2.00 | 3.00 |

Modified Dies
Brass

| 78a | 1 Paisa 2021–22 | .20 | .30 | .50 |
| 79a | 2 Paisa 2021–23 | .20 | .30 | .50 |

Bronze

| 80b | 5 Paisa 2021–23 (20.5mm) | .20 | .40 | .75 |
| 81b | 10 Paisa 2021–23 (25mm, thin) | .20 | .30 | .50 |

Bronze

| 68 | 5 Paisa 2013 | .75 | 1.25 | 2.00 |
| 69 | 10 Paisa 2013 | .25 | .50 | 1.00 |

Cupro-Nickel

82*	25 Paisa 2015–23 (19mm) 2 vars.	.50	.75	1.00
83	50 Paisa 2011–23 (25mm) 2 vars.	.50	.75	1.00
84	1 Rupee 2011–12 (29.5mm)	2.00	3.00	5.00
84a	1 Rupee 2012–23 (28.5mm) 2 vars	1.00	2.00	3.00

Cupro-Nickel

70	25 Paisa 2013	.50	.75	1.25
71*	50 Paisa 2013	1.00	1.25	1.75
72	1 Rupee 2013	1.00	2.00	3.00

Gold

73	F40 ⅙ Rupee 2013	50.00	60.00	75.00
76	F39 ½ Rupee 2013	125.00	150.00	200.00
77	F38 1 Rupee 2013	225.00	275.00	300.00

Gold

| 85 | F37 ⅕ Rupee 2012 (2.33gr.) | 50.00 | 75.00 | 100.00 |

86	*F36* ¼ Rupee 2012			
	(2.91gr.)	75.00	90.00	125.00
87	*F35* ½ Rupee 2012–19	125.00	150.00	200.00
88	*F34* 1 Rupee 2012–19	250.00	300.00	350.00
89	*F33* 2 Rupees 2012	500.00	600.00	700.00

Later issues in *Current Coins of the World*.

NETHERLANDS (Koningrijk der Nederlanden)

A constitutional hereditary monarchy in western Europe between Germany and Belgium. Much of the land is below sea level and a system of dikes has been constructed to reclaim land and control the North Sea. It is the most densely populated country in the world. Over 50 percent of the land is in holdings of 10 acres or less. Most important exports are industrial and various food products. Land area: 15,800 square miles. Language: Dutch. Capital: *Amsterdam*.

Monetary System:
100 Cents = 1 Gulden

GENERAL COINAGE

Copper

1	½ Cent 1850–77	25.00	40.00	75.00
	1852 . . . 85 1855 . . . 225 1861,77 . . . 40			
2	1 Cent 1860–77	10.00	20.00	35.00
	1860–64 . . . 25 1873,75 . . . 15			

Nos. 1 and 2 are identical to coins struck 1817–47 for Willem I and II.

Bronze

Obv: With KONINGRIJK

3	½ Cent 1878–1901	10.00	15.00	25.00
	1883 . . . 175 1886 . . . 80 1898 . . . 70			
	1900 . . . 30			
4	1 Cent 1877–1901	6.00	12.50	25.00
	1896,97 . . . 35			
5	2½ Cent 1877–98	10.00	25.00	40.00
	1883 . . . 65 1886,90 . . . 30		1894 . . . 80
	1898..45			

Obv: With KONINKRIJK

4a	1 Cent 1901	8.00	17.50	30.00

Modified Dies

3c	½ Cent 1903, 06	6.00	10.00	15.00
4c	1 Cent 1902–07	5.50	15.00	27.50
	1907 . . . 45			
5c	2½ Cent 1903–06	7.50	15.00	25.00

WILLEM III 1849–1890

Silver

6	5 Cents 1850–87	12.50	20.00	40.00
	1853 . . . 650 1868 . . . 100 1876,79 . . . 30			
	1887 . . . 65			
7	10 Cents 1849–90	40.00	75.00	115.00
	1853,55,62 . . . 110 1868 . . . 225			
	1874 . . . 125			
8	25 Cents 1849–90	225.00	400.00	500.00
9	½ Gulden 1853–68	30.00	55.00	100.00
	1853 . . . 750 1866 . . . 90			
10	1 Gulden 1851–66	40.00	80.00	130.00
	1853 . . . 375			
11	2½ Gulden 1849–74	25.00	45.00	85.00
	1849,53 . . . 225 1856,60,61 . . . 130			
	1863 . . . 1000			

Nos. 9–10 dated 1850 are patterns.

Gold

12	*F18* 5 Gulden 1851	1000.	1500.	2000.
13*	*F17* 10 Gulden 1851	1500.	2000.	2500.
14	*F16* 20 Gulden 1851, 53	2000.	2500.	3000.
	1853 . . . 3500.			

Nos. 12–14 dated 1850 are patterns.

Rev: Date at top

B16	*F19* 10 Gulden 1875	110.00	120.00	130.00

Rev: Date at bottom

A16	*F19* 10 Gulden 1876–89	110.00	120.00	130.00
	1880,85,86,87 . . . 175 1888 . . . 450			

Trade Coins

Gold

15* 1 Dukaat 1849–1975   50.00   60.00   75.00
16   *F20* 2 Dukaat 1854, 67   Rare

No. 15 was struck for foreign trade, and was used extensively in the Netherlands East Indies. See Friedberg, GOLD COINS OF THE WORLD, Neth. East Indies, Nos. 17–22; and Netherlands, No. 26a.

WILHELMINA 1890–1948
First Coinage
Nos. 3–5 were continued into this period

Silver

Obv: Child head
Rev: Value in wreath

20 10 Cents 1892–97   20.00   40.00   60.00
     1895 . . . 90
21 25 Cents 1892–97   50.00   80.00 110.00
     1896 . . . 110

22 1 Gulden 1892–97   35.00   70.00 110.00
     1896 . . . 350

Gold

28   *F20–22* 10 Gulden
     1892–97   115.00 125.00 150.00
       1892,95 . . . Rare

Second Coinage

Cupro-Nickel

33 5 Cents 1907–09   17.50   25.00   45.00
     1909 . . . 80

Silver

Obv: Young head
23 10 Cents 1898, 1901   60.00 100.00 150.00
     (small head, divided legend)
23a 10 Cents 1903, large
     head   30.00   50.00   85.00
23b 10 Cents 1904–06   25.00   45.00   85.00
     (small head, continuous legend)
24 25 Cents 1898–1906   50.00   80.00 130.00
     1898 . . . 500

25   ½ Gulden 1898   60.00 100.00 150.00
     "50C" below arms
25a ½ Gulden 1904–09   27.50   50.00   90.00
       "50C" omitted 1904, 06 . . . 90
26* 1 Gulden 1898, 1901   75.00 130.00 200.00
     "100C" below arms
26a 1 Gulden 1904–09   35.00   70.00 110.00
     "100C" omitted
       1906 . . . 400
27   2½ Gulden 1898   350.00 600.00 900.00

Gold

29   *F23* 10 Gulden 1898   300.00 400.00 500.00

Third Coinage

Bronze

35	½ Cent 1909–40	5.00	8.00	12.50
	1921,22 . . . 30			
36	1 Cent 1913–41	3.00	6.00	9.00
	1913,31 . . . 25 1924 . . . 65			
37	2½ Cents 1912–41	6.00	10.00	15.00
	1912,14,19 . . . 25			

For coins like No. 36 dated 1942–60, see listings for colonial use following No. 52.

Cupro-Nickel

34	5 Cents 1913–40	7.50	12.50	20.00
	1933 . . . 85 1932 . . . 25 1934,36 . . . 15			

For a similar coin dated 1943, see No. 34a in listings for colonial use.

Silver

Obv: Adult head

39	10 Cents 1910–25	10.00	15.00	25.00
	1910 . . . 90 1911–13 . . . 35			
40	25 Cents 1910–25	20.00	35.00	80.00
	1910 . . . 125 1911–13 . . . 65			
41	½ Gulden 1910–19	20.00	40.00	85.00
	1910,12 . . . 40			
42	1 Gulden 1910–17	25.00	55.00	90.00
	1910,11 . . . 125 1916,17 . . . 60			

Gold

31	*F25* 5 Gulden 1912	100.00	140.00	200.00
30	*F24* 10 Gulden 1911–17	110.00	120.00	140.00

Fourth Coinage

Silver

Obv: Older head

43	10 Cents 1926–45	2.50	4.50	7.50
	1934 . . . 40 1944D . . . Rare 1945P . . . 500			

44	25 Cents 1926–45	4.00	7.00	10.00
	1926 . . . 50 1945P . . . 300			

Nos. 43 and 44 dated 1941 or 1943 must have a caduceus or acorn mintmark, respectively. For identical 1941–43 coins with palm tree mintmark, see listings for colonial use below.

Rev: Similar to Nos. 41–42

45	½ Gulden 1921–30	4.00	8.00	12.50
46	1 Gulden 1922–45	6.50	10.00	14.50
	1944 . . . 70 1945 . . . 850			
47	2½ Gulden 1929–40	12.50	15.00	25.00
	1940 . . . 100			

For 1943 coins like Nos. 46–47. but with palm tree mintmark, see Nos. 46a–47a under colonial issues below.

Gold

32	*F26* 10 Gulden 1925–33	110.00	120.00	140.00

World War II Nazi Occupation

Zinc

48	1 Cent 1941–44	1.50	2.50	5.00
	1941,44 . . . 12			

49	2½ Cents 1941–42	8.00	12.00	25.00
	1942 . . . Rare			

50	5 Cents 1941–43	5.50	10.00	20.00
	1943 . . . 35			

Unless otherwise noted, prices are for coins in very fine, extremely fine, and uncirculated condition.

51 10 Cents 1941–43   1.75   3.50   8.00

54 5 Cents 1948   1.00   2.00   9.50

Nickel

55 10 Cents 1948   1.00   2.00   7.50
56 25 Cents 1948   1.00   2.00   9.50

52 29 Cents 1941–43   3.50   8.00   17.50
     1943 . . . 20

JULIANA 1948–1980

Bronze

Netherlands Types for Colonial Use Only

Note: Coins dated 1941–43 (except No. 34a) must have a palm tree mintmark to be colonial. For these dates with caduceus or acorn mintmark, see Nos. 34–36 above.

Rev: Like Nos. 53–54

57 1 Cent 1950–80   .25   .50   .75
58 5 Cents 1950–80   .25   .50   .75

A. For Surinam and Curacao
Bronze

36b 1 Cent 1942, 57–60   2.50   4.00   7.50
     1942 . . . 12.50

Nickel
Rev: Like Nos. 55–56

59 10 Cents 1950–80   .25   .50   .75
60 25 Cents 1950–80   .25   .50   .75

Brass

36a 1 Cent 1943 (for Surinam only)   6.00   12.50   20.00

Silver

61 1 Gulden 1954–67   2.00   4.00   7.50
62 2½ Gulden 1959–66   4.00   10.00   12.50
     1963,64 . . . 20

Later issues in *Current Coins of the World.*

Copper-Nickel-Zinc

34a 5 Cents 1943   5.00   10.00   17.50

Silver
Palm tree mintmark

43a 10 Cents 1941–43   10.00   17.50   25.00
44a 26 Cents 1941–43   6.50   12.50   20.00

B. For Netherlands East Indies
Silver

46a 1 Gulden 1943   6.50   10.00   17.50
47a 2½ Gulden 1943   10.00   15.00   25.00

NETHERLANDS ANTILLES
(Nederlandse Antillen)

Made up of two groups of islands in the West Indies. Of the total area of 394 square miles, the island of Curacao comprises almost half. Principal industries are oil refining and tourism. Languages: Dutch, Papiamento, English, Spanish. Capital: *Willemstad.*

Monetary System:
100 Cents = 1 Gulden

Postwar Issues

Bronze

53 1 Cent 1948   .50   1.50   7.50

JULIANA 1948–1980
Bronze

1	1 Cent 1952–68	2.00	3.00	4.00
2	2½ Cents 1956, 65	2.00	4.00	6.00

Cupro-Nickel

3	5 Cents 1957–70	3.00	4.00	5.00

Silver

4	¹⁄₁₀ Gulden 1954–70	3.00	4.00	5.00
5	¼ Gulden 1954–70	5.00	10.00	15.00

6*	1 Gulden 1952–70	10.00	15.00	20.00
7	2½ Gulden 1964	15.00	20.00	25.00

Later issues in *Current Coins of the World.*

NETHERLANDS INDIES
(Nederlandsch Indie)

A group of four large and some 3,000 small islands between southeast Asia and Australia. The home of earlier Buddhist and Hindu cultures, it became Islamic after the 12th century, and was gradually taken over by the Dutch in the 17th century. Following Japanese occupation during World War II, it became the independent Republic of Indonesia in 1945. Area: 736,000 square miles. Languages: Malay dialects, Dutch. Capital: *Batavia (now Jakarta).*

Monetary System:
100 Cents (Sen) = 1 Gulden (Roepiah)

First Coinage
Copper

Rev: Malay and Javanese legends

1	½ Cent 1856–1909	2.00	3.00	4.00
	1855 . . . 80			
2	1 Cent 1855–1912	3.00	4.00	6.00
	1855 . . . 50			
3	2½ Cents 1856–1913	4.00	8.00	15.00
	1856 . . . 10			

Silver

4	¹⁄₂₀ Gulden 1854–55	10.00	15.00	25.00
	1854 . . . 200			
5	¹⁄₁₀ Gulden 1854–1901	3.00	6.00	10.00
	1885 . . . 15			
6	¼ Gulden 1854–1901	8.00	12.00	17.50
	1882–85 . . . 20			

7	¹⁄₁₀ Gulden 1903–09	3.00	6.00	10.00
8	¼ Gulden 1903–09	8.00	15.00	20.00

Gold Trade Coin
For Netherlands trade ducats, which were used in the Netherlands Indies, see Netherlands, Nos. 15 and 16.

Second Coinage
Silver
Wide rims both sides

14	¹⁄₁₀ Gulden 1910–30	2.00	4.00	6.00
15	¼ Gulden 1910–30	3.00	5.00	8.00

Narrow rims both sides

14a	¹⁄₁₀ Gulden 1937–45	1.00	2.00	4.00
15a	¼ Gulden 1937–45	1.50	3.00	5.00

1 and 2½ Gulden types dated 1943 were made for the Indies (see Netherlands Nos. 46a and 47a).

Cupro-Nickel

| 17 | 5 Cents 1913–22 | 2.00 | 4.00 | 6.00 |

Bronze

18	½ Cent 1914–45	1.00	2.00	4.00
19	1 Cent 1914–29	.50	1.00	3.00
20	2½ Cents 1914–45	1.00	2.00	4.00

| 21 | 1 Cent 1936–45 | .50 | 1.00 | 3.00 |

WORLD WAR II
Japanese Occupation Issues
Dated in the Japanese Calendar
Aluminum

| 22 | 1 Sen 2603–04 (1943–44) | 75.00 | 100.00 | 150.00 |

Tin Alloy

Obv: Native puppet

23 5 Sen 2603 –
Not issued to circulation
24 10 Sen 2603–04   75.00 100.00 150.00
For later issues see INDONESIA.

NEW BRUNSWICK —
see CANADA

NEW CALEDONIA
(Nouvelle Caledonie)

An island halfway between Australia and the Fiji Islands. One of the many French possessions in the South Pacific. Area: 8,548 square miles. Languages: French and Melanesian dialects. Capital: *Noumea.*

Monetary System:
100 Centimes = 1 Franc

Aluminum

1	50 Centimes 1949	.25	.75	2.50
2	1 Franc 1949	.15	.50	2.00
3	2 Francs 1949	.15	.75	2.50
4	5 Francs 1952	.15	.50	2.00

NEWFOUNDLAND —
see CANADA

NEW GUINEA

The world's second largest island, situated north of Australia near the equator. In 1884 Germany annexed a section, retaining it until World War I. The League of Nations mandated it to Australia in 1920; independence along with the Papua area came in 1975. Its economy is mostly agricultural. Area: 183,540 square miles. Capital: *Port Moresby.*

Monetary System:
12 Pence = 1 Shilling

GEORGE V 1910–1936
Cupro-Nickel

| 1 | ½ Penny 1929 | 350.00 550.00 750.00 Proof . . . 900.00 |
| 2 | 1 Penny 1929 | 350.00 550.00 750.00 Proof . . . 900.00 |

| 3 | 3 Pence 1935 | 5.00 7.50 25.00 Proof . . . 250.00 |

4 6 Pence 1935

6.00 9.00 30.00
Proof . . . 250.00

Silver

10 1 Shilling 1938, 45

3.50 5.00 8.00

Silver

5 1 Shilling 1935–36

3.50 5.00 9.50

EDWARD VIII 1936

Bronze

6 1 Penny 1936

2.50 4.00 7.50
Proof . . . 300.00

GEORGE VI 1936–1952

7 1 Penny 1938, 44

3.00 5.00 10.00

Cupro-Nickel

8 3 Pence 1944

3.50 6.00 28.50

9 6 Pence 1943

7.00 12.00 38.50

NEW ZEALAND

Lying east of Australia, New Zealand comprises two large islands plus many smaller dependencies lying southeast of Australia. It is a self-governing member of the British Commonwealth. Exports: sheep, dairy products. Area: 103,736 square miles. Languages: English, Maori. Capital: *Wellington.*

Monetary System:
12 Pence = 1 Shilling
2 Shillings = 1 Florin
5 Shillings = 1 Crown
20 Shillings = 1 Pound

GEORGE V 1910–1936

Silver

1 3 Pence 1933–36
1935 . . . 95

3.50 12.50 25.00
Proof . . . 400.00

2 6 Pence 1933–36
1935 . . . 10

4.50 35.00 60.00
Proof . . . 400.00

3 1 Shilling 1933–35
1935 . . . 12

7.50 30.00 75.00
Proof . . . 400.00

4 1 Florin 1933–36
1936 . . . 50

10.00 45.00 100.00
Proof . . . 400.00

Unless otherwise noted, prices are for coins in very fine, extremely fine, and uncirculated condition.

5 ½ Crown 1933–35   15.00   75.00 150.00
                                   Proof . . . 500.00

25th Year of Reign

Rev: Treaty of Waitangi (1840)
6 1 Crown 1935   1500.   2200.   2800.
                                Proof . . . 3500.

GEORGE VI 1936–1952

Bronze

7 ½ Penny 1940–47   2.00   4.50   9.00
    1942 . . . 5   Proof . . . 300.00

8 1 Penny 1940–47   1.50   4.50   9.00
    1941–42 . . . 6   Proof . . . 300.00

Silver

Rev: Designs like Nos. 1–5

9	3 Pence 1937–46	1.50	4.50	7.50
	1941 . . . 7		Proof . . .	400.00
10	6 Pence 1937–46	3.00	9.00	18.50
	1941,42 . . . 10		Proof . . .	400.00
11	1 Shilling 1937–46	3.50	15.00	30.00
	1937–42 . . . 7		Proof . . .	400.00
12	1 Florin 1937–46	7.00	25.00	45.00
	1940 . . . 30			
13	½ Crown 1937–46	7.00	30.00	75.00
	1944 . . . 25		Proof . . .	700.00

Centennial of British Settlement

14 ½ Crown 1940   15.00   25.00   50.00
                                Proof . . . 800.00

Cupro-Nickel
Rev: Designs like Nos. 1–5

9a	3 Pence 1947	1.50	4.50	8.00
			Proof . . .	400.00
10a	6 Pence 1947	3.00	9.00	20.00
			Proof . . .	425.00
11a	1 Shilling 1947	4.50	25.00	40.00
			Proof . . .	550.00
12a	1 Florin 1947	10.00	75.00	225.00
			Proof . . .	650.00
13a	½ Crown 1947	7.50	40.00	125.00
			Proof . . .	750.00

New Legend:
KING GEORGE THE SIXTH
Designs similar to Nos. 7–13

Bronze

20	½ Penny 1949–52	.75	2.50	7.50
			Proof . . . 300.00	
21	1 Penny 1949–52	.75	1.50	6.00
			Proof . . . 300.00	

Cupro-Nickel

22	3 Pence 1948–52	.25	1.50	7.50
			Proof . . . 300.00	
23	6 Pence 1948–52	.75	2.00	7.50
			Proof . . . 300.00	
24	1 Shilling 1948–52	3.50	15.00	30.00
			Proof . . . 400.00	
25	1 Florin 1948–51	3.50	7.50	25.00
			Proof . . . 400.00	
26	½ Crown 1948–51	1.50	7.50	15.00
	1948 . . . 8		Proof . . . 500.00	

Proposed Royal Visit

Silver

27	1 Crown 1949	15.00	25.00	40.00
			Proof . . . 1000.	

ELIZABETH II 1952–

Bronze

28	½ Penny 1953–65	.15	.25	.45
	1953–55 . . . 2		Proof . . . 2.50	

29	1 Penny 1953–65	.15	.30	.75
	1954 . . . 3		Proof . . . 4.50	

Cupro-Nickel
Rev: Designs like Nos. 1–5

30	3 Pence 1953–65	.15	.25	.75
			Proof . . . 1.50	
31	6 Pence 1953–65	.30	.40	.75
			Proof . . . 2.50	
32	1 Shilling 1953–65	.40	.75	1.50
			Proof . . . 3.25	
33	1 Florin 1953–65	.50	.75	1.50
			Proof . . . 4.25	
34	½ Crown 1953–65	.75	1.50	3.00
	1953 . . . 7.50		Proof . . . 5.00	

35	1 Crown 1953	7.50	10.00	12.50

NICARAGUA

Located in the middle of Central America, it is bounded on the north by Honduras, on the south by Costa Rica. Chief products: gold, coffee, cattle, mahogany, bananas, fruit. Area: 57,145 square miles. Languages: Spanish, English. Capital: *Managua.*

Monetary System:
100 Centavos = 1 Peso to 1912
100 Centavos = 1 Cordoba 1912–

Cupro-Nickel

1	1 Centavo 1878	8.00	20.00	60.00

2	5 Centavos 1898 (ES-TADO)	2.00	8.00	30.00

Unless otherwise noted, prices are for coins in very fine, extremely fine, and uncirculated condition.

3 5 Centavos 1899
(REPCA)   2.00   8.00   30.00

Silver

4	5 Centavos 1880	10.00	30.00	100.00
5	10 Centavos 1880	7.00	25.00	100.00
6	20 Centavos 1880	12.00	35.00	150.00

7	5 Centavos 1887	4.00	12.00	50.00
8	10 Centavos 1887	5.00	15.00	60.00
9	20 Centavos 1887	7.00	22.00	100.00

Bronze

10	½ Centavo 1912–37	2.00	5.00	15.00
11	1 Centavo 1912–40	2.00	5.00	10.00

Cupro-Nickel

12	5 Centavos 1912–40	2.00	5.00	20.00

Silver

13	10 Centavos 1912–36	3.00	6.00	14.00

14	25 Centavos 1912–36	4.00	8.00	18.00
15	50 Centavos 1912, 29	10.00	30.00	60.00
16	1 Cordoba 1912	70.00	150.00	600.00

Cupro-Nickel

Obv: Edge: Lettered BNN

17	5 Centavos 1946–56	.20	.50	2.00
18	10 Centavos 1939–56	.25	1.00	3.00
19	25 Centavos 1939–56	.30	1.00	5.00
20	50 Centavos 1939–56	.50	2.00	7.00

Brass

21	1 Centavo 1943	1.00	3.00	6.00

Designs similar to Nos. 17–19
Reeded Edge

22	5 Centavos 1943 (21mm)	3.00	5.00	12.00
23	10 Centavos 1943 (24mm)	4.00	8.00	25.00
24	25 Centavos 1943 (27mm)	4.00	8.00	20.00

Later issues in *Current Coins of the World.*

NIGERIA

Nigeria, on the Gulf of Guinea, came under British control in the late 1800's and was made a colony in 1914. Full independence within the Commonwealth came in 1960, and a Republic was proclaimed in 1963. An important oil producer, Nigeria also exports agricultural products and minerals. Area: 356,699 square miles. Languages: English, native tongues. Capital: *Lagos.*

Monetary System:
12 Pence = 1 Shilling
20 Shilling = 1 Pound

See British West Africa for earlier coinage, and Biafra for civil war issues.

ELIZABETH II 1952–1963

Bronze

1	½ Penny 1959	.10	.20	.30

2 1 Penny 1959   .10   .20   .30

Nickel-Brass

3 3 Pence 1959   .15   .25   .75

Cupro-Nickel

4 6 Pence 1959   .25   .50   1.00
5 1 Shilling 1959–62   .50   1.00   1.50

Safety or reeded edge
6 2 Shillings 1959   .50   1.00   2.00
1959 Proof Set . . . 50.00

Later issues in *Current Coins of the World.*

NORTH KOREA —
see KOREA
NORTH VIET NAM —
see VIET NAM

NORWAY (Norge)

West section of the Scandinavian peninsula in northern Europe. It is a constitutional hereditary monarchy with legislative power vested in a two-house "Storting," or legislature. It is primarily a maritime nation since less than a third of its land is cultivated. Its merchant marine ranks third in the world.

Area: 125,064 square miles. Languages: Norwegian, Lappish dialect. Capital: Oslo.

Monetary System:
120 Skilling = 1 Speciedaler to 1873
100 Ore = 1 Krone 1873–

UNION WITH SWEDEN —
CARL XV 1859–1872

Copper

1 ½ Skilling 1863   20.00 30.00 65.00

2 ½ Skilling 1867   4.50   9.50 20.00
3 1 Skilling 1870   7.00 15.00 35.00

Billon

4 2 Skilling 1870–71   7.00 13.00 26.50
5 3 Skilling 1868–69   10.00 22.50 45.00
6 4 Skilling 1871   15.00 25.00 45.00

Silver

7	12 Skilling 1861–62	450.00	775.00	1300.
8	24 Skilling 1861–62	400.00	700.00	1200.
	1861 . . . 1200			
9*	½ Speciedaler 1861–62	275.00	375.00	600.00
	1861 . . . 950			
10	1 Speciedaler 1861–62	475.00	625.00	1000.
	Obv: Larger head			
7a	12 Skilling 1865	110.00	180.00	325.00
8a	24 Skilling 1865	120.00	250.00	500.00
9a	½ Speciedaler 1865	950.00	1650.	2350.
10a	1 Speciedaler 1864–69	435.00	600.00	825.00
	1867 . . . 600			

Unless otherwise noted, prices are for coins in very fine, extremely fine, and uncirculated condition.

OSCAR II 1872–1905
First Coinage
Billon

11 3 Skilling 1872–73   12.00 22.00 45.00

Silver

12 12 Skilling 1873   90.00 140.00 250.00
13 ½ Speciedaler 1873   1300. 2000. 3000.

Second Coinage
Transition to Decimal System
Silver

14 10 Ore/3 Skilling
        1874–75   20.00 35.00 60.00
          1875 . . . 35.00

15 50 Ore/15 Skilling
        1874–75   65.00 90.00 160.00
16 1 Krone/30 Skilling 1875 175.00 245.00 400.00

Gold

17 *F16* 10 Kroner/2½ Spe-
        ciedaler 1874   400.00 600.00 775.00
18 *F15* 20 Kroner/5 Spe-
        ciedaler 1874–75   250.00 450.00 600.00

Third Coinage
Decimal System
Bronze

19 1 Ore 1876–1902   5.00 15.00 35.00
          1877 . . . 25 1878 . . . 45 1885 . . . 110

20 2 Ore 1876–1902   5.00 15.00 35.00
21 5 Ore 1875–1902   7.00 23.00 55.00
          1857 . . . 32 1878 . . . 15

Silver

22 10 Ore 1875–1903   12.00 22.50 45.00
          1875,77 . . . 65 1878–80 . . . 40
          1883,88 . . . 30
23 25 Ore 1876   25.00 50.00 100.00

24 25 Ore 1896–1904   25.00 50.00 100.00

25 50 Ore 1877–1904   30.00 75.00 165.00
          1880,85,1904 . . . 125
26 1 Krone 1877–1904   45.00 100.00·215.00
          1878 . . . 400 1879–88,1904 . . . 85
27 2 Kroner 1878–1904   65.00 140.00 260.00
          1885–88 . . . 375 1892 . . . 150

Gold

28 *F18* 10 Kroner 1877,
        1902   275.00 450.00 625.00
29 *F17* 20 Kroner
        1876–1902   215.00 365.00 450.00
          1883 . . . 1500

INDEPENDENT NORWAY
HAAKON VII 1905–57
First Coinage
Bronze

30 1 Ore 1906–07   5.00 11.00 27.50

31	2 Ore 1906–07	6.00	20.00	40.00
32	5 Ore 1907	11.00	30.00	70.00

Independence Commemorative

Silver

33	2 Kroner 1906	27.50	40.00	65.00
33a	2 Kroner 1907, smaller shield	40.00	65.00	110.00

"Watch on the Border" Commemorative

34	2 Kroner 1907	150.00	200.00	300.00

Second Coinage

Bronze

35	1 Ore 1908–52	.50	1.50	5.00
	1908,15,21,23 . . . 15			
36	2 Ore 1909–52	.50	2.50	6.00
	1909–10 . . . 20 1911–12,15 . . . 12			
37	5 Ore 1908–52	1.00	2.00	7.50
	1908 . . . 35			
	1911–12,15–16,21–23,29,32–33 . . . 10			

Silver

38	10 Ore 1909–19	4.00	7.00	10.00
	1909–12,14 . . . 11			

39	25 Ore 1909–19	10.00	17.50	30.00
	1912 . . . 65 1909–17 . . . 20			

40	50 Ore 1909–19	9.00	15.00	30.00
	1912 . . . 70 1909,11,13 . . . 40			
	1915 . . . 30 1914,16 . . . 15			

41	1 Krone 1908–17	25.00	37.50	75.00
	1910 . . . 95 1912–13 . . . 70			
42	2 Kroner 1908–17	20.00	35.00	70.00
	1910,12,16 . . . 50			

Gold

43	*F20* 10 Kroner 1910	140.00	200.00	300.00
44	*F19* 20 Kroner 1910	150.00	225.00	350.00

Constitution Centennial

Silver

45	2 Kroner 1914	17.50	22.50	40.00

Unless otherwise noted, prices are for coins in very fine, extremely fine, and uncirculated condition.

World War I Issues

Iron

35a	1 Ore 1918–21	6.00	12.00	30.00
	1921 . . . 35			
36a	2 Ore 1917–20	25.00	35.00	65.00
	1917 . . . 120 1918 . . . 45			
37a	5 Ore 1917–20	35.00	50.00	80.00
	1918 . . . 175 1920 . . . 45			

Third Coinage

Cupro-Nickel

46	10 Ore 1920–23	13.00	19.00	35.00
47	25 Ore 1921–23	14.00	20.00	40.00
	1923 . . . 25			

48	50 Ore 1920–23	17.50	25.00	45.00
	1920 . . . 45 1923 . . . 80			

47a	25 Ore 1921–23	5.00	22.50	55.00
48a	50 Ore 1920–23	7.00	25.00	60.00
	1920 . . . 50			

Nos. 47a–48a are Nos. 47–48 reissued with a center hole in 1924.

Fourth Coinage

Cupro-Nickel

49	10 Ore 1924–51	.50	2.00	6.00
	1927 . . . 12			

50	25 Ore 1924–50	1.00	4.00	9.00
	1929 . . . 8			
51	50 Ore 1926–49	1.00	5.00	15.00
	1929 . . . 15			

52	1 Krone 1925–51	.50	4.00	15.00

World War II Issues
German Occupation

Iron

53	1 Ore 1941–45	.75	3.00	6.00
	1945 . . . 12			
54	2 Ore 1943–45	1.00	4.00	10.00
	1945 . . . 5			
55	5 Ore 1941–45	2.00	6.00	13.00
	1945 . . . 120			

Zinc

56	10 Ore 1941–45	1.00	3.00	9.00
	1944–45 . . . 11			
57	25 Ore 1943–45	2.00	6.00	13.00
	1944 . . . 12			
58	50 Ore 1941–45	5.00	12.00	25.00
	1943–44 . . . 25 1945 . . . 150			

Government in Exile

(Struck in London)
Nickel-Brass

49a	10 Ore 1942	40.00	60.00	95.00

50a 25 Ore 1942   40.00   60.00   95.00

51a 50 Ore 1942   40.00   60.00   95.00

PAKISTAN

When India was given independence in 1947, the two predominantly Muslim areas were separated to form the dominion of Pakistan. It became a republic within the British Commonwealth in 1956. The eastern section broke away in late 1971 to form Bangladesh, whereupon West Pakistan left the Commonwealth. The economy is primarily agricultural. Area (to 1971): 365,529 square miles. Languages: Urdu, Bengali. Capital: *Islamabad*.

Monetary System:
3 Pies = 1 Pice
4 Pice = 1 Anna
16 Annas = 1 Rupee

Postwar Issues

Bronze

59 1 Ore 1952–57	.25	1.00	3.00
60 2 Ore 1952–57	.50	2.00	6.00
61 5 Ore 1952–57	.50	3.00	8.00

Bronze

1 1 Pice 1948–52   .15   .25   .50
                            Proof . . . 1.50

Cupro-Nickel

62 10 Ore 1951–57	.50	3.00	7.00
63 25 Ore 1952–57	.50	3.00	8.00

Cupro-Nickel

2 ½ Anna 1948–51   .15   .25   .50
                            Proof . . . 1.50

64 50 Ore 1953–57	.75	5.00	12.00
1954 . . . 10			
65 1 Krone 1951–57	.75	5.00	20.00

Later issues in *Current Coins of the World.*

Rev: Crescent to right

3 1 Anna 1948–52   .25   .45   .60
                            Proof . . . 1.50

4 2 Annas 1948–51
     (square)   .25   .45   .60
                            Proof . . . 1.50

Rev: Crescent to left

3a 1 Anna 1950	3.00	5.00	9.00
4a 2 Annas 1950	4.00	6.00	10.00

NOVA SCOTIA — see CANADA

Unless otherwise noted, prices are for coins in very fine, extremely fine, and uncirculated condition.

Nickel

Rev: Crescent to right

5	¼ Rupee 1948–51	.25	.45	.60
			Proof . . . 3.00	
6	½ Rupee 1948–51	.50	.75	1.00
			Proof . . . 2.50	
7	1 Rupee 1948–49	1.00	2.50	4.00
			Proof . . . 5.00	

Rev: Crescent to left

5a	¼ Rupee 1950	15.00	25.00	60.00

Bronze

8	1 Pie 1951–56	.30	.50	1.00
			Proof . . . 1.50	

Nickel-Brass

9	1 Pice 1953–59	.20	.30	.40
			Proof . . . 1.50	

10	½ Anna 1953–58	.20	.30	.40

Cupro-Nickel

11	1 Anna 1953–58	.15	.25	.40
			Proof . . . 1.50	

12	2 Annas 1953–59	.15	.25	.50
			Proof . . . 1.50	

Later issues in *Current Coins of the World.*

PALESTINE

From the earliest times this area has been the bridge between Asia and Africa. The Turks lost it in 1917 during World War I and in 1920 the League of Nations placed it under British administration. After long and bitter disputes between Jews and Arabs, the UN in 1948 divided the country: ⁴/₅ became the new state of Israel, and the remainder was split between Jordan and Egypt. Capital: *Jerusalem.*

Monetary System:
1000 Mils = 1 Pound

Hebrew-English-Arabic Legends
Bronze

1	1 Mil 1927–47	1.00	4.00	15.00
	1937 . . . 3 1940 . . . 12 1947 . . . Rare			
2	2 Mils 1927–47	1.50	5.00	20.00
	1945 . . . 3 1946 . . . 10 1947 . . . Rare			

Cupro-Nickel

3	5 Mils 1927–47	1.00	6.00	25.00
	1934,41 . . . 10 1947 . . . Rare			
4	10 Mils 1927–47	2.00	15.00	100.00
	1933,34,46 . . . 11 1941 . . . 15 1947 . . . Rare			
5	20 Mils 1927–47	5.00	15.00	100.00
	1934 . . . 75 1941 . . . 60			

Bronze

3a	5 Mils 1942–44	1.00	5.00	20.00
4a	10 Mils 1942–43	5.00	15.00	150.00
5a	20 Mils 1942–44	5.00	75.00	150.00

Silver

6 50 Mils 1927–42   5.00   10.00   40.00
    1931,34 . . . 25

7 100 Mils 1927–42   10.00   25.00   75.00
    1931 . . . 60   1933 . . . 40   1934 . . . 95

PANAMA

The Isthmus of Panama joining Central and South America. It is bisected by the Canal Zone. It became an independent nation in 1903. Exports: bananas, pineapple, cocoa, coconuts, sugar. Area: 30,641 square miles. Languages: English, Spanish. Capital: *Panama City*.

Monetary System:
100 Centesimos = 1 Balboa

Cupro-Nickel

1 ½ Centesimo 1907   2.00   4.00   10.00

2 2½ Centesimos 1907,
    MEDIOS   3.00   6.00   30.00
2a 2½ Centesimos 1916,
    MEDIO   4.00   10.00   60.00

3 2½ Centesimos 1929   4.00   15.00   80.00

4 5 Centesimos 1929, 32   4.00   8.00   50.00

Silver

5 2½ Centesimos 1904   8.00   15.00   25.00
No. 5 is commonly called the "Panama Pill" due to its small size.
6 5 Centesimos 1904, 16   5.00   10.00   35.00
    1916 . . . 120.
7 10 Centesimos 1904   7.00   15.00   45.00
8* 25 Centesimos 1904   12.00   25.00   75.00
9 50 Centesimos 1904–05   18.00   40.00   150.00
    1905 . . . 40.

New Coinage

Bronze

10 1 Centesimo 1935, 37   3.00   8.00   25.00

11* 1¼ Centesimos 1940   1.00   3.00   6.00

Cupro-Nickel
12 2½ Centesimos 1940   1.00   3.00   8.00

Silver

13* ¹/₁₀ Balboa 1930–47, 62   1.50   2.00   4.00
14 ¼ Balboa 1930–47, 62   3.00   3.50   6.00
    1931 . . . 50.

Unless otherwise noted, prices are for coins in very fine, extremely fine, and uncirculated condition.

15 ½ Balboa 1930–47, 62   6.00   7.00   8.00
Because new dies were cut at the London Mint, design details are more distinct on the 1962 issues of Nos. 13–15.

16 1 Balboa 1931–47   12.00 13.00 20.00

50th Anniversary of Independence
(Nos. 17–21)

Bronze

17 1 Centesimo 1953   .25   1.00   4.00

Silver

18	¹⁄₁₀ Balboa 1953	1.50 2.00 7.00
19*	¼ Balboa 1953	3.00 4.00 10.00
20	½ Balboa 1953	6.00 6.50 8.00
21	1 Balboa 1953 (rev. similar to No. 16)	12.00 15.00 25.00

Later issues in *Current Coins of the World.*

PARAGUAY

An inland country of South America. Products include oranges, timber, tobacco, beef products, corn and cotton. Area: 157,000 square miles. Languages: Spanish and Guarani. Capital: *Asuncion.*

Monetary System:
100 Centesimos = 1 Peso
100 Centavos = 1 Peso
100 Centimos = 1 Guarani

Copper

1 ¹⁄₁₂ Real 1845   10.00 25.00 100.00

2	1 Centesimo 1870	4.00 8.00 30.00
3	2 Centesimos 1870	5.00 10.00 35.00
4	4 Centesimos 1870	7.00 15.00 75.00
4a	4 Centesimos 1870, crude local issue	100.00 200.00 –
	with "SAEZ"	500.00 – –

Silver

5 1 Peso 1889   85.00 150.00 300.00

Cupro-Nickel

6	5 Centavos 1900, 03	3.00 7.00 25.00
	1900 . . . 10.	
7	10 Centavos 1900, 03	3.00 7.00 25.00
8	20 Centavos 1900, 03	4.00 8.00 30.00

24 50 Centimos 1944, 51   .50   2.00   8.00

9	5 Centavos 1908	10.00	20.00	40.00
10	10 Centavos 1908	5.00	10.00	25.00
11	20 Centavos 1908	5.00	10.00	35.00
12	50 Centavos 1925	1.00	4.00	10.00
13	1 Peso 1925	1.00	4.00	10.00
14	2 Pesos 1925	2.00	5.00	10.00
15	5 Pesos 1939	2.00	5.00	10.00
16	10 Peso 1939	2.00	5.00	10.00

Aluminum

17	50 Centavos 1938	1.00	2.00	5.00
18	1 Peso 1938	1.00	2.00	6.00
19	2 Pesos 1938	1.00	3.00	8.00

25	10 Centimos 1953	.05	.10	.50
26	15 Centimos 1953	.05	.10	.50
27	25 Centimos 1953	.05	.10	.50
28	50 Centimos 1953	.05	.10	.50

Later issues in *Current Coins of the World.*

PERSIA — see IRAN

PERU

On the west coast of South America, it encompasses some of the highest peaks in the Andes Mountains. Its exports include cotton, petroleum, sugar and copper. Peru, which had been Spain's foremost colony in the New World, won its independence in 1824. Area: 514,-059 square miles. Languages: Spanish and Indian. Capital: *Lima.*

Monetary System:
16 Reales = 1 Escudo to 1863
10 Centavos = 1 Dinero
100 Centavos = 1 Sol
10 Soles = 1 Libra (Pound)

New Coinage

Aluminum-Bronze

20 1 Centimo 1944–50   .10   .50   1.00

21 5 Centimos 1944, 47   .15   1.00   3.00

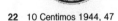

22 10 Centimos 1944, 47   .20   1.00   4.00

Transition to Decimal System 1858–1863

Silver

1*	½ Real 1858	8.00	20.00	40.00
2	50 Centimos 1858	20.00	45.00	100.00

23 25 Centimos 1944–51   .25   2.00   5.00

3 ½ Real 1859–61   5.00   10.00   30.00

Unless otherwise noted, prices are for coins in very fine, extremely fine, and uncirculated condition.

4	1 Real 1859–61	6.00	12.00	40.00
5*	25 Centavos 1859	45.00	80.00	250.00
6	50 Centavos 1858–59	25.00	60.00	150.00

Gold
Design similar to Nos. A19–19

7	F69 4 Escudos 1863	750.00	1200.	2500.
8	F68 8 Escudos 1862–63	500.00	650.00	1200.

Decimal System 1863–
First Coinage

Cupro-Nickel

Obv: Date at top

9	1 Centavo 1863–64	4.00	10.00	25.00
10	2 Centavos 1863–64	4.00	10.00	30.00

Bronze

9a	1 Centavo 1875–78, 1919	2.00	3.00	6.00
10a	2 Centavos 1876–95, 1919	2.00	5.00	10.00

Obv: Date at bottom
Thick planchet

11*	1 Centavo 1901–41, CENTAVO straight	.50	2.00	5.00
	1904 . . . 10.			
12	1 Centavo 1909–37, CENTAVO curved	.50	2.00	6.00
	1909, 34, 35, 39 . . . 10.			
13	2 Centavos 1916–41	1.00	4.00	10.00
	1917–18 . . . 10.			

Silver

Lima Mint

14	½ Dinero 1863–1917	2.00	5.00	12.00
	1893 . . . 75.			
15	1 Dinero 1863–1916	3.00	6.00	15.00
	1872 . . . 100. 1888 . . . 75.			
	1894 . . . 60. 1909 . . . 10.			
16*	⅕ Sol 1863–1917	4.00	7.00	18.00
	1914 . . . 8. 1915 . . . 35. 1917 . . . 15.			
17	½ Sol 1864–1917	6.00	8.00	18.00
	1908 . . . 12			
18	1 Sol 1864–1916	12.00	20.00	35.00
	1880 . . . 35.			

Nos. 14–18 contain many die varieties.

Branch mints

14a	½ Dinero 1885 Cuzco	150.00	500.00	1500.
15a*	1 Dinero 1886 Cuzco	40.00	90.00	500.00
16a	⅕ Sol 1885 Arequipa	1000.	–	–

Gold

A19*	F72 5 Soles 1863	125.00	160.00	250.00
B19	F71 10 Soles 1863	300.00	450.00	700.00
19	F70 20 Soles 1863	450.00	600.00	1000.

20	F75 ⅕ Libra 1906–69	25.00	30.00	40.00
21	F74 ½ Libra 1902–69	65.00	70.00	80.00
22*	F73 1 Libra 1898–1969	120.00	130.00	140.00

Silver

23	1 Sol 1910	12.00	25.00	40.00

Gold

24* *F76* 5 Soles 1910   60.00 80.00 150.00

Provisional Issues

Cupro-Nickel

25	5 Centavos 1879-80	2.00	3.00	8.00
26	10 Centavos 1879-80	2.00	5.00	12.00
27	20 Centavos 1879	10.00	20.00	75.00

Silver

28 ½ Real 1882 Ayacucho   800.00 1200. 2000.
Note: Holed or plugged pieces of No. 28 are worth 25%
of the listed price.

29*	1 Peseta 1880 Lima	6.00	15.00	35.00
30	5 Pesetas 1880 Lima	20.00	35.00	100.00
30a	5 Pesetas 1881-82 Aya-cucho	150.00	350.00	600.00
	1881 . . . 600.			

Second Coinage

Cupro-Nickel

Dates spelled out in Spanish

31	5 Centavos 1918-41	1.00	3.00	10.00
32	10 Centavos 1918-41	2.00	4.00	15.00
33	20 Centavos 1918-41	3.00	5.00	25.00

Silver

34 ½ Sol 1922-35   4.00 5.00 10.00

35	1 Sol 1923, no fineness shown	20.00	80.00	250.00
36	1 Sol 1923-35, fineness 5 Decimos	7.00	12.00	25.00

Gold

37 *F77* 50 Soles 1930-69   575.00 650.00 750.00

Third Coinage

Bronze

Thin planchet

11a*	1 Centavo 1941-44, CENTAVO straight	1.00	3.00	10.00
	1944 . . . 10.			
12a	1 Centavo 1941-49, CENTAVO curved	.15	.50	2.00
13a	2 Centavos 1941-49	.25	1.00	3.00

Brass

Dates spelled out in Spanish

31a	5 Centavos 1942-44	2.00	5.00	15.00
32a	10 Centavos 1942-44	3.00	8.00	35.00
33a	20 Centavos 1942-44	5.00	12.00	50.00

Unless otherwise noted, prices are for coins in very
fine, extremely fine, and uncirculated condition.

Brass

Dates in numerals

38	5 Centavos 1945–51	.50	1.50	4.00
39	10 Centavos 1945–51	.50	1.50	6.00
	1951 . . . 6.			
40	20 Centavos 1942–51 (2 vars.)	.50	2.00	8.00

Zinc

41	1 Centavo 1950–65	.35	1.00	2.00
42*	2 Centavos 1950–58	.40	1.50	4.00

Brass

38a	5 Centavos 1951–65	.05	.15	.50
39a	10 Centavos 1951–65	.05	.15	.50
40a	20 Centavos 1951–65	.10	.20	.50

Central Reserve Bank

43	½ Sol 1935–65	.10	.20	.50
44	1 Sol 1943–65	.10	.25	.65

Castilla Commemoratives

Brass

45	5 Centavos 1954	1.00	2.00	5.00
46	10 Centavos 1954	1.00	3.00	8.00
47	20 Centavos 1954	2.00	5.00	15.00

Bullion Issues

Gold

48	*F82*	5 Soles 1956–68	35.00	40.00	50.00
49	*F81*	10 Soles 1956–68	60.00	70.00	80.00

50	*F80*	20 Soles 1950–68	120.00	130.00	150.00
51	*F79*	50 Soles 1950–70	300.00	325.00	350.00
52	*F78*	100 Soles 1950–70	600.00	650.00	700.00
		1952, 58 UNC . . . 1000.			

Later issues in *Current Coins of the World.*

PHILIPPINES (Filipinas)

A Spanish colony until 1898, it was bought by the American government following the Spanish-American War. It was invaded by the Japanese in December, 1941, and recognized as an independent nation on July 4, 1946. Exports: pineapples, sugar, copra, lumber, iron and tobacco. Languages: Pilipino, English, Spanish. Area: 115,758 square miles. Capital: *Manila.*

Monetary System:
100 Centimos = 1 Peso to 1898
100 Centavos = 1 Peso 1903–1906

I. SPANISH COLONY to 1898.
ISABEL II 1833–1868

Silver

3	10 Centimos 1864–68	15.00	30.00	200.00
	1864–67 . . . 40			

| 12 | 20 Groszy 1923 | 1.00 | 1.50 | 2.50 |
| 13 | 50 Groszy 1923 | 1.00 | 1.50 | 3.00 |

Silver

| 15 | 1 Zloty 1924–25 | 4.00 | 10.00 | 17.50 |
| 16 | 2 Zlote 1924–25 | 5.00 | 12.50 | 35.00 |

| 17 | 5 Zlotych 1925 | 300.00 | 400.00 | 700.00 |

No. 17 not issued to circulation.

900th Anniversary
Death of Boleslaus I

Gold

| 32 | F45 | 10 Zlotych 1925 | 70.00 | 90.00 | 145.00 |
| 33 | F44 | 20 Zlotych 1925 | 100.00 | 125.00 | 165.00 |

Second Coinage

Nos. 8a–10a were continued through this period.

Nickel

| 14 | 1 Zloty 1929 | 1.00 | 2.00 | 5.00 |

Silver

| 18 | 5 Zlotych 1928–32 | 25.00 | 50.00 | 150.00 |
| | 1932 . . . 65 | | | |

Centennial of First
Revolt Against Russians

| 19 | 5 Zlotych 1930 | 25.00 | 35.00 | 125.00 |

Third Coinage

Nos. 8a–10a were continued through this period.

Silver

20	2 Zlote 1932–34	2.00	5.00	12.50
21	5 Zlotych 1932–34	5.00	10.00	20.00
22	10 Zlotych 1932–33	10.00	20.00	30.00

Obv: Jozef Pilsudski, Head of State 1926–35
Rev: Date below eagle

27	2 Zlote 1934–36	5.00	8.00	15.00
	1936 . . . 25			
28	5 Zlotych 1934–38	5.00	8.00	15.00
29	10 Zlotych 1934–39	12.50	20.00	35.00
	1934,38,39 . . . 20			

Unless otherwise noted, prices are for coins in very
fine, extremely fine, and uncirculated condition.

30	2 Zlote 1936	2.00	5.00	10.00
31	5 Zlotych 1936	5.00	10.00	17.50

250th Anniversary
Relief of Vienna

Rev: Jan III Sobieski, King 1674–96

23	10 Zlotych 1933	25.00	40.00	75.00

70th Anniversary
Second Revolt Against Russians

Rev: Romuald Traugutt, patriot leader

24	10 Zlotych 1933	25.00	45.00	75.00

20th Anniversary
Founding of Rifle Corps

Obv: Pilsudski, date at right
Rev: Badge below eagle

25	5 Zlotych 1934	10.00	15.00	30.00
26	10 Zlotych 1934	20.00	30.00	50.00

WORLD WAR II
GERMAN OCCUPATION

Zinc

34	1 Grosz 1939	1.00	3.00	5.00
35	5 Groszy 1939	3.00	5.00	7.50

36	10 Groszy 1923	.50	.75	1.50
37	20 Groszy 1923	.50	.75	1.50

Nos. 36–37 were struck ca. 1941–44.

Nickel-Plated Iron

38	50 Groszy 1938	2.00	4.00	5.00

POSTWAR ISSUES

Aluminum

39	1 Grosz 1949	.10	.20	.30

40	2 Grosze 1949	.10	.20	.30

Bronze

41	5 Groszy 1949	.75	1.00	1.25

Cupro-Nickel

42	10 Groszy 1949	.50	.75	1.25
43	20 Groszy 1949	.75	1.00	1.50

44	50 Groszy 1949	1.00	1.75	2.50

45	1 Zloty 1949	2.00	3.00	4.00

Aluminum

41a	5 Groszy 1949	.75	1.00	1.25
42a	10 Groszy 1949	.20	.30	.75
43a	20 Groszy 1949	.30	.50	.75
44a	50 Groszy 1949	.50	.60	.90
45a	1 Zloty 1949	.50	.75	1.25

Later issues in *Current Coins of the World.*

PORTUGAL

Western section of the Iberian peninsula facing the Atlantic Ocean. A kingdom until 1910 when, following a revolution, a republic was established. Exports: cork and wines. Area: 34,500 square miles. Language: Portuguese. Capital: *Lisbon.*

Monetary System:
1000 Reis = 1 Milreis to 1910
100 Centavos = 1 Escudo 1912–

LUIS I 1861–1889

Copper

1	III Reis 1868–75	7.00	10.00	15.00
2	V Reis 1867–79	2.00	5.00	10.00
3	X Reis 1867–77	4.00	8.00	15.00
4	XX Reis 1867–74	10.00	15.00	25.00

For other similar copper coins of 1865–80, see AZORES.

Bronze

5	V Reis 1882–86	1.00	3.00	6.00

6	X Reis 1882–86	2.00	4.00	10.00
7	XX Reis 1882–86	2.00	5.00	20.00

Silver

8	50 Reis 1862–89	2.00	6.00	15.00

9	100 Reis 1864–89	4.00	7.00	20.00
10	200 Reis 1862–63	25.00	40.00	80.00

10a	200 Reis 1865–88, diff. head	5.00	8.00	25.00
11	500 Reis 1863–89	10.00	15.00	45.00
	1872,76 . . . Rare.			

Gold
Rev: Arms in wreath

A12	*F130* 2000 Reis 1864–66	100.00	150.00	200.00
A13	*F129* 5000 Reis 1862–63	125.00	200.00	275.00

Rev: Mantled arms

12	*F133* 2000 Reis 1868–88	100.00	150.00	225.00
13	*F132* 5000 Reis 1867–89	135.00	200.00	275.00
14	*F131* 10,000 Reis 1878–89	200.00	350.00	475.00

Unless otherwise noted, prices are for coins in very fine, extremely fine, and uncirculated condition.

CARLOS I 1889–1908

Bronze

15	5 Reis 1890–1906	1.00	2.00	5.00
16	10 Reis 1891–92	1.00	2.00	5.00
17	20 Reis 1891–92	2.00	3.00	7.00

For bronze coins of 1901 with coat of arms replacing portrait, see AZORES.

Cupro-Nickel

18	50 Reis 1900	1.00	2.00	4.00
19	100 Reis 1900	1.00	2.00	6.00

Silver

20	50 Reis 1893	2.00	4.00	15.00

21	100 Reis 1890–98	3.00	8.00	22.00
	1894 EF . . . 100.			
22	200 Reis 1891–1903	5.00	10.00	30.00
	1901 EF . . . 100.			

23	500 Reis 1891–1908	10.00	16.00	45.00
	1894, 1904 . . . Rare.			

24	1000 Reis 1899	25.00	35.00	75.00

400th Anniversary of Voyages of Discovery 1498–1898

25	200 Reis 1898	8.00	12.00	25.00
26	500 Reis 1898	15.00	20.00	40.00
27	1000 Reis 1898	25.00	50.00	125.00

EMANUEL II 1908–1910

Bronze

28	5 Reis 1910	1.00	2.00	6.00

Silver

29	100 Reis 1909–10	4.00	6.00	12.00
30	200 Reis 1909	4.00	6.00	18.00
31	500 Reis 1908–09	12.00	18.00	35.00

COMMEMORATIVE ISSUES
Peninsular War Centennial

32	500 Reis 1910	40.00	75.00	250.00
33	1000 Reis 1910	50.00	100.00	350.00

Marquis de Pombal

34	500 Reis 1910	25.00	45.00	75.00

REPUBLIC 1910–
First Coinage
Silver

48	10 Centavos 1915	2.00	4.00	12.00
49	20 Centavos 1913–16	4.00	6.00	15.00
50	50 Centavos 1912–16	5.00	8.00	18.00
51	1 Escudo 1915–16	17.50	25.00	40.00

Birth of Republic
5th October 1910
Silver

47	1 Escudo 1910 (struck 1914)	20.00	35.00	75.00

World War I Provisional Issue
Iron

35	2 Centavos 1918	45.00	100.00	200.00

Second Coinage
Bronze

36	1 Centavo 1917–21	.50	1.00	5.00
	1922 . . . Rare.			
37	2 Centavos 1918–21	.50	1.00	6.00
	1921 EF . . . 10.			
38	5 Centavos 1920–22	.50	2.00	9.00
	1920 UNC . . . 20. 1922 . . . Rare.			

Cupro-Nickel

42	4 Centavos 1917–19	.50	1.00	8.00
43	10 Centavos 1920–21	.50	1.00	10.00
44	20 Centavos 1920–22	.50	2.00	12.00
	1922 UNC . . . 250.			

Unless otherwise noted, prices are for coins in very fine, extremely fine, and uncirculated condition.

Third Coinage

Bronze

39	5 Centavos 1924–27	.50	1.00	6.00
40	10 Centavos 1924–40	.50	1.00	10.00
41	20 Centavos 1924–25	.50	1.00	12.00

Aluminum-Bronze

45	50 Centavos 1924–26	.50	2.00	10.00
	1925 . . . Rare.			
46	1 Escudo 1924–26	1.00	3.00	12.00
	1926 UNC . . . 50.			

Bronze

60	X Centavos 1942–69	.25	.40	.75
61	XX Centavos 1942–69	.25	.40	.75

Nickel-Bronze

54	50 Centavos 1927–68	.10	.25	.50
55	1 Escudo 1927–68	.25	.50	2.00
	1935 UNC . . . 100.			

Silver

57	2½ Escudos 1932–51	2.00	4.00	10.00
	1937 UNC . . . 50			

58	5 Escudos 1932–51	3.00	4.00	15.00
	1937 UNC . . . 40.			
59	10 Escudos 1932–48	5.00	10.00	20.00
	1937 UNC . . . 75. 1942 . . . Rare.			

63	10 Escudos 1954–55	4.00	6.00	10.00

Battle of Ourique 1139

Obv: Alfonso I, King 1140–85

56	10 Escudos 1928	15.00	25.00	60.00

25 Years of Financial Reform

62	20 Escudos 1953	8.00	12.00	20.00

500th Anniversary
Death of Henry the Navigator
Silver

64	5 Escudos 1960	3.00	5.00	8.00
65	10 Escudos 1960	6.00	9.00	20.00
66	20 Escudos 1960	12.00	18.00	40.00

Later issues in *Current Coins of the World*.

PORTUGUESE GUINEA
(Guine)

This part of West Africa's Guinea coast was claimed by Portugal in 1446. An early slave trading center, it was little settled by Europeans. It became an Overseas Province in 1962. After it proclaimed independence in 1973, it was formally recognized in 1974 as the Republic of Guinea-Bissau. Its economy is primarily agricultural. Area: 14,000 square miles. Languages: Portuguese, native tongues. Capital: *Bolama (to 1941), Bissau (since 1941)*.

Monetary System:
100 Centavos = 1 Escudo

Bronze

1	5 Centavos 1933	4.00	9.00	17.50
2	10 Centavos 1933	6.00	10.00	30.00
3	20 Centavos 1933	3.50	7.50	17.50

Nickel-Bronze

4	50 Centavos 1933	8.00	20.00	150.00
5	1 Escudo 1933	8.50	25.00	200.00

500th Anniversary of Discovery
Bronze

6	50 Centavos 1946	1.00	3.00	8.00
7	1 Escudo 1946	1.00	3.00	9.00

Decree of Dec. 29, 1951
Bronze

8	50 Centavos 1952	.25	.50	2.50

Cupro-Nickel

9	2½ Escudos 1952	1.00	3.00	10.00

Silver

10	10 Escudos 1952	4.00	7.50	22.50
11	20 Escudos 1952	5.00	10.00	27.50

Later issues in *Current Coins of the World*.

PORTUGUESE INDIA
(India Portugueza,
Estado da India

Three small areas — Goa, Damao and Diu — on the west coast of India. They contain many salt and manganese mines. India occupied these enclaves in 1962.

Capital: Pangim.

Monetary System:
50 Reis = 1 Tanga (Indian Anna)
16 Tangas = 1 Rupia

Unless otherwise noted, prices are for coins in very fine, extremely fine, and uncirculated condition.

LUIS I 1861–1889
Copper

1	3 Reis 1871	10.00	20.00	40.00
2	5 Reis 1871	12.50	20.00	50.00
3	10 Reis 1871	15.00	20.00	55.00

4	¼ Tanga/15 Reis 1871	15.00	25.00	75.00
5	½ Tanga/30 Reis 1871	20.00	35.00	75.00
6	1 Tanga/60 Reis 1871	35.00	65.00	200.00

7*	⅛ Tanga 1881–86	5.00	10.00	25.00
8	¼ Tanga 1881–86	6.00	12.00	35.00
	1888 . . . 75.			

Silver

11	⅛ Rupia 1881	8.00	15.00	45.00
12	¼ Rupia 1881	9.00	17.50	50.00
13*	½ Rupia 1881–82	11.00	20.00	60.00
14	1 Rupia 1881–82	11.00	20.00	60.00

CARLOS I 1889–1908
Bronze

Obv: Date in Roman numerals

15	¹⁄₁₂ Tanga 1901, 03	3.00	10.00	25.00
16	⅛ Tanga 1901, 03	4.00	10.00	25.00
17	¼ Tanga 1901, 03	4.00	10.00	17.50
18	½ Tanga 1901, 03	5.00	12.50	40.00

Silver

19	1 Rupia 1903–04	10.00	18.00	60.00

PORTUGUESE REPUBLIC
ISSUES 1910–1961
Silver

20	1 Rupia 1912	22.50	45.00	95.00

Bronze

21	1 Tanga 1934	4.00	8.00	22.50

Cupro-Nickel

22	2 Tangas 1934	4.50	9.00	25.00
23*	4 Tangas 1934	4.50	11.00	35.00

Silver

24	½ Rupia 1936	8.00	15.00	30.00
25	1 Rupia 1935	7.50	12.50	25.00

4	20 Centimos 1864–68	10.00	20.00	275.00
	1864–67 . . . 45			
5	50 Centimos 1865–68	20.00	45.00	300.00
	1865 . . . 95 1866,67 . . . 300			

Gold

6	*F3* 1 Peso 1861–68	100.00	125.00	175.00
7	*F2* 2 Pesos 1861–68	125.00	150.00	225.00
8	*F1* 4 Pesos 1861–68	150.00	175.00	275.00

ALFONSO XII 1875–1885

Silver

9	10 Centimos 1880–85	7.50	11.00	55.00
	1880 . . . 550 1884 . . . 300			
10	20 Centimos 1880–85	9.00	15.00	75.00
	1880 . . . 60 1884 . . . 50			
11	50 Centimos 1880–85	10.00	20.00	75.00
	1880,84 . . . 200			

Gold

12	*F4* 4 Pesos 1880–85	150.00	175.00	275.00
	1880,81,82 . . . Rare			

ALFONSO XIII 1886–1898

Silver

13	1 Peso 1897	35.00	50.00	200.00

II. U.S. TERRITORY 1898–1935

Bronze

14	½ Centavo 1903–08	.75	1.50	10.00
	1905–08 Proof . . . 45			

15	1 Centavo 1903–36	.75	3.00	9.00
	1906,08 Proof . . . 45		Proof . . . 25.00	

Dates after 1904 of No. 14 not for circulation.

Cupro-Nickel

16	5 Centavos 1903–28	.75	1.50	15.00
	1905,06,08 Proof . . . 75 1916 . . . 15			
			Proof . . . 35.00	

16a	5 Centavos 1918, rev. of			
	No. 23 (error)	125.00	250.00	750.00

**Unless otherwise noted, prices are for coins in very
fine, extremely fine, and uncirculated condition.**

Reduced Size

17	5 Centavos 1930–35	1.50	3.00	25.00

Silver

18	10 Centavos 1903–06	2.00	3.00	20.00
	1905,06 Proof . . . 100 1903–S . . . 10			
			Proof . . . 50.00	
19	20 Centavos 1903–06	3.75	4.50	25.00
	1903–S . . . 10 1905,06 Proof . . . 100			
			Proof . . . 75.00	
20	50 Centavos 1903–06	10.00	13.50	45.00
	1904 . . . 20 1905,06 Proof . . . 225			
			Proof . . . 85.00	
21	1 Peso 1903–06	12.00	16.00	95.00
	1905,06 Proof . . . 475 1904 . . . 50			
	1906–S . . . 125		Proof . . . 250.00	

Reduced Size

22	10 Centavos 1907–35	1.00	2.00	20.00
	1908 Proof . . . 150 1909 . . . 15 1915–S . . . 9.			
23	20 Centavos 1907–29	2.00	3.50	20.00
	1908 Proof . . . 150 1909–13 . . . 8			

23a	20 Centavos 1928, rev. of			
	No.16	7.50	40.00	200.00
24	50 Centavos 1907–21	5.00	10.00	25.00
	1908 Proof . . . 250			
25	1 Peso 1907–12	9.00	12.00	35.00
	1908 Proof . . . 475 1911–12 . . . 20			

III. COMMONWEALTH
1935–1946.
Establishment of the Commonwealth
Silver

Obv: Murphy and Quezon

26	50 Centavos 1936	20.00	40.00	95.00

Obv: Roosevelt and Quezon

27	1 Peso 1936	50.00	75.00	200.00

Obv: Murphy and Quezon

28	1 Peso 1936	50.00	75.00	200.00

Regular Issues
Bronze

29	1 Centavo 1937–44	.15	.20	1.50

Cupro-Nickel

| 30 | 5 Centavos 1937–41 | 1.00 | 2.00 | 8.50 |

Copper-Nickel-Zinc

| 30a | 5 Centavos 1944–45 | .10 | .15 | .45 |

Silver

31	10 Centavos 1937–45	.45	1.00	1.50
32	20 Centavos 1937–45	.85	1.50	2.25
33	50 Centavos 1944–45	3.50	5.00	6.00

REPUBLIC 1946–
MacArthur Commemoratives

Silver

| 34 | 50 Centavos 1947 | 3.75 | 6.00 | 8.00 |
| 35 | 1 Peso 1947 | 5.50 | 8.00 | 12.50 |

Central Bank Issues 1958–1966

Bronze

| 36 | 1 Centavo 1958–63 | – | .05 | .10 |

Brass

| 37 | 5 Centavos 1958–66 | .05 | .10 | .15 |

Nickel-Brass

| 38 | 10 Centavos 1958–66 | .05 | .10 | .15 |
| 39 | 25 Centavos 1958–66 | .10 | .15 | .35 |

| 40 | 50 Centavos 1958, 64 | .25 | .45 | .75 |

Centennial Birth of Dr. Jose Rizal

Silver

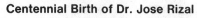

| 41 | ½ Peso 1961 | 3.50 | 5.00 | 7.50 |

| 42 | 1 Peso 1961 | 6.50 | 8.00 | 13.00 |

Unless otherwise noted, prices are for coins in very fine, extremely fine, and uncirculated condition.

Centennial Birth of Andres Bonifacio

43	1 Peso 1963	6.50	8.00	13.00

Centennial Birth of Apolinario Mabini

44	1 Peso 1964	6.50	8.00	13.00

25th Anniversary Fall of Bataan and Corregidor

45	1 Peso 1967	6.50	8.00	13.00

Later issues in *Current Coins of the World*.

POLAND
(Rzeczpospolita Polska)

A central European republic bordering the Baltic Sea between Russia and Czechoslovakia. Its great deposits of coal and iron have made it valuable conquest for other countries. It has been controlled by Austria, Germany, Prussia and Russia. It declared its independence after World War I, but was invaded by Germany and Russia in 1939. In 1945 it ceded about 70,000 square miles in the eastern section of Russia, in return getting some 40,000 square miles of German territory. Language: Polish. Capital: *Warszawa (Warsaw)*.

Monetary System:
100 Groszy = 1 Zloty

World War I Issues

A. German Military Coinage
See Germany, Nos. A18–C18 for iron 1,2 and 3 Kopeks 1916 used in eastern Poland, Russia, and the Baltic countries.

B. Regency Under Germany and Austria 1917–18.
100 Fenigow (Pfennig) = 1 Marka

Iron

4	1 Fenig 1918	5.00	10.00	20.00
5	5 Fenigow 1917–18	2.00	2.50	4.00
6	10 Fenigow 1917–18	2.00	3.00	10.00
7	20 Fenigow 1917–18	3.00	5.00	7.50

Zinc

6a	10 Fenigow 1917	50.00	90.00	175.00
7a	20 Fenigow 1917	75.00	125.00	250.00

REPUBLIC 1919–
First Coinage

Brass

8	1 Grosz 1923	12.50	20.00	45.00
9	2 Grosze 1923	1.00	3.00	7.00
10	5 Groszy 1923	1.00	2.00	5.00

Bronze

8a	1 Grosz 1923–39	.50	1.00	4.50
9a	2 Grosze 1923–39	.50	1.00	3.50
	1923 . . . 6			
10a	5 Groszy 1923–39	.50	1.00	4.00
	1923 . . . 15 1934 . . . 10			

Nickel

11	10 Groszy 1923	.50	1.00	1.75

12	20 Groszy 1923	1.00	1.50	2.50
13	50 Groszy 1923	1.00	1.50	3.00

Silver

15	1 Zloty 1924–25	4.00	10.00	17.50
16	2 Zlote 1924–25	5.00	12.50	35.00

17	5 Zlotych 1925	300.00	400.00	700.00

No. 17 not issued to circulation.

900th Anniversary
Death of Boleslaus I

Gold

32	F45	10 Zlotych 1925	70.00	90.00	145.00
33	F44	20 Zlotych 1925	100.00	125.00	165.00

Second Coinage
Nos. 8a–10a were continued through this period.

Nickel

14	1 Zloty 1929	1.00	2.00	5.00

Silver

18	5 Zlotych 1928–32	25.00	50.00	150.00
	1932 . . . 65			

Centennial of First
Revolt Against Russians

19	5 Zlotych 1930	25.00	35.00	125.00

Third Coinage
Nos. 8a–10a were continued through this period.

Silver

20	2 Zlote 1932–34	2.00	5.00	12.50
21	5 Zlotych 1932–34	5.00	10.00	20.00
22	10 Zlotych 1932–33	10.00	20.00	30.00

Obv: Jozef Pilsudski, Head of State 1926–35
Rev: Date below eagle

27	2 Zlote 1934–36	5.00	8.00	15.00
	1936 . . . 25			
28	5 Zlotych 1934–38	5.00	8.00	15.00
29	10 Zlotych 1934–39	12.50	20.00	35.00
	1934,38,39 . . . 20			

Unless otherwise noted, prices are for coins in very
fine, extremely fine, and uncirculated condition.

| 30 | 2 Zlote 1936 | 2.00 | 5.00 | 10.00 |
| 31 | 5 Zlotych 1936 | 5.00 | 10.00 | 17.50 |

WORLD WAR II
GERMAN OCCUPATION

Zinc

| 34 | 1 Grosz 1939 | 1.00 | 3.00 | 5.00 |
| 35 | 5 Groszy 1939 | 3.00 | 5.00 | 7.50 |

250th Anniversary
Relief of Vienna

Rev: Jan III Sobieski, King 1674–96

| 23 | 10 Zlotych 1933 | 25.00 | 40.00 | 75.00 |

| 36 | 10 Groszy 1923 | .50 | .75 | 1.50 |
| 37 | 20 Groszy 1923 | .50 | .75 | 1.50 |

Nos. 36–37 were struck ca. 1941–44.

Nickel-Plated Iron

| 38 | 50 Groszy 1938 | 2.00 | 4.00 | 5.00 |

70th Anniversary
Second Revolt Against Russians

Rev: Romuald Traugutt, patriot leader

| 24 | 10 Zlotych 1933 | 25.00 | 45.00 | 75.00 |

POSTWAR ISSUES

Aluminum

| 39 | 1 Grosz 1949 | .10 | .20 | .30 |

| 40 | 2 Grosze 1949 | .10 | .20 | .30 |

Bronze

| 41 | 5 Groszy 1949 | .75 | 1.00 | 1.25 |

20th Anniversary
Founding of Rifle Corps

Obv: Pilsudski, date at right
Rev: Badge below eagle

| 25 | 5 Zlotych 1934 | 10.00 | 15.00 | 30.00 |
| 26 | 10 Zlotych 1934 | 20.00 | 30.00 | 50.00 |

Cupro-Nickel

| 42 | 10 Groszy 1949 | .50 | .75 | 1.25 |
| 43 | 20 Groszy 1949 | .75 | 1.00 | 1.50 |

44	50 Groszy 1949	1.00	1.75	2.50

45	1 Zloty 1949	2.00	3.00	4.00

Aluminum

41a	5 Groszy 1949	.75	1.00	1.25
42a	10 Groszy 1949	.20	.30	.75
43a	20 Groszy 1949	.30	.50	.75
44a	50 Groszy 1949	.50	.60	.90
45a	1 Zloty 1949	.50	.75	1.25

Later issues in *Current Coins of the World.*

PORTUGAL

Western section of the Iberian peninsula facing the Atlantic Ocean. A kingdom until 1910 when, following a revolution, a republic was established. Exports: cork and wines. Area: 34,500 square miles. Language: Portuguese. Capital: *Lisbon.*

Monetary System:
1000 Reis = 1 Milreis to 1910
100 Centavos = 1 Escudo 1912–

LUIS I 1861–1889
Copper

1	III Reis 1868–75	7.00	10.00	15.00
2	V Reis 1867–79	2.00	5.00	10.00
3	X Reis 1867–77	4.00	8.00	15.00
4	XX Reis 1867–74	10.00	15.00	25.00

For other similar copper coins of 1865–80, see AZORES.

Bronze

5	V Reis 1882–86	1.00	3.00	6.00

6	X Reis 1882–86	2.00	4.00	10.00
7	XX Reis 1882–86	2.00	5.00	20.00

Silver

8	50 Reis 1862–89	2.00	6.00	15.00

9	100 Reis 1864–89	4.00	7.00	20.00
10	200 Reis 1862–63	25.00	40.00	80.00

10a	200 Reis 1865–88, diff. head	5.00	8.00	25.00
11	500 Reis 1863–89	10.00	15.00	45.00
	1872,76 . . . Rare.			

Gold
Rev: Arms in wreath

A12	*F130* 2000 Reis			
	1864–66	100.00	150.00	200.00
A13	*F129* 5000 Reis			
	1862–63	125.00	200.00	275.00

Rev: Mantled arms

12	*F133* 2000 Reis			
	1868–88	100.00	150.00	225.00
13	*F132* 5000 Reis			
	1867–89	135.00	200.00	275.00
14	*F131* 10,000 Reis			
	1878–89	200.00	350.00	475.00

Unless otherwise noted, prices are for coins in very fine, extremely fine, and uncirculated condition.

CARLOS I 1889–1908

Bronze

15	5 Reis 1890–1906	1.00	2.00	5.00
16	10 Reis 1891–92	1.00	2.00	5.00
17	20 Reis 1891–92	2.00	3.00	7.00

For bronze coins of 1901 with coat of arms replacing portrait, see AZORES.

Cupro-Nickel

18	50 Reis 1900	1.00	2.00	4.00
19	100 Reis 1900	1.00	2.00	6.00

Silver

20	50 Reis 1893	2.00	4.00	15.00

21	100 Reis 1890–98	3.00	8.00	22.00
	1894 EF . . . 100.			
22	200 Reis 1891–1903	5.00	10.00	30.00
	1901 EF . . . 100.			

23	500 Reis 1891–1908	10.00	16.00	45.00
	1894,1904 . . . Rare.			

24	1000 Reis 1899	25.00	35.00	75.00

400th Anniversary of Voyages of Discovery 1498–1898

25	200 Reis 1898	8.00	12.00	25.00
26	500 Reis 1898	15.00	20.00	40.00
27	1000 Reis 1898	25.00	50.00	125.00

EMANUEL II 1908–1910

Bronze

28	5 Reis 1910	1.00	2.00	6.00

Silver

29	100 Reis 1909–10	4.00	6.00	12.00
30	200 Reis 1909	4.00	6.00	18.00
31	500 Reis 1908–09	12.00	18.00	35.00

COMMEMORATIVE ISSUES
Peninsular War Centennial

32	500 Reis 1910	40.00	75.00	250.00
33	1000 Reis 1910	50.00	100.00	350.00

Marquis de Pombal

34	500 Reis 1910	25.00	45.00	75.00

REPUBLIC 1910–
First Coinage
Silver

48	10 Centavos 1915	2.00	4.00	12.00
49	20 Centavos 1913–16	4.00	6.00	15.00
50	50 Centavos 1912–16	5.00	8.00	18.00
51	1 Escudo 1915–16	17.50	25.00	40.00

Birth of Republic
5th October 1910
Silver

47	1 Escudo 1910 (struck 1914)	20.00	35.00	75.00

World War I Provisional Issue
Iron

35	2 Centavos 1918	45.00	100.00	200.00

Second Coinage
Bronze

36	1 Centavo 1917–21	.50	1.00	5.00
	1922 . . . Rare.			
37	2 Centavos 1918–21	.50	1.00	6.00
	1921 EF . . . 10.			
38	5 Centavos 1920–22	.50	2.00	9.00
	1920 UNC . . . 20. 1922 . . . Rare.			

Cupro-Nickel

42	4 Centavos 1917–19	.50	1.00	8.00
43	10 Centavos 1920–21	.50	1.00	10.00
44	20 Centavos 1920–22	.50	2.00	12.00
	1922 UNC . . . 250.			

Unless otherwise noted, prices are for coins in very fine, extremely fine, and uncirculated condition.

Third Coinage

Bronze

39	5 Centavos 1924–27	.50	1.00	6.00
40	10 Centavos 1924–40	.50	1.00	10.00
41	20 Centavos 1924–25	.50	1.00	12.00

Aluminum-Bronze

45	50 Centavos 1924–26	.50	2.00	10.00
	1925 . . . Rare.			
46	1 Escudo 1924–26	1.00	3.00	12.00
	1926 UNC . . . 50.			

Bronze

60	X Centavos 1942–69	.25	.40	.75
61	XX Centavos 1942–69	.25	.40	.75

Nickel-Bronze

54	50 Centavos 1927–68	.10	.25	.50
55	1 Escudo 1927–68	.25	.50	2.00
	1935 UNC . . . 100.			

Silver

57	2½ Escudos 1932–51	2.00	4.00	10.00
	1937 UNC . . . 50			

58	5 Escudos 1932–51	3.00	4.00	15.00
	1937 UNC . . . 40.			
59	10 Escudos 1932–48	5.00	10.00	20.00
	1937 UNC . . . 75. 1942 . . . Rare.			

63	10 Escudos 1954–55	4.00	6.00	10.00

Battle of Ourique 1139

Obv: Alfonso I, King 1140–85

56	10 Escudos 1928	15.00	25.00	60.00

25 Years of Financial Reform

62	20 Escudos 1953	8.00	12.00	20.00

500th Anniversary
Death of Henry the Navigator
Silver

64	5 Escudos 1960	3.00	5.00	8.00
65	10 Escudos 1960	6.00	9.00	20.00
66	20 Escudos 1960	12.00	18.00	40.00

Later issues in *Current Coins of the World*.

PORTUGUESE GUINEA (Guine)

This part of West Africa's Guinea coast was claimed by Portugal in 1446. An early slave trading center, it was little settled by Europeans. It became an Overseas Province in 1962. After it proclaimed independence in 1973, it was formally recognized in 1974 as the Republic of Guinea-Bissau. Its economy is primarily agricultural. Area: 14,000 square miles. Languages: Portuguese, native tongues. Capital: *Bolama (to 1941), Bissau (since 1941)*.

Monetary System:
100 Centavos = 1 Escudo

Bronze

1	5 Centavos 1933	4.00	9.00	17.50
2	10 Centavos 1933	6.00	10.00	30.00
3	20 Centavos 1933	3.50	7.50	17.50

Nickel-Bronze

4	50 Centavos 1933	8.00	20.00	150.00
5	1 Escudo 1933	8.50	25.00	200.00

500th Anniversary of Discovery
Bronze

6	50 Centavos 1946	1.00	3.00	8.00
7	1 Escudo 1946	1.00	3.00	9.00

Decree of Dec. 29, 1951
Bronze

8	50 Centavos 1952	.25	.50	2.50

Cupro-Nickel

9	2½ Escudos 1952	1.00	3.00	10.00

Silver

10	10 Escudos 1952	4.00	7.50	22.50
11	20 Escudos 1952	5.00	10.00	27.50

Later issues in *Current Coins of the World*.

PORTUGUESE INDIA (India Portugueza, Estado da India

Three small areas — Goa, Damao and Diu — on the west coast of India. They contain many salt and manganese mines. India occupied these enclaves in 1962.

Capital: Pangim.

Monetary System:
50 Reis = 1 Tanga (Indian Anna)
16 Tangas = 1 Rupia

Unless otherwise noted, prices are for coins in very fine, extremely fine, and uncirculated condition.

LUIS I 1861–1889
Copper

1	3 Reis 1871	10.00	20.00	40.00
2	5 Reis 1871	12.50	20.00	50.00
3	10 Reis 1871	15.00	20.00	55.00

4	¼ Tanga/15 Reis 1871	15.00	25.00	75.00
5	½ Tanga/30 Reis 1871	20.00	35.00	75.00
6	1 Tanga/60 Reis 1871	35.00	65.00	200.00

7*	⅛ Tanga 1881–86	5.00	10.00	25.00
8	¼ Tanga 1881–86	6.00	12.00	35.00
	1888 . . . 75.			

Silver

11	⅛ Rupia 1881	8.00	15.00	45.00
12	¼ Rupia 1881	9.00	17.50	50.00
13*	½ Rupia 1881–82	11.00	20.00	60.00
14	1 Rupia 1881–82	11.00	20.00	60.00

CARLOS I 1889–1908
Bronze

Obv: Date in Roman numerals

15	¹⁄₁₂ Tanga 1901, 03	3.00	10.00	25.00
16	⅛ Tanga 1901, 03	4.00	10.00	25.00
17	¼ Tanga 1901, 03	4.00	10.00	17.50
18	½ Tanga 1901, 03	5.00	12.50	40.00

Silver

19	1 Rupia 1903–04	10.00	18.00	60.00

PORTUGUESE REPUBLIC
ISSUES 1910–1961

Silver

20	1 Rupia 1912	22.50	45.00	95.00

Bronze

21	1 Tanga 1934	4.00	8.00	22.50

Cupro-Nickel

22	2 Tangas 1934	4.50	9.00	25.00
23*	4 Tangas 1934	4.50	11.00	35.00

Silver

24	½ Rupia 1936	8.00	15.00	30.00
25	1 Rupia 1935	7.50	12.50	25.00

Bronze

| 26 | 1 Tanga 1947 (25mm) | 1.00 | 2.50 | 7.50 |
| 26a | 1 Tanga 1952 (20mm) | .50 | 1.00 | 4.00 |

Cupro-Nickel

| 27 | ¼ Rupia 1947, 52 | 1.50 | 3.50 | 10.00 |
| 28 | ½ Rupia 1947, 52 | 1.75 | 4.00 | 12.50 |

Silver

| 29 | 1 Rupia 1947 | 6.00 | 10.00 | 20.00 |

Cupro-Nickel

| 29a | 1 Rupia 1952 | 2.50 | 6.00 | 13.50 |

NEW COINAGE SYSTEM

100 Centavos = 1 Escudo

Bronze

| 34 | 10 Centavos 1958–61 | .50 | 1.00 | 3.00 |
| 35 | 30 Centavos 1958–59 | .50 | 1.00 | 3.00 |

Copper-Nickel-Zinc

| 36 | 60 Centavos 1958–59 | .50 | 1.00 | 3.00 |

37	1 Escudo 1958–59	.50	2.00	6.00
38	3 Escudos 1958–59	1.00	2.00	7.00
39	6 Escudos 1959	2.00	5.00	10.00

PRINCE EDWARD ISLAND — see CANADA

PUERTO RICO

The farthest east of the Greater Antilles in the Atlantic Ocean. Ceded to the United States after the Spanish-American War, it is a self-governing Commonwealth of the United States. Major industry: sugar cultivation and processing. Area: 3,435 square miles. Capital: *San Juan.*

Monetary System:
100 Centavos = 1 Peso

UNDER SPAIN — ALFONSO XIII 1886–1898

Silver

| 1 | 5 Centavos 1896 | 15.00 | 20.00 | 90.00 |

2	10 Centavos 1896	20.00	35.00	125.00
3	20 Centavos 1895	25.00	40.00	150.00
4	40 Centavos 1896	150.00	250.00	800.00
5	1 Peso 1895	200.00	350.00	1200.

REUNION

A French overseas island territory in the Indian Ocean east of Madagascar. Chief exports: sugar, rum, vanilla, spices. Area: 969 square miles. Capital: *St.* Denis.

Monetary System:
100 Centimes = 1 Franc

Cupro-Nickel

| 1 | 50 Centimes 1896 | 20.00 | 35.00 | 150.00 |

Unless otherwise noted, prices are for coins in very fine, extremely fine, and uncirculated condition.

2 1 Franc 1896   35.00 60.00 250.00

Bank Tokens

Aluminum

3 5 Centimes 1920   50.00 75.00 175.00
4 10 Centimes 1920   100.00 150.00 400.00
5 25 Centimes 1920   75.00 125.00 350.00

Note: Former Nos. 6 and 7 (50 Centimes and 1 Franc 1941) have been deleted until their existence can be confirmed.

Regular Issues

Aluminum

8 1 Franc 1948–73   .25   .50   2.00
9 2 Francs 1948–73   .25   .50   3.00
10 5 Francs 1955–73   .35   .75   5.00

Aluminum-Bronze

11 10 Francs 1955–73   .25   .50   2.00
12 20 Francs 1955–73   .25   .50   2.50

Nickel
13 50 Francs 1962–73   .50   1.00   4.00
14 100 Francs 1964–73   .75   1.25   5.00

RHODESIA AND NYASALAND (Central African Federation)

This federation of three British territories began in September 1953 and was dissolved in 1963. It comprised the self-governing Colony of Southern Rhodesia and the two protectorates of Northern Rhodesia and Nyasaland.

Monetary System:
12 Pence = 1 Shilling
5 Shillings = 1 Crown

ELIZABETH II 1952–1964

Bronze

1 ½ Penny 1955–64   .10   .20   .50

2 1 Penny 1955–63   .15   .25   1.00

Cupro-Nickel

3 3 Pence 1955–64   .25   .50   2.00

4 6 Pence 1955–63   .50   1.00   3.00

5 1 Shilling 1955–57   .75   1.50   6.00

6 2 Shillings 1955–57   1.50   3.00   10.00

7 ½ Crown 1955–57   2.00   4.00   15.00
        1957 . . . 25.

Silver
1a–7a 7-piece set 1955   Proof . . . 140.00
See Southern Rhodesia for previous issues circulating in
this territory. See Malawi, Rhodesia and Zambia for
those now in use.

RHODESIA

Formerly Southern Rhodesia to 1953, a part of the Federation of Rhodesia and Nyasaland from 1953 to 1963.
Declared itself independent in 1965, and became a republic in 1970. Area: 150,333 square miles. Capital:
Salisbury. Now Zimbabwe.

Monetary System:
12 Pence = 1 Shilling
20 Shillings = 1 Pound

ELIZABETH II 1952–1970

Cupro-Nickel

A1 3 Pence 1968   .20   .30   1.00

1 6 Pence/5 Cents 1964   .25   .35   1.50

2 1 Shilling/10 Cents 1964   .35   .50   2.50

3 2 Shillings/20 Cents
        1964   .75   1.50   5.00

4 2½ Shillings/25 Cents
        1964   1.00   2.00   7.50

Gold

A5 *F3* 10 Shillings 1966   Proof . . . 175.00
B5 *F2* 1 Pound 1966   Proof . . . 300.00

C5 *F1* 5 Pounds 1966   Proof . . . 1250.

ROMANIA

A socialist industrial-agrarian state in southeast Europe,
bounded by the Black Sea, Bulgaria, Yugoslavia, Hungary and the U.S.S.R. The nation began in 1859 by the
union of Moldavia and Wallachia, and later gained other
territory including Transylvania. It became a republic late
in 1947. Area: 91,699 square miles. Language: Roma-
nian. Capital: *Bucuresti (Bucharest)*.

Monetary System:
100 Bani = 1 Leu

CAROL I
as Domnul (Prince) 1866–81
First Coinage

Bronze

1	1 Banu 1867	1.00	3.00	12.00
2	2 Bani 1867	1.00	3.00	12.00
3	5 Bani 1867	1.00	3.00	12.00
4	10 Bani 1867	1.00	5.00	15.00

Gold
Obv: Young head, sideburns

5	F1 20 Lei 1868		Rare

Second Coinage

Silver

Obv: Young head, short beard

6	1 Leu 1870	20.00	65.00	200.00

Gold

7	F2 20 Lei 1870	450.00	750.00	1500.

Third Coinage

Silver

8	50 Bani 1873, 76	5.00	25.00	50.00

9	1 Leu 1874–76	10.00	35.00	75.00
10	2 Lei 1872–76	15.00	75.00	150.00
	1874 . . . Rare.			

Fourth Coinage
Rev: ROMANIA above arms

Copper

11	2 Bani 1879–81	1.00	5.00	25.00

Silver

13	50 Bani 1881	5.00	20.00	50.00
14	1 Leu 1881	10.00	35.00	100.00
15	2 Lei 1881	15.00	50.00	125.00
16	5 Lei 1880–81 (2 vars.)	25.00	60.00	250.00

as Rege (King) 1881–1914

New Legend:
REGE replaces DOMNUL
Silver

27	5 Lei 1881, rev. of No. 16 (with ROMANIA)	30.00	60.00	150.00

Copper

Rev: ROMANIA at top removed

A17	1 Ban 1888			Rare
17	2 Bani 1882	1.00	5.00	20.00
18	5 Bani 1882–85	1.00	7.00	25.00

No. A17 was not issued to circulation.

Silver

19	50 Bani 1884–85	5.00	20.00	50.00
20	1 Leu 1884–85	10.00	40.00	125.00
23	5 Lei 1881–85, lettered edge	25.00	60.00	250.00
23a	5 Lei 1901, reeded edge	35.00	75.00	300.00

Gold

28 *F3* 20 Lei 1883–90   125.00 160.00 275.00

Copper
Rev: ROMANIA restored above arms

29 1 Ban 1900   1.00   3.00   10.00
30 2 Bani 1900   1.00   5.00   12.00

Cupro-Nickel

31 5 Bani 1900   .25   2.00   7.00
32 10 Bani 1900   .25   2.00   7.00
33 20 Bani 1900   2.00   10.00   25.00

34 5 Bani 1905–06   .25   2.00   7.00
35 10 Bani 1905–06   .25   2.00   7.00
36 20 Bani 1905–06   1.00   5.00   15.00

Silver

24 50 Bani 1894–1901   2.00   10.00   35.00
25 1 Leu 1894–1901   5.00   15.00   50.00
26 2 Lei 1894–1901   10.00   50.00   100.00

40th Anniversary of Reign
Silver

37 1 Leu 1906   7.00   20.00   40.00
38 5 Lei 1906   50.00 150.00 350.00

Gold

39 *F8* 12½ Lei 1906   135.00 225.00 300.00
40 *F7* 25 Lei 1906   225.00 325.00 400.00

41 *F5* 20 Lei 1906   150.00 250.00 325.00
42 *F4* 100 Lei 1906   850.00   1750.   3000.

43 *F6* 50 Lei 1906   375.00 550.00 850.00

Unless otherwise noted, prices are for coins in very fine, extremely fine, and uncirculated condition.

Regular Issues

Silver

| 44 | 50 Bani 1910–14 | 1.00 | 3.00 | 10.00 |

| 45 | 1 Leu 1910–14 | 2.00 | 7.00 | 20.00 |
| 46 | 2 Lei 1910–14 | 4.00 | 12.00 | 30.00 |

FERDINAND I 1914–1927

Aluminum

| 47 | 25 Bani 1921 | 1.00 | 5.00 | 12.00 |
| 48 | 50 Bani 1921 | 1.00 | 5.00 | 12.00 |

Cupro-Nickel

| 49 | 1 Leu 1924 | .50 | 2.00 | 10.00 |
| 50 | 2 Lei 1924 | .50 | 2.00 | 10.00 |

Note: Gold 20, 25, 50, and 100 Lei pieces dated 1922 exist, but their status as official issues is in dispute.

MIHAI I
First Reign 1927–1930

Nickel-Brass

| 55 | 5 Lei 1930 | 1.00 | 7.00 | 35.00 |

| 56 | 20 Lei 1930 | 1.00 | 7.00 | 35.00 |

CAROL II 1930–1940

Nickel-Brass

| 57 | 1 Leu 1938–41 | .15 | .50 | 2.00 |

| 58 | 10 Lei 1930 | .50 | 3.00 | 10.00 |
| 59 | 20 Lei 1930 | 1.00 | 5.00 | 15.00 |

Nickel

| 60 | 50 Lei 1937–38 | 1.00 | 5.00 | 15.00 |

| 61 | 100 Lei 1936, 38 | 1.00 | 7.00 | 25.00 |

Silver

| 62 | 100 Lei 1932 | 4.00 | 10.00 | 45.00 |

63   250 Lei 1935   5.00   20.00   50.00

64   250 Lei 1939–40   5.00   10.00   20.00

Centennial Birth of King Carol I

Gold

65   *F14* 20 Lei 1939 (arms)   300.00 700.00 1000.
66   *F16* 20 Lei 1939 (eagle) 300.00 700.00 1000.

67   *F13* 100 Lei 1939   –   3500. 5000.

68   *F15* 100 Lei 1939   –   3500. 5000.

Tenth Anniversary Reign of Carol II

Gold

Obv: large head, ornate border
71   *F18* 20 Lei 1940   300.00 450.00 700.00

A71 *F17* 100 Lei 1940   –   3000. 4000.

Obv: Small head, plain border
72   *F20* 20 Lei 1940   300.00 450.00 700.00
A72 *F19* 100 Lei 1940   –   3000. 4000.

MIHAI I
Second Reign 1940–1947

Zinc

73   2 Lei 1941   .25   1.00   5.00

Unless otherwise noted, prices are for coins in very
fine, extremely fine, and uncirculated condition.

74 5 Lei 1942 .50 2.00 7.00

75 20 Lei 1942–44 1.00 5.00 15.00

Nickel-Clad Steel

76 100 Lei 1943–44 1.00 3.00 10.00

Silver

77 200 Lei 1942 2.00 5.00 12.00

78 250 Lei 1941, edge lettered NIHIL SINE DEO 4.00 7.00 17.00

78a 250 Lei 1941, edge lettered TOTUL PENTRU TARA 10.00 20.00 35.00

79 500 Lei 1941 10.00 15.00 25.00

80 500 Lei 1944 5.00 7.00 15.00

Note: The 1944 gold piece (size of 20 Lei No. 71) is considered by some authorities to be a commemorative medal.

Second Coinage
Brass

81 200 Lei 1945 1.00 7.00 15.00

82 500 Lei 1945 1.00 7.00 20.00

Aluminum

83 500 Lei 1946 1.00 5.00 15.00

Brass

84 2000 Lei 1946   .50   2.00   7.00

85 10,000 Lei 1947   1.00   5.00   10.00

Silver

86 25,000 Lei 1946   6.00   10.00   17.50

87 100,000 Lei 1946   10.00   15.00   20.00

PEOPLE'S REPUBLIC 1947–1965
Currency Reform

Brass

88 50 Bani 1947   1.00   2.00   5.00

89 1 Leu 1947   1.00   2.00   3.00

Bronze

90 2 Lei 1947   1.00   2.00   3.00

Aluminum

91 5 Lei 1947   2.00   5.00   10.00

Aluminum-Bronze

92 1 Leu 1949–51   1.00   2.00   3.00

93 2 Lei 1950–51   1.00   2.00   3.00

Aluminum

92a 1 Leu 1951–52	1.50	2.50	3.50
93a 2 Lei 1951–52	2.00	3.00	5.00

94 5 Lei 1948–51   2.00   3.00   5.00

Unless otherwise noted, prices are for coins in very fine, extremely fine, and uncirculated condition.

95 20 Lei 1951   20.00 30.00 50.00

Currency Reform 1952
First Coinage

Aluminum-Bronze

Obv: No star at top of arms

96	1 Ban 1952	.20	.30	1.00
97	3 Bani 1952	.50	.75	1.50
98	5 Bani 1952	.50	.75	1.75

Cupro-Nickel

99	10 Bani 1952	.40	.75	1.25
100	25 Bani 1952	.75	1.00	1.50

Aluminum-Bronze

96a	1 Ban 1953–54	.15	.30	1.00
97a	3 Bani 1953–54	.30	.50	1.25
98a*	5 Bani 1953–54	.50	1.00	1.25

Aluminum-Bronze

Obv: With star, legend ends ROMANA

99a	10 Bani 1954	.20	.30	1.00
100a	25 Bani 1953–54	.30	.50	1.25

Obv: legend ends with ROMINA

99b	10 Bani 1955–56	.20	.30	1.00
100b	25 Bani 1955	.30	.50	1.25
101	50 Bani 1955–56	.75	1.00	2.00

Second Coinage
Nickel-Clad Steel

102	5 Bani 1963	.10	.15	.35

103	15 Bani 1960	.20	.30	.50

104	25 Bani 1960	.30	.50	.75

ROMANA legend resumed

105	1 Leu 1963	.40	.60	1.00

106	3 Lei 1963	.50	.75	1.25

Later issues in *Current Coins of the World.*

RUSSIA

The largest country in the world in area, it occupies eastern Europe and northern Asia, about one-sixth of the world's surface. The imperial Russia of the Czars was destroyed in 1917 by the Russian Revolution. Capital: *Moscow*.

Monetary System:
4 Polushka = 2 Denezhka = 1 Kopek;
100 Kopeks = 2 Poltina = 1 Ruble

CZARIST EMPIRE
General Issues
First Coinage
Obv: Six coats of arms on wings, no ribbons from crown

Copper

4	2 Kopeks 1855–59	5.00	20.00	45.00
5*	3 Kopeks 1855–59	7.00	25.00	50.00
6	5 Kopeks 1855–59	15.00	35.00	75.00
	1856BM . . . 35.			

Silver

13	5 Kopeks 1855–58	5.00	15.00	45.00
14	10 Kopeks 1855–58	5.00	15.00	50.00
	1855MW . . . 35.			
15	20 Kopeks 1855–58	5.00	20.00	60.00
	1857MW . . . 50			

16	25 Kopeks 1855–58	10.00	25.00	75.00
17*	½ Ruble 1855–58	15.00	45.00	125.00
18	1 Ruble 1855–58	35.00	65.00	150.00

Gold

A26	*F146* 5 Rubles 1855–58	125.00	175.00	250.00

Second Coinage
Obv: Eight coats of arms on wings, with ribbons from crown

Copper

4a	2 Kopeks 1859–67	5.00	20.00	45.00
5a	3 Kopeks 1859–67	7.00	25.00	50.00
	1865 . . . Rare			
6a	5 Kopeks 1859–67	15.00	35.00	75.00

9	1 Kopek 1867–1916	1.00	4.00	8.00
10	2 Kopeks 1867–1916	1.00	5.00	10.00
	1871CPB . . . 50.			
11	3 Kopeks 1867–1916	1.00	5.00	12.00
	1871CPB . . . 50.			
12	5 Kopeks 1867–1916	2.00	10.00	30.00
	1871CPB . . . 50.			

Silver

	Edge: Engrailed			
19	5 Kopeks 1859–66	1.00	5.00	15.00
20	10 Kopeks 1859–66	2.00	7.00	20.00
21	15 Kopeks 1860–66	2.00	7.00	20.00
22	20 Kopeks 1859–66	2.00	7.00	20.00
	Edge: Reeded			
19a	5 Kopeks 1867–1915	1.00	4.00	7.00
	1904 . . . Rare.			
20a	10 Kopeks 1867–1917	2.00	5.00	9.00
	1917 . . . 25.			
21a	15 Kopeks 1867–1917	2.00	5.00	10.00
	1888 . . . Rare. 1917 . . . 25.			
22a	20 Kopeks 1867–1917	2.00	5.00	12.00
	1902 . . . 20. 1917 . . . 35.			

Unless otherwise noted, prices are for coins in very fine, extremely fine, and uncirculated condition.

23 25 Kopeks 1859–85   15.00 30.00 65.00
Valuation is for 1859, 61, 77 and 78. All others are
worth $30. in VF.
24* ½ Ruble 1859–85   15.00 35.00 75.00
Valuation is for 1859, 77 and 78. All others are $40 in
VF.
25 1 Ruble 1859–85   25.00 60.00 125.00
          1859–62 . . . 75.

Gold

26 *F147* 3 Rubles 1869–85 175.00 275.00 375.00
          1882 . . . Rare.
B26 *F146* 5 Rubles 1859–85 125.00 150.00 250.00
                              Proof . . . 750.00
27 *F145* 25 Rubles 1876 5000. 8000. 13500.
                              Proof . . . 15,000.

Issues with Royal Portraits
or Monograms
ALEXANDER II 1855–1881

Copper

1 ¼ Kopek 1855–67   5.00 10.00 25.00
          1860 . . . 25.
2* ½ Kopek 1855–67   5.00 10.00 25.00
          1865 . . . 50.
3 1 Kopek 1855–67 (3
vars.)   5.00 15.00 30.00

7 ¼ Kopek 1867–81   5.00 10.00 20.00
8 ½ Kopek 1867–81   5.00 10.00 20.00

Dedication of
Nikolai I Monument

Silver

28 1 Ruble 1859   150.00 200.00 375.00
                              Proof . . . 650.00

ALEXANDER III 1881–1894
Coronation Commemorative

Silver

43 1 Ruble 1883   45.00 75.00 200.00

Copper

29 ¼ Kopek 1881–94   2.00   7.00 15.00
                              Proof . . . 65.00

30	½ Kopek 1881–94	1.00	5.00	10.00
			Proof . . . 65.00	

Silver

44	25 Kopeks 1886–94	35.00	85.00	150.00
	1889 . . . 100.			
45*	50 Kopeks 1886–94	45.00	100.00	200.00
	1889 . . . 100.			
46	1 Ruble 1886–94	35.00	125.00	275.00
	1889 . . . 200.		Proof . . . 1250.	

Gold

42	F151	5 Rubles 1886–94	145.00	185.00	300.00
				Proof . . . 1250.	
A42	F150	10 Rubles 1886–94	300.00	500.00	1100.
				Proof . . . 1750.	

NIKOLAI II 1894–1917

Copper

47	¼ Kopek 1894–1916	1.00	3.00	7.00
	1894 . . . 30.		Proof . . . 40.00	
48	½ Kopek 1894–1916	1.00	3.00	7.00
	1894 . . . 25.		Proof . . . 40.00	

Silver

57	25 Kopeks 1895–1901	15.00	35.00	75.00
	1901 . . . 200.			
58	50 Kopeks 1895–1914	5.00	15.00	45.00
	1898, 1903 . . . Rare		Proof . . . 250.00	
59	1 Ruble 1895–1915	20.00	50.00	150.00
	1903–06, 13 . . . 75.		Proof . . . 700.00	

Coronation Commemorative

60	1 Ruble 1896	45.00	75.00	200.00
			Proof . . . 600.00	

Dedication of Alexander II Monument

61	1 Ruble 1898	275.00	500.00	1000.

Centennial Defeat of Napoleon

68	1 Ruble 1912	100.00	175.00	350.00

Unless otherwise noted, prices are for coins in very
fine, extremely fine, and uncirculated condition.

Dedication of
Alexander III Monument

69 1 Ruble 1912   450.00 700.00 1250.

300th Anniversary
of Romanoff Dynasty

70 1 Ruble 1913   25.00 35.00 60.00
Early strikes are in low relief.

200th Anniversary
Battle of Gangut

Obv: Peter I (The Great), Emperor 1682–1725
71 1 Ruble 1914   600.00 1200. 1750.

Gold

A61 *F157* 5 Rubles 1895–96   Rare
A63 *F155* 10 Rubles 1895–97   Rare
A65 *F153* 25 Rubles 1896,
     1908   –   –   8500.
This series was for presentation only, and was not released to circulation.

Reduced Weight Gold

62 *F162* 5 Rubles
     1897–1911   65.00 85.00 150.00
        1906, 07 . . . Rare   Proof . . . 500.00
63* *F160* 7½ Rubles 1897   125.00 175.00 250.00

64 *F161* 10 Rubles
     1898–1911   125.00 150.00 200.00
        1906 . . . Rare   Proof . . . 700.00
65 *F159* 15 Rubles 1897   150.00 200.00 300.00
B65 *F152* 37½ Rubles 1902   –   –   8500.
No. B65 was for presentation only.

World War I Issues

Iron

For 1, 2 and 3 Kopeks 1916 (obv. German legend; rev. Russian value in cross) used during German occupation of northwest Russia, see GERMANY Nos. A18–C18.

Gold

85	*F163* 1 Chervonetz (10 Rubles)		
	a. 1923	175.00 275.00 375.00	
	b. 1975–80	– – 125.00	

U.S.S.R. (C.C.C.P.) (Union of Soviet Socialist Republics)

A confederacy of Soviet republics in eastern Europe and Asia. Government resulted from the overthrow of the Czarist regime in 1917. The Soviet Union has become a superpower through intensified development of its vast resources. Area: 8,649,490 square miles. Languages: Russian, many other dialects. Capital: *Moscow*

For Armavir issues, formerly Nos. 71–73, see Russian Caucasia.

First Coinage

Legend: PCOCP
Silver

80	10 Kopeks 1921–23	1.00	5.00	10.00
		Proof . . . 65.00		
81	15 Kopeks 1921–23	1.00	5.00	10.00
		Proof . . . 75.00		
82	20 Kopeks 1921–23	1.00	5.00	10.00
		Proof . . . 75.00		

83	50 Kopeks 1921–22	5.00	10.00	35.00
		Proof . . . 125.00		
84	1 Ruble 1921–22	15.00	25.00	60.00
		Proof . . . 250.00		

Second Coinage

New Legend: C.C.C.P.
Bronze

75	½ Kopek 1925–28	7.00	15.00	25.00

76	1 Kopek 1924–25	5.00	10.00	35.00
		Proof . . . 100.00		
77	2 Kopeks 1924–25	5.00	10.00	35.00
	1925 . . . 75.			
78	3 Kopeks 1924	5.00	15.00	40.00
		Proof . . . 150.00		
79	5 Kopeks 1924	10.00	20.00	45.00
		Proof . . . 200.00		

Silver

86	10 Kopeks 1924–31	1.00	3.00	10.00
	1931 . . . Rare.	Proof . . . 65.00		
87	15 Kopeks 1924–31	1.00	3.00	10.00
	1931 . . . Rare	Proof . . . 70.00		
88	20 Kopeks 1924–31	1.00	3.00	10.00
	1931 . . . Rare	Proof . . . 75.00		

Unless otherwise noted, prices are for coins in very fine, extremely fine, and uncirculated condition.

| 89 | 50 Kopeks 1924–27 | 5.00 | 10.00 | 35.00 |

Proof . . . 175.00

| 90 | 1 Ruble 1924 | 10.00 | 20.00 | 40.00 |

Proof . . . 250.00

Third Coinage

Aluminum-Bronze

91	1 Kopek 1926–35	1.00	2.00	7.00
92	2 Kopeks 1926–35	1.00	2.00	7.00
	1927 . . . Rare			
93	3 Kopeks 1926–35	1.00	2.00	10.00
	1927 . . . 25.			
94	5 Kopeks 1926–35	1.00	3.00	12.00

Cupro-Nickel

95	10 Kopeks 1931–34	1.00	2.00	7.00
96	15 Kopeks 1931–34	1.00	2.00	7.00
97	20 Kopeks 1931–34	1.00	2.00	7.00
	1934 . . . Rare.			

Fourth Coinage

Aluminum-Bronze

Obv: Three ribbons each side of wreath

98	1 Kopek 1935–36	2.00	5.00	15.00
99	2 Kopeks 1935–36	2.00	5.00	15.00
100	3 Kopeks 1935–36	2.00	5.00	15.00
101	5 Kopeks 1935–36	5.00	15.00	35.00

Cupro-Nickel

102	10 Kopeks 1935–36	1.00	3.00	10.00
103	15 Kopeks 1935–36	1.00	3.00	10.00
104	20 Kopeks 1935–36	1.00	3.00	10.00

Fifth Coinage

Aluminum-Bronze

Obv: Five ribbons each side of wreath

105	1 Kopek 1937–46	.25	.50	2.00
106	2 Kopeks 1937–46	.35	.75	3.00
107	3 Kopeks 1937–46	.50	1.00	5.00
108	5 Kopeks 1937–46	.50	1.00	5.00

Cupro-Nickel

109	10 Kopeks 1937–46	.50	1.00	4.00
110	15 Kopeks 1937–46	.50	1.00	4.00
111	20 Kopeks 1937–46	.50	1.00	4.00

Sixth Coinage
Aluminum-Bronze

Obv: 8 and 7 ribbons on wreath

112	1 Kopek 1948–56	.25	.50	2.00
113	2 Kopeks 1948–56	.25	.50	2.00
114	3 Kopeks 1948–56	.25	.50	2.00
115	5 Kopeks 1948–56	.35	.75	3.00

Cupro-Nickel

116	10 Kopeks 1948–56	.35	.75	3.00
117	15 Kopeks 1948–56	.35	.75	3.00
118	20 Kopeks 1948–56	.35	.75	3.00

Seventh Coinage
Aluminum-Bronze

Obv: 7 and 7 ribbons on wreath

119	1 Kopek 1957	.50	1.00	4.00
120	2 Kopeks 1957	.50	1.00	4.00
121	3 Kopeks 1957	.50	1.00	5.00
122	5 Kopeks 1957	.50	1.00	5.00

Cupro-Nickel

123	10 Kopeks 1957	.50	1.00	4.00
124	15 Kopeks 1957	.50	1.00	5.00
125	20 Kopeks 1957	.50	1.00	5.00

Later issues in *Current Coins of the World.*

RUSSIAN CAUCASIA

This mountainous region lies just north of Turkey and Iran, between the Black Sea and the Caspian Sea. Northern Caucasia is separated from Transcaucasia by the Greater Caucasus Mountains.

CITY OF ARMAVIR

A trade center in northwestern Caucasia, Armavir issued provincial coins and notes after coming under Soviet control in early 1918. The coins listed here formerly appeared as Russia, Nos. 72–74.

Copper

1	1 Ruble 1918 (24mm)	150.00 200.00 350.00

2	3 Rubles 1918 (28mm)	85.00 125.00 250.00
3	5 Rubles 1918 (32mm)	250.00 300.00 450.00

Pieces with larger diameters and/or in different metals are now thought to be patterns.

AMIRATE OF DAGHISTAN
(Dagestan)

An Islamic state in North Caucasia, Dagestan came under Russian domination in 1877. It regained independence for a few months during the Russian Revolution in 1919–20. Mint town: Vedeno.

Amir Uzun-Chadji
AH 1338 (1919–20)

Brass

1	2½ Toman	–	–	–
2	5 Toman AH 1338	–	–	–

3	10 Toman 1338	–	–	–

Unless otherwise noted, prices are for coins in very fine, extremely fine, and uncirculated condition.

Copper

3a 10 Toman 1338 (struck
over Russia No. 10)   –   –   –

RUSSIAN TURKESTAN

The south-central area of Russia, lying north of Iran and
Afghanistan, and stretching from Sinkiang in the east to
the Caspian Sea in the west. Serving traders and con-
querors as the bridge between Eastern and Western
worlds, it was one of the earliest centers of civilization.

**Prices below are for coins in Fine condi-
tion.**

KHANATE OF KHIVA
(Khwarezm)

A former Islamic state between Iran and the Aral Sea. It
was independent until becoming a Russian protectorate
in 1873, regaining independence in 1918. In 1920, it
became the Khwarezm Soviet People's Republic (see
below). Capital: Khiva.

Sayyid Muhammad Khan
AH 1272–1282 (1856–1865)

Copper

1 1 Pul AH 1274 (1857) (15mm)   25.00

Silver
2 1 Tenga 1275–81 (2 vars.)   25.00

Sayyid Muhammad Rahim
AH 1282–1328 (1865–1910)

Copper
3 1 Pul AH1302–11 (1884–93),
   17mm   25.00
4 2½ Tenga 1303 (26mm)   25.00
5 5 Tenga 1303 (30mm)   30.00

Silver
6 1 Tenga 1284–1313
   (1867–95)   15.00

Gold
7 1 Tilla AH–   –

Sayyid Abdullah Khan
and Djunaid Khan
AH 1337–38 (1918–20)

Copper
8   1 Tenga AH 1337   50.00
9   2½ Tenga 1337 (21mm)   30.00
10 5 Tenga 1337 (28mm)   40.00

KHWAREZM SOVIET
PEOPLE'S REPUBLIC

The successor to the Khanate of Khiva was formed by
Bolshevik factions early in 1920. Four years later it was
divided between the Uzbek and Turkmen Soviet Socialist Republics.

Bronze or Brass

1   20 Rubles AH 1338–39
    (1920–21)   50.00

2   25 Rubles 1339   25.00

3   100 Rubles 1339   25.00

4   500 Rubles 1339 (25mm)   75.00
4a* 500 Rubles 1339–40 (19mm)   30.00

EMIRATE OF BUKHARA

A former Islamic state situated north of Afghanistan and east of Khiva. Falling under Russian protection in 1868, it was again briefly independent from 1920 to 1924. In the latter year it was divided between the Uzbek, Turkmen and Tadzhik Soviet Socialist Republics. Capital: *Bukhara*.

Sayyid Abdul Ahad
AH 1303–1329 (1885–1911)

Copper

1	1 Falus AH 1322, 24 (1904, 06), 15mm	15.00

Silver

2	1 Tenga 1304–22 (1886–1904), 2 vars.	15.00

Gold

3	1 Tilla 1303–28 (21–23mm)	90.00

Alim ibn Sayyid Mir Amin
AH 1329–38 (1911–1920)

Bronze

4	1 Falus AH 1331–36 (1913–18), 15–16mm	5.00
5	4 Falus 1333–34 (15mm)	10.00
A5	8 Falus 1335 (16mm)	12.00

6	1 Tenga 1336 (15mm)	20.00

6a	1 Tenga 1336–37 (17–18mm)	25.00

Bronze or Brass

7	2 Tenga 1337	25.00

8*	3 Tenga 1336–37	25.00

9	4 Tenga 1336 (30mm)	40.00
10	5 Tenga 1336–37 (27mm)	35.00

11	10 Tenga 1337	15.00

12	20 Tenga 1336–37	35.00

RWANDA and BURUNDI

Formerly the Belgian U.N. Trusteeship of Ruanda-Urundi, united administratively with the Belgian Congo, these districts were renamed in 1960 and became officially independent in 1962.

Legend: B.E.R.B. (Banque d'Emission du Rwanda et du Burundi)
Brass

1	1 Franc 1960–64	.50	1.00	1.50

See Burundi and Rwanda for later issues.

Unless otherwise noted, prices are for coins in very fine, extremely fine, and uncirculated condition.

SAARLAND

An important mining region between France and Germany. Taken from Germany and united economically to France after both World Wars by way of reparation. In 1935, and again in 1957, the inhabitants (mostly German) voted to return to Germany. Area: 991 square miles. Capital: *Saarbrucken.*

Monetary System:
100 Centimen = 1 Frank

Aluminum-Bronze

1	10 Franken 1954	2.00	5.00	10.00
2	20 Franken 1954	2.00	5.00	10.00
3	50 Franken 1954	7.50	17.50	35.00

Cupro-Nickel

4	100 Franken 1955	6.00	10.00	25.00

ST. PIERRE AND MIQUELON (Saint-Pierre et Miquelon)

Barren islands off the southwest coast of Newfoundland belonging to France. Inhabited by fishermen, the only exports are cod and other fish products. Capital: *St. Pierre.*

Monetary System:
100 Centimes = 1 Franc

Aluminum

1	1 Franc 1948	1.00	3.00	5.00
2	2 Francs 1948	2.00	4.00	6.00

ST. THOMAS AND PRINCE (St. Tome e Principe)

Two islands in the Gulf of Guinea off the west coast of Africa. Discovered by Portugal in the fifteenth century, they produce important crops of cocoa and coffee. Independence was granted in 1975. Area: 372 square miles. Language: Portuguese. Capital: *Sao Tome.*

Monetary System:
100 Centavos = 1 Escudo

Nickel-Bronze

1	10 Centavos 1929	2.00	5.50	17.50
2	20 Centavos 1929	3.00	7.50	20.00
3	50 Centavos 1928–29	10.00	25.00	300.00

Cupro-Nickel

4	1 Escudo 1939	8.50	20.00	75.00

Nickel-Bronze

5	50 Centavos 1948	5.00	12.50	50.00
6	1 Escudo 1948	5.00	12.50	50.00

Silver

7	2½ Escudos 1939, 48	8.00	20.00	55.00
	1939 UNC . . . 75.			

8	5 Escudos 1939, 48	10.00	20.00	55.00
	1939 UNC . . . 75.			
9	10 Escudos 1939	17.50	32.50	75.00

COLONIA DE omitted
Cupro-Nickel

| 10 | 50 Centavos 1951 | 7.00 | 13.50 | 62.50 |
| 11 | 1 Escudo 1951 | 17.50 | 32.50 | 100.00 |

Silver

12	2½ Escudos 1951	8.00	15.00	35.00
13	5 Escudos 1951	7.00	16.00	37.50
14	10 Escudos 1951	7.50	17.50	40.00

Later issues in *Current Coins of the World*.

SAN MARINO

The world's smallest republic, situated in Italy. Products: cattle and wines.

Area: 24 square miles. Language: Italian. Capital: San Marino

Monetary System
100 Centesimi = 1 Lira

First Coinage
Copper

| 1 | 5 Centesimi 1864–94 | 10.00 | 15.00 | 70.00 |
| 2 | 10 Centesimi 1875–94 | 10.00 | 15.00 | 40.00 |

Silver

3	50 Centesimi 1898	10.00	20.00	40.00
4	1 Lira 1898, 1906	10.00	15.00	25.00
5	2 Lire 1898, 1906	30.00	70.00	125.00

| 6 | 5 Lire 1898 | 100.00 | 150.00 | 300.00 |

Second Coinage
Bronze

| 14 | 5 Centesimi 1935–38 | 2.00 | 5.00 | 10.00 |
| 15 | 10 Centesimi 1935–38 | 2.00 | 5.00 | 10.00 |

Silver

| 9 | 5 Lire 1931–38 | 5.00 | 10.00 | 15.00 |

| 10 | 10 Lire 1931–38 | 15.00 | 25.00 | 35.00 |
| | 1938 . . . 100. | | | |

11 20 Lire 1931–36 (15 gr.) 100.00 150.00 250.00
11a 20 Lire 1935–38 (20 gr.) 125.00 175.00 300.00
　　 1937, 38 150.00 250.00 500.00

Gold

12 *F2* 10 Lire 1925 300.00 500.00 700.00
13 *F1* 20 Lire 1925 500.00 700.00 1500.
Later issues in *Current Coins of the World.*

SARAWAK

A territory on the northwest coast of Borneo, Sarawak was given by the Sultan of Brunei to an Englishman, James Brooke, in 1841. Brooke and his descendants were known as the "White Rajahs." Following World War II, Sarawak became a British colony in 1946, and in 1963 it joined Malaya, Sabah and Singapore in the formation of Malaysia. Area: 48,250 square miles. Languages: Malay and Chinese dialects, English. Capital: *Kuching.*

Monetary System:
100 Cents = 1 Dollar

J. BROOKE, RAJAH 1841–68

Copper or Brass

1 1 Doit Sept. 24, 1841 750.00 1000. 1500.

Regular Coinage

Copper

2 ¼ Cent 1863 65.00 125.00 250.00
　　 Proof . . . 350.00
3 ½ Cent 1863 20.00 35.00 125.00
　　 Proof . . . 250.00
4 1 Cent 1863 10.00 20.00 75.00
　　 Proof . . . 175.00

C. BROOKE, RAJAH
1868–1917

Copper

5 ¼ Cent 1870, 96 20.00 35.00 75.00
　　 Proof . . . 350.00
6 ½ Cent 1870–96 15.00 25.00 75.00
　　 Proof . . . 350.00
7 1 Cent 1870–91 8.00 15.00 50.00
　　 Proof . . . 175.00

8 1 Cent 1892–97 8.00 15.00 60.00
　　 Proof . . . 175.00

Silver

9 5 Cents 1900–15 45.00 65.00 125.00
　　 Proof . . . 400.00
10 10 Cents 1900–15 35.00 50.00 100.00
　　 Proof . . . 400.00

11	20 Cents 1900–15	50.00	100.00	200.00
			Proof . . .	650.00
12	50 Cents 1900, 06	50.00	100.00	200.00
			Proof . . .	1750.

Except where noted, prices are for coins in Extremely Fine condition.

CHARLES VYNER BROOKE, RAJAH 1917–1946

Bronze

13	½ Cent 1933	1.00	2.00	5.00
14	1 Cent 1927–41	1.00	2.00	5.00
	1941 . . . 500.		Proof . . .	250.00

Cupro-Nickel

15	1 Cent 1920	10.00	15.00	25.00
16	5 Cents 1920, 27	5.00	10.00	50.00
17	10 Cents 1920–34	5.00	10.00	25.00

Silver

18	5 Cents 1920	45.00	65.00	90.00
19	10 Cents 1920	20.00	35.00	60.00
20	20 Cents 1920, 27	5.00	10.00	15.00
	1920 . . . 85.			
21	50 Cents 1927	20.00	35.00	150.00
			Proof . . .	350.00

SAUDI ARABIA

An absolute monarchy covering most of the Arabian peninsula comprising the former sultanate of Nejd and Kingdom of Hejaz in western Asia. Mostly desert area, the country is hot and dry. Its greatest wealth is in its oil fields. Area: 873,000 square miles. Language: Arabic. Capital: *Riyadh.*

Monetary System:
20 Ghirsh = 1 Riyal
1 Gold Guinea = 40 Riyals, Silver (1959)

ABD AL-AZIZ IBN SA'UD 1926–1953

Copper

1	¼ Ghirsh AH 1343 (1925)	VF . . . 15.00
2*	½ Ghirsh AH1343	VF . . . 15.00

These copper coins were struck in occupied Mecca, Hejaz Mint in 1925 by Ibn Sa'ud while establishing his dual kingdom.

Bronze

A3	½ Ghirsh 1344	15.00

Title: King of Hejaz and Sultan of Nejd
Cupro-Nickel

3	¼ Ghirsh AH 1344 (1926)	1.50
4	½ Ghirsh 1344	1.50
5*	1 Ghirsh 1344	1.25

Title: King of Hejaz, Nejd and its Dependencies
Cupro-Nickel

6	¼ Ghirsh AH 1346 (1928)	1.00
7	½ Ghirsh 1346	1.10
8	1 Ghirsh 1346	1.25

Modified Dies

6a	¼ Ghirsh 1348 (1930)	1.00
7a	½ Ghirsh 1348	1.10
8a	1 Ghirsh 1348	1.25

Unless otherwise noted, prices are for coins in very fine, extremely fine, and uncirculated condition.

Silver

12	¼ Riyal 1346, 48 (1928, 30), 24mm	40.00
13*	½ Riyal 1346, 48 (27mm)	25.00
14	1 Riyal 1346, 48 (37mm)	40.00

Title: King of Saudi Arabia
Cupro-Nickel

Edge: Plain

9*	¼ Ghirsh 1356 (1937)	.75
10	½ Ghirsh 1356	.75
11	1 Ghirsh 1356	.85

Edge: Reeded

9a	¼ Ghirsh 1356	.35
10a	½ Ghirsh 1356	.50
11a	1 Ghirsh 1356	.75

Silver

18	¼ Riyal 1354 (1935)	1.75
19*	½ Riyal 1354	3.00
20	1 Riyal 1354–70	4.00

Cupro-Nickel

A21, B21, C21 ¼, ½, and 1 Ghirsh pieces counter-stamped with Arabic "65" to break moneychanger's monopoly on small coins in AH 1365 (1946) 2.50

Gold

21	*USA F108* (1 Sovereign) ND (1947) .2354 Troy ounces fine gold	200.00
22	*USA F107* (4 Sovereigns) ND (1945–46), gross weight 493.1 grains	400.00

Nos. 21–22 were struck at Philadelphia, and although often considered bullion pieces only, are said to have circulated briefly. Counterfeits exist.

23	*F1* 1 Guinea 1370 (1951)	UNC . . . 150.00

SA'UD IBN ABDUL AZIZ
1953–1964

Bronze

30	1 Halala 1383 (1964)	UNC 25

Cupro-Nickel

A23	1 Ghirsh 1376, 78 (1957, 59)	UNC 20
24*	2 Ghirsh 1376, 79	UNC 35
25	4 Ghirsh 1376, 78	UNC 65

Silver

26	¼ Riyal 1374 (1955)	UNC . . . 2.00
27*	½ Riyal 1374	UNC . . . 5.00

28 1 Riyal 1374   UNC . . . 6.00

Gold

29 *F2* 1 Guinea 1377 (1957–58)   UNC . . . 150.00
Later issues in *Current Coins of the World*.

SERBIA

Now a part of Yugoslavia. For 500 years Serbia was a vassal principality of Turkey. It gained its freedom in 1878. After World War I it joined with other Slavic states to form what is now Yugoslavia. Capital: Belgrade. Area: 18,782 square miles.

Monetary System:
100 Para = 1 Dinar

MICHAEL, OBRENOVICH III
1839–42, 1860–68

Bronze

1	1 Para 1868	2.00	7.00	20.00
2	5 Para 1868	5.00	15.00	35.00
3	10 Para 1868	7.50	20.00	50.00

MILAN, OBRENOVICH IV
as Prince 1868–82

Silver

Obv: Young head, no moustache

4	50 Para 1875	12.50	25.00	85.00
5	1 Dinar 1875	15.00	30.00	100.00
6	2 Dinara 1875	40.00	80.00	250.00

Bronze

Obv: Older head with moustache

7	5 Para 1879	5.00	10.00	25.00
8	10 Para 1879	5.00	14.00	40.00

Silver

4a	50 Para 1879	10.00	20.00	50.00
5a	1 Dinar 1879	12.50	30.00	100.00
6a	2 Dinara 1879	15.00	45.00	150.00
9	5 Dinara 1879	55.00	150.00	500.00

Gold

10	*F3* 20 Dinara 1879	200.00	350.00	700.00

as King Milan I 1882–89

Gold

11	*F5* 10 Dinara 1882	100.00	150.00	275.00
12	*F4* 20 Dinara 1882	150.00	200.00	350.00

GENERAL COINAGE

Nos. 13–16 were issued without the name of the ruler through successive reigns.

Bronze

13	2 Pare 1904	1.00	5.00	20.00

Unless otherwise noted, prices are for coins in very fine, extremely fine, and uncirculated condition.

Cupro-Nickel

14	5 Para 1883–1917	2.00	4.00	10.00
	1917 . . . 5.			
15	10 Para 1883–1917	2.00	4.00	15.00
	1917 . . . 12.50			
16	20 Para 1883–1917	2.50	5.00	12.50

ALEXANDER I 1889–1902
Silver

17	1 Dinar 1897	5.00	12.50	35.00
18	2 Dinara 1897	10.00	20.00	50.00

PETAR I 1903–1918
Silver

Obv: Designer's name SCHWARTZ below neck				
19	50 Para 1904–15	2.00	5.00	10.00
20	1 Dinar 1904–15	4.00	7.00	15.00
21	2 Dinara 1904–15	7.50	9.00	25.00
Obv: Without name below neck				
19a	50 Para 1915	10.00	15.00	35.00
20a	1 Dinar 1915	10.00	17.50	40.00
21a	2 Dinara 1915	10.00	15.00	30.00

Centennial First Uprising Against Turks

22	5 Dinara 1904	50.00	100.00	350.00

WORLD WAR II
German Formed State
Zinc

23	50 Para 1942	1.00	5.00	12.00

24	1 Dinar 1942	1.00	2.50	5.00
25	2 Dinara 1942	1.50	2.50	7.50

26	10 Dinara 1943	4.00	6.00	12.50

SEYCHELLES

A tropical archipelago in the Indian Ocean some 1000 miles east of Kenya. Formerly a British colony, it became independent within the Commonwealth in 1976. Its economy is based on agricultural products, fishing and tourism. Area: 100 square miles. Languages: English, Creole. Capital: *Victoria*.

Monetary System:
100 Cents = 1 Rupee

GEORGE VI 1936–1952
Cupro-Nickel

1	10 Cents 1939–44	3.00	8.00	30.00

2	25 Cents 1939–44	5.00	10.00	40.00
3	½ Rupee 1939	7.50	15.00	60.00
4	1 Rupee 1939	7.50	15.00	80.00

New Legend:
KING GEORGE THE SIXTH
Bronze

5	1 Cent 1948	.25	.50	1.00

| 6 | 2 Cents 1948 | .25 | .50 | 1.00 |
| 7 | 5 Cents 1948 | .50 | 1.00 | 1.50 |

Cupro-Nickel

| 8 | 10 Cents 1951 | 3.00 | 5.00 | 7.00 |

| 9 | 25 Cents 1951 | 2.00 | 5.00 | 20.00 |

ELIZABETH II 1952–

Bronze

| 14 | 1 Cent 1959–69 | .50 | 1.00 | 2.00 |
| 15 | 2 Cents 1959–69 | 1.00 | 2.00 | 3.00 |

| 16 | 5 Cents 1964–71 | .50 | 1.00 | 3.00 |

Nickel-Brass

| 10 | 10 Cents 1953– | .50 | 1.00 | 2.00 |

Cupro-Nickel

11	25 Cents 1954–	1.00	2.00	4.00
12	½ Rupee 1954–	1.00	2.00	5.00
13	1 Rupee 1954–	1.00	2.00	5.00

Later issues in *Current Coins of the World.*

SIAM — see THAILAND

SOMALIA

Part of the northeast horn of Africa, this independent republic was set up in July, 1960 with the union of the former British Somaliland Protectorate and the former Italian trust territory of Somalia. The largely nomadic population is primarily engaged in cattle-raising. Languages: Somali, Arabic, English, Italian. Area: 262,000 square miles. Capital: *Mogadiscio.*

Monetary System:
100 Centesimi = 1 Somalo

Italian Trust Territory Issue

Bronze

1	1 Centesimo 1950	.20	.30	.50
2	5 Centesimi 1950	.20	.50	1.00
3	10 Centesimi 1950	.25	.75	1.50

Billon

| 4 | 50 Centesimi 1950 | 2.50 | 3.50 | 6.50 |
| 5 | 1 Somalo 1950 | 2.00 | 4.00 | 6.00 |

Later issues in *Current Coins of the World.*

SOUTH AFRICAN REPUBLIC
(Zuid-Afrikaansche Republiek)

Boer republic in the Transvaal, now part of the Republic of South Africa. Capital: *Pretoria*.

Monetary System:
12 Pence = 1 Shilling
20 Shillings = 1 Pond

THOMAS FRANCOIS BURGERS
President 1872–1877

Gold

A1 *F1* 1 Pond 1874 (2 vars.)   5000.   8000. 12000.

PAUL KRUGER
President 1883–1902

Bronze

1 1 Penny 1892–98   2.00   4.00   15.00
  1893 . . . 75.

Silver

2 3 Pence 1892–97   5.00   10.00   35.00
3 6 Pence 1892–97   4.00   8.00   25.00

4 1 Shilling 1892–97   5.00   15.00   40.00
  1893 . . . 75.

5 2 Shillings 1892–97   10.00   30.00   85.00
  1893 . . . 85.

6 2½ Shillings 1892–97   15.00   35.00   90.00
  1893 . . . 85.
7 5 Shillings 1892, single
  shaft on wagon   150.00 300.00 1000.
7a 5 Shillings 1892, double
  shaft   250.00 450.00 1200.

Gold

Rev: Single shaft on wagon
8 *F3* ½ Pond 1893–97   125.00 250.00 750.00
1893 . . . 1500.
9* *F2* 1 Pond 1892–1900 150.00 250.00 400.00
1892 single shaft . . . 1000.
Rev: Double shaft on wagon
8a *F3* ½ Pond 1892   175.00 300.00 500.00
9a *F2* 1 Pond 1892   200.00 300.00 650.00

The Veld Pond

Obv: ZAR monogram
10 *F4* 1 Pond 1902   2000. 3500. 6000.
Many dangerous counterfeits exist.

UNION OF SOUTH AFRICA
(Zuid-Afrika, Suid-Afrika)

The Union was formed by Britain after the Boer War, May 31, 1910. Settled in the 1800's by the Dutch, the government is still controlled by their descendants (Afrikaaners). The country became a republic and left the Commonwealth in May, 1961. Has the world's largest gold and diamond mines. Other exports: coal, asbestos, copper. Area: 472,360 square miles. Languages: English, Afrikaans. Administrative capital: *Pretoria*.

Monetary System:
12 Pence = 1 Shilling
2 Shillings = 1 Florin
20 Shillings = 1 Pound

GEORGE V 1910–1936
Legend: ZUID-AFRIKA
Bronze

11	¼ Penny 1923–25 (¼ Penny ¼)	3.00	7.00	15.00
11a	¼ Penny 1926–31 (¼ Penny)	2.00	5.00	12.00
	1926 . . . 5000.			

12	½ Penny 1923–26 (½ Penny ½)	25.00	50.00	125.00
12a	½ Penny 1928–31 (½ Penny)	10.00	25.00	75.00
13	1 Penny 1923–24 (1 Penny 1)	12.50	25.00	50.00
13a	1 Penny 1926–30 (Penny)	5.00	15.00	45.00

Silver

Rev: Value in wreath

15	3 Pence 1923–25	15.00	35.00	75.00
16	6 Pence 1923–24	20.00	50.00	110.00

Rev: Flower in frame

17	3 Pence 1925–30	5.00	15.00	50.00
18	6 Pence 1925–30	10.00	25.00	70.00

19	1 Shilling 1923–24 (1 Shilling 1)	15.00	50.00	125.00
19a	1 Shilling 1926–30 (Shilling)	20.00	75.00	250.00
	1926 . . . 150.			

20	1 Florin 1923–30	15.00	50.00	125.00
	1925 . . . 600.			
21	2½ Shillings 1923–25 (2½ Shillings 2½)	15.00	45.00	125.00
21a	2½ Shillings 1926–30 (2½ Shillings)	25.00	125.00	300.00

Gold

Same as British Sovereign, but with Pretoria mintmark, "SA"

A21	F6 ½ Sovereign 1923–26	75.00	125.00	300.00
	1923 Proof only . . . 1000.			
22	F5 1 Sovereign 1923–32	130.00	145.00	175.00
	1924 . . . 3000.			

New Spelling: SUID-AFRIKA
Bronze

"D" for Penny

23 ¼ Penny 1931–36   2.00   5.00   15.00
     1933,34,36 . . . 2000.
24 ½ Penny 1931–36   8.00   20.00   45.00
     1931 Proof only . . . 2,000.
24 1 Penny 1931–36   2.00   10.00   35.00

Silver

26 3 Pence 1931–36   3.00   12.00   40.00
     1931 . . . 3000.
27 6 Pence 1931–36   5.00   20.00   55.00
     1931 . . . 250.

28 1 Shilling 1931–36   8.00   25.00   60.00
     1931 . . . 250.
29 2 Shillings 1931–36   10.00   25.00   75.00
     1931 . . . 800.
30 2½ Shillings 1931–36   12.00   25.00   75.00
     1931 . . . 1200.

GEORGE VI 1936–1952

Bronze

31 ¼ Penny 1937–47   .25   .50   3.00

32 ½ Penny 1937–47   .50   1.00   7.00
33 1 Penny 1937–47   .50   1.00   8.00

Silver

34 3 Pence 1937–47   1.00   2.00   9.00

35 6 Pence 1937–47   1.00   2.50   10.00
     1939 Proof only . . . 5000.

36 1 Shilling 1937–47   2.00   4.00   15.00
     1939 Proof only . . . 5000.

37 2 Shillings 1937–47   4.00   6.00   20.00

38 2½ Shillings 1937–47   5.00   7.00   25.00

Royal Visit Commemorative

39 5 Shillings 1947   8.00   10.00   25.00

New Legend:
GEORGIUS SEXTUS REX
Designs similar to Nos. 31–39
Rev: SOUTH AFRICA — SUID-AFRIKA

Bronze

40 ¼ Penny 1948–50   .25   .50   2.00

41 ½ Penny 1948–52   .50   1.00   3.00
42 1 Penny 1948–50   .50   1.00   5.00

Silver

43   3 Pence 1948–50   1.00   2.50   8.00
43a 3 Pence 1950–52   1.00   1.50   4.00
44   6 Pence 1948–50   1.50   2.00   7.00

45   1 Shilling (value spelled
       out) 1948–50   3.00   5.00   15.00
       1949 Proof only . . . 300.
45a* 1 Shilling (value 1 S)
       1951–52   1.50   3.00   5.00
46   2 Shillings 1948–50   8.00   20.00   50.00
       1950 . . . 60.
47   2½ Shillings (value
       spelled out) 1948–50   75.00 150.00 250.00
47a 2½ Shillings (value 2½ S)
       1951–52   5.00   7.00   15.00

48 5 Shillings 1948–50   8.00   10.00   25.00

Gold

57 *F8* ½ Pound 1952   Proof . . . 125.00

All Values Abbreviated
Rev: SUID-AFRIKA — SOUTH AFRICA
Beginning in 1951, the following denominations used the transposed reverse legend, while the other denominations continued to place the English name first. The change was intended to give the Afrikaans language equal status with English

Bronze

49 ¼ Penny 1951–52   .25   .50   2.00
50 1 Penny 1951–52   .50   1.00   3.00

Silver

51 6 Pence 1951–52   1.00   2.00   4.00

52 2 Shillings (value 2 S)
     1951–52   2.50   4.00   8.00

60	½ Penny 1953–60	.25	.50	2.00
61	1 Penny 1953–60	.25	.50	2.50

53 5 Shillings (value 5 S)
1951   6.00   8.00   25.00

Silver

62	3 Pence 1953–60	.50	1.00	3.00

Third Centennial of Founding of Capetown

63	6 Pence 1953–60	.75	1.50	3.00
64	1 Shilling 1953–60	1.50	2.00	4.00
65	2 Shillings 1953–60	3.00	4.00	8.00
66	2½ Shillings 1953–60	4.00	5.00	10.00
67	5 Shillings 1953–59	6.00	7.50	15.00

56 5 Shillings 1952   6.00   8.00   15.00

Gold

Gold

68	*F10* ½ Pound 1953–60		Proof . . . 100.00
69	*F9* 1 Pound 1953–60		Proof . . . 175.00

58 *F7* 1 Pound 1952   Proof . . . 175.00

ELIZABETH II 1952–61

50th Anniversary of Union

Silver

Legend:
SOUTH AFRICA — SUID-AFRIKA
on Nos. 60, 62, 64, 66 and 68
SUID-AFRIKA — SOUTH AFRICA
on all other numbers 59–70
Bronze

59 ¼ Penny 1953–60   .25   .50   1.00

70 5 Shillings 1960   5.00   7.50   12.00

REPUBLIC 1961–
Decimal System
100 Cents = 1 Rand

Brass

71 ½ Cent 1961–64 .10 .25 .50

72 1 Cent 1961–64 .10 .35 1.00

Silver

73 2½ Cents 1961–64 .50 1.00 3.00

74 5 Cents 1961–64 .50 .75 2.00
75 10 Cents 1961–64 1.00 1.50 3.00

76 20 Cents 1961–64 2.00 3.00 5.00

77 50 Cents 1961–64 6.00 8.00 10.00

Gold

78 *F12* 1 Rand 1961– 60.00 65.00 75.00
79 *F11* 2 Rand 1961– 120.00 130.00 150.00
Later issues in *Current Coins of the World.*

SOUTH KOREA —
see KOREA, South
SOUTH VIETNAM —
see VIETNAM

SOUTHERN RHODESIA

From 1953 to 1963 a part of the Central African Federation, in south central Africa. Victoria Falls on the Zambesi River is one of the world's largest waterfalls. Agriculture and mining are important industries. Area: 150,333 square miles. Languages: English, Shona, Ndebele. Capital: *Salisbury.*

Monetary System:
12 Pence = 1 Shilling
2 Shillings = 1 Florin
5 Shillings = 1 Crown
20 Shillings = 1 Pound

GEORGE V 1910–1936

Cupro-Nickel

1	½ Penny 1934–36	3.00	6.00	30.00
2	1 Penny 1934–36	2.00	5.00	35.00

Silver

3	3 Pence 1932–36		4.00	15.00	50.00

4	6 Pence 1932–36		5.00	20.00	70.00

5	1 Shilling 1932–36	6.00	20.00	75.00
6	2 Shillings 1932–36	10.00	25.00	100.00

7	½ Crown 1932–36	12.00	35.00	150.00

GEORGE VI 1936–1952

Cupro-Nickel

8	½ Penny 1938–39	2.00	5.00	35.00
9	1 Penny 1937–42	1.50	4.00	25.00

Bronze

8a	½ Penny 1942–44	1.00	3.00	8.00
9a	1 Penny 1942–47	1.00	2.50	15.00

EMPEROR to right of head
Silver

Rev: Designs like Nos. 3–7

12	3 Pence 1937	5.00	12.50	50.00
13	6 Pence 1937	6.00	15.00	75.00
14	1 Shilling 1937	7.00	15.00	75.00
15	2 Shillings 1937	15.00	30.00	100.00
16	½ Crown 1937	12.50	25.00	125.00

KING EMPEROR to right of head
Rev: Designs like Nos. 3–7

17	3 Pence 1939–46	3.00	6.00	50.00
	1939 . . . 20.			
18	6 Pence 1939–46	4.00	12.00	60.00
	1945 . . . 40.			
19	1 Shilling 1939–46	5.00	15.00	75.00
20	2 Shillings 1939–46	10.00	25.00	100.00
	1939 . . . 150. 1946 . . . 300.			
21	½ Crown 1938–46	10.00	20.00	85.00

Cupro-Nickel

17a	3 Pence 1947	1.00	3.00	15.00
18a	6 Pence 1947	2.00	5.00	25.00
19a	1 Shilling 1947	2.50	6.00	40.00
20a	2 Shillings 1947	7.00	20.00	70.00
21a	½ Crown 1947	5.00	10.00	35.00

New Legend:
KING GEORGE THE SIXTH
Bronze

27	½ Penny 1951–52	1.00	2.00	8.00
28	1 Penny 1949–52	1.00	2.00	10.00

Cupro-Nickel

29	3 Pence 1948–52	.50	3.00	15.00
30	6 Pence 1948–52	1.00	3.50	20.00
31	1 Shilling 1948–52	1.50	5.00	30.00
32	2 Shillings 1948–52	2.00	6.00	35.00
33	½ Crown 1948–52	3.00	7.00	35.00

ELIZABETH II 1952–

Centennial
Birth of Cecil Rhodes
Silver

34	1 Crown 1953	8.00	15.00	25.00
			Proof . . .	150.00

Regular Issues

Bronze

35	½ Penny 1954	1.00	3.00	40.00
36	1 Penny 1954	3.00	10.00	75.00

Cupro-Nickel

37	2 Shillings 1954	75.00	200.00	1000.

38	½ Crown 1954	10.00	25.00	125.00

See Rhodesia and Nyasaland for later issues.

SPAIN (Espana)

A monarchy covering most of the Iberian peninsula in southwest Europe. Primarily an agricultural nation, it exports wines, cork, wheat, olives, fruits and many other products. Area: 195,504 square miles. Languages: Spanish, Catalan, Basque. Capital: *Madrid.*

Monetary System:
34 Maravedis = 1 Real

ISABEL II 1833–1868
First Decimal Coinage
10 Decimas = 1 Real 1848–55

Silver

Rev: Arms in order chain

13	20 Reales 1850	90.00	300.00	600.00

Copper

15	Media Decima (= ¹/₂₀) de Real 1852–53	8.00	14.00	25.00
16	Decima (= ¹/₁₀) de Real 1850–53	6.00	12.00	25.00

Unless otherwise noted, prices are for coins in very fine, extremely fine, and uncirculated condition.

17 Doble Decima (= ⅕) de
Real 1853   15.00 150.00 300.00
18 ½ Real 1848–53   8.00 20.00 50.00

Silver

Rev: Arms without pillars

19 1 Real 1850–55   10.00 17.00 22.00
20 2 Reales 1852–55   12.00 20.00 40.0
21 4 Reales 1852–55   15.00 30.00 50.00

Rev: Arms flanked by pillars

22 10 Reales 1851–56   20.00 40.00 100.00
23 20 Reales 1850–55   60.00 95.00 160.00

Gold

A23 *F179–180a* 1 Doblon
(100 Reales) 1850–51   200.00 250.00 450.00

B23 *F181* 100 Reales
1851–55   185.00 225.00 375.00

Second Decimal Coinage
100 Centimos = 1 Real 1854–64

Copper

24 5 Centimos de Real
1854–64   6.00 20.00 50.00

---

25 10 Centimos 1854–64   5.00 20.00 45.00
26 25 Centimos 1854–64   6.00 30.00 65.00
Nos. 24–25 dated 1854 are believed to be patterns.

Silver

Rev: Arms without pillars

27 1 Real 1857–64   10.00 15.00 25.00
28 2 Reales 1857–64   12.00 20.00 30.00
29 4 Reales 1856–64   10.00 20.00 30.00

Rev: Arms flanked by pillars

30 10 Reales 1857–64   20.00 35.00 75.00
31 20 Reales 1856–64   50.00 80.00 125.00

Gold

Rev: Oval arms on cartouche

32 *F184* 20 Reales
1861–63   150.00 225.00 300.00
33 *F183* 40 Reales
1861–63   90.00 125.00 200.00
35 *F182* 100 Reales
1856–62   150.00 200.00 350.00
Rev: Mantled arms
A35 *F186* 40 Reales 1864   80.00 115.00 165.00
B35 *F185* 100 Reales
1863–64   150.00 200.00 275.00

Third Decimal Coinage
100 Centimos = 1 Escudo 1864–68

Bronze

431

36	½ Centimo de Escudo			
	1866–68	7.00	15.00	25.00
37	1 Centimo 1866–68	5.00	10.00	20.00
38*	2½ Centimos 1866–68	6.00	12.00	30.00
39	5 Centimos 1866–68	8.00	17.00	40.00

Nos. 37–39 dated 1865 are patterns.

Silver

40	10 Centimos 1864–68	10.00	30.00	60.00
41	20 Centimos 1865–68	20.00	50.00	100.00
42	40 Centimos 1864–68	10.00	20.00	60.00
	Rev. Arms flanked by pillars			
43	1 Escudo 1865–68	15.00	25.00	60.00
44	2 Escudos 1865–68	50.00	80.00	125.00
	1865,66 . . . Rare.			

For similar silver coins 1864–68 with values in Centimos de Peso, see PHILIPPINES.

Gold

45	F189 2 Escudos 1865	125.00	225.00	300.00
46	F188 4 Escudos			
	1865–68	90.00	125.00	200.00
47	F187 10 Escudos			
	1865–68	150.00	200.00	300.00

PROVISIONAL ISSUES 1868–1870
(Nos. A50–60)

Battle of Alcolea Bridge

Bronze

A50	25 Milesimas de Escudo			
	1868	35.00	70.00	190.00

Dates on Spanish Coins
Beginning in 1868 (starting with 1868 dates of Nos. 41–47) most Spanish coins bear two dates. The large, obvious date is the year of authorization, and does not necessarily correspond to the year of coinage. True dates of coinage appear as tiny incuse numerals on the *six-pointed stars* found on most types. In the following listings the large dates are shown in normal fashion. Coinage dates are indicated by * within parentheses.

Coins in this catalog which do *not* have stars with small incuse dates are Nos. A50–54, 63–67, 69–70, 100–107, 103–106, 109–112.

New Coinage System
100 Centimos = 1 Peseta 1869–

Bronze

51	1 Centimo 1870	.50	5.00	10.00
52	2 Centimos 1870	.50	5.00	10.00
53*	5 Centimos 1870	.60	10.00	35.00
54	10 Centimos 1870	.50	10.00	50.00

Obv. legend: GOBIERNO PROVISIONAL
Silver

A55	1 Peseta 1869 (*69)	15.00	50.00	225.00

New obv. legend: ESPANA
Silver

55	20 Centimos 1869–70			
	(*69–70)	225.00	600.00	850.00
56	50 Centimos 1869–70			
	(*69–70)	25.00	100.00	300.00
58	1 Peseta 1869–70			
	(*69–73)	10.00	30.00	150.00
59	2 Pesetas 1869–70			
	(*69–75)	9.00	30.00	100.00
60	5 Pesetas 1869–70			
	(*69–71)	25.00	60.00	175.00
	1869 . . . Rare.			

Unless otherwise noted, prices are for coins in very fine, extremely fine, and uncirculated condition.

AMADEO I 1871–1873

61 5 Pesetas 1871 (*71–75)   25.00 60.00 150.00

REPUBLIC 1873–1874
Cartagena Mint
Silver

64 10 Reales (2½ Pesetas)
   1873   150.00 225.00 350.00
63 5 Pesetas 1873   125.00 175.00 225.00
Former No. 62, 2 Pesetas 1873 is thought to be a fantasy struck later for collectors.

CARLOS VII, Pretender
1872–1876, 1885
Bronze

66 5 Centimos 1875   20.00 40.00 100.00
67 10 Centimos 1875   20.00 50.00 100.00
Silver coins of Carlos VII 1874–85 are fantasies struck later for collectors.

ALFONSO XII 1875–1885
First Coinage

Silver
Obv: Legend REY DE ESPANA
74 5 Pesetas 1875–76
   (*75–76)   20.00 50.00 150.00

Second Coinage

Bronze

69 5 Centimos 1877–79   6.00 30.00 60.00
70 10 Centimos 1877–79   6.00 30.00 60.00

Silver

Obv: Legend POR LA G. DE DIOS
B75 1 Peseta 1876 (*76)   20.00 90.00 200.00
75 5 Pesetas 1877–82
   (*77–82)   25.00 90.00 200.00

Gold

77 F194 10 Pesetas
   1878–79 (*78–79,
   1961–62)   150.00 225.00 350.00
78 F193 25 Pesetas
   1876–80 (*76–80, 1962) 170.00 225.00 275.00

Third Coinage

Silver

Obv: Head with sideburns, moustache

A76 50 Centimos 1880–85
   (*80–86)   4.00   10.00   20.00
B76 1 Peseta 1881–85
   (*81–86)   20.00   50.00 125.00
C76 2 Pesetas 1879–84
   (*79–84)   20.00   40.00 100.00
76 5 Pesetas 1882–85
   (*82–87)   25.00 100.00 250.00

Gold

A78 *F195* 25 Pesetas
   1881–85 (*81–86)   170.00 225.00 275.00
1885 . . . Rare.

ALFONSO XIII 1886–1931
First Coinage

Silver

79 50 Centimos 1889, 92
   (*89, 92)   4.00   10.00   20.00
80 1 Peseta 1889, 91 (*89,
   91)   20.00   60.00 150.00
81 2 Pesetas 1889–92
   (*89–92)   30.00   60.00 200.00
82* 5 Pesetas 1888–92
   (*88–92)   25.00 100.00 200.00

Gold

A82 *F196* 20 Pesetas
   1887–90 (*89–90,
   1961–62)   175.00 250.00 350.00

Second Coinage
Silver

83 50 Centimos 1894 (*94)   30.00   80.00 130.00
84 1 Peseta 1893–94
   (*93–94)   35.00 100.00 225.00
85 2 Pesetas 1894 (*94)   100.00 225.00 500.00
86 5 Pesetas 1892–94
   (*92–94)   30.00 130.00 250.00

Gold

A86 *F197* 20 Pesetas 1892
   (*92)   1000.   1700.   2500.

Third Coinage
Silver

87 50 Centimos 1896, 1900
   (*96,00)   4.00   10.00   20.00
88 1 Peseta 1896–1902
   (*96–02)   15.00   30.00   65.00
89 5 Pesetas 1896–99
   (*96–99)   20.00   40.00   90.00

Gold

Unless otherwise noted, prices are for coins in very fine, extremely fine, and uncirculated condition.

A89 *F199* 20 Pesetas 1896,
99 (*99, 1961–62)   170.00 250.00 350.00
90 *F198* 100 Pesetas 1897
(*97, 1961–62)   900.00 1200. 2000.

Fourth Coinage

Bronze

96 1 Centimo 1906 (*6)   1.00   3.00   6.00
97 2 Centimos 1904–05
(*04–05)   1.00   3.00   6.00

Silver

92 50 Centimos 1904 (*04,
10)   4.00   10.00   20.00
94 1 Peseta 1903–05 (*03,
05)   12.50   25.00   50.00
95 2 Pesetas 1905 (*05)   8.00   12.00   20.00

Gold

91 *F200* 20 Pesetas 1904
(*04)   1000. 1700. 2250.

Fifth Coinage
Bronze

98 1 Centimo 1911–13
(*1–3)   1.00   3.00   6.00

---

99 2 Centimos 1911–12
(*11–12)   1.00   3.00   6.00

Silver

93 50 Centimos 1910 (*10)   4.00   10.00   20.00

Sixth Coinage

Nickel-Brass

100 25 Centimos 1925   1.50   4.00   15.00

Cupro-Nickel

101 25 Centimos 1927   1.00   3.00   10.00

Silver

102 50 Centimos 1926   4.00   9.00   15.00

REPUBLIC 1931–1938

(Republica Espanola)

First Coinage

Nickel-Bronze

107 25 Centimos 1934   1.00   3.00   7.00

Silver

108 1 Peseta 1933 (*34)   7.00   15.00   22.00

Second Coinage

Iron

103 5 Centimos 1937   3.00   6.00   12.00
The iron 10 Centimos 1938 is a pattern.

Copper

104 25 Centimos 1938   4.00   12.00   20.00

105 50 Centimos 1937 (*34,
36)   2.00   8.00   15.00

Brass

106 1 Peseta 1937   1.00.   6.00   10.00

NATIONALIST
GOVERNMENT 1937–1947
Monarchy declared under regency of Franco, 1947.

First Coinage

Cupro-Nickel

109 25 Centimos 1937   .50   4.00   10.00

Aluminum

110 5 Centimos 1940–53   .50   5.00   15.00
111 10 Centimos 1940–53   .30   5.00   15.00

Aluminum-Bronze

112 1 Peseta 1944   .80   5.00   15.00

Second Coinage

Cupro-Nickel

Rev: Arrows pointing down
115 20 Centimos 1949 (*51)   3.50   10.00   17.50

Rev: Arrows pointing up
116 50 Centimos 1949, 63
(*51–65)   .50   3.00   8.00

Unless otherwise noted, prices are for coins in very
fine, extremely fine, and uncirculated condition.

Aluminum-Bronze

113 1 Peseta 1947–63
(*48–67)   .60   4.00   10.00
114 2½ Pesetas 1953
(*54–71)   1.00   4.00   9.00

Nickel

117 5 Pesetas 1949 (*49–50)   5.00   10.00   15.00
Later issues in *Current Coins of the World.*

VISCAYAN REPUBLIC (Euzkadi)
A province of Spain of the Bay of Biscay, autonomous in 1936–37. Capital and chief port: Bilbao.

Nickel

1 1 Peseta 1937   3.00   9.00   15.00
2 2 Pesetas 1937   3.00   9.00   15.00

STRAITS SETTLEMENTS

A British Crown Colony until 1946 when it was dissolved to form the Malayan Federation. Much of the United States' tin and rubber was imported from the Straits. Taken by Japan during World War II, it was returned to Britain in 1945. Capital and chief port: Singapore.

Monetary System:
100 Cents = 1 Dollar

VICTORIA 1837–1901

Legend:
EAST INDIA COMPANY
Copper

1 ¼ Cent 1845   10.00   18.50   45.00
2 ½ Cent 1845   10.00   25.00   50.00
3 1 Cent 1845   8.00   22.50   50.00

Legend Changed: INDIA STRAITS

4 ¼ Cent 1862   50.00 100.00 225.00
                         Proof . . . 450.00
5 ½ Cent 1862   30.00   75.00 125.00
                         Proof . . . 400.00
6 1 Cent 1862   12.50   35.00   75.00
                         Proof . . . 250.00

New Legend: STRAITS SETTLEMENTS

Edge: Plain
7 ¼ Cent 1872–84   8.00   20.00   45.00
      1873 . . . 120. 1883 . . . 400. Proof . . . 185.00
8 ½ Cent 1872–84   9.00   35.00   75.00
      1873 . . . 60. 1883 . . . 100. Proof . . . 375.00
9 1 Cent 1872–86   5.00   15.00   35.00
      1878 . . . 125.   Proof . . . 175.00
Edge: Reeded
7a ¼ Cent 1889–1901   5.00   15.00   40.00
      1898 Proof only . . . 200.
8a ½ Cent 1889–91   20.00   45.00   75.00
      1890–91 Proof only . . . 400.
9a 1 Cent 1887–1901   3.00   15.00   40.00
      1898 . . . 10.   Proof . . . 175.00

Silver

13 5 Cents 1871–1901   3.50   9.00   30.00
      1871 . . . 400.   1873 . . . 700.   Proof . . . 300.00
      1876 . . . 600.   1877 . . . 400.
14 10 Cents 1871–1901   3.25   8.00   28.50
      1883-H . . . 100.   Proof . . . 200.00
15 20 Cents 1871–1901   5.00   12.50   30.00
      1871 . . . 525.   1873 . . . 500.   Proof . . . 325.00
16 50 Cents 1886–1901   40.00   80.00   200.00
      1889 . . . 875.   1893 . . . 550.

EDWARD VII 1901–1910

Copper
Rev: Designs like Nos. 10–12

17 ¼ Cent 1904–08   5.00   15.00   40.00
      1904 Proof only . . . 450.
18 ½ Cent 1904, 08   4.50   12.50   30.00
      1904 Proof only . . . 300.
19 1 Cent 1903–08   3.00   9.00   25.00
      Proof . . . 200.00

Silver

20 5 Cents 1902–10   3.00   7.00   10.00
      Proof . . . 225.00
21 10 Cents 1902–10   2.50   4.00   10.00
      Proof . . . 175.00
22 20 Cents 1902–10   5.00   12.50   30.00
      Proof . . . 225.00
23 50 Cents 1902–05
      (31mm)   50.00 100.00 175.00
      Proof . . . 800.00

Note: in 1909 the fineness of Nos. 20–22 was reduced
from .800 to .600.

24 50 Cents/½ Dollar
      1907–08 (28mm)   10.00   20.00   40.00
      Proof . . . 175.00

25* 1 Dollar 1903–04 (37mm)   20.00   35.00   60.00
      Proof . . . 750.00
25a 1 Dollar 1907–09 (34mm)   12.50   20.00   50.00
      Proof . . . 475.00

GEORGE V 1910–1936

Copper

27 ¼ Cent 1916   3.00   4.50   8.00
      Proof . . . 200.00
28 ½ Cent 1916   3.00   5.00   10.00
      Proof . . . 275.00

Bronze

29 ½ Cent 1932   1.75   4.50   9.50
      Proof . . . 200.00
30 1 Cent 1919–26   .75   3.50   10.00
      Proof . . . 100.00

Cupro-Nickel

31 5 Cents 1920   10.00   35.00   75.00
      Proof . . . 200.00

**Unless otherwise noted, prices are for coins in very
fine, extremely fine, and uncirculated condition.**

Silver

32	5 Cents 1918–20	2.00	5.00	10.00
	1920 . . . 125.			
32a	5 Cents 1926, 35, modified obv.	1.00	3.00	5.00
	Proof . . . 200.00			
34	10 Cents 1916–27	1.00	2.00	3.00
	Proof . . . 175.00			
35	20 Cents 1916–35	3.00	5.00	9.50
	Proof . . . 200.00			
36	50 Cents 1920–21	3.50	5.00	6.50
	Proof . . . 175.00			

Note: Nos. 34 and 35 were struck in both .600 and .400 silver.

37	1 Dollar 1919–26	18.50	25.00	45.00
	1925–26 Proof only . . . 1200.			

Modern restrikes exist.

See MALAYA for later issues.

THE SUDAN

The Sudan, located along the Nile River in northeastern Africa, is the continent's largest country. First conquered and unified by Egypt in the early 19th century, it revolted in 1881 and issued its first coinage. The country was retaken in 1898 and was made a joint British-Egyptian protectorate. Full independence came in 1956. Primarily an agricultural nation, its main exports are cotton, gum arabic and livestock. Area: 967,500 square miles. Languages: Arabic and native dialects. Capital: *Khartoum.*

Monetary System:
40 Para = 1 Ghirsh (Piastre) 1885–98
10 Millim = 1 Ghirsh 1956–

Prices for Nos. 1–32 are for Very Fine Coins

EL MAHDI 1881–1885

Silver

1	10 Ghirsh AH 1302 (1885)	–
2*	20 Ghirsh 1302	300.00

No. 1 was reliably reported in 1894, but its existence today is unconfirmed.

Gold

3	100 Ghirsh AH 1255, Yr. 2 (1840)	–

No. 3 is a crude copy, including date, of the same Egyptian coin.

KHALIFA ABDULLAH
1885–1898
Copper

3	5 Para 1308 (1891)	–
4	10 Para 1308	–

Nos. 3 and 4 are now thought to be patterns.

Silver or Billon

Borders of double crescents

6*	5 Ghirsh 1304, 11 (1887, 94)	35.00
7	10 Ghirsh 1304, 11	125.00
8	20 Ghirsh 1304, 09	50.00

Plain borders

9	1 Ghirsh 1304, 11	125.00
10	2 Ghirsh 1310–11	100.00
12*	5 Ghirsh 1310	75.00
13	10 Ghirsh 1310	125.00

Copper or Billon

Borders of crescents, stars and roses

16	2½ Ghirsh 1312 (1895)	50.00
17	5 Ghirsh 1311	50.00
19*	20 Ghirsh 1310 (?)–12	20.00

30	10 Ghirsh 1310	150.00
31*	20 Ghirsh 1310–15, spears on rev.	15.00
32	20 Ghirsh 1312–15, spears on obv.	10.00

Borders of crescents only

22	2½ Ghirsh 1312	60.00
23	5 Ghirsh 1311	75.00
24	20 Ghirsh 1311–12, rev. legend as No. 19	35.00
25*	20 Ghirsh 1312, rev. legend as No.12	25.00

REPUBLIC 1956–69

The following valuations are for Uncirculated coins
Bronze

34	1 Millim 1956–69	.20

35	2 Millim 1956–69	.25
36*	5 Millim 1956–69 (scalloped)	.30
37	10 Millim 1956–96	.35

Cupro-Nickel

27	2 Ghirsh 1311	50.00

38*	2 Ghirsh 1956 (17.5mm)	.80

Unless otherwise noted, prices are for coins in very fine, extremely fine, and uncirculated condition.

38a 2 Ghirsh 1963–69 (20mm)   .50
39 5 Ghirsh 1956–69   .75
40 10 Ghirsh 1956–69   1.25
41 20 Ghirsh 1967–69   Proof . . . 12.50

F.A.O. Coinage

42 25 Ghirsh 1968   Proof . . . 12.50
Later issues in *Current Coins of the World.*

SWEDEN (Sverige)

A constitutional monarchy in the eastern part of the Scandinavian peninsula of Northern Europe. Its main exports are iron ore and wood products. About ⅕ of its total production is for foreign trade. Area: 173,378 square miles. Language: Swedish. Capital: *Stockholm.*

Monetary System:
100 Ore = 1 Riksdaler Riksmynt to 1873
100 Ore = 1 Krona 1873–

CARL XV 1859–1872
Bronze

1 ½ Ore 1867   12.50 27.50 55.00

2 1 Ore 1860–72   3.00 5.00 12.00
    1860 . . . 40.
3 2 Ore 1860–72   5.00 10.00 25.00
    1860 . . . 30.
4 5 Ore 1860–72   11.00 27.50 55.00
    1860 . . . 70

Silver

5 10 Ore 1861–71   7.00 17.50 35.00
    1862 . . . 1400.

6 25 Ore 1862–71   25.00 50.00 100.00
    1862 . . . 1700.
7 50 Ore 1862   1200. 1800. 2650.

8 1 Riksdaler Riksm.
    1860–71   80.00 160.00 275.00
    1862 . . . 1700.
9* 2 Riksdaler Riksm.
    1862–71   275.00 550.00 900.00
    1862 . . . 3500.
10 4 Riksdaler Riksm.
    1861–71   250.00 350.00 500.00

Gold
B10 *F68* 1 Dukat 1860–68   300.00 600.00 1000.
1867 . . . 600.

A10 *F69* 1 Carolin/10 Francs
    1868–72   250.00 350.00 500.00
1871–72 . . . 450.

OSCAR II 1872–1907
First Coinage
Bronze

11 1 Ore 1873   8.50 17.00 40.00
12 2 Ore 1873   19.00 45.00 70.00
13 5 Ore 1873   35.00 70.00 140.00

Silver

| 17 | 10 Ore 1872–73 | 9.00 | 12.00 | 18.00 |
| 18 | 1 Riksdaler Riksm. 1873 | 450.00 | 725.00 | 1050. |

Second Coinage
Bronze

14	1 Ore 1874–77, sm. letters	12.50	25.00	55.00
	1876–77 . . . 35.			
14a	1 Ore 1877–79, med. letters	12.50	25.00	65.00
	1877–78 . . . 30.			
14b	1 Ore 1879–1905, lg. letters	2.50	6.00	12.00
	1879 . . . 250. 1892 . . . 70.			
15	2 Ore 1874–78	10.00	35.00	70.00
	1876,77 . . . 20. 1878 . . . 90.			
15a	2 Ore 1877–1905, diff. lettering	4.00	10.00	35.00
	1877–78, 80 . . . 25.			
16	5 Ore 1874–89	25.00	60.00	150.00
	1877, 79 . . . 85. 1880 . . . 55.			
16a	5 Ore 1888–1905, diff. lettering	6.00	18.00	55.00
	1888 . . . 250.			

Silver

19	10 Ore 1874–76	30.00	60.00	120.00
	1875 . . . 100.			
20	25 Ore 1874–78	30.00	60.00	180.00
	1875 . . . 80. 1878 . . . 130.			
21	50 Ore 1875–99	30.00	60.00	180.00
	1877 . . . 180. 1878–81 . . . 60.			

| 27 | 10 Ore 1880–1904 | 5.00 | 12.50 | 50.00 |
| | 1880–82 . . . 50. 1883–91 . . . 20 | | | |

| 28 | 25 Ore 1880–1905 | 5.00 | 12.50 | 50.00 |
| | 1880–81 . . . 12.50. | | | |

Obv: Legend SVERIGES O. NORGES

| 22 | 1 Krona 1875–76 | 45.00 | 150.00 | 375.00 |
| 23 | 2 Kronor 1876–80 | 95.00 | 350.00 | 825.00 |

Gold

25	*F71* 10 Kronor 1873–76	75.00	125.00	200.00
26	*F70* 20 Kronor 1873–76	225.00	335.00	525.00
27	*F70* 20 Kronor 1876–77, modified arms	225.00	335.00	525.00

Silver
Obv: Legend SVERIGES OCH NORGES

22a	1 Krona 1877–89	60.00	150.00	550.00
	1879, 87–88 . . . 120.			
23a	2 Kronor 1878, 80	145.00	500.00	1200.
	1878 . . . 1000.			

Gold

| 24 | *F72* 5 Kronor 1881–99 | 75.00 | 125.00 | 190.00 |
| | 1882, 83 . . . 140. | | | |

25a	*F71* 10 Kronor 1876–95	85.00	140.00	225.00
26a	*F70* 20 Kronor 1877–99	185.00	265.00	450.00
	1879, 81, 87 . . . 425. 1885..1750.			

Silver

Obv: Older head

Unless otherwise noted, prices are for coins in very
fine, extremely fine, and uncirculated condition.

29	1 Krona 1890–1904	30.00	90.00	215.00
30	2 Kronor 1890–1904	50.00	180.00	350.00
	1890, 93, 1903 . . . 120.			

Gold

24a	*F72* 5 Kronor 1901	75.00	125.00	190.00
25b	*F71* 10 Kronor 1901	70.00	120.00	175.00
26b	*F70* 20 Kronor 1900–02	245.00	300.00	500.00

25th Year of Reign

Silver

31	2 Kronor 1897	8.50	15.00	35.00

Third Coinage

Bronze

32	1 Ore 1906–07	1.00	3.00	12.00
	1906 . . . 12.			
33*	2 Ore 1906–07	1.00	8.00	25.00
	1906 . . . 10.			
34	5 Ore 1906–07	3.00	15.00	50.00

Billon

35	10 Ore 1907	2.50	9.00	25.00

Silver

36	25 Ore 1907	3.50	15.00	45.00
37	50 Ore 1906–07	3.00	15.00	55.00

38	1 Krona 1906–07	17.50	50.00	170.00
39	2 Kronor 1906–07	25.00	95.00	250.00
	1900 . . . 50.			

Golden Wedding Anniversary

40	2 Kronor 1907	8.50	15.00	40.00

GUSTAF V 1907–1950
Regular Issues

Bronze

44	1 Ore 1909–50	.50	1.00	5.00
	1909, 22 . . . 7.			
45	2 Ore 1909–50	.50	2.50	6.00
	1912 . . . 10.			
46	5 Ore 1909–50	1.00	5.00	15.00
	1910 . . . 300. 1927 . . . 200.			

Billon

47	10 Ore 1909–19, 27–42	1.00	1.50	7.00
	1909–16 . . . 5			

Silver

48	25 Ore 1910–19, 27–41	1.00	2.00	9.00

49 50 Ore 1911–19, 27–39   2.50   8.00   22.00
        1911–19 . . . 15.

Nickel-Bronze

55 10 Ore 1920–47   .50   2.00   9.00
        1925 . . . 6

56 25 Ore 1921–47   .75   5.00   20.00
        1921 . . . 8.
57 50 Ore 1920–47   1.50   6.00   30.00
        1920, 24 . . . 9 1921 . . . 25.

Silver

50 1 Krona 1910–42   3.50   6.00   12.50
        1910–28 . . . 10. 1942 . . . 80.
51 2 Kronor 1910–40   6.50   7.50   13.00
        1910–30, 37 . . . 11.

Gold

62 *F74* 5 Kronor 1920   85.00 130.00 190.00

63 *F73* 20 Kronor 1925   550.00 850.00 1100.

WORLD WAR I ISSUES
Designs of Nos. 44–46

Iron

52 1 Ore 1917–19   2.50   5.00   12.00
53 2 Ore 1917–19   3.00   10.00   25.00
        1919 . . . 12.
54 5 Ore 1917–19   15.00   30.00   70.00
        1918, 19 . . . 25.

COMMEMORATIVE ISSUES
400th Anniversary of Political Liberty

Silver

Obv: King Gustaf Vasa, 1521–60

58 2 Kronor 1921   7.00   11.00   20.00

300th Anniversary Death of Gustaf II Adolf

59 2 Kronor 1932   8.00   12.00   25.00

Unless otherwise noted, prices are for coins in very fine, extremely fine, and uncirculated condition.

500th Anniversary of the Riksdag

60	5 Kronor 1935	12.00 15.00 25.00	

300th Anniversary of Delaware Settlement

61	2 Kronor 1938	6.50 8.50 17.50	

Regular Issues

Billon

64	10 Ore 1942–50	.50	1.25	5.00
65	25 Ore 1943–50	.50	1.25	5.00
66	50 Ore 1943–50	1.00	3.50	15.00

67	1 Krona 1942–50	1.50	2.50	10.00
68	2 Kronor 1942–50	2.50	3.50	11.00
	1943 . . . 6.			

World War II Issues

Iron

69	1 Ore 1942–50	.25	1.00	4.50
70	2 Ore 1942–50	.50	2.00	10.00
71	5 Ore 1942–50	1.00	4.50	15.00

GUSTAF VI ADOLF 1950–1973

Bronze

72	1 Ore 1952–71	.10	.15	.50
73	2 Ore 1952–71	.10	.15	.50
74	5 Ore 1952–71	.10	.25	.50

Billon

75	10 Ore 1952–62	.50	1.00	4.50
76	25 Ore 1952–61	.50	1.00	6.00
77	50 Ore 1952–61	1.00	5.00	18.00

Silver

78 1 Krona 1952–68   1.50   2.00   4.50

79 2 Kronor 1952–66   3.00   4.00   6.00

80 5 Kronor 1954–71   4.00   5.00   7.50

Clad Cupro-Nickel

78a 1 Krona 1968–73   .10   .25   1.00

Cupro-Nickel

79a 2 Kronor 1968–71   .75   1.00   1.50

King's 70th Birthday
Silver

81 5 Kronor 1952   15.00   25.00   45.00

Sesquicentennial
Constitution of 1809
Silver

82 5 Kronor 1959   5.00   10.00   15.00
Later issues in *Current Coins of the World*.

SWITZERLAND
(Helvetia,
Confoederatio Helvetica)

A confederated republic bounded by Germany, France, Austria, Liechtenstein and Italy. It forms no military alliances and is not a member of the United Nations. It is noted for its cheese, precision instruments and wines. Area: 15,944 square miles. Languages: German, French, Italian. Capital: *Berne*.

Unless otherwise noted, prices are for coins in very fine, extremely fine, and uncirculated condition.

Monetary System:
100 Rappen (Centimes) = 1 Frank (Franc)

SHOOTING FESTIVAL COINS
Silver

1-S 4 Franken 1842, Chur   850.00   1050.   2250.

4-S 5 Franken 1857, Bern   300.00 475.00   1000.

2-S 40 Batzen 1847, Glarus   1800.   3150.   4000.

5-S 5 Franken 1859, Zurich   200.00 315.00 850.00

3-S 5 Franken 1855, Soloth-
    urn   1200.   2000.   5000.
(Design as No. 29)

6-S	5 Franken 1861, Nidwalden	275.00	375.00	750.00
7-S	5 Franken 1863, La Chaux-de-Fonds	275.00	375.00	750.00
8-S	5 Franken 1865, Schaffhausen	125.00	250.00	450.00
9-S	5 Franken 1867, Schwyz	125.00	225.00	525.00
10-S	5 Franken 1869, Zug	200.00	275.00	725.00
11-S	5 Franken 1872, Zurich	125.00	175.00	425.00
12-S	5 Franken 1874, St. Gallen	100.00	125.00	325.00
13-S	5 Franken 1876, Lausanne	90.00	120.00	325.00
14-S	5 Franken 1879, Basel	85.00	110.00	325.00

15-S	5 Francs 1881, Fribourg	85.00	110.00	325.00
16-S	5 Franken 1883, Lugano	75.00	85.00	325.00
17-S	5 Franken 1885, Bern	85.00	120.00	325.00

Modern Series

44	5 Francs 1934, Fribourg	30.00	50.00	110.00
47	5 Francs 1939, Luzern	50.00	75.00	110.00

Gold

45	*F11* 100 Francs 1934, Fribourg	1500.	2250.	3000.
48	*F12* 100 Franken 1939, Luzern	500.00	700.00	950.00

Regular Issues

Bronze

18	1 Centime 1850–1941	.50	1.00	4.00

1855 . . . 90. 1863 . . . 225.
1864 . . . 240. 1896 . . . Rare.

19	2 Centimes 1850–1941	.75	1.50	3.00

1870 . . . 45. 1896 . . . Rare.

Zinc

18a	1 Centime 1942–46	.50	1.00	5.00
19a	2 Centimes 1942–46	.75	1.50	7.50

Billon

20	5 Centimes 1850–77	15.00	27.50	75.00

1851 . . . 400.

21	10 Centimes 1850–76	45.00	70.00	100.00

1851 . . . 60. 1875 . . . 700.

22	20 Centimes 1850–59	20.00	45.00	125.00

1851 . . . 150.

Cupro-Nickel

23	5 Centimes 1879–1931, 1940–	.20	.50	1.00

1896 . . . Rare.

24	10 Centimes 1879–1931, 1940–	.20	.50	1.00

1896 . . . Rare

25	20 Centimes 1939–	.25	.60	1.25

Nickel

23a	5 Centimes 1932–41	.35	1.00	5.00
24a	10 Centimes 1932–39	.25	1.00	10.00
25a	20 Centimes 1881–1938	.35	1.50	12.50

Brass

23b	5 Centimes 1918	20.00	22.50	30.00
24b	10 Centimes 1918–19	27.50	37.50	50.00

1919 . . . 90.

Unless otherwise noted, prices are for coins in very fine, extremely fine, and uncirculated condition.

Silver

26	½ Franc 1850–51	120.00	225.00	500.00
27	1 Franc 1850–61	165.00	300.00	550.00
	1857 . . . Rare. 1860 . . . 225.			
28	2 Francs 1850–63	120.00	225.00	650.00
	1850, 63 . . . 225. 1857 . . . Rare.			
29	5 Francs 1850–74	225.00	285.00	500.00
	1873 . . . 900.			

36	5 Francs 1931–69, smaller size	7.50	11.00	15.00
	1952 . . . 60. 1968 . . . Rare.			

30	½ Franc 1875–1967	1.50	2.50	3.50
	1875 . . . 90 1877, 78 . . . 120.			
	1879 . . . 75 1896 . . . Rare.			
31	1 Franc 1875–1967	3.00	4.50	6.00
	1875, 80 . . . 100. 1896 . . . Rare.			
32	2 Francs 1874–1967	5.00	9.00	12.50
	1896 . . . Rare 1901 . . . 225.			

Gold

40	*F5* 20 Francs 1883, reeded edge	125.00	185.00	300.00
40a	*F5* 20 Francs 1886–96, lettered edge	125.00	185.00	275.00

41	*F7* 20 Francs 1897–1935, stars on edge	100.00	115.00	145.00
41a	*F7* 20 Francs 1947, 49, lettered edge	100.00	115.00	145.00

33	5 Francs 1888–1916	200.00	350.00	650.00
	1896, 1912 . . . Rare 1916 . . . 850.			

Obv: Like No. 36

34	5 Fr (ancs) 1922–23	95.00	140.00	250.00
34a	5 FR (ancs) 1924–28	175.00	240.00	350.00
	1924 . . . 350. 1928 . . . Rare.			

42	*F9–10* 10 Francs
	1911–22	100.00 120.00 140.00
	1911 . . . 200.
43	*F8* 100 Francs 1925	5000. 7000. 9500.

COMMEMORATIVE ISSUES
Armament Fund
Silver

| 46 | 5 Francs 1936 | 25.00 40.00 50.00 |

600th Anniversary
Battle of Laupen

| 49 | 5 Francs 1939 | 300.00 400.00 500.00 |

Zurich Exposition

| 50 | 5 Francs 1939 | 50.00 100.00 150.00 |

650th Anniversary of
Confederation 1291–1941

| 51 | 5 Francs 1941 | 40.00 65.00 85.00 |

500th Anniversary Battle of
St. Jakob an der Birs

| 52 | 5 Francs 1944 | 40.00 65.00 85.00 |

Centennial of
Swiss Confederation

| 53 | 5 Francs 1948 | 40.00 65.00 85.00 |

Regular Issues

Bronze

| 54 | 1 Centime 1948– | .10 | .20 | .30 |
| 55 | 2 Centimes 1948– | .10 | .20 | .30 |

Later issues in *Current Coins of the World.*

Unless otherwise noted, prices are for coins in very
fine, extremely fine, and uncirculated condition.

SYRIA

In western Asia, bordered by Turkey on the north. It was part of the Turkish Empire until 1920, when it was made an independent state under French mandate. In 1944 it was given complete independence and proclaimed a republic. On February 21, 1958 Syria joined Egypt as part of the United Arab Republic.

It broke away and declared itself independent again on September 29, 1961. The principal industries are farming and cattle raising. Area: 72,234 square miles.

Languages: Arabic, French. Capital: Damascus.

Monetary System:
100 Ghirsh (Piastres) = 1 Lira (Pound)

Prices, except where noted, are for coins in Very Fine condition.

First Coinage
Cupro-Nickel

1	½ Piastre 1921	1.00

Second Coinage
Nickel-Bronze

4	½ Piastre 1935–36	1.25

5	1 Piastre 1929–36	.75

Zinc
5a	1 Piastre 1940	.75

Aluminum-Bronze

2	2 Piastres 1926	5.00
3	5 Piastres 1926–40	.75
6	2½ Piastres 1940, like No. 5	.75

Silver

7	10 Piastres 1929	5.00
8*	25 Piastres 1929–37	3.00
9	50 Piastres 1929–37	7.50

World War II Issues
Brass

10	1 Piastre ND	1.50

Aluminum
11*	2½ Piastres ND	5.00

REPUBLIC 1944–1958
Cupro-Nickel

12	2½ Piastres 1948–56	.25

13	5 Piastres 1948, 56	.60
14*	10 Piastres 1948, 56	.60

Silver

15	25 Piastres 1947	2.00
16	50 Piastres 1947	2.25

17 1 Lira 1950   3.50

Gold

18* F2 ½ Pound 1950   UNC . . . 75.00
19 F1 1 Pound 1950   UNC . . . 175.00

UNITED ARAB REPUBLIC
1958–1961

Silver

A19 25 Ghirsh 1958   UNC . . . 2.00

B19 50 Ghirsh 1958   UNC . . . 3.00

Founding of the Republic

20 50 Ghirsh 1959   UNC . . . 7.00

Regular Issues

Aluminum-Bronze

21 2½ Ghirsh 1960   UNC . . .25

22 5 Ghirsh 1960   UNC 35

23 10 Ghirsh 1960   UNC 50
Later issues in *Current Coins of the World*.

TARIM and GHURFAH —
see ARABIAN
SULTANATES

THAILAND (Siam)

A constitutional monarchy in southeast Asia, extending
down onto the Malay Peninsula. The name was officially
changed to Thailand in 1939. Exports: rice, teak, tungsten, rubber and tin. Area: 200,148 square miles. Capital: *Bangkok*.

Monetary System
to 1908:
8 Att = 1 Fuang
2 Fuang = 1 Salung
4 Salung = 1 Baht (Tical)
1897 and 1908 on:
100 Satang = 1 Baht

Thai Numerals

Western	1	2	3	4	5
Thai	๑	๒	๓	๔	๕

6	7	8	9	0	10
๖	๗	๘	๙	๐	๑๐

For details of dating system see Introduction in front of book.

Modern Coins of the Bangkok Dynasty
PHRA CHOM KLAO (MONGKUT) 1851–1868

Tin Compostion

5	¹⁄₁₆ Fuang ND (1862), 23mm	5.00	7.50	15.00
6*	⅛ Fuang ND	5.00	10.00	25.00

Contemporary counterfeits of Nos. 5–6 are common and are usually heavier than originals.

Cast Copper, Thick Flan (3mm)

1	¼ Fuang ND (1865), 22mm	30.00	50.00	100.00
2	½ Fuang ND (28mm)	30.00	50.00	100.00

Thin Flan (1.5mm)

3	¼ Fuang ND (1865)	40.00	60.00	125.00
4	½ Fuang ND	50.00	90.00	150.00

Silver

7	¹⁄₁₆ Baht ND (1860), 13mm	30.00	40.00	65.00
8	⅛ Baht ND (15mm)	5.00	10.00	20.00
9	¼ Baht ND (20mm)	25.00	50.00	100.00
10*	½ Baht ND	50.00	100.00	175.00
11	1 Baht ND (31mm)	15.00	40.00	85.00
12	2 Baht ND (37mm)	250.00	350.00	700.00
A12	4 Baht ND, rev. Chinese inscr.			Rare

Gold

13	2 Baht ND (1863, 95), as No.8	400.00	500.00	600.00

14	4 Baht ND (1863, 95)	300.00	400.00	600.00
15*	8 Baht ND (1863, 95)	500.00	750.00	950.00

Nos. 13–15 have reeded edges. Similar gold pieces with plain edges are presentation strikings of Nos. 7–A12.

Contemporary counterfeits of Nos. 7–15, A34 and 39 were made primarily to be worn as religious charms.

PHRA MAHA CHULALONGKORN 1868–1910
First Coinage

Tin

16	¹⁄₁₆ Fuang ND (1868)	10.00	20.00	40.00

Silver

Obv: Parasols in plain field

28	1 Fuang ND (1868)	5.00	10.00	20.00
29*	1 Salung ND	15.00	20.00	50.00
31	1 Baht ND	20.00	45.00	80.00

Second Coinage
Copper

17	½ Att CS 1236, 44 (1874, 82)	1.00	4.00	10.00

18*	1 Att 1236–44	2.00	4.00	8.00
19	2 Att 1236–44	4.00	6.00	12.00
20	4 Att 1238 (1876)	15.00	30.00	60.00

Bronze

21	½ Att CS 1249, RS 109–124 (1897–1905)	2.00	5.00	10.00
22	1 Att 1249, RS 109–124	2.00	4.00	8.00
23*	2 Att CS 1249, RS 109–124	2.00	5.00	10.00

Cupro-Nickel

24	2½ Satang RS 116 (1897)	2.00	4.00	6.00
25	5 Satang 116	10.00	15.00	20.00
26*	10 Satang 116	20.00	30.00	40.00
27	20 Satang 116	10.00	15.00	25.00

Silver

32	1 Fuang ND (1876–1902)	3.00	5.00	7.50
33*	1 Salung ND	5.00	10.00	20.00
34	1 Baht ND	10.00	15.00	35.00
	Rev: Date at bottom			
32a	1 Fuang RS 121–127 (1902–08)	3.00	5.00	7.50
33a	1 Salung RS 120–127	4.00	7.00	12.50
34a	1 Baht RS 120–126	10.00	15.00	35.00

Gold
Designs like Nos. 32–34

A34	2 Baht ND (1876)	–

Third Coinage
Silver

39	1 Baht RS 127 (1908)	125.00	175.00	225.00

Smaller coins of this design are patterns.

General Coinage
Nos. 35–37 were struck during four reigns without regal identification.

Bronze

50*	½ Satang BE 2480 (1937)	.50	1.00	2.00

35	1 Satang RS 127–130, BE 2456–80 (1908–37)	.75	1.00	2.00

Nickel

36	5 Satang RS 127–31, BE 2456–80	1.00	2.00	4.00
37	10 Satang RS 127–31, BE 2456–80	1.00	2.00	3.00

VAJIRAVUDH 1910–1925
Silver

43	1 Salung BE 2458–68 (1915–25)	2.00	4.00	6.00
44*	2 Salung 2458–64	4.00	6.00	8.50
45	1 Baht 2456–61	10.00	15.00	20.00

Unless otherwise noted, prices are for coins in very fine, extremely fine, and uncirculated condition.

PRAJADHIPOK 1925–1935

Silver

48	25 Satang BE 2472 (1929)	4.00	7.50	12.50
49*	50 Satang 2472	5.00	10.00	15.00

ANANDA MAHIDOL 1935–1946

Beginning with No. 51 coins bear a longer legend because of the change in name from Siam to Thailand.

Bronze

51	1 Satang BE 2482 (1939)	1.00	3.00	5.00

54*	1 Satang BE 2484 (1941)	.50	1.00	2.00

Silver

55	5 Satang 2484	2.00	3.00	4.00
56	10 Satang 2484	4.00	6.00	8.00
A56	20 Satang 2485	7.00	10.00	15.00

Tin Alloy

57	1 Satang 2485 (not holed)	.25	.50	1.00

No. 57 was restruck for circulation in 1969–71.

58*	5 Satang 2485	.75	1.50	3.00
59	10 Satang 2485	1.00	2.00	4.00

Values and B.E. Dates in "Western" numerals

60	1 Satang BE 2487 (not holed)	.15	.30	.60

Thick planchet

61	5 Satang BE 2487–88	.50	1.00	2.50
62	10 Satang 2487	1.00	2.00	3.00

Thin planchet

61a	5 Satang 2488	.50	1.00	2.50
62a	10 Satang 2488	1.00	2.00	4.00
63*	20 Satang 2488	1.00	2.00	4.00

Obv: Child bust of Ananda

64	5 Satang BE 2489 (1946)	.50	1.00	2.00
65	10 Satang 2489	.50	1.00	2.00
66*	20 Satang 2489	2.00	4.00	6.00
67	50 Satang 2489	10.00	30.00	60.00

Obv: Older bust

68	5 Satang 2489	.20	.50	1.00
69	10 Satang 2489	.50	.75	1.00
70	25 Satang 2489	.20	.50	1.00
71*	50 Satang 2489	1.00	1.25	1.75

PHUMIPHOL ADULYADET 1946–

Tin

Obv: Large bust, one medal on uniform

72	5 Satang BE 2493 (1950)	.50	1.00	2.00
73	10 Satang 2493	.50	1.00	1.50

Aluminum-Bronze

72a	5 Satang 2493	.25	.75	1.50
73a	10 Satang 2493	.50	1.00	2.00
76*	25 Satang 2493	1.00	2.00	3.00
77	50 Satang 2493	1.00	2.00	3.00

Later issues in *Current Coins of the World.*

5*	1 Sho ND (1908), 22mm	50.00	–	–
6	2 Sho ND (25mm)	125.00	–	–

Copper

A7	⅛ Sho Yr. 1 (1909), as No. 9, (22mm)		VF	100.00
B7	¼ Sho Yr. 1, as No. 9 (26mm)	100.00	–	–

Silver

8	5 Sho Yr. 1		–	–
9*	1 Srang Yr. 1, reeded edge	250.00	–	–

Varieties of No. 9 with plain edge are thought to be counterfeit.

TIBET

Until recent times this country high in the Himalaya and Kunlin Mountains of Central Asia was forbidden territory to strangers. It is now under the government of the People's Republic of China. The average altitude of the country is 16,000 feet. Area: 475,000 square miles. Capital: *Lhasa.*

Monetary System:
10 Skar = 1 Shokang
15 Skar = 1 Tangka
10 Sho = 1 Srang
3 Tangka = 1 Indian Rupee

In the Lhasa dialect, "srang" is pronounced "sang;" and "skar" is pronounced "kar" or "karma."

Most earlier issues are seldom encountered in grades above Very Fine. When found, they command substantial premiums.

CHINESE ISSUES
KUANG HSU 1875–1908

Struck in Szechuan Province for Tibet
Silver

1	¼ Rupee ND (ca. 1903), 19mm	50.00	75.00	125.00
2*	½ Rupee ND (ca. 1903), 24mm	60.00	90.00	150.00
3	1 Rupee ND (ca. 1903–38), vars.	20.00	30.00	60.00

HSUAN T'UNG 1908–1911

Copper

A4	½ Skar ND (1908), as No. 5	75.00	–	–
4	1 Skar ND, sim. (27mm)	125.00	–	–

Silver

TANGKA SYSTEM

Silver

A13	1 Tangka (1890–91)	10.00	20.00	–

13	1 Tangka ND (ca. 1840–1925)	4.00	6.00	–

Many varieties exist of No. 13. They all average about 4.4 grams.

14*	1 Tangka ND (1909)	5.00	10.00	–
15	2 Tangka ND (1912), as No. 13; 9.3 gr.		VF	200.00

Unless otherwise noted, prices are for coins in very fine, extremely fine, and uncirculated condition.

SRANG SYSTEM
First Coinage
Copper

| | 19 | 5 Skar (1918–25) | 4.00 | 8.00 | – |

	10*	2½ Skar (1909) 22mm	–	–	–
	A10	5 Skar (1909) 25mm	–	–	–
	11	7½ Skar (1909) 28mm	–	–	–

| 20 | 7½ Skar (1918–25) | 3.00 | 6.00 | – |

Silver

| 12 | 1 Srang (1909), plain edge | 250.00 | – | – |

| 21 | 1 Sho (1918–28), central legend horizontal on reverse | 1.00 | 1.50 | 3.00 |

Second Coinage
Copper

| 16 | 2½ Skar (1913–18) | 15.00 | – | – |
| 17* | 5 Skar (1913–18) | 5.00 | 12.00 | – |

| 21a | 1 Sho (1918–23), central legend vertical on rev. | 1.00 | 2.00 | 5.00 |

Silver

| 18 | 5 Sho (1913–27), as No. 12 | 50.00 | – | – |
| A18 | 1 Srang (1914–19), as No. 12, reeded edge. | VF 350.00 | | |

| 32 | 5 Sho ND (ca. 1928–29), 27mm | – | – | – |
| 32a | 5 Sho 1930 (24mm) | – | – | – |

Third Coinage
Copper

Gold

| A19 | 2½ Skar (1918–21) | 75.00 | – | – |

22 *F1* 20 Srang (1918–21)   400.00 500.00 700.00

Fourth Coinage

Copper

23   1 Sho (1932–38)   3.00   5.00   12.50

27   3 Sho (1946)   10.00   15.00   30.00

Silver

24   1½ Srang (1935–46)   5.00   10.00   25.00

25   3 Srang (1933–34)   10.00   20.00   50.00

26   3 Srang (1935–46)   10.00   15.00   40.00

Fifth Coinage

Copper

28   5 Sho (1947–50), 2 suns
         on obv.   2.00   3.00   5.00
28a 5 Sho (1949–53), moon
         and sun   2.00   3.00   5.00

Billon

29   10 Srang (1948–49), 2
         suns on obv., 2 vars. 6.00   12.00   40.00
29a 10 Srang (1950–52),
         moon and sun on obverse 10.00 20.00 55.00
Modern copies exist in gold, silver and cupro-nickel.

30   10 Srang (1950–51)   10.00   20.00   45.00

31   5 Srang ND (Ca.
         1947–48)   5.00   10.00   25.00

Unless otherwise noted, prices are for coins in very
fine, extremely fine, and uncirculated condition.

32 5 Srang (1953), 26mm,
sim. to No. 24   –   –   –

TIMOR

An island off the coast of Australia, the eastern part belonging to Portugal, the western to Indonesia. Exports: coffee, sandalwood, copra. Area: 7,330 square miles. Capital: *Dili.*

Monetary System:
100 Avos = 1 Pataca to 1957
100 Centavos = 1 Escudo

Bronze

1 10 Avos 1945–51   1.00   2.00   6.00

Nickel-Bronze

2 20 Avos 1945   15.00   35.00 100.00

Silver

3 50 Avos 1945–51   6.00   10.00   20.00
        1945 UNC . . . 50.

Bronze

4	10 Centavos 1958	1.00	3.00	15.00
5	30 Centavos 1958	1.00	2.00	6.00

Cupro-Nickel

6	60 Centavos 1958	1.00	2.00	5.00
7	1 Escudo 1958	1.00	3.00	10.00

Silver

8	3 Escudos 1958	2.00	5.00	12.00
9	6 Escudos 1958	5.00	10.00	17.00
10	10 Escudos 1964	6.00	10.00	20.00

Later issues in *Current Coins of the World.*

TOGO

After World War I the German colony of Togoland in West Africa on the Gulf of Guinea was split up and administered for the League of Nations and UNO by Britain and France. The British section is now part of Ghana. The coinage here is that of the French section, which became the independent Republic of Togo in 1960. Area: 20,400 square miles. Languages: French, local dialects. Capital: *Lome.*

Monetary System:
100 Centimes = 1 Franc

Aluminum-Bronze

1	50 Centimes 1924–26	3.00	7.50	25.00
2	1 Franc 1924–25	3.00	7.50	25.00
3	2 Francs 1924–25	5.00	10.00	35.00

Aluminum

4	1 Franc 1948	5.00	10.00	25.00
5	2 Francs 1948	6.00	12.50	35.00

Aluminum-Bronze

6 5 Francs 1956, diff. head   1.00   2.00   5.00
See FRENCH WEST AFRICA for integrated coinage, 1957.

TONKIN (Tongking)

Formerly a French protectorate in Indo-China, now a part of Vietnam. Capital: *Hanoi.*

Zinc

1 ¹⁄₆₀₀ Piastre 1905   10.00 20.00 30.00
Counterfeits are common, but most are cast rather than struck.

TUNISIA (Tunisie)

Formerly a monarchy on the Mediterranean coast of Africa, Tunisia was a French protectorate from 1881 to 1956. An independent kingdom was proclaimed in 1956, but was changed to a republic in 1957. Although the economy is mainly agricultural, mineral ores, petroleum and tourism are significant. Area: 63,378 square miles. Languages: Arabic, French. Capital: *Tunis.*

Monetary System:
16 Kharubs = 1 Piastre (Sebili) to 1891
100 Centimes = 1 Franc 1891–1958

MUHAMMAD AL-SADIQ
BEY 1859–1882

Under French Protectorate 1881–82
Designs similar to Nos. 5–9

Silver

1	8 Kharubs AH 1299			
	(1882)	200.00	–	–
2	1 Piastre 1299	250.00	–	–
3	2 Piastres 1299	300.00	–	–

Gold

4*	*F5* 25 Piastres 1298,			
	1300	150.00	200.00	–
A4	*F3* 50 Piastres 1299	500.00	850.00	–

ALI BEY 1882–1902
First Coinage

Silver

5*	8 Kharubs AH 1301–07			
	(1884–90), 17.5mm	40.00	80.00	–
6	1 Piastre 1303–08			
	(22.5mm)	50.00	75.00	–
7	2 Piastres 1307–08			
	(27mm)	75.00	150.00	–
8	4 Piastres 1305–08			
	(31mm)	85.00	175.00	–

Gold

9	*F9* 25 Piastres 1300, 02	150.00	200.00	–
A10	50 Piastres 1304	–	–	–
B10	100 Piastres 1303	–	–	–
10	*F10–11* 25 Piastres/15			
	Fr. 1304–08	150.00	200.00	–

Second Coinage

Note: All current silver and gold denominations were coined annually from 1891 to the late 1930's. In years when large quantities were not needed for circulation, limited numbers (20 to 1000 pieces) of each denomination were struck, probably to be used as gifts by the Bey.

Bronze

11	1 Centime 1891	3.50	6.50	15.00
12	2 Centimes 1891	2.50	5.00	10.00
13	5 Centimes 1891–93	2.00	5.00	12.50
14	10 Centimes 1891–93	1.00	5.00	10.00

Unless otherwise noted, prices are for coins in very fine, extremely fine, and uncirculated condition.

Silver

15	50 Centimes 1891–1902	2.50	5.00	20.00
16	1 Franc 1891–1902	3.00	6.00	22.50
17	2 Francs 1891–1902	7.00	12.50	25.00

Dates after 1891 of No. 15 and after 1892 of Nos. 16–17 were not struck for circulation.

Gold

18	*F13* 10 Francs 1891–1902	60.00	80.00 120.00
19	*F12* 20 Francs 1891–1902	120.00	140.00 180.00

Dates after 1891 of No. 18 and after 1901 of No. 19 were not struck for circulation.

MUHAMMAD AL-HADI BEY 1902–1906
Obv: Name of Bey
Rev: Designs like Nos. 13–19

Bronze

20	5 Centimes 1903–04	3.00	9.00	17.50
21	10 Centimes 1903–04	2.00	7.50	15.00

Silver

22	50 Centimes 1903–06			Rare
23	1 Franc 1903–06	6.00	12.00	20.00
24	2 Francs 1903–06	10.00	15.00	25.00

No. 22, and dates other than 1904 of Nos. 23 and 24 were not struck for circulation.

Gold

25	*F13* 10 Francs 1903–06		Rare
26	*F12* 20 Francs 1903–06	120.00 140.00	180.00

No. 25, and dates 1905–06 of No. 26 were not struck for circulation.

MUHAMMAD AL-NASR BEY 1906–1922
First Coinage
Obv: Name of Bey
Rev: Designs like Nos. 13–19

Bronze

27	5 Centimes 1907–17	2.00	5.00	10.00
28	10 Centimes 1907–17	1.00	5.00	10.00

Silver

29	50 Centimes 1907–21	1.50	2.50	15.00
30	1 Franc 1907–21	4.00	6.00	15.00
31	2 Francs 1907–21	10.00	15.00	25.00

Dates after 1917, 1918, and 1916 of Nos. 29, 30 and 31 respectively, were not struck for circulation.

Gold

32	*F13* 10 Francs 1907–21		Rare
33	*F12* 20 Francs 1907–21		Rare

Nos. 32–33 were not struck for circulation.

Second Coinage

Cupro-Nickel

34	5 Centimes 1918–20 (19mm)	.35	1.50	4.00
34a	5 Centimes 1920 (17mm)	2.00	5.00	15.00
35	10 Centimes 1918–20	.35	1.00	2.00
36	25 Centimes 1918–20	.50	1.50	3.50

General Coinage
Issued without name of ruler through successive reigns

Aluminum-Bronze

37	50 Centimes 1921–45	.25	.50	2.50
38	1 Franc 1921–45	.40	.60	3.00
39	2 Francs 1921–45	.60	1.00	3.00

MUHAMMAD AL-HABIB
BEY 1922–1929
Obv: Name of Bey
Rev: Designs like Nos. 35, 15–19

Cupro-Nickel

40	10 Centimes 1926	3.00	5.00	15.00

Silver

41	50 Centimes 1923–28	100.00	150.00	250.00
42	1 Franc 1923–28	150.00	200.00	300.00
43	2 Francs 1923–28	200.00	225.00	350.00

Nos. 41–43 not struck for circulation.

Gold

44	*F13* 10 Francs 1922–28		Rare
45	*F12* 20 Francs 1922–28		Rare

Nos. 44–45 were not struck for circulation.

AHMED BEY 1929–1942

Cupro-Nickel
Obv: Name of Bey
Rev: Designs like Nos. 34a–36

46	5 Centimes 1931–38	1.00	2.00	4.00
47	10 Centimes 1931–38	1.50	3.00	9.00
48	25 Centimes 1931–38	2.00	5.00	12.00

Silver

49	10 Francs 1930–34	20.00	40.00	80.00
50	20 Francs 1930–34	45.00	75.00	115.00

51	5 Francs AH 1353–57			
	(1934–38)	2.50	5.00	10.00
52	10 Francs AH 1353–57	10.00	20.00	50.00
53	20 Francs AH 1353–57	10.00	20.00	50.00

Dates after 1355 of No. 51, and after 1353 of Nos. 52–53 were not struck for circulation.

54	5 Francs 1939	2.50	5.00	10.00
55	10 Francs 1939	4.50	10.00	15.00
56	20 Francs 1939	15.00	40.00	85.00

Gold

57	*F14* 100 Francs		
	1930–37	125.00 175.00 250.00

Dates after 1934 or 1935 of No. 57 were not struck for circulation.

Zinc

58	10 Centimes 1941–42	1.00	2.00	3.00
59	20 Centimes 1942	2.00	3.00	7.50

MUHAMMAD AL-AMIN
BEY 1943–1957
Zinc

| 60 | 10 Centimes 1945 | 30.00 | 50.00 | 70.00 |
| 61 | 20 Centimes 1945 | 35.00 | 60.00 | 75.00 |

Aluminum-Bronze

| 62 | 5 Francs 1946 | 1.25 | 2.00 | 10.00 |

Cupro-Nickel

63	5 Francs 1954, 57	.20	.35	.75
64	20 Francs 1950, 57	.20	.35	.75
65	50 Francs 1950, 57	.30	.50	1.00
66	100 Francs 1950, 57	.75	1.25	4.50

Later issues in *Current Coins of the World.*

TURKEY
(Turkiye Cumhuriyeti)

A republic in both Europe and Asia, between the Mediterranean and Black Seas. The Ottoman Empire was destroyed after World War I and was reduced in area from 710,224 square miles to 296,500 square miles. The republic was formed in 1923. The country is the foremost chrome producer in the world. Capital: *Ankara.*

Monetary System:
40 Para = 1 Kurus (Kurush, Piastre)
100 Kurus = 1 Lira

The accession date of the ruler appears in Arabic numerals on the lower reverse of each coin. The regnal year (year of issue), also in Arabic, is usually found below the toughra (monogram of the ruler).

Valuations are for coins in Very Fine condition.

ABDUL AZIZ 1861–1876

(Accession Date AH 1277 on Coins)
Copper

1*	5 Para Yr. 1 (1861)	3.50
2	10 Para Yr. 1	2.00
3	20 Para Yr. 1	3.00

4	5 Para Yr. 4 (1864)	1.25
5	10 Para Yr. 4	1.25
6*	20 Para Yr. 4	1.25
7	40 Para Yr. 4	1.75

Silver

8	20 Para Yrs. 1–7	3.50
9	1 Kurus Yrs. 1–7	2.25
10*	2 Kurus Yrs. 1–5	30.00

11	5 Kurus Yrs. 1–15	3.50
12*	10 Kurus Yrs. 1–2	75.00
13	20 Kurus Yrs. 1–15	20.00

Gold

16	F27	25 Kurus Yrs. 1–12	30.00
A16	F26	50 Kurus Yrs. 1–9	62.50
17*	F25	100 Kurus Yrs. 1–14	125.00
A17	F24	250 Kurus Yrs. 1–9	300.00
B17	F23	500 Kurus Yrs. 1–13	600.00

MURAD V 1876

(Accession Date AH 1293 on Coins)
Designs similar to Nos. 9–17
Obv: No flower to right of toughra

Silver

18 1 Kurus Yr. 1 (1876)   110.00

20 5 Kurus Yr. 1   60.00
22* 20 Kurus Yr. 1   70.00

Gold

A22 *F33* 25 Kurus Yr. 1   200.00
B22 *F32* 50 Kurus Yr. 1   –
C22 *F31* 100 Kurus Yr. 1   135.00

ABDUL HAMID II 1876–1909

(Accession Date AH 1293 on Coins)

First Coinage
Obv: Flower at right of toughra

Copper

23 5 Para Yrs. 3–4   1.00

Silver

26 20 Para Yrs. 1, 4   35.00

27* 1 Kurus Yrs. 1–4   45.00
28 2 Kurus Yrs. 1   325.00

29 5 Kurus Yrs. 1–4   9.00
30* 10 Kurus Yrs. 1–3   15.00
31 20 Kurus Yrs. 1–3   25.00

Gold

A31 *F38* 25 Kurus Yrs. 3–6   35.00
B31 *F37* 50 Kurus Yrs.1–6   55.00
C31* *F36* 100 Kurus Yrs. 1–6   125.00
D31 *F35* 250 Kurus Yrs. 1–2   –
E31 *F34* 500 Kurus Yrs. 1–2   600.00

Second Coinage
Obv: "El-Ghazi" (the Victorious) at right of toughra

Billon

24 5 Para Yrs. 25–30   .85
25* 10 Para Yrs. 25–30   .25

Silver

F31 20 Para Yr. 8   12.50

32 1 Kurus Yrs. 8–34   .65
33* 2 Kurus Yrs. 8–34   .85

Unless otherwise noted, prices are for coins in very
fine, extremely fine, and uncirculated condition.

34* 5 Kurus Yrs. 8–34   2.50
     Yr. 34 . . . 25.
35 10 Kurus Yrs. 12–33   6.00
     Yr. 19 . . . 20.

Gold

A40	F49	12½ Kurus Yrs. 25, 30	30.00
B40	F48	25 Kurus Yrs. 26–34	35.00
C40	F47	50 Kurus Yrs. 25–33	55.00
D40	F46	100 Kurus Yrs. 23–33	125.00
41	F45	250 Kurus Yrs. 24–33	275.00
42*	F44	500 Kurus Yrs. 26–33	550.00

36	F43	25 Kurus Yrs. 7–32	35.00
37	F42	50 Kurus Yrs. 7–34	55.00
38	F41	100 Kurus Yrs. 6–34	125.00
39	F40	250 Kurus Yrs. 7–32	275.00
40*	F39	500 Kurus Yrs. 7–32	550.00

Gold Presentation Pieces
(Monnaie de Luxe)

MOHAMMED RESHAT V
1909–1918

(Accession Date AH 1327 on Coins)

First Coinage
Obv: "Reshat" at right of toughra

Nickel

43 5 Para Yrs. 2–7   .35
     Yr. 7 . . . 30.
44 10 Para Yrs. 2–7   .30
45 20 Para Yrs. 2–6   .40
46* 40 Para Yrs. 3–5   .50

Silver

47 1 Kurus Yrs. 1–3   1.00
48* 2 Kurus Yrs. 1–6   1.25

49* 5 Kurus Yrs. 1–7 — 2.50
50 10 Kurus Yrs. 1–7 — 10.00
    Yr. 3 . . . Rare.

Gold

A51 *F54* 25 Kurus Yrs. 1–6 — 30.00
B51 *F53* 50 Kurus Yrs. 2–5 — 60.00
C51 *F52* 100 Kurus Yrs. 1–7 — 125.00
D51 *F51* 250 Kurus Yrs. 1–6 — 275.00
E51* *F50* 500 Kurus Yrs. 1–4 — 550.00
Some gold and silver coins struck in 1910 and 1911 have names of cities visited by Mohammed V. Some are rare. Monnaies de Luxe were also issued during this reign. See Friedberg, GOLD COINS OF THE WORLD.

Second Coinage
Obv: "El-Ghazi" (the Victorious) at right of toughra

Nickel
43a 5 Para Yr. 7 — 30.00
44a 10 Para Yrs. 7–8 — .50

Cupro-Nickel
46a 40 Para Yrs.8–9 — .50

Silver

A50 2 Kurus Yrs. 7–9 — 25.00
    Yr. 9 . . . 50.

B50 5 Kurus Yrs. 7–9 — 8.50
    Yr. 9 . . . 30.
C50 10 Kurus Yrs. 7–10 — 8.00
51* 20 Kurus Yrs. 8–10 — 12.00

Gold

Obv: "El-Ghazi" at right of toughra
53 *F59* 25 Kurus Yr. 7 — 35.00
54 *F58* 50 Kurus Yr. 9 — 60.00
55* *F57* 100 Kurus Yrs. 7–10 — 125.00
56 *F56* 250 Kurus Yr. 7 — 275.00
57 *F55* 500 Kurus Yr. 10 — 550.00

MOHAMMED VI 1918–1922

(Accession Date AH 1336 on Coins)
Designs similar to Nos. 43–57

Cupro-Nickel

58* 40 Para Yr. 4 (1921) — .60

Silver
59 2 Kurus Yrs. 1–2 — 100.00
60 5 Kurus Yrs. 1–2 — 80.00
61 10 Kurus Yrs. 1–2 — 200.00
62 20 Kurus Yrs. 1–2 — 100.00

Gold

63 *F74* 25 Kurus Yrs. 1–2 — 30.00
64 *F73* 50 Kurus Yrs. 1, 5 — 125.00

Unless otherwise noted, prices are for coins in very fine, extremely fine, and uncirculated condition.

65* *F72* 100 Kurus Yr. 1–2   125.00
66   *F71* 250 Kurus Yr. 1   300.00
67   *F70* 500 Kurus Yrs. 1–3   575.00
Gold Monnaies de Luxe also struck; see Friedberg, GOLD COINS OF THE WORLD.

REPUBLIC 1923–

A. H. Dating System
Aluminum-Bronze

68   100 Para AH 1340–41
     (1922–24)   .35
69   5 Kurus 1340–41   .50
70   10 Kurus 1340–41   .65

Nickel

71* 25 Kurus 1341   1.50

Western Dating System
Aluminum-Bronze

68a 100 Para 1926   .35
69a 5 Kurus 1926   .50
70a 10 Kurus 1926   .65

Nickel

71a 25 Kurus 1926, 28   1.50

Gold

72   *F83* 25 Kurus 1926–28   50.00
73   *F82* 50 Kurus 1926–28   65.00
74   *F81* 100 Kurus 1926–29   150.00
75* *F80* 250 Kurus 1926–28   300.00
76   *F79* 500 Kurus 1926–29   600.00

Monnaies de Luxe

77* *F88* 25 Kurus 1927–28
     (23mm)   60.00
78   *F87* 50 Kurus 1927–28
     (28mm)   100.00
79   *F86* 100 Kurus 1927–28
     (35mm)   150.00
80   *F85* 250 Kurus 1927–28
     (45mm)   300.00
81   *F84* 500 Kurus 1927–28
     (49mm)   600.00

NEW SYSTEM 1933–

Western Dates and Numerals
100 Kurus = 1 Lira

Silver

Obv: President Ataturk (1923–38)

82   100 Kurus 1934   10.00

Cupro-Nickel

87   1 Kurus 1935–37   .50
88   5 Kurus 1935–43   .60
89   10 Kurus 1935–40   .75

Silver

83	25 Kurus 1935–37	5.00
84	50 Kurus 1935–37	6.00
85	1 Lira 1937–39	10.00

Obv: President Inonu (1938–50)

86	1 Lira 1940–41	13.50

Cupro-Nickel

90	1 Kurus 1938–44	.60

Aluminum-Bronze

91	10 Para 1940–42	.35

Nickel-Brass

92	25 Kurus 1944–46	.50

New Coinage

Prices are for Uncirculated coins.
Brass

A92	½ Kurus 1948	250.00
93	1 Kurus 1947–51	.35
94	2½ Kurus 1948–51	.50

No. A92 was not issued to circulation.

95	5 Kurus 1949–57	.25
96	10 Kurus 1949–56	.35
97	25 Kurus 1948–56	.45

Silver

98	50 Kurus 1947–48	7.50
99	1 Lira 1947–48	8.00

Gold

Rev: President Inonu (1938–50)

A99	*F103* 25 Kurus Yrs. 20–25 (1943–49), 15mm	30.00
B99	*F102* 50 Kurus Yrs. 20–27 (18mm)	60.00
C99	*F101* 100 Kurus Yrs. 20–25 (22mm)	120.00
D99	*F100* 250 Kurus Yrs. 20–23 (27mm)	250.00
E99*	*F99* 500 Kurus Yrs. 20–24 (35mm)	500.00

Rev: President Ataturk (1923–38)

100	*F93* 25 Kurus Yrs. 20– (1943–)	25.00
101*	*F92* 50 Kurus Yrs. 20–	50.00
102	*F91* 100 Kurus Yrs.20–	100.00
103	*F90* 250 Kurus Yrs. 20–	250.00
104	*F89* 500 Kurus Yrs. 20–	500.00

Gold Monnaies de Luxe with portraits of Inonu and Ataturk were issued in the same denominations as above, but larger and thinner, with ornate borders. See Friedberg, GOLD COINS OF THE WORLD.

Later issues in *Current Coins of the World*.

TUVA
(Tannu Tuva People's Republic)

Tuva, located north of Mongolia in central Asia, broke away from the Chinese Empire in 1911 and later became a Russian protectorate. An independent People's Republic was proclaimed in 1921, and the country was annexed by the U.S.S.R. as an autonomous region in 1944. The major occupation is livestock herding, and rich mineral resources are still little exploited. Area: 65,-830 square miles. Language: Tuvan. Capital: *Kyzyl*.

Monetary System:
100 Kopejek (Kopek) = 1 Aksha

Prices are for coins in Very Fine condition.
Aluminum-Bronze

1	1 Kopejek 1934	50.00
2	2 Kopejek 1934	55.00
3	3 Kopejek 1934	50.00
4	5 Kopejek 1934	55.00

Cupro-Nickel

5	10 Kopejek 1934	55.00
6	15 Kopejek 1934	55.00
7	20 Kopejek 1934	55.00

UNITED STATES
OF AMERICA

Continental area 2,977,128 square miles. Capital: Washington, D.C. The prices shown are for the commonest date and mint. For a detailed catalog of all dates, mint marks and principal varieties of each coin type, we recommend *A Guide Book of United States Coins* by R.S. Yeoman, which is revised annually. Note with respect to conditions: uncirculated and proof issues are for typical pieces in MS-60 or proof-60 states of preservation.

Monetary System:
10 Cents = 1 Dime
100 Cents = 1 Dollar

Cupro-Nickel

1	1 Cent 1856–58	30.00 60.00 250.00	
		Proof . . . 1700.00	

Rev: Laurel wreath

2	1 Cent 1859	20.00 60.00 275.00
		Proof . . . 850.00

Rev: Oak wreath and shield

2a	1 Cent 1860–64	10.00 17.50 100.00
		Proof . . . 350.00

Bronze

2b	1 Cent 1864–1909	1.50 17.50 100.00
		Proof . . . 350.00

3	2 Cents 1864–73	12.50 30.00 175.00
		Proof . . . 350.00

Silver
Obv: No lines around star

4	3 Cents 1851–53	22.50 50.00 225.00

Obv: 3 outlines to star
Rev: Olive sprig, arrows added

4a	3 Cents 1854–58	30.00 80.00 350.00
		Proof . . . 900.00

Obv: 2 outlines to star

4b 3 Cents 1859–73   30.00   50.00 225.00
        Proof . . . 425.00

Cupro-Nickel

5   3 Cents 1865–89   7.50   15.00 100.00
        Proof . . . 250.00

Rev: Rays between stars

6   5 Cents 1866–67   30.00   75.00 275.00
        Proof . . . 2500.

Rev: Rays omitted

6a 5 Cents 1867–83   12.50   27.50 125.00
        Proof . . . 250.00

Liberty Seated Series

Silver

Obv: Without stars

7   ½ Dime 1837–38   85.00 175.00 450.00
8   1 Dime 1837–38   125.00 295.00 725.00

Obv: Stars around border

7a ½ Dime 1838–59   20.00   50.00 295.00
        Proof . . . 800.00

8a 1 Dime 1838–60   20.00   50.00 195.00
        Proof . . . 1000.

9   ¼ Dollar 1838–65   22.50   50.00 375.00
        Proof . . . 425.00
10   ½ Dollar 1839–66   35.00   55.00 500.00
        Proof . . . 525.00
11   1 Dollar 1840–65   200.00 275.00 750.00
        Proof . . . 950.00

Obv: Arrows at date
Rev: Rays around eagle

9a* ¼ Dollar 1853   35.00 125.00 850.00
10a ½ Dollar 1853   80.00 225.00 750.00

Obv: Arrows at date

7b ½ Dime 1853–55   15.00   45.00 265.00
        Proof . . . 1500.
8b 1 Dime 1853–55   15.00   45.00 300.00
        Proof . . . 3000.
9b ¼ Dollar 1854–55   25.00   75.00 675.00
10b ½ Dollar 1854–55   40.00   95.00 800.00
        Proof . . . 4000.

Obv: Legend replaces stars
Rev: Modified wreath

7c ½ Dime 1860–73   12.50   27.50 225.00
        Proof . . . 325.00
8c 1 Dime 1860–91   7.50   20.00 175.00
        Proof . . . 300.00

Rev: Motto on ribbon above eagle

9c* ¼ Dollar 1866–91   20.00   50.00 325.00
        Proof . . . 375.00
10c ½ Dollar 1866–91   27.50   50.00 500.00
        Proof . . . 500.00
11a 1 Dollar 1866–73   200.00 275.00 775.00
        Proof . . . 900.00

**Unless otherwise noted, prices are for coins in very
fine, extremely fine, and uncirculated condition.**

Obv: Arrows at date

8d 1 Dime 1873–74   40.00 100.00 700.00
                           Proof . . . 625.00

9d ¼ Dollar 1873–74   55.00 150.00 850.00
                           Proof . . . 725.00

10d ½ Dollar 1873–74   80.00 225.00 900.00
                           Proof . . . 900.00

12 20 Cents 1875–78   85.00 165.00 675.00
                           Proof . . . 950.00

1877, 78 not for circulation.

TRADE DOLLAR

Struck for circulation in the Orient only; still legal tender.

13 1 Dollar 1873–85   80.00 150.00 600.00
                           Proof . . . 850.00

Dates after 1878 not for circulation.

Liberty Head Series

Cupro-Nickel

14 V (Cents) 1883, rev. with-
    out CENTS   5.00   7.50   40.00
                           Proof . . . 300.00

14a V Cents 1883–1912, with
     CENTS   5.00   15.00 110.00
          Silver   Proof . . . 225.00

15 1 Dime 1892–1916   7.50   20.00 125.00
                           Proof . . . 275.00

16 ¼ Dollar 1892–1916   15.00   40.00 225.00
                           Proof . . . 375.00

17 ½ Dollar 1892–1915   40.00 125.00 550.00
                           Proof . . . 500.00

18 1 Dollar 1878–1921   15.00   22.50   45.00
                           Proof . . . 650.00

Gold
Obv: Liberty head

19 *F1–5* 1 Dollar 1849–54   200.00 225.00 700.00

Obv: Indian head

20 *F6–10* 1 Dollar 1854–56,
small head   325.00 500.00 2500.

20a *F11–14* 1 Dollar
1856–89, large head   200.00 225.00 700.00
                                     Proof . . . 1500.

21 *F41–44* 3 Dollars
1854–89   550.00 800.00 2500.
                                     Proof . . . 4000.

22 *F31–36* 2½ Dollars
1840–1907   225.00 250.00 650.00
                                     Proof . . . 1650.

23 *F55–59* 5 Dollars
1839–66   200.00 225.00 800.00
                                     Proof . . . 5000.

24 *F71–74* 10 Dollars
1838–66   300.00 325.00 1300.
                                     Proof . . . 10000.

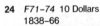

25 *F86–89* 20 Dollars
1849–66   600.00 650.00 1500.
                                     Proof . . . 8000.

Rev: Motto above eagle

23a *F60–64* 5 Dollars
1866–1908   175.00 200.00 300.00
                             Proof . . . 2500.

24a *F75–79* 10 Dollars
1866–1907   275.00 300.00 375.00
                             Proof . . . 3500.

25a *F91–93* 20 Dollars
1866–76   600.00 650.00 750.00
value TWENTY D.   Proof . . . 7000.

25b *F94–97* 20 Dollars
1877–1907   600.00 650.00 700.00
value TWENTY DOLLARS   Proof . . . 5000.

Modern Designs

Bronze

Obv: Abraham Lincoln, 16th President (1861–65)

26   1 Cent 1909–58   .05   .10   .20
                                   Proof . . . 1.50

Zinc-Coated Steel

26a 1 Cent 1943   .10   .20   1.25

Cupro-Nickel

27   5 Cents 1913, rev. value
on mound   6.50   12.50   27.50
                                   Proof . . . 2000.

27a 5 Cents 1913–38, rev.
value below line   .35   1.50   20.00
                                   Proof . . . 525.00

Unless otherwise noted, prices are for coins in very
fine, extremely fine, and uncirculated condition.

Silver

28 1 Dime 1916–45   1.25 1.50 7.50
Proof . . . 150.00

31 1 Dollar 1921–35, 64   15.00 20.00 27.50

Gold

29 ¼ Dollar 1916–17   27.50 55.00 150.00

32 *F37–38* 2½ Dollars
1908–29   200.00 225.00 335.00
Proof . . . 2500.

33 *F65–68* 5 Dollars
1908–29   275.00 300.00 925.00
Proof . . . 4000.

Rev: No motto

34 *F80–82* 10 Dollars
1907–08   475.00 550.00 900.00
Proof . . . 4500.

29a ¼ Dollar 1917–30,   12.50 25.00 100.00
modified dies

Rev: Motto added

34a *F83–85* 10 Dollars
1908–33   400.00 450.00 600.00
Proof . . . 5000.

30 ½ Dollar 1916–47   7.50 20.00 65.00
Proof . . . 300.00

Design in high relief

35 *F99* 20 Dollars MCMVII
(1907)   3500. 4750. 9000.
Proof . . . Rare

Design in low relief

35a* *F100–101* 20 Dollars
    1907–08   675.00 750.00 850.00
                          Proof . . . 12000.

Rev: Motto added above sun

35b *F102–104* 20 Dollars
    1908–32   625.00 650.00 700.00
                          Proof . . . 11000.

Current Designs

Bronze

36 1 Cent 1959–   –   –   .10
                           Proof . . . 1.25

Cupro-Nickel

Obv: Thomas Jefferson, 3rd President (1801–09)
37 5 Cents 1938–   –   .10   .15
                          Proof . . . 1.00

Billon

37a 5 Cents 1942–45   .75   .85   4.50
                          Proof . . . 125.00

Silver

Obv: Franklin Roosevelt, 32nd President (1933–45)
38 1 Dime 1946–64   1.00   1.25   1.50
                          Proof . . . 2.00

Obv: George Washington, 1st President, (1789–97)
39 ¼ Dollar 1932–64   2.50   2.75   3.00
                          Proof . . . 3.25

Obv: Benjamin Franklin, Signer of Declaration of Independence
40 ½ Dollar 1948–63   5.00   5.50 10.00
                          Proof . . . 11.00

Obv: John Kennedy, 35th President (1961–63)
41 ½ Dollar 1964   5.00   5.50   6.00
                          Proof . . . 7.50

Later issues in *Current Coins of the World.*

UNITED STATES
COMMEMORATIVE COINS
Listed Alphabetically
by Subject

**Values are for Extremely Fine
and Uncirculated specimens and for a
single coin of each type. Some proof
pieces are also known.**
Silver

C1 ¼ Dollar 1893. Columbian
      Exposition   175.00 450.00
(Isabella Quarter)

Unless otherwise noted, prices are for coins in very
fine, extremely fine, and uncirculated condition.

C2 1 Dollar 1900. Lafayette
Memorial   300.00 750.00

Half Dollars
Nos. C4–C55

C4	1921 Alabama Centennial	75.00	275.00
C5	1936 Albany, New York Charter	175.00	225.00
C6	1937 Battle of Antietam	210.00	300.00
C7	1935–39 Arkansas Centennial	50.00	80.00
C8	1936–S San Francisco-Oakland Bay Bridge	65.00	110.00
C9	1934–38 Daniel Boone Bicentennial	115.00	150.00
C10	1936 Bridgeport, Conn. Centennial	65.00	110.00
C11	1925–S California Diamond Jubilee	55.00	110.00
C12	1936 Cincinnati Musical Center	210.00	275.00
C13	1936 Cleveland, Great Lakes Exposition	45.00	85.00
C14	1936 Columbia, S.C. Sesquicentennial	175.00	225.00
C16	1892–93 Columbian Exposition	12.50	25.00
C17	1935 Connecticut Tercentenary	150.00	225.00
C18	1936 Delaware Tercentenary	150.00	200.00
C19	1936 Elgin, Illinois Centennial	150.00	175.00
C20	1936 Gettysburg Memorial	150.00	250.00
C22	1922 Centennial Birth of U.S. Grant	45.00	90.00
C23	1928 Hawaii Sesquicentennial	575.00	750.00
C24	1935 Hudson, N.Y. Sesquicentennial	375.00	525.00

C25	1924 Huguenot-Walloon Tercentenary	55.00	100.00
C26	1946 Iowa Centennial	60.00	85.00
C27	1925 Lexington-Concord Sesquicentennial	35.00	50.00
C28	1918 Lincoln-Illinois Centennial	47.50	75.00
C29	1936 Long Island Tercentenary	47.50	75.00
C30	1936 Lynchburg, Va. Sesquicentennial	125.00	175.00
C31	1920 Maine Centennial	70.00	100.00
C32	1934 Maryland Tercentenary	90.00	125.00
C34	1921 Missouri	200.00	425.00
C35	1923–S Monroe Doctrine Centennial	25.00	50.00
C36	1938 New Rochelle, N.Y.	275.00	350.00
C37	1936 Norfolk, Va. Bicentennial	250.00	335.00
C38*	1926–39 Oregon Trail Memorial	60.00	100.00
C39	1915–S Panama-Pacific Exposition	225.00	400.00
C40	1920–21 Pilgrim Tercentenary	37.50	55.00
C42	1936 Providence, R.I. Tercentenary	60.00	110.00
C43	1937 Roanoke Island, N.C. 350th Anniv.	135.00	175.00
C44	1936 Robinson-Arkansas	90.00	120.00
C45	1935–36 San Diego, Ca. Pacific Exposition	50.00	100.00
C46	1926 U.S. Independence Sesquicentennial	25.00	50.00

C47	1935 Old Spanish Trail	500.00	675.00
C48	1925 Stone Mountain Memorial	22.50	42.50
C49	1934–38 Texas Centennial	85.00	115.00
C50	1925 Fort Vancouver Centennial	250.00	450.00
C51	1927 Vermont Sesquicentennial	110.00	225.00
C52	1946–51 Booker T. Washington Memorial	10.00	15.00

C53 1951–54 Washington-
Carver   10.00   15.00

C54 1936 Wisconsin Territorial
Centennial   155.00 210.00
C55 1936 York County, Maine
Tercentenary   125.00 200.00

Commemorative Gold Coins

C56 *F20–21* 1 Dollar 1922.
Grant Memorial   550.00   1000.
C58 *F17* 1 Dollar 1904–05.
Lewis and Clark Exposi-
tion   500.00   1200.
C59 *F15* 1 Dollar 1903. Louisi-
ana Purchase-Jefferson   375.00 650.00
C60 *F16* 1 Dollar 1903. Louisi-
ana Purchase-McKinley   375.00 650.00
C61 *F19* 1 Dollar 1916–17.
McKinley Memorial   335.00 725.00
C62 *F18* 1 Dollar 1915–S.
Panama-Pacific Exposi-
tion   325.00 725.00

C63 *F39* 2½ Dollars 1915–S.
Panama-Pacific Exposi-
tion   700.00   1750.

C64 *F105* 50 Dollars 1915–S.
Panama-Pacific Exposi-
tion, Round   20000. 30000.
C65* *F106* 50 Dollars
1915–S. Panama-Pacific
Exposition, Octagonal   15000. 22500.
C66 *F40* 2½ Dollars 1926.
Philadelphia Sesquicen-
tennial   300.00 525.00

URUGUAY
(Republica Oriental
del Uruguay)

The smallest republic in South America. It declared its
independence from Brazil in 1825. Largest industry:
cattle raising. Area: 72,172 square miles.

Language: Spanish. Capital: Montevideo.

Monetary System —
To 1862:
100 Centesimos = 1 Real
8 Reales = 1 Peso
From 1862:
100 Centesimos = 1 Peso

First Coinage
Copper

1   5 Centesimos 1840–55   40.00 100.00 250.00
        1840, 44 . . . 400.   1855 . . . 250.
2   20 Centesimos 1840–55   50.00 150.00 500.00
3   40 Centesimos 1844   80.00 250.00 750.00
Nos. 1–3 occur in several minor varieties.

Unless otherwise noted, prices are for coins in very
fine, extremely fine, and uncirculated condition.

4	5 Centesimos 1857	6.00	15.00	40.00
5	20 Centesimos 1857	8.00	20.00	60.00
6	40 Centesimos 1857	10.00	25.00	100.00

Montevideo Peso
Silver

| 10 | 1 Peso 1844 | 350.00 | 800.00 | 3000. |

Second Coinage
Bronze

7	1 Centesimo 1869	3.00	5.00	25.00
8	2 Centesimos 1869	4.00	8.00	35.00
9	4 Centesimos 1869	5.00	10.00	75.00

Silver

| 11 | 10 Centesimos 1877, 93 | 4.00 | 9.00 | 30.00 |

12	20 Centesimos 1877, 93	8.00	15.00	50.00
13	50 Centesimos 1877–94	12.00	25.00	100.00
14	1 Peso 1877–95	25.00	50.00	200.00
	1878 . . . 350.			

Third Coinage
Cupro-Nickel

15	1 Centesimos 1901–36	1.00	2.00	5.00
16	2 Centesimos 1901–41	1.00	3.00	8.00
17	5 Centesimos 1901–41	2.00	4.00	10.00

Copper

| 16a | 2 Centesimos 1943–51 | .30 | 1.00 | 5.00 |
| 17a | 5 Centesimos 1944–51 | .30 | 1.00 | 5.00 |

Silver

20	20 Centesimos 1920	5.00	10.00	25.00
22	50 Centesimos 1916–17	7.00	15.00	60.00
23	1 Peso 1917	25.00	50.00	150.00

Constitution Centennial
(Nos. 18, 21, 24)

Aluminum-Bronze

| 18 | 10 Centesimos 1930 | 5.00 | 10.00 | 25.00 |

Silver

| 21 | 20 Centesimos 1930 | 5.00 | 8.00 | 25.00 |

Gold

24 *F6* 5 Pesos 1930   175.00 250.00 300.00

Fourth Coinage
Aluminum-Bronze

19 10 Centesimos 1936   4.00 8.00 22.00

Silver

25 20 Centesimos 1942   2.00 3.00 5.00

26 50 Centesimos 1943   3.00 4.00 7.00

27 1 Peso 1942   3.25 5.00 10.00

Fifth Coinage
Cupro-Nickel

28 1 Centesimos 1953   .20 .30 .50

29	2 Centesimos 1953	.20	.30	.50
30	5 Centesimos 1953	.20	.30	.50
31	10 Centesimos 1953, 59	.20	.30	.50

Silver

32 20 Centesimos 1954   1.50 2.50 5.00

Sixth Coinage
Copper-Nickel-Zinc

33	2 Centesimos 1960	.10	.20	.50
34	5 Centesimos 1960	.10	.20	.50
35	10 Centesimos 1960	.20	.30	.50

Cupro-Nickel

36	25 Centesimos 1960	.30	.40	.75
37	50 Centesimos 1960	.40	.50	.85
38	1 Peso 1960	.50	.75	1.50

Sesquicentennial
Gaucho Heroes
Silver

39 10 Pesos 1961   5.00 6.00 10.00

Later issues in *Current Coins of the World.*

Unless otherwise noted, prices are for coins in very
fine, extremely fine, and uncirculated condition.

VATICAN CITY
(Stato della Citta
del Vaticano)

The Papal States originally covered some 16,000 square miles. In 1871 the territory became part of Italy. Finally, in 1929 an independent state of the Vatican City was set up. Its present area is 108.7 acres and includes St. Peter's, the Vatican Palace and the Museum.

Monetary System:
100 Centesimi = 1 Lira

PIUS XI 1922-1939

Bronze

1	5 Centesimi 1929-38	1.00	2.00	5.00
	1938 . . . 100.			

2	10 Centesimi 1929-38	1.00	3.00	10.00
	1938 . . . 150.			

Nickel

3	20 Centesimi 1929-37	1.00	2.00	10.00
	1929 . . . 10. 1935 . . . 50.			

4	50 Centesimi 1929-37	1.00	2.00	10.00
	1929 . . . 10. 1935 . . . 50.			

5	1 Lira 1929-37	1.00	2.00	10.00
	1929 . . . 10.			
6	2 Lire 1929-37	1.00	2.00	10.00
	1929 . . . 10.			

Silver

7	5 Lire 1929-37	5.00	10.00	15.00
	1929 . . . 20.			

8	10 Lire 1929-37	5.00	10.00	20.00
	1929 . . . 20.			

Gold

9	F283 100 Lire 1929-35 (24mm)	100.00	150.00	250.00
9a	F285 100 Lire 1936-37 (21mm)	100.00	150.00	250.00
	1937 . . . 2000.			

Jubilee Issues 1933

These coins are similar to the 1929-37 types and are dated "1933-1934."

Bronze
11	5 Centesimi	1.00	5.00	10.00
12	10 Centesimi	1.00	5.00	10.00

Nickel
13	20 Centesimi	1.00	5.00	10.00
14	50 Centesimi	1.00	5.00	10.00

15	1 Lira	1.00	5.00	10.00
16	2 Lire	1.00	5.00	10.00

Silver

17	5 Lire	5.00	10.00	20.00
18	10 Lire	5.00	10.00	20.00

Gold

19	*F284* 100 Lire	100.00	150.00	200.00

SEDE VACANTE 1939

Silver

20	5 Lire 1939	10.00	15.00	25.00
21	10 Lire 1939	10.00	15.00	25.00

PIUS XII 1939–58

First Coinage
Designs like Nos. 1–6

Bronze

22	5 Centesimi 1939–41	1.00	5.00	15.00
23	10 Centesimi 1939–41	1.00	5.00	15.00

Nickel

24	20 Centesimi 1939	1.00	2.00	5.00
25	50 Centesimi 1939	1.00	2.00	5.00
26	1 Lira 1939	1.00	2.00	5.00
27	2 Lire 1939	1.00	2.00	5.00

Stainless Steel

24a	20 Centesimi 1940–41	1.00	2.00	5.00
25a	50 Centesimi 1940–41	1.00	2.00	5.00
26a	1 Lira 1940–41	1.00	2.00	5.00
27a	2 Lire 1940–41	1.00	2.00	5.00

Silver

Rev: Designs like Nos. 7–10

28	5 Lire 1939–41	5.00	10.00	15.00
29	10 Lire 1939–41	10.00	15.00	25.00

Gold

30	*F286* 100 Lire 1939–41	100.00	200.00	400.00

Second Coinage

Aluminum-Bronze

31	5 Centesimi 1942–46	1.00	2.00	5.00
	1943–46 . . . 50.			
32	10 Centesimi 1942–46	1.00	2.00	5.00
	1943–46 . . . 50.			

Stainless Steel

33	20 Centesimi 1942–46	1.00	2.00	5.00
	1943–46 . . . 50.			
34	50 Centesimi 1942–46	1.00	2.00	5.00
	1943–46 . . . 50.			
35	1 Lira 1942–46	1.00	2.00	5.00
	1943–46 . . . 50.			
36	2 Lire 1942–46	1.00	2.00	5.00
	1943–46 . . . 50.			

Silver

37	5 Lire 1942–46	10.00	20.00	25.00
	1943–46 . . . 100.			
38	10 Lire 1942–46	20.00	30.00	50.00
	1943–46 . . . 100.			

Gold

39	*F287–288* 100 Lire 1942–49	150.00	250.00	450.00

Unless otherwise noted, prices are for coins in very
fine, extremely fine, and uncirculated condition.

Third Coinage

Aluminum

40	1 Lira 1947–49	2.00	5.00	10.00
41	2 Lire 1947–49	2.00	5.00	10.00

42	5 Lire 1947–49	2.00	5.00	10.00
43	10 Lire 1947–49	2.00	5.00	10.00

Holy Year Commemoratives

Aluminum

44	1 Lira MCML (1950)	1.00	2.00	5.00

45	2 Lire MCML	2.00	4.50	9.00

46	5 Lire MCML	2.00	5.00	10.00
47	10 Lire MCML	2.00	5.00	10.00

Gold

48	*F289* 100 Lire MCML	100.00 200.00 400.00

Fourth Coinage

Aluminum

49	1 Lira 1951–58	.50	.75	1.75
50	2 Lire 1951–58	.50	.75	1.75

Obv: Bust
Rev: Justice standing

51	5 Lire 1951–58	.25	.50	1.00

52	10 Lire 1951–58	.50	1.00	2.00

Aluminum-Bronze

A52	20 Lire 1957–58	2.00	4.00	7.50

Stainless Steel

54	50 Lire 1955–58	1.50	2.50	5.00

55	100 Lire 1955–58		1.00	2.00	5.00

60	5 Lire 1959–62	1.00	2.00	3.50
61	10 Lire 1959–62	1.00	2.00	3.50

Silver

56	500 Lire 1958	7.00	12.50	25.00

Aluminum-Bronze

62	20 Lire 1959–62	1.00	2.00	5.00

Gold

53	*F290* 100 Lire 1951–56	275.00	450.00	550.00
A53	*F291* 100 Lire 1957–58,			
	Papal arms on rev.	150.00	250.00	450.00

Stainless Steel

63	50 Lire 1959–62	1.00	2.00	5.00
64	100 Lire 1959–62	1.00	2.00	5.00

1959 50, 100 and 500 Lire have A-I or AN-I (year one and later) upside down under bust. 1960 and later coins have AN-II etc. right side up.

SEDE VACANTE 1958

Silver

57	500 Lire 1958	7.00	12.50	20.00

JOHN XXIII 1958–1963

Aluminum

58	1 Lira 1959–62	1.50	3.00	7.50

Silver

65	500 Lire 1959–62	5.00	10.00	25.00

1960–62 have date under bust on obverse.

Gold

59	2 Lire 1959–62	1.50	3.00	7.50

66	*F292* 100 Lire 1959	750.00	1400.	2000.

Unless otherwise noted, prices are for coins in very fine, extremely fine, and uncirculated condition.

Ecumenical Council Commemoratives

Aluminum

67	1 Lira 1962	1.50	2.50	5.00
68	2 Lire 1962	1.50	2.50	5.00

69	5 Lire 1962	.50	1.00	2.00
70	10 Lire 1962	.50	1.00	2.00

Aluminum-Bronze

71	20 Lire 1962	1.00	2.00	5.00

Stainless Steel

72	500 Lire 1962	.50	1.00	2.00

73	100 Lire 1962	.50	1.00	2.00

Silver

74	500 Lire 1962	5.00	10.00	25.00

SEDE VACANTE 1963

75	500 Lire 1963	7.00	12.50	20.00

Later issues in *Current Coins of the World*.

VENEZUELA

A republic in northern South America. The country is divided by the Orinoco River. Exports: petroleum, coffee, iron. Area: 352,150 square miles. Languages: Spanish, Indian dialects. Capital: *Caracas*.

Monetary System:
100 Centavos = 10 Reales = 1 Peso to 1865
100 Centavos = 1 Venezolano 1865–79
100 Centimos = 1 Bolivar 1879–

REPUBLICA DE VENEZUELA
1830–1863

Copper

1	¼ Centavo 1843, 52 (19mm)	15.00	30.00	75.00
2	½ Centavo 1843, 52 (24mm)	20.00	40.00	100.00
3	1 Centavo 1843, 52 (32mm)	40.00	100.00	200.00
	1843 . . . 75			

Size Reduced

4	¼ Centavo 1852 (18mm)	20.00	40.00	100.00
5	½ Centavo 1852 (22mm)	25.00	45.00	120.00
6	1 Centavo 1852 (30mm)	10.00	20.00	50.00

Size Further Reduced

7	1 Centavo 1858–63			
	(26mm)	6.00	12.00	40.00

LIBERTAD incuse 1858, raised 1858–63.

Silver

8	''1½'' (= ½) Real 1858	400.00	800.00	1500.
9	1 Real 1858	300.00	600.00	1000.
10	2 Reales 1858	350.00	750.00	1400.
11	5 Reales 1858	500.00	1000.	2500.

Obv: President Paez
Rev: Value in wreath

A11	10 Reales 1863	4000.	8000.	12000.

No. A11 was not issued to circulation. Smaller silver coins are probably patterns; copper denominations are believed to be fantasies produced later.

ESTADOS UNIDOS DE VENEZUELA 1864–1953
First Coinage

Cupro-Nickel

25	1 Centavo 1876–77	8.00	25.00	75.00
26	2½ Centavos 1876–77	10.00	35.00	125.00

Nos. 12–17 bear no denominations, but have their weights stated in grams as shown below. Silver coins

are identical to Nos. 20–24, as only the legal names of denominations were changed in 1879.

Obv: Simon Bolivar

12	GR.1.250 (5 Centavos)			
	1874,76	25.00	50.00	125.00

13*	GR.2.500 (10 Centavos)			
	1874,76	35.00	70.00	200.00
14	GRAM.5 (20 Centavos)			
	1874,76	40.00	100.00	300.00
15	G.12,500 (50 Centavos)			
	1873–76	150.00	275.00	750.00
16	GRAM.25 (1 Venezolano)			
	1876	400.00	1250.	5000.

Gold

17	*F7* GR.8.0645 (5 Venezolanos) 1875	275.00	450.00	600.00

Second Coinage

100 Centimos = 1 Bolivar

Cupro-Nickel

27	5 Centimos 1896–1938	1.00	4.00	12.00
28	12½ Centimos 1896–1938	1.00	5.00	15.00

Silver

See note on denominations above No. 12

19	GRAM.1 (⅕ Bolivar) 1879	500.00	1000.	2000.

Unless otherwise noted, prices are for coins in very fine, extremely fine, and uncirculated condition.

20* GR.1.250 (¼ Bolivar)
1894–1948 .75 1.00 2.00
1901, 03 . . . 25.

21 GR.2.500 (½ Bolivar)
1879–1936 4.00 10.00 25.00
1879, 1903, 11 . . . 150.
1887, 88 . . . 400.
1889 . . . 2000.
22* GRAM.5 (1 Bolivar)
1879–1936 3.00 6.00 15.00
1887, 88, 89 . . . 400.
23 GRAM.10 (2 Bolivares)
1879–1936 5.00 10.00 20.00
1886, 88, 89 . . . 200.
24 GRAM.25 (5 Bolivares)
1879–1936 12.00 18.00 40.00
1879–89 . . . 65.

Gold

31 *F6* GR.3.2258 (10 Bolivares) 1930 60.00 75.00 100.00
32 *F5* GR.6.4516 (20 Bolivares) 1879–1912 110.00 125.00 165.00
33* *F2* GR.32.2580 (100 Bolivares) 1886–89 700.00 1000. 1200.

Brass

Obv: modified shield
29 5 Centimos 1944 4.00 6.00 15.00
30 12½ Centimos 1944 25.00 60.00 125.00

Cupro-Nickel

29a 5 Centimos 1945–48 .25 .50 3.00
30a 12½ Centimos 1945–48 .25 .50 3.00

Silver

Rev: Modified arms
21a GR.2.500 (½ Bolivar)
1944–46 2.00 3.00 10.00
22a* GRAM.5 (1 Bolivar)
1945 2.00 3.00 6.00
23a GRAM.10 (2 Bolivares)
1945 3.00 4.00 8.00

Silver

35 25 Centimos 1954 – 1.00 2.00
35a 25 Centimos 1960,
smaller shield – 1.00 1.75
36 50 Centimos 1954 – 1.50 3.00
36a* 50 Centimos 1960,
smaller shield – 1.50 1.75

37 1 Bolivar 1954 2.00 2.50 4.00
37a 1 Bolivar 1960, 65
smaller head and legend 2.00 2.25 3.00

A37 2 Bolivares 1960, 65   4.00   4.25   4.50

Cupro-Nickel

38 5 Centimos 1958   .10   .30   1.00

39 12½ Centimos 1958   .10   .30   1.00
Later issues in *Current Coins of the World.*

VIETNAM

Formerly part of French Indochina, Vietnam was formed
after World War II of Annam, Tonkin and Cochin China.
A provisional communist government was formed in
1945, while a French-sponsored monarchy was established in 1949. After the defeat of the French in 1954
the country was partitioned between the two rival factions. Following years of warfare, the country was unified under communist rule in 1975. Area: 126,436
square miles. Language: Vietnamese. Capitals: Hanoi
(communist), Saigon (monarchy).

Monetary System:
10 Xu = 1 Hao
100 Xu = 1 Dong

**Provisional Government
1945–1946**

Aluminum

1 20 Xu 1945   50.00 100.00 175.00

2 5 Hao 1946 (value in-
cused)   45.00   80.00 125.00
2a 5 Hao 1946 (value raised) 12.50   20.00   35.00

Obv: President Ho Chi Minh (1945–69)

3 1 Dong 1946   125.00 200.00 300.00

Bronze

4 2 Dong 1946   50.00 100.00 150.00
For later issues see NORTH and SOUTH VIETNAM,
which follow.

VIETNAM, NORTH

A part of former French Indochina. A 1954 Geneva accord separated Vietnam at the 17th parallel into North
and South Vietnam. Area: 60,156 square miles. Language: Vietnamese. Capital: *Hanoi.*

Monetary System:
10 Xu = 1 Hao
100 Xu = 1 Dong

Aluminum

| 5 | 1 Xu 1958 | 2.00 | 5.00 | 10.00 |

| 6 | 2 Xu 1958 | 2.00 | 5.00 | 10.00 |
| 7 | 5 Xu 1958 | 2.00 | 5.00 | 10.00 |

| 4 | 50 Su 1960 | .75 | 1.25 | 2.50 |

Cupro-Nickel

| 5 | 1 Dong 1960 | .25 | .50 | 1.00 |

Aluminum
| 6 | 50 Xu 1963 | .50 | 1.00 | 2.00 |

Later issues in *Current Coins of the World.*

VIETNAM, SOUTH

Southern zone of Vietnam established by 1954 Geneva accord below the 17th parallel. Formerly a part of French Indo-China. Fell to North Vietnam in 1975. Area: 65,498 square miles. Languages: Vietnamese, French, Chinese, others. Capital: *Saigon (now Ho Chi Minh City).*

Monetary System:
100 Xu (Su) = 1 Dong

Aluminum

| 1 | 10 Su 1953 | .50 | 1.00 | 1.75 |
| 2 | 20 Su 1953 | .75 | 1.25 | 2.50 |

| 3 | 50 Xu 1953 | 5.00 | 15.00 | 22.50 |

VISCAYAN REPUBLIC —

see SPAIN

YEMEN

Situated in the southwest corner of Arabia. Formerly an independent feudal kingdom, it became a republic in 1962. Exports: Coffee, cotton, salt, hides. Area: 75,000 square miles. Capitals: Taiz and San'a

Monetary System:
2 Halala = 1 Buqsha (Bogach)
2 Buqsha = 1 Ghirsh (Piastre)
40 Buqsha = 1 Imadi, Ahmadi, Riyal or Maria Theresa Thaler

Unless otherwise noted, prices are for coins in Very Fine condition.

IMAM YAHYA BIN MOHAMMED HAMID AL-DIN

As Rebel A.H. 1321 (1903–04)
Silver

| A1 | 1 Ghirsh AH 1321 | 75.00 |

As Imam and King
A.H. 1322–1367 (1904–48)
Yellow or Red Bronze

B1 ½ Halala AH 1322   60.00
Date 1322 is accession date, not issue date.
1 ½ Halala AH 1342 (1923),
crescent type   45.00

1a* ½ Halala 1342–46 (plain
type)   10.00
2 1 Halala 1322 (1904)   50.00

2a* 1 Halala 1330–61   10.00
3 1 Bogach 1341–67   9.00
There are at least five distinct varieties of No. 3.

Silver

4 $^1/_{20}$ Imadi AH 1337–66   10.00
5 $^1/_{10}$ Imadi 1337–42   10.00
5a* $^1/_{10}$ Imadi 1343–66   5.00
8 ⅛ Imadi 1339   500.00
6 ¼ Imadi 1341–43   35.00
7 1 Imadi 1344   11.00

10* ¼ Imadi AH 1344–66   12.50

AHMED HAMID AL-DIN
1948–1962
Bronze

11* 1 Halala AH 1368–86
(1949–67)   1.00
12 1 Bogach 1368–79   1.25

Aluminum

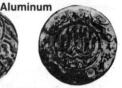

11a* 1 Halala 1374–78 (1955–59)   .70
12a 1 Bogach 1374–77   1.50

Silver

13 $^1/_{16}$ Ahmadi AH 1367–74
(1948–55)   4.00
A14 $^1/_{10}$ Ahmadi 1370   750.00
14* ⅛ Ahmadi 1367–80   2.50

14a ⅛ Ahmadi 1368, hexagonal   500.00

15* ¼ Ahmadi AH 1367–80   7.50

16 ½ Ahmadi 1367–82   12.50

Unless otherwise noted, prices are for coins in very
fine, extremely fine, and uncirculated condition.

17 1 Ahmadi (Ryal) 1367–80
(1948–61)   25.00

Aluminum

18* 1 Halala ND (1956)   .60
19 1 Bogach ND (1956)   .75
Date 1367 shown on Nos. 18–19 is accession date, not
issue date.

Gold

G15 *F4* ¼ Ahmadi "(1)"   300.00
G16* *F3* ½ Ahmadi "(2)"   500.00
G17 *F2* 1 Ahmadi "(5)"   1000.

YEMEN ARAB REPUBLIC 1962–

Brass or Bronze

Obv: Hand holding torch
20* 1 Halala AH 1382 (1963)   1.50
22 1 Bogach 1382–84   1.00

Obv: Star between two lines
Rev: Value in center
21* 1 Halala 1382, value spelled
out   4.25
32 ½ Bogach (1 Halala) 1382,
value as fraction   10.00

Silver

23 ¹/₂₀ Ryal AH 1382   4.50
24 ¹/₁₀ Ryal 1382   4.25
25* ⅕ Ryal 1382   10.00
A25 ¼ Ryal 1382   45.00
(Thick and thin varieties of Nos. 23, 24, A25.)

Later issues in *Current Coins of the World.*

YUGOSLAVIA
(Kraljevina Jugoslavija)

On the east shore of the Adriatic Sea south of Hungary.
It was formed after World War I by uniting to the kingdom of Serbia several Austro-Hungarian provinces plus
the erstwhile kingdom of Montenegro. Principal industries are agriculture, cattle-raising and forestry. Area:
98,766 square miles. Languages: Serbo-Croatian, Slo-
venian, Macedonian. Capital: Belgrade.

Monetary System:
100 Para = 1 Dinar

PETAR I 1918–1921
(Hitherto King of Serbia)

Zinc

1 5 Para 1920   5.00 10.00 25.00
2 10 Para 1920   3.00   7.00 15.00

Nickel-Bronze

3	25 Para 1920	.50	2.00	7.00

ALEXANDER I 1921–1934
First Coinage
Cupro-Nickel

4	50 Para 1925	.50	2.00	7.00
5	1 Dinar 1925	.50	2.00	7.00
6	2 Dinara 1925	1.00	3.00	10.00

Gold

10	*F1* 20 Dinara 1925	125.00	200.00	275.00

Second Coinage
Silver

7	10 Dinara 1931	5.00	10.00	20.00

8	20 Dinara 1931	7.00	15.00	35.00
9	50 Dinara 1932	10.00	25.00	85.00

There are two varieties of No. 9: with and without name below truncation of neck.

Trade Coins

Gold

A11	*F3* 1 Dukat 1931–33	60.00	100.00	135.00

12	*F2* 4 Dukata 1931–32	275.00	400.00	600.00

Nos. A11 and 12 have a small official counterstamp on obverse near rim.

PETAR II 1934–1945

Bronze

13	25 Para 1938	.40	4.00	10.00

Unless otherwise noted, prices are for coins in very fine, extremely fine, and uncirculated condition.

Aluminum-Bronze

14	50 Para 1938	.50	3.00	7.00
15	1 Dinar 1938	.50	2.00	7.00
16	2 Dinara 1938 (large crown)	.20	1.00	6.00

| 17 | 2 Dinara 1938 (small crown) | 5.00 | 10.00 | 25.00 |

Nickel

| 18 | 10 Dinara 1938 | .50 | 3.00 | 10.00 |

Silver

| 19 | 20 Dinara 1938 (head left) | 3.00 | 7.00 | 22.50 |
| 20 | 50 Dinara 1938 | 4.00 | 10.00 | 25.00 |

CROATIA

German-Formed State 1941–1944
Zinc

| 1 | 2 Kune 1941 | 5.00 | 10.00 | 25.00 |

See SERBIA for other World War II issues from this area.

FEDERATED REPUBLIC
1945–1952

Zinc

21	50 Para 1945	.75	2.00	5.00
22	1 Dinar 1945	.50	1.00	3.00
23	2 Dinara 1945	1.00	2.00	5.00

| 24 | 5 Dinara 1945 | 1.00 | 2.00 | 5.00 |

FEDERATED PEOPLE'S
REPUBLIC 1953–1962

Legend:
FEDERATIVNA NARODNA
REPUBLIKA JUGOSLAVIJA
Aluminum

25	50 Para 1953	.10	.20	.30
26	1 Dinar 1953	.10	.20	.30
27	2 Dinara 1953	.20	.30	.40
28	5 Dinara 1953	.30	.50	.75

Aluminum-Bronze

29   10 Dinara 1955   .50   1.00   1.50

30   20 Dinara 1955   1.00   1.50   2.50

31   50 Dinara 1955   2.00   3.00   4.00

SOCIALIST FEDERATED REPUBLIC 1963–

New Legend: SOCIJALISTICKA FEDERATIVNA REPUBLIKA JUGOSLAVIJA
Aluminum

32	1 Dinar 1963	.05	.10	.20
33	2 Dinara 1963	.10	.20	.30
34	5 Dinara 1963	.20	.30	.50

Aluminum-Bronze

35	10 Dinara 1963	.50	.75	1.00
A35	20 Dinara 1963	1.00	1.50	2.00
B35	50 Dinara 1963	2.00	3.00	4.00

Later issues in *Current Coins of the World*.

ZANZIBAR

The Arab Sultanate of Zanzibar and Pemba, a group of islands off the east African coast plus a narrow strip of mainland, was a possession of Muscat and Oman until becoming independent in the mid–19th century. It enjoyed prosperity as a major Indian Ocean trading center, noted for cloves and other spices, ivory and slaves. In 1890 it became a British protectorate. The Indian Rupee and Maria Theresa Thaler (ryal) were moneys of account until 1936, and in 1964 Zanzibar united with Tanganyika to form Tanzania. Area: 1,020 square miles. Languages: Swahili, English, Arabic. Capital: *Zanzibar City*.

Monetary System:
64 Pysa (Pice) = 1 India Rupee
136 Pysa = 1 Ryal to 1908
100 Cents = 1 Rupee 1908–09

Sultan Barghash ibn Sa'id 1870–1888

Copper

1   1 Pysa AH 1299 (1882)   2.00   5.00   25.00
                                       Proof . . . 250.00

2   1 Pysa AH 1304 (1887)   2.50   5.00   50.00
                                       Proof . . . 250.00

Unless otherwise noted, prices are for coins in very fine, extremely fine, and uncirculated condition.

Silver

5 1 Ryal 1299   175.00 250.00 550.00

Gold

7 *F1* 5 Ryals 1299   4500. 7000. 10000.
Other silver and gold coins dated AH 1299 (former Nos.
3, 4, 6) are patterns.

Sultan Ali Bin Hamud
1902–1911

Bronze

8* 1 Cent 1908   175.00 300.00 500.00
9 10 Cents 1908   225.00 400.00 650.00

Nickel

10 20 Cents 1908   300.00 525.00 850.00
Nos. 8–10 not released to circulation.

For later issues see EAST AFRICA.

PRECIOUS METAL CONTENT OF WORLD COINAGE 1850-1950

Compiled by Holland Wallace

Nearly all modern coins are composed of a mixture of two or more metals. This mixture, called an alloy, may be simply the traditional 90% silver and 10% copper, or something as complex as 50% silver, 40% copper, 5% zinc and 5% tin. Usually it is not important to know the exact composition of a coin; therefore, the listings in the body of this catalog indicate only the principal metals used. The heading "silver," for instance, is used for coins containing from 50% to 94½% silver (those with less than 50% silver are termed "billon"), and "gold" is applied to any coin containing enough gold to have a yellow color, from as low as 17½% to as high as 98.6%.

Normally it is only in the case of precious metals that the exact proportions of a coin's alloy become significant to the collector. Such information can be used to determine the genuineness of a given coin, or to compute its intrinsic value based on its bullion content of gold or silver.

A new interest in the bullion value of coins has arisen because of frequent changes in value of gold and silver. The metals have recently been priced at all-time highs, and because of this some coins are now valued more for their metal content than as numismatic items.

Because of today's need for more facts concerning bullion values, this special section has been added to the catalog. In the following tables almost every silver and gold coin of the world from 1850 to 1950 is listed with its gross weight, fineness and net metal content. This content has been calculated both in net grams and ounces troy of pure gold or silver.

To determine the current bullion value of a coin you need only multiply the net ounce troy figure by the daily price quotation for the metal involved. As an example, if the day's fixed price of gold is $415 per ounce, the bullion value of a sovereign is determined by multiplying $415 times .2354 ounce, giving $97.69 as the value of the gold in that coin.

The weights and finenesses in the tables are those specified by law, and do not take into account any tolerances or fluctuations caused by the manufacturing process. Such tolerances range from a fraction of a percent up to many percentage points, depending on the technical ability and the willingness of a country to adhere to its legal standards. Weights shown are, of course, for coins in substantially original condition which have not lost noticeable weight through wear.

In almost every case the weights and finenesses have been taken from official sources such as mint reports and other publications of various governments. Unofficial statistics have been used only where they seem to be highly reliable, and material from supposedly authoritative sources has sometimes been disregarded when it seemed questionable. Figures in italics indicate conflicting information from official sources, or data whose accuracy could not be completely verified. Certain coinages, for the most part those of more irregular manufacture, have been omitted due to lack of any precise official data whatever.

Because of the large volume of statistical material involved in the preparation of these tables, errors are inevitable. Further information that will increase the accuracy of the listings is invited.

PRECIOUS METAL CONTENT — SILVER

Dates	Denomination	Gross Wt., Gms.	Fineness	Silver Content Grams	Silver Content Ounces	Dates	Denomination	Gross Wt., Gms.	Fineness	Silver Content Grams	Silver Content Ounces
						1858-67	5 Kreuzer	1.3333	.375	0.5000	.0161
ALBANIA							10 Kreuzer	2.0000	.500	1.0000	.0322
1925-37 same as Latin Monetary Union (Franka Ari = Franc)						1868-72	10 Kreuzer	1.6667	.400	0.6667	.0214
1939 same as Italy (Lek = Lire)							20 Kreuzer	2.6667	.500	1.3333	.0429
ARGENTINA						1857-92	¼ Florin	5.3450	.5208	2.7837	.0895
1881-83	10 Centavos	2.5000	.900	2.2500	.0723		1 Florin	12.3457	.900	11.1111	.3572
	20 Centavos	5.0000	.900	4.5000	.1447		2 Florin	24.6914	.900	22.2222	.7144
	50 Centavos	12.5000	.900	11.2500	.3617	1892-1916	1 Krone	5.0000	.835	4.1750	.1342
	1 Peso	25.0000	.900	22.5000	.7234		2 Kronen	10.0000	.835	8.3500	.2685
AUSTRALIA							5 Kronen	24.0000	.900	21.6000	.6944
1910-45 same as Great Britain 1817-1920						1924	1 Schilling	7.0000	.800	5.6000	.1800
1946-64 same as Great Britain 1920-46						1925-38	½ Schilling	3.0000	.640	1.9200	.0617
AUSTRIA							1 Schilling	6.0000	.640	3.8400	.1235
1780 MT Thaler	28.0668	.833⅓	23.3890	.7520			2 Schilling	12.0000	.640	7.6800	.2469
1857-68	1 Vereinsthaler ..	18.5186	.900	16.6667	.5358		5 Schilling	15.0000	.835	12.5250	.4027
	2 Vereinsthaler ..	37.0371	.900	33.3333	1.0717	**BELGIUM**					
						1832-65 same as France 1803-66					

Dates	Denomination	Gross Wt., Gms.	Fineness	Silver Content Grams	Silver Content Ounces
BELGIUM (cont.)					
1865-1918	see Latin Monetary Union				
1933-35	20 Francs	11.0000	.680	7.4800	.2405
	50 Francs	22.0000	.680	14.9600	.4810
1939-40	50 Francs	20.0000	.835	16.7000	.5369
1948-60	20 Francs	8.0000	.835	6.6800	.2148
	50 Francs	12.5000	.835	10.4375	.3356
	100 Francs	18.0000	.835	15.0300	.4832
BELGIAN CONGO					
1887-96	same as Latin Monetary Union				
BOLIVIA					
1864-71	1/20 Bol/5 Cvos	1.2500	.900	1.1250	.0362
	1/10 Bol/10 Cvos	2.5000	.900	2.2500	.0723
	1/5 Bol/20 Cvos	5.0000	.900	4.5000	.1447
1873-91	½ Bol/50 Cvos	12.5000	.900	11.2500	.3617
1864-79	1 Boliviano	25.0000	.900	22.5000	.7234
1909	20 Centavos	4.0000	.833⅓	3.3333	.1072
	50 Centavos	10.0000	.833⅓	8.3333	.2679
BRAZIL					
1867-69	200 Reis	2.5000	.835	2.0875	.0671
	500 Reis	6.2500	.835	5.2188	.1678
	1000 Reis	12.5000	.835	10.4375	.3356
	2000 Reis	25.0000	.835	20.8750	.6711
1875-1900	400 Reis	5.1000	.916⅔	4.6750	.1503
	500 Reis	6.3750	.916⅔	5.8438	.1879
	1000 Reis	12.7500	.916⅔	11.6875	.3758
	2000 Reis	25.5000	.916⅔	23.3750	.7515
	4000 Reis	51.0000	.916⅔	46.7500	1.5030
1906-13	500 Reis	5.0000	.900	4.5000	.1447
	1000 Reis	10.0000	.900	9.0000	.2894
	2000 Reis	20.0000	.900	18.0000	.5787
1922	2000 Reis	8.0000	.900	7.2000	.2315
1922-35	2000 Reis	8.0000	.500	4.0000	.1286
1936-38	5000 Reis	10.0000	.600	6.0000	.1929
BRITISH GUIANA					
1888-1943	4 Pence	1.8851	.925	1.7437	.0561
1944-45	4 Pence	1.8851	.500	0.9425	.0303
BRITISH HONDURAS					
1894-1946	same as Canada 1858-1910				
BRITISH NORTH BORNEO					
1929	25 Cents	2.8276	.500	1.4138	.0455
BRITISH WEST AFRICA					
1913-20	same as Great Britain 1817-1920				
BULGARIA					
1882-1916	same as Latin Monetary Union (Stotinki/Leva = Centimes/Francs)				
1930-37	20 Leva	4.0000	.500	2.0000	.0643
	50 Leva	10.0000	.500	5.0000	.1608
	100 Leva	20.0000	.500	10.0000	.3215
CANADA					
1858-1910	5 Cents	1.1620	.925	1.0749	.0346
	10 Cents	2.3240	.925	2.1497	.0691
	20 Cents	4.6480	.925	4.2994	.1382
	25 Cents	5.8100	.925	5.3743	.1728
	50 Cents	11.6200	.925	10.7485	.3456
1910-19	5 Cents	1.1664	.925	1.0789	.0347
	10 Cents	2.3328	.925	2.1578	.0694
	25 Cents	5.8319	.925	5.3945	.1734
	50 Cents	11.6638	.925	10.7890	.3469
1920-67	5 Cents	1.1664	.800	0.9331	.0300
	10 Cents	2.3328	.800	1.8662	.0600
	25 Cents	5.8319	.800	4.6655	.1500
	50 Cents	11.6638	.800	9.3310	.3000
	1 Dollar	23.3276	.800	18.6621	.6000
NEW BRUNSWICK					
1862-64	same as Canada 1858-1910				
NEWFOUNDLAND					
1865-1912	5 Cents	1.1782	.925	1.0898	.0350
	10 Cents	2.3564	.925	2.1797	.0701

Dates	Denomination	Gross Wt., Gms.	Fineness	Silver Content Grams	Silver Content Ounces
	20 Cents	4.7127	.925	4.3592	.1401
	50 Cents	*11.7818*	.925	*10.8982*	*.3504*
1917-44	same as Canada 1910-19				
1945-47	same as Canada 1920-67				
CEYLON					
1892-1917	10 Cents	1.1664	.800	0.9331	.0300
	25 Cents	2.9160	.800	2.3328	.0750
	50 Cents	5.8319	.800	4.6655	.1500
1919-42	10 Cents	1.1664	.550	0.6415	.0206
	25 Cents	2.9160	.550	1.6038	.0516
	50 Cents	5.8319	.550	3.2075	.1031
CHILE					
1852-59	same as Peru 1863-1917(Decimo/Peso=Dinero/Sol)				
1860-80	½ Decimo	1.1500	.900	1.0350	.0333
	1 Decimo	2.3000	.900	2.0700	.0666
	20 Centavos	4.6000	.900	4.1400	.1331
1879-94	½ Decimo	1.2500	.500	0.6250	.0201
	1 Decimo	2.5000	.500	1.2500	.0402
	20 Centavos	5.0000	.500	2.5000	.0804
1891	20 Centavos	4.0000	.500	2.0000	.0643
	20 Centavos	5.0000	.200	1.0000	.0322
1853-91	50 Centavos	12.5000	.900	11.2500	.3617
	1 Peso	25.0000	.900	22.5000	.7234
1895-97	5 Centavos	1.0000	.835	0.8350	.0268
	10 Centavos	2.0000	.835	1.6700	.0537
	20 Centavos	4.0000	.835	3.3400	.1074
	1 Peso	20.0000	.835	16.7000	.5369
1899-1907	5 Centavos	1.0000	.500	0.5000	.0161
	10 Centavos	2.0000	.500	1.0000	.0322
	20 Centavos	4.0000	.500	2.0000	.0643
	50 Centavos	10.0000	.700	7.0000	.2251
	1 Peso	20.0000	.700	14.0000	.4501
1907-13	5 Centavos	1.0000	.400	0.4000	.0129
	10 Centavos	1.5000	.400	0.6000	.0193
	20 Centavos	3.0000	.400	1.2000	.0386
	40 Centavos	6.0000	.400	2.4000	.0772
	1 Peso	12.0000	.900	10.8000	.3472
1915-19	5 Centavos	1.0000	.450	0.4500	.0145
	10 Centavos	1.5000	.450	0.6750	.0217
	20 Centavos	3.0000	.450	1.3500	.0434
	1 Peso	9.0000	.720	6.4800	.2083
1919-20	same as 1907-13				
1921-27	1 Peso	9.0000	.500	4.5000	.1447
	2 Pesos	18.0000	.500	9.0000	.2894
	5 Pesos	25.0000	.900	22.5000	.7234
1932	1 Peso	6.0000	.400	2.4000	.0772
CHINA					
1932-34	1 Yuan	26.6971	.880	23.4934	.7553
1949	5 Chio	5.0000	.720	3.6000	.1157
COLOMBIA					
1872-86	5 Centavos	1.2500	.666	0.8333	.0268
	10 Centavos	2.5000	.835	2.0875	.0671
	20 Centavos	5.0000	.835	4.1750	.1342
	50 Cs/5 Ds	12.5000	.835	10.4375	.3356
1885-89	10 Centavos	2.5000	.500	1.2500	.0402
	20 Centavos	5.0000	.500	2.5000	.0804
	50 Cs/5 Ds	12.5000	.500	6.2500	.2009
1889-1908	5 Centavos	*1.2500*	*.666*	*0.8333*	*.0286*
	10 Centavos	2.5000	.666	1.6667	.0536
	20 Centavos	5.0000	.666	3.3333	.1072
	50 Centavos	12.5000	.835	10.4375	.3356
1911-42	10 Centavos	2.5000	.900	2.2500	.0723
	20 Centavos	5.0000	.900	4.5000	.1447
	50 Centavos	12.5000	.900	11.2500	.3617
1945-52	10 Centavos	2.5000	.500	1.2500	.0402
	20 Centavos	5.0000	.500	2.5000	.0804
	50 Centavos	12.5000	.500	6.2500	.2009
1953	20 Centavos	5.0000	.300	1.5000	.0482
1956	1 Peso	25.0000	.900	22.5000	.7234
COMORO ISLANDS					
1890	5 Francs	25.0000	.900	22.5000	.7234

Dates	Denomination	Gross Wt., Gms.	Fine- ness	Silver Content Grams	Ounces
COSTA RICA					
1864-93	5 Centavos *1.2680*		.750	*0.9510*	*.0306*
	10 Centavos *2.5361*		.750	*1.9021*	*.0612*
	25 Centavos *6.3402*		.750	*4.7552*	*.1529*
	50 Centavos *12.6804*		.750	*9.5103*	*.3058*
1902-14	5 Centavos 1.0000		.900	0.9000	.0289
	10 Centavos 2.0000		.900	1.8000	.0579
	50 Centavos 10.0000		.900	9.0000	.2894
1917-24	10 Centavos 2.0000		.500	1.0000	.0322
	25 Centavos 3.4500		.650	2.2425	.0721
	50 Centavos 10.0000		.500	5.0000	.1608
CRETE					
1901	same as Latin Monetary Union (Lepta/Drachmai=Centimes/Francs)				
CUBA					
1915-53	20 Centavos 5.0000		.900	4.5000	.1447
	40 Centavos ... 10.0000		.900	9.0000	.2894
	Other values: same as United States (Centavos/Pesos=Cents /Dollars)				
CURACAO					
1900-48	same as Netherlands				
CYPRUS					
1901-40	3 Piastres 1.8851		.925	1.7437	.0561
	4½ Piastres 2.8276		.925	2.6155	.0841
	9 Piastres 5.6552		.924	5.2311	.1682
	18 Piastres 11.3104		.925	10.4621	.3364
	45 Piastres 28.2759		.925	26.1552	.8409
CZECHOSLOVAKIA					
1928-37	5 Korun 7.0000		.500	3.5000	.1125
	10 Korun 10.0000		.700	7.0000	.2251
	20 Korun 12.0000		.700	8.4000	.2701
.1939-44	10 Korun 7.0000		.500	3.5000	.1125
	20 Korun 15.0000		.500	7.5000	.2411
	50 Korun 16.5000		.700	11.5500	.3713
1947-51	50 Korun 10.0000		.500	5.0000	.1608
	100 Korun 14.0000		.500	7.0000	.2251
DANISH WEST INDIES					
1859-79	3 Cents *1.0440*		.625	*0.6525*	*.0210*
	5 Cents *1.7400*		.625	*1.0875*	*.0350*
	10 Cents *3.4800*		.625	*2.1750*	*.0699*
	20 Cents *6.9600*		.625	*4.3500*	*.1399*
1905-07	50 Bit/10 Cents .. 2.5000		.800	2.0000	.0643
	1 Fr/20 Cents 5.0000		.800	4.0000	.1286
	2 Fr/40 Cents ... 10.0000		.800	8.0000	.2572
DANZIG					
1923-27	½ Gulden 2.5000		.750	1.8750	.0603
	1 Gulden 5.0000		.750	3.7500	.1206
	2 Gulden 10.0000		.750	7.5000	.2411
	5 Gulden 25.0000		.750	18.7500	.6028
1932	2 Gulden 10.0000		.500	5.0000	.1608
	5 Gulden 15.0000		.500	7.5000	.2411
DENMARK					
1874-1958	see Scandinavian Monetary Union				
DOMINICAN REPUBLIC					
1891	same as Latin Monetary Union (Centesimos/Francos=Centimes/Francs)				
1897	10 Centavos 2.5000		.350	0.8750	.0281
	20 Centavos 5.0000		.350	1.7500	.0563
	½ Peso 12.5000		.350	4.3750	.1407
	1 Peso 25.0000		.350	8.7500	.2813
1937-61	same as United States ((Centavos/Peso=Cents/Dollars)				
EAST AFRICA					
1906-19	same as Ceylon 1892-1917				
1920	25 Cents 2.9160		.500	1.4580	.0469
	50 Cents 5.8319		.500	2.9160	.0937
	1 Florin 11.6638		.500	5 8319	.1875
1921-46	50 Cents 3.8879		.250	0.9720	.0312
	1 Shilling 7.7759		.250	1.9440	.0625

Dates	Denomination	Gross Wt., Gms.	Fine- ness	Silver Content Grams	Ounces
ECUADOR					
1884-1916	same as Peru 1863-1917 (Decimos/Sucres=Dineros/Soles)				
1928-44	50 Centavos 2.5000		.720	1.8000	.0579
	1 Sucre 5.0000		.720	3.6000	.1157
	2 Sucres 10.0000		.720	7.2000	.2315
	5 Sucres 25.0000		.720	18.0000	.5787
EGYPT					
1885-1942	1 Ghirsh 1.4000		.833⅓	1.1667	.0375
	2 Ghirsh 2.8000		.833⅓	2.3333	.0750
	5 Ghirsh 7.0000		.833⅓	5.8333	.1875
	10 Ghirsh 14.0000		.833⅓	11.6667	.3751
	20 Ghirsh 28.0000		.833⅓	23.3333	.7502
1944	2 Ghirsh *2.8000*		.500	*1.4000*	*.0450*
ERITREA					
1890-96	50 Centesimi 2.5000		.835	2.0875	.0671
	1 Lira 5.0000		.835	4.1750	.1342
	2 Lire 10.0000		.835	8.3500	.2685
	5 Lire 28.1250		.800	22.5000	.7234
1918	1 Tallero 28.0668		.835	23.4358	.7535
ESTONIA					
1930-33	1 Kroon 6.0000		.500	3.0000	.0965
	2 Krooni 12.0000		.500	6.0000	.1929
ETHIOPIA					
1897-1903	1 Gersh 1.4038		.835	1.1721	.0377
	⅛ Ber 3.5094		.835	2.9303	.0942
	¼ Ber 7.0188		.835	5.8607	.1884
	½ Ber 14.0375		.835	11.7213	.3768
	1 Ber 28.0750		.835	23.4426	.7537
1944	50 Santeem *7.0307*		.800	*5.6246*	*.1808*
	50 Santeem *7.0307*		.700	*4.9215*	*.1582*
FIJI					
1934-45	same as Great Britain 1920-46				
1942-43	6 Pence 2.8276		.900	2.5448	.0818
	1 Shilling 5.6552		.900	5.0897	.1636
	1 Florin 11.3104		.900	10.1794	.3273
FINLAND					
1864-1917	25 Pennia 1.2747		.750	0.9560	.0307
	50 Pennia 2.5494		.750	1.9121	.0615
	1 Markka 5.1828		.868	4.4987	.1446
	2 Markkaa 10.3657		.868	8.9974	.2893
1951-52	500 Markkaa ... 12.0000		.500	6.0000	.1929
FRANCE					
1803-66	20 Centimes 1.0000		.900	0.9000	.0289
	25 Cmes/¼ Franc 1.2500		.900	1.1250	.0362
	50 Cmes/½ Franc 2.5000		.900	2.2500	.0723
	1 Franc 5.0000		.900	4.5000	.1447
	2 Francs 10.0000		.900	9.0000	.2894
	5 Francs 25.0000		.900	22.5000	.7234
1866-1920	see Latin Monetary Union				
1929-39	10 Francs 10.0000		.680	6.8000	.2186
	20 Francs 20.0000		.680	13.6000	.4372
FRENCH COCHIN CHINA					
1879-85	10 Centimes 2.7216		.900	2.4494	.0787
	20 Centimes 5.4431		.900	4.8988	.1575
	50 Centimes ... 13.6078		.900	12.2470	.3937
	1 Piastre 27.2156		.900	24.4940	.7875
FRENCH INDO-CHINA					
1855-95	same as French Cochin China				
1895-96	10 Centimes 2.7000		.900	2.4300	.0781
	20 Centimes 5.4000		.900	4.8600	.1562
1898-1919	10 Centimes 2.7000		.835	2.2545	.0725
	20 Centimes 5.4000		.835	4.5090	.1450
1920	10 Centimes 3.0000		.400	1.2000	.0386
	20 Centimes 6.0000		.400	2.4000	.0772
1921-37	10 Centimes 2.7000		.680	1.8360	.0590
	20 Centimes 5.4000		.680	3.6720	.1181
1896-1936	50 Centimes ... 13.5000		.900	12.1500	.3906
1895-1928	1 Piastre 27.0000		.900	24.3000	.7812
1931	1 Piastre 20.0000		.900	18.0000	.5787

Dates	Denomination	Gross Wt., Gms.	Fineness	Silver Content Grams	Silver Content Ounces

GERMAN STATES

1874-1918	2 Mark 11.1111	.900		10.0000	.3215
	3 Mark 16.6666	.900		15.0000	.4823
	5 Mark 27.7777	.900		25.0000	.8038

GERMANY

1873-1919	20 Pfennig 1.1111	.900		1.0000	.0322
	50 Pf/½ Mark ... 2.7777	.900		2.5000	.0804
	1 Mark 5.5555	.900		5.0000	.1608
1924-33	1 Mark 5.0000	.500		2.5000	.0804
	2 Mark 10.0000	.500		5.0000	.1608
	3 Mark 15.0000	.500		7.5000	.2411
	5 Mark 25.0000	.500		12.5000	.4019
1933-39	2 Mark 8.0000	.625		5.0000	.1608
	5 Mark 13.8888	.900		12.5000	.4019

GERMAN EAST AFRICA
1890-1914 same as India 1835-1939 (Rupie=Rupee)

GERMAN NEW GUINEA
1894 same as Germany and German States 1873-1919

GREAT BRITAIN

1817-1920	3 Pence 1.4138	.925		1.3078	.0420
	4 Pence 1.8851	.925		1.7437	.0561
	6 Pence 2.8276	.925		2.6155	.0841
	1 Shilling 5.6552	.925		5.2311	.1682
	1 Florin 11.3104	.925		10.4621	.3364
	½ Crown 14.1380	.925		13.0777	.4204
	2 Florin 22.6207	.925		20.9241	.6727
	1 Crown 28.2759	.925		26.1552	.8409
1895-1935	Trade Dollar 26.9568	.900		24.2611	.7800
1920-46	3 Pence 1.4138	.500		0.7069	.0227
	6 Pence 2.8276	.500		1.4138	.0455
	1 Shilling 5.6552	.500		2.8276	.0909
	2 Sh/Florin 11.3104	.500		5.6552	.1818
	½ Crown 14.1380	.500		7.0690	.2273
	1 Crown 28.2759	.500		14.1380	.4545

GREECE

1868-1911	see Latin Monetary Union (Lepta/Drachmai=Centimes/Francs)				
1930	10 Drachmai 7.0000	.500		3.5000	.1125
	20 Drachmai 11.3333	.500		5.6667	.1822

GUATEMALA

1881-99	2 Rs/25 Cvos 6.2500	.835		5.2188	.1678
1869-97	1 Peso 25.0000	.900		22.5000	.7234
1925-64	5 Centavos 1.6667	.720		1.2000	.0386
	10 Centavos 3.3333	.720		2.4000	.0772
	¼ Q/25 Cvos ... 8.3333	.720		6.0000	.1929
1925	½ Quetzal 16.6667	.720		12.0000	.3858
	1 Quetzal 33.3333	.720		24.0000	.7716
1962-63	50 Centavos 11.9444	.720		8.6000	.2765

HAITI
1881-95 same as Venezuela 1873-76 (Centimes/Gourdes=Centavos/Venezolanos)

HAWAII
1883 same as United States 1873-1964

HONDURAS

1931-58	20 Centavos 2.5000	.900		2.2500	.0723
	50 Centavos 6.2500	.900		5.6250	.1808
	1 Lempira 12.5000	.900		11.2500	.3617

HONG KONG

1863-1933	5 Cents 1.3577	.800		1.0862	.0349
	10 Cents 2.7154	.800		2.1723	.0698
	20 Cents 5.4308	.800		4.3446	.1397
1866-68	½ Dollar 13.4784	.900		12.1306	.3900
	1 Dollar 26.9568	.900		24.2611	.7800
1890-1905	50 Cents 13.5769	.800		10.8615	.3492

HUNGARY
1868-92 same as Austria 1868-92 (Krajczar/Forint=Kreuzer/Florin)
1892-1916 same as Austria 1892-1916 (Korona=Krone)

Dates	Denomination	Gross Wt., Gms.	Fineness	Silver Content Grams	Silver Content Ounces

1926-39	1 Pengo 5.0000	.640		3.2000	.1029
	2 Pengo 10.0000	.640		6.4000	.2058
	5 Pengo 25.0000	.640		16.0000	.5144
1946	5 Forint 20.0000	.833		16.6600	.5356
1947-48	5 Forint 12.0000	.500		6.0000	.1929
	10 Forint 20.0000	.500		10.0000	.3215

INDIA

1841-1917	2 Annas 1.4580	.916⅔		1.3365	.0430
1835-1943	¼ Rupee 2.9160	.916⅔		2.6730	.0859
1835-1940	½ Rupee 5.8319	.916⅔		5.3459	.1719
1835-1939	1 Rupee 11.6638	.916⅔		10.6918	.3437
1943-45	¼ Rupee 2.9160	.500		1.4580	.0469
1941-45	½ Rupee 5.8319	.500		2.9160	.0937
1940-45	1 Rupee 11.6638	.500		5.8319	.1875

IRAN

1878-1929	(3) Shahi 0.6908	.900		0.6217	.0200
	¼ Qiran 1.1513	.900		1.0362	.0333
	500 Dinar 2.3025	.900		2.0723	.0666
	1000 Dinar 4.6050	.900		4.1445	.1332
	2000 Dinar 9.2100	.900		8.2890	.2665
	5000 Dinar 23.0251	.900		20.7226	.6662
	1 Toman 46.0501	.900		41.4451	1.3325
1931-36	¼ Rial 1.2500	.828		1.0350	.0333
	½ Rial 2.5000	.828		1.0350	.0666
	1 Rial 5.0000	.828		4.1400	.1331
	2 Rial 3.2000	.600		1.9200	.0617
	5 Rial 8.0000	.600		4.8000	.1543
1943-51	1 Rial 1.6000	.600		0.9600	.0309
	2 Rial 3.2000	.600		1.9200	.0617
	5 Rial 8.0000	.600		4.8000	.1543
	10 Rial 16.0000	.600		9.6000	.3086

IRAQ

1931-53	20 Fils 3.6000	.500		1.8000	.0579
	50 Fils 9.0000	.500		4.5000	.1447
	1 Riyal 20.0000	.900		18.0000	.5787

IRELAND

1928-43	1 Shilling 5.6552	.750		4.2414	.1364
	1 Florin 11.3104	.750		8.4828	.2727
	½ Crown 14.1380	.750		10.6035	.3409

ITALY

1863-1917	see Latin Monetary Union (Centesimi/Lire=Centimes/Francs)				
1926-41	5 Lire 5.0000	.835		4.1750	.1342
	10 Lire 10.0000	.835		8.3500	.2685
1927-34	20 Lire 15.0000	.800		12.0000	.3858
1928	20 Lire commem. 20.0000	.600		12.0000	.3858
1936-41	20 Lire 20.0000	.800		16.0000	.5144

ITALIAN SOMALILAND

1910-21	same as India 1835-1939 (Rupia=Rupee)				
1925	5 Lire 6.0000	.835		5.0100	.1611
	10 Lire 12.0000	.835		10.0200	.3221

JAPAN

1870-71	5 Sen 1.2500	.800		1.0000	.0322
	10 Sen 2.5000	.800		2.0000	.0643
	20 Sen 5.0000	.800		4.0000	.1286
	50 Sen 12.5000	.800		10.0000	.3215
1873-1906	5 Sen 1.3479	.800		1.0783	.0347
	10 Sen 2.6957	.800		2.1566	.0693
	20 Sen 5.3914	.800		4.3131	.1387
	50 Sen 13.4785	.800		10.7828	.3467
1870-1914	1 Yen 26.9568	.900		24.2611	.7800
	Trade Dollar 27.2156	.900		24.4940	.7875
1906-17	10 Sen 2.2500	.720		1.6200	.0521
	20 Sen 4.0500	.800		3.2400	.1042
	50 Sen 10.1250	.800		8.1000	.2604
1922-38	50 Sen 4.9500	.720		3.5640	.1146

KOREA
1892-93 same as Japan 1873-1906 (5 Yang=1 Yen)
1901-06 same as Japan 1873-1906 } (Chon/Won=Sen/Yen)
1907-10 same as Japan 1906-1917 }

Dates	Denomination	Gross Wt., Gms.	Fine-ness	Silver Content Grams	Ounces

LATIN MONETARY UNION

The Latin Monetary Union was formed by treaties standardizing the silver and gold currencies of France, Italy, Belgium, Switzerland and Greece. Derived from the French coinage system established in 1803, the Union was formed in 1865 and dissolved in 1926. Many other countries, although not Union members, struck coinage to these standards.

Dates	Denomination	Gross Wt., Gms.	Fine-ness	Silver Content Grams	Ounces
1865-1926	20 Centimes	1.0000	.835	0.8350	.0268
	50 Cmes/½ Franc	2.5000	.835	2.0875	.0671
	1 Franc	5.0000	.835	4.1750	.1342
	2 Francs	10.0000	.835	8.3500	.2685
	5 Francs	25.0000	.900	22.5000	.7234

LATVIA

Dates	Denomination	Gross Wt., Gms.	Fine-ness	Silver Content Grams	Ounces
1924-32	1 Lats	5.0000	.835	4.1750	.1342
	2 Lati	10.0000	.835	8.3500	.2685
	5 Lati	25.0000	.835	20.8750	.6711

LEBANON

1929-52 same as Syria 1929-59

LITHUANIA

Dates	Denomination	Gross Wt., Gms.	Fine-ness	Silver Content Grams	Ounces
1925	1 Litas	2.7000	.500	1.3500	.0434
	2 Litu	5.4000	.500	2.7000	.0868
	5 Litai	13.5000	.500	6.7500	.2170
1936-38	5 Litai	9.0000	.750	6.7500	.2170
	10 Litu	18.0000	.750	13.5000	.4340

LUXEMBOURG

Dates	Denomination	Gross Wt., Gms.	Fine-ness	Silver Content Grams	Ounces
1929	5 Francs	8.0000	.625	5.0000	.1608
	10 Francs	13.3000	.750	9.9750	.3207
1946	20 Francs	8.5000	.835	7.0975	.2282
	50 Francs	12.5000	.835	10.4375	.3356
	100 Francs	25.0000	.835	20.8750	.6711

MALAYA

Dates	Denomination	Gross Wt., Gms.	Fine-ness	Silver Content Grams	Ounces
1939-41	5 Cents	1.3577	.750	1.0183	.0327
	10 Cents	2.7154	.750	2.0365	.0655
	20 Cents	5.4308	.750	4.0731	.1310
1943-45	5 Cents	1.3577	.500	0.6788	.0218
	10 Cents	2.7154	.500	1.3577	.0437
	20 Cents	5.4308	.500	2.7154	.0873

MEXICO

Dates	Denomination	Gross Wt., Gms.	Fine-ness	Silver Content Grams	Ounces
1822-69	¼ Real	0.8460	.9027	0.7637	.0246
	½ Real	1.6921	.9027	1.5275	.0491
	1 Real	3.3841	.9027	3.0548	.0982
1863-1905	5 Centavos	1.3537	.9027	1.2220	.0393
	10 Centavos	2.7073	.9027	2.4439	.0786
	20 Centavos	5.4146	.9027	4.8878	.1571
1822-1905	2 R/25 Cvos	6.7683	.9027	6.1097	.1964
	4 R/50 Cvos	13.5365	.9027	12.2194	.3929
1822-1914	8 R/1 Peso	27.0730	.9027	24.4388	.7857
1905-18	10 Centavos	2.5000	.800	2.0000	.0643
	20 Centavos	5.0000	.800	4.0000	.1286
	50 Centavos	12.5000	.800	10.0000	.3215
1918-19	10 Centavos	1.8125	.800	1.4500	.0466
	20 Centavos	3.6250	.800	2.9000	.0932
	50 Centavos	9.0625	.800	7.2500	.2331
	1 Peso	18.1250	.800	14.5000	.4662
1919-45	10 Centavos	1.6667	.720	1.2000	.0386
	20 Centavos	3.3333	.720	2.4000	.0772
	50 Centavos	8.3333	.720	6.0000	.1929
	1 Peso	16.6667	.720	12.0000	.3858
	2 Pesos	26.6667	.900	24.0000	.7716
1935	50 Centavos	7.9733	.420	3.3488	.1077
1947-49	1 Peso	14.0000	.500	7.0000	.2251
	5 Pesos	30.0000	.900	27.0000	.8681
	Troy Ounce	33.6250	.925	31.1031	1.0000

MOMBASA

1888-90 same as India 1835-1939

MONGOLIA

1925 same as Russia (Mongo/Tukhrik=Kopek/Ruble)

MONTENEGRO

1909-14 same as Austria 1892-1916 (Perpera=Kronen)

MOROCCO

Dates	Denomination	Gross Wt., Gms.	Fine-ness	Silver Content Grams	Ounces
1882-1901	½ Dirhem	1.4558	.835	1.2156	.0391
	1 Dirhem	2.9116	.835	2.4312	.0782
	2½ Dirhem	7.2790	.835	6.0780	.1954
	5 Dirhem	14.5580	.835	12.1559	.3908
	10 Dirhem	29.1160	.900	26.2044	.8425
1902-18	1/20 Rial	1.2500	.835	1.0438	.0336
	1/10 Rial	2.500	.835	2.0875	.0671
	¼ Rial	6.2500	.835	5.2188	.1678
	½ Rial	12.5000	.835	10.4375	.3356
	1 Rial	25.0000	.900	22.5000	.7234
1929-34	5 Francs	5.0000	.680	3.4000	.1093
	10 Francs	10.0000	.680	6.8000	.2186
	20 Francs	20.0000	.680	13.6000	.4372

MOZAMBIQUE

1935-51 same as Portugal

NETHERLANDS

Dates	Denomination	Gross Wt., Gms.	Fine-ness	Silver Content Grams	Ounces
1848-1945	5 Cents	0.6850	.640	0.4384	.0141
	10 Cents	1.4000	.640	0.8960	.0288
	25 Cents	3.5750	.640	2.2880	.0736
1840-1919	½ Gulden	5.0000	.945	4.7250	.1519
	1 Gulden	10.0000	.945	9.4500	.3038
	2½ Gulden	25.0000	.945	23.6250	.7595
1921-45	½ Gulden	5.0000	.720	3.6000	.1157
	1 Gulden	10.0000	.720	7.2000	.2315
	2½ Gulden	25.0000	.720	18.0000	.5787

NETHERLANDS INDIES

Dates	Denomination	Gross Wt., Gms.	Fine-ness	Silver Content Grams	Ounces
1854-1945	1/20 Gulden	0.6100	.720	0.4392	.0141
	1/10 Gulden	1.2500	.720	0.9000	.0289
	¼ Gulden	3.1800	.720	2.2896	.0736

NEW GUINEA

Dates	Denomination	Gross Wt., Gms.	Fine-ness	Silver Content Grams	Ounces
1935-45	1 Shilling	5.38	.925	4.98	.16

NEW ZEALAND

1933-49 same as Great Britain 1920-46

NICARAGUA

Dates	Denomination	Gross Wt., Gms.	Fine-ness	Silver Content Grams	Ounces
1880-1936	5 Centavos	1.2500	.800	1.0000	.0322
	10 Centavos	2.5000	.800	2.0000	.0643
	20 Centavos	5.0000	.800	4.0000	.1286
	25 Centavos	6.2500	.800	5.0000	.1608
	50 Centavos	12.5000	.800	10.0000	.3215
	1 Cordoba	25.0000	.900	22.5000	.7234

NORWAY

1874-1919 see Scandinavian Monetary Union

PALESTINE

Dates	Denomination	Gross Wt., Gms.	Fine-ness	Silver Content Grams	Ounces
1927-42	50 Mils	5.8319	.720	4.1990	.1350
	100 Mils	11.6638	.720	8.3979	.2700

PANAMA

Dates	Denomination	Gross Wt., Gms.	Fine-ness	Silver Content Grams	Ounces
1904-16	2½ Centesimos	1.2500	.900	1.1250	.0362
	5 Centesimos	2.5000	.900	2.2500	.0723
	10 Centesimos	5.0000	.900	4.5000	.1447
	25 Centesimos	12.5000	.900	11.2500	.3617
	50 Centesimos	25.000	.900	22.5000	.7234
1930-62	same as United States				

PARAGUAY

Dates	Denomination	Gross Wt., Gms.	Fine-ness	Silver Content Grams	Ounces
1889	1 Peso	25.0000	.900	22.5000	.7234

PERU

Dates	Denomination	Gross Wt., Gms.	Fine-ness	Silver Content Grams	Ounces
1863-1917	½ Dinero	1.2500	.900	1.1250	.0362
	1 Dinero	2.5000	.900	2.2500	.0723
	1/5 Sol	5.0000	.900	4.5000	.1447
	½ Sol	12.5000	.900	11.2500	.3617
	1 Sol	25.0000	.900	22.5000	.7234
1880-82	½ Real	1.2500	.900	1.1250	.0362
	1 Peseta	5.0000	.900	4.5000	.1447
	5 Pesetas	25.0000	.900	22.5000	.7234
1922-35	½ Sol	12.5000	.500	6.2500	.2009
	1 Sol	25.0000	.500	12.5000	.4019

PHILIPPINES

Dates	Denomination	Gross Wt., Gms.	Fine-ness	Silver Content Grams	Ounces
1864-80	10 Centimos	2.5960	.900	2.3364	.0751

Dates	Denomination	Gross Wt., Gms.	Fineness	Silver Content Grams	Ounces
PHILIPPINES (cont.)					
	20 Centimos	5.1920	.900	4.6728	.1502
	50 Centimos	12.9800	.900	11.6820	.3756
1881-97	10 Centimos	2.5960	.835	2.1677	.0697
	20 Centimos	5.1920	.835	4.3353	.1394
	50 Centimos	12.9800	.835	10.8383	.3485
	1 Peso	25.0000	.900	22.5000	.7234
1903-06	10 Centavos	2.6924	.900	2.4232	.0779
	20 Centavos	5.3849	.900	4.8464	.1558
	50 Centavos	13.4784	.900	12.1306	.3900
	1 Peso	26.9568	.900	24.2611	.7800
1907-47	10 Centavos	2.0000	.750	1.5000	.0482
	20 Centavos	4.000	.750	3.0000	.0965
	50 Centavos	10.0000	.750	7.5000	.2411
	1 Peso	20.0000	.800	16.0000	.5144
POLAND					
1924-25	1 Zloty	5.0000	.750	3.7500	.1206
	2 Zlote	10.0000	.750	7.5000	.2411
	5 Zlotych	25.0000	.900	22.5000	.7234
1928-32	5 Zlotych	18.0000	.750	13.5000	.4340
1932-39	2 Zlote	11.0000	.750	8.2500	.2652
	5 Zlotych	8.8000	.750	6.6000	.2122
	10 Zlotych	22.0000	.750	16.5000	.5305
PORTUGAL					
1854-1903	50 Reis	1.2500	.916⅔	1.1458	.0368
	100 Reis	2.5000	.916⅔	2.2917	.0737
	200 Reis	5.0000	.916⅔	4.5833	.1474
1908-09	100 Reis	2.5000	.835	2.0875	.0671
	200 Reis	5.0000	.835	4.1750	.1342
1854-1910	500 Reis	12.5000	.916⅔	11.4583	.3684
	1000 Reis	25.0000	.916⅔	22.9167	.7368
1912-16	10 Centavos	2.5000	.835	2.0875	.0671
	20 Centavos	5.0000	.835	4.1750	.1342
	50 Centavos	12.5000	.835	10.4375	.3356
	1 Escudo	25.0000	.835	20.8750	.6711
1932-60	2½ Escudos	3.5000	.650	2.2750	.0731
	5 Escudos	7.0000	.650	4.5500	.1463
1928-48	10 Escudos	12.5000	.835	10.4375	.3356
PORTUGUESE INDIA					
1881-1936 same as India (Rupia=Rupee)					
PUERTO RICO					
1895-96	5 Centavos	1.2500	.835	1.0438	.0336
	10 Centavos	2.5000	.835	2.0875	.0671
	20 Centavos	5.0000	.835	4.1750	.1342
	40 Centavos	10.0000	.835	8.3500	.2685
	1 Peso	25.0000	.900	22.5000	.7234
ROMANIA					
1870-1914 same as Latin Monetary Union (Bani/Lei=Centimes/Francs)					
1932-35	100 Lei	14.0000	.500	7.0000	.2251
	250 Lei	13.5000	.750	10.1250	.3255
RUSSIA					
1813-60	5 Kopek	1.0366	.868	.8998	.0289
	10 Kopek	2.0732	.868	1.7995	.0579
	20 Kopek	4.1463	.868	3.5990	.1157
1860-66	5 Kopek	1.0366	.750	0.7775	.0250
	10 Kopek	2.0732	.750	1.5549	.0500
	15 Kopek	3.1097	.750	2.3323	.0750
	20 Kopek	4.1463	.750	3.1097	.1000
1867-1931	5 Kopek	0.8998	.500	0.4499	.0145
	10 Kopek	1.7996	.500	0.8998	.0289
	15 Kopek	2.6994	.500	1.3497	.0434
	20 Kopek	3.5992	.500	1.7996	.0579
1801-85	25 Kopek	5.1829	.868	4.4988	.1446
	50 Kopek	10.3658	.868	8.9975	.2893
	1 Ruble	20.7316	.868	17.9950	.5785
1886-1931	25 Kopek	4.9987	.900	4.4988	.1446
	50 Kopek	9.9979	.900	8.9981	.2893
	1 Ruble	19.9957	.900	17.9961	.5786

Dates	Denomination	Gross Wt., Gms.	Fineness	Silver Content Grams	Ounces
ST. THOMAS & PRINCE					
1939-51	2½ Escudos	3.5000	.650	2.2750	.0731
	5 Escudos	7.0000	.650	4.5500	.1463
1939	10 Escudos	12.5000	.835	10.4375	.3356
1951	10 Escudos	12.5000	.720	9.0000	.2894
EL SALVADOR					
1892-1914	5 Centavos	1.2500	.835	1.0438	.0336
	10 Centavos	2.5000	.835	2.0875	.0671
	20 Centavos	5.0000	.835	4.1750	.1342
	25 Centavos	6.2500	.835	5.2188	.1678
	50 Centavos	12.5000	.900	11.2500	.3617
	1 Peso	25.0000	.900	22.5000	.7234
1943-44	25 Centavos	7.5000	.900	6.7500	.2170
SAN MARINO					
1898-1906 same as Latin Monetary Union (Centesimi/Lire=Centimes/Francs)					
1931-38	5 Lire	5.0000	.835	4.1750	.1342
	10 Lire	10.0000	.835	8.3500	.2685
	20 Lire	15.0000	.800	12.0000	.3858
	20 Lire	20.0000	.600	12.0000	.3858
SAUDI ARABIA					
1935-55 same as India 1835-1939 (Riyal=Rupee)					

SCANDINAVIAN MONETARY UNION

This union was formed by treaties between Denmark, Sweden and Norway to standardize their monetary systems. Although never formally terminated, it was gradually abandoned following World War I. The only issues on this standard after World War II were Danish 2 Kroner commemoratives to 1958.

Dates	Denomination	Gross Wt., Gms.	Fineness	Silver Content Grams	Ounces
1874-1958	10 Ore, Ore	1.4500	.400	0.5800	.0186
	25 Ore, Ore	2.4200	.600	1.4520	.0467
	50, Ore, Ore	5.0000	.600	3.0000	.0965
	1 Krone, Krona	7.5000	.800	6.0000	.1929
	2 Kroner, Kronor	15.0000	.800	12.0000	.3858
SERBIA					
1875-1915 same as Latin Monetary Union (Para/Dinara=Centimes/Francs)					
SEYCHELLES					
1939-44 same as India 1940-55					
SOUTH AFRICA					
1923-51	3 Pence	1.4138	.800	1.1310	.0364
	6 Pence	2.8276	.800	2.2621	.0727
	1 Shilling	5.6552	.800	4.5241	.1454
	2 Sh/Florin	11.3104	.800	9.0483	.2909
	2½ Shillings	14.1380	.800	11.3104	.3636
	5 Shillings	28.2759	.800	22.6207	.7273
1951-60 same as Great Britain 1920-46 (5 Shillings=1 Crown)					
SOUTHERN RHODESIA					
1932-42 same as Great Britain 1817-1920					
1944-46 same as Great Britain 1920-46					
SPAIN					
1850-65	1 Real	1.3146	.900	1.1831	.0380
	2 Reales	2.6291	.900	2.3662	.0761
	4 Reales	5.2582	.900	4.7324	.1521
	10 Reales	13.1455	.900	11.8310	.3804
	20 Reales	26.2910	.900	23.6619	.7607
1864-68	10 Centimos	1.2980	.810	1.0514	.0338
	20 Centimos	2.5960	.810	2.1028	.0676
	40 Centimos	5.1920	.810	4.2055	.1352
	1 Escudo	12.9800	.900	11.6820	.3756
	2 Escudos	25.9600	.900	23.3640	.7512
1869-1934 same as Latin Monetary Union (Centimos/Pesetas=Centimes/Francs)					
STRAITS SETTLEMENTS					
1871-1905 same as Hong Kong					
1907-17	5 Cents	1.3577	.600	0.8146	.0262
	10 Cents	2.7154	.600	1.6292	.0524

PRECIOUS METAL CONTENT — SILVER · GOLD

Dates	Denomination	Gross Wt., Gms.	Fineness	Silver Content Grams	Silver Content Ounces
STRAITS SETTLEMENTS (cont.)					
	20 Cents 5.4308		.600	3.2585	.1048
	50 Cents 10.1088		.900	9.0979	.2925
	1 Dollar 20.2176		.900	18.1958	.5850
1918-21	5 Cents 1.3577		.400	0.5431	.0175
	10 Cents 2.7154		.400	1.0862	.0349
	20 Cents 5.4308		.400	2.1723	.0698
	50 Cents 8.4240		.500	4.2120	.1354
	1 Dollar 16.8480		.500	8.4240	.2708
1926-35	same as 1907-17				
SWEDEN					
1874-1942	see Scandanavian Monetary Union				
1935	5 Kronor 25.0000		.900	22.5000	.7234
1942-68	10 Ore 1.4400		.400	0.5760	.0185
	25 Ore 2.3200		.400	0.9280	.0298
	50 Ore 4.8000		.400	1.9200	.0617
	1 Krona 7.0000		.400	2.8000	.0900
	2 Kronor 14.0000		.400	5.6000	.1800
SWITZERLAND					
1850-51	½, 1, 2, Francs; same as France 1803-66				
1857-63	1 Franc 5.0000		.800	4.0000	.1286
	2 Francs 10.0000		.800	8.0000	.2572
1874-1967	½, 1, 2 Francs } see Latin Monetary Union				
1850-1928	5 Francs				
1931-69	5 Francs 15.0000		.835	12.5250	.4027
SYRIA					
1929-37	10 Piastres 2.0000		.680	1.3600	.0437
	25 Piastres 5.0000		.680	3.4000	.1093
	50 Piastres 10.0000		.680	6.8000	.2186
1947-59	25 Piastres 2.5000		.600	1.5000	.0482
	50 Piastres 5.0000		.600	3.0000	.0965
	1 Lira 10.0000		.680	6.8000	.2186
TARIM & GHURFAH					
1897	6 Chamsi 0.8500		.900	0.7650	.0246
	12 Chamsi 1.5500		.900	1.3950	0.448
	24 Chamsi 3.1000		.900	2.7900	.0897
1926	4 Chamsi 0.5660		.900	0.5094	.0164
	8 Chamsi 1.0333		.900	0.9300	.0299
	15 Chamsi 1.9375		.900	1.7438	.0561
	30 Chamsi 3.8750		.900	3.4875	.1121
	45 Chamsi 5.8125		.900	5.2313	.1682
	60 Chamsi 7.7500		.900	6.9750	.2242
THAILAND					
1908-25	¼ Baht 3.7500		.800	3.0000	.0965
	½ Baht 7.5000		.800	6.0000	.1929
	1 Baht 15.0000		.900	13.5000	.4340
1929	25 Satang 3.7500		.650	2.4375	.0784
	50 Satang 7.5000		.650	4.8750	.1567
1941	5 Satang 1.5000		.650	0.9750	.0313
	10 Satang 2.5000		.650	1.6250	.0522
	20 Satang 3.0000		.650	1.9500	.0627
TIMOR					
1945-51	50 Avos 3.5000		.650	2.2750	.0731
TUNISIA					
1891-1928	same as Latin Monetary Union				
1930-39	5 Francs 5.0000		.680	3.4000	.1093
	10 Francs 10.0000		.680	6.8000	.2186
	20 Francs 20.0000		.680	13.6000	.4372
TURKEY					
1844-1919	20 Para 0.6013		.830	0.4491	.0160
	1 Kurus 1.2027		.830	0.9982	.0321
	2 Kurus 2.4055		.830	1.9966	.0642
	5 Kurus 6.0130		.830	4.9908	.1605
	10 Kurus 12.0270		.830	9.9824	.3209
	20 Kurus 24.0550		.830	19.9657	.6419
1899-1904	5 Para 1.0023		.100	0.1002	.0032
	10 Para 2.0046		.100	0.2005	.0064
1934-41	25 Kurus 3.0000		.830	2.4900	.0801
	50 Kurus 6.0000		.830	4.9800	.1601

Dates	Denomination	Gross Wt., Gms.	Fineness	Silver Content Grams	Silver Content Ounces
	100 Kurus/1 Lira 12.0000		.830	9.9600	.3202
1947-48	50 Kurus 4.0000		.600	2.4000	.0772
	1 Lira 7.5000		.600	4.5000	.1447
UNITED STATES OF AMERICA					
1851-53	3 Cents 0.8019		.750	0.6014	.0193
1853-73	3 Cents 0.7465		.900	0.6719	.0216
	½ Dime 1.2442		.900	1.1197	.0360
	1 Dime 2.4883		.900	2.2395	.0720
	¼ Dollar 6.2208		.900	5.5987	.1800
	½ Dollar 12.4416		.900	11.1974	.3600
1873-1964	1 Dime 2.5000		.900	2.2500	.0723
	20 Cents 5.0000		.900	4.5000	.1447
	¼ Dollar 6.2500		.900	5.6250	.1808
	½ Dollar 12.5000		.900	11.2500	.3617
1840-1935	1 Dollar 26.7296		.900	24.0566	.7734
1873-85	Trade Dollar 27.2156		.900	24.4940	.7875
1942-45	5 Cents 5.0000		.350	1.7500	.0563
URUGUAY					
1877-1917	same as Argentina (Centesimos = Centavos)				
1920-30	20 Centesimos ... 5.0000		.800	4.0000	.1286
1942-54	20 Centesimos ... 3.0000		.720	2.1600	.0694
	50 Centesimos ... 7.0000		.720	5.0400	.1620
	1 Peso 9.0000		.720	6.4800	.2083
VATICAN					
1929-46	same as Italy 1926-41				
VENEZUELA					
1858	½ Real 1.1500		.900	1.0350	.0333
	1 Real 2.3000		.900	2.0700	.0666
	2 Reales 4.6000		.900	4.1400	.1331
	5 Reales 11.5000		.900	10.3500	.3328
1873-1965	1/5 Bolivar 1.0000		.835	0.8350	.0268
	5 Cvos/⅕ Bol 1.2500		.835	1.0438	.0336
	10 Cvos/½ Bol ... 2.5000		.835	2.0875	.0671
	20 Cvos/1 Bol.... 5.0000		.835	4.1750	.1342
	2 Bolivares 10.0000		.835	8.3500	.2685
	50 Centavos 12.5000		.835	10.4375	.3356
	1 Ven/5 Bol 25.0000		.900	22.5000	.7234
YUGOSLAVIA					
1931-32	10 Dinara 7.0000		.500	3.5000	.1125
	20 Dinara 14.0000		.500	7.0000	.2251
	50 Dinara 22.0000		.750	16.5000	.5305
1938	20 Dinara 9.0000		.750	6.7500	.2170
	50 Dinara 15.0000		.750	11.2500	.3617
ZANZIBAR					
1882	same as United States 1873-85 (Ryal = Trade Dollar)				

GOLD

Dates	Denomination	Gross Wt., Gms.	Fineness	Content Grams	Content Ounces
ALBANIA					
1926-38	same as Latin Monetary Union (Frang Ar = Franc)				
ARGENTINA					
1881-96	½ Argentino 4.0322		.900	3.6290	.1167
	1 Argentino 8.0645		.900	7.2581	.2333
AUSTRALIA					
1852-1931	same as Great Britain				
AUSTRIA					
1857-1915	1 Dukat 3.4909		.9861	3.4424	.1107
	4 Dukaten 13.9636		.9861	13.7695	.4427
1858-66	½ Krone 5.5555		.900	5.0000	.1608
	1 Krone 11.1111		.900	10.0000	.3215
1870-92	4 Fl/10 Fr 3.2258		.900	2.9032	.0933
	8 Fl/20 Fr 6.4516		.900	5.8064	.1867
1892-1924	10 Kronen 3.3875		.900	3.0488	.0980
	20 Kronen 6.7751		.900	6.0976	.1960
	100 Kronen 33.8753		.900	30.4878	.9802
1926-38	25 Schilling 5.8811		.900	5.2930	.1702
	100 Schilling ... 23.5245		.900	21.1721	.6807

Dates	Denomination	Gross Wt., Gms.	Fine- ness	Gold Content Grams	Ounces

BELGIUM
1848-1914 see Latin Monetary Union

BRAZIL

1849-1922	5000 Reis 4.4822	.916⅔	4.1087	.1321
	10000 Reis 8.9645	.916⅔	8.2175	.2642
	20000 Reis 17.9290	.916⅔	16.4349	.5284

BULGARIA
1894-1912 same as Latin Monetary Union

CANADA
1908-19 1 Sovereign: same as Great Britain
1912-14 5,10 Dollars: same as United States

NEWFOUNDLAND

1865-88	2 Dollars 3.3284	.916⅔	3.0510	.0981

CHILE

1851-92	1 Peso 1.5253	.900	1.3728	.0441
	2 Pesos 3.0506	.900	2.7455	.0883
	5 Pesos 7.6265	.900	6.8639	.2207
	10 Pesos 15.2520	.900	13.7277	.4413
1895-1917	5 Pesos 2.9955	.916⅔	2.7459	.0883
	10 Pesos 5.9910	.916⅔	5.4918	.1766
	20 Pesos 11.9821	.916⅔	10.9836	.3531
1926-62	20 Pesos 4.0679	.900	3.6611	.1177
	50 Pesos 10.1698	.900	9.1528	.2943
	100 Pesos 20.3397	.900	18.3057	.5885

COLOMBIA
1856-78 same as Latin Monetary Union (1 Peso=5 Francs)

1885	5 Pesos 8.0645	.666	5.3763	.1728

1913-30 same as Great Britain (5 Pesos=1 Sovereign)

COSTA RICA

1864-76	1 Peso 1.4677	.875	1.2843	.0413
	2 Pesos 2.9355	.875	2.5685	.0826
	5 Pesos 7.3387	.875	6.4213	.2064
	10 Pesos 14.6774	.875	12.8427	.4129
1873	5 Pesos 8.0645	.900	7.2581	.2333
	20 Pesos 32.2581	.900	29.0323	.9334
1897-1928	2 Colones 1.5560	.900	1.4004	.0450
	5 Colones 3.8900	.900	3.5010	.1126
	10 Colones 7.7800	.900	7.0020	.2251
	20 Colones 15.5600	.900	14.0040	.4502

CUBA

1915-16	2 Pesos 3.3436	.900	3.0092	.0967
	4 Pesos 6.6872	.900	6.0185	.1935

Other values: same as United States (Pesos=Dollars)

CZECHOSLOVAKIA

1923-51	1 Dukat 3.4909	.9861	3.4424	.1107
	2 Dukaty 6.9818	.9861	6.8848	.2213
	5 Dukatu 17.4545	.9861	17.2119	.5534
	10 Dukatu 34.9089	.9861	34.4237	1.1067

DANISH WEST INDIES
1904-05 same as Latin Monetary Union
(1 Daler=5 Francs)

DANZIG
1923-30 same as Great Britain (25 Gulden=1 Sovereign)

DENMARK
1873-1931 see Scandinavian Monetary Union

ECUADOR

1899-1900	10 Sucres 8.1360	.900	7.3224	.2354
1928	1 Condor 8.3592	.900	7.5233	.2419

EGYPT

1835-1960	5 Ghirsh 0.4250	.900	0.3825	.0123
	10 Ghirsh 0.8500	.900	0.7650	.0246
	20 Ghirsh 1.7000	.900	1.5300	.0492
	25 Ghirsh 2.1250	.900	1.9125	.0615
	50 Gh/½ Lira ... 4.2500	.900	3.8250	.1230
	100 Gh/1 Lira .. 8.5000	.900	7.6500	.2459
	500 Gh/5 Lira ... 42.5000	.900	38.2500	1.2297

Dates	Denomination	Gross Wt., Gms.	Fine- ness	Gold Content Grams	Ounces

FINLAND
1878-1913 same as Latin Monetary Union (Markkaa=Francs)

1926	100 Markkaa 4.2105	.900	3.7895	.1218
	200 Markkaa 8.4211	.900	7.5789	.2437

FRANCE
1803-1914 see Latin Monetary Union

1929-36	100 Francs 6.5500	.900	5.8950	.1895

GERMANY

1871-1915	5 Mark 1.9913	.900	1.7922	.0576
	10 Mark 3.9825	.900	3.5843	.1152
	20 Mark 7.9650	.900	7.1685	.2305

GERMAN EAST AFRICA

1916	15 Rupien 7.1680	.750	5.3760	.1728

GERMAN NEW GUINEA
1895 same as Germany

GREAT BRITAIN

1817-1968	½ Sovereign 3.9940	.916⅔	3.6612	.1177
	1 Sovereign 7.9881	.916⅔	7.3224	.2354
	2 Pounds 15.9761	.916⅔	14.6448	.4708
	5 Pounds 39.9403	.916⅔	36.6119	1.1711

GREECE
1876-1967 see Latin Monetary Union (Drachmai=Francs)

GUATEMALA
1869-78 same as Latin Monetary Union (1 Peso=5 Francs)
1926 same as United States (Quetzales=Dollars)

HONDURAS
1871-1922 same as Latin Monetary Union (1 Peso=5 Francs)

HUNGARY
1870-1916 same as Austria
(Dukat/Forint/Korona=Dukat/Florin/Krone)

INDIA

1835-1918	5 Rupees 3.8879	.916⅔	3.5639	.1146
	10 Rupees 7.7759	.916⅔	7.1279	.2292
	15 R/1 Mohur .. 11.6638	.916⅔	10.6918	.3437
	2 Mohur 23.3276	.916⅔	21.3836	.6875
1918	1 Sovereign: same as Great Britain

IRAN

1879-1926	1/5 Toman 0.5749	.900	0.5174	.0166
	½ Toman 1.4372	.900	1.2935	.0416
	1 Toman 2.8744	.900	2.5870	.0832
	2 Toman 5.7488	.900	5.1739	.1663
	5 Toman 14.3720	.900	12.9348	.4159
	10 Toman 28.7440	.900	25.8696	.8317
1926-29	1 Pahlavi........ 1.9180	.900	1.7262	.0555
	2 Pahlavi 3.8360	.900	3.4524	.1110
	5 Pahlavi 9.5900	.900	8.6310	.2775
1931-	¼ Pahlavi 2.0340	.900	1.8306	.0589
	½ Pahlavi 4.0680	.900	3.6612	.1177
	1 Pahlavi 8.1360	.900	7.3224	.2354
	2½ Pahlavi 20.3400	.900	18.3060	.5885
	5 Pahlavi 40.6799	.900	36.6119	1.1771

ITALY
1861-1927 see Latin Monetary Union (Lire=Francs)

1931-36	50 Lire 4.3995	.900	3.9596	.1273
	100 Lire 8.7990	.900	7.9191	.2546
1937	100 Lire 5.1966	.900	4.6769	.1504

JAPAN

1870-97	1 Yen 1.6667	.900	1.5000	.0482
	2 Yen 3.3333	.900	3.0000	.0965
	5 Yen 8.3333	.900	7.5000	.2411
	10 Yen 16.6667	.900	15.0000	.4823
	20 Yen 33.3333	.900	30.0000	.9645
1897-1932	5 Yen 4.1667	.900	3.7500	.1206
	10 Yen 8.3333	.900	7.5000	.2411
	20 Yen 16.6667	.900	15.0000	.4823

KOREA
1906-10 same as Japan 1897-1932 (Won=Yen)

Dates	Denomination	Gross Wt., Gms.	Fineness	Gold Content Grams	Gold Content Ounces

LATIN MONETARY UNION

This Union (see silver section for explanation) struck denominations as listed below for 1865-1926, though some countries struck coins of identical standards both earlier and later. Other denominations shown below were struck prior to the Union or by nonmember states; these values have proportional weights, however, and are included here for ease of reference.

Dates	Denomination	Gross Wt., Gms.	Fineness	Gold Content Grams	Gold Content Ounces
1865-1926	5 Francs	1.6129	.900	1.4516	.0467
	10 Francs	3.2258	.900	2.9032	.0933
	20 Francs	6.4516	.900	5.8064	.1867
	50 Francs	16.1290	.900	14.5161	.4667
	100 Francs	32.2581	.900	29.0323	.9334
Other:	12½ Francs	4.0323	.900	3.6291	.1167
	25 Francs	8.0645	.900	7.2581	.2333
	40 Francs	12.9032	.900	11.6129	.3734

LIECHTENSTEIN
1898-1900 same as Austria 1892-1924
1930-52 same as Latin Monetary Union (Franken = Francs)

MEXICO

Dates	Denomination	Gross Wt., Gms.	Fineness	Gold Content Grams	Gold Content Ounces
1822-73	½ Escudo	1.6921	.875	1.4805	.0476
	1 Escudo	3.3841	.875	2.9611	.0952
	2 Escudos	6.7683	.875	5.9222	.1904
	4 Escudos	13.5365	.875	11.8444	.3808
	8 Escudos	27.0730	.875	23.6889	.7616
1870-1905	1 Peso	1.6921	.875	1.4805	.0476
	2½ Pesos	4.2301	.875	3.7014	.1190
	5 Pesos	8.4602	.875	7.4027	.2380
	10 Pesos	16.9205	.875	14.8054	.4760
	20 Pesos	33.8410	.875	29.6109	.9520
1905-59	2 Pesos	1.6667	.900	1.5000	.0482
	2½ Pesos	2.0833	.900	1.8750	.0603
	5 Pesos	4.1667	.900	3.7500	.1206
	10 Pesos	8.3333	.900	7.5000	.2411
	20 Pesos	16.6667	.900	15.0000	.4823
	50 Pesos	41.6667	.900	37.5000	1.2056

MONACO
1878-1904 same as Latin Monetary Union

MONTENEGRO
1910 same as Austria 1892-1924 (Perpera = Kronen)

NETHERLANDS

Dates	Denomination	Gross Wt., Gms.	Fineness	Gold Content Grams	Gold Content Ounces
1817-1960	1 Dukaat	3.4940	.983	3.4346	.1104
	2 Dukaat	6.9880	.983	6.8692	.2208
1819-53	5 Gulden	3.3645	.900	3.0281	.0974
	10 Gulden	6.7290	.900	6.0561	.1947
	20 Gulden	13.4580	.900	12.1122	.3894
1875-1933	5 Gulden	3.3600	.900	3.0240	.0972
	10 Gulden	6.7200	.900	6.0480	.1944

NORWAY
1874-1910 see Scandinavian Monetary Union

PERU

Dates	Denomination	Gross Wt., Gms.	Fineness	Gold Content Grams	Gold Content Ounces
1863	same as Latin Monetary Union (1 Sol = 5 Francs)				
1898-	1/5 Libra	1.5976	.916⅔	1.4645	.0471
	½ Libra	3.9940	.916⅔	3.6612	.1177
	1 Libra	7.9881	.916⅔	7.3224	.2354
1930-	50 Soles	33.4363	.900	30.0926	.9675
1950-	5 Soles	2.3404	.900	2.1064	.0677
	10 Soles	4.6807	.900	4.2126	.1354
	20 Soles	9.3614	.900	8.4253	.2709
	50 Soles	23.4036	.900	21.0632	.6772
	100 Soles	46.8071	.900	42.1264	1.3544

PHILIPPINES

Dates	Denomination	Gross Wt., Gms.	Fineness	Gold Content Grams	Gold Content Ounces
1861-85	1 Peso	1.6915	.875	1.4801	.0476
	2 Pesos	3.3830	.875	2.9602	.0952
	4 Pesos	6.7661	.875	5.9203	.1903

POLAND
1925 same as Latin Monetary Union (Zlotych = Francs)

PORTUGAL

Dates	Denomination	Gross Wt., Gms.	Fineness	Gold Content Grams	Gold Content Ounces
1855-89	1000 Reis	1.7735	.916⅔	1.6257	.0523
	2000 Reis	3.5470	.916⅔	3.2514	.1045
	5000 Reis	8.8675	.916⅔	8.1285	.2613
	10000 Reis	17.7350	.916⅔	16.2571	.5227

ROMANIA
1868-1940 same as Latin Monetary Union (Lei = Francs)

RUSSIA

Dates	Denomination	Gross Wt., Gms.	Fineness	Gold Content Grams	Gold Content Ounces
1817-85	3 Ruble	3.9264	.916⅔	3.5992	.1157
	5 Ruble	6.5440	.916⅔	5.9987	.1929
	25 Ruble	32.7200	.916⅔	29.9933	.9643
1886-97	5 Ruble	6.4519	.900	5.8067	.1867
	10 Ruble	12.9039	.900	11.6135	.3734
1896-1908	25 Ruble	32.2595	.900	29.0336	.9334
1897-1923	5 Ruble	4.3012	.900	3.8711	.1245
	7½ Ruble	6.4518	.900	5.8066	.1867
	10 Ruble	8.6024	.900	7.7422	.2489
	15 Ruble	12.9036	.900	11.6132	.3734
	37½ Ruble	32.2590	.900	29.0331	.9334

EL SALVADOR
1892 same as Latin Monetary Union (1 Peso = 5 Francs)

SAN MARINO
1925 same as Latin Monetary Union (Lire = Francs)

SAUDI ARABIA

Dates	Denomination	Gross Wt., Gms.	Fineness	Gold Content Grams	Gold Content Ounces
1945-47	1 Sovereign	7.9881	.916⅔	7.3224	.2354
	4 Sovereigns	31.9522	.916⅔	29.2895	.9417

SCANDINAVIAN MONETARY UNION
The unified currencies of Denmark, Sweden and Norway. See silver section for explanation.

Dates	Denomination	Gross Wt., Gms.	Fineness	Gold Content Grams	Gold Content Ounces
1873-1931	5 Kronor	2.2402	.900	2.0162	.0648
	10 Kroner/Kronor	4.4803	.900	4.0323	.1296
	20 Kroner/Kronor	8.9606	.900	8.0645	.2593

SERBIA
1879-82 same as Latin Monetary Union (Dinara = Francs)

SOUTH AFRICA
1874- same as Great Britain
(Sovereign = Pond, Pound, Rand)

SPAIN

Dates	Denomination	Gross Wt., Gms.	Fineness	Gold Content Grams	Gold Content Ounces
1850-64	20 Reales	1.6674	.900	1.5007	.0482
	40 Reales	3.3349	.900	3.0014	.0965
	100 Rs/1 Doblon	8.3371	.900	7.5034	.2412
1865-68	2 Escudos	1.6674	.900	1.5097	.0485
	4 Escudos	3.3548	.900	3.0193	.0971
	10 Escudos	8.3870	.900	7.5483	.2427
1876-1904	same as Latin Monetary Union (Pesetas = Francs)				

SWITZERLAND

Dates	Denomination	Gross Wt., Gms.	Fineness	Gold Content Grams	Gold Content Ounces
1883-1949	10,20 Francs	} see Latin Monetary Union			
'1925	100 Francs				
1934	100 Francs	25.9000	.900	23.3100	.7494
1939	100 Francs	17.5000	.900	15.7500	.5064

SYRIA

Dates	Denomination	Gross Wt., Gms.	Fineness	Gold Content Grams	Gold Content Ounces
1950	½ Lira	3.3793	.900	3.0414	.0978
	1 Lira	6.7586	.900	6.0827	.1956

TUNISIA

Dates	Denomination	Gross Wt., Gms.	Fineness	Gold Content Grams	Gold Content Ounces
1856-91	5 Sebili	0.9840	.900	0.8856	.0285
	10 Sebili	1.9680	.900	1.7712	.0569
	25 S/15 Francs	4.9200	.900	4.4280	.1424
	50 Sebili	9.8400	.900	8.8560	.2847
	100 Sebili	19.6800	.900	17.7120	.5694
1891-1928	same as Latin Monetary Union				
1930-37	same as France 1929-36				

TURKEY

Dates	Denomination	Gross Wt., Gms.	Fineness	Gold Content Grams	Gold Content Ounces
1844-1919	25 Kurus	1.8041	.916⅔	1.6538	.0532
	50 Kurus	3.6083	.916⅔	3.3076	.1063
	100 Kurus	7.2166	.916⅔	6.6152	.2127
	250 Kurus	18.0414	.916⅔	16.5380	.5317
	500 Kurus	36.0828	.916⅔	33.0759	1.0634

Dates	Denominations	Gross Wt., Gms.	Fine-ness	Gold Content Grams	Ounces
TURKEY (Cont.)					
1925-	regular issues: same as 1844-1919 "de Luxe:"				
	25 Kurus	1.7540	.916⅔	1.6078	.0517
	50 Kurus	3,5080	.916⅔	3.2157	.1034
	100 Kurus	7.0160	.916⅔	6.4313	.2068
	250 Kurus	17.5400	.916⅔	16.0783	.5169
	500 Kurus	35.0800	.916⅔	32.1567	1.0338
UNITED STATES OF AMERICA					
1837-1933	1 Dollar	1.6718	.900	1.5046	.0484
	2½ Dollars	4.1795	.900	3.7616	.1209
	3 Dollars	5.0154	.900	4.5139	.1451
	5 Dollars	8.3591	.900	7.5232	.2419
	10 Dollars	16.7181	.900	15.0463	.4837
	20 Dollars	33.4363	.900	30.0926	.9675
	50 Dollars	83.5906	.900	75.2316	2.4187

.Dates	Denominations	Gross Wt., Gms.	Fine-ness	Gold Content Grams	Ounces
URUGUAY					
1930	5 Pesos	8.4850	.916⅔	7.7779	.2501
VATICAN					
1929-35	same as Italy 1931-36				
1936-59	same as Italy 1937				
VENEZUELA					
1875	same as Latin Monetary Union (5 Venezolanos = 25 Francs)				
1879-1930	same as Latin Monetary Union (Bolivares = Francs)				
YUGOSLAVIA					
1925	same as Latin Monetary Union (Dinara = Francs)				
1931-33	sames as Austria 1857-1915				
ZANZIBAR					
1882	same as United States (Ryals = Dollars)				

ALPHABETICAL INDEX OF
WORLD COIN DENOMINATIONS

WORLD COIN DENOMINATIONS

FEN — China, Chinese Turkestan, Manchukuo
FENIG (Fenigow) — Poland
FILLER — Hungary
FILS — Iraq, Jordan, South Arabia
FLORIN — Australia, Austria, East Africa, Fiji, Great Britain, Ireland, Malawi, New Zealand, South Africa
FORINT — Hungary
FRANC — Algeria, Austria, Belgian Congo, Belgium, Cambodia, Cameroun, Comoro Islands, Danish West Indies, Ecuador, France, French Equatorial Africa, French Oceania, French Somaliland, French West Africa, Guadeloupe, Guinea, Hungary, Katanga, Luxembourg, Madagascar, Martinique, Monaco, Morocco, New Caledonia, Reunion, Rwanda & Burundi, St. Pierre and Miquelon, Sweden, Switzerland, Togo, Tunisia
FRANCO — Dominican Republic

FRANG — Albania, Luxembourg
FRANK (Franken) — Belgium, Liechtenstein, Saarland, Switzerland
FUANG — Thailand
FUN — Korea

GERSH — Ethiopia
GHIRSH — Egypt, Hejaz, Nejd, Saudi Arabia, Sudan, Syria, Yemen
GOURDE — Haiti
GROAT — Great Britain
GROSCHEN — Austria
GROSZ (Grosze, Groszy) — Poland
GUARANI — Paraguay
GUERCHE — Egypt
GUINEA — Saudi Arabia
GULDEN — Curacao, Danzig, Netherlands, Netherlands Indies

HABIBI — Afghanistan
HALALA — Saudi Arabia, Yemen
HALER (Halierov, Halere, Haleru) — Bohemia-Moravia, Czechoslovakia, Slovakia
HAO — China, Vietnam
HELLER — Austria, German East Africa
HSIEN — China

IMADI — Yemen

JINIA (=Guinea) — Egypt, Saudi Arabia

KAPANG — Sarawak
KHARUB — Tunisia
KOPEJEK — Tuva
KOPEK — Germany, Russia
KORI — Junagadh, Kutch
KORONA — Hungary
KORUNA (Koruny, Korun) — Bohemia-Moravia, Czechoslovakia, Slovakia
KRAJCZAR — Hungary
KRAN — see QIRAN
KREUZER — Austria
KRONA (Kronor) — Sweden
KRONA (Kronur) — Iceland
KRONE (Kroner) — Austria, Liechtenstein
KRONE (Kroner) — Denmark, Greenland, Norway
KROON (Krooni) — Estonia
KUNA (Kune) — Croatia
KURUS — Turkey
KYAT — Burma

LARIN (Lari) — Maldive Islands
LATS (Lati) — Latvia
LEI — Romania (see LEU)
LEK (Leku, Leke) — Albania
LEMPIRA — Honduras
LEPTON (Lepta) — Crete, Greece
LEU (Lei) — Romania
LEV (Leva) — Bulgaria
LI — China, Chinese Turkestan, Manchukuo
LIANG — China, Chinese Turkestan

LIBRA — Peru
LIRA (Lire) — Eritrea, Italian Somaliland, Italy, San Marino, Syria, Turkey, Vatican City
LITAS (Litu, Litai) — Lithuania

MACE — China, Chinese Turkestan
MACUTA — Angola
MAHALEK — Ethiopia
MARAVEDIS (Maravedi) — Spain
MARK — Estonia, Germany, German New Guinea
MARKKA (Markkaa) — Finland
MATONA — Ethiopia
MAZUNA — Morocco
MEI — China
MELGAREJO — Bolivia
MIL — Cyprus, Hong Kong, Israel, Palestine
MILESIMA — Spain
MILLIEME (Millim) — Egypt
MILREIS (1000 Reis) — Brazil, Portugal
MISQAL — Chinese Turkestan
MOHAR — Nepal
MOHUR — Burma, India, India Native States
MONGO — Mongolia
MUN — Korea
MUZUNA — Morocco

NAYE PAISE — India

ONZA — Costa Rica
ORE — Denmark, Faeroe Islands, Greenland, Norway
ORE — Sweden

PAHLAVI — Iran
PAI — Hyderabad
PAISA (Paise) — Afghanistan, India, India Native States, Nepal
PARA — Egypt, Hejaz, Sudan, Turkey
PARA — (Pare) — Montenegro, Serbia, Yugoslavia
PATACA — Macao, Timor
PENCE — see PENNY
PENGO — Hungary
PENNI (Pennia) — Finland
PENNY (Pence) — Australia, British Guiana, British West Africa, Ceylon, Fiji, Ghana, Great Britain, Guernsey, Ireland, Jamaica, Malawi, New Brunswick, New Guinea, New Zealand, Nigeria, Nova Scotia, Rhodesia and Nyasaland, Rhodesia, South Africa, Southern Rhodesia
PERPER (Perpera) — Montenegro
PESA — German East Africa
PESETA — Peru, Puerto Rico, Spain, Viscayan Republic
PESSA — Lahej
PESO — Argentina, Cambodia, Chile, Colombia, Costa Rica, Cuba, Dominican Republic, Guatemala, Honduras, Mexico, Paraguay, Philippines, Puerto Rico, Salvador, Uruguay
PESO BOLIVIANO — Bolivia
PFENNIG — Danzig, German New Guinea, Germany
PIASTRE — Cambodia, Cyprus, Egypt, French Cochin China, French Indo-China, Lebanon, Sudan, Syria, Tonkin, Tunisia, Turkey
PICE — Bhutan, East Africa, India, India Native States, Mombasa, Pakistan
PIE — Baroda
POND — South African Republic
POUND — Great Britain, Israel, Rhodesia, South Africa
PRUTA (Prutot) — Israel
PUFFIN — Lundy
PUL — Afghanistan, Khiva
PYSA — Zanzibar

QINDAR ARI — Albania
QINDAR LEKU — Albania
QIRAN — Afghanistan, Iran
QUARTO — Catalonia (Spain)
QUETZAL — Guatemala

RAND — South Africa
RAPPEN — Switzerland

WORLD COIN DENOMINATIONS

REAAL — Curacao
REAL (Reales) — Chile, Colombia, Dominican Republic, Ecuador, Guatemala, Honduras, Mexico, Paraguay, Peru, Salvador, Spain, Venezuela
REICHSMARK — Germany
REICHSPFENNIG — Germany
REIS — Azores, Brazil, Portugal, Portuguese India
RENTENPFENNIG — Germany
RIAL — Iran, Morocco
RIGSDALER — Denmark
RIKSDALER — Sweden
RIN — Japan
RIYAL — Iraq, Muscat & Oman, Saudi Arabia
RUBLE — Armavir, Khiva, Khwarezm, Russia
RUPEE — Afghanistan, Bhutan, Burma, Ceylon, India, India Native States, Mauritius, Mombasa, Nepal, Pakistan, Seychelles, Tibet
RUPIA — Italian Somaliland, Portuguese India
RUPIE (Rupien) — German East Africa
RYAL — Hejaz, Muscat and Oman, Nejd, Yemen, Zanzibar

SALUNG — Thailand
SANAR — Afghanistan
SANTEEM — Ethiopia
SANTIMS (Santimi, Santimu) — Latvia
SAPEQUE — Annam, French Cochin China, French Indo-China
SATANG — Thailand
SCHILLING — Austria
SCUDO — Bolivia, Peru
SEN — China, Indonesia, Japan, Netherlands Indies
SENT (Senti) — Estonia
SHAHI — Afghanistan, Iran
SHILLING — Australia, British West Africa, Cyprus, East Africa, Fiji, Ghana, Great Britain, Guernsey, Ireland, Jamaica, Jersey, Malawi, New Guinea, New Zealand, Nigeria, Rhodesia and Nyasaland, Rhodesia, South Africa, Southern Rhodesia
SHO — Tibet
SKARUNG (Skar) — Tibet
SKILLING — Denmark, Norway

SOL (Soles) — Bolivia, Peru
SOMALO — Somalia
SOVEREIGN — Australia, Canada, Great Britain, India, South Africa
SPECIEDALER — Norway
SRANG — Tibet
STOTINKA (Stotinki) — Bulgaria
STUIVER — Curacao
SU — Vietnam, South
SUCRE — Ecuador
SUELDO — Bolivia

TAEL — China, Chinese Turkestan
TALARI — Ethiopia
TALLERO — Eritrea
TANGA — Portuguese India
TANGKA — Tibet
TENGA — Bukhara, Khiva
THALER (or Taler) — Austria, Liechtenstein
THEBE — Botswana
TICAL — Thailand (Siam)
TILLA — Afghanistan, Bukhara
TOMAN — Daghistan, Iran
TRADE DOLLAR — Japan, United States
TRAMBIYA — Kutch
TUKHRIK — Mongolia

VENEZOLANO — Venezuela
VEREINSTHALER — Austria, Liechtenstein

WARK — Ethiopia
WARN — Korea
WEN — China, Chinese Turkestan
WHAN — Korea
WON — Korea

XU — Vietnam, also North and South Vietnam

YANG — Korea
YEN — Japan
YUAN — China

ZLOTY (Zlote, Zlotych) — Poland

INDEX